THE LITTLE, BROWN READER

Seventh Edition

THE LITTLE, BROWN READER

Seventh Edition

Edited by

Marcia Stubbs
Wellesley College

Sylvan Barnet
Tufts University

HarperCollins*College Publishers*

Acquisitions Editor: Patricia Rossi
Developmental Editor: Katharine Glynn
Project Coordination and Text Design: York Production Services
Photo Researcher: Nina Page
Manufacturing Manager: Hilda Koparanian
Electronic Page Makeup: R.R. Donnelly and Sons, Inc.
Printer and Binder: R.R. Donnelly and Sons, Inc.
Cover Printer: Color-Imetry Corp.

THE LITTLE, BROWN, READER 7/E.

Library of Congress Cataloging-in-Publication Data

The Little, Brown reader / edited by Marcia Stubbs, Sylvan Barnet. — 7th ed.
   p. cm.
  Includes index.
  ISBN 0-673-52429-9. — ISBN 0-673-52426-4
  1. College readers. I. Stubbs, Marcia. II. Barnet. Sylvan.
PE1122.L56 1995
808'.0427—dc20
                                                     95–24191
                                                         CIP

4 5 6 7 8 9 10 -DOC- 01 00 99 98 97

Contents

7 Teaching and Learning

* Fiction
** Poetry

8 Work and Play

* Fiction

9 Open for Business

* Fiction
** Poetry

10 Messages

** Poetry

11 Art and Life

** Poetry

feminist" because "she exposes the puritanism and
suffocating ideology of American feminism."

The dance—and particularly ballet—"appears to defeat
the laws of gravity, defy death itself."

Responding to complaints that Walt Disney's Lion King
includes material frightening to children, a pediatrician
agues against simplifying children's entertainment.

A short story about "an obstinate case."

The author tells her questioners that the "content" of her
story is not the life or death of any character but "the
deep-grained habit of love."

Arguing that "a nation absorbs its values through its art," a
former candidate for the Republican nomination for
president expresses his anger that the National Endowment
for the Arts funded an artist whose work he finds highly
offensive.

A Republican senator argues that it is not the business of
Congress to tell the National Endowment for the Arts
what it may or may not subsidize.

A philosopher, looking at congressional foes of the NEA,
argues that "It is very much in the interest of every
taxpayer that freedom be supported, even—or especially—
in its most extreme expressions."

12 Law and Order

Francisco Goya, *The Third of May, 1808*
Bernie Boston, *Flower Power*
Henri Cartier-Bresson, *Cell of a Model Prison, U.S.A., 1975*
Normal Rockwell, *The Problem We All Live With*

* Fiction

"... we have not yet, as a society, begun to face the underlying ideas about class, race, children and above all, women that the new maternities rely on."

An American woman of Japanese parentage reflects on the internment of Japanese-Americans in 1942.

13 Identities

Anonymous, *Sapolio*
Dorothea Lange, *Grandfather and Grandchildren Awaiting Evacuation Bus*
Marion Post Wolcott, *Behind the Bar, Birney, Montana*
Grant Wood, *American Gothic*

Margaret Mead, Charlotte Perkins Gilman, Simone de Beauvoir, Heather Formaini, Israel Zangwill, Lawrence Fuchs, Theodore Roosevelt, Woodrow Wilson, Vladimir I. Lenin, Joyce Carol Oates, Martin Luther King, Jr.

A distinguished writer offers an answer to the male question, "What on earth do women want?"

On the "irrelevant and highly injurious" biological labeling of women and other disadvantaged groups.

"Every time a woman looks at her daughter and thinks, 'She can be anything,' she knows in her heart, from experience, that it's a lie."

"I was baffled when the women at college accused me and my sex of having cornered the world's pleasures."

"It is very hard to imagine any concept of manliness that does not belittle women."

** Poetry

14 Classic Essays

* Fiction
** Poetry

how they may make children "sound, useful members of the commonwealth."

The women at the 1848 Seneca Falls Convention adopt a new declaration, accusing men of failures and crimes parallel to those that led Jefferson in 1776 to denounce King George III.

A writer examines the effects of property on him.

Two obstacles women must confront on entering new professions

Being alone is not the same as being lonely.

An imprisoned civil rights leader argues that victims of unjust laws have the right to break those laws as long as they use nonviolent tactics.

A philosopher argues that we have no right to eat "pieces of slaughtered nonhuman" or to experiment on nonhumans "in order to benefit humanity."

Rhetorical Contents

Analogy

Analysis or Classification

Cause and Effect

Diction

Evaluation

Exposition

Irony

Narration

Style

Preface

Books have been put to all sorts of unexpected uses. Tolstoy used Tatishef's dictionaries as a test of physical endurance, holding them in his outstretched hand for five minutes, enduring "terrible pain." Books (especially pocket-sized Bibles) have served as armor by deflecting bullets. And they have served as weapons: two hundred years ago the formidable Dr. Johnson knocked a man down with a large book.

In a course in writing, what is the proper use of the book in hand? This anthology contains some one hundred and twenty essays, together with a few poems, stories, and fables, and numerous "Short Views," that is, paragraphs and aphorisms. But these readings are not the subject matter of the course; the subject matter of a writing course is writing, particularly the writing the students themselves produce. The responsibilities we felt as editors, then, were to include selections that encourage and enable students to write well, and to exclude selections that do not.

To talk of "enabling" first: Students, like all other writers, write best when they write on fairly specific topics that can come within their experience and within their command in the time that they have available to write. A glance at the first three thematic sections of our table of contents will reveal the general areas within which, we believe, students can find topics they have already given some thought to and are likely to be encountering in other courses as well: family relationships, love and courtship; schools; work, sports, and play.

Although the next two sections ("Open for Business" and "Messages") are also on familiar subjects—entrepreneurship, language, and popular culture—the selections themselves offer ways of thinking about these subjects that may be less familiar. Television commercials and films, for example, can be thought of as networks that articulate and transmit values implicit in a culture.

The next three sections are about areas of experience that, while hardly remote from students' interest, are perhaps more difficult for all of us to grasp concretely: the relationships between life and the arts; the tension between civil rights and liberties and the need for law and order; matters of gender and ethnic identity. In these sections, therefore, we have taken particular care to exclude writing that is, for our purposes, too abstract, or too technical, or too elaborate. Finally, we conclude with "Classic Essays," ranging from Jonathan Swift to Martin Luther King, Jr.

As editors we have tried to think carefully about whether selections we were inclined to use—because they were beautifully written or on a stimulating topic—would encourage students to write. Such encouragement does not come, we feel, solely from the subject of an essay or from its excellence; it comes when the essay engenders in the reader a confidence in the writing process itself. No one quality in essays automatically teaches such confidence: not length or brevity, not difficulty or simplicity, not necessarily clarity, and almost certainly not brilliance. But essays that teach writing demonstrate, in some way, that the writers had some stake in what they were saying, took some pains to say what they meant, and took pleasure in having said it. The selections we include vary in length, complexity, subtlety, tone, and purpose. Most were written by our contemporaries, but not all. The authors include historians, sociologists, scientists, saints, philosophers, and undergraduates, as well as journalists and other professional writers. And we have included some pictures in each section. The pictures (beautiful things in themselves, we think) provide immediate or nearly immediate experiences for students to write about. (Two essays about family photographs, written by students, give some indication of ways in which one can write about pictures.) But we hope that everything here will allow students to establish helpful connections between the activities that produced the words (and pictures) in these pages and their own work in putting critical responses to them on paper.

Although any arrangement of the selections—thematic, rhetorical, alphabetical, chronological, or random—would have suited our purposes, we prefer the thematic arrangement. For one thing, by narrowing our choices it helps us to make decisions. But more important, we know that in the real world what people write about is subjects, and we don't want to miss any opportunity to suggest that what goes on in writing courses is something like what goes on outside. The thematic categories are not intended to be rigid, however, and they do not pretend to be comprehensive; some of the questions following the selections suggest that leaping across boundaries is permitted, even encouraged. And, for instructors who prefer to organize their writing course rhetorically, we have added a selective table of contents organized rhetorically. Finally, we append a glossary of terms for students of writing.

A Note on the Seventh Edition

"Never read a book that is not old." Thus Emerson. It's good advice, but we are of course pleased that when *The Little, Brown Reader* was published it immediately found a receptive audience. Second, third, fourth, fifth, and sixth editions allowed us to strengthen the book by adding some recent essays, and now the publisher has asked for a seventh edition in order to meet the needs of instructors who wish to continue to use the book but who also want something new. William Hazlitt, Emerson's older contemporary, said that he always read an old book when a new one was published. We hope that this new edition allows instructors to read both at once. We have of course retained those essays and the special features (for example the headnotes and the Topics for Critical Thinking and Writing at the end of each essay) that in our experience and in the experience of many colleagues have consistently been of value to instructors and to students, and we have also added new material. To the introductory chapters on writing, for example, we have added a chapter on **"Writing an Argument,"** with brief argumentative essays—on bilingual education, school dress codes, and cultural criticism—for students to analyze and to argue with. We have also added a new chapter on **"Art and Life,"** including a small mini-research folder on whether the government should fund the arts. And within other thematic chapters, instructors will find many new readings.

Acknowledgments

As usual, we are indebted to readers-in-residence. Morton Berman, William Burto, and Judith Stubbs have often read our material and then told us what we wanted to hear.

We are grateful also to colleagues at other institutions who offered suggestions for the seventh edition:

Betty Bamberg	University of Southern California
Peggy F. Broder	Cleveland State University
Domenick Caruso	Kingsborough Community College
Benjamin A. L. Click III	Pennsylvania State University
Geraldine DeLuca	Brooklyn College
Joanna Gibson	Texas A&M University
Shelby Grantham	Dartmouth College
Douglas Hesse	Illinois State University
Cynthia Lee Katona	Ohlone College
Robert F. Lucid	University of Pennsylvania
Cecelia Martyn	Montclair State College
Anne Matthews	Princeton University

Lori Ann Miller   University of California/Irvine
Michael G. Moran   University of Georgia
Thomas E. Recchio   University of Connecticut
William E. Rivers   University of South Carolina
Don Share   Boston University
Ronald E. Smith   University of North Alabama
Carla J. Valley   University of Wisconsin-LaCrosse
Richard J. Zbaracki   Iowa State University

People at HarperCollins have been unfailingly helpful; we would especially like to thank Katharine H. Glynne and Patricia Rossi.

We are again indebted to Virginia Creeden, who effectively handled the difficult job of obtaining permission for copyrighted material.

We thank those instructors who generously offered suggestions based on their classroom experience with the first six editions: Bonnie Alexander, Kenneth Alrutz, Marianne Antczack, Norman Sidney Ashbridge, Andrew Aung, Donald Babcock, James Barcus, Lloyd Becker, Frank Bidart, Joseph Blimm, Frank Bliss, Beverly Boone, Grant Boswell, George Branam, Eric D. Brown, Lillian Broderick, Ruth Brown, Jean Young Brunk, Beth Burch, Debra L. Burgauet, Anne Burley, Carol Burns, D. G. Campbell, J. V. Chambers, John Clifford, Ann Connor, Anne Cooney, Kenneth Cooney, Marion Copeland, Robert Cosgrove, Helene Davis, Donald DeSulis, William Devlin, John A. R. Dick, Fiona Emde, Robert Erickson, Richard Fahey, Evelyn Farbman, Michael Feehan, Linda Feldmeier, Gretchen Fillmore, Sister Jeremy Finnegan, Kathleen P. Flint, Martha Flint, William Ford, Joseph S. Frany, James French, Charles Frey, Yvonne Frey, David Gadziola, George Griffith, George D. Haich, Steve Hamelman, Bettina Hanlon, Brian O. Hannon, Hymen H. Hart, Pat Hart, Steven Harvey, Mal Haslett, Stephen Hathaway, Mark Hawkins, George Hayhoe, Zelda Hedden-Sellman, Ruth C. Hage, Kathryn Hellerstein, Dr. Elbert R. Hill, Maureen Hoal, David Hoddeson, Kathryn Holms, John Howe, William Howrath, Morris Husted, Lois B. Janzer, Johanna Jung, F. A. Kachur, Michael Kalter, Robert D. Keohan, Richard Kirchoffer, Walt Klarner, Robert Knox, Karl Kumm, Sandra M. Lee, Dorinda Lemaire, Claudia Limbert, Joyce D. Lipkis, WilLiam E. Lucas, William Lutz, Celia Martin, Marie M. McAllister, Anne McCormich, Charles McLaughlin, Garry Meritt, George Miller, John Milstead, Mary F. Minton, Chris M. Mott, Abigail Mulcahy, John Nesselhof, Robert Ohafson, Terry Otten, Jewyl Pallette, Linda Pelzer, Richard Prince, Richard Priebe, Phyllis Reed, Karyn Riedell, Leo Rockas, Duncan Rollo, Harriet Rosenblum, Ronald Ruland, Ralph St. Louis, Jack Selzer, Mary Shesgreen, Emerson Shuck, Carol Sicherman, James Smith, Larry Smith, Mark Smith, Harry Solomon, John Stahl, Judith Stanford, Carol Starikoff, Petra Steele, William B. Stone, Mary Lee Strode, William L. Stull, Tereatha Taylor, David Templeman, Elizabeth Tentarelli, Robert

Thompson, Leatrice Timmons, Pamela Topping, Marilyn Valention, J. Keith Veizer, Harvey Vetstein, Brother Roland Vigeant, Lorraine Viscardi, Anthony Vital, Carolyn Wall, Don Wall, Doug Watson, Mary Weinkauf, Mark Wenz, Michael West, Richard Whitworth, Lyn Yonack, Lee Yosha, and Thomas Young.

We owe a special debt to Professor John Harwood and other teachers in the composition program at Pennsylvania State University for suggesting ways in which *The Little, Brown Reader* can be used in a course that emphasizes persuasive writing.

Marcia Stubbs
Sylvan Barnet

THE LITTLE, BROWN READER

Seventh Edition

1
A WRITER READS

One reads well only when one reads with some personal goal in mind. It may be to acquire some power. It may be out of hatred for the author.

Paul Valéry

Good writers are also good readers—of the works of other writers and of their own notes and drafts. The habits they develop as readers of others—for instance evaluating assumptions, scrutinizing arguments, and perceiving irony—empower them when they write, read, and revise their own notes and drafts. Because they themselves are readers, when they write they have a built-in awareness of how their readers might respond. They can imagine an audience, and they write almost as if in dialogue with it.

Active reading (which is what we are describing) involves writing at the outset: annotating a text by highlighting or underlining key terms, putting question marks or brief responses in the margin, writing notes in a journal. Such reading, as you already may have experienced, helps you first of all to understand a text, to get clear what the writer seems to intend. Later, skimming your own notes will help you to recall what you have read.

But active reading also gives you confidence as a writer. It helps you to treat your own drafts with the same respect and disrespect with which you read the work of others. To annotate a text or a draft is to respect it enough to give it serious attention, but it is also to question it, to assume that the text or draft is not the last word on the topic.

But let's start at the beginning.

Previewing

By *previewing* we mean getting a tentative fix on a text before reading it closely.

If you know something about the **author,** you probably already know something about a work even before you read the first paragraph. An essay by Martin Luther King Jr. will almost surely be a deeply serious discussion centering on civil rights, and, since King was a Baptist clergyman, it is likely to draw on traditional religious values. An essay by Woody Allen or one by Annie Dillard will almost surely differ from King's in topic and tone. Allen usually writes about the arts, especially the art of film, and Dillard writes highly personal meditations, often on the sacredness of nature. All three writers are serious (though Allen also writes comic pieces), but they are serious about different things and serious in different ways. We can read all three with interest, but when we begin with any one of them, we know we will get something very different from the other two.

2

King, Allen, and Dillard are exceptionally well known, but you can learn something about all of the authors represented in *The Little, Brown Reader* because they are introduced by means of biographical notes. Make it a practice to read these notes. They will give you some sense of what to expect. You may never have heard, for example, of J. H. Plumb, but when you learn from the note that he was a professor of history at the University of Cambridge and that he also taught in U. S. universities, you can tentatively assume that the essay will have an historical dimension. Of course, you may have to revise this assumption—the essay may be about the joys of trout fishing or the sorrows of being orphaned at an early age—but in all probability the biographical note will have given you some preparation for reading the essay.

The **original organ of publication** may also give you some sense of what the piece will be about. The essays in *The Little, Brown Reader* originally were published in books, magazines, or newspapers, and these sources (specified, when relevant, in the biographical notes) may in themselves provide a reader with clues. For instance, since *The American Scholar* is published by Phi Beta Kappa and is read chiefly by college and university teachers or by persons with comparable education, articles in *The American Scholar* usually offer somewhat academic treatments of serious matters. They assume that the readers are serious and capable of sustained intellectual effort. Whereas a newspaper editorial runs about one thousand words, articles in *The American Scholar* may be fifteen or so pages long.

Some journals have an obvious political slant, and the articles they publish are to some degree predictable in content and attitude. For instance, William Buckley's *National Review* is politically conservative. Its subscribers want to hear certain things, and *National Review* tells them what they want to hear. Its readers know, too, that the essays will be lively and can be read fairly rapidly. Similarly, subscribers to *Ms.* expect highly readable essays with a strong feminist slant. When *Ms.* published an essay called "Why I Want a Wife," the very title probably aroused the reader's suspicion. The suspicion was confirmed when the reader noted that the author is a woman, but if a reader missed this clue, the first paragraph indicates the author's satiric intent. (The essay is printed in this book, on page 129.)

The **form,** or **genre** (a literary term for type or kind of literature), may provide another clue as to what will follow. For instance, you can expect a letter to the editor to amplify or contradict an editorial or to comment approvingly or disapprovingly on some published news item. It will almost surely be concerned with a current issue. Martin Luther King Jr.'s "Letter from Birmingham Jail" a response to a letter from eight clergymen, is a famous example of a letter arguing on behalf of what was then a current action.

The **title,** as we have already noted, may provide a clue. Again, King provides an example; even before studying "I Have a Dream," a reader can assume that the essay will be about King's vision of the future. Other examples of titles that announce the topic are Alexandra Armstrong's "Starting a Business" and Paul Robinson's "TV Can't Educate." These titles are straightforward and informative, but suppose you pick up an essay called "Do-It-Yourself Brain Surgery." What do you already know about the essay?

Skimming

"Some books are to be tasted, others to be swallowed, and some few to be chewed and digested." You may already have encountered this wise remark by Francis Bacon, a very good reader (and a good writer, too—though he did not write Shakespeare's plays). The art of reading includes the art of skimming, that is, the art of gliding rapidly over a piece of writing and getting its gist.

Skimming has three important uses: to get through junk mail and other lightweight stuff; to locate what is relevant to your purpose in a mass of material, as, for instance, when you are working on a research paper; and (our topic now) to get an overview of an essay, especially to get the gist of its argument. Having discovered what you can from the name of the author, the title of the work, and the place of publication, you may want to skim the essay before reading it closely.

The **opening paragraph** will often give you a good idea of the **topic** or general area of the essay (for instance, the family). And if the essay is essentially an argument, it may announce the writer's **thesis,** the point that the writer will argue (for instance, that despite the high divorce rate, the family is still in good shape). Here is an example from Barbara Ehrenreich's "The 'Playboy' Man and the American Family." (The entire essay is printed later in this chapter.)

> As a scapegoat for social pathology, feminism ranks with creeping social-ism, godless atheism, and other well-known historic threats to public or-der. We have, in the last decade alone, been accused of causing male impo-tence, encouraging sexual perversity, and undermining our colorful national tradition of sex roles. In most cases, we're happy to take the credit, but there's one charge that can still make strong women cringe: the accusation that feminism "destroyed the family" or is deeply and wickedly "antifamily" even when we are talking about wholesome do-mestic issues like child care for working parents or who folds the clothes.

Now, this paragraph may cause some difficulties—a reader may, for instance, not be clear about the meaning of "social pathology" in the first sentence; but probably the gist is clear: because the charge that "feminism 'destroyed the family'" is so often made, it needs to be discussed. Taking the opening paragraph in connection with the title—"The 'Playboy' Man and the American Family"—a reader assumes that the essay will be concerned with the man's role in the destruction of the family. The thesis is not explicitly announced, but even a skimming of this paragraph may suggest to the reader that the writer will reject the charge against feminism.

If the first paragraph does not seem especially informative (it may be a sort of warmup, akin to the speechmaker's "A funny thing happened to me on my way here"), look closely at the second. Then, as you scan subsequent paragraphs, look especially for **topic sentences** (often the first sentence in a paragraph), which summarize the paragraph, and for passages that follow **key phrases** such as "the important point to remember," "these two arguments can be briefly put thus," "in short," "it is essential to recall," and so on. Ehrenreich's second paragraph, for instance, begins by saying "The real issue . . . is . . ." The **final paragraph** probably will reformulate the writer's thesis. When you read Ehrenreich's essay, you'll notice that her final paragraph begins thus:

> The problem, and it is a big one, is that men may have won their freedom before we win our battle against sexism.

Later, when you reread her essay carefully, you'll be on the lookout for the evidence that supports this view.

As you scan an essay, you'll find it useful to highlight phrases or sentences, or to draw vertical lines in the margin next to passages that seem to be especially concise bearers of meaning. In short, even while you are skimming you are using your pen.

If the essay is divided into sections, **headings** may give you an idea of the range of coverage. You probably won't need to highlight them—they already stand out—but there's no harm in doing so.

When you skim you are seeking to get the gist of the author's **thesis or point**. But you are also getting an idea of the author's **methods** and the author's **purpose.** For instance, skimming may reveal that the author is using statistics (or an appeal to common sense, or whatever) to set forth an unusual view. When Ehrenreich begins by saying that "feminism ranks with creeping socialism, godless atheism, and other well-known historic threats to public order," she is using sarcasm. Why is she using sarcasm? For at least two reasons: to ridicule the opposition and to entertain her readers. Skimming reveals Ehrenreich's **attitude** as well as her purpose and audience. It reveals that she is probably talking to an audience of like-minded people and is chiefly giving them encouragement to maintain their view.

Another author, however, may assume that the audience needs to be educated to the real facts. Such a writer will probably take less for granted—for instance, he or she will carefully define terms—and will take pains to seem to be scrupulously fair. Or skimming may reveal that the author is not especially concerned with persuading the reader but is more concerned with sharing an emotional experience.

During this preliminary trip through a piece of writing, you may also get some idea of the writer's personality. More precisely, since you are encountering not the writer in the flesh but only the image that the writer presents in the essay, you may form an impression of the **voice,** or **persona,** that speaks in the essay. Something of Ehrenreich's persona is evident in a line such as "feminism ranks with creeping socialism, godless atheism, and other well-known historic threats to public order," where we probably hear a tone of ridicule. We will return to this important matter later, on page 20.

Let's look at an essay by J. H. Plumb, who, as you already know, was a professor of history both in England and in the United States. We suggest that in your first reading you skim it—perhaps highlighting, underlining, or drawing vertical lines next to passages that strike you as containing the chief ideas. To this extent, you are reading for information. But because you have ideas of your own and because you do not accept something as true simply because it appears in print, you may also want to put question marks or expressions of doubt ("Really?" "Check this") in the margin next to any passages that strike you as puzzling. Further, you may want to circle any words that you are not familiar with, but at this stage don't bother to look them up. In short, run through the essay, seeking to get the gist and briefly indicating your responses, but don't worry about getting every detail of the argument.

J. H. Plumb

The Dying Family

I was rather astonished when a minibus drove up to my house and out poured ten children. They had with them two parents, but not one child had them both in common as mother and father, and two of them belonged to neither parent, but to a former husband of the wife who had died. Both parents, well into middle age, had just embarked, one on his fourth, the other on her third marriage. The children, who came in all sizes, and ranged from blonde nordic to jet-haired Greek, bounded around the garden, young and old as happy as any children that I have seen. To them, as Californians, their situation was not particularly odd; most of their friends had multiple parents. Indeed to them perhaps the odd family was the one which Western culture has held up as a model for two thousand years or more—the life-long union of man and wife. But it took me a very long time to believe that they could be either happy or adjusted. And yet, were they a sign of the future, a way the world was going?

Unlike anthropologists or sociologists, historians have not studied family life very closely. Until recently we knew very little of the age at which people married in Western Europe in the centuries earlier than the nineteenth or how many children they had, or what the rates of illegitimacy might be or whether, newly wed, they lived with their parents or set up a house of their own. Few of these questions can be answered with exactitude even now, but we can make better guesses. We know even less, however, of the detailed sexual practices that marriage covered: indeed this is a subject to which historians are only just turning their attention. But we do know much more of the function of family life—its social role—particularly if we turn from the centuries to the millennia and pay attention to the broad similarities rather than the fascinating differences between one region and another: and, if we do, we realize that the family has changed far more profoundly than ever the bus load of Californians might lead us to expect.

Basically the family has fulfilled three social functions—to provide a basic labor force, to transmit property and to educate and train children not only into an accepted social pattern, but also in the work skills upon which their future subsistence would depend. Until very recent times, the vast majority of children never went to any school: their school was the family, where they learned to dig and sow and reap and herd their animals, or they learned their father's craft of smith or carpenter or potter. The unitary family was particularly good at coping with the small peasant holdings which covered most of the world's fertile regions from China to Peru. In the primitive peasant world a child of four or five could begin to earn its keep in the fields, as they still can in India and Africa: and whether Moslem, Hindu, Inca or Christian, one wife at a time was all that the bulk of the world's population could support, even though their religion permitted them more. Indeed, it was the primitive nature of peasant economy which gave the family, as we know it, its wide diffusion and its remarkable continuity.

Whether or not it existed before the neolithic revolution we shall never know, but certainly it must have gained in strength as families became rooted to the soil. Many very primitive people who live in a pre-agrarian society of hunting and food-gathering often tend to have a looser structure of marriage and the women a far greater freedom of choice and easier divorce, as with the Esquimaux, than is permitted in peasant societies. There can be little doubt that the neolithic revolution created new opportunities for the family as we know it, partly because this revolution created new property relations. More importantly it created great masses of property, beyond anything earlier societies had known. True, there were a few hunting peoples, such as the Kwakiutl Indians, who had considerable possessions—complex lodges, great pieces of copper and piles of fibre blankets, which periodically they destroyed in great battles of raging pride—but the property, personal or communal, of most primitive hunting people is usually trivial.

After the revolution in agriculture, property and its transmission lay at the very heart of social relations and possessed an actuality which we find hard to grasp. Although we are much richer, possessions are more anonymous, often little more than marks in a ledger, and what we own constantly changes. Whereas for the majority of mankind over this last seven thousand years property has been deeply personal and familial: a plot of land, if not absolute ownership over it, then valuable rights in it; sometimes a house, even though it be a hovel by our standards; perhaps no more than the tools and materials of a craft, yet these possessions were the route both to survival and to betterment. Hence they were endowed with manna, bound up with the deepest roots of personality. In all societies the question of property became embedded in every aspect of family life, particularly marriage and the succession and rights of children. Because of property's vital importance, subservience of women and children to the will of the father, limited only by social custom, became the pattern of most great peasant societies. Marriage was sanctified not only by the rites of religion, but by the transmission of property. Few societies could tolerate freedom of choice in marriage—too much vital to the success or failure of a family depended on it: an ugly girl with five cows was a far fairer prospect than a pretty girl with one. And because of the sexual drives of frail human nature, the customs of marriage and of family relationships needed to be rigorously enforced. Tradition sanctified them; religion blessed them. Some societies reversed the sexually restrictive nature of permanent marriage and permitted additional wives, but such permission was meaningless to the mass of the peasantry who fought a desperate battle to support a single family. And, as we shall see, the patterns of family life were always looser for the rich and the favored.

But a family was always more than property expressed clearly and visibly in real goods; it was for thousands of years both a school and a tribunal, the basic unit of social organization whose function in modern society has been very largely taken over by the state. In most peasant societies, life is regulated by the village community, by the patriarchs of the village, and the only officer of the central government these villagers see with any regularity is the tax-gatherer; but in societies that have grown more complex, and this is particularly true of the West during the last four hundred years, life has become regulated by the nation state or by the growth in power and importance of more generalized local communities—the town or county.

This has naturally weakened the authority of heads of families, a fact that can be symbolically illustrated by change in social custom. No child in Western Europe would sit unbidden in the presence of its parents until the eighteenth century: if it did it could be sure of rebuke and punishment. No head of a household would have thought twice about beating a recalcitrant young servant or apprentice before the end of the nineteenth century. For a younger brother to marry without the consent of his eldest brother would have been regarded as a social enormity; and sisters were disposable property. All of this power has vanished.

Indeed the family ties of all of us have been so loosened that we find it hard to grasp the intensity of family relationships or their complexity, they have disintegrated so rapidly this last hundred years. Now nearly every child in the Western world, male or female, is educated outside the family from five years of age. The skills they learn are rarely, if ever, transmitted by parents: and what is more they learn about the nature of their own world, its social structure and its relationships in time outside the family. For millennia the family was the great transmitter and formulator of social custom; but it now only retains a shadow of this function, usually for very young children only.

Although the economic and education functions of the family have 8 declined, most of us feel that it provides the most satisfactory emotional basis for human beings; that a secure family life breeds stability, a capacity not only for happiness, but also to adjust to society's demands. This, too, may be based on misjudgment, for family life in the past was not remarkable for its happiness. We get few glimpses into the private lives of men and women long dead, but when we do we often find strain, frustration, petty tyranny. For so many human beings family life was a prison from which they could not escape. And although it might create deep satisfactions here and there, the majority of the rich and affluent classes of the last four hundred years in Western Europe created for themselves a double standard, particularly as far as sex was concerned. In a few cities such as Calvin's Geneva, the purity of family life might be maintained, but the aristocracies of France, Italy and Britain tolerated, without undue concern, adultery, homosexuality and that sexual freedom which, for better or worse, we consider the hallmark of modern life. Indeed the family as the basic social group began firstly to fail, except in its property relations, amongst the aristocracy.

But what we think of as a social crisis of this generation—the rapid growth of divorce, the emancipation of women and adolescents, the sexual and educational revolutions, even the revolution in eating which is undermining the family as the basis of nourishment, for over a hundred years ago the majority of Europeans never ate in public in their lives—all of these things, which are steadily making the family weaker and weaker, are the inexorable result of the changes in society itself. The family as a unit of social organization was remarkably appropriate for a less complex world of agriculture and craftsmanship, a world which stretches back some seven thousand years, but ever since industry and highly urbanized societies began to take its place, the social functions of the family have steadily weakened—and this is a process that is unlikely to be halted. And there is no historical reason to believe that human beings could be less or more happy, less or more stable. Like any other human institution the family has always been molded by the changing needs of society, sometimes slowly, sometimes fast. And that bus load of children does no more than symbolize the failure, not of marriage, but of the role of the old-fashioned family unit in a modern, urbanized, scientific and affluent society.

Even a quick skimming reveals that Plumb offers, as you anticipated he would, a historical view. He begins with a glance at one contemporary family, but you probably noticed that by the second paragraph he speaks as a historian, tracing the origins and development of the institution of the family.

Highlighting, Underlining, Annotating

Now that you have the gist of Plumb's essay, go back and reread it; this time, highlight or underline key passages as though you were marking the text so that you might later easily review it for an examination. Your purpose now is simply to make sure that you know what Plumb is getting at. You may strongly disagree with him on details or even on large matters, and you would certainly make clear your differences with him if you were to write about his essay; but for the moment your purpose is to make sure that you know what his position is. See if in each paragraph you can find a sentence that contains the topic idea of the paragraph. If you find such sentences, mark them.

Caution: Do not allow yourself to highlight or underline whole paragraphs. Before you start to mark a paragraph, read it to the end, and then go back and mark what you now see as the key word, phrase, or passage. If you simply start marking a paragraph from the beginning, you may end up marking the whole; and thus you will defeat your purpose which is to make highly visible the basic points of the essay.

You may also want to jot down, in the margins, questions or objections and you may want to circle any words that puzzle you.

Time's up. Let's talk about the underlinings and highlightings.

No two readers of the essay will make exactly the same annotations. To take a small example, a reader in Alaska would probably be more likely to mark the passage about "the Esquimaux" in paragraph 4 than would a reader in St Louis, but here is what one reader produced.

note first person ⟨I⟩was rather astonished when a minibus drove up to my house and out poured <u>ten children</u>. They had with them two parents, but <u>not one child had them both</u> <u>in common as mother and father</u>, and two of them be- *new (California) style* longed to neither parent, but to a former husband of the wife who had died. Both parents, well into middle age, had just embarked, one on his fourth, the other on her third marriage. The children, who came in all sizes, and ranged from blonde nordic to jet-haired Greek, bounded around the garden, young and old as happy as any children that (I) have seen. To them, as Californians, their situation was not particularly odd; most of their friends had multiple parents. Indeed to them perhaps the odd family was the one which Western culture has held up as a model for two thousand years or more—the lifelong union of man and wife. But it took me a very long time to believe that they could be either happy or adjusted. And yet, were they a sign of the future, a way the world was going?

old style

who says they are happy?

Unlike anthropologists or sociologists, (historians) have not studied family life very closely. Until recently we knew very little of the age at which people married in Western Europe in the centuries earlier than the nineteenth or how many children they had, or what the rates of illegitimacy might be or whether, newly wed, they lived with their parents or set up a house of their own. Few of these questions can be answered with exactitude even now, but we can make better guesses. We know even less, however, of the detailed sexual practices that marriage covered: indeed this is a subject to which historians are only just turning their attention. But we do know much more of the function of family life—its social role—particularly if we turn from the centuries to the millennia and pay attention to the broad similarities rather than the fascinating differences between one region and another: and, if we do, we realize that the family has changed far more profoundly than even the bus load of Californians might lead us to expect.

first person again, but less "personal"

change

Basically the family has fulfilled three social functions—to provide a basic labor force, to transmit property and to educate and train children not only into an accepted social pattern, but also in the work skills upon which their future subsistence would depend. Until very recent times, the vast majority of children never went to any school: their school was the family, where they learned to dig and sow and reap and herd their animals, or they learned their father's craft of smith or carpenter or potter. The (unitary) family was particularly good at coping with the small peasant holdings which covered most of the world's fertile regions from China to Peru. In the primitive peasant world a child of four or five could begin to earn its keep in the fields, as they still can in India and Africa; and whether Moslem, Hindu, Inca or Christian,

3 functions

1. provides labor

2. transmits property

3. educates children

?

one wife at a time was all that the bulk of the world's *? couldn't wives earn their keep?*
population could support, even though their religion
permitted them more. Indeed, it was the primitive nature of peasant economy which gave the family, as we
know it, its wide diffusion and its remarkable continuity.

not also religious teachings?

Whether or not it existed before the neolithic revo- *?*
lution we shall never know, but certainly it must have
gained in strength as families became rooted to the soil.
Many very primitive people who live in a pre-agrarian
society of hunting and food-gathering often tend to
have a looser structure of marriage and the women a
far greater freedom of choice and easier divorce, as with
the Esquimaux, than is permitted in peasant societies.
There can be little doubt that the neolithic revolution
created new opportunities for the family as we know
it, partly because this revolution created new property
relations. More importantly it created great masses
of property, beyond anything earlier societies had
known. True, there were a few hunting peoples, such
as the Kwakiutl Indians, who had considerable possessions—complex lodges, great pieces of copper
and piles of fibre blankets, which periodically they destroyed in great battles of raging pride—but the
property, personal or communal, of most primitive
hunting people is usually trivial.

Of course different readers will find different passages of special interest and importance. Our personal histories, our beliefs, our preconceptions, our current preoccupations, to some extent determine how we
read. For instance, when they come to the fifth paragraph some readers
may mark Plumb's sexist language ("mankind"), and some may highlight the assertion that "Marriage was sanctified not only by the rites of
religion, but by the transmission of property." Readers who are especially interested in class relations might also highlight and underline
this sentence:

The patterns of family life were always looser for the rich and the favored.

Notice, by the way, that although Plumb makes this assertion he does
not offer a value judgment. A reader might mark the sentence and add
in the margin: *Still true, and outrageous!* Or, conversely, a reader may feel
that the statement is false, and might write, *Really???*, or even *Not the
rich, but the poor (free from bourgeois hangups) are sexually freer.*

As these last examples indicate, even when you simply set out to
make a few notes that will help you to follow and to remember the
essayist's argument, you may well find yourself making notes that
record your **responses** (where you agree, what you question), notes
that may start you thinking about the validity of the argument.

As we have already said, *what* you annotate will partly depend on what interests you, what your values are, and what your purpose is. True, you have read the essay because it was assigned, but Plumb's original readers read it for other reasons. It appeared first in a magazine and then in a collection of Plumb's essays. The original readers, then, were people who freely picked it up because they wanted to learn about the family or perhaps because they had read something else by Plumb, liked it, and wanted to hear more from this author.

Imagine yourself, for a moment, as a reader encountering this essay in a magazine that you have picked up. If you are reading because you want to know something about the family in an agrarian society, you'll annotate one sort of thing; if you are reading because as a child of divorced parents you were struck and possibly outraged by his first paragraph, you'll annotate another sort of thing; if you are reading because you admire Plumb as a historian, you'll annotate another sort of thing; and if you are reading because you dislike Plumb, you'll annotate something else. We remind you of a comment by Paul Valéry, quoted at the beginning of this chapter: "One reads well only when one reads with some quite personal goal in mind. It may be to acquire some power. It can be out of hatred for the author." An exaggeration, of course, but there is something to it. (In the Book of Job, Job wishes that his "adversary had written a book.")

Summarizing and Outlining

In your effort to formulate a brief version of what an essayist is saying, you may want to write a summary, especially if you found the essay difficult. A good way to begin is to summarize each paragraph in a sentence or two, or in some phrases. By summarizing each paragraph, you compile—without doing any additional work—an outline of the essay. Here is a student's outline of Plumb's essay.

```
1.    Minibus in California: 10 children and 2 parents,
      but not one child was child of both adults. Differ-
      ent from traditional family. Sign of the way the
      world is going.
2.    Many things not known about the past (age of mar-
      riage, sexual practices), but something known of
      the function of family life.
3.    Three functions: providing a labor force, transmit-
      ting property, educating and training children.
      Peasant families today.
4, 5. After neolithic (agricultural?) revolution, family
      strengthened because people rooted to the soil
      (produced masses of property: land, house, or tools
```

```
                of a craft). Transmission of property sanctified
                marriage.
6, 7.  Family was also school and basic social unit. Head
                of the household ruled (chose the mate for a child,
                etc.). In modern societies government has taken
                over many functions of patriarchs.
8.     Despite loss of functions, most of us still feel
                that a family breeds stability, happiness. May be a
                misjudgment; family often was a prison. And for
                last 400 years the rich created a double standard,
                at least for sex.
9.     Decline of family (divorce, emancipation of women
                and adolescents, etc.) is result of historic change
                in society itself. Family appropriate for agricul-
                tural society but less in industrial and urban so-
                cieties. Busload of kids symbolizes not the failure
                of marriage but the loss of role for old-fashioned
                family in a modern society.
```

Especially if an essay is complex, writing a summary of this sort can help you to follow the argument. Glancing over your notes, you probably can see, fairly easily, what the writer's *main* points are, as distinct from the *subordinate* points and the examples that clarify the points. Furthermore, since your summary is now a paragraph outline, you can look it over to see not only what it adds up to, but also how the writer shaped the material. Producing a summary, then, may be an activity that is useful to you when you are *reading* an essay. It will almost surely help you to grasp the essay and to remember its argument. And if you are *writing* about the essay—perhaps to take issue with it or to amplify a point that it makes—you may have to include in your essay a brief summary so that your readers will know what you are writing about.

How long should the summary be? Just long enough to give readers what they need in order to follow your essay. If in a fairly long essay you are going to take issue with several of Plumb's points, you may want to give a fairly detailed summary—perhaps a page long.

For a short essay, however, something like the following passage might be appropriate:

```
     In "The Dying Family," J. H. Plumb argues that when
society was primarily agricultural, the family provided
education and training, a labor force, and a way of
transmitting property. In today's industrialized society,
however, these functions are largely provided by the gov-
ernment, and the traditional family is no longer func-
tional.
```

(For further discussion of summaries, see the entry on pages 801–02 of this book, in "A Writer's Glossary.")

Questioning the Text

We have already said that you will probably find yourself putting question marks in the margins next to words that you don't know and that don't become clear in the context, and next to statements that you find puzzling or dubious. These marks will remind you to take action—perhaps to check a dictionary, to reread a paragraph, or to jot down your objection in the margin or at greater length in a journal.

But analytic readers also engage in another sort of questioning, though they may do so almost unconsciously. They are almost always asking themselves—or rather asking the text— several questions. You'll notice that these questions concern not only the writer's point but also the writer's craft. By asking such questions, you will learn about subject matter (for instance, about the history of the family in Plumb's essay) and also about some of the tricks of the writer's trade (for instance, effective ways of beginning). If you read actively, asking the following questions, you will find that reading is *not* a solitary activity; you are conversing with a writer.

- What is the writer's thesis?
- How does the writer support the thesis?
- What is the writer's purpose (to persuade, to rebut, to entertain, to share an experience, or whatever)?
- How do the writer's audience and purpose help shape the writing? (The place of publication is often a clue to the audience.) For instance, does the writer use humor or, on the other hand, speak earnestly? Are terms carefully defined, or does the writer assume that the audience is knowledgeable and does not need such information?
- What is the writer's tone?

These questions will help you to understand what you are reading and how writers go about their business. But you are also entitled to evaluate what you are reading, hence some other questions, of a rather different sort:

- How successful is the piece? What are its strengths and weaknesses? What do I especially like or dislike about it? Why?

We recommend that when you read an essay you ask each of these questions—not, of course, during an initial skimming, but during a second and third reading, after you have some sense of the essay.

These questions almost can be boiled down to one question:

What is the writer up to?

That is, a reader who is not content merely to take what the writer is handing out asks such questions as, Why *this* way of opening? Why *this* way of defining the term? Of course, the assumption that the writer has a purpose may be false. (We are reminded of a comment that Metternich, the keenly analytic Austrian statesman and diplomat, uttered when he learned that the Czar had died: "I wonder why he did that.") Yes, the writer may just be blundering along, but it's reasonable to begin with the assumption that the writer is competent. If under questioning the writer fails, you have at least learned that not everything in print is worthy.

A Second Essay

Let's look at the whole of an essay we excerpted earlier, "The 'Playboy' Man and the American Family," by Barbara Ehrenreich, coauthor of *Remaking Love* and author of *The Hearts of Men: American Dreams and the Flight from Commitment*. The essay first appeared in *Ms.* in June 1983. (You'll notice that some of the statistics are out of date, especially the statement in paragraph 8 that women's earnings average only a little more than $10,000 a year.) We suggest that you read it once straight through to get the gist and then reread it carefully, highlighting or underlining key passages and jotting queries and comments in the margins or on a piece of paper. And then, either to clarify your understanding of the essay or simply as an exercise, write a summary of each paragraph.

Barbara Ehrenreich

The "Playboy" Man and the American Family

As a scapegoat for social pathology, feminism ranks with creeping socialism, godless atheism, and other well-known historic threats to public order. We have, in the last decade alone, been accused of causing male impotence, encouraging sexual perversity, and undermining our colorful national tradition of sex roles. In most cases, we're happy to take the credit, but there's one charge that can still make strong women cringe: the accusation that feminism "destroyed the family" or is deeply and wickedly "antifamily" even when we are talking about wholesome domestic issues like child care for working parents or who folds the clothes.

The real issue in the debate over the family, it turns out, is *marriage* (heterosexual, monogamous, and so on), and when the critics charge feminists with being "antifamily," they mean we are responsible for "broken" homes, the 50 percent divorce rate, unwed mothers, and sometimes the entire "me generation."

The notion that women, and feminists in particular, have been waging war on matrimony departs so far from common experience and cultural memory as to deserve the status of whimsy. True, many women initiate divorces, and not only because their husbands are drunks and batterers. True, too, that a few brave women, from Emma Goldman on, have taken a principled stand against marriage as an unwelcome intrusion of government into their private lives. But the truth is that if either sex has been in revolt against marriage, it is men, and that the male revolt against marriage started long before our own rebellion as feminists.

When I was growing up in the 1950s, male hostility to marriage and the responsibilities of breadwinning was an accepted fact of life. In the comics, Daisy Mae kept in training all year to catch L'il Abner on Sadie Hawkins Day, and poor, beaten-down Dagwood slaved away at the office to keep Blondie supplied with new hats. From a male perspective, which was pretty much the only one around, marriage was a "trap" for men and a lifelong sinecure for women. Even after they were "caught," men tried to escape in minor ways—into baseball, golf, hunting, bowling, poker games, or the ideal, female-free world of Westerns.   4

This flight from "maturity," as concerned psychiatrists dubbed it, is one of the most venerable themes in American literary culture. In American mythic tradition, women are the civilizers and entrappers; men the footloose adventurers. Our heroes chase across the sea after great white whales, raft down the Mississippi, or ride off into the sunset on horseback. Cooper's *Deerslayer* traveled light; Davy Crockett didn't fuss over mortgage payments; and Rip Van Winkle, not quite so enterprising, went to sleep for 20 years to escape a nagging wife.

But it was in the 1950s that male hostility to marriage began to take a more urgent and articulate tone. There were low rumblings against gray-flannel "conformity"—a code word for male acquiescence to marriage and breadwinning—but in an America that was busily purging itself of Communists, bohemians, and similar deviants, no viable alternative was offered. Until Hugh Hefner's *Playboy*, which began publication in 1953. From the first feature article in the very first issue, *Playboy*'s writers railed against "gold-digging women"—wives, ex-wives, and would-be wives—all of them bent on crushing "man's adventurous, freedom-loving spirit." Marriage was an "estate in which the sexes . . . live half-slave and half-free," the slave-half being, of course, the husbands who toiled away while their wives spent their time "relaxing, reading, watching TV, playing cards, socializing. . . ." No man had to put up with this, *Playboy* told its readers: Why sign on for a life contract with one woman when there were so many Bunnies to sample? Why settle for "conformity, togetherness . . . and slow death" when you could have a bachelor apartment, a stereo, and a life of sybaritic thrills? By 1956, nearly a million loyal male readers were getting this manifesto of the male revolt.

All this, I emphasize, was going on at a time when there were fewer open feminists in the entire land than there are today in, say, the executive ranks of the Mormon Church. Married women by the thousands felt trapped and desperate too, but they weren't seething with a subversive zeal to "destroy the family" or smash the institution of marriage. In fact, when it came to marriage, Hefner was the radical; Friedan the conservative. Her manifesto of female discontent (*The Feminine Mystique*, published a full 10 years after the first issue of *Playboy*) argued that wider opportunities for women would strengthen marriage, since divorce reflected "the growing aversion and hostility that men have for the feminine millstones hanging around their necks. . . ." Friedan, and most of the feminists who followed, wanted a more equal, companionate marriage; Hefner and his followers simply wanted *out*.

There should be no mystery why, over the years, women have had 8 a disproportionate investment in marriage. Women's earnings average out to a little more than $10,000 a year each—nowhere near enough to support a single in a swinging lifestyle, much less a single mother and her children. For most women, the obvious survival strategy has been to establish a claim on some man's more generous wage, i.e., to marry him. For men, on the other hand, as *Playboy*'s writers clearly saw, the reverse is true: not counting love, home-cooked meals, or other benefits of the married state, it makes more sense for a man to keep his paycheck for himself, rather than sharing it with an underpaid or unemployed woman and her no doubt unemployed children. A recent study by Stanford University sociologist Lenore J. Weitzman suggests the magnitude of men and women's divergent interests: upon divorce, a woman's standard of living falls, on the average, by 73 percent for the first year, while the standard of living of her ex-husband *rises* by 42 percent. For men, the alternative to marriage might be loneliness and TV dinners; for women it is, all too often, poverty.

By the standards of the 1950s, today's men are in many respects "free" at last: 7.3 million of them live alone (nearly half of them in the "never married" category) compared to 3.5 million in 1970. (The number of women living alone has also increased, but at a much lower rate, because single women are far more likely to live with children than single men.) If a man remains single until he is 28 or even 38, he may be criticized by girlfriends for his "fear of commitment," but he will no longer be suspected of an unhealthy attachment to his mother or a latent tendency to you-know-what. If he divorces his middle-aged wife for some sweet young thing, he may be viewed not as a traitor to the

American way, but as a man who has a demonstrated capacity for "growth."

At the risk of sounding "antifamily," I must say that I do not think these changes, and the male revolt that inspired them, are an altogether bad thing. As feminists, we have always stood for men's as well as for women's liberation, which includes their right to be something other than husbands and breadwinners. As my son's mother, I know that I want him to grow up to be a loving and responsible adult, but I also know that it would be heartbreaking to see him "tied down," as the expression goes, to a lifetime of meaningless, uncreative jobs in order to support a family. So my purpose in recalling the recent history of men's revolt is not to say, "So there, blame *them*!"

The problem, and it is a big one, is that men may have won their freedom before we win our battle against sexism. Women might like to be free-spirited adventurers too, but the female equivalent of "playboy" does not work well in a culture still riddled with misogyny. We still earn less than men, whether or not we have men to help support us. Which is only to say that the feminist agenda is as urgent as ever, and those who are concerned about "the family" should remember that we—and our sisters and daughters and mothers—are members of it also.

Let's assume that you have read Ehrenreich's essay at least twice and that you have written a paragraph outline. You'll recall that earlier we suggested a reader may profitably put certain questions to the text. Here, again, are those questions.

- What is the writer's thesis?
- How does the writer support the thesis?
- What is the writer's purpose (to persuade, to rebut, to entertain, to share an experience, or whatever)?
- How does the writer shape the purpose to the audience? (The place of publication is often a clue to the audience.) Does the writer use humor, or on the other hand does the writer speak earnestly? Are terms carefully defined, or does the writer assume that the audience is knowledgeable and does not need elementary information?
- What is the writer's tone?
- How successful is the piece? What are its strengths and weaknesses? What do I especially like or dislike about it?

Here are a few additional questions, which this time specifically refer to Ehrenreich's essay. You might jot down your responses and later compare them with those of another reader.

- *Ms.*, in which this essay originally appeared, addresses primarily women's issues. Is Ehrenreich's tone hospitable to male readers as well? Or is she likely to offend them?
- Ehrenreich calls attention to the hostility to marriage displayed in comic strips and in *Playboy*. Do you think that such writings are to be taken seriously, or are they merely harmless jokes? On what do you base your response?
- Reread the essay closely and jot down some brief notes concerning the precautions Ehrenreich takes to make her position appear reasonable. If you can't find such material, do you regard her position as unreasonable?

If there are fundamental differences between your responses and those of a classmate, try to account for them. (The differences are probably due to your different personalities and interests, but you may find that you have fewer disagreements after discussion.)

A Note about Tone and Persona

Perhaps you know the line from Owen Wister's novel, *The Virginian*: "When you call me that, smile." Words spoken with a smile mean something different from the same words spoken through clenched teeth. But while speakers can communicate by facial gestures, body language, and changes in tone of voice, writers have only words in ink on paper. Somehow the writer has to help us to know whether, for instance, he or she is solemn or joking or joking in earnest.

Consider again the first paragraph of Barbara Ehrenreich's "The 'Playboy' Man and the American Family":

> As a scapegoat for social pathology, feminism ranks with creeping socialism, godless atheism, and other well-known historic threats to public order. We have, in the last decade alone, been accused of causing male impotence, encouraging sexual perversity, and undermining our colorful national tradition of sex roles. In most cases, we're happy to take the credit, but there's one charge that can still make strong women cringe: the accusation that feminism "destroyed the family" or is deeply and wickedly "antifamily" even when we are talking about wholesome domestic issues like child care for working parents or who folds the clothing.

Let's look at this paragraph, sentence by sentence. Ehrenreich *could* have begun,

> It is the view of some people that feminism is no less a cause of evils in our society than is a tendency toward socialism, the loss of religious faith, and other forces that in the course of history have caused harm to the commonweal.

Notice, for a start, the difference between "feminism is no less a cause . . . than is . . ." and Ehrenreich's "feminism ranks with . . ." The verb *ranks* gives her version an energy that the revision, with its colorless *is*, does not have.

The colorless or, we might say, voiceless revision is perhaps something that a reader might encounter in a sociology textbook, but it is not the sort of writing that people willingly read. What are some things that can be said about the voice evident in the original paragraph?

- The words *social pathology* (roughly, diseases of society) indicate an educated speaker, someone familiar with academic language. The terms *creeping socialism* and *godless atheism* are clichés, words used in past decades by right-wing journalists and speakers. We might for a moment be surprised to find these canned terms in the mouth of an academic speaker, until we realize that they are used jokingly. Since *Ms.* is, roughly speaking, a liberal publication (at least so far as right-wingers see it), the words must be used ironically. In fact, even if the essay had not appeared in *Ms.,* a reader would know that the writer was being ironic; anyone who today uses these old-fashioned words must be speaking with tongue in cheek.

- In the second sentence when the speaker says "We have . . . been accused," by *we* she of course means women who are feminists—women such as those who read *Ms.*—and so she is establishing a comforting bond between herself and her readers. This bond is strengthened when she lists the (in her view) absurd charges that she and her readers have been accused of—causing "male impotence, [and] encouraging sexual perversity. . . ." In the words "undermining our colorful national tradition of sex roles" we again hear irony, for feminists find conventional American sex roles oppressive rather than "colorful."

- In the third sentence, in simple and direct language the speaker further emphasizes the bond with her feminist readers ("In most cases, we're happy to take the credit"), but she also jokes a bit. When she says that one accusation "can still make strong women cringe," she is playfully using a cliché commonly used of men ("can make strong men cringe"). But by the end of the paragraph she makes it clear that, for all of her joking, she is serious about serious matters, such as "child care for working parents."

What sort of person is Ms. Ehrenreich? Or, more accurately, what sort of persona does she convey in the essay? (As a person she presumably is many things. She may, for instance, be a loving parent, a careful editor of other people's prose, a good—or a bad—cook, and so on. Since we don't know her, we can't presume to say what sort of person she may be, but we can say what sort of *persona* she conveys in the essay.) But first, how do readers form an impression of a persona? By listening, so to speak, with a third ear, listening for the writer's attitude toward: 1) himself or herself, 2) the subject, and 3) the audience. Still, different readers will, of course, respond differently. To take a simple example, readers who do not wish to hear arguments criticizing certain male attitudes will almost surely find the writer of the essay unfair, unwomanly, naive, crude, hysterical, or all of the above. But we think that most readers will agree with us in saying that Ehrenreich conveys the persona of someone who is: 1) educated, 2) at least moderately witty, 3) not inclined to put up with nonsense, and 4) eager to address an important issue. It's our guess, too, that Ehrenreich hoped to be seen as this sort of person. If readers of her first paragraph conclude that she is conceited, unfunny, hostile to all men, a liberal who doesn't know what she is talking about, a threat to society, and so on, she has failed terribly, because she has turned her readers away.

There is a lesson for writers, too. When you reread your own drafts and essays, try to get out of yourself and into the mind of an imagined reader, say a classmate. Try to hear how your words will sound in this other person's ear; that is, try to imagine what impression this reader will form of your attitude toward yourself, your subject, and your reader.

2
A READER WRITES

All there is to writing is having ideas. To learn to write is to learn to have ideas.

Robert Frost

So far, the only writing that we have suggested you do is in the form of annotating, summarizing, and responding to some basic and some specific questions about the essayist's thesis and methods. All of these activities help you to think about what you are reading. "It is thinking," the philosopher John Locke wrote, "that makes what we read ours." But, of course, ultimately your thoughts will manifest themselves in your own essays, which probably will take off from one or more of the essays that you have read. Before we discuss writing about more than one essay, let's look at another essay, this one by C. S. Lewis (1898–1963).

Lewis taught English literature at Oxford and at Cambridge, but he is most widely known not for his books on literature but for his books on Christianity (*The Screwtape Letters* is one of the most famous), his children's novels (collected in a seven-volume set called *The Chronicles of Narnia*), and his science fiction (for instance, *Perelandra*). Lewis also wrote autobiographical volumes and many essays on literature and on morality. The essay printed here—the last thing that he wrote—was published in *The Saturday Evening Post* in December 1963, shortly after his death.

C. S. Lewis

We Have No "Right to Happiness"

After all," said Clare, "they had a right to happiness."

We were discussing something that once happened in our own neighborhood. Mr. A. had deserted Mrs. A. and got his divorce in order to marry Mrs. B., who had likewise got her divorce in order to marry Mr. A. And there was certainly no doubt that Mr. A. and Mrs. B. were very much in love with one another. If they continued to be in love, and if nothing went wrong with their health or their income, they might reasonably expect to be very happy.

It was equally clear that they were not happy with their old partners. Mrs. B. had adored her husband at the outset. But then he got smashed up in the war. It was thought he had lost his virility, and it was known that he had lost his job. Life with him was no longer what Mrs. B. had bargained for. Poor Mrs. A., too. She had lost her looks—and all her liveliness. It might be true, as some said, that she consumed herself by bearing his children and nursing him through the long illness that overshadowed their earlier married life.

You mustn't, by the way, imagine that A. was the sort of man who   4
nonchalantly threw a wife away like the peel of an orange he'd sucked dry. Her suicide was a terrible shock to him. We all knew this, for he told us so himself. "But what could I do?" he said. "A man has a right to happiness. I had to take my one chance when it came."

I went away thinking about the concept of a "right to happiness."

At first this sounds to me as odd as a right to good luck. For I believe—whatever one school of moralists may say—that we depend for a very great deal of our happiness or misery on circumstances outside all human control. A right to happiness doesn't, for me, make much more sense than a right to be six feet tall, or to have a millionaire for your father, or to get good weather whenever you want to have a picnic.

I can understand a right as a freedom guaranteed me by the laws of the society I live in. Thus, I have a right to travel along the public roads because society gives me that freedom; that's what we mean by calling the roads "public." I can also understand a right as a claim guaranteed me by the laws, and correlative to an obligation on someone else's part. If I have a right to receive £100 from you, this is another way of saying that you have a duty to pay me £100. If the laws allow Mr. A. to desert his wife and seduce his neighbor's wife, then, by definition, Mr. A. has a legal right to do so, and we need bring in no talk about "happiness."

But of course that was not what Clare meant. She meant that he had   8
not only a legal but a moral right to act as he did. In other words, Clare is—or would be if she thought it out—a classical moralist after the style of Thomas Aquinas, Grotius, Hooker and Locke. She believes that behind the laws of the state there is a Natural Law.[1]

I agree with her. I hold this conception to be basic to all civilization. Without it, the actual laws of the state become an absolute, as in Hegel. They cannot be criticized because there is no norm against which they should be judged.

The ancestry of Clare's maxim, "They have a right to happiness," is august. In words that are cherished by all civilized men, but especially by Americans, it has been laid down that one of the rights of man is a right to "the pursuit of happiness." And now we get to the real point.

What did the writers of that august declaration mean?

---

[1]**Thomas Aquinas ... Natural Law** Lewis names some philosophers and theologians from the thirteenth through the eighteenth century who believed that certain basic moral principles are evident to rational people in all periods and in all cultures. (Editors' note)

It is quite certain what they did not mean. They did not mean that   12
man was entitled to pursue happiness by any and every means—
including, say, murder, rape, robbery, treason and fraud. No society
could be built on such a basis.

They meant "to pursue happiness by all lawful means"; that is, by
all means which the Law of Nature eternally sanctions and which the
laws of the nation shall sanction.

Admittedly this seems at first to reduce their maxim to the tautology that men (in pursuit of happiness) have a right to do whatever they
have a right to do. But tautologies, seen against their proper historical
context, are not always barren tautologies. The declaration is primarily
a denial of the political principles which long governed Europe: a challenge flung down to the Austrian and Russian empires, to England
before the Reform Bills, to Bourbon France.[2] It demands that whatever
means of pursuing happiness are lawful for any should be lawful for
all; that "man," not men of some particular caste, class, status or religion, should be free to use them. In a century when this is being unsaid
by nation after nation and party after party, let us not call it a barren
tautology.

But the question as to what means are "lawful"—what methods of
pursuing happiness are either morally permissible by the Law of
Nature or should be declared legally permissible by the legislature of a
particular nation—remains exactly where it did. And on that question I
disagree with Clare. I don't think it is obvious that people have the
unlimited "right to happiness" which she suggests.

For one thing, I believe that Clare, when she says "happiness,"   16
means simply and solely "sexual happiness." Partly because women
like Clare never use the word "happiness" in any other sense. But also
because I never heard Clare talk about the "right" to any other kind.
She was rather leftist in her politics, and would have been scandalized
if anyone had defended the actions of a ruthless man-eating tycoon on
the ground that his happiness consisted in making money and he was
pursuing his happiness. She was also a rabid teetotaler; I never heard
her excuse an alcoholic because he was happy when he was drunk.

A good many of Clare's friends, and especially her female friends,
often felt—I've heard them say so—that their own happiness would be
perceptibly increased by boxing her ears. I very much doubt if this
would have brought her theory of a right to happiness into play.

Clare, in fact, is doing what the whole western world seems to me
to have been doing for the last forty-odd years. When I was a youngster, all the progressive people were saying, "Why all this prudery? Let

---

[2]**England . . . France** England before the bills that liberalized representation in Parliament
in the nineteenth century, and France before the French Revolution of 1789–99 (Editors'
note)

us treat sex just as we treat all our other impulses." I was simple-minded enough to believe they meant what they said. I have since discovered that they meant exactly the opposite. They meant that sex was to be treated as no other impulse in our nature has ever been treated by civilized people. All the others, we admit, have to be bridled. Absolute obedience to your instinct for self-preservation is what we call cowardice; to your acquisitive impulse, avarice. Even sleep must be resisted if you're a sentry. But every unkindness and breach of faith seems to be condoned provided that the object aimed at is "four bare legs in a bed."

It is like having a morality in which stealing fruit is considered wrong—unless you steal nectarines.

And if you protest against this view you are usually met with chatter about the legitimacy and beauty and sanctity of "sex" and accused of harboring some Puritan prejudice against it as something disreputable or shameful. I deny the charge. Foam-born Venus . . . golden Aphrodite . . . Our Lady of Cyprus[3] . . . I never breathed a word against you. If I object to boys who steal my nectarines, must I be supposed to disapprove of nectarines in general? Or even of boys in general? It might, you know, be stealing that I disapproved of.   20

The real situation is skillfully concealed by saying that the question of Mr. A.'s "right" to desert his wife is one of "sexual morality." Robbing an orchard is not an offense against some special morality called "fruit morality." It is an offense against honesty. Mr. A.'s action is an offense against good faith (to solemn promises), against gratitude (toward one to whom he was deeply indebted) and against common humanity.

Our sexual impulses are thus being put in a position of preposterous privilege. The sexual motive is taken to condone all sorts of behavior which, if it had any other end in view, would be condemned as merciless, treacherous and unjust.

Now though I see no good reason for giving sex this privilege, I think I see a strong cause. It is this.

It is part of the nature of a strong erotic passion—as distinct from a transient fit of appetite—that it makes more towering promises than any other emotion. No doubt all our desires make promises, but not so impressively. To be in love involves the almost irresistible conviction that one will go on being in love until one dies, and that possession of the beloved will confer, not merely frequent ecstasies, but settled, fruitful, deep-rooted, lifelong happiness. Hence *all* seems to be at stake. If we miss this chance we shall have lived in vain. At the very thought of such a doom we sink into fathomless depths of self-pity.   24

[3]**Foam-born Venus . . . Aphrodite . . . Cyprus** The Roman goddess Venus was identified with the Greek goddess of love, Aphrodite. Aphrodite sprang from the foam (*aphros*), and was especially worshipped in Cyprus. (Editors' note)

Unfortunately these promises are found often to be quite untrue. Every experienced adult knows this to be so as regards all erotic passions (except the one he himself is feeling at the moment). We discount the world-without-end pretensions of our friends' amours easily enough. We know that such things sometimes last—and sometimes don't. And when they do last, this is not because they promised at the outset to do so. When two people achieve lasting happiness, this is not solely because they are great lovers but because they are also—I must put it crudely—good people; controlled, loyal, fairminded, mutually adaptable people.

If we establish a "right to (sexual) happiness" which supersedes all the ordinary rules of behavior, we do so not because of what our passion shows itself to be in experience but because of what it professes to be while we are in the grip of it. Hence, while the bad behavior is real and works miseries and degradations, the happiness which was the object of the behavior turns out again and again to be illusory. Everyone (except Mr. A. and Mrs. B.) knows that Mr. A. in a year or so may have the same reason for deserting his new wife as for deserting his old. He will feel again that all is at stake. He will see himself again as the great lover, and his pity for himself will exclude all pity for the woman.

Two further points remain.

One is this. A society in which conjugal infidelity is tolerated must always be in the long run a society adverse to women. Women, whatever a few male songs and satires may say to the contrary, are more naturally monogamous than men; it is a biological necessity. Where promiscuity prevails, they will therefore always be more often the victims than the culprits. Also, domestic happiness is more necessary to them than to us. And the quality by which they most easily hold a man, their beauty, decreases every year after they have come to maturity, but this does not happen to those qualities of personality—women don't really care twopence about our *looks*—by which we hold women. Thus in the ruthless war of promiscuity women are at a double disadvantage. They play for higher stakes and are also more likely to lose. I have no sympathy with moralists who frown at the increasing crudity of female provocativeness. These signs of desperate competition fill me with pity.

Secondly, though the "right to happiness" is chiefly claimed for the sexual impulse, it seems to me impossible that the matter should stay there. The fatal principle, once allowed in that department, must sooner or later seep through our whole lives. We thus advance toward a state of society in which not only each man but every impulse in each man claims *carte blanche*.[4] And then, though our technological skill may help us survive a little longer, our civilization will have died at heart, and will—one dare not even add "unfortunately"—be swept away.

[4]*Carte blanche* full permission to act (French for "blank card") (Editors' note)

Responding to an Essay

After you have read Lewis's essay at least twice, you may want to jot down your responses to the basic questions that we introduced on page 16 and reprinted on page 19 after Barbara Ehrenreich's essay. Here they are yet again, slightly abbreviated:

- What is the writer's thesis?
- How does the writer support the thesis?
- What is the writer's purpose?
- How does the writer shape the purpose to the audience?
- What is the writer's tone?
- How successful is the piece? What are its strengths and weaknesses?

And here, to help you to think further about Lewis's essay, are some specific questions:

- Having read the entire essay, look back at Lewis's first five paragraphs and point out the ways in which he is not merely recounting an episode but is already conveying his attitude and seeking to persuade.
- Lewis argues that we do not have a "right to (sexual) happiness." What *duty* or *duties* do we have, according to Lewis?
- In paragraph 25 Lewis writes:

  When two people achieve lasting happiness, this is not solely because they are great lovers but because they are also—I must put it crudely—good people; controlled, loyal, fairminded, mutually adaptable people.

  If you know of a couple who in your opinion have achieved "lasting happiness," do you agree with Lewis's view that their achievement is largely due to the fact that they are "good people"?
- Evaluate Lewis's comment in paragraph 28 on the differences between men and women.

If you find yourself roughing out responses to any of these questions, you may be on the way toward writing a first draft of an essay.

The Writing Process

An essay is a response to experience. J. H. Plumb saw (or says that he saw) a busload of people and was prompted to think about them and ultimately to write an essay on the family (page 6); Barbara Ehrenreich heard people complaining about feminism and was prompted to write a response (page 16); C. S. Lewis heard (or says that he heard) someone utter a comment about a right to happiness, and he was set to thinking and then to writing about it (page 24). Their essays came out of their experience. By *experience* we do not mean only what they actually saw (since we can suspect that Plumb and Lewis may have invented the episodes they use at the start of their essays); their experience included things they had read about and had reflected on. After all, Plumb's bus, Ehrenreich's report of antifeminist objections, and Lewis's report of Clare's remark were at most only triggers, so to speak. A good deal of previous experience and a good deal of later experience—chiefly in the form of reading and of thinking about what they had read—went into the production of their essays.

In short, writers record their responses to experience. You have been actively reading their responses—engaging in a dialogue with these authors—and so you have been undergoing your own experiences. You have things to say, though on any given topic you probably are not yet certain of *all* that you have to say or of how you can best say it. You need to get further ideas, to do further thinking. How do you get ideas? The short answer is that you will get ideas if you engage in an imagined dialogue with the authors whom you are reading. When you read an essay, you will find yourself asking such questions as: What evidence supports this assertion? Is the writer starting from assumptions with which I don't agree? Why do I especially like (or dislike) this essay?

Many writers—professionals as well as students—have found it useful to get their responses down on paper, either as annotations in the margins or as entries in a journal, or both. Here, as a sample, are the annotations that one student jotted next to Lewis's third and fourth paragraphs.

It was equally clear that they were not happy with their old partners. Mrs. B. had adored her husband at the outset. But then he got smashed up in the war. It was thought he had lost his virility, and it was known that he had lost his job. Life with him was no longer what Mrs. B. had <u>bargained</u> for. Poor Mrs. A., too. She had lost her looks—and all her liveliness. It might be true, as some said, that she consumed herself by bearing his children and nursing him through the long illness that overshadowed their earlier married life.

Loaded word. Makes her too calculating

These examples are caricatures They really defeat L's purpose

You mustn't, by the way, imagine that A. was the sort of man who nonchalantly threw a wife away like the peel of an orange he'd sucked dry. Her suicide was a terrible shock to him. We all knew this, for <u>he told us so himself.</u> "But what could I do?" he said. "A man has a right to happiness. I had to take my one chance when it came."

Is CSL making him too awful?

Annotations of this sort often are the starting point for entries in a journal.

Keeping a Journal

A journal is not a diary, a record of what the writer did during the day ("Today I read Lewis's "We Have No 'Right to Happiness'""). Rather, a journal is a place to store some of the thoughts that you may have scribbled on a bit of paper or in the margin of the text—for instance, your initial response to the title of an essay or to something you particularly liked or disliked. It is also a place to jot down further reflections. You can record your impressions as they come to you in any order—almost as though you are talking to yourself. Since no one else is going to read your notes, you can be entirely free and at ease. The student whose annotations we reproduced a moment ago wrote the following entry in his journal:

```
I find Lewis's writing is very clear and in its way per-
suasive, but I also think that his people—A. and B. and
Clare—are not real people. They are almost caricatures.
Anyway, he certainly has chosen people (or invented
them?) who help him make his case. What if Mrs. B.'s hus-
band had been a wife-beater, or maybe someone who mo-
lested their daughter? Would Lewis still think Mrs. B.
was wrong to leave Mr. B.?
```

A second student wrote a rather different entry in her journal:

```
Lewis at first seems to be arguing against a "right to
happiness," but really he is arguing against adultery and
divorce, against what we can call the Playboy morality.
He's talking about what Barbara Ehrenreich talked about
when she said that in the Playboy world if a man "di-
vorces his middle-aged wife for some sweet young thing,
he may be viewed not as a traitor to the American way,
but as a man who has a demonstrated capacity for growth."
```

Here is a third entry:

```
Terrific. That story about A and B really got to me. But
is it true? Does it matter if it isn't true? Probably
not; there are people like the A's and the B's. Lewis re-
ally is awfully good at holding my interest. And I was
really grabbed by that business about a right to happi-
ness being as strange as a right to be six feet tall. But
my question is this: I agree that we don't have a right
to be six feet tall, but why, then, do we have any
rights? Lewis talks about Natural Law, but what is that?
```

```
Is the idea of one husband and one wife "Natural Law"? If
so, how come so many societies don't obey it? When
Bertrand Russell talks about natural instincts and emo-
tions "which we inherit from our animal ancestors," is
this like Natural Law?
```

```
Still, I think Lewis is terrific. And I think he is prob-
ably right about the difference between men and women. It
seems obvious to me that men care more about a woman's
looks than women care about a man's looks. How can this
be checked?
```

You might even make a journal entry in the form of a letter to the author or in the form of a dialogue. Or you might have Mr. A. and Mrs. B. give *their* versions of the story that Clare reports.

Questioning the Text Again

We have already suggested that one way to increase your understanding of an essay and to get ideas that you may use in an essay of your own is to ask questions of the selection that you have read. Let's begin by thinking about the questions we asked following C. S. Lewis's "We Have No 'Right to Happiness'" (page 24). All of these could provide topics for your own essays. Some were questions that might be asked of any essay, you'll recall—about the author's thesis, the way in which the author supports the thesis, the author's purpose, the author's persona or tone, and your evaluation of the essay. And there were questions specifically about Lewis's essay, concerning Lewis's comments on rights and his comments about the differences between men and women.

Probably the most obvious topic for an essay such as Lewis's is

What is the author's thesis, and how sound is it?

One student formulated the thesis as follows:

```
We not only do not have a "right" to sexual happiness,
but we probably cannot achieve lasting happiness if we
allow sex to govern behavior that otherwise "would be
condemned as merciless, treacherous and unjust."
```

An essay concerning Lewis's thesis might be narrowed, for example, to

Does Lewis give a one-sided view of divorce?

or

Does Lewis underestimate (or overestimate) the importance of
sexual satisfaction?

But other topics easily come to mind, for instance:

- Lewis's methods as a writer.
- The logic of Lewis's argument.

Take the first of these three, Lewis's methods, a topic of special interest
if you are trying to become a better writer. One student who planned to
write about this topic made the following notes.

Jottings and Lists

(Parenthetic numbers refer to Lewis's paragraphs.)

1.   Purpose is obviously to persuade. How does he do it?
2.   Very informal manner:
      a. Begins by telling of a conversation he had (1).
      b. Often uses "I"; for instance, "I went away think-
         ing" (5); "this sounds to me" (6); "I can under-
         stand" (7); "I was simple-minded enough to
         believe" (18). So the tone is personal, as if he
         and the reader were having a conversation.
3.   Though informal, seems very educated:
      a. Cites authorities, apparently philosophers, in
         par. 8 (check these names); refers to Austrian,
         Russian, English, and French history (14).
      b. Educated vocabulary ("tautologies" in par. 14).
4.   But also uses easy examples: Mr. and Mrs. A. and Mr.
      and Mrs. B. in first paragraph; stealing fruit
      (19-21).
5.   Makes the abstract clear by being concrete. In par.
      18, when he says that our impulses have to be con-
      trolled, he says, "Absolute obedience to your
      instinct for self-preservation is what we call cow-
      ardice. . . ."
6.   Sentences are all clear. Some are very short ("I
      agree with her" 9), but even the long sentences—
      several lines of type—are clear. Give one (or maybe
      two) examples?
7.   In next-to-last par., frankly speaks as a male: "do-
      mestic happiness is more necessary to them [that is,
      women] than to us." And "the quality by which they
      [that is, women] most easily hold a man," and "women
      don't really care twopence about our <u>looks</u>" (all in

```
28). Sense of a man talking heart-to-heart to men.
But how might it strike a woman? Sexist? Ask Jane
and Tina.
```

You may prefer to record your thoughts in the form of lists:

```
Methods:
     Examples
     Anecdote about A. and B. (par. 1)
     Stealing fruit (19-21)
Informal style:
     Uses "I" (many places)
     Also uses "we"
Clear sentences (give examples)
Vocabulary:
     Usually simple words
     A few hard words ("tautologies" in par. 14)
Beginning: an individual listening
End: rather authoritative: generalizes about men vs
     women
```

Further thinking and further readings of Lewis's essay produced more evidence, and of course the material then had to be reorganized into a clear and effective sequence, but these notes and lists were highly promising. The student who wrote them was well on the way to writing a strong first draft.

After converting his notes into a draft and then revising the draft, an interesting—yet rather common—thing happened. The student found himself dissatisfied with his point. He now felt that he wanted to say something rather different. The annotations and the drafts, it turned out, were a way of helping him to get to a deeper response to Lewis's essay, and so he rewrote his essay, changing his focus. But we are getting ahead of our story.

Getting Ready to Write a Draft

After jotting down notes (and further notes stimulated by rereading and further thinking), you probably will be able to formulate a tentative thesis, a point such as "Lewis argues with great skill," or "Lewis does not make clear the concept of Natural Law," or "Lewis generalizes too freely," or "Lewis has a narrow idea of why people divorce." At this point most writers find it useful to clear the air by glancing over their preliminary notes and by jotting down the thesis and a few especially promising notes—brief statements of what they think their key points may be. These notes may include some key quotations that the writer thinks will help support the thesis.

Draft of an Essay

On "We Have No 'Right to Happiness'"

When I first read the title of C. S. Lewis's essay, I was interested and also somewhat resistant. Without having given much thought to it, I believe that I do have a right to happiness. I don't want to give up this right or this belief. Still I was intrigued to know what Lewis had to say. After reading the essay, it seemed entirely reasonable to say that if there is a right to happiness there are also limits to it. So I decided to look at how Lewis managed to make me change my mind--at least part way.

C. S. Lewis is persuasive, especially because of three things. First, although Lewis (a professor) is obviously very learned, he uses an informal manner that sounds very natural and honest. Second, he gives clear examples. Three, his sentences are always clear. This is true even when they are not especially short. All of these things combine together to make his essay clear and interesting. Lewis is an Englishman, not an American.

Lewis's informal manner, especially seen in his use of the first-person pronoun, appears right away. In the second sentence, when he says "We were discussing something. . . ." He uses "I" in the fifth paragraph and in many later paragraphs.

Another sign of Lewis's informality is his use of such expressions as "It might be true, as some said," and "You mustn't, by the way, imagine," and "for one thing." It sounds like an ordinary person talking, even though Lewis also mentions the names of philosophers in paragraph 8, and in paragraph 14 mentions several historical matters.

Next I will deal with Lewis's examples. The examples help him to be clear to the reader. The essay begins with a story about four people. Two said they had a "right to happiness." In this story Lewis lets us see two people (Mr. A. and Mrs. B.) who behave very badly. They justify their behavior simply by saying they have a right to happiness. They behave so badly--Mr. A. deserts the wife who nursed him through a long illness, and Mrs. B. deserts her husband, who is a wounded veteran--that just to hear them talk about a "right to happiness" is almost enough to make you say they should not be happy and they certainly do not have a right to happiness. The example of Mr. and Mrs. A. and Mr. and Mrs. B. is the longest example that Lewis gives, but Lewis several times gives short examples. These short examples make his point clear. For instance, when he wants to show how silly it is to treat sex differently from all other impulses, he says that it is "like having a morality in which stealing fruit is considered wrong--unless you steal nectarines."

Another thing Lewis does to persuade the reader is to write very clear sentences. Some of his sentences are long--about three lines of print--but the reader has no trouble with them. Here is an example of this sort of sentence.

```
A right to happiness doesn't, for me, make much more

sense than a right to be six feet tall, or to have a

millionaire for your father, or to get good weather

whenever you want to have a picnic.


The only thing that causes any trouble is a few

unfamiliar words such as "tautologies" (paragraph 14) and

"tycoon" (paragraph 16), but you can understand the essay

even without looking up such words.
```

Revising and Editing a Draft

To write a good essay you must be a good reader not only of the essay you are writing about but also of the essay you yourself are writing. We're not talking about proofreading or correcting spelling errors, though of course you must engage in those activities as well.

Revising. In revising their work, writers ask themselves such questions as:

> Do I mean what I say?
> Do I say what I mean? (Answering this question will cause you to ask yourself such questions as: Do I need to define my terms, add examples to clarify, reorganize the material so that a reader can grasp it?)

During this part of the process of writing, you do your best to read the draft in a skeptical frame of mind. In taking account of your doubts, you will probably unify, organize, clarify, and polish the draft.

- **Unity** is achieved partly by eliminating irrelevancies. In the second paragraph of the draft, for example, the writer says that "Lewis is an Englishman, not an American," but the fact that Lewis is English is not clearly relevant to the student's argument that Lewis writes persuasively. The statement should be deleted—or its relevance should be demonstrated.
- **Organization** is largely a matter of arranging material into a sequence that will assist the reader to grasp the point. If you reread your draft and jot down a paragraph outline of the sort shown on page 33, you can then see if the draft has a reasonable organization—a structure that will let the reader move easily from the beginning to the end.

- **Clarity** is achieved largely by providing concrete details, examples, and quotations to support generalizations and by providing helpful transitions ("for instance," "furthermore," "on the other hand," "however").
- **Polish** is small-scale revision. For instance, one deletes unnecessary repetitions. In the first sentence of the second paragraph, "C. S. Lewis" can effectively be changed to "Lewis"—there really is no need to repeat his initials—and in the second sentence of the second paragraph "Lewis" can be changed to "he." Similarly, in polishing, a writer combines choppy sentences into longer sentences and breaks overly long sentences into shorter sentences.

Editing. After producing a draft that seems good enough to show to someone, writers engage in yet another activity. They edit; that is, they check the accuracy of quotations by comparing them with the original, check a dictionary for the spelling of doubtful words, check a handbook for doubtful punctuation—for instance, whether a comma or a semicolon is needed in a particular sentence.

A Revised Draft

Persuasive Strategies in C.S. Lewis's
On "~~We~~ Have No 'Right to Happiness'"

When I first read the title of C. S. Lewis's essay I was interested and also somewhat resistant. Without having given much thought to it, I believe that I do have a right to happiness. I don't want to give up this right or this belief. Still I was intrigued to know what Lewis has to say. After reading the essay it seemed entirely reasonable to say that if there is a right to happiness there are also limits to it. So I decided to look at how Lewis managed to make me change my mind, at least part way.

C.S. Lewis's "We Have No 'Right to Happiness'" is surprisingly persuasive — "surprisingly" because I believe in the right to happiness which is mentioned in the Declaration of Independence. Lewis, an Englishman writing in an American magazine, probably knew he was facing an audience who did not hold his view, and he apparently decided to begin by stating his position as directly as possible in his title, "We Have No 'Right to Happiness'." How does he win his reader over?

C.S. Lewis is persuasive because in addition to thinking carefully, he writes effectively. Three features of his writing especially contribute to his effectiveness.

~~C. S. Lewis is persuasive especially because of three things.~~ First, although Lewis (a professor) is obviously very learned, he uses an informal manner *helps to establish a bond between him and his reader* that ~~sounds very natural and honest~~. Second, he gives clear examples. *Third* ~~Third~~, his sentences are always clear. This is true even when they are not especially short. All of these things combine together to make his essay clear and interesting. ~~Lewis is an Englishman, not an American.~~

Lewis's informal manner, especially seen in his use of the first person pronoun, appears right away/ *in* ~~In~~ the second sentence, when he says "We were discussing something...." He uses "I" in the fifth paragraph and in many later paragraphs.

Another sign of Lewis's informality is his use
of such expressions as "It might be true, as some
said," and "You mustn't, by the way, imagine," and
"for one thing." It sounds like an ordinary person
talking, even though Lewis also mentions the names
of philosophers in paragraph 8, and in paragraph 14
mentions several historical matters.

As for
Next I will deal with Lewis's examples, The *which*
the story of Mr & Mrs. A and
examples help him to be clear, to the reader. The
Mr & Mrs. B is a good illustration. *Mr. A & Mrs. B*
essay begins with a story about four people. Two
both of whom believed they
said they had a "right to happiness," In this story
Lewis lets us see two people (Mr. A and Mrs. B) who
behave very badly. They justify their behavior simply by saying they have a right to happiness. They
behave so badly—Mr. A deserts the wife who nursed
him through a long illness, and Mrs. B deserts her
husband, who is a wounded veteran--that just hear
them talk about a "right to happiness" is almost
doubt that there can be such a right
enough to make you say they should not be happy and
they certainly do not have a right to happiness. The
example of Mr. and Mrs. A and Mr. and Mrs. B is the
he
longest example that Lewis gives, but Lewis several
that
times gives short examples, These short examples
make his point clear. For instance, when he wants to
show how silly it is to treat sex differently from
all other impulses, he says that it is "like having
a morality in which stealing fruit is considered
wrong—unless you steal nectarines."

Lewis's third persuasive technique

~~Another thing Lewis does to persuade the reader~~
is to write very clear sentences. Some of his sentences are long--about three lines of print--but the
reader has no trouble with them. Here is an example
of this sort of sentence.

> A right to happiness doesn't, for me, make much
> more sense than a right to be six feet tall, or
> to have a millionaire for your father, or to get
> good weather whenever you want to have a picnic.

*The sentence is fairly long, partly because
the second half gives three examples, but
because these examples are given in a
parallel construction ("to be," "or to have,"
"or to get") the reader easily follows the
thought.*

True,
~~The only thing that causes any trouble is~~ a few
unfamiliar words such as <u>tautologies</u> (paragraph
may cause a bit of trouble
14) and <u>tycoon</u> (paragraph 16), but ~~you~~ can under-
a reader
stand the essay even without looking up such words.

*Of course Lewis has not absolutely proved
that there is no "right to happiness," but
he has made a good, clear case. The
clarity, in fact, is part of the case.
Everything that Lewis says here seems so
obvious that a reader is almost
persuaded by Lewis's voice alone.*

Rethinking the Thesis: Preliminary Notes

You'll probably agree that the student improved his draft, for instance by deleting the original first paragraph and replacing it with a more focused paragraph. But, as we mentioned earlier, when the student thought further about his revision, he was still dissatisfied with it because he no longer fully believed his thesis.

He found that although he continued to admire Lewis's persuasive techniques, he remained unpersuaded by Lewis's argument. He therefore felt obliged to change the thesis of his essay from (approximately) "Lewis's chief persuasive techniques are . . ." to "Although Lewis is highly skilled as a persuasive writer, even his rhetorical skill cannot overcome certain weaknesses in his thesis."

Here are some of the annotations that the student produced after he recognized his dissatisfaction with his revised draft.

Mr. and Mrs. A. and B. may or may not be real people, but
    they certainly <u>seem</u> UNREAL: too neatly suited (all
    good or bad) to L's purpose.

> <u>The villains:</u> Mr. A. (he tosses out his wife
> after she loses her looks, despite the fact
> that she wore herself out with his children
> and nursed him through long illness; even
> after wife commits suicide he doesn't see that
> he continues to talk selfishly); Mrs. B. (she
> leaves her husband when he gets wounded and he
> loses his "virility" and loses his job).
> Aren't these people a bit too awful? Are they
> really typical of people who divorce?
>
> <u>The heroes--or saints?</u> Mrs. A. (nursed husband
> through long illness, wore self out with the
> children); Mr. B. (injured in war; loses job).

    Clare: She also seems too suited to CSL's thesis;
    she's pretty terrible, and stupid too.

Lewis on Divorce: He seems to think it is always moti-
    vated by a desire for sex, and that it is always
    wrong. But what if a husband abuses his wife--maybe
    physically, or maybe verbally and emotionally? Maybe
    chronic alcoholic, refuses treatment, etc.? Or what
    if wife abuses husband--probably not physically, but
    verbally, and maybe she assaults kids? Or take an-
    other angle: what if woman married at too young an
    age, inexperienced, married to escape from an awful
    family, and now finds she made a mistake? Should she

stay married to the man for life? In short, does Lewis see divorce from enough angles?

First five paragraphs are extremely interesting, but are unfair for three reasons:

1. Lewis <u>loads the dice</u>, showing us goodies and baddies, and then says (par. 5) that they set him to thinking about the "right to happiness";
2. He <u>overemphasizes the importance of sex</u>, neglects other possible reasons why people divorce;
3. His discussion of <u>"Natural Law,"</u> is not convincing to me. I simply am not convinced that there is a "Law of Nature" that "eternally sanctions" certain things.

Sexist??? Although CSL seems to be defending women (esp. par. 28, in which he says that promiscuity puts women at a double disadvantage), there is something sort of sexist in the essay, and I imagine that this will turn off women, and maybe even men. I know that <u>I'm</u> a little bothered by it.

The Final Version

We won't take you through the drafts that the student wrote, but in reading the final version, below, you will notice that although some of the points from the draft are retained, the thesis, as we said, has shifted. Notice, for instance, that the first paragraph of the revised draft is used in the final version but with two significant changes: in the first sentence the student now adds that he finds Lewis's essay "finally unconvincing," and in the last sentence of the paragraph he implies that he will discuss why the essay is "not finally convincing."

Jim Weinstein
Professor Valdez
English Composition 12
2 February 1995

Style and Argument:
An Examination of C. S. Lewis's
"We Have No 'Right to Happiness'"

C. S. Lewis's "We Have No 'Right to Happiness'" is, though finally unconvincing, surprisingly persuasive-- "surprisingly" because I believe in the right to happiness, which is mentioned in the Declaration of Independence. Lewis, an Englishman writing in an American magazine, probably knew he was facing an audience who did not hold his view, and he apparently decided to begin by stating his position as directly as possible in his title: "We Have No 'Right to Happiness.'" How does he nearly win his reader over? And why is he not finally convincing?

Lewis is highly (though not entirely) persuasive because he writes effectively. Three features of his writing especially contribute to his effectiveness. First, although Lewis (a professor) is obviously very learned, he uses an informal manner that helps to establish a bond between him and his reader. Second, he gives clear examples. Third, his sentences are always clear, even when they are not especially short. All of these things combine to make his essay clear and interesting--and almost convincing.

His informal manner, especially his use of the first-person pronouns, appears right away in the second sentence, when he says "We were discussing something. . . ." He uses "I" in the fifth paragraph and in many later paragraphs. Another sign of his informality is his use of such expressions as "It might be true, as some said," and "You mustn't, by the way, imagine." It sounds like an ordinary person talking.

Most of his examples, too, seem ordinary. They make his points seem almost obvious. For instance, when he wants to show how silly it is to treat sex differently from all other impulses, he says that it is "like having

a morality in which stealing fruit is considered wrong--
unless you steal nectarines" (p. 27). The touch of humor
drives the point home.

Still, although Lewis seems thoughtful and he makes
his argument very clear, the essay somehow does not
finally persuade. The trouble may largely be Mr. and Mrs.
A. and B., but there are other difficulties, too.

Mr. and Mrs. A. and B. are just too simple a case,
too neat an illustration. Lewis of course wanted to make a
clear-cut case, but a reader does not really believe in
these people. They are caricatures: Mr. A. tosses out his
wife after she loses her looks (and she lost them not only
through the natural process of aging but through taking
care of the family), and Mrs. B. leaves her husband, a
wounded veteran. Of course it is conceivable that there
really were a Mr. A. and a Mrs. B., but surely the pros
and cons of divorce ought not to be based on cases like
this, where it is so clear that Mr. A. and Mrs. B. are
irresponsible. They are, one might say, as morally stupid
as Clare is. But the fact that these people are selfish
and stupid and that they each get a divorce does not prove
that only selfish and stupid people seek divorce.

Nor do the experiences of the A's and the B's show
that people who seek a divorce always are seeking sexual
pleasure. We can imagine, for instance, a woman married
to a wife-beater. Does she not have a right to be free of
her abusive husband, a "right to happiness"? Nor need we
limit our case to physical abuse. A husband (or a wife)
can abuse a spouse verbally and emotionally and can be
impossibly neglectful of the children. Or we can imagine

a couple who married when very young--perhaps partly for the sake of defying their parents, or maybe in order to escape from a bad family situation. In any case, we can imagine that one member of the couple now sees that a bad mistake was made. Need they stay tied to each other?

Lewis's essay is powerful, partly because it clearly advances a thesis that must seem strange to many Americans; and it is interesting, partly because Lewis makes his points clearly and he seems to be such a thoughtful and decent person. But in the end, the essay is not convincing. It is just a little too simple in its examples and in its suggestion that people who claim a right to happiness are really just saying that they want to get divorced so they can live legally with another sexual partner.

[New page]

Work Cited

Lewis, C.S. "We Have No 'Right to Happiness'." The Little Brown Reader. Eds. Marcia Stubbs and Sylvan Barnet. New York: HarperCollins, 1996. 24-28.

_____

A Brief Overview of the Final Version

- First, a mechanical matter: The student has added a footnote, telling the reader where the essay can be found and explaining that all quotations are from this source.
- The title, though not especially engaging, is informative—more so than, say, "On an Essay by C. S. Lewis." Readers know that the writer will discuss Lewis's style and argument in a particular essay.

- The student's final essay is *not* simply a balanced debate, a statement of the pros and cons that remains inconclusive. Rather, the student argues a thesis: although Lewis's essay is in some ways admirable, it remains unconvincing.
- The student's thesis is stated early, in fact in the first paragraph. It's almost always a good idea to let your reader know early where you will be going.
- Quotations are used as evidence, not as padding. See, for example, paragraphs 3 and 4.
- The writer has kept his reader in mind. He has not summarized Lewis's essay in needless detail, but, on the other hand, he has not assumed that the reader knows the essay inside out. For instance, he does not simply assert that Mr. A. behaves very badly; rather, he reminds us that Mr. A. rejects his wife after she loses her looks. When he uses a quotation, he guides the reader to where in Lewis's essay the quotation can be found.
- He also keeps the reader in mind by using helpful transitions. In paragraph 2 notice "First," "Second," and "Third"; in paragraph 5, "Still" indicates a reversal of direction. Notice, too, that key words and phrases are repeated. Repetition of this sort, like transitions, makes it easy for the reader to follow the writer's train of thought. In the second paragraph, for example, he cites Lewis's "informal manner" as the first of three points of style. His next paragraph begins, "His informal manner. . . ." Similarly, the last sentence of paragraph 3 contains the words "ordinary person." The next paragraph begins, "Most of his examples, too, seem ordinary."
- So far we have talked about what is in the essay. But what is *not* in it is also worth comment. In the final essay, the student does *not* include all of the points he jotted down in his preliminary notes. He does not take up either Natural Law or the issue of sexism, probably because he felt unsure about both. Notes are points of departure; if when you get going you find you are going down a blind alley, don't hesitate to go back and drop the point.

✓ A Checklist for Analyzing and Evaluating an Essay That You Are Writing About

When you read, try to read sympathetically, opening yourself to the writer's vision of things. But when you have finished a sympathetic reading—and an attentive reading—and you have made various sorts of notes, probably including an outline and a summary of the essay you are reading, you are ready to *analyze* the writer's methods and to *evaluate* the piece.

In **analyzing,** you will examine the relationships between the parts; that is, you will ask such questions as:

What is the *topic* of the essay? Try to state it, preferably in writing, as specifically as possible. For example, broadly speaking, one might say that the subject of Lewis's essay is the right to happiness; but within this subject his topic, more specifically, is sexual freedom. Plumb's subject is the family, and his topic is the historical changes that the family has undergone.

What is the essay's *thesis* (either stated or implied)? If you have located a *thesis sentence* in the essay, underline it and write *thesis* in the margin. If the thesis is implied, try to formulate it in a sentence of your own.

What does the title do? What *purpose* does it suggest the writer holds?

What is the function of the opening paragraph (or paragraphs)? What claim on our attention or beliefs does it make?

What speaker or *persona* (see page 20) does the writer create, and how does the writer create it?

What is the tone? Does the tone (page 20) shift as the essay progresses? If so, why?

What *audience* is the writer addressing? The general, literate public, or a more specialized group?

How is the argument set forth? By logic? By drawing on personal experience? What evidence is there that the writer is an authority on the topic? Are there other appeals to authority? What other kinds of evidence support the essay's claim? What are the author's underlying assumptions? Are they stated or implied, and are they acceptable to you, or can you challenge them?

If there is a formal, explicit conclusion, underline or restate it. If the conclusion is not stated but is implied, what does the writer want us to conclude?

In **evaluating,** you will ask such questions as:

Is the essay as clear as it can be, given the complexity of the material? For instance, do specific examples help to make the generalizations clear? Are crucial terms adequately defined? If the thesis is not explicitly stated, is the essay unclear or is it perhaps better because of the indirectness?

If the conclusion is not stated but implied, why does the writer not state it?

Is the argument (if the essay is chiefly an argument) convincing, or is it marred by faulty thinking? If statistics are used, are they sound and relevant? If authorities are quoted, are they indeed authorities (rather than just big names) on this topic?

Is the essay interesting? If so, in what ways, and if not, why not—which gets us back to analysis. If there are passages of undisguised argument, for instance, are they clear without being repetitious and boring? Do specific examples clarify and enliven general assertions?

If the essay includes narrative or descriptive passages, are they pertinent? Should they have been amplified, or should they have been reduced or even deleted?

How is the essay organized? Is the organization effective? Does the essay build to a climax?

Another way of thinking about the criteria for evaluating an essay is to ask:

Is the essay persuasive (whether because of its logic or because of the power of the speaker's personality)? and,

Does the essay give pleasure?

Don't hesitate to demand that an essay give you pleasure. The author probably thought that he or she was writing well, and certainly hoped to hold your interest throughout the essay and to make you feel that you were learning something of interest. In short, the author hoped that you would like the essay. You have every right to evaluate the essay partly by considering the degree of pleasure that it affords. Of course, in your essay you cannot simply say that you enjoyed an essay or that you were bored by it. You will have to support your assertions with reasons based on evidence. To support your assertions you must have read the writer's words carefully, so we are back to an earlier point: the first thing to do if you are going to write about a piece of writing is to read it attentively, pen or pencil in hand.

As you read and reread the material that you are writing about, subjecting it to the kinds of questions we have mentioned, your understanding of it will almost surely deepen. You will probably come to feel that it is better—or worse—than you had thought at first, or in any case that it is somewhat different.

As you prepare to write your own essay and as you draft it, you are learning, feeling your way toward a considered analysis. All writers are in the position of the little girl who, told by an adult that she should think before she spoke, replied, "How do I know what I think until I say it?" But once having said something—whether in a mental question to yourself or in a note or a draft—you have to evaluate your thought and improve it if it doesn't stand up under further scrutiny.

3
A WRITER COMPARES VIEWPOINTS

Writing about Opposed Arguments

Your instructor will probably ask you to read more than one essay in some section of this book. The chief reason for such an assignment, of course, is to stimulate you to think about some complex issue. After all, no one essay on any topic of significance can claim to say all that needs to be said about the topic. Essays that advocate similar positions on, say, capital punishment may, because of slightly different emphases, usefully supplement one another; and even two radically opposed essays may both contain material that you find is essential to a thoughtful discussion of the topic.

Let's say that you read an essay supporting the death penalty. Perhaps, as an aid to grasping the author's argument, you prepared a summary of the essay, and you notice that the writer's chief points are these:

1. The death penalty serves as a deterrent.
2. Justice requires that murderers pay an appropriate price for their crimes.

These basic points probably are supported by some evidence, but you have been reading critically, and you have wondered whether this or that piece of evidence is compelling. You have also wondered if more can't be said on the other side—not only by specific refutation of certain arguments, but perhaps also by arguments that the first essayist has not raised. You turn to a second essayist, someone who opposes the death penalty, and who (you find when you summarize the essay) in effect offers these arguments:

1. The death penalty does not serve as a deterrent.
2. If the death penalty is inflicted mistakenly, the error cannot be corrected.
3. The death penalty is imposed unequally; statistics indicate that when blacks and whites are guilty of comparable offences, blacks are more likely to be sentenced to death.

It is now evident that the two writers are and are not talking about the same thing. They are talking about the death penalty, but for the most part they are not confronting the same issues. On only one issue—deterrence—do they face each other. On this issue you will want to think hard about the evidence that each offers. Possibly you will decide that one author makes a compelling case at least on this issue, but it is also possible that you will decide that the issue cannot be resolved. Or you may find that you can make a better case than did either writer.

Think about the other arguments offered—on the one hand that justice requires the death penalty, and on the other hand that it can be mistakenly inflicted and is awarded unequally. You will not only want to think hard about each of these points, but you will also wonder why only one of the two essayists took them up. Is one or the other argument so clearly mistaken that it is not worth discussing? Or is a particular argument one that can't be proved either true of false? Or are the writers working from different **assumptions** (unexamined beliefs). For instance, the writer who argues that the death penalty is capriciously enforced may assume that race prejudice cannot be overcome, whereas a writer who rejects the argument may assume that the courts can and will see to it that the death penalty is imposed impartially. As a critical reader, you will want to be alert to the assumptions that writers make. You'll have to ask yourself often, *What assumption lies beneath this assertion?* That is, what belief is so firmly held, and is assumed to be so self-evident, that the writer does not bother to assert it? Do I share this assumption? Why?

If you are asked to compare two opposed essays, you probably will want to point out where the two face each other and where they don't. You probably will want also to offer an evaluation of the two. Or, depending on the assignment, you may use the two merely as a point of departure for your own essay on the topic. That is, you may want to draw on one or both—giving credit, of course—and then offer your own argument.

Writing about Essays Less Directly Related

Let's assume that your instructor has asked you to read Plumb's "The Dying Family" (p. 6), Ehrenreich's "The 'Playboy' Man and the American Family" (p. 16), and Lewis's "We Have No 'Right to Happiness'" (p. 24), and has asked you to compare two of the three. These essays all concern family relationships, but they do not take distinctly different positions on a single controversial topic.

Notes and Journal Entries

Let's say that you settle on Plumb and Lewis, specifically on their attitudes toward their material. Perhaps your first thought is that Lewis very obviously offers value judgments, whereas Plumb, as a historian, simply reports what has happened in history.

On rereading the two essays, you may find yourself making notes somewhat like these notes that a student made:

```
1.  Some of Plumb's assumptions:
      Family evolves: history a process (not static, not
          cyclical).
      Idea of parents wedded until death no longer needed
          in our urban, industrial society.
```

Happiness not increasing or decreasing.

2. I'm surprised to find so many assumptions in the writings of a historian. I thought history was supposed to be an account, the "story" of what happened: in Social Studies we learned history is "value-free."

3. Some of Lewis's assumptions:
   Lewis very clearly makes assumptions, for instance, belief in the existence of "Natural Law" (par. 8) and belief that "domestic happiness is more necessary to them than to us" (to women, than to men), par. 28. Also assumes that women don't care much about men's looks (28)--but is this true? How might someone be able to prove it?

4. Big difference between Plumb and Lewis on assumptions. I think that Plumb makes assumptions but is hardly aware of them, whereas Lewis makes them and puts them right up front. With Lewis we know exactly where he stands. For instance, he obviously believes that we can use our free will to behave in ways that he considers proper. He even talks about "good people; controlled, loyal, fairminded" (25). (It's hard to imagine Plumb talking about "good people"; he only talks about whether people are "happy" or "stable.") Lewis pretty clearly believes not only that it's our job to act decently but that we <u>can</u> act decently. Seems not to accept the idea that we can be overwhelmed by passion or by the unconscious. Probably very anti-Freud. Anyway, his position is clear (and I agree with it). With Plumb we can hardly argue--at least I can't-- since I'm not a historian. I don't know if what he says about the past really is true. but his opening paragraph strikes me as completely made up.

5. Attitudes toward change in family:
   For Lewis, a moralist, breakdown of family is a disaster; for Plumb, a fact of social evolution.

One student, whose thoughts were something like those that we have just presented, wrote two entries in his journal.

Plumb: As I see it, he makes assumptions that pretty much go against what Lewis is arguing. Plumb looks at this family in California, and he says they are happy and he thinks everything is just fine. Well, maybe not fine, but at least he says that these children seem "as happy as any children that I have seen." I'm not so sure they are as happy as most. I <u>know</u> (from my own experience and from what I hear from friends) what divorced kids go through. Divorce may be normal (common, ordinary), but is it

<u>right</u>? It seems to lead to so much unhappiness (for par-
ents <u>and</u> children). Putting aside my own feelings, I can
certainly see that my parents aren't especially happy
with their new families. But there is Plumb, with his
happy busload. Is he kidding? Or trying to fool us?

Lewis: Lewis says we have no right to happiness--no right
to divorce, remarry several times, and have families like
that busload of people Plumb talks about. Lewis seems to
be saying that divorce is morally wrong. Why? What are
his reasons? I think he gives two: 1) it makes people unhappy (for instance, Mr. B., the wounded veteran, must
have been miserable when Mrs. B. left him), and 2) it is
against "Natural Law." But come to think of it, what <u>is</u>
Natural Law? What makes divorce contrary to Natural Law?
Is it really "<u>unnatural</u>"? Why? Lots of religions--maybe
most of them--accept divorce. And certainly governments
accept it. So what makes it unnatural? What is it that
Bertrand Russell said about our animal instinct? Check
this.

The next day, after rereading Lewis's essay and the two entries, he
wrote two additional entries in his journal:

I think that I agree with Lewis that we don't have a
right to happiness, just as we don't have a right to be
rich and handsome. But I wish Lewis had given some clear
reasons instead of just saying that we have to remain for
life with one spouse--even if we see that we have made a
bad choice--because "Natural Law" tells us that we can't
change. Come to think of it, Lewis <u>does</u> give some reasons
against giving sex a special privilege: we hurt others,
and we kid ourselves if we think each passion will last.

Both Lewis and Plumb use short stories to make their
points: Plumb's busload of Californians, Lewis's Mr. and
Mrs. A. and Mr. and Mrs. B. Suppose these stories aren't
true and Lewis and Plumb made these stories up. Does that
matter?

The Final Version

Drawing on this material, the student drafted and revised an essay and
then submitted it to peer review. Then, in the light of the comments and
further thinking, he wrote the final version, which we give here. Our
marginal comments summarize some of the strengths that we find in

the finished essay. (*Note:* The original essay was, of course, double-spaced.)

Title gives a clue to topic.

Two Ways of Thinking
about Today's Families

Opening paragraph names authors and essays, and indicates thesis—that the essays strongly differ.

    J. H. Plumb in "The Dying Family" and C. S. Lewis in "We Have No 'Right to Happiness'" both note that today's families often consist of adults who have been divorced. But that is about as much as they would agree on. Judging from an example Plumb gives of a minibus with ten happy children, none of whom had both parents in common, Plumb thinks there is no reason to regret, much less to condemn, the behavior that presumably has produced this sort of family. And judging from the examples Lewis gives of Mrs. B who left her wounded husband and of Mr. A who left his worn-out wife, Lewis thinks that the pursuit of happiness--sexual happiness at the expense of marriage--is immoral.

Clear transition ("Despite these great differences").

    Despite these great differences, there are interesting similarities in the essays. The essays are both by Englishmen, are about the same length, were both written around the middle of the twentieth century, and both begin with an example. Plumb begins with his minibus of ten children and two adults, Lewis with his Mr. and Mrs. A. and Mr. and Mrs. B. Certainly both examples are striking. I'm not sure that, on rereading the essays, I believe either example is real, but they caught my attention. I must say, however, that I have more trouble believing in Plumb's happy busload than in Lewis's two couples. Putting aside my own experience as the child of divorced parents (each of whom has remarried), ten children--not <u>two</u> of whom have the same two parents-- just seems like too many.

Details support generalization.

Again a clear transition ("In addition to").

    In addition to these relatively superficial resemblances, there is also a deeper resemblance. Plumb and Lewis are both talking about the great change in sexual behavior that came about in the twentieth century, especially in the middle of the century when divorce became respectable and common. But there is a big difference in their response. Plumb, writing as a historian, tries to understand why the change came about. Having concluded that the family no longer serves the purposes that it served in earlier periods, Plumb is not disturbed by the change. He ends his essay by saying, "And that bus load of children does no more than symbolize the failure, not of marriage, but of the role of the old-fashioned family unit in a modern, urbanized, scientific and affluent society" (11). Lewis, on the other hand, writes as a moralist. He tries to understand why the A's and B's of this world do what they do, and he sees that they behave as they do because of "the sexual impulse" (32). But Lewis does more than see what they do; he <u>judges</u> what they do, in particular he judges behavior against what he calls "Natural Law" (29) and "the Law of Nature" (30). And he makes it clear that he is not speaking only of sexual behavior. After saying that women are at a disadvantage in a society that tolerates conjugal infidelity, he makes a final point that goes far beyond matters of sex:

> Secondly, though the "right to happiness" is chiefly claimed for the sexual impulse, it seems to me impossible that the matter should stay there. The fatal principle, once allowed in that department, must sooner or later seep through the whole of our lives. (33)

For Plumb, then, the family is something produced by history, and it changes as history goes on. For Lewis, the family—two adults wedded for life—is something in accordance with Natural Law, and since this law does not change, the nature of the family does not change, or, rather, <u>should not</u> change. This difference between the essays, of course, is far more important than all of the similarities. Each essay is interesting to read, and maybe each is even convincing during the moments that someone is reading it. But finally the essays are strongly opposed to each

**Side notes (left margin):**

Quotation is used as evidence to support student's assertion that Plumb "is not disturbed."

Cites evidence.

Quotation of more than four lines is indented five spaces at left.

Transition ("For Plumb, then") by means of brief summary.

Parallel construction ("For Plumb ... For Lewis") highlights similarities and differences.

other, and it is impossible to agree with both of them.

Student briefly offers objections to each essay.

How is a reader to decide between the two essays? Doubtless the earlier experience of a reader predisposes that reader to believe certain things and not to believe other things. Reading Plumb's essay, I find, drawing on my experience, that I cannot believe in his busload of happy children. Plumb does not seem to be aware that children are greatly pained by the divorce and remarriage of their parents. In short, Plumb seems to me to be too satisfied that everything is just fine and that we need not regret the loss of the old-style family. On the other hand, Lewis does not think that everything is just fine with the family. He sees the selfishness behind the "right to [sexual] happiness" that for the most part has destroyed the old-fashioned family. But Lewis rests his case entirely on Natural Law, something that perhaps not many people today believe in.

Discloses reasons.

Student imaginatively extends the discussion.

I can imagine Lewis and Plumb meeting and having a debate. Lewis points out to Plumb that divorce causes more unhappiness than Plumb has admitted, and Plumb points out to Lewis that if modern divorce causes much suffering, there must also have been much suffering when parents did <u>not</u> get divorced. Plumb and Lewis each grant the truth of these objections, and then, in my imagined debate, Plumb says to Lewis, "Furthermore, you build your case on 'Natural Law,' but I don't think there really is any such thing. I will grant that Mr. A. and Mrs. B. seem irresponsible, but I won't grant that married adults must for their entire lives remain with each other." Lewis replies: "If you don't think that some things are right--<u>always</u> right--and that some things are wrong--<u>always</u> wrong--what guides actions? You seem to care whether or not people are happy. But isn't it clear to you that some people seek their own happiness at the expense of others? What gives them such a right? If you don't believe in Natural Law, what do you believe in? Where do 'rights' come from?"

Transition and conclusion about the two essays.

> And so the debate ends, not so much because they differ about whether people today are happier than people in the past, but because they differ in their assumptions. Plumb's assumption that history determines the rightness or wrongness of the family is unacceptable to Lewis, and Lewis's assumption that the family is based on Natural Law is unacceptable to Plumb.

Student introduces a personal note, but relates it closely to the two readings.

> What is my own position? For the moment, I find <u>both</u> assumptions unacceptable. Intellectually I feel the force of Plumb's argument, but my experience tells me that he accepts the change in the family too easily. Intellectually I feel the force of Lewis's argument, but somehow I cannot convince myself that there is such a thing as Natural Law. Still, of the two writers, I feel that Lewis has a clearer

Concludes with succinct references to both essays.

> picture of what people are like. I do know lots of people like Mr. and Mrs. A and Mr. and Mrs. B, but I don't know that busload of California kids.

Works Cited

Documentation

Lewis, C. S. "We Have No 'Right to Happiness.'" <u>The Little, Brown Reader</u>. Ed. Marcia Stubbs and Sylvan Barnet. 7th ed. New York: HarperCollins, 1996. 24-28.

Plumb, J. H. "The Dying Family." <u>The Little, Brown Reader</u>. Ed. Marcia Stubbs and Sylvan Barnet. 7th ed. New York: HarperCollins, 1996. 6-10.

Using Quotations

Our marginal comments briefly call your attention to the student's use of quotations, but here we remind you of procedures for using quotations. These procedures are not noteworthy when handled properly, but they become noticeable and even ruinous to your essay when bungled. Read over the following reminders, check them against the student's essay that you have just read, and consult them again the first few times you write about an essay.

- *Quote.* Quotations from the work under discussion provide indispensable support for your argument.

- *Don't overquote.* Most of your essay should consist of your own words.
- *Quote briefly.* Use quotations as evidence, not as padding.
- *Comment on what you quote*—immediately before or immediately after the quotation. Make sure your reader understands why you find the quotation relevant. Don't count on the quotation to make your point for you.
- *Take care with embedded quotations* (quotations within a sentence of your own). A quotation must make good sense and must fit grammatically into the sentence of which it is a part.

Incorrect:

```
Plumb says he was "astonished when a minibus drove up to
my house."
```

(In this example, the shift from Plumb to "my" is bothersome, especially since the student uses the first person in his essay.)

Improved:

```
Plumb says that he was "astonished" when he saw a minibus
arrive at his house.
```

Or:

```
Plumb says, "I was astonished when a minibus drove up to
my house."
```

Incorrect:

```
Plumb implies he is well read because "Unlike anthropolo-
gists or sociologists, historians have not studied family
life very closely."
```

Improved:

```
Plumb implies he well read in his assertion that "Un-
like anthropologists or sociologists, historians have not
studied family life very closely."
```

- Don't try to fit a long quotation into the middle of one of your own sentences. It is almost impossible for the reader to come out of the quotation and pick up the thread of your sentence. It is better to lead into a long quotation with "Plumb says," followed by a colon, and then, after quoting, to begin a new sentence of your own.
- *Quote exactly.* Any material that you add (to make the quotation coherent with your sentence) must be in square brackets. Thus:

```
Plumb says that he "was rather astonished when a minibus
drove up to [his] house and out poured ten children."
```

An ellipsis (any material that you omit from a quotation) must be indicated by three spaced periods:

```
Plumb says he "was rather astonished when a minibus drove
up . . . and out poured ten children."
```

If you end the quotation before the end of the author's sentence, add a period and then three spaced periods to indicate the omission:

```
Plumb says he "was rather astonished when a minibus drove
up. . . ."
```

- *Quote fairly.* It would not be fair, for instance, to say that Lewis says, "After all, . . . they had a right to happiness." The words do in fact appear in Lewis's essay, but he is quoting them in order, ultimately, to refute them.
- *Identify the quotation* clearly for your reader. Use such expressions as "Lewis says," "Plumb argues."
- *Identify the source of quotations* in a list called "Works Cited."
- *Check your punctuation.* Remember: Periods and commas go *inside* the closing quotation marks, semicolons and colons go outside. Question marks and exclamation points go inside if they are part of the quotation, outside if they are your own.

✓ A Checklist for Editing: Thirteen Questions to Ask Yourself

- Is the title of my essay at least moderately informative?
- Do I identify the subject of my essay (author and title) early?
- What is my thesis? Do I state it soon enough (perhaps even in the title) and keep it in view?
- Is the organization reasonable? Does each point lead into the next, without irrelevancies and without anticlimaxes?
- Is each paragraph unified by a topic sentence or a topic idea? Are there adequate transitions from one paragraph to the next?
- Are generalizations supported by appropriate concrete details, especially by brief quotations from the text?
- Is the opening paragraph interesting and, by its end, focused on the topic? Is the final paragraph conclusive without being repetitive?
- Is the tone appropriate? No sarcasm, no apologies, no condescension?
- If there is a summary, is it as brief as possible, given its purpose?

- Are the quotations accurate? Do they serve a purpose other than to add words to the essay?
- Is documentation provided where necessary?
- Are the spelling and punctuation correct? Are other mechanical matters (such as margins, spacing, and citations) in correct form? Have I proofread carefully?
- Is the paper properly identified—author's name, instructor's name, course number, and date?

4
WRITING AN ARGUMENT

Although in common usage an **argument** can be a noisy wrangle ("You could hear them arguing a block away"), in this chapter we mean a discourse that uses *reasons*—rather than, say, appeals to pity, or, for that matter, threats—in order to persuade readers to hold the writer's opinion, or at least to persuade readers that the writer's opinion is thoughtful and reasonable.

What distinguishes argument from **exposition** (for instance, the explanation of a process) is this: argument and exposition both consist of statements, but in argument some statements are offered as *reasons* for other statements. Another characteristic of argument is that argument assumes there may be a substantial disagreement among informed readers. Exposition assumes that the reader is unfamiliar with the subject matter, but it does *not* assume that the reader holds a different opinion. The writer of an argument, however, seeks to overcome a disagreement by offering reasons that are convincing or at least worth considering carefully. Here, for instance, is Supreme Court Justice Louis Brandeis concluding a justly famous argument that government may not use evidence illegally obtained by wiretapping:

> Decency, security, and liberty alike demand that government officials shall be subjected to the same rules of conduct that are commands to the citizen. In a government of laws, existence of the government will be imperilled if it fails to observe the law scrupulously. Our Government is the potent, the omnipresent teacher. For good or for ill, it teaches the whole people by its example. Crime is contagious. If the Government becomes a lawbreaker, it breeds contempt for law; it invites every man to become a law unto himself; it invites anarchy. To declare that in the administration of the criminal law the end justifies the means—to declare that the Government may commit crimes in order to secure the conviction of a private criminal—would bring terrible retribution. Against that pernicious doctrine the Court should resolutely set its face.

Notice here that Brandeis's reasoning is highlighted by his forceful style. Note the resonant use of parallel constructions ("Decency, security, and liberty," "For good or for ill," "it breeds . . . it invites," "To declare . . . to declare"), which convey a sense of dignity and authority. Notice, too, the effective variation between short and long sentences. The sentences range from three words ("Crime is contagious"—forceful because of its brevity and its alliteration) to thirty-seven words (the next-to-last sentence—impressive because of its length and especially because the meaning is suspended until the end, when we get the crucial verb and its object, "would bring terrible retribution"). Later in our discussion of argument we will talk about the importance of the writer's style.

The Aims of an Argumentative Essay

The aim might seem obvious—to persuade the reader to accept the writer's opinion. In fact, often there are other aims. First, writers draft argumentative essays partly in order to find out what they believe. In drafting a paper they come to see that certain of their unformed beliefs can't really be supported or that their beliefs need to be considerably modified. This point should not come as a surprise; in earlier chapters we have said that writers get ideas and refine their beliefs by the act of writing. Second, if you read argumentative essays in, say, *National Review* (a conservative magazine), in *The New Republic* (a liberal magazine), in *Ms.* (a feminist magazine), or in just about any magazine, you will see that much of the writing is really a matter of preaching to the converted. Good arguments may be offered, but they are offered not to persuade readers but to reassure them that the views they already hold are sound. After all, few liberals read *National Review,* few conservatives read *The New Republic,* few male chauvinists read *Ms.,* and so on.

When you write an argumentative essay, although of course you may hope to convince all readers to adopt your view, you probably also realize that the subject is complex, and that other opinions are possible. What you want to do is to set forth your viewpoint as effectively as possible, not because you believe all readers will say "Yes, of course, you have converted me," but because *you want your view to be given a hearing. You want to show that it is one that can be held by a reasonable person.* Because you are a person of good will, with an open mind, you realize that most issues are very complicated. You have formed some ideas, and now you are taking a stand and arguing on its behalf. However, you probably are not saying that no other view can possibly have the tiniest scrap of merit. As Virginia Woolf put it (with perhaps a bit of self-irony),

> When a subject is highly controversial . . . one cannot hope to tell the truth. One can only show how one came to hold whatever opinion one does hold. One can only give one's audience the chance of drawing their own conclusions as they observe the limitations, the prejudices, the idiosyncrasies of the speaker.

Again, we want to say that in drafting the paper your chief aim is to educate yourself; in offering it to readers your chief aim is to let others know that your views are worth considering because they are supported by reason. If you persuade your readers to accept your views, great; but you should at least persuade them that a reasonable person can hold these views.

Making Reasonable Claims

You have only a little time—perhaps only a week, at most a few weeks—to think about and to support your claim. Within that time, you probably cannot come up with a comprehensive health-care program, evaluate whether our planet has or has not been undergoing a greenhouse effect, or determine whether elephants are so endangered that a ban on the sale of ivory is needed in order to preserve the species.

On the other hand, maybe you can. You may find, after reading a few related essays in this book, that indeed you do have a pretty good sense of the pros and cons of, say, capital punishment. You may rightly feel that you are in a position to offer your own point of view, to make a reasonable and perhaps a novel claim.

We want also to mention that what may at first seem to be an unreasonable claim may, after some reflection, become reasonable. Not much more than a century ago it seemed unreasonable to many intelligent people to argue that slavery was immoral. Issues such as those regarding women in the priesthood or in combat roles in the armed forces, gay people in the military, and the use of animals in scientific experimentation are still matters on which one can take a stand that others may regard as utterly unreasonable.

It happens that on the day we are writing these pages, the newspaper includes an account of Andrew Martinez, "the Naked Guy," a junior at the University of California, Berkeley, who strolls the campus naked except for his peace-sign, shoes, and socks (and on cool days a sweatshirt), eats naked in the dining hall, and attends class naked. Campus police arrested the Naked Guy, but the state of California refused to prosecute him because nudity without "lewd behavior" is not illegal. The university then passed a ban on campus nudity—addressed specifically at Martinez—and suspended him. He hopes to take the matter to the courts. The university's arguments include the charge that his behavior constitutes sexual harassment of women and creates intolerable conditions for students in the "workplace." On the other hand, Martinez says that clothing is part of a middle-class, body-hating, repressive, consumerist society. Can one make a reasonable case for nudism? Can one make a reasonable case against nudism?

Claims of Fact

We can usually distinguish between two kinds of claims, claims of fact and claims of value, and we can sometimes distinguish these from a third kind of claim, claims of policy. **Claims of fact** assert that something is or was or will be. They include, for instance, arguments about cause and effect, correlation, probability, and states of affairs.

> Vanilla is the most popular flavor of ice cream in the United States.

> Pornography, by providing release through fantasy, reduces violence against women.

> Pornography stimulates violence against women.

> Capital punishment reduces crime.

Capital punishment does not reduce crime.

Racial integration of the armed forces was achieved with very little conflict during the Korean War.

To support a claim of this sort, in your essay you will want to

- Define terms that may be in dispute (*pornography* and *violence* need to be defined).
- Provide information (for instance, statistics, examples, the testimony of authorities, or your own experience).

Even if the claim has to do with the future, (let's say the claim that gun control will not reduce crime), one tries to offer information—for example, information about the experiences of other countries, or even of certain states, that have adopted strict regulations concerning the sale of guns.

Claims of Value

Claims of value concern what is right or wrong, good or bad, better or worse than something else:

Country music deserves to be taken seriously.

Rock is better than country music.

Capital punishment is barbaric.

Euthanasia is immoral.

We make such claims every day, for instance when we recommend one movie or one course over another. In a sense, we *live* such claims almost every moment of our waking lives, when we buy one pair of jeans rather than another or choose to spend our time doing one thing rather than something else. We are almost always making choices based on the feeling that one thing or one course of action is better than another. But some distinctions must be made here. First, we can put to one side matters of taste, such as "Vanilla is better than chocolate." The word *better* makes this statement seem to be a claim of value, but the sentence probably really means only "I like vanilla more than I like chocolate." If indeed the speaker is talking about a personal preference rather than asserting (for instance) that vanilla is more healthful than chocolate, or that one should eat vanilla in order to give employment to persons who grow vanilla beans, it is hard to imagine how one could go about supporting such a claim—or how someone else could refute it. Probably the best one can do is to reply with the Latin proverb, "*De gustibus non est disputandum*" ("there is no disputing about tastes"). Notice, however, that the claim that vanilla is better than chocolate is quite different from the claim that most Americans prefer vanilla to chocolate. This last statement is a claim of fact, not of value, and it can be proved or disproved with information—for example with information provided by the makers of ice cream.

Are all assertions of **aesthetic value**—"*Hamlet* is greater than *Romeo and Juliet*," or "Sandra Cisneros's new collection of stories is far superior to her first collection"—really nothing more than disguised statements of preference, deceptive or inflated ways of saying "I prefer vanilla to chocolate"? Probably not. When we say we prefer vanilla to chocolate, we are not suggesting that our preference can be checked against any **standard,** anything outside of our own heads. We are in effect saying only, "Well, that's my *opinion*" rather than "That's my *judgment*." When we make an aesthetic judgment—that is, when we say that a book, a film, a work of art, or a performer is better than something comparable—we are suggesting that we have thought about the matter and that there are external standards (things out there, so to speak) against which we can measure the works or the performers.

We do *not* mean to suggest that by saying "This is my opinion," one is also implying "and I cannot support it." After all, a judge might say "It is my carefully considered opinion that . . . ," and in fact the courts hand down what are called "legal opinions." What we mean is this: One can make a distinction between **opinions,** which we are defining here as statements that are unsupported and that do not require support, such as "In my opinion vanilla is the best flavor," and **judgments,** which are statements that imply a standard and that can be supported—or rebutted—by reasons.

For instance, if we say that a film is good, we probably can go on to give our reasons: the characters are psychologically interesting and physically attractive; the acting is convincing; the setting is exotic; the special effects are impressive, and so on. (Of course we can quarrel with these standards. Furthermore, different standards or criteria are offered for different kinds of works of art. If we are talking about a comedy, we will ask how funny it is, whether the humor is racist, etc.; if we are talking about a mystery, we will ask how ingenious the solution is.)

What are some of the standards commonly used in judging aesthetic works? Among them are: 1) truth (i.e., resemblance to reality), 2) morality, 3) complexity, and 4) craftsmanship. (Again, different standards apply to different forms. No one asks a farce to be "true," or a symphony to be "moral.") Let's look at a very short poem by Robert Herrick (1591–1674), "Divination by Daffodil." (Divination is the art of foretelling future events.)

> When a daffodil I see,
> Hanging down his head towards me,
> Guess I may, what I must be:
> First, I shall decline my head;
> Secondly, I shall be dead;
> Lastly, safely buried.

Can we go beyond saying "I like it [or I don't like it], but that's just my opinion"? Can we support our preference with reasons? One student who like the poem offered the following reasons:

```
1.    Since I am interested in the occult--and in fact I
      read tea leaves and tarot cards--the title especially
      interested me. The poem turned out not to be what I
      expected, but I was pleasantly surprised by this un-
      usual sort of "divination." I think the idea of com-
      paring a daffodil to a dying person who cannot hold
      her head up is unusual and, in a way, encouraging,
      since it compares the person to a beautiful object,
      not to something ugly.
2.    I also like the idea that death is natural and that
      we are part of the natural world. Just as the flower
      returns to the earth and is "safely buried," so we
      return to the earth and to safety. After death we
      will no longer be in any sort of danger.
```

These reasons interest us, even though we do not happen to share the student's interest in the occult. That is, we are interested to hear this *reason* given for the student's preference. We can say, "Well, that makes sense; I understand how you feel—even though I happen not to share this interest."

A student who did *not* like the poem and who was encouraged to give reasons rather than simply to say "I don't like it," came up with these notes:

```
1.    The title at first puzzled me, and even now that it
      has been explained I still don't really see that this
      is about "divination."
2.    I think the poem is too jingly. And this jingliness
      seems to me to be inappropriate in a poem about a
      serious subject like death.
3.    Chiefly my objection is that I don't enjoy reading
      about (or thinking about) death. It seems to me to be
      morbid for writers to write about it, unless of
      course they have recently experienced a death in
      their family.
```

All five statements (the two favorable statements and the three unfavorable ones) offer reasons; they make assertions that can be thought about and discussed. It is even conceivable that if the two students were to exchange ideas, one or both might undergo a change of mind— at least to some small degree.

Let's now briefly discuss claims of value about matters other than aesthetics. Such claims—for instance claims of morality—of course need to be supported by appeals to standards ("Such-and-such a proposal is bad *because* governments should not restrict the rights of individuals"). In supporting claims of value, writers usually appeal to standards that they believe are acceptable to their readers. For example:

> Sex-education programs in schools are inappropriate *because* aspects of moral education should be given only by parents.
>
> Sex-education programs in schools are appropriate *because* society has a duty to provide what most parents obviously are reluctant to provide.
>
> Doctors should be permitted to end a patient's life if the patient makes such a request, *because* each of us should be free to make the decisions that most concern us.
>
> Euthanasia is unacceptable *because* only God can give or take life.

In arguing a claim of value, you will probably want to:

- Specify your standards.
- Perhaps explain *why* you hold these standards.
- Explain (if the issue is of morality rather than aesthetics) how adherence to these standards will be beneficial.

Claims of Policy

Claims of policy (which are not always distinct from claims of value) assert that something should be done—a policy, law, or custom should be initiated, altered, or dropped. In short, claims of policy make a proposal. Usually they are characterized by words like *should, ought* and *must.*

> Children should be allowed to vote if they wish to.
>
> A course in minority cultures ought to be required.
>
> The federal tax on gasoline must be raised.

In defending an unfamiliar claim of policy you may want to begin by pointing out that there is a problem that is usually overlooked. For instance, if you urgently believe that children should have the right to vote—a view almost never expressed—you'll probably first have to convince your audience that there really is an arguable issue here, an issue concerning children's rights that deserves serious thought.

In defending a claim of policy you will probably find yourself providing information, just as you would do in support of a claim of fact. For instance, if your topic is children and the vote, you might point out that until 1920 women could not vote in the United States, the usual arguments being that they were mentally unfit and that they would vote the way their men told them to vote. Experience has proved the error of thus underestimating the capabilities of the disenfranchised.

But in defending a claim of policy you will probably have to consider *values* as well as *facts.* Thus, in arguing for an increase in the gasoline tax, you might want not only to provide factual information about how much money a five-cent-per-gallon tax would raise, but also to argue that such an increase is *fairer* than an alternative such as reducing Social Security benefits.

In short, in an argument about policy you probably will do the following:

- Inform the reader of a problem (usually this means explaining why something must be done).
- Indicate the policy you are recommending or rejecting.
- Give reasons, with supporting evidence, for your proposal.
- Recognize other proposals and show why you find them less satisfactory than yours.

Three Kinds of Evidence: Examples, Testimony, Statistics

Writers of arguments seek to persuade by offering evidence. The chief forms of evidence used in argument are:

Examples

Testimony (the citation of authorities)

Statistics

We'll briefly consider each of these.

Examples

Example is from the Latin *exemplum,* which means "something taken out." An **example** is the sort of thing, taken from among many similar things, that one selects and holds up for view, perhaps after saying "for example" or "for instance."

Three sorts of examples are especially common in written arguments:

Real examples

Invented instances

Analogies

Real examples are just what they sound like—instances that have occurred. If, for example, we are arguing that gun control won't work, we point to those states that have adopted gun control laws and that nevertheless have had no reduction in crimes using guns. Or, if one wants to support the assertion that a woman can be a capable head of state, one may find oneself pointing to women who have actually served as heads of state, such as Cleopatra, Queen Elizabeth I of England, Golda Meir (prime minister of Israel), Indira Ghandi (prime minister of India), and Margaret Thatcher (prime minister of England).

The advantage of using real examples is, clearly, that they are real. Of course, an opponent might stubbornly respond that the persons whom you name could not, for some reason or other, function as the head of state in *our* country. One might argue, for instance, that the case of Golda Meir proves nothing, since the role of women in Israeli society is different from the role of women in the United States (a country in which a majority of the citizens are Christians). And one might argue that much of Mrs. Gandhi's power came from her being the daughter of Nehru, an immensely popular Indian statesman. Even the most compelling real example inevitably will be in some ways special or particular, and in the eyes of some readers may not seem to be a fair example.

Consider, for instance, a student who is arguing that peer review should be part of the writing course, pointing out that he or she found it of great help in high school. An opponent argues that things in college are different: college students should be able to help themselves, even highly gifted college students are not competent to offer college-level instruction, and so on. Still, as the feebleness of these objections (and the objections against Meir and Gandhi indicate), real examples can be very compelling.

Invented instances are exempt from the charge that, because of some detail or other, they are not relevant as evidence. Suppose, for example, you are arguing against capital punishment, on the grounds that if an innocent person is executed, there is no way of even attempting to rectify the injustice. If you point to the case of X, you may be met with the reply that X was not in fact innocent. Rather than get tangled up in the guilt or innocence of a particular person, it may be better to argue that we can suppose—we can imagine—an innocent person convicted and executed, and we can imagine that evidence later proves the person's innocence.

Invented instances have the advantage of presenting an issue clearly, free from all of the distracting particularities (and irrelevancies) that are bound up with any real instance. But invented instances have the disadvantage of being invented, and they may seem remote from the real issues being argued.

Analogies are comparisons pointing out several resemblances between two rather different things. For instance, one might assert that a government is like a ship, and in times of stress—if the ship is to weather the storm—the authority of the captain must not be questioned.

But don't confuse an analogy with proof. An analogy is an extended comparison between two things: it can be useful in exposition, for it explains the unfamiliar by means of the familiar: "A government is like a ship, and just as a ship has a captain and a crew, so a government has . . ."; "Writing an essay is like building a house; just as an architect must begin with a plan, so the writer must. . . . " Such comparisons can be useful, helping to clarify what otherwise might be obscure, but their usefulness goes only so far. Everything is what it is, and not something else. A government is not a ship, and what is true of a captain's power need not be true of a president's power; and a writer is not an architect. Some of what is true about ships may be roughly true of governments, and some of what is true about architects may be (again, roughly) true of writers, but there are differences too. Consider the following analogy between a lighthouse and the death penalty:

> The death penalty is a warning, just like a lighthouse throwing its beams out to sea. We hear about shipwrecks, but we do not hear about the ships the lighthouse guides safely on their way. We do not have proof of the number of ships it saves, but we do not tear the lighthouse down.

> J. Edgar Hoover

How convincing is Hoover's analogy as an argument, that is, as a reason for retaining the death penalty?

Testimony

Testimony, or the citation of authorities, is rooted in our awareness that some people are recognized as experts. In our daily life we constantly turn to experts for guidance: we look up the spelling of a word in the dictionary, we listen to the weather forecast on the radio, we take an ailing cat to the vet for a checkup. Similarly, when we wish to become informed about controversial matters, we often turn to experts, first to help educate ourselves and then to help convince our readers.

Don't forget that *you* are an authority on many things. For example, today's newspaper includes an article about the cutback in funding for teaching the arts in elementary and secondary schools. Educators are responding that arts education is not a frill, and that in fact the arts provide the analytical thinking, teamwork, motivation, and self-discipline that most people agree are needed to reinvigorate American schools. If you have studied the arts in school—for instance, if you painted pictures or learned to play a musical instrument—you are in a position to evaluate these claims. Similarly, if you have studied in a bilingual educational program, your own testimony will be invaluable.

There are at least two reasons for offering testimony in an argument. The obvious reason is that expert opinion does (and should) carry some weight with the audience; the less obvious one is that a change of voice (if the testimony is not your own) in an essay may afford the reader a bit of pleasure. No matter how engaging our own voice may be, a fresh voice—whether that of Thomas Jefferson, Albert Einstein, or Barbara Jordan—may provide a refreshing change of tone.

But, of course, there are dangers. The chief dangers are that the words of authorities may be taken out of context or otherwise distorted, or that the authorities may not be authorities on the topic at hand. We are concerned quite rightly with what the framers of the U.S. Constitution said, but it is not entirely clear that their words can be fairly applied, on one side or the other, to such an issue as abortion. We are concerned quite rightly with what Einstein said, but it is not entirely clear that his eminence as a physicist qualifies him as an authority on, say, world peace. In a moment, when we discuss errors in reasoning, we'll have more to say about the proper and improper use of authorities.

Statistics

Statistics, another important form of evidence, are especially useful in arguments concerning social issues. If we want to argue for (or against) raising the driving age, we will probably do some research in the library, and will offer statistics about the number of accidents caused by people in certain age groups.

But a word of caution: the significance of statistics may be difficult to assess. For instance, opponents of gun control legislation have pointed out, in support of the argument that such laws are ineffectual, that homicides in Florida *increased* after Florida adopted gun control laws. Supporters of gun control laws cried "foul," arguing that in the years after adopting these laws Miami became (for reasons having nothing to do with the laws) the cocaine capital of the United States, and the rise in homicide was chiefly a reflection of murders involved in the drug trade. That is, a significant change in the population has made a comparison of the figures meaningless. This objection seems plausible, and probably the statistics therefore should carry little weight.

How Much Evidence Is Enough?

If you allow yourself ample time to write your essay, you probably will turn up plenty of evidence to illustrate your arguments, such as examples drawn from your own experience and imagination, from your reading, and from your talks with others. Examples will not only help to clarify and to support your assertions but will also provide a concreteness that will be welcome in a paper that might be, on the whole, fairly abstract. Your sense of your audience will have to guide you in making your selection of examples. Generally speaking, a single example may not fully illuminate a difficult point, and so a second exam-ple—a clincher—may be desirable. If you offer a third or fourth exam-ple you probably are succumbing to a temptation to include something that tickles your fancy. If it is as good as you think it is, the reader prob-ably will accept the unnecessary example and may even be grateful. But before you pile on examples, try to imagine yourself in your read-er's place, and ask if an example is needed. If not, ask yourself if the reader will be glad to receive the overload.

One other point: on most questions—say on the value of bilingual education or on the need for rehabilitation programs in prisons—it's not possible to make a strictly logical case, in the sense of an absolutely airtight proof. Don't assume that it is your job to make an absolute proof. What you are expected to do is to offer a reasonable argument. Remember Virginia Woolf's words: "When a subject is highly contro-versial . . . one cannot hope to tell the truth. One can only show how one came to hold whatever opinion one does hold."

Avoiding Fallacies

Let's further examine writing reasonable arguments by considering some obvious errors in reasoning. In logic these errors are called **fallac-ies** (from a Latin verb meaning "to deceive"). As Tweedledee says in *Through the Looking-Glass,* "If it were so, it would be; but as it isn't, it ain't. That's logic."

To persuade readers to accept your opinions you must persuade them that you are reliable; if your argument includes fallacies, thoughtful read-ers will not take you seriously. More important, if your argument includes fallacies, you are misleading yourself. When you search your draft for fal-lacies, you are searching for ways to improve the quality of your thinking.

1. False Authority. Don't try to borrow the prestige of authorities who are not authorities on the topic in question—for example, a heart surgeon speaking on politics. Similarly, some former authorities are no longer authorities because the problems have changed or because later knowledge has superseded their views. Adam Smith, Thomas Jeffer-son, Eleanor Roosevelt, and Albert Einstein remain persons of genius, but an attempt to use their opinions when you are examining modern issues—even in their fields—may be questioned. Remember the last words of John B. Sedgwick, a Union Army general at the Battle of Spot-sylvania in 1864: "They couldn't hit an elephant at this dist—."

In short, before you rely on an authority, ask yourself if the person in question *is* an authority on the topic. And don't let stereotypes influ-ence your idea of who is an authority. There is an apt Yiddish proverb: "A goat has a beard, but that doesn't make him a rabbi."

2. False Quotation. If you do quote from an authority, don't mis-quote. For example, you may find someone who grants that "there are strong arguments in favor of abolishing the death penalty"; but if she goes on to argue that, on balance, the arguments in favor of retaining it seem stronger to her, it is dishonest to quote her words so as to imply that she favors abolishing it.

3. Suppression of Evidence. Don't neglect evidence that is contrary to your own argument. You owe it to yourself and your reader to present all the relevant evidence. Be especially careful not to assume that every question is simply a matter of *either/or.* There may be some truth on both sides. Take the following thesis: "Grades encourage unwholesome competition and should therefore be abolished." Even if the statement about the evil effect of grading is true, it may not be the whole truth, and therefore it may not follow that grades should be abolished. One might point out that grades do other things, too: they may stimulate learning, and they may assist students by telling them how far they have progressed. One might nevertheless conclude, on balance, that the fault outweighs the benefits. But the argument will be more persuasive now that the benefits of grades have been considered.

Concede to the opposition what it deserves and then outscore the opposition. Failure to confront the opposing evidence will be noticed; your readers will keep wondering why you do not consider some particular point, and may consequently dismiss your argument. However, if you confront the opposition, you will almost surely strengthen your own argument. As Edmund Burke said two hundred years ago, "He that

"*Look, maybe you're right, but for the sake of argument let's assume you're wrong and drop it.*"

Drawing by Mankoff; © 1983 The New Yorker Magazine,Inc.

wrestles with us strengthens our nerves, and sharpens our skill. Our antagonist is our helper."

4. *Generalization from Insufficient Evidence.* In rereading a draft of an argument that you have written, try to spot your own generalizations. Ask yourself if a reasonable reader is likely to agree that the generalization is based on an adequate sample.

A visitor to a college may sit in on three classes, each taught by a different instructor, and may find all three stimulating. That's a good sign, but can we generalize and say that the teaching at this college is excellent? Are three classes a sufficient sample? If all three are offered by the Biology Department, which includes only five instructors, perhaps we can tentatively say that the teaching of biology at this institution is good. If the Biology Department contains twenty instructors, perhaps we can still say—though more tentatively—that this sample indicates that the teaching of biology is good. But what does the sample say about the teaching of other subjects at the college? It probably does say something—the institution may be much concerned with teaching across the board—but then again it may not say a great deal, since the Biology Department may be exceptionally concerned with good teaching.

5. *The Genetic Fallacy.* Don't assume that something can necessarily be explained in terms of its birth or origin. "He wrote the novel to make money, so it can't be any good" is not a valid inference. The value of a novel does not depend on the author's motivations in writing it. Indeed, the value or worth of a novel needs to be established by reference to other criteria. Neither the highest nor the lowest motivations guarantee the quality of the product. Another example: "Capital punishment arose in days when men sought revenge, so now it ought to be abolished." Again, an unconvincing argument: capital punishment may have some current value; for example, it may serve as a deterrent to crime. But that's another argument, and it needs evidence if it is to be believed. Be on guard, too, against the thoughtless tendency to judge people by their origins: Mr. X has a foreign accent, so he is probably untrustworthy or stupid or industrious.

6. *Begging the Question and Circular Reasoning.* Don't assume the truth of the point that you should prove. The term "begging the question" is a trifle odd. It means, in effect, "You, like a beggar, are asking me to grant you something at the outset."

Examples: "The barbaric death penalty should be abolished"; "This senseless language requirement should be dropped." Both of these statements assume what they should prove—that the death penalty is barbaric, and that the language requirement is senseless. You can, of course, make such assertions, but you must go on to prove them.

Circular reasoning is usually an extended form of begging the question. What ought to be proved is covertly assumed. Example: "X is the best-qualified candidate for the office, because the most informed people say so." Who are the most informed people? Those who recognize X's superiority. Circular reasoning, then, normally includes intermediate steps absent from begging the question, but the two fallacies are so closely related that they can be considered one. Another example: "I feel sympathy for her because I identify with her." Despite the "because," no reason is really offered. What follows "because" is merely a restatement, in slightly different words, of what precedes; the shift of words, from *feel sympathy* to *identify with* has misled the writer into thinking she is giving a reason. Other examples: "Students are interested in courses when the subject matter and the method of presentation are interesting"; "There cannot be peace in the Middle East because the Jews and the Arabs will always fight." In each case, an assertion that ought to be proved is reasserted as a reason in support of the assertion.

7. *Post hoc ergo propter hoc.* Latin: "after this, therefore because of this." Don't assume that because X precedes Y, X must cause Y. For example: "He went to college and came back a boozer; college corrupted him." He might have taken up liquor even if he had not gone to college. Another example: "When a fifty-five-mile-per-hour speed limit was imposed in 1974, after the Arab embargo on oil, the number of auto fatalities decreased sharply, from 55,000 deaths in 1973 to 46,000 in 1974. Therefore, it is evident that a fifty-five-mile-per-hour speed limit—still adhered to in some states—saves lives." Not quite. Because gasoline was expensive after the embargo, the number of miles traveled decreased. The number of fatalities *per mile* remained constant. The price of gas, not the speed limit, seems responsible for the decreased number of fatalities. Moreover, the national death rate has continued to fall. Why? Several factors are at work: seat-belt and child-restraint laws, campaigns against drunk driving, improved auto design, and improved roads. Medicine, too, may have improved, so that today doctors can save accident victims who in 1974 would have died. In short, it probably is impossible to isolate the correlation between speed and safety.

8. *Argumentum ad hominem.* Here the argument is directed toward the person (*hominem* is Latin for *man*) rather than toward the issue. Don't shift from your topic to your opponent. A speaker argues against legalizing abortions, and her opponent, instead of facing the merits of the argument, attacks the character or the associations of the opponent: "You're a Catholic, aren't you?"

9. *False Assumption.* Consider the Scot who argued that Shakespeare must have been a Scot. Asked for his evidence, he replied, "The ability of the man warrants the assumption." Or take such a statement as "She goes to Yale, so she must be rich." Possibly the statement is based on faulty induction (the writer knows four Yale students, and all four are rich), but more likely he is just passing on a cliché. The Yale student in question may be on a scholarship, may be struggling to earn the money, or may be backed by parents of modest means who for eighteen years have saved money for her college education. Other examples: "I haven't heard him complain about French 10, so he must be satisfied";

"She's a writer, so she must be well read." A little thought will show how weak such assertions are; they *may* be true, but they may not.

The errors we have discussed are common. In revising your writing, try to spot them and eliminate or correct them. You have a point to make, and you should make it fairly. If you can only make it unfairly, you are doing an injustice to your reader and yourself; you should try to change your view of the topic. You don't want to be like the politician whose speech had a marginal note: "Argument weak; shout here."

Drafting an Argument

Choosing a Topic

If the topic is assigned, write on it. If the choice is left to you, keep the following points in mind in selecting a topic.

- The topic must contain *some* degree of controversy. One can hardly argue, for instance, that schools should educate and should not be mere warehouses for young people. After all, who could possibly believe otherwise? Similarly, one cannot argue that George

"Please forgive Edgar. He has no verbal skills."

Drawing by Lorenz; © 1980 The New Yorker Magazine, Inc.

Washington did indeed chop down a cherry tree and say "I cannot tell a lie." No one holds this view, because there is absolutely no evidence to support it.

- The topic should not be so vast that it cannot possibly be treated in a short paper. Example: heredity rather than culture is the origin of most of our behavior.
- The topic should be something you are genuinely interested in—perhaps something where your own experience is relevant.

Imagining an Audience

A writer's job is made easier if the audience is known. Thus, if you are writing for the college newspaper, you can assume that your readers know certain things, and you can adopt a moderately familiar tone. Similarly, if you are writing a letter to the college trustees, you can assume that they know certain things—you will not have to tell them that the institution is a small, coeducational, undergraduate college located in northern Georgia—but you will probably adopt a somewhat more formal tone than you would use in writing for your fellow students.

Your instructor may tell you to imagine a particular audience—readers of the local newspaper, alumni, high school students, your representative in Congress, or any other group. But if your instructor does not specify an audience, you will probably do best if you imagine one of two possibilities: either write for the general reader (the person who reads *Time* or *Newsweek*) or for your classmates. Although these two audiences are similar in many respects, there is a significant difference. All of your classmates may be of the same gender or the same religion, they may be of approximately the same age, and they may come from the same area. In your essay, then, you may not have to explain certain things that you will indeed have to explain if you are writing for the general reader. To cite an obvious example: if the school is specialized (for instance, if it is a religious school or a military school), you can assume that your readers know certain things and share certain attitudes that you cannot assume in the general public.

Getting Started

If your essay is related to one or more of the readings in this book, of course you will read the essay(s) carefully—perhaps highlighting, underlining, annotating, summarizing, and outlining, as we suggest in our first chapter. You will question the text, and you probably will make entries in a journal, as we suggest in the second and third chapters. These entries may be ideas that come to you out of the blue, or they may emerge from conscious, critical thinking, perhaps in conversations with some of your classmates. (Critical thinking means, among other things, that you will question your own assumptions and evaluate your evidence as objectively as possible.)

Discussions—with yourself and with others—will of course help you to improve your ideas. At this stage, you will probably have some ideas that you did not have when you began thinking about the topic, and you will probably want to abandon some of your earlier ideas which now seem less strong than you had originally thought.

Writing a Draft

By now you probably have a fair idea of what your thesis—your claim—is and what reasons you will offer to support it. You also probably have at hand some of the supporting evidence—for instance, examples, statements by authorities, or personal experiences—that you intend to offer as support.

Some people, at this point—especially if they are writing on a word processor—like to sit down and write freely, pouring out their ideas. They then print out the material and, on rereading, highlight what seems useful, perhaps indicating in the margins how the material should be reorganized. They then (again, we are speaking of writing on a word processor) move blocks of material into some reasonable organization.

Our own preference (even though we also use a word processor when we write a first draft) is to prepare a rough outline on paper—really a list of topics. Then, after further thought, we add to it, circling items on the list and indicating (by means of arrows) better positions for these items. Next, when we have a rough outline (perhaps a list of five or six chief items, under each of which we have written a word or phrase indicating how the point might be developed), we start writing on the word processor. It happens that our rough outline (later, much changed) for this section ran thus:

audience

    assigned? or general? or classmates?

choosing topic

    must be controversial

    not impossibly big

starting

    annotating, journal? Refer to earlier chapters?

writing

    brainstorming? outline first, then word processor?

Revising

Revising a Draft

After you have written a first draft, you will read it and, almost surely, make extensive revisions. Some points will now strike you as not really worth making; others that do survive the cut you will now see as needing to be developed. You may also see that the organization needs improvement. For instance, if you notice that a point you have made in the second paragraph is pretty much the same as one in the sixth paragraph, the two should be combined, rewritten, and perhaps put into an entirely new position.

Reorganizing, and providing the transitional words and phrases that make the organization clear to the reader ("moreover," "a second example," "on the other hand"), are usually not difficult, especially if you outline your draft. When you look at the outline of what you have written, you will probably see that portions of the draft have to be moved around or (in some cases) amplified or deleted, and new transitions written. Organizing an argument is so important that we will treat it separately, at some length, in a moment.

In revising, think carefully about how you use **quotations.** Keep in mind the following principles:

- Most quotations should be brief; present a long quotation only if it is extremely interesting and cannot be summarized effectively.
- Let the reader know who wrote the quotation. Identify an author who is not widely known, for example: "Judith Craft, a lawyer who specializes in constitutional matters, argues . . . "; "The warden of a maximum security prison, John Alphonso, testified that . . . "; "Anne Smith, a lesbian who has given birth to one child and adopted a second, suggests that families headed by lesbians . . . . " This sort of lead-in gives authority to the quotation.
- Let the reader know how the quotation was originally used. Examples: "Hillary Clinton argues . . . "; "Senator Dole summarizes his party's view when he says . . . "; "The Pope rejects this view, saying . . . "; "Dr. Joycelyn Elders interprets the statistics as indicating that . . . "
- Use the present tense: "*X* says," *not* "*X* said," though of course if you are treating the passage as something from the past, use the past tense: "*X* wrote, twenty years ago, that . . . , but today he argues that. . . . "

After revising your draft, you may want to show it to some classmates or friends; they will doubtless give you helpful advice if you make it clear that you really do want their assistance.

Organizing an Argument

The writer of a persuasive essay almost always has to handle, in some sequence or other, the following matters:

- The background (for instance, the need to consider the issue).
- The readers' preconceptions.
- The thesis (claim).
- The evidence that supports the claim.
- The counterevidence.
- Responses to counterclaims and counterevidence (perhaps a refutation, or perhaps a concession that there *is* merit in the counterclaims although not as much as in the writer's thesis).
- Some sort of reaffirmation—for instance that the topic needs attention, that the thesis advanced is the most plausible or the most workable or the most moral, or that the ball is now in the readers' court.

Three methods of organizing arguments are fairly common; one or another may suit an essay you're working on.

1. Begin first with the background, then set forth the thesis statement; next work from the simplest argument up to the most complex. Such an arrangement will keep your reader with you, step by step.
2. Begin by setting forth the background and your thesis, then set forth the arguments in order of increasing strength. The danger in following this plan, however, is that you may lose the reader fairly early, because you begin with a weak argument. Avoid the danger by telling your reader that indeed the first argument is relatively weak (if it is *terribly* weak, it isn't an argument at all—so scrap it!), but that you offer it for the sake of completeness or because it is given often, and indicate that you will soon give the reader far stronger arguments. Face the opposition to this initial argument, grant that opposition as much as it deserves, and salvage what is left of the argument. Then proceed to the increasingly strong arguments, devoting at least one paragraph to each. Be sure to introduce each argument with an appropriate transition ("another reason," "even more important," "most convincing of all"). State the argument briefly, summarize the opposing view, and then show the limitations of this opposition. With this organization, your discussion of each of your own arguments will end affirmatively.

An argumentative essay usually has *one* big point, one chief argument. Why? Because our belief is usually founded on one point that we take to be decisive. Of course there are many reasons why, for instance, guns should or should not be restricted, but probably most of us hold the attitude we do because of a single factor. For example, a writer opposing gun control may build the case chiefly on the constitutional argument ("the right of the people to keep and bear arms shall not be infringed"); a writer favoring gun control may build the case chiefly on the accidental deaths resulting from keeping firearms in the home. Such writers probably will mention other arguments but only briefly—either in the introductory paragraphs or near the end, where they will point out that although there *are* other arguments, such as *X* and *Y*, the main argument is of primary importance.

3.   After sketching the background and stating your thesis in an introductory paragraph, mass all of the opposing arguments—perhaps weakest to strongest—and then respond to them one by one.

In short, when you a) think you have done your initial thinking and your rethinking, b) have (if appropriate) consulted some published sources, c) have talked with friends and perhaps with experts, and d) have moved from random notes and lists to fairly full drafts, you are still not quite done. You then must check what you hope is your last draft to see if you have found the best possible order for the arguments, given effective examples, and furnished transitions. That is, you must check to see if you have produced an argument that will strike a reasonable reader as courteous, clear, concrete, and thoughtful.

A Word about Beginnings and Endings

In the **introduction** (the first paragraph or first few paragraphs) you will usually indicate what the issue is, why it is of significance, and what your thesis is. You will also, through your tone, introduce yourself—which is to say that you will convey some sort of personality to the reader. Obviously, it is in your interest to come across as courteous, reasonable, and well informed. We will talk about this matter in a moment, when we discuss the writer's persona.

In the **ending** you probably will offer a paragraph of summary, but try to make it interesting by including something new. You might, for instance, include an interesting quotation, reexamine a phrase from your opening paragraph in a new light, or suggest that it is now time for the reader to act.

Persona and Style

In Chapter 1 we talked about the writer's **persona**—the personality that the writer conveys through his or her words. More exactly, the persona is the image of the writer that *the readers* imagine. The writer tries to convey a certain image (courteous, fair-minded, authoritative, or all of the above, and more); but if readers find the writer discourteous, well, the writer *is* discourteous (or mean-spirited, or uninformed). It won't do for the writer, hearing of the readers' response, to insist that he or she did not mean to be discourteous (is not mean-spirited or is well-informed).

The persona is created, of course, by the impression that the words make—both the individual words and the kinds of sentences (long or short, complex or simple) in which they appear. For instance, a writer who says something like "It behooves us to exert all of our mental capacities on what I deem the primary issue of our era" will strike readers as a pompous ass. The writer may have a heart of gold and be well-informed, but he or she will still strike readers as a pompous ass—and the writer's argument will not get a very attentive hearing. A writer who uses many short sentences, much direct address to the reader, and lots of colloquial diction ("Let's get down to nuts and bolts. You've got to stop kidding yourselves. We all know what the problem is") probably will strike readers as aggressive—someone they are not keen on associating with. In short, the wrong persona can alienate readers. Even though arguments are thoughtful, the readers will be put off. We would live in a better world if we could listen objectively and separate the argument (very good) from the speaker (very unpleasant), but we can't usually do so. A hundred years ago Samuel Butler put it this way (he is overstating the case, but there is much to what he says): "We are not won by arguments that we can analyze but by tone and temper, by the manner which is the man himself."

Now, in fact one often *does* find aggressive writing in magazines, but this writing is, as we said earlier, a sermon addressed to the converted. The liberal readers of *The New Republic* derive pleasure from seeing conservatives roughed up a bit, just as the conservative readers of *National Review* derive pleasure from seeing liberals similarly handled. But again, these writers are not trying to gain a hearing for their ideas; rather, they are reassuring their readers that the readers' ideas are just fine.

What kind of persona should you, as the writer of an argument, try to project? Of course you will want to be (you will *have to be*) yourself. But, just as you have different kinds of clothes, suitable for different purposes, you have several or even many selves—for instance, the self you are with a close friend, the self you are with your teachers, the self you are with customers (if you have a job), and so forth. The self that you will present in your essays—the self that you hope the readers will see from the words you put down on the page—will probably include certain specific qualities. You probably want your readers to see that you are informed and fair and are presenting a thoughtful case. You want them to be interested in hearing what you have to say. If you browse through the essays in this book, you will of course hear different voices. Although some may have an academic tone and some may sound folksy, almost all of them have one thing in common: they are the voices of people whom we would like to get to know. For instance, Noel Perrin, arguing on behalf of what he calls "part-time marriage," begins thus:

> When my wife told me she wanted a divorce, I responded like any normal college professor. I hurried to the college library. I wanted to get hold of some books on divorce and find out what was happening.

Perrin begins with a humorous episode, in which he laughs a bit at himself. Since most of us like a joke, and we like people who can make jokes at their own expense, we probably find Perrin attractive, and we want to hear what he has to say.

But of course there are other ways of opening, and other voices. Elizabeth Joseph, arguing on behalf of polygamy, has a different voice:

> I married a married man. In fact, he had six wives when I married him 17 years ago. Today, he has nine.

There really is no need for us to cite additional examples. If you browse in this book, you will see that the voices range widely; no one voice or one technique is required. You do want to get your argument across, and you would like your readers to come around to your point of view. However, you are writing not so much to convert readers as to show them that your belief is interesting, can be held by a thoughtful person, and can be supported by compelling reasons.

An Overview: An Examination of an Argument

Now that we have covered the ground from a more or less theoretical point of view, let's look at a specific argument. That is, let's see how one writer went about arguing her case. The writer is Barbara Mujica, a professor of Spanish at Georgetown University, in Washington, D.C. The essay originally appeared as an op-ed piece (i.e., opposite the editorial page) in *The New York Times* in 1995.

Barbara Mujica

No Comprendo

Last spring, my niece phoned me in tears. She was graduating from high school and had to make a decision. An outstanding soccer player, she was offered athletic scholarships by several colleges. So why was she crying?

My niece came to the United States from South America as a child. Although she had received good grades in her schools in Miami, she spoke English with a heavy accent and her comprehension and writing skills were deficient. She was afraid that once she left the Miami environment she would feel uncomfortable and, worse still, have difficulty keeping up with class work.

Programs that keep foreign-born children in Spanish-language classrooms for years are only part of the problem. During a visit to my niece's former school, I observed that all business, not just teaching, was conducted in Spanish. In the office, secretaries spoke to the administrators and the children in Spanish. Announcements over the public-address system were made in an English so fractured that it was almost incomprehensible.

I asked my niece's mother why, after years in public schools, her daughter had poor English skills. "It's the whole environment," she replied. "All kinds of services are available in Spanish or Spanglish. Sports and after-school activities are conducted in Spanglish. That's what the kids hear on the radio and in the street."   4

Until recently, immigrants made learning English a priority. But even when they didn't learn English themselves, their children grew up speaking it. Thousands of first-generation Americans still strive to learn English, but others face reduced educational and career opportunities because they have not mastered this basic skill they need to get ahead.

According to the 1990 census, 40 percent of the Hispanics born in the U.S. do not graduate from high school, and the Department of Education says that a lack of proficiency in English is an important factor in the drop-out rate.

People and agencies that favor providing services only in foreign languages want to help people who do not speak English, but they may be doing them a disservice by condemning them to a linguistic ghetto from which they can not easily escape.

And my niece? She turned down all of her scholarship opportunities, deciding instead to attend a small college in Miami, where she will never have to put her English to the test.   8

Let's go through Mujica's argument, step by step, beginning with her title.

We think the title—Spanish for "I don't understand"—is effective. For the general reader, the term is associated with Spanish-speaking people who are weak in English. For instance, an English-speaking tourist visiting Chicago stops someone on the street to ask where the bus station is, and the local resident replies "No comprendo." For the readers of *The New York Times* the effect of Mujica's title is perhaps slightly comic. We want to know what this professor (who is writing in an English-language newspaper) does not understand and why she is using Spanish

The first paragraph sets forth, very briefly, a personal experience that gets our attention—especially because it is puzzling: if the niece was offered several scholarships, why was she crying? In short, the paragraph gains our interest by giving us the start of a story, and it implies that this essay will be about something urgent, something that can make a young woman cry.

The second paragraph enlightens us: now we know exactly why the niece was crying, and we doubtless feel some sympathy for her. We may also become indignant with the school system, since Mujica tells us that the girl received "good grades" even though "her comprehension and writing skills were deficient." By the time we finish the essay, we can easily see that Mujica indeed is telling us that there is something wrong with the system, not with the girl.

The third paragraph openly blames programs "that keep foreign-born children in Spanish-language classrooms for years," but it goes even further, calling our attention to the fact that "all business, not just teaching, was conducted in Spanish." Mujica supports her point with concrete details: the secretaries spoke to administrators and children in Spanish, and public announcements were "made in an English so fractured that it was almost incomprehensible." (Actually this last point, about the public announcements in fractured English, somewhat undermines her statement that "all business . . . was conducted in Spanish," but perhaps the idea is that this "fractured" English really was "Spanish," English with a heavy admixture of Spanish.)

Thus far we can say that the evidence Mujica offers is largely personal. She does not tell us that 92 percent of the students in the school have such-and-such a degree of proficiency in English, or that a committee of independent investigators reported such-and-such. The evidence is the first-hand observation of the writer—her interaction with her niece and her experience as a visitor to the school. This evidence is compelling: Mujica's story, thus far, seems both truthful and moving (the niece's tears touch our hearts). On the other hand, we must realize that Mujica's essay is not addressing the arguments offered by those who support bilingual programs. (The chief argument, briefly, is that students who are not competent in English can hardly expect to do well in courses in, say, biology, if they are taught in English. Therefore, biology courses should be taught in the students' native language while they are also acquiring competence in English.)

The fourth paragraph adds the authority of the girl's mother. That is, Mujica in effect says, "I'm not the only one who blames the girl's poor English on the omnipresence of "Spanish or Spanglish. Look, her mother says 'That's what the kids hear on the radio and in the street.'"

The fifth paragraph, glancing at the past, asserts that immigrants used to make learning English "a priority." The assumption here is that today's immigrants can and ought to do what immigrants of the past could and did do. However, notice that Mujica cautiously modifies this view a bit by adding that even if the earlier immigrants themselves didn't learn English, their children did. Her modification is necessary, because in fact many of the earlier immigrants did not learn English. Mujica wisely avoids overstating her case.

There are at least two other things to notice in this paragraph. First, Mujica is careful not to chastise *all* of today's first-generation immigrants. She doubtless knows that if one generalizes too broadly one loses one's audience; readers will simply dismiss a writer who claims to speak unpleasant truths about whole classes of people. Second, she quietly introduces the suggestion that the school system is damaging the students *materially*; the students "face reduced . . . career opportunities. . . ." So, among other things, we are talking about serious economic matters.

The sixth paragraph—more or less continuing this point about career opportunities—tells us that the drop-out rate is high, and that, according to the Department of Education, "a lack of proficiency in English is an important factor in the drop-out rate." What is one to make of this? Mujica cites an authority—the Board of Education—but a skeptic might say that the Board of Education says many things and its countless reports are not always convincing. Our own feeling is that there must be something to her point, but we also feel, uneasily, that her argument is weakened by the almost meaningless words, "an important factor." How important? We aren't told. We would be more impressed if we were told something like this: "The Department of Education, in a report endorsed by the governors of forty states, said that 'the chief cause of dropping out is lack of proficiency in English.'" *That* would have some weight. Still, though scarcely compelling, Mujica's statement cannot be simply brushed aside. Anyone responding to her would have to face the argument that the Department of Education sees lack of competence in English as "an important factor."

The seventh paragraph assumes that the people who are damaging the students are in fact people of good will, people who "want to help them," but (and here the economic argument returns) these people are "condemning [the students] to a linguistic ghetto." It is almost always appropriate to assume that people who hold views opposed to yours are acting from honorable intentions. First of all, they probably *do* have honorable intentions; second, by making such an assumption, you come across to your reader as a decent, fair-minded person.

The eighth (final) paragraph returns nicely to the anecdote with which the essay began, thus effectively rounding off or completing the essay. The anecdote is a sad one (or at least this is Mujica's point). But the very fact that it is sad makes it especially appropriate as a part of the argument. After all, if the niece had chosen to go, let's say, to the University of Wisconsin, Mujica's argument would collapse. The moral of such a story would be, "Even if a school keeps the student from mastering English, no great harm is done, since the student will go to a mainstream college or university anyway."

In short, although Mujica makes use of statistics and authority when (in her sixth paragraph) she mentions the Department of Education, chiefly she builds her case on personal experience. The implication is that she knows what she is talking about because she has seen it. But is personal experience enough to bring us around to her side? Perhaps so—if the person is someone of good will. Mujica shows that she is such a person at the outset, when she reveals herself to be a concerned aunt, and especially in paragraph 7, when she concedes that the opponents mean well.

One last thought. We think that up to this point readers will agree with our analysis of Mujica's arguments and strategies, but now we want to raise a more controversial issue. When readers finish the essay, and reach the closure provided by the end of the anecdote, perhaps their minds go back to the beginning of the essay and to the title, "No Comprendo," "I don't understand." Mujica is saying, or seems to be saying, "I don't understand. After all, the people who run these bilingual programs are decent, well-meaning people, but it's obvious that students like my niece are being harmed. I don't understand how people can do this—how they can go on with these programs. I just don't understand." But (and here we get to the point that we think our readers may find controversial) perhaps the reader of Mujica's essay says, "Yes, she is right; the programs are harmful, but there are obvious reasons—*bad* reasons—why some people support the programs. The people who support them are (say) unduly chauvinistic, or maybe they are more concerned about getting teaching jobs for their Spanish-speaking friends than they are concerned about the welfare of the children." Our point, then, is this: Mujica says, by means of her title, that she doesn't understand. This position allows her to present her case and *not* to confront the opposition directly. Indeed it allows her, as we have seen, to speak highly (if very briefly) of the opposition. If we are right, her strategy is to let *the reader* make the most serious charges against her opposition. The reader is drawn to say, "Yes, I agree with you that the programs damage students, but I think I know why these programs exist—and the reasons that they exist are bad."

You may of course have a very different response to Mujica's essay and to our discussion of it—especially to our remarks in the preceding paragraph. Perhaps you will even be stimulated to write an argument showing that we have misread the essay. Or you may be stimulated to write an argument opposing Mujica's position.

A Checklist for Revising Drafts of Arguments

- Does the introduction let the audience know what the topic is, why the topic is of some importance, and what your thesis is?
- Are the terms clearly defined?
- Are the assumptions likely to be shared by your readers? If not, are they reasonably argued rather than merely asserted?
- Are the facts verifiable? Is the evidence reliable? (No out-of-date statistics, no generalizations from insufficient evidence?)

- Is the reasoning sound?
- Are the authorities really authorities on this matter?
- Are quotations no longer than they need to be, are they introduced with useful lead-ins, and do they make good reading?
- Are all of the substantial counterarguments recognized and effectively responded to?
- Is the organization effective? Does the essay begin interestingly, keep the thesis in view, and end interestingly?
- Is the tone appropriate? (Avoid sarcasm, present yourself as fair-minded, and assume that people who hold views opposed to yours are also fair-minded.)

An Argument for Analysis

Mark Mathabane

Mark Mathabane, born in South Africa in 1960, is the author of Kaffir Boy: The True Story of a Black Youth's Coming of Age in Apartheid South Africa *(1986). Mathabane, from an impoverished family, was inspired by seeing the African-American tennis player Arthur Ashe when Ashe toured South Africa. The boy took up tennis and won a tennis scholarship offered by an American school. The book ends with him getting on a plane headed for the United States.*

We reprint an essay that originally was published in The New York Times, *in 1993.*

Appearances Are Destructive

As public schools reopen for the new year, strategies to curb school violence will once again be hotly debated. Installing metal detectors and hiring security guards will help, but the experience of my two sisters makes a compelling case for greater use of dress codes as a way to protect students and promote learning.

Shortly after my sisters arrived here from South Africa I enrolled them at the local public school. I had great expectations for their educational experience. Compared with black schools under apartheid, American schools are Shangri-Las, with modern textbooks, school buses, computers, libraries, lunch programs and dedicated teachers.

But despite these benefits, which students in many parts of the world only dream about, my sisters' efforts at learning were almost derailed. They were constantly taunted for their homely outfits. A couple of times they came home in tears. In South Africa students were required to wear uniforms, so my sisters had never been preoccupied with clothes and jewelry.

They became so distraught that they insisted on transferring to different schools, despite my reassurances that there was nothing wrong with them because of what they wore.   4

I have visited enough public schools around the country to know that my sisters' experiences are not unique. In schools in many areas, Nike, Calvin Klein, Adidas, Reebok and Gucci are more familiar names to students than Zora Neale Hurston, Shakespeare and Faulkner. Many students seem to pay more attention to what's on their bodies than in their minds.

Teachers have shared their frustrations with me at being unable to teach those students willing to learn because classes are frequently disrupted by other students ogling themselves in mirrors, painting their fingernails, combing their hair, shining their gigantic shoes or comparing designer labels on jackets, caps and jewelry.

The fiercest competition among students is often not over academic achievements, but over who dresses most expensively. And many students now measure parental love by how willing their mothers and fathers are to pamper them with money for the latest fads in clothes, sneakers and jewelry.

Those parents without the money to waste on such meretricious   8
extravagances are considered uncaring and cruel. They often watch in dismay and helplessness as their children become involved with gangs and peddle drugs to raise the money.

When students are asked why they attach so much importance to clothing, they frequently reply that it's the cool thing to do, that it gives them status and earns them respect. And clothes are also used to send sexual messages, with girls thinking that the only things that make them attractive to boys are skimpy dresses and gaudy looks, rather than intelligence and academic excellence.

The argument by civil libertarians that dress codes infringe on freedom of expression is misleading. We observe dress codes in nearly every aspect of our lives without any diminution of our freedoms—as demonstrated by flight attendants, bus drivers, postal employees, high school bands, military personnel, sports teams, Girl and Boy Scouts, employees of fast-food chains, restaurants and hotels.

In many countries where students outperform their American counterparts academically, school dress codes are observed as part of creating the proper learning environment. Their students tend to be neater, less disruptive in class and more disciplined, mainly because their minds are focused more on learning and less on materialism.

It's time Americans realized that the benefits of safe and effective   12
schools far outweigh any perceived curtailment of freedom of expression brought on by dress codes.

Topics for Critical Thinking and Writing

1. What is the problem that Mathabane is addressing—and do you agree that there really is a problem?
2. What solution does he offer, and exactly what arguments (reasons) does he offer in support of this solution?

3. Mathabane draws on personal experience. Do you find this evidence impressive, or of no weight, or somewhere in between? Explain.
4. Does Mathabane recognize possible objections to his proposal? If so, where? What objections can *you* think of?
5. Evaluate Mathabane's final paragraph as the concluding paragraph to an argument. If you think he should have said something else, write the paragraph that you think he should have written. If, on the other hand, you think the paragraph is effective, explain to a reader *why* it is an effective ending.
6. If you disagree with Mathabane, draft a letter of about 250 words telling him why you disagree. If you agree with him, draft a letter to the principal of the elementary school that you attended, explaining why you think he or she should consider Mathabane's proposal. (In your letter you will have to summarize the proposal, but keep the summary down to a sentence or two.)

Two Debates for Analysis

"Three Strikes"—Two Views

Mario Cuomo

Mario Cuomo, during his last term as governor of New York, proposed a "three strikes" crime law in his 1994 State of the State message. This essay, along with the opposing essay by Mimi Silbert, was published in The New York Times, *29 January 1994.*

Harsh, Sure, But Fair

Violence has shattered the order of our civilized life like a bullet through the living room window. In response, political leaders across the country have offered a spectrum of tough new laws. One in particular has gained attention everywhere. In New York, we call it "three strikes and you're in." It would put those convicted of three violent felonies behind bars for life, with no possibility of parole.

Nearly 30 states are considering some version of this law, and President Clinton in his State of the Union address proposed such a measure for violent Federal offenses. In all its many variations, the idea has received widespread support, and on both sides of the political aisle.

It is imperative that we act forcefully to help the American people regain their basic sense of security, and a well-formulated "three strikes" law can be part of the answer. But we should not give in to the appeal of a solution with a snappy name and a gratifying harshness, only to create a rigid law that won't do much good or will come back to bite us with unintended costs or consequences.

The merits of the law are clear, so long as it is carefully written to   4
focus on the worst offenders. Studies by criminologist Marvin Wolf-gang and others have shown that 15 percent of offenders account for 85 percent of personal-injury offenses. A "three strikes" law would give us a heavy hammer to use against these career criminals. The law would not only protect us from the most violent criminals, it would surely have a powerful deterrent effect. While it will be years before we can know the full effects of "three strikes" laws, for many prisoners not even execution is more frightening than the idea of spending the rest of their lives behind bars.

Despite the strength of the "three strikes" idea, others have raised legitimate questions about its consequences. One objection is that the law would not affect enough criminals to do any good. In 1992, of 25,000 offenders imprisoned in New York State, only 286 were sentenced as three time violent offenders. Thus a "three strikes" law would have kept "only" 286 murderers, rapists, armed robbers and other violent felons off our streets.

If that number seems small, imagine the public outcry if we announced that instead of locking these felons up for life, we intended to release that many. If a "three strikes" law prevented only one rape, one murder, one assault, it would have been worth the trouble to pass the legislation.

Other critics suggest that the law will cost too much money by producing long and expensive trials. Experience tells us that most violent crime is committed by relatively young people and that even repeat felons tend to get less violent as they get older. Thus, the argument goes, we would be spending money to incarcerate people who would eventually cease to pose much of a threat.

But the number of potential cases is relatively small, so the criminal   8
justice system could absorb the consequences of appeals and delays without difficulty, especially since the alternative—releasing these offenders on parole—would likely result in more arrests and trials for future offenses.

More importantly, all too many incorrigible offenders never drop their violent behavior, and our criminal justice system doesn't provide an adequate way to keep them off our streets. Surely we can afford the price of incarceration—even for a life term—if it means protecting our citizens from serious harm and pervasive fear.

Certainly, no single proposal will end violence in our society. To stop the tide of violent crime, we will need to take aggressive steps on many fronts—tough gun control, tough law enforcement, tough love and a society that offers young people real economic opportunity. But a "three strikes" law can be part of an intelligent, comprehensive answer to one of the most urgent problems of our time.

Topics for Critical Thinking and Writing

1. In paragraph 4 Cuomo says that "for many prisoners not even execution is more frightening than the idea of spending the rest of their lives behind bars." Do you think he should have supported this assertion, for instance with a reference to a statistical study? Or do you think it is self-evident and in need of no support? Explain your position.
2. List the arguments that Cuomo offers *against* his own position. How satisfactory are his responses to each? What other significant arguments, if any, can you think of against his position?
3. How would you characterize Cuomo's tone? Smug? Earnest? Or what? (Your response may require more than one word, of course.) Specify passages that seem to you to establish his overall tone.
4. Read the next argument, by Mimi Silbert, and then—in so far as you can put yourself into Cuomo's mind—write his response to her. (Probably you will assume that she has not convinced him. If you do find her argument compelling, you may want to assume that Cuomo too is convinced—in which case you will write an essay in which he sets forth reasons for abandoning his earlier position.)

Mimi Silbert

Mimi Silbert is president of the Delancey Street Foundation in San Francisco, an organization that helps felons to help themselves. This essay, paired with the preceding essay by Mario Cuomo, originally appeared in The New York Times, *29 January 1994.*

The Need to Change

At ten years old, Albert had already distinguished himself as the youngest member of his barrio gang. Recruited into gang life by his mother, he sold drugs diligently and remained loyal to his gang as he was shipped from one foster home to another during his mother's various prison terms.

Like many children, Albert had a dream. He dreamed of being in San Quentin Prison by his 18th birthday. He missed by a year. Albert went to San Quentin at 19, by which time he had been arrested for 27 armed robberies and fathered two children. He returned to prison several times for drug sales, robbery and burglary.

One glance at Albert's record would convince anyone that he was incorrigible, a career criminal and a menace to society. Had "three strikes and you're out" been a law then, Albert would have gone to prison for life.

Instead, today Albert is a polite, well-dressed gentleman with a mild and courteous demeanor. At 36, he has been crime-free, drug-   4 free and violence-free for many years. He works as a plumber and substitute teacher, pays his taxes and worries about his children's schooling.

Our justice system works in extremes. Either we excuse the criminal ("poor Albert had no mommy or daddy") and put him back on the streets, or we give up on him ("bad Albert is a menace"), lock him up and throw away the key. As with any extremes, these work for only a few.

A few criminals can turn themselves around with only a hand and a hug; most cannot. A few criminals need to be in prison forever; most do not. For most, we need a tightly structured community to control criminals, hold them responsible, get them off drugs and alcohol and teach them to be decent citizens.

In the past 23 years, 10,000 former felons, including Albert, have turned their lives around in just such a community. The Delancey Street Foundation in San Francisco is the nation's largest self-help organization for felons and drug addicts. It accepts no government funds and has no paid staff. The entire organization is run by its residents; the foundation supports itself primarily through a number of training schools, which provide vocational skills and generate the organization's income.

In today's climate, it's fashionable to reject such an approach as "soft on crime." But life here is anything but soft; new residents long for prison, where virtually nothing is expected of them. Prisoners are not required to work, confront their problems or change. Taxes pay for everything, drugs are easy to come by, and the daily routine can consist of watching television and pumping iron. Fights and gangs are considered normal. 8

At Delancey Street, on the other hand, Albert had to live cooperatively with others, learn to read, admit responsibility for the harm he caused, earn his keep and make restitution to society. Not everyone here succeeds, of course, but most do: graduates include realtors, contractors, a deputy sheriff and even a member of the San Francisco Board of Supervisors.

Every person "three strikes and you're out" puts behind bars would cost the taxpayers about $1 million (assuming a 35-year stay), and that is only the direct cost of building the cell and caring for the prisoner. We will also pay to support their children on welfare. Every person at Delancey Street costs the taxpayers nothing, and residents learn to care for their own children and pay their own taxes.

If building more prisons made our streets safe, it would merit a large investment. But it has failed to do so. In the last decade, California's prison population has increased 400 percent, its corrections budget 500 percent, yet violent crime is up 40 percent. No credible study concludes that more imprisonment means less crime.

We are no longer dealing with a few bad apples. Too many people   12
are now too many generations into criminal behavior. Prison will not
deter them, because they do not consider the consequences of their
actions. They have been inculcated by abuse, violence and poverty at
every level. This does not excuse their behavior; it intensifies the need
to change it.

The only tough and smart response to crime is to break the cycle of
it. The more responsible and productive people we can build now, the
fewer prisons we will have to build later.

Topics for Critical Thinking and Writing

1. Silbert's first four paragraphs form an introductory unit. Do you think
   they make an effective beginning for her argument? Explain.
2. In paragraph 11 Silbert cites statistics from California: the prison population is up, the budget for corrections is up, and yet violent crime is
   also up. *Why* does she offer these statistics? Assuming the truth of the
   statistics, how do you interpret them?
3. What are Silbert's basic arguments (her *reasons* for taking the position
   she takes)? To what degree do you find her reasons convincing? Does
   she take sufficient account of opposing arguments? Explain.
4. In her final paragraph Silbert suggests that we need to "build" people
   who are "responsible and productive." Presumably, this means offering
   educational programs of various sorts—ranging perhaps from better
   kindergartens to counseling and vocational training for ex-convicts. Do
   you agree with Silbert? If you do, would you agree that taxes must be
   raised to support such programs? Explain.
5. Imagine that you are Silbert and that you have just read Mario
   Cuomo's essay. Write a letter from Silbert to Cuomo.
6. Examine paragraph 6 and comment on its rhetoric, sentence by sentence. Does the first sentence of the paragraph strike you as effective?
   Why, or why not? The second? The third?

Censoring Creativity—Two Views

These two opposing essays, by Michael Kinsley and Barbara Ehrenreich, appeared in *Time* magazine. The essays concern *Cop Killer*, a song
by Ice-T, a rapper—but of course the issue of censorship goes beyond
the particular work in question.

When the song was released on Ice-T's album, *Body Count* (1992),
some people argued that since it seemed to urge the hearers to murder
police, Time Warner should have refused to publish it. On the other
hand, defenders argued that it was an artistic representation of what
has come to be called "black rage."

Michael Kinsley

Michael Kinsley holds a law degree, but he earns his living as a commentator on social issues. He is a contributing editor of The New Republic, *and one of the two hosts on CNN's* Crossfire.

Ice-T: The Issue Is Social Responsibility

How did the company that publishes this magazine come to produce a record glorifying the murder of police?

> I got my 12-gauge sawed off
> I got my headlights turned off
> I'm 'bout to bust some shots off
> I'm 'bout to dust some cops off . . .
> Die, Die, Die, Pig, Die!

So go the lyrics to *Cop Killer* by the rapper Ice-T on the album *Body Count.* The album is released by Warner Bros. Records, part of the Time Warner media and entertainment conglomerate.

In a *Wall Street Journal* op-ed piece laying out the company's position, Time Warner co-CEO Gerald Levin makes two defenses. First, Ice-T's *Cop Killer* is misunderstood. "It doesn't incite or glorify violence . . . It's his fictionalized attempt to get inside a character's head . . . *Cop Killer* is no more a call for gunning down the police than *Frankie and Johnny* is a summons for jilted lovers to shoot one another." Instead of "finding ways to silence the messenger," we should be "heeding the anguished cry contained in his message."

This defense is self-contradictory. *Frankie and Johnny* does not pre- 4 tend to have a political "message" that must be "heeded." If *Cop Killer* has a message, it is that the murder of policemen is a justified response to police brutality. And not in self-defense, but in premeditated acts of revenge against random cops. ("I know your family's grievin'—f—'em.")

Killing policemen is a good thing—that is the plain meaning of the words, and no "larger understanding" of black culture, the rage of the streets or anything else can explain it away. This is not Ella Fitzgerald telling a story in song. As in much of today's popular music, the line between performer and performance is purposely blurred. These are political sermonettes clearly intended to endorse the sentiments being expressed. Tracy Marrow (Ice-T) himself has said, "I scared the police, and they need to be scared." That seems clear.

The company's second defense of *Cop Killer* is the classic one of free expression: "We stand for creative freedom. We believe that the worth of what an artist or journalist has to say does not depend on preapproval from a government official or a corporate censor."

Of course Ice-T has the right to say whatever he wants. But that doesn't require any company to provide him an outlet. And it doesn't relieve a company of responsibility for the messages it chooses to promote. Judgment is not "censorship." Many an "anguished cry" goes unrecorded. This one was recorded, and promoted, because a successful artist under contract wanted to record it. Nothing wrong with making money, but a company cannot take the money and run from the responsibility.

The founder of Time, Henry Luce, would snort at the notion that   8 his company should provide a value-free forum for the exchange of ideas. In Luce's system, editors were supposed to make value judgments and promote the truth as they saw it. Time has moved far from its old Lucean rigidity—far enough to allow for dissenting essays like this one. That evolution is a good thing, as long as it's not a handy excuse for abandoning all standards.

No commercial enterprise need agree with every word that appears under its corporate imprimatur. If Time Warner now intends to be "a global force for encouraging the confrontation of ideas," that's swell. But a policy of allowing diverse viewpoints is not a moral free pass. Pro and con on national health care is one thing; pro and con on killing policemen is another.

A bit of sympathy is in order for Time Warner. It is indeed a "global force" with media tentacles around the world. If it imposes rigorous standards and values from the top, it gets accused of corporate censorship. If it doesn't, it gets accused of moral irresponsibility. A dilemma. But someone should have thought of that before deciding to become a global force.

And another genuine dilemma. Whatever the actual merits of *Cop Killer,* if Time Warner withdraws the album now the company will be perceived as giving in to outside pressure. That is a disastrous precedent for a global conglomerate.

The Time-Warner merger of 1989 was supposed to produce corporate "synergy": the whole was supposed to be more than the sum of the parts. The *Cop Killer* controversy is an example of negative synergy. People get mad at *Cop Killer* and start boycotting the movie *Batman Returns.* A reviewer praises *Cop Killer* ("Tracy Marrow's poetry takes a switchblade and deftly slices life's jugular," etc.), and TIME is accused of corruption instead of mere foolishness. Senior Time Warner executives find themselves under attack for—and defending—products of their company they neither honestly care for nor really understand, and doubtless weren't even aware of before controversy hit.

Anyway, it's absurd to discuss *Cop Killer* as part of the "confrontation of ideas"—or even as an authentic anguished cry of rage from the ghetto. *Cop Killer* is a cynical commercial concoction, designed to titillate its audience with imagery of violence. It merely exploits the authentic anguish of the inner city for further titillation. Tracy Marrow is in business for a buck, just like Time Warner. *Cop Killer* is an excellent joke on the white establishment, of which the company's anguished apologia ("Why can't we hear what rap is trying to tell us?") is the punch line.

Topics for Critical Thinking and Writing

1. In his fifth paragraph Kinsley says that "In much of today's popular music, the line between performer and performance is purposely blurred." If you agree, cite instances that support his point.
2. In paragraph 6 Kinsley summarizes Time Warner's second argument, and in paragraph 7 he rejects it, arguing that "a company cannot take the money and run from the responsibility." Exactly why not?
3. In his final paragraph Kinsley makes vigorous assertions, such as "Tracy Marrow is in business for a buck," and it is "absurd" to "discuss *Cop Killer* as part of the 'confrontation of ideas'—or even as an authentic anguished cry of rage from the ghetto." Has Kinsley done enough to *demonstrate* the truth of these assertions, or are they so obvious that they do not need to be demonstrated? Explain.
4. What do you think are Kinsley's strongest arguments? What are his weakest?
5. If you are familiar with a song that deals with violence, offer arguments why disk jockeys should or should not play it.

Barbara Ehrenreich

The following essay appeared in Time *magazine, along with the preceding essay by Michael Kinsley. Barbara Ehrenreich, born in 1941 in Butte, Montana, and educated at Reed College and at Rockefeller University, is the author of several books concerning social issues.*

Ice-T: The Issue Is Creative Freedom

Ice-T's song *Cop Killer* is as bad as they come. This is black anger—raw, rude and cruel—and one reason the song's so shocking is that in postliberal America, black anger is virtually taboo. You won't find it on TV, not on the *McLaughlin Group* or *Crossfire*, and certainly not in the placid features of Arsenio Hall or Bernard Shaw. It's been beaten back into the outlaw subcultures of rap and rock, where, precisely because it is taboo, it sells. And the nastier it is, the faster it moves off the shelves. As Ice-T asks in another song on the same album, "Goddamn what a brotha gotta do/To get a message through/To the red, white and blue?"

But there's a gross overreaction going on, building to a veritable paroxysm of white denial. A national boycott has been called, not just of the song or Ice-T, but of all Time Warner products. The President himself has denounced Time Warner as "wrong" and Ice-T as "sick." Ollie

North's Freedom Alliance has started a petition drive aimed at bringing Time Warner executives to trial for "sedition and anarchy."

Much of this is posturing and requires no more courage than it takes to stand up in a VFW hall and condemn communism or crack. Yes, *Cop Killer* is irresponsible and vile. But Ice-T is as right about some things as he is righteous about the rest. And ultimately, he's not even dangerous—least of all to the white power structure his songs condemn.

The "danger" implicit in all the uproar is of empty-headed, suggestible black kids, crouching by their boom boxes, waiting for the word. But what Ice-T's fans know and his detractors obviously don't is that *Cop Killer* is just one more entry in pop music's long history of macho hyperbole and violent boast. Flip to the classic-rock station, and you might catch the Rolling Stones announcing "the time is right for violent revoloo-shun!" from their 1968 hit *Street Fighting Man*. And where were the defenders of our law-enforcement officers when a white British group, the Clash, taunted its fans with the lyrics: "When they kick open your front door/How you gonna come/With your hands on your head/Or on the trigger of your gun?"   4

"Die, Die, Die Pig" is strong speech, but the Constitution protects strong speech, and it's doing so this year more aggressively than ever. The Supreme Court has just downgraded cross burnings to the level of bonfires and ruled that it's no crime to throw around verbal grenades like "nigger" and "kike." Where are the defenders of decorum and social stability when prime-time demagogues like Howard Stern deride African Americans as "spear chuckers"?

More to the point, young African Americans are not so naive and suggestible that they have to depend on a compact disc for their sociology lessons. To paraphrase another song from another era, you don't need a rap song to tell which way the wind is blowing. Black youths know that the police are likely to see them through a filter of stereotypes as miscreants and potential "cop killers." They are aware that a black youth is seven times as likely to be charged with a felony as a white youth who has committed the same offense, and is much more likely to be imprisoned.

They know, too, that in a shameful number of cases, it is the police themselves who indulge in "anarchy" and violence. The U.S. Justice Department has received 47,000 complaints of police brutality in the past six years, and Amnesty International has just issued a report on police brutality in Los Angeles, documenting 40 cases of "torture or cruel, inhuman or degrading treatment."

Menacing as it sounds, the fantasy in *Cop Killer* is the fantasy of the powerless and beaten down—the black man who's been hassled once too often ("A pig stopped me for nothin'!"), spread-eagled against a police car, pushed around. It's not a "responsible" fantasy (fantasies seldom are). It's not even a very creative one. In fact, the sad thing about *Cop Killer* is that it falls for the cheapest, most conventional image of rebellion that our culture offers: the lone gunman spraying fire from   8 his AK–47. This is not "sedition"; it's the familiar, all-American, Holly-wood-style pornography of violence.

Which is why Ice-T is right to say he's no more dangerous than George Bush's pal Arnold Schwarzenegger, who wasted an army of cops in *Terminator 2*. Images of extraordinary cruelty and violence are marketed every day, many of far less artistic merit than *Cop Killer.* This is our free market of ideas and images, and it shouldn't be any less free for a black man than for other purveyors of "irresponsible" sentiments, from David Duke to Andrew Dice Clay.

Just, please, don't dignify Ice-T's contribution with the word sedi-tion. The past masters of sedition—men like George Washington, Tous-saint-Louverture, Fidel Castro or Mao Zedong, all of whom led and won armed insurrections—would be unimpressed by *Cop Killer* and probably saddened. They would shake their heads and mutter words like "infantile" and "adventurism." They might point out that the cops are hardly a noble target, being, for the most part, honest working stiffs, who've got stuck with the job of patrolling ghettos ravaged by eco-nomic decline and official neglect.

There is a difference, the true seditionist would argue, between a rev-olution and a gesture of macho defiance. Gestures are cheap. They feel good, they blow off some rage. But revolutions, violent or otherwise, are made by people who have learned how to count very slowly to 10.

Topics for Critical Thinking and Writing

1. Make a list of the arguments Ehrenreich offers in defence of Ice-T, and evaluate each one. Are some of her arguments stronger than others? If so, explain the strengths and the weaknesses. (For instance, in para-graph 4 she argues that today's defenders of law and order did not object to the lyrics sung by British groups in past years. Is this a strong or a weak argument? Why?)
2. In paragraph 9 Ehrenreich suggests that *Cop Killer* has "artistic merit." If you are familiar with the piece and you agree with this evaluation, argue the case. (On arguing aesthetic evaluations, see pages 67–69.)
3. In paragraph 9 Ehrenreich reports that Ice-T says he is no more danger-ous than Arnold Schwarzenegger. What replies, if any, can be offered to this comparison?
4. Why do you suppose Ehrenreich didn't end with her ninth paragraph? What do the last two paragraphs (10–11) do for the essay?
5. Do you find any areas of agreement between Kinsley and Ehrenreich? If so, what are they?
6. Putting aside, if possible, your own view of whether the song should be aired, which of the two essays do you think offers the stronger argu-ments? Explain.

5
A NOTE ON READING (AND WRITING ABOUT) PICTURES

I am after the one unique picture whose composition possesses such vigor and richness, and whose content so radiates outwards from it, that this single picture is a whole story in itself.

Henri Cartier-Bresson

The Language of Pictures

It may sound odd to talk about "reading" pictures and about the "language" of pictures, but pictures, like words, convey messages. Advertisers know this, and that's why their advertisements for soft drinks include images of attractive young couples frolicking at the beach. The not-so-hidden message is that consumers of these products are healthy, prosperous, relaxed, and strongly attractive to people of the opposite sex.

Like compositions made of words—stories, poems, even vigorous sentences—many paintings are carefully constructed things, built up in a certain way in order to make a statement. To cite an obvious example, in medieval religious pictures Jesus or Mary may be shown larger than the surrounding figures to indicate their greater spiritual status. But even in realistic paintings the more important figures are likely to be given a greater share of the light or a more central position than the lesser figures. Such devices of composition are fairly evident in paintings, but we occasionally forget that photographs too are almost always constructed things. The photographer—even the amateur just taking a candid snapshot—adjusts a pillow under the baby's head, or asks the subject to smile or to lean against a tree, and then the photographer backs up a little and bends his or her knees before clicking the shutter. Even when photographing something inanimate, the photographer searches for the best view, waits for a cloud to pass, and perhaps pushes out of the range of the camera some trash that would spoil the effect of a lovely fern growing beside a rock. Minor White was speaking for almost all photographers when he said, "I don't take pictures, I make them."

And we often make our photographs for a particular purpose—perhaps to have a souvenir of a trip, or to show what we look like in uniform or at our job, or to show grandma what the new baby looks like. We take pictures of all sorts of subjects for a variety of reasons, but because most of the photographs that amateurs take are of family members, this chapter will include two essays in which students analyze family pictures. Before we give these essays, however, we want first to set forth some questions that may help you think about pictures. Then, as an example of reading the language of pictures, we reproduce a famous photograph by Dorothea Lange along with some students' comments on it.

What are some of the basic things to look for in understanding the language of pictures? One can begin almost anywhere, but let's begin with the relationship among the parts:

Do the figures share the space evenly, or does one figure over-power another, taking most of the space or the light?

Are the figures harmoniously related, perhaps by a similar stance or shared action? Or are they opposed, perhaps by diagonals thrusting at each other? Generally speaking, diagonals may sug-gest instability, except when they form a triangle resting on its base. Horizontal lines suggest stability, as do vertical lines when connected by a horizontal line. Circular lines are often associat-ed with motion, and sometimes—especially by men—with the female body and fertility. These simple formulas, however, must be applied cautiously, for they are not always appropriate.

In a landscape, what is the relation between humans and nature? Are the figures at ease in nature, or are they dwarfed by it? Are they earthbound, beneath the horizon, or (because the view-point is low) do they stand out against the horizon and perhaps seem in touch with the heavens, or at least with open air? Do the natural objects in the landscape somehow reflect the emo-tions of the figures in it?

If the picture is a portrait, how do the furnishings and the back-ground and the angle of the head or the posture of the head and body (as well, of course, as the facial expression) contribute to our sense of the person portrayed?

What is the effect of light in the picture? Does it produce sharp contrasts, brightly illuminating some parts and throwing others into darkness? Or does it, by means of gentle gradations, unify most or all of the parts? Does the light seem theatrical or nat-ural, disturbing or comforting? If the picture is in color, is the color realistic or is it expressive, or both?

You can stimulate responses to pictures by asking yourself two kinds of questions:

1. *What is this doing?* Why is this figure here and not there, why is this tree so brightly illuminated, why are shadows omitted, why is this seated figure leaning forward like that?
2. *Why do I have this response?* Why do I find this figure pathetic, this landscape oppressive, this child revoltingly sentimental but that child fascinating?

The first of these questions, "What is this doing?" requires you to iden-tify yourself with the artist, wondering perhaps whether the fence or the side of the house is the better background for this figure, or whether both figures should sit or stand. The second question, "Why do I have this response?" requires you to trust your feelings. If you are amused, repelled, unnerved, or soothed, assume that these responses are appropriate and follow them up—at least until further study of the work provides other responses.

Thinking about Dorothea Lange's
Migrant Mother, Nipomo, California

Let's look now at a photograph by Dorothea Lange, an American photographer who made her reputation with photographs of migrant farmers in California during the depression that began in 1929. Lange's *Migrant Mother, Nipomo, California* (1936) is probably the best-known image of the period. One of our students made the following entry in his journal. (The student was given no information about the photograph other than its title.)

```
This woman seems to be thinking. In a way, the picture
reminds me of a statue called The Thinker, of a seated
man who is bent over, with his chin resting on his fist.
But I wouldn't say that this photograph is really so much
about thinking as it is about other things. I'd say that
it is about several other things. First (but not really
in any particular order), fear. The children must be
afraid, since they have turned to their mother. Second,
the picture is about love. The children press against
their mother, sure of her love. The mother does not actu-
ally show her love--for instance, by kissing them, or
even hugging them--but you feel she loves them. Third,
the picture is about hopelessness. The mother doesn't
seem to be able to offer any comfort. Probably they have
very little food; maybe they are homeless. I'd say the
picture is also about courage. Although the picture seems
to me to show hopelessness, I also think the mother, even
though she does not know how she will be able to help her
children shows great strength in her face. She also has a
lot of dignity. She hasn't broken down in front of the
children: she is going to do her best to get through the
day and the next day and the next.
```

Another student wrote:

```
I remember from American Lit that good literature is not
sentimental. (When we discussed the word, we concluded
```

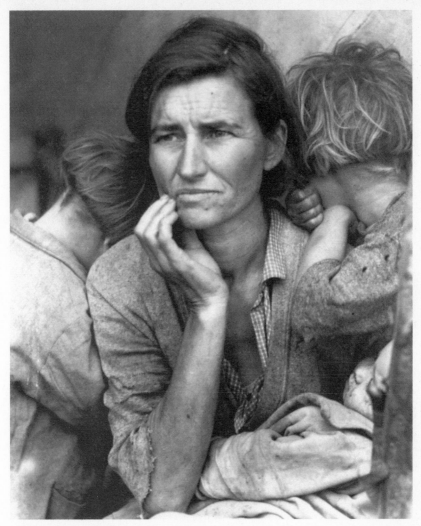

FSA Photo/Library of Congress

that "sentimental" meant "sickeningly sweet.") Some people might think that Lange's picture, showing a mother
and two little children, is sentimental, but I don't
think so. Although the children must be upset, and maybe
they even are crying, the mother seems to be very strong.
I feel that with a mother like this, the children are in
very good hands. She is not "sickeningly sweet." She may
be almost overcome with despair, but she doesn't seem to
ask us to pity her.

A third student wrote:

```
It's like those pictures of the homeless in the newspa-
pers and on TV. A photographer sees some man sleeping in
a cardboard box, or a woman with shopping bags sitting in
a doorway, and he takes their picture. I suppose the pho-
tographer could say that he is calling the public's at-
tention to "the plight of the homeless," but I'm not con-
vinced that he's doing anything more than making money by
selling photographs. Homeless people have almost no pri-
vacy, and then some photographer comes along and invades
even their doorways and cardboard houses. Sometimes the
people are sleeping, or even if they are awake they may
be in so much despair that they don't bother to tell the
photographer to get lost. Or they may be mentally ill and
don't know what's happening. In the case of this picture,
the woman is not asleep, but she seems so preoccupied
that she isn't aware of the photographer. Maybe she has
just been told there is no work for her, or maybe she has
been told she can't stay if she keeps the children.
Should the photographer have intruded on this woman's
sorrow? This picture may be art, but it bothers me.
```

All of these entries seem to us to be thoughtful, interesting, and help-ful, though of course even taken together they do not provide the last word. Here are a few additional points. First, it happens that Lange has written about the picture. She said that she had spent the winter of 1935–36 taking photographs of migrants, and now, in March, she was preparing to drive five hundred miles to her home when she noticed a sign that said, "Pea-Pickers Camp." Having already taken hundreds of pictures, she drove on for twenty miles, but something preyed on her mind, and she made a U-turn and visited the camp. Here is part of what she wrote.

> I saw and approached the hungry and desperate mother, as if drawn by a magnet. I do not remember how I explained my presence or my camera to her, but I do remember she asked me no questions. I made five exposures, working closer and closer from the same direction. I did not ask her name or her history. She told me her age, that she was thirty-two. She said that they had been living on frozen vegetables from the surrounding fields, and birds that the children killed. She had just sold the tires from her car to buy food. There she sat in that lean-to tent with her children huddled around her, and seemed to know that my pictures might help her, and so she helped me. There was a sort of equality about it. . . . What I am trying to tell other photographers is that had I not been deeply involved in my undertaking on that field trip, I would not have had to turn back. What I am trying to say is that I believe this inner compulsion to be the vital in-gredient in our work.

Lange does not say anything about posing the woman and her child, and we can assume that she had too much decency to ask a woman and children in these circumstances to arrange themselves into an interesting pictorial composition. Furthermore, it seems obvious that unlike, say, a figure in a wedding portrait, the woman is not striking a pose. She has not deliberately prepared herself for a picture that will represent her to the public. Nevertheless, the composition—the way things are put together—certainly contributes to the significance of the picture. Of course the subject matter, a mother with children, may suggest the traditional Madonna and Child of the Middle Ages and the Renaissance, but the resemblance is not just in the subject matter. Lange's photograph may remind us of paintings in which the Madonna and the infant Jesus form a unified composition, their heads and limbs harmonizing and echoing each other. The photograph, with its near-balance—a child on each side, the mother's bare left arm balanced by the child's bare arm, the mother's hand at one side of her neck echoed by the child's hand at the other side—achieves a stability, or harmony, that helps make the painfulness of the subject acceptable. That is, although the subject may be painful, it is possible to take some pleasure in the way in which it is presented. That the faces of the children are turned away probably helps make the subject acceptable. If we saw not only the woman's face but also the faces of two hungry children, we might feel that Lange was tugging too vigorously at our heartstrings. Finally, speaking of faces, it is worth mentioning that the woman does not look at us. Of course we don't know why, but we can guess that she takes no notice of us because she is preoccupied with issues far beyond us.

Writing about Family Photographs: Two Essays by First-year Students

You may take a course in college that is partly or largely concerned with reading images. Art history courses obviously have this concern, but other courses too may ask you to study pictures. A sociology course may ask you to examine such a topic as the images of brides in popular magazines, a religion course may ask you to examine images of deities in a certain culture, and a course in advertising will certainly ask you to write about visual ads. It may be mentioned, too, that much of what we know about the past—for instance about Pre-Columbian society in the New World—depends on the interpretation of images. And, of course, some careers are based on the interpretation of images—for instance, of aerial photographs and of x-rays. There are good reasons, then, to develop some skill in analyzing pictures, but perhaps the best reason is that it's fun to think about pictures.

At the beginning of each thematic chapter of this text, you'll find four pictures, which we hope you will enjoy looking at and thinking about. Like the Short Views, which also introduce each chapter, the pictures offer occasions for reflecting on the chapter's theme—family, education, work, business, and so on—and you may find yourself referring to them in journal entries or essays that you write. Or they may themselves be subjects of essays—a good way to practice consciously reading images.

Another good way to practice thinking about images is to analyze a snapshot or family photograph that you own, the sort of picture many of us took with us when we left home for college, or carry with us in our wallets. The two essays that we print below are students' analyses of family photographs. They were written in response to an assignment by Nadia Medina, the instructor in a writing class whose theme, like that of our first thematic chapter, was the family.

First, the assignment:

Select a family photograph and write a paper in which you both analyze and describe the relationship of the people as they are revealed in the picture. You are welcome, indeed encouraged, to use your personal knowledge of the circumstances under which the photograph was taken, or the occasion that it celebrates, to add to your analysis. Any other material can be included (as, for example, what happened afterwards), but your paper should be anchored in the photograph itself.

Cheryl Lee
February 17, 1992
Writing 1250
Medina

The Story behind the Gestures: A Family Photograph

At the close of my graduation ceremony, my entire
family gathered together to immortalize the special moment
on film. No one escaped the flash of my mother's camera
because she was determined to document every minute of the
occasion at every possible angle. My mother made sure that
she took pictures of me with my hat on, with my hat off,
holding the bouquet, sitting, standing, and in countless
other positions. By the time this family picture was taken,
my smile was intact, frozen on my face. This is not to say
that my smile was anything less than genuine, for it truly
was a smile of thankfulness and joy. It is just that after
posing for so many pictures, what initially began as a
spontaneous reaction became a frozen expression.

The viewer should, however, consider not so much
the frozen expressions of those in the photograph, but
rather the fact that the picture is posed. A posed picture supposedly shows only what the people in the picture
want the viewer to see--in this case, their happiness.
But ironically the photograph reveals much more about its
subjects than the viewer first imagines. The photograph
speaks of relationships and personalities. It speaks
about the more intimate details that first seem invisible
but that become undeniable through the study of gestures.

In the photograph, the most prominent and symbolic of
gestures is the use and position of the arms. Both my

father and mother place an arm around me and in turn around
each other. Their encircling arms, however, do more than
just show affection: they unify the three figures into a
close huddle that leads the viewer's eye directly to them
as opposed to the background or the periphery. The slightly
bended arms that rest at their sides act as arrows that not
only reinforce the three figures as the focal point but
also exclude the fourth figure, my brother, from sharing
the "spotlight." Unlike the other members of the family,
whose arms and hands are intertwined, Edwin stands with
both hands down in front of him, latching onto no one. The
lack of physical contact between the huddled figures and
Edwin is again emphasized as he positions himself away from
the viewer's eye as he stands in the periphery.

Edwin's position in the photograph is indicative of
him as a person, for he always seems to isolate himself
from the spotlight, from being the center of attention.
Thus, it is his decision to escape public scrutiny, not
the force of my parents' arms that drives him to the
side. His quiet, humble nature directs him away from even
being the focal point of a picture and leads him towards
establishing his own individuality and independence in
privacy. His long hair and his "hand-me-down" clothes are
all an expression of his simply being himself. The reason
behind his physical independence is the emotional independence that he already possesses at the age of sixteen.
He stands alone because he can stand alone.

While Edwin stands apart from the other three figures, I stand enclosed and protected. The lock of arms as
well as the bouquet restrain me; they dissuade me from
breaking away in favor of independence. Although my moth-

er wants me to achieve the same kind of independence that Edwin has achieved, she works to delay the time when I actually will move away to the periphery. Perhaps my being the only daughter, the only other female in the family, has something to do with my mother's desire to keep me close and dependent as long as possible. Her arm reaches out with bouquet in hand as if to shield me from the world's unpleasantness. Even though my father also holds onto me with an encircling arm, it is my mother's firm grip that alone persuades me to stay within the boundary of their protective arms.

Her grip, which proves more powerful than my father's hold, restrains not only me but also my father. In the picture, he falls victim to the same outstretched hand, the same touch of the bouquet. Yet this time, my mother's bouquet does more than just restrain; it seems to push my father back "into line" or into his so-called place. The picture illustrates this exertion of influence well, for my mother in real life does indeed assume the role of the dominant figure. Although my father remains the head of the household in title, it is my mother around whom the household revolves; she oversees the insignificant details as well as the major ones. But my father doesn't mind at all. Like me, he also enjoys the protection her restraining arm offers. It is because of our mutual dependence on my mother that my father and I seem to draw closer. This dependence in turn strengthens both of our relationships with my mother.

I seriously doubt that at the time the picture was taken, my mother realized the significance of her position in the picture or the import of her gestures. All of us in fact seem too blinded by the festivity of the occasion to realize that this photograph would show more than just a happy family at a daughter's graduation. The family photograph would inevitably become a telling portrait of each member of the family. It would, in a sense, leave us vulnerable to the speculative eyes of the viewer, who in carefully examining the photograph would recognize the secrets hidden in each frozen expression.

In thinking about Cheryl Lee's essay, you might ask yourself these questions:

1. Is the essay devoted chiefly to analyzing a picture, or is it devoted chiefly to exploring Lee's feelings about the picture?
2. What is the function of Lee's opening paragraph? What is your response to her statement that the family gathered together "to immortalize" her graduation? What is the effect of "with my hat on, with my hat off"? How would you characterize the writer of this paragraph?
3. Do you think that Lee's interpretation is probably sound, or do you think that she reads too much (or too little) into the picture? Support your view.
4. Evaluate the final paragraph as a final paragraph.

Here is an essay by a second student, writing on the same assignment.

Samantha Campbell
Writing 1250
April 9, 1991

My Father's Photograph

I am asleep. And very little; little and asleep. I am on my back, my little head turned to the side and on my face is the emotionless solemnity of baby dreams. My left hand rests on a little stuffed kangaroo doll, and my

right hand is open so you can see all my pretty little
fingers. I am wearing a little white terrycloth suit that
snaps all the way up the front. My hair looks dark in the
black-and-white photograph, but I am told it was quite
red when I was just born.

I am the only person in this picture; without the
background collage it would be a boring shot, documenting
that indeed I did sleep as a newborn child. The precise
rows of small photographs on which I lie are what makes
the person flipping through my baby book stop to look
more closely. There are seven slightly tilted horizontal
rows of these identical pictures. If you stare at them
long enough they become a series of black-and-white patterns, an oddly frenetic patchwork quilt. They are leftover birth announcements showing the photograph taken in
the delivery room minutes after I was born, picturing my
mother, my father, and me. In each tiny picture mother is

lying down and holding me up; she is smiling at the camera, looking a bit tired but genuinely pleased. My father, standing, rests his hand on her long, straight, dark hair, and peers down through his glasses at me, the little baby. He wears antiseptic surgical garb so that he will not breathe on me or transmit to me any unclean particles that I should be spared, at least for a while.

It is a nice picture, the birth announcement photo. The doctor apparently had a good sense of artistic composition: the arrangement is circular, the figures appear interwoven, bonded and linked. And the entire shot, me resting on this careful grid-work, is interesting too. Pretty creative of my father (the biological one)!

But I've never liked it, and I love looking at old pictures of myself and my family. This photo has always disturbed me in a vague sort of way. It's hard and it's cold. It's all stark and unflinching lines. The background must have taken an awfully long time to lay out: I can just see my father, squinting, leaning over the floor, meticulously spacing the old announcements so that they are equidistant and straight. Like his bottles of vitamins and his comb and his brush and his toothbrush and his dental floss and his lotions and his after-shave all perfectly aligned near the bathroom sink that whenever I see them make me want to scream and pound the counter so hard they all jiggle and vibrate and maybe fall over and then finally settle disrupted and just a little just a little bit crooked.

I can see him taking me out of my crib when I'm sleeping and gingerly putting me down, very very careful not to disturb his delicate configuration (but I can see that the photo right under my cheek is the tiniest bit misaligned). I'm sure he put the kangaroo under my hand, reached quickly for the camera and took picture after picture. I know he changed my position, gave me different toys to hold, because I have seen similar shots where I, the composition, and the angle have been manipulated, very slightly. One roll of film, two? Photograph after photograph of a little baby asleep on a crafted crazed collage. I don't like it.

It must be the feeling behind it, because in a way I can appreciate the originality. Objectively I like the pictures. But I cannot be objective when it comes to my father because I do not like what he does and I do not like who he is. I have been physically separated from him most of my life, and I grow more apart from him every year. But I cannot be objective because I do not like his constantly calculating mind, his absolute egomania, his entire system of values. And I do not like the way he uses me and talks to me and has ideas about me.

"Blood, Samantha," he says, strong gravelly voice. "That's what it's all about. You see, you can have your friends, that's good, friends are important and other people are important. But you have only one mother and one father. You are connected to your family, your real family, by blood. That's forever, kid." I've heard variations on a blood theme for years and years, especially since my mother remarried and I gained not only a stepfather but also his entire family, to whom I have been very close.

So I know my father loves this picture, because it is dripping with blood. He repeats himself over and over here. "This is you with your mother and father, this is

you with your father and mother, this is blood. There you
are in the midst of it, on top of it, you sleep with it.
This is it." Here is what I say: "No. This is not me who
I am, this is me what I was, which is an infant who can
be (damn it) used to do whatever a parent wants to do.
No, it's not me. And I don't care about the integration
of figures here, the circular image of mother father
child. I don't care that I have mother's birth blood on
my body or yours running through my veins or half your
chromosomes or eyebrows shaped like yours I don't care I
really don't. And you can't make me."

This is not a picture of love, of adoration of a
child just born. It is a picture of cold cleverness and
colder ideas. It is manipulated, I am manipulated. I feel
used, like I have been before: as a weapon against my
mother when he took me away from her (twice), or as the
smiling, blond, childish centerpiece of a casual business
meeting. He likes to show me off, to show people what
he has created, his own blood. This is not love. People
tell me, "But he really loves you, look what he sent you,
see how he calls you all the time and wants to see you
and. . . ." I can't make them understand that this is not
love; I know it is not.

If you really look at the birth announcement photograph, you see that the circle is not perfect. My mother
is the one who holds me. My father, masked, is not touching me; his hand drops to his side. My mother looks out-
ward towards the photographer; she's not trapped here in
this circle. And me, well, I'm just a baby. A new, little
thing of flesh and yes, blood, but it is me what I was
and not me who I am. And I am not part of this photo-

```
graph, this dead collage with the living child on top of
it. This perfect, pretty, artful creation of a man who is
only my father.
```

We can ask of this essay questions similar to those we asked of Cheryl Lee's essay.

1.   Is the essay chiefly devoted to analyzing a picture, or is it chiefly devoted to exploring Campbell's feelings about the picture?
2.   What is the function of Campbell's opening paragraph? What is the effect on you of the first sentence—very short—and of the second— also short, and marked by the repetition of "little." Notice, too, that except for the second sentence, all of the sentences in this paragraph begin with "I am," or with "My." How would you characterize the writer of this paragraph?
3.   Do you think that Campbell's interpretation is probably sound, or do you think that she reads too much (or too little) into the picture? Or do you think that our opinion about the validity of the interpretation is irrelevant? Support your view.
4.   Evaluate the final paragraph as a final paragraph.

Last Words

If your instructor asks you to write about a picture—perhaps one in this book—and if even after thinking about the questions on pages 105–106 you don't quite know where to begin, you may want to think about it partly in terms of one of the following remarks by distinguished photographers. (But remember: a remark need not be true just because it was made by someone who is highly regarded as a photographer.)

> A great photograph is a full expression of what one feels about what is being photographed in the deepest sense, and is, thereby, a true expression of what one feels about life in its entirety.
>
> Ansel Adams

> It's the subject-matter that counts. I'm interested in revealing the subject in a new way to intensify it.
>
> Harry Callahan

> Documentary photography records the social scene of our time. It mirrors the present and documents for the future. Its focus is man in his relations to mankind.
>
> Dorothea Lange

Photography is the simultaneous recognition, in a fraction of a second, of the significance of an event as well as of the precise organization of forms which give that event its proper expression.

Henri Cartier-Bresson

I am a passionate lover of the snapshot because of all photographic images it comes closest to truth. The snapshot is a specific spiritual moment. . . . What the eye sees is different from what the camera records. Whereas the eye sees in three dimensions, images are projected on a surface of two dimensions, which for every image-maker is a great problem. The snap-shooter disregards this problem, and the result is that his pictures have an apparent disorder and imperfection, which is exactly their appeal and their style. . . . Out of this imbalance, and out of this not knowing, and out of this real innocence toward the medium comes an enormous vitality and expression of life.

Lisette Model

Or you might begin by thinking about a statement by Janet Malcolm, who in *Diana and Nikon* (a book about photography) said:

If "the camera can't lie," neither is it inclined to tell the truth, since it can reflect only the usually ambiguous, and sometimes outright deceitful sur-face of reality.

6
ALL IN THE FAMILY

Sonia
Joanne Leonard, 1966

Mrs. Brown and Catherine
Faith Ringgold, 1973

Short Views

After a certain age, the more one becomes oneself, the more obvious one's family traits become.

Marcel Proust

All happy families resemble one another; every unhappy family is unhappy in its own fashion.

Leo Tolstoy, *Anna Karenina*

On Tuesday, March 31, he and I dined at General Paoli's. A question was started, whether the state of marriage was natural to man. Johnson. "Sir, it is so far from being natural for a man and woman to live in a state of marriage, that we find all the motives which they have for remaining in that connection, and the restraints which civilized society imposes to prevent separation, are hardly sufficient to keep them together." The General said, that in a state of nature a man and woman uniting together would form a strong and constant affection, by the mutual pleasure each would receive; and that the same causes of dissension would not arise between them, as occur between husband and wife in a civilized state. Johnson. "Sir, they would have dissensions enough, though of another kind. One would choose to go a hunting in this wood, the other in that; one would choose to go a fishing in this lake, the other in that; or, perhaps, one would choose to go a hunting, when the other would choose to go a fishing; and so they would part. Besides, Sir, a savage man and a savage woman meet by chance; and when the man sees another woman that pleases him better, he will leave the first."

James Boswell

Marriage is the best of human statuses and the worst, and it will continue to be. And that is why, though its future in some form or other is as assured as anything can be, this future is as equivocal as its past. The demands that men and women make on marriage will never be fully met; they cannot be.

Jessie Bernard

A slavish bondage to parents cramps every faculty of the mind; and Mr. Locke very judiciously observes, that "if the mind be curbed and humbled too much in children, if their spirits be abased and broken much by too strict an hand over them, they lose all their vigour and industry." This strict hand may in some degree account for the weakness of women; for girls, from various causes, are more kept down by their parents, in every sense of the word, than boys. The duty expected from them is, like all the duties arbitrarily imposed on women, more from a sense of propriety, more out of respect for decorum, than reason; and thus taught slavishly to submit to their parents, they are prepared for the slavery of marriage. I may be told that a number of women are not slaves in the marriage state. True, but they then become tyrants; for it is not rational freedom, but a lawless kind of power resembling the authority exercised by the favourites of absolute monarchs, which they obtain by debasing means.

      Mary Wollstonecraft

Nobody who has not been in the interior of a family can say what the difficulties of any individual of that family may be.

      Jane Austen, *Emma*

When I was young enough to still spend a long time buttoning my shoes in the morning, I'd listen toward the hall: Daddy upstairs was shaving in the bathroom and Mother downstairs was frying the bacon. They would begin whistling back and forth to each other up and down the stairwell. My father would whistle his phrase, my mother would try to whistle, then hum hers back. It was their duet. I drew my buttonhook in and out and listened to it—I knew it was "The Merry Widow." The difference was, their song almost floated with laughter: how different from the record, which growled from the beginning, as if the Victrola were only slowly being wound up. They kept it running between them, up and down the stairs where I was now just about ready to run clattering down and show them my shoes.

      Eudora Welty

Lewis Coser

Lewis Coser, born in Berlin in 1913, was educated at the Sorbonne in Paris and at Columbia University, where he received a Ph.D. in sociology in 1954. For many years he taught at the State University of New York, Stony Brook, where he held the title Distinguished Professor. The passage given below is from a textbook designed for college students.

The Family

Following the French anthropologist Claude Lévi-Strauss, we can define the family as a group manifesting these characteristics: it finds its origin in marriage; it consists of husband, wife and children born in their wedlock—though other relatives may find their place close to that nuclear group; and the members of the group are united by moral, legal, economic, religious, and social rights and obligations. These include a network of sexual rights and prohibitions and a variety of socially patterned feelings such as love, attraction, piety, awe, and so on.

The family is among the few universal institutions of mankind. No known society lacks small kinship groups of parents and children related through the process of reproduction. But recognition of the universality of this institution must immediately be followed by the acknowledgment that its forms are exceedingly varied. The fact that many family organizations are not monogamic, as in the West, led many nineteenth-century observers to the erroneous conclusion that in "early" stages of evolution there existed no families, and that "group marriage," institutionalized promiscuity, prevailed. This is emphatically not the case; even though patterned wife-lending shocked the sensibilities of Victorian anthropologists, such an institution is evidently predicated on the fact that men have wives in the first place. No matter what their specific forms, families in all known societies have performed major social functions—reproduction, maintenance, socialization, and social placement of the young.

Families may be monogamous or polygamous—there are systems where no man is entitled to several wives and others where several husbands share one wife. A society may recognize primarily the small nuclear, conjugal unit of husband and wife with their immediate descendants or it may institutionalize the large extended family linking several generations and emphasizing consanguinity more than the conjugal bond. Residence after marriage may be matrilocal, patrilocal or neolocal; exchanges of goods and services between families at the time of marriage may be based on bride price, groom price or an equal exchange; endogamous or exogamous regulations may indicate who is and who is not eligible for marriage; the choice of a mate may be controlled by parents or it may be left in large measure to the young persons concerned. These are but a few of the many differences which characterize family structures in variant societies.

Topics for Critical Thinking and Writing

1.   At the end of paragraph 2, Coser writes: "No matter what their specific forms, families in all known societies have performed major social functions—reproduction, maintenance, socialization, and social placement of the young." What does "socialization" mean? How does it differ from "social placement of the young"? What specific forms does each take in our society?
2.   What examples can you give of "moral, legal, economic, religious, and social rights and obligations" (paragraph 1) that unite members of a family?
3.   Compare Coser and Plumb (pages 6–10) on the social functions of the family. According to Plumb, what responsibility does the family in our society have in performing the social functions Coser lists? How do other institutions compete with the family in performing some of these functions?
4.   As you read other selections in this chapter what variations in form of the family do you encounter? Are there any variations in form Coser did not mention or anticipate?

Judy Brady

Judy Brady was born in San Francisco in 1937. She received a bachelors degree from the University of Iowa in 1960 and wanted to do the graduate work that would qualify her for teaching in a university but her male teachers discouraged her. "Why I Want a Wife" originally appeared in the first issue of Ms.

Why I Want a Wife

I belong to that classification of people known as wives. I am A Wife. And, not altogether incidentally, I am a mother.

Not too long ago a male friend of mine appeared on the scene fresh from a recent divorce. He had one child, who is, of course, with his ex-wife. He is looking for another wife. As I thought about him while I was ironing one evening, it suddenly occurred to me that I, too, would like to have a wife. Why do I want a wife?

I would like to go back to school so that I can become economically independent, support myself, and, if need be, support those dependent upon me. I want a wife who will work and send me to school. And while I am going to school I want a wife to take care of my children. I want a wife to keep track of the children's doctor and dentist appointments. And to keep track of mine, too. I want a wife to make sure my children eat properly and are kept clean. I want a wife who will wash the children's clothes and keep them mended. I want a wife who is a good nurturant attendant to my children, who arranges for their schooling, makes sure that they have an adequate social life with their peers, takes them to the park, the zoo, etc. I want a wife who takes care of the children when they are sick, a wife who arranges to be around when the children need special care, because, of course, I cannot miss classes at school. My wife must arrange to lose time at work and not lose the job. It may mean a small cut in my wife's income from time to time, but I guess I can tolerate that. Needless to say, my wife will arrange and pay for the care of the children while my wife is working.

I want a wife who will take care of *my* physical needs. I want a wife   4
who will keep my house clean. A wife who will pick up after my children, a wife who will pick up after me. I want a wife who will keep my clothes clean, ironed, mended, replaced when need be, and who will see to it that my personal things are kept in their proper place so that I can find what I need the minute I need it. I want a wife who cooks the meals, a wife who is a *good* cook. I want a wife who will plan the menus, do the necessary grocery shopping, prepare the meals, serve them pleasantly, and then do the cleaning up while I do my studying. I want a wife who will care for me when I am sick and sympathize with my pain and loss of time from school. I want a wife to go along when our family takes a vacation so that someone can continue to care for me and my children when I need a rest and change of scene.

I want a wife who will not bother me with rambling complaints about a wife's duties. But I want a wife who will listen to me when I feel the need to explain a rather difficult point I have come across in my course of studies. And I want a wife who will type my papers for me when I have written them.

I want a wife who will take care of the details of my social life. When my wife and I are invited out by my friends, I want a wife who will take care of the babysitting arrangements. When I meet people at school that I like and want to entertain, I want a wife who will have the house clean, will prepare a special meal, serve it to me and my friends, and not interrupt when I talk about things that interest me and my friends. I want a wife who will have arranged that the children are fed and ready for bed before my guests arrive so that the children do not bother us. I want a wife who takes care of the needs of my guests so that they feel comfortable, who makes sure that they have an ashtray, that they are passed the hors d'oeuvres, that they are offered a second helping of the food, that their wine glasses are replenished when necessary, that their coffee is served to them as they like it. And I want a wife who knows that sometimes I need a night out by myself.

I want a wife who is sensitive to my sexual needs, a wife who makes love passionately and eagerly when I feel like it, a wife who makes sure that I am satisfied. And, of course, I want a wife who will not demand sexual attention when I am not in the mood for it. I want a wife who assumes the complete responsibility for birth control, because I do not want more children. I want a wife who will remain sexually faithful to me so that I do not have to clutter up my intellectual life with jealousies. And I want a wife who understands that *my* sexual needs may entail more than strict adherence to monogamy. I must, after all, be able to relate to people as fully as possible.

If, by chance, I find another person more suitable as a wife than the wife I already have, I want the liberty to replace my present wife with another one. Naturally, I will expect a fresh, new life; my wife will take the children and be solely responsible for them so that I am left free.   8

When I am through with school and have a job, I want my wife to quit working and remain at home so that my wife can more fully and completely take care of a wife's duties.

My God, who *wouldn't* want a wife?

Topics for Critical Thinking and Writing

1. Does the second sentence of the essay mean anything different from the first? If so, what? If not, why is it there?
2. Describing a recently divorced man, Brady says in paragraph 2: "He had one child, who is, of course, with his ex-wife." What information does "of course" convey? What attitude or tone?
3. If the constant repetition of "I want a wife who . . ." is not boring, what keeps it from being boring?
4. Brady is attacking sexual stereotyping. Do you find in her essay any assumptions or details that limit the stereotyping to an economic class or to an ethnic or racial group? Explain.

Diane Medved

Diane Medved was born in 1951 in Los Angeles and educated (B.A., M.A., and Ph.D.) at the University of California, Los Angeles. She is a licensed clinical therapist and the author of three books: Children, To Have or Have Not? *(1982, under the name of Diane C. Elvenstar),* First Comes Love: Deciding Whether or Not to Get Married *(1983, also under the name of Elvenstar), and (under the name of Medved)* The Case against Divorce *(1989, in which the material that we reprint here appears.*

The Case against Divorce

I have to start with a confession: This isn't the book I set out to write.

I planned to write something consistent with my previous professional experience—helping people with decision making. In ten years as a psychologist, I've run scores of workshops that specialized in weighing the pros and cons of major life choices. I've even published books on two of life's major turning points: whether or not to have a child and whether or not to get married. When I conceptualized this book on divorce, it was in that mold—a guide to help people decide if separation is appropriate.

I based this concept on some firmly held assumptions and beliefs. For example, I started this project believing that people who suffer over an extended period in unhappy marriages ought to get out. In my private practice, I'd seen plenty of struggling couples, and in every case, I anguished along with them when they described manipulation, lack of attention, or emotional dissatisfaction. I knew from their stories, as well as from my own experience, the heart-wrenching desperation that precedes separating and the liberation that leaving represents. I originally thought that staying together in turmoil was ultimately more traumatic than simply making the break.

I was convinced that recent no-fault divorce laws were a praiseworthy step toward simplifying a legally, psychologically, and emotionally punishing process. I thought that striking down taboos about divorce was another part of the ongoing enlightenment of the women's, civil rights, and human potential movements of the last twenty-five years. I had learned early in my graduate school training that crisis fosters growth, and therefore I assumed that the jolt of divorce almost always brings beneficial psychological change. 4

To my utter befuddlement, the extensive research I conducted for this book brought me to one inescapable and irrefutable conclusion: I had been wrong. The statistics and anecdotes I gathered forced me to scuttle my well-prepared plans. I had to face the fact that writing a "morally neutral" book showing divorce to be just another option—a life choice no better or worse than staying married—would be irreparably damaging to the audience I wanted to help.

The change came as I shifted my focus from still-married couples in conflict, who made up the bulk of my practice, to now-single individuals who had already received their decrees.

I asked questions—and got some predictable answers: Are you glad you divorced? Yes. Do you regret getting your divorce? No. I was pleased that the responses to these two questions confirmed my original thinking.

But then I plumbed beneath the surface: What kind of contact do 8
you have with your ex-spouse? How has the divorce affected your children? What kinds of experiences have you had in the dating world since your divorce? How has your style of living changed?

"Oh, everything's fine, fine," the respondents at first insisted. Everyone was without a doubt stronger and more hearty than ever.

But my questions kept coming. And the truth was difficult to avoid. Often in a rush of tears, they described the suffering and anguish they had endured—nights of fantasies about the husband or wife who left them; days of guilt after abandoning a once-devoted mate. They talked about the nuts-and-bolts of daily life, of uprooting, of shifting to an apartment and splitting possessions, of balancing parental duties with now-pressing work demands. They spoke of changing relationships with their children, who moved from innocent babes to confidants to arbitrators and sometimes to scapegoats.

And they mourned a part of themselves never to be recaptured. The part they had once invested in a marital or family unit was now destroyed. Wearily, they told of the transformation of the optimism and enthusiasm they had devoted to the now-crushed marriage to bitterness, skepticism, and self-preservation. "Never again," echoed my respondents. "Never again will I combine my income with another's." "Never again will I trust my spouse away overnight." "Never again will I believe someone when he says 'I'll take care of you.'"

I didn't want to hear it. I wanted to hear that they got past their   12
divorces and emerged better for it. And while the women and men I spoke to were more sure of themselves and capable of living independently, I also heard that they had gained this self-reliance out of painful necessity, not out of free choice.

For given a choice, they preferred to be married. Everyone said he or she wanted to find somebody new. Many women were panic-stricken, afraid they would not find the "right" man before their childbearing years were lost. Others had become so jaded that they lamented the sobering truth that they were unlikely to find another mate at all. With their newfound strength, they all said they would survive; all said they were perfectly content with themselves and the lives they'd recently reconstructed. Still, there was regret. "Looking back now, do you think that you could have made it work with your first husband?" I asked.

"Well, he was crazy," they'd begin. "He was a slob. He was unromantic. He only thought of himself and his career. But knowing what I know now . . . yes, I probably could have made it work."

I was aghast. But the more I heard these or similar words, and the more I read from the library, the more I was forced to concede that the ruinous stories of my divorced clients and interviewees were true. Divorce was catastrophic—but not in the commonly acceptable terms of a simple year or two thrown away. I found that the mere contemplation of divorce—the acceptance of it as an imminent option (rather than dedication to working on a wounded marriage) is debilitating. The process of evaluating the injuries—of cajoling and pleading and threatening—is emotionally exhausting. The physical act of packing a bag and moving out is traumatic. And from there the trauma escalates.

Quite simply, I discovered in my research that the process and   16
aftermath of divorce is so pervasively disastrous—to body, mind, and spirit—that in an overwhelming number of cases, the "cure" that it brings is surely worse than marriage's "disease."

Of course, there are exceptions. There are times when divorce is clearly the only recourse. When physical or mental abuse exists. When emotional cruelty or neglect becomes intolerable. When one partner adamantly refuses to stay in the marriage or withdraws to the point where in reality you're alone.

I used to think that the range of situations when divorce is appropriate encompassed quite a bit more than that. But when I look at the balance of the bad and the good that divorced individuals endure, my only possible conclusion is that people could be spared enormous suffering if they scotched their permissive acceptance of divorce and viewed marriage as a serious, lifelong commitment, a bond not to be entered into—or wriggled out of—lightly.

The old wedding vows read "for better or for worse . . . until death do us part." They now commonly intone, "through good times and bad . . . as long as our love shall last." Until recently, I nodded at the "improvement"; now I soberly acknowledge the wisdom in the message of the past.

Too Late for Marleen

The grim stories of crippled couples whom I interviewed for this book [20] got me thinking about the permanent distrust, anguish, and bitterness divorce brings. But the catalyst coalescing these thoughts was a simple workaday lunch with a friend I've known for about eight years. Marleen Gaines, a school district administrator, is a handsome woman of forty who wears sophisticated silks, renews season tickets to the symphony, and stays sharp on the decisions of the courts, cabinet, and city council. When a mutual friend originally introduced us, I instantly clicked into Marleen's quick wit, upbeat attitude, and direct, self-confident zest. But as we sat down to salads at a café near my office, her usual sunny veneer gave way to a depressing monotone of desolation.

Three years ago, Marleen startled her friends by suddenly walking out of her nine-year marriage. At the time she left him, her husband Bob, now forty-two, seemed unbearably boring, uneducated, and unmotivated to achieve. Marleen wanted more of a dynamo, a brilliant intellectual she could admire, successful in his career. She met lots of these stimulating men at the office, and casual flirtations suggested to her that once she was free to pursue them, she would have plenty of opportunities for a more satisfying marriage.

But after three years single, she has found only frustration—and the humiliating realization that at her age, she is considered witty and glib but not especially desirable. There were a couple of flings with married men and an unrequited crush on her self-absorbed boss, who encouraged her attention merely to further inflate his swollen ego. She fell in love with a coworker, who treasured her company so much he told her every excruciating detail of his romantic exploits and eventual engagement. Meanwhile, her three closest friends remarried one by one and had stylishly late-in-life babies.

Now alone in a rambling house in San Bernardino with only her three dogs for companionship, she yearns for the simple warmth of Bob's presence. Though he was a college dropout and works now as a supermarket manager, Bob had his virtues. Always gentle and good-natured, he doted on Marleen and provided consistent encouragement. He may not have been the go-getter she desired, but he had an intuitive intelligence and a good, steady income to maintain their comfortable lifestyle.

It took all this time for Marleen to realize her mistake. At first, Bob had begged her to return; rebuked, he rebounded into one, then another serious relationship. He now lives with a woman who's pushing for marriage, and he's grown quite fond of her two teenage sons. When they speak every few weeks, Bob confesses to Marleen that his current companion "can be a pain" and swears that Marleen is the only woman he's ever "really" loved. Now Marleen has asked for a reconciliation, but weak-willed Bob is too dominated in his new world to leave, and Marleen, realizing that "possession is nine-tenths of the law," has resigned herself to the fact that he's not coming back.

Divorces Are Forever

Sitting in the restaurant trying to console my friend, I was struck by the frequency with which I've heard stories similar to hers—not only in my workshops and clinical psychology practice, but increasingly in everyday social chatter. It's a well-known U.S. Census Bureau statistic that half of all marriages fail; equally well-publicized is how both men and women suffer financially as a result. Sociologist Leonore Weitzman found that women's standard of living declines by a whopping 73 percent in the first year after divorce, and those who are mothers are further saddled with additional child care and logistics chores.

While everyone laments the immediate trauma of "going through a divorce," more discomfiting is the alarming news of its lingering emotional and psychological effects. Research by the California Children of Divorce Project headed by Judith Wallerstein, for example, shows an especially dismal future for women forty and over—even ten years after the divorce. Half of the women studied at that distant point could be diagnosed as "clinically depressed," and all were moderately or severely lonely, despite the fact that 50 percent of them had initiated the divorce themselves. Exacerbating their malaise might be alarming new statistics on their chances of finding another husband—chances *Newsweek* magazine (June 1986) claims are so low that these women face a greater likelihood of being struck by a terrorist!

Uncovering these facts during the preparation of this book only made me determined to probe reactions to divorce further. I jotted down some ideas and then developed an informal questionnaire that I distributed to an unscientific but diverse sample of two hundred people who had been separated or divorced. The results brought home undeniably that the effects of divorce last a lifetime. And they are in actuality far worse than we care to confront.

Everyone has some understanding of the pain of divorce. And yet, in these days of disposable marriage, at one time or another every married person contemplates separation. It may be in the heat of an argument, or during a fantasy about a more perfect mate. It may appear amid recurrent minor irritations, or it may come as the cumulative result of larger problems stored away for years. Everyone in the throes of a flirtation or affair considers the possibility of chucking the safe and boring for the exciting and glamorous. And people on the cusp of new success are tempted to leave reminders of the less glorious past and begin anew.

Clashing with this casual attitude toward divorce is America's reclaiming of traditional values. Religion has gained renewed respectability. Women who cried "career first" are now honoring their maternal instincts and realizing they may not be able to "have it all." Conservative politics have recently attracted many of yesterday's liberals. And college students, once esoterically majoring in philosophy and sociology, are taking the most direct routes to their MBAs.

Personal lives are more conservative as well, due to the sheer terror provoked by the specter of AIDS. People are practicing "safe sex" not only with frank conversation prior to intimacy and with the use of condoms, but through definite changes in outlook toward recreational sex. A 1987 bestseller, taken seriously enough to be the subject of a day's discussion on the Oprah Winfrey television talk show and a return appearance by the author, advocated sexual abstinence before marriage. In addition, a representative national survey of twelve hundred college students undertaken by *Glamour* magazine revealed that "the AIDS epidemic is a serious damper on sexual activity: about half of all college students say the threat of AIDS has caused them to change their sexual habits."

The AIDS scare and the broader shift toward conservative attitudes, however, seem distant to couples in the throes of conjugal combat. In the midst of a shouting match, a gloriously portrayed single life and freedom from the oppression of a particular spouse call much more loudly. Unfortunately, veterans of divorce like my friend Marleen, who yearn for families and secure, permanent relationships, now see that they have been sadly duped by those compelling myths, which suggest that divorce "can open up new horizons," that the dating scene is exciting, and that bright, attractive people will always find new partners with whom to share their lives.

It's finally time to renounce—openly and clearly—these self-serving platitudes about independence and fulfillment and look at the reality of divorce. We act too frequently as if every infirm marriage deserves to die, based simply upon the emotional report of one distressed partner. Rather than viewing a separation first with alarm, we're full of sympathy for a divorcing friend, and we offer understanding of the temporary insanity involved in severing old ties.

Still influenced by the "do your own thing" era, we don't act constructively. We don't take the husband (or wife) by the shoulders and shake him. We don't shout in his ear that he might be making a disastrous mistake. Even if we care immensely about him, we feel it's too intrusively "judgmental" to do more than step back and say, "Okay, if that's what you want," and close our eyes to the consequences. My research suggests that this is more cruelty than friendship.

Even Winners Pay the Price

Some people who know me well ask how I could take this position, having been divorced and then happily remarried myself. It is partially because I have faced divorce that I can speak with some authority. It is true that I am one of the very lucky few who entered the chancy world of potential happiness or permanent pain and was ultimately given a break. But there are so many others—just as bright, just as desirable or more so—who bitterly ask why their "best years" must be spent alone. Even though I found a satisfying relationship, I am still paying the price of my divorce.

It is difficult for me to discuss something as personal as my own divorce, partially because I now invest so much in the new life I have created. I also don't like writing about my divorce because I am embarrassed and ashamed, and those feelings are painful to express.

Though my ex-husband and I were constitutionally quite different, we were nevertheless also the same in many ways, or at least had grown that way over the years. And because we shared our adolescence and formative adult period, we had a bond I found excruciating to discard. Unfortunately, like almost all of the divorced couples I have seen and researched, we cannot manage that ridiculous myth of being "just friends." So in becoming divorced, I severed an important extension of myself, negating a crucial and memorable chunk of my history and development. It is an enormous loss.

I am humiliated and mortified at failing in a relationship others at one time held exemplary. My divorce clashes with the self-image I work earnestly to cultivate: that I am triumphant in my endeavors, that the things I attempt are not only worthwhile but likely to succeed. By divorcing, I have proven myself inept—at least once—in perhaps the most crucial arena, one which by profession is my stock-in-trade—the ability to analyze choices and proceed wisely.

My divorce would have been bad enough were I able to keep my downfall a secret, like the dieter who sneaks a bag of cookies while driving on the anonymous freeway. But I am embarrassed further because of the public discredit and the possibility that former admirers now view me as diminished. Whether or not my associates really do see my character as smirched, or whether they are truly forgiving, is not as relevant as the fact that I *feel* I am now less worthy of their regard.

For those who do go on to build a second life, the future, built more on hope than confidence, may falter. Only about half of those I interviewed who remarried stayed with the second spouse or reported conjugal satisfaction; many found themselves reeling from their first marriages years later and admitted repeating the same mistakes.

The book *Crazy Time* by Abigail Trafford describes the weeks and months after separation, when typically people replay those crushing moments over and over in their minds. The one who is rejected remembers the years together in measured fragments, dissecting every retort, every misplaced movement, for signs of failure or symbols of flawed passion.

The one who leaves in search of something better is so wracked by guilt and remorse that he can do nothing more than look ahead, shielding himself from the overwhelming self-loathing and embarrassment of looking at his past. Like Pharaoh, who refused the Jews' pleas for freedom even when confronted by the convincing pressure of the ten plagues, a spouse who negates his marriage must harden his heart against it. He must bury all the love that still exists for his partner, even if he realizes that it is love shaped by gratitude rather than attraction. The safe and cozy, welcoming home that the estranged partner once provided must be temporarily barred from consciousness. Years of striving together for the success of the other, for the enhancement of the unit, must be eliminated from the mind.

No one ever emerges from a divorce unscathed—he or she is inevitably permanently harmed.

That the divorced end up even more unhappy is not their fault. They're told by innumerable subtle and direct messages that they ought to be "mad as hell and unwilling to take it anymore," to paraphrase the inciteful slogan of the movie *Network*. They're encouraged by magazines sold at checkout stands to dissect their relationships. They're led by business-seeking shrinks to believe they can't possibly be fulfilled unless they're undergoing turmoil and instigating change.

I've read more than fifty books off my local public library shelves that comfort and cheer on those involved in divorce. These volumes take you step-by-step through the court procedure and tell you what stages of distress your "normal" child will endure. These books ease you like silk into the singles game and tout your "new freedom" as if it, rather than marriage, is the ultimate means toward fulfillment.

I write this book as a counterbalance, to shake a few shoulders, with hopes that I might spare some children helplessness and some partners pain. I want to expose the forces that strive to hide the damage of divorce. Too many people think "If only I could be out of this marriage . . ." and conclude that sentence with their own private miracles. To repeat: It's not their fault; they're victims of propaganda. But the lure lets them down, for after they buy it they inevitably remain the same people, with the same problem-solving skills, values, and styles of relating to another. And so they can't help but choose and shape new relationships into duplications of their spoiled romance. How can they be expected to see that divorce is, with very few exceptions, the wrong way to improve their lives?

And so this book is for everyone who is now focusing on some infuriating characteristic of their mate and thinking, "I can't take this much longer." It is for those who have already packed and moved out, either physically or emotionally, who look ahead and therefore can't see that their brightest path lies behind them. It is for those who have been hurt, whose wounds are so painful that they simply want to run away, and for others who see signs and want to prevent a breakup before the repairs become too overwhelming.

Perhaps you or someone you know has uttered something similar to one or more of these lines:

> "Our fights are getting so fierce, the good times don't seem worth the arguments anymore."
> "Sure I love him. But I know I could do better."
> "I've found the love of my life—I have to get out of my marriage because I just can't end this affair and give up such a good thing."
> "I've been smothered in this marriage too long—I need to go off on my own and prove myself."
> "I don't respect or admire her anymore."
> "He's been bugging me for a long time. I've just stuck it out for the sake of the children."

When any of these statements are used long after the fact—years 48 beyond a final decree—there's nothing to be done. But in many other cases, it may not be too late. I've found that none of these sentiments automatically signals an irreparable tear in the basic fiber of a marriage. If you hear someone for whom you have any feeling at all hinting at separation, instead of tacitly endorsing the move, instantly protest. Nearly every marriage has something worth preserving, something that can be restored. Revitalizing a relationship brings triumph and ongoing reward; and as you'll see, avoiding divorce spares those concerned from the greatest trauma of their lives.

The Case against Divorce

Of course, nobody *wants* to get divorced. Or does he? Joseph Epstein, in *Divorced in America,* recognizes the respectability of divorce: "In some circles, not to have gone through a divorce seems more exceptional than having gone through one; here living out one's days within the confines of a single marriage might even be thought to show an insufficiency of imagination, evidence that one is possibly a bit callow emotionally."

God forbid we appear emotionally callow! How dare we assume that those in the same dreary marriage they claim to have treasured for years could have gotten a lot out of it! The unspoken popular wisdom declares that only by undergoing this rite of psychological passage can anyone mature. I've heard the tales of postdivorce development: people who finally find themselves; who finally learn to be self-sufficient; who finally achieve independence. It is true that after divorce women especially, and men to some extent, report emotional growth. But they won't admit that they might have blossomed even more had they gathered the gumption to stick with and heal the marriage.

Of course, it's useless to speculate about what might have been accomplished in any particular relationship. But some things we *do* know—and these comprise the major arguments in the case against divorce:

1. *Divorce hurts you.* Divorce brings out selfishness, hostility, and vindictiveness. It ruins your idealism about marriage. It leaves emotional scars from which you can never be free. It costs a bunch of money—and significantly reduces your standard of living.
2. *Divorce hurts those around you.* It devastates your children for at least two years and probably for life. It hurts your family by splitting it in two; both family and friends are compelled to take sides. It forces you to be hardened against people you once loved. It rips the fabric of our society, each divorce providing another example of marriage devalued.
3. *The single life isn't what it's cracked up to be.* Ask anyone—the "swinging singles" life is full of frustration, rejection, and disappointment. The Mr. and Ms. Right you assume waits for you may be only a futile fantasy. Even a successful affair that bridges you from one marriage to another often becomes merely a second failure.
4. *Staying married is better for you.* You don't have to disrupt your life for two to seven years; instead, solving marital problems provides a sense of teamwork and stands as a concrete accomplishment that enhances problem-solving skills in the larger world. Marriage is statistically proven to be the best status for your health, divorce the worst. Marriage gives you something to show for your time on earth—children (usually) and a bond built on continuity and history.

I don't expect that everyone will agree with what I've found. It's largely a matter of values and also one of semantics. For example, I write that a family is worth preserving, and therefore it is worth compromising your goals or habits to save your marriage. Others holding different values might say that no marriage is worth burying your "true self" by dashing the goals you truly desire or stifling your personal inclinations. Obviously, it's not so easy to make a marriage work. But few achievements are as major or lasting.

Topics for Critical Thinking and Writing

1. Looking at the "ruinous stories of [her] divorced clients and interviewees" (paragraph 15) Medved calls divorce "catastrophic." Who were her "divorced clients and interviewees," or what can we guess about them? And what does Medved mean here by "catastrophic"?
2. In paragraph 27 Medved describes distributing a questionnaire to an "unscientific but diverse sample of two hundred people who had been separated or divorced." What, in your opinion, would a *scientific* sample have been? If the sample were "diverse" would it have crossed racial, ethnic, and class lines? Do we know if Medved's sample crossed such lines?
3. Why, according to Medved, has she written her book? In your opinion, do you think that she will succeed?
4. Medved calls her essay "The Case against Divorce." What case does she offer here?
5. Putting aside your own personal feelings if you oppose divorce, in 250 words set forth the strongest case you can imagine *in favor of* divorce.

Julie Matthaei

Julie Matthaei teaches economics at Wellesley College and is active with the Economic Literacy Project of Women for Economic Justice of Boston. She is the author of An Economic History of Women in America *and is working on a book entitled* Beyond Sex and Blood: Economy, Family, and the Breakdown of the "Natural" Family.

Political Economy and Family Policy

O*ur current, "natural" family system, based on biological similarities and differences, is in crisis. Not only are its institutions breaking down, they are also under attack as unjust, unequal, and unfree. The "natural" family system needs to be replaced by a consciously social family system; this means socializing parenting costs and pursuing policies which attack the sexual division of Labor and better integrate economic and family life.*

The family plays a central role in the distribution of income and wealth in our society, reproducing class, race, and gender inequalities.

This paper will 1) present a radical and feminist analysis of the "traditional" family system, 2) discuss the recent breakdown of this system, 3) present a radical and feminist critique of the traditional family system, and 4) indicate social policies which would build a family system more consistent with the principles of equality, freedom, and social justice.

The "Natural" Family

The development of capitalism and wage labor in the nineteenth-century U.S. brought with it new familial institutions. The family continued to be patriarchal—ruled by the husband/father—but was less defined by and involved in commodity production, either as a family firm, or as a family enslaved to producing for others. The family emerged as an increasingly personal and feminine sphere, physically separate and distinct from the competitive and masculine economy (Matthaei 1982). Since, in the nineteenth century, "scientific" explanations of social life were replacing the former religious ones, the new familial institutions were viewed as "natural," and stress was placed on their determination by biological similarities and differences. This "natural"[1] family system has three, interconnected parts:

1. *"Natural" Marriage.* Marriage is seen as a union of naturally different and complementary beings: men/males and women/females (biological sex and social gender are equated). Men and women are believed to be instinctually heterosexual; those who form homosexual liaisons are viewed as unnatural and perverted.[2] Men are seen as natural bread-winners, competing in the economy, and women as natural homemakers, caring for their husbands and children in the home, and segregated into dead-end, low paid "women's jobs." Forced into this sexual division of labor, men and women need one another to be socially complete, and in order to undertake the essential function of marriage, which is seen as . . .

2. *"Natural" Parenting.* Parenting is seen as the biological production of offspring, a process in which adults pass on their identities and wealth to their children, to "their own flesh and blood." Children are seen as the responsibility and property of their parents. Women/females are seen as naturally endowed with special maternal instincts which make them more qualified than men/males for parenting.

3. *"Natural" Community.* Connected to the view of family life as natural is a white racist view of society which divides people into races and views whites as the biologically superior race. Whites rationalize their political and economic domination of people of color not only as

---

[1]*Natural* is in quotes because the "natural" family system is actually a social product.
[2]In contrast, previous times viewed homosexual attractions as natural (and shared by all) but immoral and not to be acted on (Weeks 1979).

natural but also as part of "white man's burden to civilize the savages."[3] Races and white supremacy are perpetuated as social entities by the prohibition of racial intermarriage; by the passing down of wealth or poverty, language and culture to one's children; and by racially segregated institutions such as housing and job markets.

The Breakdown of the "Natural" Family System

In the last fifteen years, the "natural" family system has been breaking down and coming under increasing attack by feminists and others.

1. *Married women have entered the labor force and "men's jobs" in growing numbers, challenging the "natural" sexual division of labor.* Now over half of married women are in paid jobs at any one time. Women are demanding entry into the better-paid "men's jobs," and pressing their husbands to do "women's work" in the home. The "natural" marriage union between a bread-winning husband and a homemaking wife has become the exception rather than the rule, characterizing only 29% of husband/wife couples in 1985 (Current Population Reports March 1985).

2. *Married women's labor force participation has created a crisis in day care: there is a severe shortage of day care facilities, especially affordable ones.* In New York, for example, between 830,000 and 1.2 million preschool and school-age children vie for the fewer than 135,000 available licensed child care placements (Select Committee on Children 1987). The shortage of day care, combined with the absence of flexible jobs, forces parents to use make-shift arrangements: 2.1 million or 7% of 5–13 year olds whose mothers work outside the home are admittedly left unsupervised; actual numbers are much higher (Children's Defense Fund 1987).

3. *Growing numbers are not living in husband/wife families;* only 57% of all households include married couples. Adults are marrying later, spending more time living alone (23.4% of all households) or with friends or lovers. Homosexuality appears to be on the rise, and gays are coming out of the closet and demanding their rights. Marriages have become very unstable; divorce rates more than tripled between 1960 and 1982, more than doubling the number of female-headed households (1986 and 1987 Statistical Abstracts).

4. *"Natural" parenting is on the wane.* Divorces create "unnatural" female-headed households, most with dependent children. Unwed mothering has increased to comprise 1 in 5 births and over half of all births among blacks (1987 Statistical Abstract). Remarriages create

8

---

[3]Similarly, whites in the Eugenics movement argued that poor whites had inferior genes, and worked to limit their reproduction (Gould 1981).

"unnatural" families, with step-parents and -siblings. More "unnatural" is the trend for sterile couples, gays, and singles to obtain children through artificial insemination, surrogate mothers, and inter-country inter-racial adoptions.

What do these trends mean? Members of the so-called Moral   12
Majority interpret them as the breakdown of *the* family; their solution, embodied in the Family Protection Act of the late 1970s and early 1980s, is to put the "natural" family back together: encourage marriage; discourage divorce, unwed mothering, homosexuality; and get married women out of men's jobs and back into the home. The radical perspective is the opposite; the "natural" family is only one of many possible family systems, a very oppressive and ineffective one at that, as the next section will show. Growing numbers are rejecting the "natural" family system, and trying to create alternative family structures. What society needs is a radical family policy to focus and facilitate this process of dismantling of the old family system and constructing a new and more liberated one.

The Radical Critique of the "Natural" Family

The radical critique of the "natural" family has many prongs. All of these are underlain by a common claim—the "natural" family is not natural, necessary, or optimal, and a more adequate family system needs to be developed.

1. *The "natural" family system is not natural.* Biological differences in skin color or sex organs, and biological similarities between parent and child, do not necessitate a particular family form, or hierarchy and difference between the sexes and races. Past family systems have been very different from the "natural" family.[4] It is not nature but our society which is producing and reproducing the "natural" family, and its associated institutions of gender and race difference and inequality, through parenting practices, laws, labor market structures, and culture.

2. *The "natural" family system is classist and racist.* The conception of the "natural" family is generated by the dominant culture of upper-class, native-born whites, who then claim it applies to all. Since being a man means bread-winning and supporting a homebound homemaker

[4]Among the Rangiroa, adopted children were given equal status and rights as biological offspring, and considered "one belly" (from the same mother) with one another and with their other siblings (Sahlins 1976). In the New England and Southern colonies, mothering among the wealthy was essentially biological, producing one's husband's children, who were then nursed and cared for by poor white or slave women. Mead (1935) found societies where men and women shared the early care of children. Many societies see polygamy as the norm for marriage; others have allowed females to live as men and take wives after having cross-sex dreams (Blackwood 1984). Among the ancient Greeks, the highest form of love for an adult man was homosexual love for a younger man.

and children, men without "family wage" jobs due to unemployment, class, or race discrimination are seen (and often see themselves) as less than manly. Black women, forced into the labor force to compensate for their husbands' lack of economic opportunity, are viewed as unfeminine, castrating "matriarchs," and the extended and chosen family system which blacks have developed to combat poverty and economic insecurity is condemned as deviant (Stack 1974). The inability of the poor to properly parent their children because of their meager resources is seen as a fault in their characters, and they are criticized for having children at all, as if the poor do not have a right to parent.

3. *The "natural" family system impoverishes female-headed households.*   16
Women and children face high risks of poverty. Married women are to specialize in unpaid homemaking and mothering, complementing their husbands' bread-winning. Divorce or widowhood leaves women with little access to income, but with major if not full emotional and financial responsibility for the children.[5] "Women's jobs" do not pay enough to cover child care and keep female households with young children out of poverty. The present welfare system (Aid to Families with Dependent Children), structured to support the "natural" family system, does not even provide female-headed families with poverty-level income. The result: the majority of black and Hispanic female-headed families (50 and 53%, respectively), and 27% of white female-headed families, are poor. Children are penalized the most: 54% of children in such families are poor (Current Population Reports 1985).

4. *"Natural" marriage creates inequality between the sexes.* Since wives are relegated to unpaid housework and low paid jobs, they are economically dependent upon their husbands. Fear of losing this financial support can force women into subservience to their husbands, and into staying in unsatisfying marriages. Indeed, some feminists see "natural" marriage as a struggle in which men have gained the upper hand by monopolizing the higher-paid jobs (Hartmann 1981). Whatever its origins, "natural" marriage is clearly unequal, making mutual love and respect difficult.

5. *"Natural" parenting is oppressive and unjust.* Along with financial responsibility, parents are given almost total power over children. Children have no rights, and no system through which they can complain about mistreatment or find alternative parents (Rodham 1976). In a society where most men are under the power of bosses, and women under that of their husbands, parenting provides an arena where adults have total power and authority. It is easy to forget one's children's needs and use or abuse them to fill one's own needs. What results is not

---

[5]In 1983, only 35% of mothers caring for their children with absent fathers received any child support, and the average yearly payment was only $2,341; only 6% of separated or divorced women received any alimony (1987 Statistical Abstract).

only an epidemic of child physical and sexual abuse,[6] but also the training of each child to accept and participate in hierarchical and authoritarian systems, from schools to workplaces to politics (Miller 1981).

6. *The "natural" family perpetuates inequality between families* through the generations, because parents pass down their economic position to their children. Inheritance keeps ownership of the means of production in the hands of a few, mostly white, families.[7] Children born into higher-income families receive better nutrition, housing, health care, and schooling than their poor counterparts, have the "insurance" of wealthy relatives to back them up and encourage risk-taking, and can expect to inherit wealth. On the other hand, 11 million children (one in five) must live without even the most basic goods and services (Current Population Reports 1985). This is not only unjust but also irrational: it is in society's interest to guarantee quality health care and education to its future workers and citizens.

7. *The "natural" family system discourages the formation of alternative families, while forcing many into unwanted "natural" families.* Its broad and virulent anti-gay discrimination from education, employment, housing, and marriage laws to media images—makes it very difficult for people to love and share their lives with people of the same sex. It discriminates against couples who are unable to have children biologically by treating adoption and artificial insemination as "unnatural" and undesirable options. On the other hand, the "natural" family's equation of sex, reproduction, and marriage creates unwanted children by creating opposition to sex education, birth control for unmarried teens, and abortion. Forty percent of all births are mistimed or unwanted—for those under 24, a disastrous 53%—forcing millions of women into premature or unwanted motherhood and/or marriages (1987 Statistical Abstract).

Conceptualizing a Social Family System

The "natural" family system is inadequate, oppressive, and is coming apart at the seams. At the same time, all need the love and warmth and sharing and parenting which family relationships provide.[8] Hence criticism is not enough; an *alternative* and better vision of family life needs to be delineated, along with a set of concrete policies to bring such a new family system into being.

---

[6]The media have focussed on child abuse by strangers—on day care scandals and missing children—whereas the vast majority of children are abused by their parents or relatives (Eliasoph 1986).

[7]The wealthiest 2.4% of households owns 65% of the income-producing wealth (Edwards, Reich, Weisskopf 1986).

[8]Some feminists and gays have taken an "anti-family" position, as if the "natural" family is the only family form (Barrett and McIntosh 1982); however they usually advocate some alternative, family-like institutions.

The oppressiveness of the "natural" family system was accepted because its institutions were seen as natural and inevitable. Our new family system would be a *consciously* social one, its institutions developed through study, discussion, struggle and compromise, and continually criticized and improved so as to maximize freedom, equality, self-fulfillment, democracy, and justice. Here are some of the central principles of such a system; while it may appear utopian, many are living out parts of this vision now.

Social Marriage. Marriage would become a symmetrical relationship between whole, equal, and socially independent human beings, each participating in a similar range of familial, economic and political activities.[9] Its basis would be mutual love of the other, i.e., liking of, respect for, and sexual attraction to the person the other is, as providing the reason for intimate sharing of lives and living spaces and, if desired, parenting. Couples would not be expected to stay together "for better or for worse . . . as long as ye both shall live"; nor would they need to, since each would have earnings.

Social Parenting. Parenting would be recognized as a quintessentially social activity which, by shaping our unconsciousnesses, bodies, and minds, shapes the future of our society. Society would ensure that each child is well cared for and educated, since the upbringing of children as physically and psychologically healthy, creative, educated, and socially-conscious citizens is essential both to society's well-being, and to our belief in equal opportunity. This would include providing children and their parents with economic and institutional support, as well as seeking out optimal parenting practices and educating prospective parents in them.

Social Community. Cultural and economic differences between groups of people would be acknowledged to be social rather than natural products. All human beings would be recognized as equally human citizens of the world, and a concept of basic human rights, both political and economic, developed. Intercultural marriages would be encouraged to further social understanding.

Bringing the Social Family into Being: A Policy Checklist

Although the "natural" family system is in decline, the social family system cannot replace it unless there are many changes in our economic and social institutions. Here are some of the policies which will help bring about these changes; many are now in place in other countries.

1. *Policies which socialize parenting*

---

[9] If this seems far-fetched, an October 1977 CBS–*New York Times* National Survey found that 50% of 30–44 year olds, and 67% of 18–29 year olds, preferred a symmetrical marriage (of a man and woman who both had jobs, did housework, and cared for the children) over the traditional, complementary one.

a. *Policies which establish the right of all adults to choose when and if* 28
they wish to parent. Universal sex education and parenting training for
adolescents, as well as access of all to free, safe, 100% effective birth
control, abortions, and adoption placement, are needed to make every
child a wanted child. At the same time, society must recognize the right
of those who are infertile, gay, or single to parent, and support the
development of alternative modes of obtaining children from adoption
to artificial insemination and in-vitro fertilization.[10] The right to parent
must also be protected by programs to help low-income parents with
the costs of child-rearing (see 1b). Finally, the right to parent must be
seen as socially established, rather than inhering in the genetic connection between a parent and a child; parenting rights must be revocable if
a parent neglects or abuses a child, and society should seek to prevent
child abuse through an effective system of child advocates and parenting support and training.

b. *Policies which ensure a basic, social inheritance for every child.* The
best way to ensure healthy and provided-for children is to ensure this
health and income to all families through a system of national health
insurance and a combination of anti-poverty measures, from full
employment, to comparable worth, to a guaranteed annual income. In
addition, since having children does increase a family's poverty risk,
family allowances should be provided to parents according to need.[11]
Furthermore, all children need to have access to high quality, free or
sliding-scale education, from preschool day care when their parents are
at work, to elementary and secondary school and college. This "social
inheritance" program would be paid for by high inheritance taxes and
very progressive income and/or luxury taxes. Such taxes would, in
themselves, help reduce the present gross inequalities of opportunity
among children.[12]

c. *Policies which socialize child-care costs: government- and business-
subsidized day care.* Making quality child care available and affordable to
all should be the joint financial responsibility of business and government, since it benefits both employers and society at large. A few trend-
setting employers now provide child-care benefits to their workers,

---

[10]Most doctors refuse to artificially inseminate single or lesbian women. The developing
practice of surrogate mothering is very controversial among feminists and radicals. Since
eggs can be fertilized outside of a womb, and embryos can be raised in incubators from
the age of a few months, there are many other possibilities, including impregnating men,
or even producing infants entirely outside of human bodies, as Marge Piercy (1976) and
Shulamith Firestone (1970) have envisioned.

[11]Sweden and France give housing allowances to parents (Kamerman and Kahn 1979);
many European countries have national health insurance and family allowances.
Swedish policy is to guarantee all citizens a minimum standard of living (Ibid.); in the
U. S., the needy only receive support through "entitlement" programs, which require certain qualifications (such as being a female household head with children) other than
being poor, and which do not, in any event, raise incomes up to the poverty level.

[12]See Chester (1982) for a review of Western thought on inheritance.

having found that these more than pay for themselves by decreasing worker absenteeism, increasing productivity, and attracting top workers (Blau and Ferber 1986). Current federal funding through Title 20 is woefully inadequate; many states are serving less than 30% of their eligible populations (Select Committee on Children 1987). One survey found that ¼ of all full-time homemakers, and ½ of all single parents, were kept from employment and training programs by the unavailability of child care (Cal. Governor's Task Force on Child Care 1986). Again, Sweden provides the example to follow: the government pays 90% of the child-care costs of public day care centers, which are used by over half of children with employed mothers (Blau and Ferber 1986).

On the other hand, to permit parents with job commitments to spend more time with their children, especially their infants, a system of paid leaves from work without loss of one's job or seniority must be established. The U.S. does not even have laws guaranteeing prospective parents an *unpaid* leave when they have or adopt a child.[13] In a few states, women can use their temporary disability insurance to pay for 4 to 10 weeks of pregnancy/infant care leave (Kamerman et al. 1983). Again, Sweden is the model in this area, with: 1) paid, year-long parental leaves, 2) up to 60 days a year paid leave to care for sick children, and 3) the right for all full-time employed parents with children under 8 to reduce their work weeks (with reduced pay) to 30 hours a week (Ginsberg 1983). Radicals have advocated a shorter work week without reduction in pay as a solution to unemployment and low productivity, for it would create more jobs, reduce unemployment, and increase output (Bowles, Gordon, and Weisskopf 1983); a consideration of the needs of parents makes such policies even more desirable. Other innovations which allow adults to combine work with parenting are flex-time and flex-place (working at home); the extension of health, pension, and other benefits to part-time workers; and the cafeteria benefit plan, which allows dual-career couples to eliminate doubly-covered benefits in favor of more of other benefits, such as leaves or child-care support (Farley 1983; Kamerman and Hayes 1982).

2. *Policies to support egalitarian, symmetrical marriages* in which partners participate equally in parenting, housework, the labor force, and political life.[14]

a. *Comparable worth, affirmative action, increased unionization.* Comparable worth would increase the pay of women's jobs to that of men's jobs requiring comparable skill, effort, and responsibility. Affirmative action encourages women to enter into traditionally masculine jobs.

[13]Kamerman and Kingston (in Kamerman and Hayes 1982) found that paid maternity leave was available to fewer than one-third of all employed women in 1978, and averaged only about six weeks of benefits.
[14]Cuba encourages such marriages through its "Family Code," adopted in 1975 (Randall 1981); however, it still discriminates against gay couples.

Women need to organize in unions to fight for the above, and for general wage increases; one platform is "solidarity wages," again practiced in Sweden, in which workers agree to take part of their wage increase to reduce inequalities among them. Together these policies would stop the segregation of women into low-paid, dead end, less-satisfying jobs, reduce women's economic dependence upon men, and encourage more similar work and family participation by the sexes.

b. *Socialization of parenting* (see #1 above) would support symmetrical marriage, for it would allow adults to combine parenting with labor force commitments, reducing the pressure to specialize as in "natural" marriage.

c. *Repeal of the laws that discourage formation of "unnatural" marriages and non-traditional households.* This includes repealing sodomy laws and advocating legislation prohibiting discrimination against gays in employment, housing, insurance, foster parenting, adoption, and other areas.[15] Gay relationships must be legitimized in marriage laws, to give spouses health insurance, pension, inheritance, and other benefits and rights enjoyed by heterosexual spouses.[16] The repeal of co-residence laws, which in many states prohibit the cohabitation of more than two unrelated adults, is needed to allow the formation of non-biologically-based extended families.

d. *Individual rather than joint taxation of married couples.* Our present income tax system is progressive and married couples are discouraged from entering the labor force since, when a woman's earnings raise the household's tax bracket, much of her earnings are paid to the government in taxes.[17] Taxing adults individually (as is currently done in Sweden), rather than jointly, would instead encourage both members of a couple to participate in the labor force.

e. *Policies to aid the casualties of the "natural" marriage system.* Until the above changes are achieved, women and children will continue to face high poverty risks when they live in female-headed households. Many feminists advocate the strengthening of alimony and child-support laws; however, this both reinforces the "natural" marriage notion that husbands should be the main providers, and reproduces class and race inequality, because wives' and children's incomes depend on that

15Sodomy laws, which outlaw forms of "unnatural sex" (e.g., anal intercourse and oral/genital sex, either heterosexual or homosexual), still exist in many states, and were recently upheld by the Supreme Court, although they are seldom enforced. Many cities and a few states have passed gay rights legislation, and more and more employers have extended their non-discrimination policy to include sexual preference or orientation.

16In June 1987, the Swedish Parliament approved a bill which gave gay couples the same rights as heterosexuals married by common law; it will allow couples to sign housing leases as couples, regulate the division of property after a break-up, and grant lovers the right to inherit property in the absence of a will (*Gay Community News*, June 14–20, 1987).

17Even though the recent tax reform reduced the progressivity of the tax system, and a 1983 reform exempted 10% of the income of the lower-earning partner from taxation, the "marriage penalty" persists (Blau and Ferber 1986).

of their husbands/fathers. Extensive welfare reform, combined with the policies above, is a better solution.

3. *Policies to create social community.* Labor market reforms (2a) must always aim at eliminating both race and sex segregation and discrimination. These, along with social inheritance policies, will go far in stopping the economic reproduction of racial inequality in the U.S. The decline of "natural" parenting views of children as "one's own flesh and blood" will foster, and in turn be fostered by, the decline of conceptions of race, as both are replaced by a view of a human community reproduced through social parenting.

Bibliography

Barrett, Michele, and McIntosh, Mary. 1982. *The Anti-Social Family.* London: New Left Books.

Blackwood, Evelyn. 1984. Sexuality and Gender in Certain Native Tribes: The Case of Cross-Gender Females. *Signs* 10(1):27–42.

Blau, Francine, and Ferber, Marianne. 1986. *The Economics of Women, Men, and Work.* Englewood Cliffs, N.J.: Prentice-Hall.

Bowles, Samuel, David M. Gordon, and Thomas E. Weisskopf. 1983. *Beyond the Wasteland: A Democratic Alternative to Economic Decline.* New York: Anchor Doubleday.

Chester, Ronald. 1982. *Inheritance, Wealth, and Society.* Bloomington: Indiana University Press.

Children's Defense Fund. 1987. Unpublished paper.

Edwards, Richard, Reich, Michael, and Weisskopf, Thomas. 1986. *The Capitalist System.* Englewood Cliffs, N.J.: Prentice-Hall. Third Edition.

Eliasoph, Nina. 1986. Drive-In Mortality, Child Abuse, and the Media. *Socialist Review* #90, 16(6):7–31.

Farley, Jennie, ed. 1983. *The Woman in Management,* New York: ILR Press.

Firestone, Shulamith. 1970. *The Dialectic of Sex.* New York: Morrow.

Ginsberg, Helen. 1983. *Full Employment and Public Policy: The United States and Sweden.* Lexington, Mass.: D.C. Heath and Co.

Gould, Stephen J. 1981. *The Mismeasure of Man.* New York: Norton.

Hartmann, Heidi. 1981. The Unhappy Marriage of Marxism and Feminism. In *Women and Revolution: A Discussion of the Unhappy Marriage of Marxism and Feminism,* Lydia Sargent (ed.), pp. 1–41. Boston: South End Press.

Kamerman, Sheila, and Kahn, Alfred. 1979. *Family Policy: Government and Families in Fourteen Countries.* New York: Columbia University Press.

Kamerman, Sheila, and Hayes, Cheryl, eds. 1982. *Families That Work: Children in a Changing World.* Washington: National Academy Press.

Kamerman, Sheila, et al., eds. 1983. *Maternity Policies and Working Women.* New York: Columbia University Press.

Matthaei, Julie. 1982. *An Economic History of Women in America: Women's Work, the Sexual Division of Labor, and the Development of Capitalism.* New York: Schocken Books.

Mead, Margaret. 1935. *Sex and Temperament in Three Primitive Societies.* New York: William Morrow and Co.

Miller, Alice. 1981. *The Drama of the Gifted Child.* trans. by Ruth Ward. New York: Basic Books.

Piercy, Marge. 1976. *Woman on the Edge of Time.* New York: Fawcett.

Randall, Margaret. 1981. *Women in Cuba: Twenty Years Later.* New York: Smyrna Press.

Rodham, Hillary. 1976. Children under the Law. In *Rethinking Childhood* Arlene Skolnick (ed.). Boston: Little, Brown and Co.

Sahlins, Marshall. 1976. *The Use and Abuse of Biology: An Anthropological Critique of Sociobiology.* Ann Arbor: University of Michigan Press.

Select Committee on Children, Youth and Families, U.S. House of Representatives. 1987. Fact Sheet: Hearing on Child Care, Key to Employment in a Changing Economy. March 10.

Stack, Carol. 1974. *All Our Kin.* New York: Harper & Row.

U.S. Bureau of the Census, Current Population Reports. 1985. Household and Family Characteristics: March 1985.

—. 1985. Money Income and Poverty Status of Families and Persons in the United States.

—. 1986, 1987. Statistical Abstract of the United States.

Weeks, Jeffrey. 1979. *Coming Out: Homosexual Politics in Britain, from the Nineteenth Century to the Present.* London: Quartet Books.

Topics for Critical Thinking and Writing

1. What, if anything, strikes you as "radical" in Matthaei's "radical analysis" of the "'natural' family" (paragraph 3)? Do any parts of this analysis strike you as unfair, misleading, or wrong? If so, which parts, and what do you find wrong with them?

2. In paragraph 7 Matthaei says that "adults are marrying later." Assuming this statement to be true, what do you think are the causes? What do you think may be the consequences, good and bad?

3. In paragraph 10 Matthaei denies that the "natural" family is natural. Do you think she proves her case? If not, in what way(s) does she fail?

4. Matthaei argues (paragraph 15) that the idea of the "natural" family can lead easily to child abuse. Can one argue in response that the "natural" family is better suited to assist children in growing into healthy, responsible, happy adults than is any conceivable alternative arrangement? If you think so, what arguments might you offer? (For an interesting argument that children should be granted legal rights to escape impossible families, see "Confessions of an Erstwhile Child," pages 80–84.)

5. In paragraph 17 Matthaei argues that the idea of the "natural" family "discriminates against couples who are unable to have children biologically." Is she saying that all adults—including the sterile, the infertile,

and those who do not wish to engage in heterosexual sex—have a right to have children? If she is saying this, on what might she base this right? In her next paragraph she says, "All need the love and warmth and sharing and parenting which family relationships provide." Is this need perhaps the basis for a right—possessed by all adults—to have children? (See also the discussion in paragraph 24.)

6. Much of the essay is devoted to arguing on behalf of various kinds of equality. For example, in paragraph 20, in discussing "social marriage," Matthaei says that "marriage would become a symmetrical relationship between whole, equal, and socially independent human beings." The two persons involved would participate "in a similar range of familial, economic, and political activities." But what if both persons do not share an interest in, for example, political activities? Should they therefore not marry? (For an argument that it is better for a couple *not* to share their interests around the clock and seven days a week, see the essay by Perrin, pages 169–71.) Or suppose that one person enjoyed the world of paid work and the other preferred to engage, at least for a while, chiefly in the role of parenting and housekeeping. Do you think such a marriage would be inherently unstable?

7. In point 1b of paragraph 24, Matthaei argues for programs and policies that would redistribute wealth—for example, a guaranteed annual income. Suppose someone argued (or at least asserted) that he or she saw no reason to support the families of the poor. What reply might you make?

8. Matthaei apparently sees marriage as involving only two adults. Do you assume that she rejects polygamy (a practice not unknown in the United States and elsewhere)? And what about polyandry (one woman with two or more husbands)? If you accept Matthaei's arguments, or most of them, how do *you* feel about polygamy and polyandry? Arguments for polygamy can be found in the essay by Elizabeth Joseph (pages 167–68). What argument(s) for polyandry can you imagine?

Florence Trefethen

Florence Trefethen holds degrees from Bryn Mawr and the University of Cambridge. She has taught English at Tufts University and now is executive editor for books published by the Council on East Asian Studies at Harvard University. Her poems and short stories appear frequently. This essay was originally published in the Washington Post.

Points of a Lifelong Triangle
Reflections of an Adoptive Mother

I have a friend who's a social worker. Her clients include a group of women who've given up a child for adoption. Their ages range widely, and the moment of surrender may have been long ago or last year. They form a birth mothers' support group.

My friend says their meetings are suffused with sorrow, sometimes bitterness. They describe their lost children and the new parents as ambling through life happily, selfishly, and with never a thought for the origins left behind. As an adoptive mother, I find that picture distorted.

I think of the biological father rarely, envisioning him as the dashing young fellow he must have been at the time he sired our daughter. But scarcely a day goes by when the birth mother is not in my thoughts, growing older as I do.

She's been with me from the start. When Gwyned was placed with   4 us on probation, there was always the threat that the birth mother might change her mind and snatch our baby back. She loomed as a fearsome adversary. I pictured her wild-eyed, manic, appearing in the courtroom a moment before the final decree, shouting, "She's mine, and her name is Monica!" Our papers were approved, however, without incident.

Those papers contain my signature and my husband's. The birth parents' signatures were folded under so that we never learned their names. The papers are dated Dec. 30, 1953, and are locked away in a Maryland court house, apparently inviolate. We received a "birth certificate" proclaiming that Gwyned was born to me and my husband on May 8, 1953, in Garfield Memorial Hospital, Washington, D.C.

What is a birthday like for an adopted daughter who's 1 or 4 or 10 or 16 or all the years between and after? Just like birthdays for other children—parties, presents, friends and family gathered to celebrate. But for me there was always a special poignancy when lighting the candles on the cake. I, the mother in residence, would think of that first mother, wondering where she was, knowing she was remembering the day. I wanted to call out to her and say, "Look how delightful Gwyned is! Thank you." My hands always shook as I carried the cake to the table, trying not to quaver as I started singing "Happy Birthday."

Gwyned didn't seem to care. She grew up in a neighborhood and attended a school where there were several adopted children. No big deal, she said. In fact, she implied that there was a special cachet to being "selected." Though she knew better, I think she fantasized about our walking down an aisle lined with bassinets until we came to her and said, "That's the one!"

When Gwyned acquired a figure, it turned out to be more svelte   8 than the figures in my family; I imagined the birth mother trim in bikinis, mini skirts and other fashions I avoided. Gwyned took to singing in choruses, acting in plays; the birth mother became the repository of performing talents I'd never possessed. Gwyned liked skiing and running and in college elected "self defense" in gym; the birth mother assumed the dimensions of a sportswoman, perhaps Olympics material.

With the approach of Gwyned's wedding, I grew restless, then frantic. Ought we try to contact that birth mother, to assure her everything had turned out well, possibly to invite her to the marriage? I struggled with these questions through sleepless nights and finally consulted a psychiatrist. He offered a common-sense suggestion I wish I'd thought of in my anxiety: "Why don't you ask Gwyned?" I did. She said she'd just as soon leave things as they were. She spoke as though that issue was closed. But later in life she changed her mind. After giving birth to her own children, she began to wonder about physical traits and medical histories.

At the same time, large-scale changes were in motion. Mothers were locating long-lost children; adult adoptees were searching for parents, combing registers, placing ads; associations were established to facilitate these investigations and, it was hoped, ultimate reunions. Some agencies and some states offered help to the searchers. Others clung to the conditions in force at the time of adoption—usually an unbreachable barrier between birth parents and adoptive parents.

"Can't I get the name of at least one of my parents?" Gwyned asked. "With a name, I could search." She presented herself at the adoption agency; they declined to reveal that information. She petitioned the court and had a hearing before the judge; he said he did not want "to disturb the birth mother." In the hope that our support might be useful, my husband and I wrote to both agency and judge, to no avail.

It's difficult to sort out the rights and wrongs in a case like this.   12
Gwyned feels compelled to close a loop that's been open all her life. She gets encouragement from support groups but also pain, since they usually include happy birth mothers and adult adoptees who have found each other. My heart aches as I observe her thus far futile efforts to pinpoint anyone who can help her, any clue that might lead to success. Sometimes I feel guilty for having failed, in the initial wonder of acquiring a marvelous child, to anticipate that the secrecy then imposed might one day frustrate us all.

Yet we can understand the adamance of the adoption agency and the court. They are simply adhering to the rules in force nearly four decades ago when the decree became final. They were parties to a contract and are loath to break it. Perhaps they may even feel they are sparing us grief. Indeed, the birth mother, if located, might not wish to be disturbed, might reject Gwyned. Or she could prove to be a disappointment.

I doubt it, though. She's been in my mind and my mind's eye for 37 years, and I'm convinced she's a sad but lovely lady. Whatever her name, and whether or not we ever find her, she, Gwyned and I are the points of a triangle that will endure all our lives.

Topics for Critical Thinking and Writing

1. Do you agree with the decisions made by the adoption agency and the judge? Why or why not? Do you know of any instances of reunions between the birth parent and a child? If so, how do they influence your

opinion about the advisability of agencies and courts facilitating such reunions?

2. The father is mentioned only briefly, in the first sentence of the third paragraph, and to our knowledge is rarely the parent sought by adopted children. Nor do we hear or read of adopted sons seeking their birth parents. What do you make of this phenomenon? Or do you know of exceptions to our generalizations?

3. The essay is about a controversial point—should agencies and courts reveal the names of birth parents to the children whom they surrendered? But it is also about Gwyned, about the birth mother, and about the author. How would you characterize the author? What do you think the author's purposes in writing the essay were?

4. Consider the title (including the subtitle) and the opening and the concluding paragraphs. What does the title lead you to expect? What does the first paragraph suggest about birth mothers and the author's attitude toward them? How does the concluding paragraph change or enrich your reading (or rereading) of the title and the first paragraph?

5. Imagine that you are one of Gwyned's birth parents—since you are imagining, you can choose either gender—and you have happened on this article. What do you imagine you would feel or would do? Write a letter (but don't, of course, mail it) to Florence or Gwyned Trefethen, or to the editor of *The Washington Post* (you can ask to have your name withheld), explaining what you feel and what you plan or do not plan to do.

Letty Cottin Pogrebin

Letty Cottin Pogrebin (b. 1939) is the author of Growing Up Free, *a book about the need to resist the sexist cultural programming of television, books, and schools. The essay that we reprint originally appeared in* The New York Times.

Consequences

In 1958, I had an illegal abortion. I was 19, a senior in college, an English major. Marriage was not an option: the boyfriend was my age but he was a sophomore majoring in basketball. When I met him after practice and told him I was pregnant, the panic in his eyes infuriated me. I assured him I didn't want to get married. The panic remainded. The poor guy was terified for my sake but he didn't know what to say or do. He started to cry, then caught himself and punched the cinder-block wall of the gym, breaking his hand and getting himself benched for the season.

I didn't know what to do, either. In all honesty, I wasn't even sure how I'd gotten into this fix. Many women of my generation believed you could get pregnant from a toilet seat but were never quite clear about how you got pregnant from a man. Our sexual gospel was full of axioms like "you can't get pregnant if you do it standing up" and "no one gets pregnant the first time." I needed two missed periods to believe that it had happened to me.

Finally I told my roommate. She was as innocent as I was of such matters, but she persuaded me to confide in our dorm counselor, a kindly woman who coached girls' field hockey. The coach hugged me as I sobbed, but didn't lecture me; she let me vent my misery, answered my questions and made sure I understood my options and their repercussions. In biology texts, I'd seen that at this stage a pregnancy is a mass of cells, not a "child." I told her I had decided to have an abortion, an early, immediate abortion.

She was nonjudgmental, but given the criminal penalties at the time was afraid to get involved in my search for a doctor. She convinced me to have a pregnancy test, at least, to confirm my suspicions. The test came back positive. For about 48 hours, I thought about killing myself.

For those who didn't live through the 50's, it's hard to believe the suffocating terror of sexual shame and the coercive power of social propriety. In those years, etiquette demanded that women not wear white before Memorial Day or after Labor Day, so you can imagine the moral absolutes. For a well-bred middle-class girl, pregnancy "out of wedlock" was the ultimate disgrace, and in the Jewish community in which I grew up, it was a *shonda,* a scandal discussed in contemptuous whispers behind closed doors.

The category "single mothers" did not exist then. A woman could be a married mother, a widow with children or a "divorcee" with children, but unless her body was legitimized by marriage, the fruit of her womb was "illegitimate," and she herself forfeited the right to travel in polite company or win a respectable husband in the future. As a result, young pregnant women were quickly pressed into "shotgun" marriages or else, under a canopy of lies—"she's caring for a sick aunt in Cleveland"—were spirited away to "homes for unwed mothers" where they disappeared from view, like lepers, until the pregnancy ran its course. Until they gave birth among strangers and left their babies to be adopted by strangers.

I could not tolerate that idea. It seemed wrong to make pregnancy the punishment for my sexual activity (especially when, for the same activity, the young man would get off with some angst and a broken hand). And it seemed crazy to consider adoption a "solution." I would not carry a child for a full nine months, feel it move inside my body, endure morning sickness, swollen legs and the pain of labor only to have my baby taken away from me. I could never live in a world where a child of mine was being raised by someone else.

I wanted to be a mother, someday. I wanted to create a new life and give it the same loving, well-fed childhood my mother gave me. But I would not be an accidental mother, an ashamed mother, an impoverished mother, a hostile mother or what today is termed a "birth mother"—one who brings a child into the world but cannot share its life.

Even in 1958, I did not confuse my capacity to breed with my capability to mother. One day, I thought, I will be a terrific parent, but at 19 I was still raising myself out of adolescence, four years after my own mother died. She was my model of sensitivity, understanding and patience. Because of her, I had great respect for what it takes to be a good parent. I wanted to be worthy of the job. I would not be a mother before I could be an adult.

With single parenthood and adoption out of the question, abortion was my choice, the only choice for me. But where could I turn for money and help?

My father, a lawyer, subscribed to traditional gender roles except when it came to me and money. Earning his own living at an early age had been the making of him, he said, and he insisted it would be character-building for me, even though I was a girl. He paid for college, but I had to earn my spending money, which I did by taking summer jobs, tutoring athletes and working for the Hillel rabbi on campus. For all my bootstrap efforts, $12 was what I had left in the bank after I paid for the pregnancy test. I had to ask my father for help; there was no one else.

He was the sort of man who could talk about French conjugations or   12 the First Amendment but not about problems or emotions. Paralyzed with fear, I finally breathed out the words: "Daddy, I'm pregnant, and I can't afford an abortion." His expression never changed; there was no moralizing, no scolding, but also no comfort. Nurturing wasn't his style. He went straight for the practical issues: who, when and how much. He said he would take care of the arrangements and lend me the money.

Although I had been warned about kitchen-table hacks, my father found a real doctor who did abortions on the side. Late one night, I hurried into a darkened medical office, accompanied by my father and his new wife. I hated having her along, but he insisted we might need a woman in case there were complications.

There were no complications.

These memories came flooding back last December, when a friend stunned me with the news that she'd just heard from the child she gave up for adoption 32 years ago. I know this woman's 28-year-old son, but I never knew about the secret daughter, the one who got born because a bogus abortionist took an unsuspecting young woman's money and left her pregnant. Now the baby she last saw in the delivery room was coming for Christmas with *her* baby.

"I'm excited to be a grandmother," my friend told me, "but I feel   16 such regret, loss and guilt about my daughter that it overpowers all my other feelings."

I hope my friend's reunion story ends well. All I know is what it aroused in me. Relief. Waves of God-grateful relief. Had I not been able to terminate that pregnancy in 1958, I might now have a 32-year-old daughter (or son) looking for *me,* and surely I would be a very different me for having carried the misery that burdened my friend all these years.

It's never simple. That's why public policy on abortion and adoption must be filtered through the experiences of women like us. When adoption is heralded as the answer to unwanted pregnancy, the targets of concern are infertile parents, not the woman, her feelings, her body and her future—or the future feelings of the child she must give away.

I was grateful I never had to leave a child of mine with strangers or unwittingly pass a legacy of rejection to an infant at birth. If such a child existed today, no matter how happy our reunion, I would forever mourn the 32 lost years.

The fact that I was able to choose abortion made possible the life   20
that was and is. Above all, the child-who-wasn't made possible the three wanted children who are my family today.

Topics for Critical Thinking and Writing

1. In paragraph 10, Pogrebin writes: "With single parenthood and adoption out of the question, abortion was my choice, my only choice." How has she attempted to persuade us, up to this point in the essay, that single parenthood and adoption were "out of the question"?
2. How does her account of her mother in paragraph 8, her father in paragraphs 11 and 12, and the abortion in paragraph 13, further attempt to persuade? What further issue begins to appear in paragraph 15?
3. Although the essay is largely a personal narrative, it is also an argument. Which arguments are stated and which are implied? Overall, which arguments do you find most persuasive and which least? Try to explain why.
4. What arguments for or against abortion has she not touched on in this essay? Should she have?
5. Paragraph 14 consists of a single sentence. What is the effect? Notice also the fragment that concludes paragraph 6. Can you justify the use of a fragment here?
6. Pogrebin seems to assume that an adopted child retains a "legacy of rejection" (paragraph 19). Do you find this a valid assumption? Why or why not?
7. To what does the essay's title refer? Write a paragraph in which you explain the title to someone who has not read the essay.
8. Compare Pogrebin and Trefethen (pages 153–55) on their characterization and depiction of "birth mothers" and their attitudes toward the search by adopted children for their birth parents.

Dorsett Bennett

Dorsett Bennett is an attorney in Roswell, New Mexico. His essay was originally published in the "My Turn" section of Newsweek, *on 4 July 1994.*

I, Too, Am a Good Parent

Divorce is a fact of modern life. A great number of people simply decide that they do not wish to stay married to their spouse. A divorce is not a tremendously difficult situation unless there are minor children born to the couple. If there are no minor children you simply divide the assets and debts. But you cannot divide a child. The child needs to be placed with the appropriate parent.

In my own case, my former wife chose not to remain married to me. That is her right and I do not fault her decision. My problem is that I do not believe it is her right to deny me the privilege of raising our children. Some fathers want to go to the parent/teacher conferences, school plays, carnivals and to help their kids with homework. I have always looked forward to participating on a daily basis in my children's lives. I can no longer enjoy that privilege—the children live with their mother, who has moved to a northern Midwest state.

I tried so hard to gain custody of my children. I believe the evidence is uncontradicted as to what an excellent father (and more important, parent) I am. My ex-wife is a fairly good mother, but unbiased opinions unanimously agreed I was the better parent. Testimonials were videotaped from witnesses who could not attend the out-of-state custody hearing. I choose to be a father. When I was three years old, my own father left my family. While I've loved my father for many years, I did and still do reject his parental pattern.

A couple of centuries ago, a father and mother might have shared equally in the care and raising of children above the age of infancy. But with the coming of the Industrial Revolution the father went to work during the day, leaving the full-time care of the young to the mother, who stayed at home. It was easier to decide who should get child custody under those circumstances. That would be true today even if the mother were put into the position of working outside the home after the divorce.

Now, a majority of married mothers are in the workplace—often because the family needs the second income to survive. With the advent of the working mother, we have also seen a change in child care. Not only have we seen an increase in third-party caregivers; there is a decided difference in how fathers interact with their children. Fathers are even starting to help raise their children. I admit that in a great many families there is an uneven distribution of child-care responsibil-

4

ities. But there are fathers who do as much to raise the children as the mother, and there are many examples where men are full-time parents.

But, because we have this past history of the mother being the principal child caregiver, the mother has almost always been favored in any contested child-custody case. The law of every state is replete with decisions showing that the mother is the favored custodial parent. The changes in our lifestyles are now being reflected in our laws. In most, if not all, states, the legislature has recognized the change in child-care responsibilities and enacted legislation that is gender blind. The statutes that deal with child custody now say that the children should be placed with the parent whose care and control of the child will be in the child's best interest.

This legislation is enlightened and correct. Society has changed. We no longer bring up our children as we did years ago. But it is still necessary to have someone make the choice in the child's best interest if the parents are divorcing and cannot agree on who takes care of the kids. So we have judges to make that enormous decision.

The state legislature can pass laws that say neither parent is favored because of their gender. But it is judges who make the ultimate choice. And those judges are usually *older males* who practiced law during the time when mothers were the favored guardians under the law. These same judges mostly come from a background where mothers stayed home and were the primary caregivers. By training and by personal experience they have a strong natural bias in favor of the mother in a child-custody case. That belief is regressive and fails to acknowledge the changed realities of our present way of life. Someone must be appointed to render a decision when parents cannot agree. I would ask that those judges who make these critical decisions re-examine their attitudes and prejudices against placing children with fathers. 8

After the videotaped testimony was completed, one of my lawyers said he had "never seen a father put together a better custody case." "But," he asked me, "can you prove she is unfit?" A father should not be placed in the position of having to prove the mother is unfit in order to gain custody. He should not have to prove that she has two heads, participates in child sacrifice or eats live snakes. The father should only have to prove that he is the more suitable parent.

Fathers should not be discriminated against as I was. It took me three years to get a trial on the merits in the Minnesota court. And Minnesota has a law directing its courts to give a high priority to child-custody cases. What was even worse was that the judge seemed to ignore the overwhelming weight of the evidence and granted custody to my ex-wife. At the trial, her argument was, "I am their mother." Other than that statement she hardly put on a case. Being the mother of the children was apparently deemed enough to outweigh evidence that all the witnesses who knew us both felt I was the better parent; that those witnesses who knew only me said what an excellent parent I was; that our children's behavior always improved dramatically after spending time with me; that my daughter wished to live with me, and that I had a better child-custody evaluation than my wife.

So I say to the trial judges who decide these cases: "Become part of the solution to this dilemma of child custody. Don't remain part of the problem." It is too late for me. If this backward way of thinking is changed, then perhaps it won't be too late for other fathers who should have custody of their children.

Topics for Critical Thinking and Discussion

1. How would you characterize Bennett—that is, what persona emerges from the essay?
2. According to Bennett, why do judges usually give the mother the custody of the children? Evaluate his explanation.
3. Do you agree with Bennett's assertion (paragraph 9) that a father "should only have to prove that he is the more suitable parent"? Explain.
4. Are you aware of a custody decision that seems to you to be clearly wrong? If so, summarize the situation, and (if possible) explain why the judge probably made the wrong decision. (Do not use real names.)

Andrew Sullivan

Andrew Sullivan grew up in England, but he earned a doctorate in government at Harvard University. Sullivan is now the editor of The New Republic, *where the following essay was originally published in 1989.*

Here Comes the Groom
A (Conservative) Case for Gay Marriage

Last month in New York, a court ruled that a gay lover had the right to stay in his deceased partner's rent-control apartment because the lover qualified as a member of the deceased's family. The ruling deftly annoyed almost everybody. Conservatives saw judicial activism in favor of gay rent control: three reasons to be appalled. Chastened liberals (such as the *New York Times* editorial page), while endorsing the recognition of gay relationships, also worried about the abuse of already stretched entitlements that the ruling threatened. What neither side quite contemplated is that they both might be right, and that the way to tackle the issue of unconventional relationships in conventional society is to try something both more radical and more conservative than putting courts in the business of deciding what is and is not a family. That alternative is the legalization of civil gay marriage.

The New York rent-control case did not go anywhere near that far, which is the problem. The rent-control regulations merely stipulated that a "family" member had the right to remain in the apartment. The judge ruled that to all intents and purposes a gay lover is part of his lover's family, inasmuch as a "family" merely means an interwoven social life, emotional commitment, and some level of financial interdependence.

It's a principle now well established around the country. Several cities have "domestic partnership" laws, which allow relationships that do not fit into the category of heterosexual marriage to be registered with the city and qualify for benefits that up till now have been reserved for straight married couples. San Francisco, Berkeley, Madison, and Los Angeles all have legislation, as does the politically correct Washington, D.C. suburb, Takoma Park. In these cities, a variety of interpersonal arrangements qualify for health insurance, bereavement leave, insurance, annuity and pension rights, housing rights (such as rent-control apartments), adoption and inheritance rights. Eventually, according to gay lobby groups, the aim is to include federal income tax and veterans' benefits as well. A recent case even involved the right to use a family member's accumulated frequent-flier points. Gays are not the only beneficiaries; heterosexual "live-togethers" also qualify.

There's an argument, of course, that the current legal advantages   4 extended to married people unfairly discriminate against people who've shaped their lives in less conventional arrangements. But it doesn't take a genius to see that enshrining in the law a vague principle like "domestic partnership" is an invitation to qualify at little personal cost for a vast array of entitlements otherwise kept crudely under control.

To be sure, potential DPs have to prove financial interdependence, shared living arrangements, and a commitment to mutual caring. But they don't need to have a sexual relationship or even closely mirror old-style marriage. In principle, an elderly woman and her live-in nurse could qualify. A couple of uneuphemistically confirmed bachelors could be DPs. So could two close college students, a pair of seminarians, or a couple of frat buddies. Left as it is, the concept of domestic partnership could open a Pandora's box of litigation and subjective judicial decision-making about who qualifies. You either are or are not married; it's not a complex question. Whether you are in a "domestic partnership" is not so clear.

More important, the concept of domestic partnership chips away at the prestige of traditional relationships and undermines the priority we give them. This priority is not necessarily a product of heterosexism.

Consider heterosexual couples. Society has good reason to extend legal advantages to heterosexuals who choose the formal sanction of marriage over simply living together. They make a deeper commitment to one another and to society; in exchange, society extends certain benefits to them. Marriage provides an anchor, if an arbitrary and weak one, in the chaos of sex and relationships to which we are all prone. It provides a mechanism for emotional stability, economic security, and the healthy rearing of the next generation. We rig the law in its favor not because we disparage all forms of relationships other than the nuclear family, but because we recognize that not to promote marriage would be to ask too much of human virtue. In the context of the weakened family's effect upon the poor, it might also invite social disintegration. One of the worst products of the New Right's "family values" campaign is that its extremism and hatred of diversity has disguised this more measured and more convincing case for the importance of the marital bond.

The concept of domestic partnership ignores these concerns, indeed directly attacks them. This is a pity, since one of its most important objectives—providing some civil recognition for gay relationships—is a noble cause and one completely compatible with the defense of the family. But the way to go about it is not to undermine straight marriage; it is to legalize old-style marriage for gays.

The gay movement has ducked this issue primarily out of fear of division. Much of the gay leadership clings to notions of gay life as essentially outsider, antibourgeois, radical.[18] Marriage, for them, is co-optation into straight society. For the Stonewall generation, it is hard to see how this vision of conflict will ever fundamentally change. But for many other gays—my guess, a majority—while they don't deny the importance of rebellion twenty years ago and are grateful for what was done, there's now the sense of a new opportunity. A need to rebel has quietly ceded to a desire to belong. To be gay and to be bourgeois no longer seems such an absurd proposition. Certainly since AIDS, to be gay and to be responsible has become a necessity.

Gay marriage squares several circles at the heart of the domestic partnership debate. Unlike domestic partnership, it allows for recognition of gay relationships, while casting no aspersions on traditional marriage. It merely asks that gays be allowed to join in. Unlike domestic partnership, it doesn't open up avenues for heterosexuals to get benefits without the responsibilities of marriage, or a nightmare of definitional litigation. And unlike domestic partnership, it harnesses to an already established social convention the yearnings for stability and acceptance among a fast-maturing gay community.

8

[18]The Stonewall Inn was a gay bar in New York City. When the police closed it in June 1966, the gays did not submit (as they had done in the past) but attacked the police. The event is regarded as a turning point in gay history.

Gay marriage also places more responsibilities upon gays: It says for the first time that gay relationships are not better or worse than straight relationships, and that the same is expected of them. And it's clear and dignified. There's a legal benefit to a clear, common symbol of commitment. There's also a personal benefit. One of the ironies of domestic partnership is that it's not only more complicated than marriage, it's more demanding, requiring an elaborate statement of intent to qualify. It amounts to a substantial invasion of privacy. Why, after all, should gays be required to prove commitment before they get married in a way we would never dream of asking of straights?

Legalizing gay marriage would offer homosexuals the same deal society now offers heterosexuals: general social approval and specific legal advantages in exchange for a deeper and harder-to-extract-yourself-from commitment to another human being. Like straight marriage, it would foster social cohesion, emotional security, and economic prudence. Since there's no reason gays should not be allowed to adopt or be foster parents, it could also help nurture children. And its introduction would not be some sort of radical break with social custom. As it has become more acceptable for gay people to acknowledge their loves publicly, more and more have committed themselves to one another for life in full view of their families and their friends. A law institutionalizing gay marriage would merely reinforce a healthy social trend. It would also, in the wake of AIDS, qualify as a genuine public health measure. Those conservatives who deplore promiscuity among some homosexuals should be among the first to support it. Burke[19] could have written a powerful case for it.

The argument that gay marriage would subtly undermine the   12
unique legitimacy of straight marriage is based upon a fallacy. For heterosexuals, straight marriage would remain the most significant—and only legal—social bond. Gay marriage could only delegitimize straight marriage if it were a real alternative to it, and this is clearly not true. To put it bluntly, there's precious little evidence that straights could be persuaded by any law to have sex with—let alone marry—someone of their own sex. The only possible effect of this sort would be to persuade gay men and women who force themselves into heterosexual marriage (often at appalling cost to themselves and their families) to find a focus for their family instincts in a more personally positive environment. But this is clearly a plus, not a minus: Gay marriage could both avoid a lot of tortured families and create the possibility for many happier ones. It is not, in short, a denial of family values. It's an extension of them.

Of course, some would claim that any legal recognition of homosexuality is a de facto attack upon heterosexuality. But even the most hardened conservatives recognize that gays are a permanent minority

[19]Edmund Burke (1729–97), conservative British politician.

and aren't likely to go away. Since persecution is not an option in a civilized society, why not coax gays into traditional values rather than rail incoherently against them?

There's a less elaborate argument for gay marriage: It's good for gays. It provides role models for young gay people who, after the exhilaration of coming out, can easily lapse into short-term relationships and insecurity with no tangible goal in sight. My own guess is that most gays would embrace such a goal with as much (if not more) commitment as straights. Even in our society as it is, many lesbian relationships are virtual textbook cases of monogamous commitment. Legal gay marriage could also help bridge the gulf often found between gays and their parents. It could bring the essence of gay life—a gay couple—into the heart of the traditional straight family in a way the family can most understand and the gay offspring can most easily acknowledge. It could do as much to heal the gay-straight rift as any amount of gay rights legislation.

If these arguments sound socially conservative, that's no accident. It's one of the richest ironies of our society's blind spot toward gays that essentially conservative social goals should have the appearance of being so radical. But gay marriage is not a radical step. It avoids the mess of domestic partnership: it is humane; it is conservative in the best sense of the word. It's also practical. Given the fact that we already allow legal gay relationships, what possible social goal is advanced by framing the law to encourage those relationships to be unfaithful, undeveloped, and insecure?

Topics for Critical Thinking and Writing

1. In his second paragraph Sullivan summarizes a judge's definition of a family. How satisfactory do you find the definition? Explain.
2. What is "conservative"—Sullivan's word, in his title—about this case for gay and lesbian marriages?
3. A common argument in support of the financial privileges that the state awards to the traditional family is that it is in the state's interest for children to be brought up by adults committed to each other. However, divorce is now common, and, of course, many married couples do not have children, for one reason or another. Can any justification, then, be offered for allowing a spouse—but not an unmarried heterosexual or homosexual lover—to inherit without payment of taxes the partner's share of property jointly held?
4. In Sullivan's view why is marriage better than mere cohabitation? What is your view of this matter?
5. In paragraph 11 Sullivan says that "there's no reason gays should not be allowed to adopt or be foster parents." This issue is highly controversial. Construct the strongest argument you can, on one side or the other. (Remember, a strong argument faces the opposing arguments.)

6. In his next-to-last paragraph Sullivan says that "legal gay marriages could also help bridge the gulf often found between gays and their parents." If you are aware of gays who are separated from their parents by a "gulf," do you think that legal marriage might reduce that gulf? Explain.

Elizabeth Joseph

Elizabeth Joseph, a lawyer, lives in Big Water, Utah. This essay appeared in The New York Times *in 1991.*

My Husband's Nine Wives

I married a married man. In fact, he had six wives when I married him 17 years ago. Today, he has nine.

In March, the Utah Supreme Court struck down a trial court's ruling that a polygamist couple could not adopt a child because of their marital style. Last month, the national board of the American Civil Liberties Union, in response to a request from its Utah chapter, adopted a new policy calling for the legalization of polygamy.

Polygamy, or plural marriage, as practiced by my family is a paradox. At first blush, it sounds like the ideal situation for the man and an oppressive one for the women. For me, the opposite is true. While polygamists believe that the Old Testament mandates the practice of plural marriage, compelling social reasons make the life style attractive to the modern career woman.

Pick up any women's magazine and you will find article after article about the problems of successfully juggling career, motherhood and marriage. It is a complex act that many women struggle to manage daily; their frustrations fill up the pages of those magazines and consume the hours of afternoon talk shows.

In a monogamous context, the only solutions are compromises. The kids need to learn to fix their own breakfast, your husband needs to get used to occasional microwave dinners, you need to divert more of your income to insure that your pre-schooler is in a good day care environment.

I am sure that in the challenge of working through these compromises, satisfaction and success can be realized. But why must women only embrace a marital arrangement that requires so many trade-offs?

When I leave for the 60-mile commute to court at 7 A.M., my two-year-old daughter, London, is happily asleep in the bed of my husband's wife, Diane. London adores Diane. When London awakes,

4

about the time I'm arriving at the courthouse, she is surrounded by family members who are as familiar to her as the toys in her nursery.

My husband Alex, who writes at night, gets up much later. While   8
most of his wives are already at work, pursuing their careers, he can almost always find one who's willing to chat over coffee.

I share a home with Delinda, another wife, who works in town government. Most nights, we agree we'll just have a simple dinner with our three kids. We'd rather relax and commiserate over the pressures of our work day than chew up our energy cooking and doing a ton of dishes.

Mondays, however, are different. That's the night Alex eats with us. The kids, excited that their father is coming to dinner, are on their best behavior. We often invite another wife or one of his children. It's a special event because it only happens once a week.

Tuesday night, it's back to simplicity for us. But for Alex and the household he's dining with that night, it's their special time.

The same system with some variation governs our private time   16
with him. While spontaneity is by no means ruled out, we basically use an appointment system. If I want to spend Friday evening at his house, I make an appointment. If he's already "booked," I either request another night or if my schedule is inflexible, I talk to the other wife and we work out an arrangement. One thing we've all learned is that there's always another night.

Most evenings, with the demands of career and the literal chasing after the needs of a toddler, all I want to do is collapse into bed and sleep. But there is also the longing for intimacy and comfort that only he can provide, and when those feelings surface, I ask to be with him.

Plural marriage is not for everyone. But it is the life style for me. It offers men the chance to escape from the traditional, confining roles that often isolate them from the surrounding world. More important, it enables women, who live in a society full of obstacles, to fully meet their career, mothering and marriage obligations. Polygamy provides a whole solution. I believe American women would have invented it if it didn't already exist.

Topics for Critical Thinking and Writing

1. In her fourth paragraph Joseph suggests that "compelling social reasons" make polygamy "the life style attractive to the modern career woman." How does she support this assertion? Do you think that she adequately supports it? Why, or why not?

2. Try to imagine advantages that Joseph does not discuss for women in polygamy, for example for women who are divorced or widowed. Whether or not you support polygamy, make the strongest arguments for these advantages that you can (and then, if you wish, answer them).

3. Joseph does not suggest or discuss any problems in polygamous marriages. What problems occur to you? Why should she or should she not have discussed them?
4. Many societies have practiced (and continue to practice) plural marriage, but it is illegal in the United States. Do you think that plural marriage should be a legal option? Why, or why not?
5. Does Joseph's article provide an answer to Brady's "Why I Want a Wife"? Read the essay (pages 129–31), imagine you are Brady, and answer this question. Or, imitating Joseph, write an article supporting polyandry (the practice of having more than one husband at a time).

Noel Perrin

Noel Perrin (b 1927) was educated at Williams College, Duke University, and Cambridge University. He has written on a wide variety of subjects, for instance on Thomas Bowdler (the editor of an expurgated edition of Shakespeare, and hence the source of the word bowdlerize, *"to expurgate prudishly") and on the introduction of guns to Japan in the sixteenth century. Since 1959 he has taught English at Dartmouth College.*

A Part-time Marriage

When my wife told me she wanted a divorce, I responded like any normal college professor. I hurried to the college library. I wanted to get hold of some books on divorce and find out what was happening to me.

Over the next week (my wife meanwhile having left), I read or skimmed about 20. Nineteen of them were no help at all. They offered advice on financial settlements. They told me my wife and I should have been in counseling. A bit late for *that* advice.

What I sought was insight. I especially wanted to understand what was wrong with me that my wife had left, and not even for someone else, but just to be rid of *me*. College professors think they can learn that sort of thing from books.

As it turned out, I could. Or at least I got a start. The twentieth book   4
was a collection of essays by various sociologists, and one of the pieces took my breath away. It was like reading my own horoscope.

The two authors had studied a large group of divorced people much like my wife and me. That is, they focused on middle-class Americans of the straight-arrow persuasion. Serious types, believers in marriage for life. Likely to be parents—and, on the whole, good parents. Likely to have pillar-of-the-community potential. But, nevertheless, all divorced.

Naturally there were many different reasons why all these people had divorced, and many different ways they behaved after divorce. But there was a dominant pattern, and I instantly recognized myself in it. Recognized my wife, too. Reading the essay told me not only what was wrong with me, but also with her. It was the same flaw in both of us. It even gave me a hint as to what my postdivorce behavior was likely to be, and how I might find happiness in the future.

This is the story the essay told me. Or, rather, this is the story the essay hinted at, and that I have since pieced together with much observation, a number of embarrassingly personal questions put to divorced friends, and to some extent from my own life.

Somewhere in some suburb or town or small city, a middle-class   8
couple separate. They are probably between 30 and 40 years old. They own a house and have children. The conscious or official reason for their separation is quite different from what it would have been in their parents' generation. Then, it would have been a man leaving his wife for another, and usually younger, woman. Now it's a woman leaving her husband in order to find herself.

When they separate, the wife normally stays in the house they occupied as a married couple. Neither wants to uproot the children. The husband moves to an apartment, which is nearly always going to be closer to his place of employment than the house was. The ex-wife will almost certainly never see that apartment. The husband, however, sees his former house all the time. Not only is he coming by to pick up the children for visits; if he and his ex-wife are on reasonably good terms, he is apt to visit them right there, while she makes use of the time to do errands or to see a friend.

Back when these two were married, they had an informal labor division. She did inside work, he did outside. Naturally there were exceptions: She gardened, and he did his share of the dishes, maybe even baked bread. But mostly he mowed the lawn and fixed the lawn mower; she put up any new curtains, often enough ones she had made herself.

One Saturday, six months or a year after they separated, he comes to see the kids. He plans also to mow the lawn. Before she leaves, she says, "That damn overhead garage door you got is off the track again. Do you think you'd have time to fix it?" Apartment life makes him restless. He jumps at the chance.

She, just as honorable and straight-arrow as he, has no idea of ask-   12
ing for this as a favor. She invites him to stay for an early dinner. She may put it indirectly—"Michael and Sally want their daddy to have supper with them"—but he is clear that the invitation also proceeds from her.

Provided neither of them has met a really attractive other person yet, they now move into a routine. He comes regularly to do the outside chores, and always stays for dinner. If the children are young enough, he may read to them before bedtime. She may wash his shirts.

One such evening, they both happen to be stirred not only by physical desire but by loneliness. "Oh, you might as well come upstairs," she says with a certain self-contempt. He needs no second invitation; they are upstairs in a flash. It is a delightful end to the evening. More delightful than anything they remember from their marriage, or at least from the later part of it.

That, too, now becomes part of the pattern. He never stays the full night, because, good parents that they are, they don't want the children to get any false hopes up—as they would, seeing their father at breakfast.

Such a relation may go on for several years, may even be inter-   16
rupted by a romance on one side or the other and then resume. It may even grow to the point where she's mending as well as washing his shirts, and he is advising her on her tax returns and fixing her car.

What they have achieved postdivorce is what their marriage should have been like in the first place. Part-time. Seven days a week of marriage was too much. One afternoon and two evenings is just right.

Although our society is even now witnessing de facto part-time arrangements, such as the couple who work in different cities and meet only on weekends, we have no theory of part-time marriage, at least no theory that has reached the general public. The romantic notion still dominates that if you love someone, you obviously want to be with them all the time.

To me it's clear we need such a theory. There are certainly people who thrive on seven-day-a-week marriages. They have a high level of intimacy and they may be better, warmer people than the rest of us. But there are millions and millions of us with medium or low levels of intimacy. We find full-time family membership a strain. If we could enter marriage with more realistic expectations of what closeness means for us, I suspect the divorce rate might permanently turn downward. It's too bad there isn't a sort of glucose tolerance test for intimacy.

As for me personally, I still do want to get married again. About   20
four days a week.

Topics for Critical Thinking and Writing

1. In the model that Perrin dicusses, what is the cause for divorce?
2. Judging from what you have seen around you, do you think many divorces proceed from the cause Perrin cites?
3. Does Perrin's behavior (and that of his wife) strike you as immoral? As bad for themselves, bad for the children, and bad for society? Or, on the other hand, should this sort of arrangement be recognized as a type of satisfactory family arrangement?
4. In paragraph 19 Perrin argues that a need exists for part-time marriages. Does he persuade you, or do you think he is rationalizing his own shortcomings or sense of failure?
5. Did you enjoy reading the essay? Why, or why not? If some passages especially pleased you—perhaps because they were amusing or notably insightful—examine them to see why they impressed you.

6. Perrin begins his essay as a first-person narrative: "When my wife told me she wanted a divorce. . . ." Beginning with paragraph 8 he shifts into a third-person narrative: "Somewhere in some suburb or town or small city, a middle-class couple separate." Can you suggest reasons for this shift? Does it work—that is, does the shift retain or heighten your interest? If you have first-hand knowledge of divorce, try telling about it through a third-person narrative.

Laura Cunningham

Laura Cunningham was born in 1947. Orphaned at the age of eight, she was brought up by two unmarried uncles, both of whom were writers. She says that she became a writer because she didn't know that one could become anything else. Had she known of other possibilities, she says, she would have become a ballerina. The essay that we reprint appeared originally in The New York Times.

The Girls' Room

When I heard she was coming to stay with us I was pleased. At age eight I thought of "grandmother" as a generic brand. My friends had grandmothers who seemed permanently bent over cookie racks. They were a source of constant treats and sweets. They were pinchers of cheeks, huggers and kissers. My own grandmother had always lived in a distant state; I had no memory of her when she decided to join the household recently established for me by my two uncles.

But with the example of my friends' grandmothers before me, I could hardly wait to have a grandmother of my own—and the cookies would be nice too. For while my uncles provided a cuisine that ranged from tuna croquettes to Swedish meatballs, they showed no signs of baking anything more elegant than a potato.

My main concern on the day of my grandmother's arrival was: How soon would she start the cookies? I remember her arrival, my uncles flanking her as they walked down the apartment corridor. She wore a hat, a tailored navy blue suit, an ermine stole. She held, tucked under her arm, the purple leather folder that contained her work in progress, a manuscript entitled "Philosophy for Women." She was preceded by her custom-made white trunk packed with purses, necklaces, earrings, dresses and more purple-inked pages that stress "the spiritual above the material."

She was small—at five feet one inch not much taller than I was—   4
thin and straight, with a pug nose, one brown eye (the good eye) and one blue eye (the bad eye, frosted by cataracts). Her name was "Esther

in Hebrew, Edna in English, and Etka in Russian." She preferred the Russian, referring to herself as "Etka from Minsk." It was not at once apparent that she was deaf in her left ear (the bad ear) but could hear with the right (the good ear). Because her good ear happened to be on the opposite side from the good eye, anyone who spoke to her had to run around her in circles, or sway to and fro, if eye contact and audibility were to be achieved simultaneously.

Etka from Minsk had arrived not directly from Minsk, as the black-eyed ermine stole seemed to suggest, but after many moves. She entered with the draft of family scandal at her back, blown out of her daughter's home after assaults upon her dignity. She held the evidence: an empty-socketed peacock pin. My cousin, an eleven-year-old boy, had surgically plucked out the rhinestone eyes. She could not be expected to stay where such acts occurred. She had to be among "human beings," among "real people" who could understand. We seemed to understand. We—my two uncles and I—encircled her, studied her vandalized peacock pin and vowed that such things would never happen with "us."

She patted my head—a good sign—and asked me to sing the Israeli national anthem. I did, and she handed me a dollar. My uncles went off to their jobs, leaving me alone with my grandmother for the first time. I looked at her, expecting her to start rolling out the cookie dough. Instead she suggested: "Now maybe you could fix me some lunch?"

It wasn't supposed to be this way, I thought, as I took her order: "toasted cheese and a sliced orange." Neither was she supposed to share my pink and orange bedroom, but she did. The bedroom soon exhibited a dual character—stuffed animals on one side, a hospital bed on the other. Within the household this chamber was soon referred to as "the girls' room." The name, given by Uncle Abe, who saw no incongruity, only the affinity of sex, turned out to be apt, for what went on in the girls' room could easily have been labeled sibling rivalry if she had not been eighty and I eight. I soon found that I had acquired not a traditional grandmother but an aged kid sister.

The theft and rivalry began within days. My grandmother had given me her most cherished possession, a violet beaded bag. In return I gave her my heart-shaped "ivory" pin and matching earrings. That night she stole back the purse but insisted on keeping the pin and earrings. I turned to my uncles for mediation and ran up against unforeseen resistance. They thought my grandmother should keep the beaded bag; they didn't want to upset her.

I burned at the injustice of it and felt the heat of an uncomfortable truth: where I once had my uncles' undivided indulgence, they were now split as my grandmother and I vied for their attention. The household, formerly geared to my little-girl needs, was rearranged to accommodate hers. I suffered serious affronts—my grandmother, in a fit of frugality, scissored all the household blankets, including what a

8

psychiatrist would have dubbed my "security" blanket, in half. "Now," she said, her good eye gleaming, "we have twice as many." I lay under my narrow slice of blanket and stared hopelessly up at the ceiling. I thought evilly of ways of getting my grandmother out of the apartment.

Matters worsened, as more and more of my trinkets disappeared. One afternoon I came home from school to find her squeezed into my unbuttoned favorite blouse. Rouged and beribboned, she insisted that the size 3 blouse was hers. Meanwhile, I was forced to adapt to her idiosyncracies: she covered everything black—from the dog to the telephone—with white doilies. She left saucers balanced on top of glasses. She sang nonstop. She tried to lock my dog out of the apartment.

The word that explained her behavior was "arteriosclerosis." She had forgotten so much that sometimes she would greet me with "You look familiar." At other times she'd ask, "What hotel is this?" My answer, shouted in her good ear, was: "We're not in a hotel! This is our apartment!" The response would be a hoot of laughter: "Then why are we in the ballroom?"

Finally we fought: arm-to-arm combat. I was shocked at her grip, 12 steely as the bars that locked her into bed at night. Her good eye burned into mine and she said, "I'll tell." And she did. For the first time I was scolded. She had turned their love to disapproval, I thought, and how it chafed. Eventually our rivalry mellowed into conspiracy. Within months we found we had uses for each other. I provided the lunches and secret, forbidden ice cream sundaes. She rewarded me with cold cash. She continued to take my clothes; I charged her competitive prices. I hated school; she paid me not to go. When I came home for lunch I usually stayed.

Our household endured the status quo for eight years: my uncles, my grandmother and I. Within the foursome rivalries and alliances shifted. I became my grandmother's friend and she became mine. We were the source of all the family comedy. When she said she wanted a college diploma we gave her one—with tinfoil stars and a "magna magna summa summa cum laude" inscription. We sang and performed skits. With talcum-powdered hair and wearing one of her old dresses, I would appear as her "long-lost friend." We had other themes, including a pen pal, "The Professor."

Of course, living with an elderly person had its raw aspects. When she was ill our girls' room took on the stark aura of a geriatrics ward. I imagined, to my shame, that neighbors could stare in through curtainless windows as I tended to my grandmother's most personal needs.

Yet, in these times of age segregation, with grandmothers sent off to impersonal places, I wonder if the love and the comedy weren't worth the intermittent difficulties. Certainly I learned what it might be to become old. And I took as much comfort as my grandmother did in a nightly exchange of Russian endearments—"Ya tebya lyublyu," "Ya tebya tozhe lyublyu—I love you," "I love you, too."

If I sold my grandmother blouses and baubles, maybe she gave me the truth in exchange. Once, when we were alone in the girls' room, she turned to me, suddenly lucid, her good eye as bright as it would ever be—a look I somehow recognized as her "real" gaze—and said, "My life passes like a dream."

Topics for Critical Thinking and Writing

1. In the second sentence, what does Cunningham mean by "a generic brand"?
2. What is the title of Esther's manuscript? What is it about? Do you detect any irony in the way Cunningham conveys this information? Explain.
3. In the second sentence of paragraph 4, what is conveyed by putting the names within quotation marks?
4. Is paragraph 4—about Esther's physical disabilities—in bad taste? Explain.
5. In her last paragraph Cunningham says that perhaps her grandmother gave her "the truth." What does she mean?
6. "I burned at the injustice of it and felt the heat of an uncomfortable truth." Where in the narrative does Cunningham say this? What was the "truth"? If you remember a similar experience, write a narrative that discloses both the experience and the truth on which it was based. Or, write an essay of five hundred words on your own most potent experience of living with or near an elderly person.

Black Elk

Black Elk, a wichasha wakon *(holy man) of the Oglala Sioux, as a small boy witnessed the battle of the Little Bighorn (1876). He lived to see his people all but annihilated and his hopes for them extinguished. In 1931, toward the end of his life, he told his life story to the poet and scholar John G. Neihardt to preserve a sacred vision given him.*

"High Horse's Courting" is a comic interlude in Black Elk Speaks, *a predominantly tragic memoir.*

High Horse's Courting

You know, in the old days, it was not very easy to get a girl when you wanted to be married. Sometimes it was hard work for a young man and he had to stand a great deal. Say I am a young man and I have seen a young girl who looks so beautiful to me that I feel all sick when I think about her. I cannot just go and tell her about it and then get married if she is willing. I have to be a very sneaky fellow to talk to her at all, and after I have managed to talk to her, that is only the beginning.

Probably for a long time I have been feeling sick about a certain girl because I love her so much, but she will not even look at me, and her parents keep a good watch over her. But I keep feeling worse and worse all the time; so maybe I sneak up to her tepee in the dark and wait until she comes out. Maybe I just wait there all night and don't get any sleep at all and she does not come out. Then I feel sicker than ever about her.

Maybe I hide in the brush by a spring where she sometimes goes to get water, and when she comes by, if nobody is looking, then I jump out and hold her and just make her listen to me. If she likes me too, I can tell that from the way she acts, for she is very bashful and maybe will not say a word or even look at me the first time. So I let her go, and then maybe I sneak around until I can see her father alone, and I tell him how many horses I can give him for his beautiful girl, and by now I am feeling so sick that maybe I would give him all the horses in the world if I had them.   4

Well, this young man I am telling about was called High Horse, and there was a girl in the village who looked so beautiful to him that he was just sick all over from thinking about her so much and he was getting sicker all the time. The girl was very shy, and her parents thought a great deal of her because they were not young any more and this was the only child they had. So they watched her all day long, and they fixed it so that she would be safe at night too when they were asleep. They thought so much of her that they had made a rawhide bed for her to sleep in, and after they knew that High Horse was sneaking around after her, they took rawhide thongs and tied the girl in bed at night so that nobody could steal her when they were asleep, for they were not sure but that their girl might really want to be stolen.

Well, after High Horse had been sneaking around a good while and hiding and waiting for the girl and getting sicker all the time, he finally caught her alone and made her talk to him. Then he found out that she liked him maybe a little. Of course this did not make him feel well. It made him sicker than ever, but now he felt as brave as a bison bull, and so he went right to her father and said he loved the girl so much that he would give two good horses for her—one of them young and the other one not so very old.

But the old man just waved his hand, meaning for High Horse to go away and quit talking foolishness like that.

High Horse was feeling sicker than ever about it; but there was another young fellow who said he would loan High Horse two ponies and when he got some more horses, why, he could just give them back for the ones he had borrowed.

Then High Horse went back to the old man and said he would give   8
four horses for the girl—two of them young and the other two not hard-

ly old at all. But the old man just waved his hand and would not say anything.

So High Horse sneaked around until he could talk to the girl again, and he asked her to run away with him. He told her he thought he would just fall over and die if she did not. But she said she would not do that; she wanted to be bought like a fine woman. You see she thought a great deal of herself too.

That made High Horse feel so very sick that he could not eat a bite, and he went around with his head hanging down as though he might just fall down and die any time.

Red Deer was another young fellow, and he and High Horse were great comrades, always doing things together. Red Deer saw how High Horse was acting, and he said: "Cousin, what is the matter? Are you sick in the belly? You look as though you were going to die."

Then High Horse told Red Deer how it was, and said he thought   12
he could not stay alive much longer if he could not marry the girl pretty quick.

Red Deer thought awhile about it, and then he said: "Cousin, I have a plan, and if you are man enough to do as I tell you, then everything will be all right. She will not run away with you; her old man will not take four horses; and four horses are all you can get. You must steal her and run away with her. Then afterwhile you can come back and the old man cannot do anything because she will be your woman. Probably she wants you to steal her anyway."

So they planned what High Horse had to do, and he said he loved the girl so much that he was man enough to do anything Red Deer or anybody else could think up. So this is what they did.

That night late they sneaked up to the girl's tepee and waited until it sounded inside as though the old man and the old woman and the girl were sound asleep. Then High Horse crawled under the tepee with a knife. He had to cut the rawhide thongs first, and then Red Deer, who was pulling up the stakes around that side of the tepee, was going to help drag the girl outside and gag her. After that, High Horse could put her across his pony in front of him and hurry out of there and be happy all the rest of his life.

When High Horse had crawled inside, he felt so nervous that he   16
could hear his heart drumming, and it seemed so loud he felt sure it would 'waken the old folks. But it did not, and afterwhile he began cutting the thongs. Every time he cut one it made a pop and nearly scared him to death. But he was getting along all right and all the thongs were cut down as far as the girl's thighs, when he became so nervous that his knife slipped and stuck the girl. She gave a big, loud yell. Then the old folks jumped up and yelled too. By this time High Horse was outside, and he and Red Deer were running away like antelope. The old man and some other people chased the young men but they got away in the dark and nobody knew who it was.

Well, if you ever wanted a beautiful girl you will know how sick High Horse was now. It was very bad the way he felt, and it looked as though he would starve even if he did not drop over dead sometime.

Red Deer kept thinking about this, and after a few days he went to High Horse and said: "Cousin, take courage! I have another plan, and I am sure, if you are man enough, we can steal her this time." And High Horse said: "I am man enough to do anything anybody can think up, if I can only get that girl."

So this is what they did.

They went away from the village alone, and Red Deer made High   20
Horse strip naked. Then he painted High Horse solid white all over, and after that he painted black stripes all over the white and put black rings around High Horse's eyes. High Horse looked terrible. He looked so terrible that when Red Deer was through painting and took a good look at what he had done, he said it scared even him a little.

"Now," Red Deer said, "if you get caught again, everybody will be so scared they will think you are a bad spirit and will be afraid to chase you."

So when the night was getting old and everybody was sound asleep, they sneaked back to the girl's tepee. High Horse crawled in with his knife, as before, and Red Deer waited outside, ready to drag the girl out and gag her when High Horse had all the thongs cut.

High Horse crept up by the girl's bed and began cutting at the thongs. But he kept thinking, "If they see me they will shoot me because I look so terrible." The girl was restless and kept squirming around in bed, and when a thong was cut, it popped. So High Horse worked very slowly and carefully.

But he must have made some noise, for suddenly the old woman   24
awoke and said to her old man: "Old Man, wake up! There is somebody in this tepee!" But the old man was sleepy and didn't want to be bothered. He said: "Of course there is somebody in this tepee. Go to sleep and don't bother me." Then he snored some more.

But High Horse was so scared by now that he lay very still and as flat to the ground as he could. Now, you see, he had not been sleeping very well for a long time because he was so sick about the girl. And while he was lying there waiting for the old woman to snore, he just forgot everything, even how beautiful the girl was. Red Deer who was lying outside ready to do his part, wondered and wondered what had happened in there, but he did not dare call out to High Horse.

Afterwhile the day began to break and Red Deer had to leave with the two ponies he had staked there for his comrade and girl, or somebody would see him.

So he left.

Now when it was getting light in the tepee, the girl awoke and the   28
first thing she saw was a terrible animal, all white with black stripes on it, lying asleep beside her bed. So she screamed, and then the old

woman screamed and the old man yelled. High Horse jumped up, scared almost to death, and he nearly knocked the tepee down getting out of there.

People were coming running from all over the village with guns and bows and axes, and everybody was yelling.

By now High Horse was running so fast that he hardly touched the ground at all, and he looked so terrible that the people fled from him and let him run. Some braves wanted to shoot at him, but the others said he might be some sacred being and it would bring bad trouble to kill him.

High Horse made for the river that was near, and in among the brush he found a hollow tree and dived into it. Afterwhile some braves came there and he could hear them saying that it was some bad spirit that had come out of the water and gone back in again.

That morning the people were ordered to break camp and move   32
away from there. So they did, while High Horse was hiding in his hollow tree.

Now Red Deer had been watching all this from his own tepee and trying to look as though he were as much surprised and scared as all the others. So when the camp moved, he sneaked back to where he had seen his comrade disappear. When he was down there in the brush, he called, and High Horse answered, because he knew his friend's voice. They washed off the paint from High Horse and sat down on the river bank to talk about their troubles.

High Horse said he never would go back to the village as long as he lived and he did not care what happened to him now. He said he was going to go on the war-path all by himself. Red Deer said: "No, cousin, you are not going on the war-path alone, because I am going with you."

So Red Deer got everything ready, and at night they started out on the war-path all alone. After several days they came to a Crow camp just about sundown, and when it was dark they sneaked up to where the Crow horses were grazing, killed the horse guard, who was not thinking about enemies because he thought all the Lakotas were far away, and drove off about a hundred horses.

They got a big start because all the Crow horses stampeded and it   36
was probably morning before the Crow warriors could catch any horses to ride. Red Deer and High Horse fled with their herd three days and nights before they reached the village of their people. Then they drove the whole herd right into the village and up in front of the girl's tepee. The old man was there, and High Horse called out to him and asked if he thought maybe that would be enough horses for his girl. The old man did not wave him away that time. It was not the horses that he wanted. What he wanted was a son who was a real man and good for something.

So High Horse got his girl after all, and I think he deserved her.

Topics for Critical Thinking and Writing

Although High Horse's behavior is amusing and at times ridiculous, how does Black Elk make it clear that he is not ridiculing the young man, but is instead in sympathy with him? Consider the following questions:

1. What is the effect of the first three paragraphs? Think about the first two sentences, and then the passage beginning "Say I am a young man . . ." and ending ". . . I would give him all the horses in the world if I had them."
2. Describe the behavior of the young girl and of her father and mother. How do they contribute to the comedy? How does their behavior affect your understanding of Black Elk's attitude toward High Horse?
3. What is the function of Red Deer?
4. The narrative consists of several episodes. List them in the order in which they occur and then describe the narrative's structure. How does this structure affect the tone?

Anonymous

The anonymous author of this essay has revealed only that he was forty when he wrote it, is married, and is the father of three children. The essay originally appeared in The New Republic, *a magazine regarded by some as liberal.*

Confessions of an Erstwhile Child

Some years ago I attempted to introduce a class of Upward Bound students to political theory via More's *Utopia.* It was a mistake: I taught precious little theory and earned More a class full of undying enemies on account of two of his ideas. The first, that all members of a Utopian family were subject to the lifelong authority of its eldest male. The second, the Utopian provision that should a child wish to follow a profession different from that of his family, he could be transferred by adoption to a family that practiced the desired trade. My students were not impressed with my claim that the one provision softened the other and made for a fair compromise—for what causes most of our quarrels with our parents but our choice of life-patterns, of occupation? In objecting to the first provision my students were picturing themselves as children, subject to an unyielding authority. But on the second provision they surprised me by taking the parents' role and arguing that this form of ad lib adoption denied them a fundamental right of ownership over their children. It occurred to me that these reactions were two parts of the same pathology: having suffered the discipline of unreasonable parents, one has earned the right to be unreasonable in turn to one's children. The phenomenon has well-known parallels, such as frantic martinets who have risen from the ranks. Having served time as property, my Upward Bound students wanted theirs back as proprietors. I shuddered. It hardly takes an advanced course in Freudian psychology to realize that the perpetuation, generation after generation, of psychic lesions must go right to this source, the philosophically dubious notion that children are the property of their biological parents, compounded with the unphilosophic certitude so many parents harbor, that their children must serve an apprenticeship as like their own as they can manage.

The idea of the child as property has always bothered me, for personal reasons I shall outline. I lack the feeling that I own my children and I have always scoffed at the idea that what they are and do is a continuation or a rejection of my being. I like them, I sympathize with them, I acknowledge the obligation to support them for a term of years—but I am not so fond or foolish as to regard a biological tie as a lien on their loyalty or respect, nor to imagine that I am equipped with preternatural powers of guidance as to their success and happiness. Beyond inculcating some of the obvious social protocols required in civilized life, who am I to pronounce on what makes for a happy or successful life? How many of us can say that we have successfully managed our own lives? Can we do better with our children? I am unimpressed, to say no more, with parents who have no great track record, presuming to oracular powers in regard to their children's lives.

The current debate over the Equal Rights Amendment frequently turns to custody questions. Opponents of ERA have made the horrifying discovery that ERA will spell the end of the mother's presumed rights of custody in divorce or separation cases, and that fathers may begin custody rights. Indeed a few odd cases have been so settled recently in anticipation of the ratification of ERA. If ratified, ERA would be an extremely blunt instrument for calling the whole idea of custody into question, but I for one will applaud anything that serves to begin debate. As important as equal rights between adults may be, I think that the rights of children are a far more serious and unattended need. To me, custody by natural parents, far from being a presumed right only re-examined in case of collapsing marriages, should be viewed as a privilege.

At this point I have to explain why I can so calmly contemplate the   4 denial of so-called parental rights.

I am the only child of two harsh and combative personalities who married, seemingly, in order to have a sparring partner always at hand. My parents have had no other consistent or lasting aim in life but to win out over each other in a contest of wills. They still live, vigorous and angry septuagenarians, their ferocity little blunted by age or human respect. My earliest memories—almost my sole memories—are of unending combat, in which I was sometimes an appalled spectator, more often a hopeless negotiator in a war of no quarter, and most often a bystander accused of covert belligerency on behalf of one side or the other, and frequently of both! I grew up with two supposed adults who were absorbed in their hatreds and recriminations to the exclusion of almost all other reality. Not only did I pass by almost unnoticed in their struggle, the Depression and World War II passed them by equally unnoticed. I figured mainly as a practice target for sarcasm and invective, and occasionally as the ultimate culprit responsible for their unhappiness. ("If it weren't for you," my mother would sometimes say, "I could leave that SOB," a remark belied by her refusal to leave the SOB during these 20 long years since I left their "shelter.")

The reader may ask, "How did you survive if your parents' house was all that bad?" I have three answers. First, I survived by the moral equivalent of running away to sea or the circus, i.e., by burying myself in books and study, especially in the history of faraway and (I thought) more idealistic times than our own, and by consciously shaping my life and tastes to be as different as possible from those of my parents (this was a reproach to them, they knew, and it formed the basis of a whole secondary area of conflict and misunderstanding). Second, I survived because statistically most people "survive" horrible families, but survival can be a qualified term, as it is in my case by a permanently impaired digestive system and an unnatural sensitivity to raised voices. And third, though I found solace in schooling and the rationality, cooperation and basic fairness in teachers that I missed in my parents, I must now question whether it is healthy for a child to count so heavily on schooling for the love and approval that he deserves from his home and family. Even if schooling can do this well, in later life it means that one is loyal and affectionate toward schooling, not toward parents, who may in some sense need affection even if they don't "deserve" it. I am not unaware that however fair and rational I may be in reaction to my parents' counter-examples, I am a very cold-hearted man. I might have done better transferred to a new family, not just by receiving love, but through learning to give it—a lack I mourn as much or more than my failure to receive.

It is little wonder then that I have an acquired immunity to the notion that parental custody is by and large a preferable thing. In my case, almost anything else would have been preferable, including even a rather callously run orphanage—anything for a little peace and quiet. Some people are simply unfit, under any conditions, to be parents, even if, indeed especially if, they maintain the charade of a viable marriage. My parents had no moral right to custody of children, and I cannot believe that my experience is unique or particularly isolated. There are all too many such marriages, in which some form of horror, congenial enough to adults too sick or crazed to recognize it, works its daily ruination on children. Surely thousands of children conclude at age 10 or 11, as I did, that marriage is simply an institution in which people are free to be as beastly as they have a mind to, which may lead either to a rejection of marriage or to a decision to reduplicate a sick marriage a second time, with another generation of victims. It is time to consider the rights of the victims.

How to implement a nascent theory of justice for children is diffi- 8 cult to say. One cannot imagine taking the word of a five-year-old against his parents, but what about a ten- or twelve-year-old? At *some* point, children should have the right to escape the dominance of impossible parents. The matter used to be easier than it has been since World War I. The time-honored solution—for boys—of running away from home has been made infeasible by economic conditions, finger-prints, social security and minimum wage laws. No apprenticeship sys-tem exists any more, much less its upper-class medieval version—with required exchange of boys at puberty among noble families to serve as pages and so forth. The adoption system contemplated in More's *Utopia* is a half-remembered echo of a medieval life, in which society, wiser than its theory, decreed a general exchange of children at or just before puberty, whether through apprenticeship or page-service, or more informal arrangements, like going to a university at 14 or running away with troubadors or gypsies.

Exchanging children is a wisely conceived safety valve against a too traumatic involvement between the biological parent and the child. Children need an alternative to living all their formative life in the same biological unit. They should have the right to petition for release from some sorts of families, to join other families, or to engage in other sorts of relationships that may provide equivalent service but may not be organized as a family. The nuclear family, after all, is not such an old or proven vehicle. Phillippe Aries' book, *Centuries of Childhood*, made the important point that the idea of helpless childhood is itself a notion of recent origin, that grew up simultaneously in the 16th and 17th cen-turies with the small and tight-knit nuclear family, sealed off from the world by another recent invention, "privacy." The older *extended* fami-ly (which is the kind More knew about) was probably more authoritar-ian on paper but much less productive of dependency in actual opera-tion. There ought to be more than one way a youngster can enter adult society with more than half of his sanity left. At least no one should be forced to remain in a no-win game against a couple of crazy parents for 15–18 years. At 10 or 12, children in really messy situations should have the legal right to petition for removal from impossible families, and those rights should be reasonably easy to exercise. (This goes on de facto among the poor, of course, but it is not legal, and usually carries both stigma and danger.) The minimum wage laws should be modified to exempt such persons, especially if they wish to continue their educa-tion, working perhaps for public agencies, if they have no other means of support. If their parents can support them, then the equivalent of child support should be charged them to maintain their children, not in luxury, but adequately. Adoption of older children should be facilitated by easing of legal procedures (designed mainly to govern the adoption of *infants*) plus tax advantages for those willing to adopt older children on grounds of goodwill. Indeed children wishing to escape impossible family situations should be allowed a fair degree of initiative in finding and negotiating with possible future families.

Obviously the risk of rackets would be very high unless the exact terms of such provisions were framed very carefully, but the possibility of rackets is less frightening to anyone who thinks about it for long than the dangers of the present situation, which are evident and unrelieved by any signs of improvement. In barely a century this country has changed from a relatively loose society in which Huckleberry Finns were not uncommon, to a society of tense, airless nuclear families in which unhealthy and neurotic tendencies, once spawned in a family, tend to repeat themselves at a magnifying and accelerating rate. We may soon gain the distinction of being the only nation on earth to need not just medicare but "psychi-care." We have invested far too heavily in the unproved "equity" called the nuclear family; that stock is about to crash and we ought to begin finding escape options. In colonial days many New England colonies passed laws imposing fines or extra taxes on parents who kept their children under their own roofs after age 15 or 16, on the sensible notion that a person of that age ought to be out and doing on his own, whether going to Yale or apprenticing in a foundry. Even without the benefit of Freud, the colonial fathers had a good sense of what was wrong with a closely bound and centripetal family structure—it concentrates craziness like compound interest, and so they hit it with monetary penalties, a proper Protestant response, intolerant at once of both mystery and excuses. But this was the last gasp of a medieval and fundamentally Catholic idea that children, God help them, while they may be the children of *these* particular parents biologically, spiritually are the children of God, and more appositely are the children of the entire community, for which the entire community takes responsibility. The unguessed secret of the middle ages was not that monasteries relieved parents of unwanted children; more frequently, they relieved children of unwanted parents!

Topics for Critical Thinking and Writing

1. What is the author's thesis? (Quote the thesis sentence.) Apart from his own experience, what evidence or other means does he offer to persuade you to accept his thesis?
2. What part does the *tone* of his article play in persuading you to agree with him or in alienating you? Does his tone strike you, perhaps, as vigorous or belligerent, as ironic or bitter, as reasonable or hysterical?

3. The author admits (paragraph 6) that he is "a very cold-hearted man."
    Do you remember your initial reaction to that sentence? What was it?
    Overall, does the author strengthen or jeopardize his argument by this
    admission? Explain.
4. If you did not find the article persuasive, did you find it interesting? Can
    you explain why?

Celia E. Rothenberg

*Celia E. Rothenberg graduated from Wellesley College in 1991. A history major with a special
interest in the lives of Middle Eastern women, she was awarded a Marshall fellowship and is
now studying modern Middle Eastern history at Oxford. She has served as an intern in an
Israeli-Palestinian women's peace group in Jerusalem, and she plans to continue working for
understanding between these two groups.*

Rothenberg wrote the following essay while she was an undergraduate

Child of Divorce

Over this past winter vacation my parents, brother, and I
spent a few days together—a rare event now that the four of us live in
four different states. As I watched my parents and brother engage in
our usual laughter and reminiscing, accompanied by an occasional tear
at a past both bitter and sweet, I listened more closely than ever before
to what is a frequent topic of discussion, our relationship as a family.

Perhaps because my parents divorced when I was a small child, it
seems to surprise my friends that my family's recollections of those
years are filled with many pleasant memories. After all, those who
don't know my family have reason to assume that the memories of
growing up with divorced parents in some tough economic times
might be rather dreary. In fact, however, my memories center on the
results of the thoughtfulness and conscious effort exerted by both my
parents to create a sense of love and protection for my brother and me.
I have always felt that my family was a team, a team that sometimes
fumbled, and sometimes seemed to have two, three, or even four captains, and a team that underwent a change in plan mid-game, but a
team nevertheless. It is only recently, however, that I have realized how
much patience and understanding went into achieving that sense of
belonging and love, and how achieving it was part of the long and often
painful process for us of divorce and healing.

My parents divorced, after fifteen years of marriage, when I was
six. I have nearly no memories of living in a two-parent household.
From the time of my earliest memories, my mother has always studied
or worked full time. Immediately after the divorce, she, like many
women who find themselves single after many years as a "housewife,"

went back to school. My brother at the time was twelve. Although I remember my Cinderella-shaped cake for my seventh birthday, a few of my favorite pets, and a well-loved school teacher, I remember very little of my mom's return to school, or my own or brother's adjustment to our new surroundings. Perhaps the gaps in my memory serve as some kind of mental defense mechanism to protect me from the reality of the harder times; no matter the reason for my memory voids, however, my brother's recollections are so vivid, and my mom and dad so open about those years, that my scattered memories have been augmented by their story-telling—to the point that I often confuse my memories with theirs.

It is only recently, in fact, that I have realized how difficult the initial years following the divorce were for my mother, brother and father.   4
Over this past winter vacation, my mom told me for the first time how taxing even the simplest tasks seemed to be. For example, locking the doors to our new, small house conjured up all the difficulties and sadnesses of this new beginning. Because my dad had customarily locked up, she had rarely been the one to lock each lock and turn off each light. Doing these tasks in a new house in a new city was a constant reminder of her changed circumstances. Late in the evening she would carefully plot the order in which to turn off the lights, so as not to be alone in the dark. She would lock a door, and then a window, pausing in between the locks to distract her mind from the task at hand—and the frightening and lonely feelings these new responsibilities brought with them.

My family now openly recalls that those years were a difficult time of adjustment to new schools, a new city, and a new life. We had moved from a small suburb of St. Louis to Champaign-Urbana, a community largely centered on the life of the University of Illinois. Our first house in Champaign and my mom's tuition for the Master's degree in Library and Information Science were largely financed by the sale of the lovely Steinway baby grand piano that had graced my parents' living room since before I was born. Before the divorce, my father was an attorney until he found himself in legal difficulties, which ultimately led him to give up the practice of law. His reduced income and my mom's tuition bills placed us under a great financial strain.

My brother, who was twelve at the time of the divorce, particularly recalls how difficult communication was between the three of us and my father, and at times even among the three of us. To help ease the tension of my dad's monthly visits and maintain a relationship which included some fun, my brother and dad played checkers through the mail. They carefully conceived of a plan of multiple paper copies of the checker board and colored pencils for their game. One of my few early memories of those years focusses on the checker board we set up on the dining room table to represent the game my brother and dad played on paper. One evening, the cat we brought with us from (as my mother often said) our "other life," jumped on the board, knocking the pieces all over the table. Steve was inconsolable, and only a prolonged long-distance phone call to figure out where each piece belonged resolved the situation.

That first year my brother escaped into a world of books, often reading fiction and plays when he should have been doing homework, a coping behavior he practiced until he was nearly through high school.

But even the deepest hurts can heal over time. With encouragement and support from both my parents, Steve channeled his considerable energy and anger into planning for an early graduation from high school and a year in Israel between high school and college. The only conditions set were that he had to earn enough money to buy his own plane ticket and he had to have a college acceptance letter in hand before he left. These goals gave him something to work for at a time when he felt that he had lost friends and status in coming to a new, very different, and less comfortable environment than had been part of his early days.

As for me, perhaps because I was six years younger, I appeared to go blithely along, oblivious to most of the tensions and strains that Steve seemed to feel. With my mother studying for her classes and Steve spending almost all his time reading, I became an avid reader myself, almost in self defense. I found new friends and reveled in my new elementary school, a magnet school where we studied French every day. I wrote long, detailed stories of a young girl who lived on a farm with both parents and a dozen brothers and sisters and a beautiful horse. Perhaps I, too, was seeking some consolation in an imaginary life far removed from our little house.

It can take years for wounds to heal, and I am happy to say that my family healed more quickly than most. Perhaps we got past that initial phase early on because my parents did not make too many mistakes. They avoided some common pitfalls of divorcing families. The divorce was quick—the process was completed a few months after my parents sold their house and moved to their new homes—there were no court battles, no screaming fights, no wrenching decisions that we children were required to make. Steve and I were never asked—or allowed—to choose sides or express a preference for one parent over the other. Although my own memories are blurry, the few recollections I have of those first five years focus on my dad's regular monthly visits (he lived a few hours away by car). By the time I was ten, he was spending nearly every weekend with us at the house, a pattern which continued for the next decade, until I was out of high school and off to Wellesley.

Nothing worthwhile, my mother has always told me, is ever easy. It could not have always been easy for either of my parents to spend so much of their free time together when they had chosen to create separate lives, but at the time Steve and I rarely saw anything but civility and fondness. As parents they were determined not to let their children suffer for mistakes they may have made in their marriage. It is one of their greatest gifts to Steve and me, for it was the ultimate lesson in learning about the commitment and cost of love and the lifelong responsibilities of family.

The stories we have accumulated over the years have become more   12
hilarious as I have grown older. My dad, determined not to be a "Disneyland daddy," showing up on the weekends for shopping and dinners out, was not uncomfortable in our new home. In fact, he helped us figure out how to do various home improvement projects. Under his direction, we rewired our house (and nearly electrocuted Steve in the process), insulated our attic (the family story lingers that we nearly blew off the roof), and painted the house (and, of course, ourselves). Our projects probably didn't save us very much money, since we seemed to spend as much money on fixing the mistakes we made as on the project itself, yet we were not merely building the house, or growing gardens, or mowing the lawn. We were rebuilding our lives, making memories, and creating a sense of togetherness.

My own clear and more complete memories begin at the age of eleven, when my mother, brother, and I began a new life-style, which reflected a newly achieved flexibility and confidence in our ability to manage our lives. When my brother entered the University of Illinois, we moved into a big old house and I began high school. The house was what a real estate broker fondly calls a "fixer-upper," and was perfect for my mom's income (she worked for the University after she finished her Master's degree) and our need for space for friends of mine and Steve's. Steve, in particular, brought home countless Jewish college students whom he knew from his involvement in the campus Jewish student organization. They often needed a good meal, a shoulder to lean on, an opinion on a paper, or a good night's sleep.

I remember our dining room on Shabbos, furnished with a dining room set probably beautiful in my grandmother's day but battered after three generations of use, packed with college students eating dinner. I remember vividly the talk and the laughter, the jesting and the endless debates. My mom was not only an intellectual support for those students but also an inspiration, someone who had experienced a marriage gone bad, the trials and tribulations of parenting alone (at least during the week), and the tough economics of a single-parent household. Conversations stretched from the abstract to the concrete, from the politics of the Eastern bloc to the intricacies of love and sex.

Over the years it has become clear that the divorce, although traumatic, opened our minds, enriched our relationships with each other, and loosened restraints we did not know we were subject to. I vividly remember my high school years as a busy time full of my friends and my brothers' who simply enjoyed being around the house. The slightly chaotic, easy-going atmosphere of the house was fostered in large part by our mom; she had disliked the isolated feeling of life in suburbia when she was married. She wanted to create a different atmosphere for Steve and me, a place where young people were comfortable to come and go.

My friends in high school were fascinated by my home, and I enjoyed it as much as they did. My dad was able to watch us grow and change from weekend to weekend, his place secure and comfortable at the head of the Shabbos table surrounded by students. He helped us with science projects, participated in countless car-pools, and, most of all, was there when we needed him. Although from the point of view of the Census Bureau we were a "single parent household," in actuality we were a *family* that happened to have divorced parents. Perhaps our experience was not typical of some families in which there has been a divorce, but the labels obscure our understanding of the needs and hopes of all families, which I think are probably the same, divorced or not. My parent's expectations for Steve and me were not altered by their marital status, nor do I think that Steve and I let them get away with very much on the excuse that they were divorced!

I have always loved my family, but I find that I admire each of them increasingly as time goes on. Now, when we gather from different corners of the country and world during vacations a few times a year, we admit that the best and the worst, but always the most precious times, were when we were together on the weekends in that big old house, sometimes with the students and sometimes with only each other. On special occasions, we have a (very patient) long-distance operator connect the four of us on the same phone line, and we talk as if there is no tomorrow. We are fiercely proud of one another; I often have to restrain myself from blurting out the merits of my exceptional family to my unsuspecting friends.

At times I wonder how different we would be if we had not gone through the divorce, but for that question I can conjure up no really meaningful speculation. I know that we immensely value our time together, freely share our money (or, I should say, our student loans, as my brother is now in law school, my mom is a full-time doctoral student and my father shoulders the Wellesley burden), and exorbitantly rejoice in each other's company. What more could any of us want from family? So often, it seems to me, I see families that do not realize they possess a great wealth—time. They are together all the time. They don't miss the moments of their mother/father/brother/sister's lives that are irreplacable.

There is no question that it is often difficult to be a family. My own family's life took a path with an unexpected curve. We weathered times of tough adjustments, economic difficulties, and typical adolescent rebellion. Through it all, though, there was a guiding (if unspoken until many years later) principle of life: family is family forever, and there is no escaping either the trials or the rewards. My parents expect my brother and me to extend ourselves and do work that in some way will bring more light into the world. I have parents who, on modest incomes and

16

budgets, have endowed me with dreams and a sense that the impossible is possible. I have parents for whom I am extremely grateful.

When I told my family that Wellesley asked me to write an article   20
on growing up in a single parent household, they responded in their typical chaotic fashion. My brother forced each of us to sit and write a page about the "Single-Parent Thing" before he let us eat dinner. My mother began plotting a book made up of chapters written from the different perspectives of mother, father, son, and daughter in the single-parent household. My dad insisted we discuss it over dinner (and promised to write his page immediately after dessert). In the end, I took their contributions with me back to Wellesley and wrote down my own feelings, late at night in Munger Hall.

Topics for Critical Thinking and Writing

1. What are your earliest memories of your family? How would you account for the fact that Rothenberg has "nearly no memories of living in a two-parent household"?
2. Rothenberg calls her family "exceptional." What do you find to be her strongest evidence for this claim?
3. In paragraph 2 Rothenberg refers to assumptions that her friends make about a child who grew up with divorced parents. What are or were your assumptions? On what are (or were) they based?
4. A highly personal essay runs the risk of being of little interest to persons other than the author. If you found this essay interesting, try to account for its appeal.

Jamaica Kincaid

Jamaica Kincaid was born in 1949 in St. Johns, Antigua, in the West Indies. She was educated at the Princess Margaret School in Antigua and, briefly, at Westchester Community College and Franconia College. Since 1974 she has been a contributor to The New Yorker *where "Girl" first was published. "Girl" was later included in the first of Kincaid's four books,* At the Bottom of the River. *Her most recent book is a short novel about a young black woman who comes to the United States from the West Indies.*

Ms. Kincaid informs us that "benna," mentioned early in "Girl," refers to "songs of the sort your parents didn't want you to sing, at first calypso and later rock and roll."

Girl

Wash the white clothes on Monday and put them on the stone heap; wash the color clothes on Tuesday and put them on the clothesline to dry; don't walk barehead in the hot sun; cook pumpkin fritters in very hot sweet oil; soak your little clothes right after you take them off; when buying cotton to make yourself a nice blouse, be sure that it doesn't have gum on it, because that way it won't hold up well after a wash; soak salt fish overnight before you cook it; is it true that you sing benna in Sunday school?; always eat your food in such a way that it won't turn someone else's stomach; on Sundays try to walk like a lady and not like the slut you are so bent on becoming; don't sing benna in Sunday school; you mustn't speak to wharf-rat boys, not even to give directions; don't eat fruits on the street—flies will follow you; *but I don't sing benna on Sundays at all and never in Sunday school*; this is how to sew on a button; this is how to make a buttonhole for the button you have just sewed on; this is how to hem a dress when you see the hem coming down and so to prevent yourself from looking like the slut I know you are so bent on becoming; this is how you iron your father's khaki shirt so that it doesn't have a crease; this is how you iron your father's khaki pants so that they don't have a crease; this is how you grow okra—far from the house, because okra tree harbors red ants; when you are growing dasheen, make sure it gets plenty of water or else it makes your throat itch when you are eating it; this is how you sweep a corner; this is how you sweep a whole house; this is how you sweep a yard; this is how you smile to someone you don't like too much; this is how you smile to someone you don't like at all; this is how you smile to someone you like completely; this is how you set a table for tea; this is how you set a table for dinner; this is how you set a table for dinner with an important guest; this is how you set a table for lunch; this is how you set a table for breakfast; this is how to behave in the presence of men who don't know you very well, and this way they won't recognize immediately the slut I have warned you against becoming; be sure to wash every day, even if it is with your own spit; don't squat down to play marbles—you are not a boy, you know; don't pick people's flowers—you might catch something; don't throw stones at blackbirds, because it might not be a blackbird at all; this is how to make a bread pudding; this is how to make doukona; this is how to make pepper pot; this is how to make a good medicine for a cold; this is how to make a good medicine to throw away a child before it even becomes a child; this is how to catch a fish; this is how to throw back a fish you don't like, and that way something bad won't fall on you; this is how to bully a man; this is how a man bullies you; this is how to love a man, and if this doesn't work there are other ways, and if they don't work don't feel too bad about giving up; this is how to spit up in the air if you feel like it, and this is how to move quick so that it doesn't fall on you; this is how to make ends meet; always squeeze bread to make sure it's fresh; *but what if the baker won't let me feel the bread?*; you mean to say that after all you are really going to be the kind of woman who the baker won't let near the bread?

Topic for Critical Thinking and Writing

In a paragraph, identify the two characters whose voices we hear in this story. Explain what we know about them (their circumstances and their relationship). Cite specific evidence from the text. For example, what is the effect of the frequent repetition of "this is how"? Are there other words or phrases frequently repeated?

Sharon Olds

Sharon Olds was born in San Francisco in 1942 and was educated at Stanford University and Columbia University. She has published several volumes of poetry and has received major awards.

I Go Back to May 1937

I see them standing at the formal gates of their colleges,
I see my father strolling out
under the ochre sandstone arch, the
red tiles glinting like bent   4
plates of blood behind his head, I
see my mother with a few light books at her hip
standing at the pillar made of tiny bricks with the
wrought-iron gate still open behind her, its   8
sword-tips black in the May air,
they are about to graduate, they are about to get married,
they are kids, they are dumb, all they know is they are
innocent, they would never hurt anybody.   12
I want to go up to them and say Stop,
don't do it—she's the wrong woman,
he's the wrong man, you are going to do things
you cannot imagine you would ever do,   16
you are going to do bad things to children,
you are going to suffer in ways you never heard of,
you are going to want to die. I want to go
up to them there in the late May sunlight and say it,   20
her hungry pretty blank face turning to me,
his pitiful beautiful untouched body,
his arrogant handsome blind face turning to me,
his pitiful beautiful untouched body,   24
but I don't do it. I want to live. I
take them up like the male and female
paper dolls and bang them together
at the hips like chips of flint as if to   28

strike sparks from them, I say
Do what you are going to do, and I will tell about it.

[1987]

Topics for Critical Thinking and Writing

1. Having read the poem, how do you understand its title? How does Olds seem to define "I"? What does she mean by "Go Back to"? And why "May 1937"?
2. In the first line Olds says, "I see them." *How* does she see them? Actually? In imagination? In photographs? Or can't we know?
3. Consider the comparisons, such as the simile in lines 4–5 ("red tiles glinting like bent/plates of blood") and the metaphor in lines 8–9 (the uprights of the wrought-iron fence are "sword-tips"). What do they tell us about the speaker's view of things?
4. Observe where the sentences of the poem begin and end. Can you explain these sentence boundaries? What shifts of meaning or mood accompany the end of one sentence and the beginning of the next?
5. How are the mother and father characterized when young? Are these characterizations consistent or inconsistent with the violent emotions of lines 13–19?
6. How do you read the last line? Do you feel that the speaker is, for example, angry, or vengeful, or sympathetic, or resigned? How do you interpret "and I will tell about it"? To whom will she "tell about it," and how?

7
TEACHING AND LEARNING

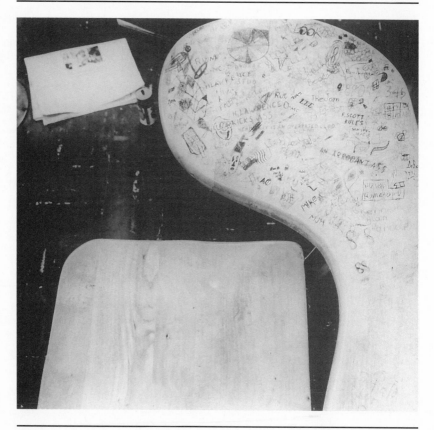

The Target Collection of American Photography, museum purchase with funds provided by Target Stores, Museum of Fine Arts, Houston, © Catherine Wagner

The Lesson—Planning a Career
Ron James, 1963

Ets J. E. Bulloz

Short Views

Knowledge is power.
Francis Bacon

Hard students are commonly troubled with gouts, catarrahs, rheums, cachexia, bradypepsia, bad eyes, stone, and collick, crudities, oppilations, vertigo, winds, consumptions, and all such diseases as come by over-much sitting: they are most part lean, dry, ill-colored . . . and all through immoderate pains and extraordinary studies.
Robert Burton

In my opinion, the only justification for high schools is as therapeutic halfway houses for the deranged. Normal adolescents can find themselves and grow further only by coping with the jobs, sex, and chances of the real world—it is useless to feed them curricular imitations. I would simply abolish the high schools, substituting apprenticeships and other alternatives and protecting the young from gross exploitation by putting the school money directly in their pockets. The very few who have authentic scholarly interests will gravitate to their own libraries, teachers, and academies, as they always did in the past, when they could afford it. In organic communities, adolescents cluster together in their own youth houses, for their fun and games and loud music, without bothering sober folk. I see no reason whatsoever for adults to set up or direct such nests or to be there at all unless invited.
Paul Goodman

I can judge one of the main effects of personal grading by the attitudes of students who land in my remedial course in college. They hate and fear writing more than anything else they have had to do in school. If they see a blank sheet of paper on which they are expected to write something, they look as though they want to scream. Apparently they have never written anything that anyone thought was good. At least, no one ever told them that anything in their writing was good. All their teachers looked for were mistakes, and there are so many kinds of mistakes in writing that their students despair of ever learning to avoid them.

The attitude toward writing that these students have developed is well illustrated by a story told by the Russian writer Chekhov about a kitten that was given to his uncle. The uncle wanted to make the kitten a champion killer of mice, so while it was still very young, he showed it a live mouse in a cage. Since the kitten's hunting instinct had not yet developed, it examined the mouse curiously but without any hostility. The uncle wanted to teach it that such fraternizing with the enemy was wrong, so he slapped the kitten, scolded it, and sent it away in disgrace. The next day the same mouse was shown to the kitten again. This time the kitten regarded it rather fearfully but without any aggressive intent. Again the uncle slapped it, scolded it, and sent it away. This treatment went on day after day. After some time, as soon as the kitten saw or smelled that mouse, it screamed and tried to climb up the walls. At that point the uncle lost patience and gave the kitten away, saying that it was stupid and would never learn. Of course the kitten had learned perfectly, and had learned exactly what it had been taught, but unfortunately not what the uncle intended to teach. "I can sympathize with that kitten," says Chekhov, "because that same uncle tried to teach me Latin."

Paul B. Diederich

A woman came to Rabbi Israel, the great maggid or teacher in Koznitz, and told him, with many tears, that she had been married a dozen years and still had not borne a son. "What are you willing to do about it?" he asked her. She did not know what to say. "My mother," so the maggid told her, "was aging and still had no child. Then she heard that the holy Baal Shem was stopping over in Apt in the course of a journey. She hurried to his inn and begged him to pray she might bear a son. 'What are you willing to do about it?' he asked. 'My husband is a poor book-binder,' she replied, 'but I do have one fine thing that I shall give to the rabbi.' She went home as fast as she could and fetched her good cape, her 'Katinka,' which was carefully stowed away in a chest. But when she returned to the inn with it, she heard that the Baal Shem had already left for Mezbizh. She immediately set out after him and since she had no money to ride, she walked from town to town with her 'Katinka' until she came to Mezbizh. The Baal Shem took the cape and hung it on the wall. 'It is well,' he said. My mother walked all the way back, from town to town, until she reached Apt. A year later, I was born."

"I, too," cried the woman, "will bring you a cape of mine so that I may get a son."

"That won't work," said the maggid. "You heard the story. My mother had no story to go by."

Hasidic Tale

You go to a great school not for knowledge so much as for arts and habits; for the habit of attention, for the art of expression, for the art of assuming at a moment's notice a new intellectual posture, for the art of entering quickly into another person's thought, for the habit of submitting to censure and refutation, for the art of indicating assent or dissent in graduated terms, for the habit of regarding minute points of accuracy, for the habit of working out what is possible in a given time, for taste, for discrimination, for mental courage and mental soberness. Above all, you go to a great school for self-knowledge.

William Cory

How people keep correcting us when we are young! There's always some bad habit or other they tell us we ought to get over. Yet most bad habits are tools to help us through life.

Johann Wolfgang von Goethe

Supposing anyone were to suggest that the best results for the individual and society could be derived through compulsory feeding, would not the most ignorant rebel against such a stupid procedure? And yet the stomach has far greater adaptability to almost any situation than the brain. With all that, we find it quite natural to have compulsory mental feeding.

Indeed, we actually consider ourselves superior to other nations, because we have evolved a compulsory brain tube through which, for a certain number of hours every day, and for so many years, we can force into the child's mind a large quantity of mental nutrition.

. . . The great harm done by our system of education is not so much that it teaches nothing worth knowing, that it helps to perpetuate privileged classes, that it assists them in the criminal procedure of robbing and exploiting the masses; the harm of the system lies in its boastful proclamation that it stands for true education, thereby enslaving the masses a great deal more than could an absolute ruler.

Emma Goldman

The education of women should always be relative to that of men. To please, to be useful to us, to make us love and esteem them, to educate us when young, to take care of us when grown up; to advise, to console us, to render our lives easy and agreeable. These are the duties of women at all times, and what they should be taught in their infancy.

Jean Jacques Rousseau, *Emile*

If Johnny can't learn because he is hungry, that's the fault of poverty. But if Johnny can't pay attention because he is sleepy, that's the fault of parents.

What does it matter if we have a new book or an old book, if we open neither?
> Jesse Jackson

Universities are, of course, hostile to geniuses.
> Ralph Waldo Emerson

The man who can make hard things easy is the educator.
> Ralph Waldo Emerson

It is perhaps idle to wonder what, from my present point of view, would have been an ideal education. If I could provide such a curriculum for my own children they, in their turn, might find it all a bore. But the fantasy of what I would have liked to learn as a child may be revealing, since I feel unequipped by education for problems that lie outside the cloistered, literary domain in which I am competent and at home. Looking back, then, I would have arranged for myself to be taught survival techniques for both natural and urban wildernesses. I would want to have been instructed in self-hypnosis, in *aikido* (the esoteric and purely self-defensive style of judo), in elementary medicine, in sexual hygiene, in vegetable gardening, in astronomy, navigation, and sailing; in cookery and clothesmaking, in metalwork and carpentry, in drawing and painting, in printing and typography, in botany and biology, in optics and acoustics, in semantics and psychology, in mysticism and yoga, in electronics and mathematical fantasy, in drama and dancing, in singing and in playing an instrument by ear; in wandering, in advanced daydreaming, in prestidigitation, in techniques of escape from bondage, in disguise, in conversation with birds and beasts, in ventriloquism, in French and German conversation, in planetary history, in morphology, and in classical Chinese. Actually, the main thing left out of my education was a proper love for my own body, because one feared to cherish anything so obviously mortal and prone to sickness.
> Alan Watts

Education! Which of the various me's do you propose to educate, and which do you propose to suppress?
> D. H. Lawrence

Think about the kind of world you want to live and work in. What do you need to know to build the world? Demand that your teachers teach you that.
> Prince Kropotkin

The entire object of true education is to make people not merely *do* the right things, but *enjoy* the right things.

John Ruskin

Learning without thought is labor lost; thought without learning is dangerous.

Confucius

Nan-in, a Japanese master during the Meiji era (1868–1912), received a university professor who came to inquire about Zen.

Nan-in served tea. He poured his visitor's cup full, and then kept on pouring.

The professor watched the overflow until he no longer could restrain himself. "It is overfull. No more will go in!"

"Like this cup," Nan-in said, "you are full of your own opinions and speculations. How can I show you Zen unless you first empty your cup?"

Anonymous Zen Anecdote

I think [Raymond Weaver] first attracted my attention as someone worth watching when, while we were both new instructors, I heard from a bewildered freshman about the quiz he had just given. The first question written on the blackboard was, "Which of the required readings in this course did you find least interesting?" Then, after members of the class had had ten minutes in which to expatiate on what was certainly to many a congenial topic, he wrote the second question: "To what defect in yourself do you attribute this lack of interest?"

Joseph Wood Krutch

Plato

Plato (427–347 B.C.), born in Athens, the son of an aristocratic family, wrote thirty dialogues in which Socrates is the chief speaker. Socrates, about twenty-five years older than Plato, was a philosopher who called himself a gadfly to Athenians. For his efforts at stinging them into thought, the Athenians executed him in 399 B.C. "The Myth of the Cave" is the beginning of Book VII of Plato's dialogue entitled The Republic. Socrates is talking with Glaucon.

For Plato, true knowledge is philosophic insight or awareness of the Good, not mere opinion or the knack of getting along in this world by remembering how things have usually worked in the past. To illustrate his idea that awareness of the Good is different from the ability to recognize the things of this shabby world, Plato (through his spokesman Socrates) resorts to an allegory: men imprisoned in a cave see on a wall in front of them the shadows or images of objects that are really behind them, and they hear echoes, not real voices. (The shadows are caused by the light from a fire behind the objects, and the echoes by the cave's acoustical properties.) The prisoners, unable to perceive the real objects and the real voices, mistakenly think that the shadows and the echoes are real, and some of them grow highly adept at dealing with this illusory world. Were Plato writing today, he might have made the cave a movie theater: we see on the screen in front of us images caused by an object (film, passing in front of light) that is behind us. Moreover, the film itself is an illusory image, for it bears only the traces of a yet more real world—the world that was photographed—outside of the movie theater. And when we leave the theater to go into the real world, our eyes have become so accustomed to the illusory world that we at first blink with discomfort—just as Plato's freed prisoners do when they move out of the cave—at the real world of bright day, and we long for the familiar darkness. So too, Plato suggests, dwellers in ignorance may prefer the familiar shadows of their unenlightened world ("the world of becoming") to the bright world of the eternal Good ("the world of being") that education reveals.

We have just used the word education. You will notice that the first sentence in the translation (by Benjamin Jowett) says that the myth will show "how far our nature is enlightened or unenlightened." In the original Greek the words here translated enlightened and unenlightened are paideia and apaideusia. No translation can fully catch the exact meanings of these elusive words. Depending on the context, paideia may be translated as enlightenment, education, civilization, culture, knowledge of the good.

The Myth of the Cave

And now, I said, let me show in a figure how far our nature is enlightened or unenlightened—Behold! human beings living in an underground den, which has a mouth open toward the light and reaching all along the den; here they have been from their childhood, and have their legs and necks chained so that they cannot move, and can only see before them, being prevented by the chains from turning round their heads. Above and behind them a fire is blazing at a distance, and between the fire and the prisoners there is a raised way; and you will see, if you look, a low wall built along the way, like the screen which marionette players have in front of them, over which they show the puppets.

I see.

And do you see, I said, men passing along the wall carrying all sorts of vessels, and statues and figures of animals made of wood and stone and various materials, which appear over the wall? Some of them are talking, others silent.

You have shown me a strange image, and they are strange prisoners.   4

Like ourselves, I replied; and they see only their own shadows, or the shadows of one another, which the fire throws on the opposite wall of the cave?

True, he said; how could they see anything but the shadows if they were never allowed to move their heads?

And of the objects which are being carried in like manner they would only see the shadows?

Yes, he said.   8

And if they were able to converse with one another, would they not suppose that they were naming what was actually before them?

Very true.

And suppose further that the prison had an echo which came from the other side, would they not be sure when one of the passersby spoke that the voice which they heard came from the passing shadow?

No question, he replied.   12

To them, I said, the truth would be literally nothing but the shadows of the images.

That is certain.

And now look again, and see what will naturally follow if the prisoners are released and disabused of their error. At first, when any of them is liberated and compelled suddenly to stand up and turn his neck round and walk and look toward the light, he will suffer sharp pains; the glare will distress him, and he will be unable to see the realities of which in his former state he had seen the shadows; and then conceive some one saying to him, that what he saw before was an illusion, but that now, when he is approaching nearer to being and his eye is turned toward more real existence, he has a clearer vision—what will be his reply? And you may further imagine that his instructor is pointing to the objects as they pass and requiring him to name them—will he not be perplexed? Will he not fancy that the shadows which he formerly saw are truer than the objects which are now shown to him?

Far truer.   16

And if he is compelled to look straight at the light, will he not have a pain in his eyes which will make him turn away to take refuge in the objects of vision which he can see, and which he will conceive to be in reality clearer than the things which are now being shown to him?

True, he said.

And suppose once more, that he is reluctantly dragged up a steep and rugged ascent, and held fast until he is forced into the presence of the sun himself, is he not likely to be pained and irritated? When he approaches the light his eyes will be dazzled, and he will not be able to see anything at all of what are now called realities.

Not all in a moment, he said.   20

He will require to grow accustomed to the sight of the upper world. And first he will see the shadows best, next the reflections of men and other objects in the water, and then the objects themselves; then he will gaze upon the light of the moon and the stars and the spangled heaven; and he will see the sky and the stars by night better than the sun or the light of the sun by day?

Certainly.

Last of all he will be able to see the sun, and not mere reflections of him in the water, but he will see him in his own proper place, and not in another; and he will contemplate him as he is.

Certainly.   24

He will then proceed to argue that this is he who gives the season and the years, and is the guardian of all that is in the visible world, and in a certain way the cause of all things which he and his fellows have been accustomed to behold?

Clearly, he said, he would first see the sun and then reason about him.

And when he remembered his old habitation, and the wisdom of the den and his fellow-prisoners, do you not suppose that he would felicitate himself on the change, and pity them?

Certainly, he would.   28

And if they were in the habit of conferring honors among themselves on those who were quickest to observe the passing shadows and to remark which of them went before, and which followed after, and which were together; and who were therefore best able to draw conclusions as to the future, do you think that he would care for such honors and glories, or envy the possessors of them? Would he not say with Homer,

> Better to be the poor servant of a poor master,

and to endure anything, rather than think as they do and live after their manner?

Yes, he said, I think that he would rather suffer anything than entertain these false notions and live in this miserable manner.

Imagine once more, I said, such an one coming suddenly out of the sun to be replaced in his old situation; would he not be certain to have his eyes full of darkness?

To be sure, he said.   32

And if there were a contest, and he had to compete in measuring the shadows with the prisoners who had never moved out of the den, while his sight was still weak, and before his eyes had become steady (and the time which would be needed to acquire this new habit of sight might be very considerable), would he not be ridiculous? Men would say of him that up he went and down he came without his eyes; and that it was better not even to think of ascending; and if any one tried to loose another and lead him up to the light, let them only catch the offender, and they would put him to death.

No question, he said.

This entire allegory, I said, you may now append, dear Glaucon, to the previous argument; the prison-house is the world of sight, the light of the fire is the sun, and you will not misapprehend me if you interpret the journey upwards to be the ascent of the soul into the intellectual world according to my poor belief, which, at your desire, I have expressed—whether rightly or wrongly God knows. But, whether true or false, my opinion is that in the world of knowledge the idea of good appears last of all, and is seen only with an effort; and, when seen, is also inferred to be the universal author of all things beautiful and right, parent of light and of the lord of light in this visible world, and the immediate source of reason and truth in the intellectual; and that this is the power upon which he who would act rationally either in public or private life must have his eye fixed.

I agree, he said, as far as I am able to understand you.   36

Moreover, I said, you must not wonder that those who attain to this beatific vision are unwilling to descend to human affairs; for their souls are ever hastening into the upper world where they desire to dwell; which desire of theirs is very natural, if our allegory may be trusted.

Yes, very natural.

And is there anything surprising in one who passes from divine contemplations to the evil state of man, misbehaving himself in a ridiculous manner; if, while his eyes are blinking and before he has become accustomed to the surrounding darkness, he is compelled to fight in courts of law, or in other places, about the images or the shadows of images of justice, and is endeavoring to meet the conceptions of those who have never yet seen absolute justice?

Anything but surprising, he replied.   40

Any one who has common sense will remember that the bewilderments of the eyes are of two kinds, and arise from two causes, either from coming out of the light or from going into the light, which is true of the mind's eye, quite as much as of the bodily eye; and he who remembers this when he sees any one whose vision is perplexed and weak, will not be too ready to laugh; he will first ask whether that soul of man has come out of the brighter life, and is unable to see because unaccustomed to the dark, or having turned from darkness to the day is dazzled by excess of light. And he will count the one happy in his condition and state of being, and he will pity the other; or, if he have a mind to laugh at the soul which comes from below into the light, there will be more reason in this than in the laugh which greets him who returns from above out of the light into the den.

That, he said, is a very just distinction.

But then, if I am right, certain professors of education must be wrong when they say that they can put a knowledge into the soul which was not there before, like sight into blind eyes.

They undoubtedly say this, he replied.   44

Whereas, our argument shows that the power and capacity of learning exists in the soul already; and that just as the eye was unable to turn from darkness to light without the whole body, so too the instrument of knowledge can only by the movement of the whole soul be turned from the world of becoming into that of being, and learn by degrees to endure the sight of being, and of the brightest and best of being, or in other words, of the good.

Very true.

And must there not be some art which will effect conversion in the easiest and quickest manner; not implanting the faculty of sight, for that exists already, but has been turned in the wrong direction, and is looking away from the truth?

Yes, he said, such an art may be presumed.

And whereas the other so-called virtues of the soul seem to be akin to bodily qualities, for even when they are not originally innate they can be implanted later by habit and exercise, the virtue of wisdom more than anything else contains a divine element which always remains, and by this conversion is rendered useful and profitable; or, on the other hand, hurtful and useless. Did you never observe the narrow intelligence flashing from the keen eye of a clever rogue—how eager he is, how clearly his paltry soul sees the way to his end; he is the reverse of blind, but his keen eyesight is forced into the service of evil, and he is mischievous in proportion to his cleverness?

Very true, he said.

But what if there had been a circumcision of such natures in the days of their youth; and they had been severed from those sensual pleasures, such as eating and drinking, which, like leaden weights, were attached to them at their birth, and which drag them down and turn the vision of their souls upon the things that are below—if, I say, they had been released from these impediments and turned in the opposite direction, the very same faculty in them would have seen the truth as keenly as they see what their eyes are turned to now.

Very likely.

Yes, I said; and there is another thing which is likely, or rather a necessary inference from what has preceded, that neither the uneducated and uninformed of the truth, nor yet those who never make an end of their education, will be able ministers of State; not the former, because they have no single aim of duty which is the rule of all their actions, private as well as public; nor the latter, because they will not act at all except upon compulsion, fancying that they are already dwelling apart in the islands of the blest.

Very true, he replied.

Then, I said, the business of us who are the founders of the State will be to compel the best minds to attain that knowledge which we have already shown to be the greatest of all—they must continue to ascend until they arrive at the good; but when they have ascended and seen enough we must not allow them to do as they do now.

48

52

What do you mean?   56

I mean that they remain in the upper world: but this must not be allowed; they must be made to descend again among the prisoners in the den, and partake of their labors and honors, whether they are worth having or not.

But is not this unjust? he said; ought we to give them a worse life, when they might have a better?

You have again forgotten, my friend, I said, the intention of the legislator, who did not aim at making any one class in the State happy above the rest; the happiness was to be in the whole State, and he held the citizens together by persuasion and necessity, making them benefactors of the State, and therefore benefactors of one another; to this end he created them, not to please themselves, but to be his instruments in binding up the State.

True, he said, I had forgotten.   60

Observe, Glaucon, that there will be no justice in compelling our philosophers to have a care and providence of others; we shall explain to them that in other States, men of their class are not obliged to share in the toils of politics: and this is reasonable, for they grow up at their own sweet will, and the government would rather not have them. Being self-taught, they cannot be expected to show any gratitude for a culture which they have never received. But we have brought you into the world to be rulers of the hive, kings of yourselves and of the other citizens, and have educated you far better and more perfectly than they have been educated, and you are better able to share in the double duty. Wherefore each of you, when his turn comes, must go down to the general underground abode, and get the habit of seeing in the dark. When you have acquired the habit, you will see ten thousand times better than the inhabitants of the den, and you will know what the several images are, and what they represent, because you have seen the beautiful and just and good in their truth. And thus our State which is also yours will be a reality, and not a dream only, and will be administered in a spirit unlike that of other States, in which men fight with one another about shadows only and are distracted in the struggle for power, which in their eyes is a great good. Whereas the truth is that the State in which the rulers are most reluctant to govern is always the best and most quietly governed, and the State in which they are most eager, the worst.

Quite true, he replied.

And will our pupils, when they hear this, refuse to take their turn at the toils of State, when they are allowed to spend the greater part of their time with one another in the heavenly light?

Impossible, he answered; for they are just men, and the commands   64 which we impose upon them are just; there can be no doubt that every one of them will take office as a stern necessity, and not after the fashion of our present rulers of State.

Yes, my friend, I said; and there lies the point. You must contrive for your future rulers another and a better life than that of a ruler, and then you may have a well-ordered State; for only in the State which offers this, will they rule who are truly rich, not in silver and gold, but in virtue and wisdom, which are the true blessings of life. Whereas if they go to the administration of public affairs, poor and hungering after their own private advantage, thinking that hence they are to snatch the chief good, order there can never be; for they will be fighting about office, and the civil and domestic broils which thus arise will be the ruin of the rulers themselves and of the whole State.

Most true, he replied.

And the only life which looks down upon the life of political ambition is that of true philosophy. Do you know of any other?

Indeed, I do not, he said.   68

And those who govern ought not to be lovers of the task? For, if they are, there will be rival lovers, and they will fight.

No question.

Who then are those whom we shall compel to be guardians? Surely they will be the men who are wisest about affairs of State, and by whom the State is best administered, and who at the same time have other honors and another and a better life than that of politics?

They are the men, and I will choose them, he replied.   72

And now shall we consider in what way such guardians will be produced, and how they are to be brought from darkness to light—as some are said to have ascended from the world below to the gods?

By all means, he replied.

The process, I said, is not the turning over of an oyster-shell,[1] but the turning round of a soul passing from a day which is little better than night to the true day of being, that is, the ascent from below which we affirm to be true philosophy?

Quite so.   76

Topics for Critical Thinking and Writing

1. Plato is not merely reporting one of Socrates' conversations; he is teaching. What advantages does a dialogue have over a narrative or an essay as a way of teaching philosophy? How is the form of a dialogue especially suited to solving a problem?
2. If you don't know the etymology of the word *conversion*, look it up in a dictionary. How is the etymology appropriate to Plato's idea about education?
3. In paragraph 19, describing the prisoner as "reluctantly dragged" upward and "forced" to look at the sun, Socrates asks: "Is he not likely

---

[1]An allusion to a game in which two parties fled or pursued according as an oyster shell that was thrown into the air fell with the dark or light side uppermost. (Translator's note)

to be pained and irritated?" Can you recall experiencing pain and irritation while learning something you later were glad to have learned?
Can you recall learning something new *without* experiencing pain and
irritation?
4. "The State in which rulers are most reluctant to govern is always the
best and most quietly governed, and the State in which they are most
eager, the worst" (paragraph 61). What does Socrates mean? Using
examples from contemporary politics, defend this proposition or argue
against it.
5. Can you account for the power of this myth or fable? In our introductory comment (page 205), we tried to clarify the message by saying that
a movie theater might serve as well as a cave. But, in fact, if the story
were recast using a movie theater, would the emotional power be the
same? Why or why not?
6. The metaphors of education as conversion and ascent are linked by
the metaphor of light. Consider such expressions as "I see" (meaning "I
understand") and "Let me give an illustration" (from the Latin *in* = in,
and *lustrare* = to make bright). What other expressions about light are
used metaphorically to describe intellectual comprehension?

Richard Rodriguez

*Richard Rodriguez, the son of immigrants from Mexico, was born in San Francisco in 1944.
He was educated at Stanford University, Columbia University, and the University of California,
Berkeley, where he specialized in English literature of the Renaissance. In his book,* The
Hunger of Memory *(1982), he reports how his progress in the Anglo world was accompa-
nied by estrangement from the Spanish-speaking world. We print an excerpt from the book;
the title of the excerpt is our own.*

Public and Private Language

Supporters of bilingual education today imply that students like me miss a great deal by not being taught in their family's language. What they seem not to recognize is that, as a socially disadvantaged child, I considered Spanish to be a private language. What I
needed to learn in school was that I had the right—and the obligation—
to speak the public language of *los gringos*. The odd truth is that my
first-grade classmates could have become bilingual, in the conventional sense of that word, more easily than I. Had they been taught (as
upper-middle-class children are often taught early) a second language
like Spanish or French, they could have regarded it simply as that:
another public language. In my case such bilingualism could not have
been so quickly achieved. What I did not believe was that I could speak
a single public language.

Without question, it would have pleased me to hear my teachers address me in Spanish when I entered the classroom. I would have felt much less afraid. I would have trusted them and responded with ease. But I would have delayed—for how long postponed?—having to learn the language of public society. I would have evaded—and for how long could I have afforded to delay?—learning the great lesson of school, that I had a public identity.

Fortunately, my teachers were unsentimental about their responsibility. What they understood was that I needed to speak a public language. So their voices would search me out, asking me questions. Each time I'd hear them, I'd look up in surprise to see a nun's face frowning at me. I'd mumble, not really meaning to answer. The nun would persist, "Richard, stand up. Don't look at the floor. Speak up. Speak to the entire class, not just to me!" But I couldn't believe that the English language was mine to use. (In part, I did not want to believe it.) I continued to mumble. I resisted the teacher's demands. (Did I somehow suspect that once I learned public language my pleasing family life would be changed?) Silent, waiting for the bell to sound, I remained dazed, diffident, afraid.

Because I wrongly imagined that English was intrinsically a public   4
language and Spanish an intrinsically private one, I easily noted the difference between classroom language and the language of home. At school, words were directed to a general audience of listeners. ("Boys and girls.") Words were meaningfully ordered. And the point was not self-expression alone but to make oneself understood by many others. The teacher quizzed: "Boys and girls, why do we use that word in this sentence? Could we think of a better word to use there? Would the sentence change its meaning if the words were differently arranged? And wasn't there a better way of saying much the same thing?" (I couldn't say. I wouldn't try to say.)

Three months. Five. Half a year passed. Unsmiling, ever watchful, my teachers noted my silence. They began to connect my behavior with the difficult progress my older sister and brother were making. Until one Saturday morning three nuns arrived at the house to talk to our parents. Stiffly, they sat on the blue living room sofa. From the doorway of another room, spying the visitors, I noted the incongruity—the clash of two worlds, the faces and voices of school intruding upon the familiar setting of home. I overheard one voice gently wondering, "Do your children speak only Spanish at home, Mrs. Rodriguez?" While another voice added, "That Richard especially seems so timid and shy."

That Rich-heard!

With great tact the visitors continued, "Is it possible for you and your husband to encourage your children to practice their English when they are home?" Of course, my parents complied. What would they not do for their children's well-being? And how could they have questioned the Church's authority which those women represented? In an instant, they agreed to give up the language (the sounds) that had revealed and accentuated our family's closeness. The moment after the visitors left, the change was observed. "*Ahora*, speak to us *en inglés*," my father and mother united to tell us.

At first, it seemed a kind of game. After dinner each night, the family gathered to practice "our" English. (It was still then *inglés*, a language foreign to us, so we felt drawn as strangers to it.) Laughing, we would try to define words we could not pronounce. We played with strange English sounds, often over-anglicizing our pronunciations. And we filled the smiling gaps of our sentences with familiar Spanish sounds. But that was cheating, somebody shouted. Everyone laughed. In school, meanwhile, like my brother and sister, I was required to attend a daily tutoring session. I needed a full year of special attention. I also needed my teachers to keep my attention from straying in class by calling out, *Rich-heard*—their English voices slowly prying loose my ties to my other name, its three notes. *Ri-car-do*. Most of all I needed to hear my mother and father speak to me in a moment of seriousness in broken—suddenly heartbreaking—English. The scene was inevitable: One Saturday morning I entered the kitchen where my parents were talking in Spanish. I did not realize that they were talking in Spanish however until, at the moment they saw me, I heard their voices change to speak English. Those *gringo* sounds they uttered startled me. Pushed me away. In that moment of trivial misunderstanding and profound insight, I felt my throat twisted by unsounded grief. I turned quickly and left the room. But I had no place to escape to with Spanish. (The spell was broken.) My brother and sisters were speaking English in another part of the house. 8

Again and again in the days following, increasingly angry, I was obliged to hear my mother and father: "Speak to us *en inglés*." (*Speak*). Only then did I determine to learn classroom English. Weeks after, it happened: One day in school I raised my hand to volunteer an answer. I spoke out in a loud voice. And I did not think it remarkable when the entire class understood. That day, I moved very far from the disadvantaged child I had been only days earlier. The belief, the calming assurance that I belonged in public, had at last taken hold.

Shortly after, I stopped hearing the high and loud sounds of *los gringos*. A more and more confident speaker of English, I didn't trouble to listen to *how* strangers sounded, speaking to me. And there simply were too many English-speaking people in my day for me to hear American accents anymore. Conversations quickened. Listening to persons who sounded eccentrically pitched voices, I usually noted their sounds for an initial few seconds before I concentrated on *what* they were saying. Conversations became content-full. Transparent. Hearing someone's *tone* of voice—angry or questioning or sarcastic or happy or sad—I didn't distinguish it from the words it expressed. Sound and word were thus tightly wedded. At the end of a day, I was often bemused, always relieved, to realize how "silent," though crowded with words, my day in public had been. (This public silence measured and quickened the change in my life.)

At last, seven years old, I came to believe what had been technically true since my birth: I was an American citizen.

But the special feeling of closeness at home was diminished by   12
then. Gone was the desperate, urgent, intense feeling of being at home: rare was the experience of feeling myself individualized by family intimates. We remained a loving family, but one greatly changed. No longer so close; no longer bound tight by the pleasing and troubling knowledge of our public separateness. Neither my older brother nor sister rushed home after school anymore. Nor did I. When I arrived home there would often be neighborhood kids in the house. Or the house would be empty of sounds.

Following the dramatic Americanization of their children, even my parents grew more publicly confident. Especially my mother. She learned the names of all the people on our block. And she decided we needed to have a telephone installed in the house. My father continued to use the word *gringo*. But it was no longer charged with the old bitterness or distrust. (Stripped of any emotional content, the word simply became a name for those Americans not of Hispanic descent.) Hearing him, sometimes, I wasn't sure if he was pronouncing the Spanish word *gringo* or saying gringo in English.

Matching the silence I started hearing in public was a new quiet at home. The family's quiet was partly due to the fact that, as we children learned more and more English, we shared fewer and fewer words with our parents. Sentences needed to be spoken slowly when a child addressed his mother or father. (Often the parent wouldn't understand.) The child would need to repeat himself. (Still the parent misunderstood.) The young voice, frustrated, would end up saying, "Never mind"—the subject was closed. Dinners would be noisy with the clinking of knives and forks against dishes. My mother would smile softly between her remarks; my father at the other end of the table would chew and chew at his food, while he stared over the heads of his children.

My *mother!* My *father!* After English became my primary language, I no longer knew what words to use in addressing my parents. The old Spanish words (those tender accents of sound) I had used earlier— *mamá* and *papá*—I couldn't use anymore. They would have been too painful reminders of how much had changed in my life. On the other hand, the words I heard neighborhood kids call *their* parents seemed equally unsatisfactory. *Mother* and *Father; Ma, Papa, Pa, Dad, Pop* (how I hated the all-American sound of that last word especially)—all these terms I felt were unsuitable, not really terms of address for *my* parents. As a result, I never used them at home. Whenever I'd speak to my parents, I would try to get their attention with eye contact alone. In public conversations, I'd refer to "my parents" or "my mother and father."

My mother and father, for their part, responded differently, as their   16
children spoke to them less. She grew restless, seemed troubled and anxious at the scarcity of words exchanged in the house. It was she who
would question me about my day when I came home from school. She
smiled at small talk. She pried at the edges of my sentences to get me to
say something more. (What?) She'd stopped her children's talking. By
contrast, my father seemed reconciled to the new quiet. Though his English improved somewhat, he retired into silence. At dinner he spoke
very little. One night his children and even his wife helplessly giggled at
his garbled English pronunciation of the Catholic Grace before Meals.
Thereafter he made his wife recite the prayer at the start of each meal,
even on formal occasions, when there were guests in the house. Hers
became the public voice of the family. On official business, it was she,
not my father, one would usually hear on the phone or in stores, talking
to strangers. His children grew so accustomed to his silence that, years
later, they would speak routinely of his shyness. (My mother would
often try to explain: Both his parents died when he was eight. He was
raised by an uncle who treated him like little more than a menial servant. He was never encouraged to speak. He grew up alone. A man of
few words.) But my father was not shy, I realized, when I'd watch him
speaking Spanish with relatives. Using Spanish, he was quickly effusive.
Especially when talking with other men, his voice would spark, flicker,
flare alive with sounds. In Spanish, he expressed ideas and feelings he
rarely revealed in English. With firm Spanish sounds, he conveyed confidence and authority English would never allow him.

The silence at home, however, was finally more than a literal
silence. Fewer words passed between parent and child, but more profound was the silence that resulted from my inattention to sounds. At
about the time I no longer bothered to listen with care to the sounds of
English in public, I grew careless about listening to the sounds family
members made when they spoke. Most of the time I heard someone
speaking at home and didn't distinguish his sounds from the words
people uttered in public. I didn't even pay much attention to my parents' accented and ungrammatical speech. At least not at home. Only
when I was with them in public would I grow alert to their accents.
Though, even then, their sounds caused me less and less concern. For I
was increasingly confident of my own public identity.

I would have been happier about my public success had I not
sometimes recalled what it had been like earlier, when my family had
conveyed its intimacy through a set of conveniently private sounds.
Sometimes in public, hearing a stranger, I'd hark back to my past. A
Mexican farmworker approached me downtown to ask directions to
somewhere. "Hijito . . . ?" he said. And his voice summoned deep longing. Another time, standing beside my mother in the visiting room of a
Carmelite convent, before the dense screen which rendered the nuns
shadowy figures, I heard several Spanish-speaking nuns—their busy,

singsong overlapping voices—assure us that yes, yes, we were remembered, all our family was remembered in their prayers. (Their voices echoed faraway family sounds.) Another day, a dark-faced old woman—her hand light on my shoulder—steadied herself against me as she boarded a bus. She murmured something I couldn't quite comprehend. Her Spanish voice came near, like the face of a never-before-seen relative in the instant before I was kissed. Her voice, like so many of the Spanish voices I'd hear in public, recalled the golden age of my youth. Hearing Spanish then, I continued to be a careful, if sad, listener to sounds. Hearing a Spanish-speaking family walking behind me, I turned to look. I smiled for an instant, before my glance found the Hispanic-looking faces of strangers in the crowd going by.

Topics for Critical Thinking and Writing

1. We have called this selection from Richard Rodriguez's *The Hunger of Memory* "Public and Private Language," and, indeed, the words occur often in the text. But, from reading these pages, how would you identify what is "public language" and what is "private"? What words and images would you associate with each?
2. In his first paragraph Rodriquez identifies himself as a "socially disadvantaged child." What does he mean?
3. At the end of his second paragraph Rodriguez identifies "the great lesson of school," that he "had a public identity." What does Rodriguez mean by his "public identity," and would you say that your elementary school also aided you in achieving one? Explain.
4. In his eleventh and twelfth paragraphs Rodriguez comes "to believe what had been technically true since [his] birth"—he was now an "American citizen." He seems to associate this truth with a change in his family relationships. Was there a period in your life when you felt such a change in your family—with or without a change in language? If so, how would you characterize it?

David Gelernter

David Gelernter, a professor of computer science at Yale University, originally published this essay in The New Republic *in 1994.*

Unplugged

Over the last decade an estimated $2 billion has been spent on more than 2 million computers for America's classrooms. That's not surprising. We constantly hear from Washington that the schools are in trouble and that computers are a godsend. Within the education establishment, in poor as well as rich schools, the machines are awaited with nearly religious awe. An inner-city principal bragged to a teacher friend of mine recently that his school "has a computer in every classroom . . . despite being in a bad neighbor-hood!"

Computers should be in the schools. They have the potential to accomplish great things. With the right software, they could help make science tangible or teach neglected topics like art and music. They could help students form a concrete idea of society by displaying on-screen a version of the city in which they live—a picture that tracks real life moment by moment.

In practice, however, computers make our worst educational night-mares come true. While we bemoan the decline of literacy, computers discount words in favor of pictures and pictures in favor of video. While we fret about the decreasing cogency of public debate, comput-ers dismiss linear argument and promote fast, shallow romps across the information landscape. While we worry about basic skills, we allow into the classroom software that will do a student's arithmetic or correct his spelling.

Take multimedia. The idea of multimedia is to combine text, sound   4
and pictures in a single package that you browse on screen. You don't just *read* Shakespeare; you watch actors performing, listen to songs, view Elizabethan buildings. What's wrong with that? By offering chil-dren candy-coated books, multimedia is guaranteed to sour them on unsweetened reading. It makes the printed page look even more boring than it used to look. Sure, books will be available in the classroom, too—but they'll have all the appeal of a dusty piano to a teen who has a Walkman handy.

So what if the little nippers don't read? If they're watching Olivier instead, what do they lose? The text, the written word along with all of its attendant pleasures. Besides, a book is more portable than a com-puter, has a higher-resolution display, can be written on and dog-eared and is comparatively dirt cheap.

Hypermedia, multimedia's comrade in the struggle for a brave new classroom, is just as troubling. It's a way of presenting documents on screen without imposing a linear start-to-finish order. Disembodied paragraphs are linked by theme; after reading one about the First World War, for example, you might be able to choose another about the technology of battleships, or the life of Woodrow Wilson, or hemlines in the '20s. This is another cute idea that is good in minor ways and terri-ble in major ones. Teaching children to understand the orderly unfold-ing of a plot or a logical argument is a crucial part of education. Authors don't merely agglomerate paragraphs; they work hard to make the nar-rative read a certain way, prove a particular point. To turn a book or a document into hypertext is to invite readers to ignore exactly what counts—the story.

The real problem, again, is the accentuation of already bad habits. Dynamiting documents into disjointed paragraphs is one more expression of the sorry fact that sustained argument is not our style. If you're a newspaper or magazine editor and your readership is dwindling, what's the solution? Shorter pieces. If you're a politician and you want to get elected, what do you need? Tasty sound bites. Logical presentation be damned.

Another software species, "allow me" programs, is not much better. These programs correct spelling and, by applying canned grammatical and stylistic rules, fix prose. In terms of promoting basic skills, though, they have all the virtues of a pocket calculator.   8

In Kentucky, as *The Wall Street Journal* recently reported, students in grades K–3 are mixed together regardless of age in a relaxed environment. It works great, the *Journal* says. Yes, scores on computation tests have dropped 10 percent at one school, but not to worry: "Drilling addition and subtraction in an age of calculators is a waste of time," the principal reassures us. Meanwhile, a Japanese educator informs University of Wisconsin mathematician Richard Akey that in his country, "calculators are not used in elementary or junior high school because the primary emphasis is on helping students develop their mental abilities." No wonder Japanese kids blow the pants off American kids in math. Do we really think "drilling addition and subtraction in an age of calculators is a waste of time"? If we do, then "drilling reading in an age of multimedia is a waste of time" can't be far behind.

Prose-correcting programs are also a little ghoulish, like asking a computer for tips on improving your personality. On the other hand, I ran this article through a spell-checker, so how can I ban the use of such programs in schools? Because to misspell is human; to have no idea of correct spelling is to be semiliterate.

There's no denying that computers have the potential to perform inspiring feats in the classroom. If we are ever to see that potential realized, however, we ought to agree on three conditions. First, there should be a completely new crop of children's software. Most of today's offerings show no imagination. There are hundreds of similar reading and geography and arithmetic programs, but almost nothing on electricity or physics or architecture. Also, they abuse the technical capacities of new media to glitz up old forms instead of creating new ones. Why not build a time-travel program that gives kids a feel for how history is structured by zooming you backward? A spectrum program that lets users twirl a frequency knob to see what happens?

Second, computers should be used only during recess or relaxation   12
periods. Treat them as fillips, not as surrogate teachers. When I was in

school in the '60s, we all loved educational films. When we saw a movie in class, everybody won: teachers didn't have to teach, and pupils didn't have to learn. I suspect that classroom computers are popular today for the same reasons.

Most important, educators should learn what parents and most teachers already know: you cannot teach a child anything unless you look him in the face. We should not forget what computers are. Like books—better in some ways, worse in others—they are devices that help children mobilize their own resources and learn for themselves. The computer's potential to do good is modestly greater than a book's in some areas. Its potential to do harm is vastly greater, across the board.

Topics for Critical Thinking and Writing

1. If you used computers in your elementary or secondary school, evaluate their contribution to your education. (This need not be an all-or-nothing issue; it may be that computers were useless in some courses, moderately useful in others, and highly useful in still others.)
2. One of Gelernter's complaints (paragraph 3) is that "computers discount words in favor of pictures and pictures in favor of video." Is this true—and if it is true, is it necessarily a bad thing? Explain.
3. Paragraph 9 touches on whether "drilling addition and subtraction in an age of calculators is a waste of time." Your views?

Ernest van den Haag

Ernest van den Haag, born in 1914 in The Hague, Netherlands, came to the United States in 1940 and became a U.S. citizen in 1947. During a long and highly productive career, he practiced psychoanalysis and taught psychology, sociology, and law at several universities. Though he is now retired as a psychoanalyst and as a teacher, he continues to write.

In the following essay, reprinted from the National Review, *van den Haag offers several steps to help youngsters learn more—the first of which is for adults to decide that children ought to learn.*

Why Do American Kids Learn So Little?

American children learn far less in school than European and Japanese children do, although America spends far more per pupil. Why is so little education achieved for so much money? The answer may lie in a major oddity in the American creed.

Europeans have always regarded children as barbarians to be painfully civilized by schooling. Childhood is thought to be merely, or mainly, a means to adult achievement. Children are apprentice adults. Schools are to teach them what they will need, even if they cannot see the use of it: language (including grammar), arithmetic, science, history, classics. In Europe there are hardly any of those undemanding classes so frequent in the U.S., such as current events, or home economics.

Of course, the young have never liked the stern demands the schools made. They have preferred to enjoy being young—*gaudeamus igitur juvenes dum sumus,*[1] the students sang—instead of using their young years to prepare for adult careers. But the young could sing all they wanted (in the Latin they learned in school), they had little choice. Without parental support—inheritance and connections—they could never hope to make their way in the world, for which the schools served as gatekeepers. Thus, in Europe—and in Japan, which has swallowed the European idea hook, line, and sinker—the power of the older generation is used to make children spend most of their time doing schoolwork. Occasionally they have rebelled, but, on the whole, they have submitted, become literate, and gone on their way.

In America, however, youth is seen as an end in itself, never merely a means to adult achievement. Children rarely are expected to work at anything they don't enjoy. Teachers are expected to "motivate" their students and to make learning a pleasure, even if this means going easy on unavoidably tedious stretches. The young themselves tend to see adulthood as a hard-to-avoid postscript, almost a decline. Many adults nostalgically agree.   4

Parents seldom can make unwilling children do homework, and teachers wisely don't ask for what they can't get. To demand vexatious schoolwork of children seems almost immoral in the American context.

Unlike Europeans, Americans do not expect their children to continue in their own social position: they regard their children as the hope of the future. Far from imposing the civilization of the past, education is to help the young to "find themselves," to unfold their innate creativity. The young will do better if less encumbered by the past. Margaret Mead even told parents that they must learn from the young, who "have the knowledge."

To most Americans the future always has been more real than the past. This notion makes teaching hard, for teaching requires, at least temporarily, submission to the authority of ancient ideas, and of teachers who transmit them. All learning initially must rest on the authority of the past; after all, the past is all that can be learned.

Pupils must first accept the teachers' authority. Teachers cannot explain to an eight-year-old why words are spelled as they are, or why two and two make four, not five. It is only after much material has been absorbed by rote—children fortunately like learning by rote, although   8

---

[1]*Gaudeamus igitur juvenes dum sumus,* let us be joyful while we are young (Latin, from a medieval university song).

progressive teachers don't like to let them—that students can begin to examine critically and usefully what they are learning. If the authority of the older generation is weak, little knowledge will be absorbed.

We largely let students elect the classes they prefer, assuming that they know enough to fashion their own curriculum, although they cannot yet have learned how to evaluate the importance of various kinds of knowledge. Of course, they elect the easy classes, sometimes of dubious value. They get the same credit toward a diploma for easy classes as they get for harder ones, the same for Contemporary Drama as for Advanced Algebra.

Via Media[2]

There must be a reasonable middle way between a joyous childhood and an exclusively instrumental use of it, a way of combining the civilizing influence of science, history, and literature with the enjoyment of youth. The young must learn to learn as well as to play. Some even may enjoy learning once they try it. Is there anything that can be done to bring about the necessary changes? Consider some beginning steps.

Public schools currently have a monopoly on tax money, which they jealously guard, and because public schools do not compete with one another—pupils are assigned—each public school is in a near monopoly position. The usual effects of monopoly occur: shoddy products at high cost to the involuntary purchasers (taxpayers). A voucher system, entitling parents to choose any public school in the state for their children—and, later on, any approved private school as well—would introduce some competition and might eliminate the worst effects of the monopoly. Schools never should be subsidized; *schooling* should be, by granting vouchers to parents.

Other monopoly features should be dismantled as well. Currently   12
nobody, however capable, is allowed to teach without first attending courses in education. This functions as a barrier to entry, strengthening the entrenched monopoly defended by unions. Private schools hire teachers able to teach their subjects well, in spite (or because) of not having attended a school of education. Usually these teachers are much less well paid than public-school teachers; yet their students, on the average, learn more according to all available tests.

In other countries children spend more time in school. It has been suggested therefore that the school day should be lengthened and summer vacations shortened. I doubt that this will help much. It is not that children spend too little time in school; rather, they learn too little in the time they spend. More homework might indeed help, if only marginally.

What ails American schools is not lack of money. We spend much more per pupil (adjusted for inflation) than we did in the past, and far

[2]*Via Media*, the middle way (Latin).

more than other countries do. But the returns in learning are remarkably low. Where does the money go? Far too much goes into non-teaching activities. There is far too much administration, as can be shown irrefutably by comparing the ratio of teaching to non-teaching personnel in private and public schools. I do not claim that these administrators, counselors, et al. do not work hard. Rather, the work doesn't contribute much to the education of children. They keep each other busy.

Then there is the quality of the teachers themselves. Children cannot learn much from teachers who do not command basic skills. Scandalously few do.

Teachers have some reasonable complaints. They get many children from homes to which learning is as alien as discipline. Still, most children can learn to spell and to read, can learn elementary grammar and arithmetic—if teachers are allowed to impose the necessary discipline, as they are not now. There are some things that can be learned by doing—in fact, only by doing: carefulness, punctuality, manners, discipline are among them. Anybody can acquire these; but schools make little effort to help. They do not feel they are charged with helping to forge the character of students, many of whom graduate functionally illiterate, with slovenly work habits and manners.

Minimum requirements for a high-school diploma (to which each school should be able to add its own) should be imposed by every state, fulfilled only by passing examinations, including essay tests, graded by teachers from schools other than the one attended by the student.

Public schools also should be allowed to expel students unwilling to learn (or to submit to discipline), as private schools are now. Contrary to much opinion, not only would the schools be better off, the expelled students themselves are likely to do better by not being kept when schooling is unproductive for them.

We should stop assuming complacently that our children are being educated just because we have many schools with lots of teachers and myriad administrators. Currently they learn very little, not because they are stupid, but because they are taught very little. It is easier that way for everybody, the kids, the teachers, the parents. But we can't afford it any longer. If we want to avoid a rapid decline of America we must make sure that our children are educated rather than just entertained and kept in school. This will require more changes than I proposed. But we have to begin somewhere.

Topics for Critical Thinking and Writing

1. Do you agree with van den Haag (paragraph 2) that courses in current events and home economics are necessarily "undemanding"? Explain.
2. In paragraph 4 van den Haag speaks of "unavoidably tedious stretches," and in paragraph 5 of "vexatious schoolwork." Do you agree that there must be such things? If so, how would you as a teacher proceed? Or do you assume that material is "tedious" and "vexatious" only

because it is not properly taught? If so, give an example of how a skilled teacher presented material that might otherwise have been tedious or vexatious and made it exciting or enjoyable.

3. In paragraph 6 van den Haag quotes what he implies is a wrong-headed statement by Margaret Mead, to the effect that parents must learn from their young, who "have the knowledge." He does not cite his source, but do you think that he has said enough to indicate that the idea is preposterous? Or on the other hand do you think that the young do indeed have certain kinds of "knowledge" and that their parents can learn some things from them? Explain.

4. Do you agree with the remarks in paragraph 8 about authority and rote learning? If not, explain your position.

5. In paragraph 9 van den Haag dismisses the idea of youngsters electing courses. Drawing on your own experience in secondary school, evaluate his reason.

6. As you look back on your elementary or high school education, what do you think were the greatest strengths? The greatest weaknesses? (You may want to compare one kind of schooling with the other.)

7. Van den Haag implies that many teachers "do not command basic skills." Drawing on your experience, do you agree? (If you write about particular teachers, do not use their real names.)

8. In paragraph 16 van den Haag suggests that schools should teach "carefulness, punctuality, manners, discipline"—in short, aspects of character. Do you agree? Did some or all of your teachers teach any or all of these things? Explain.

9. Consider the strategies that van den Haag uses in his final paragraph. Do you think it provides a good ending for this argumentative essay? Explain.

Diane Ravitch

Diane Ravitch (b. 1938) has taught history and education at Teachers College, Columbia University. In 1991 she was appointed an Assistant Secretary of Education in the George Bush administration. The essay that we print here appeared in 1991 in The Key Reporter, *a newsletter published by Phi Beta Kappa, a national academic society.*

Multiculturalism
E Pluribus Plures[1]

Questions of race, ethnicity, and religion have been a perennial source of conflict in American education. The schools have often attracted the zealous attention of those who wish to influence the future, as well as those who wish to change the way we view the past.

---

[1]*E Pluribus Plures,* Latin for "Out of Many, Many" (a variant on a motto of the United States, *E Pluribus Unum,* "Out of Many, One").

In our history, the schools have been not only an institution in which to teach young people skills and knowledge, but an arena where interest groups fight to preserve their values, or to revise the judgments of history, or to bring about fundamental social change.

Given the diversity of American society, it has been impossible to insulate the schools from pressures that result from differences and tensions among groups. When people differ about basic values, sooner or later those disagreements turn up in battles about how schools are organized or what the schools should teach. Sometimes these battles remove a terrible injustice, like racial segregation. Sometimes, however, interest groups politicize the curriculum and attempt to impose their views on teachers, school officials, and textbook publishers. When groups cross the line into extremism, advancing their own agendas without regard to reason or to others, they threaten public education itself, making it difficult to teach any issues honestly and making the entire curriculum vulnerable to political campaigns.

For many years, the public schools attempted to neutralize controversies over race, religion, and ethnicity by ignoring them. The textbooks minimized problems among groups and taught a sanitized version of history. Race, religion, and ethnicity were presented as minor elements in the American saga; slavery was treated as an episode, immigration as a sidebar, and women were largely absent. The textbooks concentrated on presidents, wars, national politics, and issues of state. An occasional "great black" or "great woman" received mention, but the main narrative paid little attention to minority groups and women.

With the ethnic revival of the 1960s, this approach to the teaching of history came under fire, because the history of national leaders—virtually all of whom were white, Anglo-Saxon, and male—ignored the place in American history of those who were none of the above. The traditional history of elites had been complemented by an assimilationist view of American society, which presumed that everyone in the American melting pot would eventually lose or abandon those ethnic characteristics that distinguished each from mainstream Americans. The ethnic revival demonstrated that many groups did not want to be assimilated or melted. Ethnic studies programs popped up on campuses to teach not only that "black is beautiful," but also that every other variety of ethnicity is "beautiful" as well; everyone who had "roots" began to look for them so that they, too, could recover that ancestral part of themselves that had not been homogenized.

As ethnicity became an accepted subject for study in the late 1960s, textbooks were assailed for their failure to portray blacks accurately; within a few years, the textbooks in wide use were carefully screened to eliminate bias against minority groups and women. At the same time, new scholarship about the history of women, blacks, and various ethnic minorities found its way into the textbooks. Today's history textbooks routinely incorporate the experiences of women, blacks, American Indians, and various immigrant groups.

As a result of the political and social changes of recent decades, cultural pluralism is now generally recognized as an organizing principle of this society. In contrast to the idea of the melting pot, which promised to erase ethnic and group differences, children now learn that variety is the spice of life. They learn that America has provided a haven for many different groups and has allowed them to maintain their cultural heritage or to assimilate, or—as is often the case—to do both; the choice is theirs, not the state's. They learn that cultural pluralism is one of the norms of a free society; that differences among groups are a national resource rather than a problem to be solved. Indeed, the unique feature of the United States is that its common culture has been formed by the interaction of its subsidiary cultures. It is a culture that has been influenced over time by immigrants, American Indians, Africans (slave and free) and by their descendants. American music, art, literature, language, food, clothing, sports, holidays, and customs all show the effects of the commingling of diverse cultures in one nation. Paradoxical though it may seem, the United States has a common culture that is multicultural.

This understanding of the pluralistic nature of American culture has taken a long time to forge. It is based on sound scholarship and has led to major revisions in what children are taught and what they read in school. The new history is—indeed, must be—a warts-and-all history; it demands an unflinching examination of racism and discrimination in our history. Making these changes is difficult, raises tempers, and ignites controversies, but gives a more interesting and accurate account of American history. Accomplishing these changes is valuable, because there is also a useful lesson for the rest of the world in America's relatively successful experience as a pluralistic society. Throughout human history, the clash of different cultures, races, ethnic groups, and religions has often been the cause of bitter hatred, civil conflict, and international war. The ethnic tensions that now are tearing apart Lebanon, Sri Lanka, Kashmir, and various republics of the Soviet Union remind us of the costs of unfettered group rivalry. Thus, it is a matter of more than domestic importance that we closely examine and try to understand that part of our national history in which different groups competed, fought, suffered, but ultimately learned to live together in relative peace and even achieved a sense of common nationhood.

Particularism

Alas, these painstaking efforts to expand the understanding of American culture into a richer and more varied tapestry have taken a new turn, and not for the better. Almost any idea, carried to its extreme, can be made pernicious, and this is what is happening now to multicultur- 8 alism. Today, pluralistic multiculturalism must contend with a new, particularistic multiculturalism. The pluralists seek a richer common culture; the particularists insist that no common culture is possible or desirable.

The new particularism is entering the curriculum in a number of school systems across the country. Advocates of particularism propose an ethnocentric curriculum to raise the self-esteem and academic achievement of children from racial and ethnic minority backgrounds. Without any evidence, they claim that children from minority backgrounds will do well in school *only* if they are immersed in a positive, prideful version of their ancestral culture. If children are of, for example, Fredonian ancestry, they must hear that Fredonians were important in mathematics, science, history, and literature. If they learn about great Fredonians and if their studies use Fredonian examples and Fredonian concepts, they will do well in school. If they do not, they will have low self-esteem and will do badly.

The particularistic version of multi-culturalism is unabashedly filiopietistic[2] and deterministic. It teaches children that their identity is determined by their "cultural genes"—that something in their blood or their racial memory or their cultural DNA defines who they are and what they may achieve; that the culture in which they live is not their own culture, even though they were born here; that American culture is "Eurocentric," and therefore hostile to anyone whose ancestors are not European. Perhaps the most insidious implication of particularism is that racial and ethnic minorities are not and should not try to be part of American culture; it implies that American culture belongs only to those who are white and European; it implies that those who are neither white nor European are alienated from American culture by virtue of their race or ethnicity; it implies that the only culture they do belong to or can ever belong to is the culture of their ancestors, even if their families have lived in this country for generations.

The pluralist approach to multiculturalism promotes a broader interpretation of the common American culture and seeks due recognition for the ways that the nation's many racial, ethnic, and cultural groups have transformed the national culture. The pluralists say, in effect, "American culture belongs to us, all of us; the United States is us, and we remake it in every generation." But particularists have no interest in extending or revising American culture; indeed, they deny that a common culture exists. Particularists reject any accommodation among groups, any interactions that blur the distinct lines between them. The brand of history that they espouse is one in which everyone is a descendant of victims or oppressors. By taking this approach, they fan and re-create ancient hatreds in each new generation.

---

[2]**Filiopietistic,** excessively reverential of ancestors.

Particularism has its intellectual roots in the ideology of ethnic sep-   12
aratism and in the black nationalist movement. In the particularist
analysis, the nation has five cultures: African American, Asian American, European American, Latino/Hispanic, and American Indian. The
huge cultural, historical, religious, and linguistic differences within
these categories are ignored, as is the considerable intermarriage
among these groups, as are the linkages (like gender, class, sexual orientation, and religion) that cut across these five groups. No serious
scholar would claim that all Europeans and white Americans are part
of the same culture, or that all Asians are part of the same culture, or
that all people of Latin American descent are of the same culture, or
that all people of African descent are of the same culture. Any catego-
rization this broad is essentially meaningless and useless.

Particularism is a bad idea whose time has come. It is also a fashion
spreading like wildfire through the education system, actively promoted by organizations and individuals with a political and professional
interest in strengthening ethnic power bases in the university, in the
education profession, and in society itself. One can scarcely pick up an
educational journal without learning about a school district that is converting to an ethnocentric curriculum in an attempt to give "self-
esteem" to children from racial minorities. A state-funded project in a
Sacramento high school is teaching young black males to think like
Africans and to develop the "African Mind Model Technique," in order
to free themselves of the racism of American culture. A popular black
rap singer, KRS-One, complained in an op-ed article in the *New York
Times* that the schools should be teaching blacks about their cultural
heritage, instead of trying to make everyone Americans. "It's like trying
to teach a dog to be a cat," he wrote. KRS-One railed about having to
learn about Thomas Jefferson and the Civil War, which had nothing to
do (he said) with black history.

Ethnomathematics

Pluralism can easily be transformed into particularism, as may be seen
in the potential uses in the classroom of the Mayan contribution to
mathematics. The Mayan example was popularized in a movie called
Stand and Deliver, about a charismatic Bolivian-born mathematics
teacher in Los Angeles who inspired his students (who are Hispanic) to
learn calculus. He told them that their ancestors invented the concept of
zero; but that wasn't all he did. He used imagination to put across
mathematical concepts. He required students to do homework and to
go to school on Saturdays and during the Christmas holidays, so that
they might pass the advanced placement mathematics examination.
The teacher's reference to the Mayans' mathematical genius was a valid

instructional device: It was an attention-getter and would have interested even students who were not Hispanic. But the Mayan example would have had little effect without the teacher's insistence that the class study hard for a difficult examination.

Ethnic educators have seized on the Mayan contribution to mathematics as the key to simultaneously boosting the ethnic pride of Hispanic children and attacking Eurocentrism. One proposal claims that Mexican-American children will be attracted to science and mathematics if they study Mayan mathematics, the Mayan calendar, and Mayan astronomy. Children in primary grades are to be taught that the Mayans were first to discover the zero and that Europeans learned it long afterward from the Arabs, who had learned it in India. This will help students see that Europeans were latecomers in the discovery of great ideas. Botany is to be learned by study of the agricultural techniques of the Aztecs, a subject of somewhat limited relevance to children in urban areas. Furthermore, "ethnobotanical" classifications of plants are to be substituted for the Eurocentric Linnaean system. At first glance, it may seem curious that Hispanic children are deemed to have no cultural affinity with Spain; but to acknowledge the cultural tie would confuse the ideological assault on Eurocentrism.

This proposal suggests some questions: Is there any evidence that   16
the teaching of "culturally relevant" science and mathematics will draw Mexican-American children to the study of these subjects? Will Mexican-American children lose interest or self-esteem if they discover that their ancestors were Aztecs or Spaniards, rather than Mayans? Are children who learn in this way prepared to study the science and mathematics that are taught in American colleges and universities and that are needed for advanced study in these fields? Are they even prepared to study the science and mathematics taught in *Mexican* universities? If the class is half Mexican-American and half something else, will only the Mexican-American children study in a Mayan and Aztec mode or will all the children? But shouldn't all children study what is culturally relevant for them? How will we train teachers who have command of so many different systems of mathematics and science?

The interesting proposal to teach ethnomathematics comes at a time when American mathematics educators are trying to overhaul present practices, because of the poor performance of American children on national and international assessments. Mathematics educators are attempting to change the teaching of their subject so that children can see its uses in everyday life. There would seem to be an incipient conflict between those who want to introduce real-life applications of mathematics and those who want to teach the mathematical systems used by ancient cultures. I suspect that most mathematics teachers would enjoy doing a bit of both, if there were time or student interest. But any widespread movement to replace modern mathematics with ancient ethnic mathematics runs the risk of disaster in a field that is struggling to up-date existing curricula. If, as seems likely, ancient mathematics is taught mainly to minority children, the gap between them and middle-class white children is apt to grow. It is worth noting that children in Korea, who score highest in mathematics on international assessments, do not study ancient Korean mathematics.

Particularism is akin to cultural Lysenkoism[3] for it takes as its premise the spurious notion that cultural traits are inherited. It implies a dubious, dangerous form of cultural predestination. Children are taught that if their ancestors could do it, so could they. But what happens if a child is from a cultural group that made no significant contribution to science or mathematics? Must children find a culturally appropriate field in which to strive? How does a teacher find the right cultural buttons for children of mixed heritage? And how in the world will teachers use this technique when the children in their classes are drawn from many different cultures, as is usually the case? By the time that every culture gets its due, there may be no time left to teach the subject itself. This explosion of filiopietism (which, we should remember, comes from adults, not from students) is reminiscent of the period some years ago when the Russians claimed that they had invented everything first; as we now know, this nationalistic braggadocio did little for their self-esteem and nothing for their economic development. We might reflect, too, on how little social prestige has been accorded in this country to immigrants from Greece and Italy, even though the achievements of their ancestors were at the heart of the classical curriculum.

In school districts where most children are black and Hispanic, there has been a growing tendency to embrace particularism rather than pluralism. Many of the children in these districts perform poorly in academic classes and leave school without graduating. They would fare better in school if they had well-educated and well-paid teachers, small classes, good materials, encouragement at home and school, summer academic programs, protection from the drugs and crime that ravage their neighborhoods, and higher expectations of satisfying careers upon graduation. These are expensive and time-consuming remedies that must also engage the large society beyond the school. The lure of particularism is that it offers a less complicated anodyne, one in which the children's academic deficiencies may be addressed— or set aside—by inflating their racial pride. The danger of this remedy is that it will detract attention from the real needs of schools and the real interests of children, while simultaneously arousing distorted race pride in the children of all races, increasing racial antagonism and producing fresh recruits for white and black racist groups.

---

[3]**Lysenkoism,** named for T. F. Lysenko (1898–1976), a Soviet geneticist who claimed that acquired characteristics can be inherited.

The Effects of Particularism

The rising tide of particularism encourages the politicization of all cur- 20
ricula in the schools. If education bureaucrats bend to the political and
ideological winds, as is their wont, we can anticipate a generation of
struggle over the content of the curriculum in mathematics, science, literature, and history. Demands for "culturally relevant" studies, for eth-
nostudies of all kinds, will open the classroom to unending battles over
whose version is taught, who gets credit for what, and which ethno-
interpretation is appropriate.

The spread of particularism throws into question the very idea of
American public education. Public schools exist to teach children the
general skills and knowledge that they need to succeed in American
society, and the specific skills and knowledge that they need in order to
function as American citizens. They receive public support because
they have a public function. Historically, the public schools were
known as "common schools" because they were schools for all, even if
the children of all the people did not attend them. Over the years, the
courts have found that it was unconstitutional to teach religion in the
common schools, or to separate children on the basis of their race in the
common schools. In their curriculum, their hiring practices, and their
general philosophy, the public schools must not discriminate against or
give preference to any racial or ethnic group. Yet they are permitted to
accommodate cultural diversity by, for example, serving food that is
culturally appropriate or providing library collections that emphasize
the interests of the local community. They should not, however, be
expected to teach children to view the world through an ethnocentric
perspective that rejects or ignores the common culture.

For generations, those groups that wanted to inculcate their religion or their ethnic heritage have instituted private schools—after
school, on weekends, or on a full-time basis. There, children learn with
others of the same group—Greeks, Poles, Germans, Japanese, Chinese,
Jews, Lutherans, Catholics, and so on—and are taught by people from
the same group. Valuable as this exclusive experience has been for
those who choose it, this has not been the role of public education. One
of the primary purposes of public education has been to create a national community, a definition of citizenship and culture that is both expansive and *inclusive.*

The multicultural controversy may do wonders for the study of
history, which has been neglected for years in American schools. At
this time, only half of our high school graduates ever study any world
history. Any serious attempt to broaden students' knowledge of
Africa, Europe, Asia, and Latin America will require at least two, and
possibly three, years of world history (a requirement thus far only in
California). American history, too, will need more time than the one-
year high-school survey course. Those of us who have insisted for

years on the importance of history in the curriculum may not be ready to assent to its redemptive power, but hope that our new allies will ultimately join a constructive dialogue that strengthens the place of history in the schools.

Some Solutions

As cultural controversies arise, educators must adhere to the principle of "E Pluribus Unum." That is, they must maintain a balance between the demands of the one—the nation of which we are common citizens—and the many—the varied histories of the American people. It is not necessary to denigrate either the one or the many. Pluralism is a positive value, but it is also important that we preserve a sense of an American community—a society and a culture to which we all belong. If there is no overall community with an agreed upon vision of liberty and justice, if all we have is a collection of racial and ethnic cultures, lacking any common bonds, then we have no means to mobilize public opinion on behalf of people who are not members of our particular group. We have, for example, no reason to support public education. If there is no larger community, then each group will want to teach its own children in its own way, and public education ceases to exist.

24

History should not be confused with filiopietism. History gives no grounds for race pride. No race has a monopoly on virtue. If anything, a study of history should inspire humility, rather than pride. People of every racial group have committed terrible crimes, often against others of the same group. Whether one looks at the history or Europe or Africa or Latin America or Asia, every continent offers examples of inhumanity. Slavery has existed in civilizations around the world for centuries. Examples of genocide can be found around the world, throughout history, from ancient times right through to our own day. Governments and cultures, sometimes by edict, sometimes simply following tradition, have practiced not only slavery, but human sacrifice, infanticide, cliterodectomy, and mass murder. If we teach children this, they might recognize how absurd both racial hatred and racial chauvinism are.

What must be preserved in the study of history is the spirit of inquiry, the readiness to open new questions and to pursue new understandings. History, at its best, is a search for truth. The best way to portray this search is through debate and controversy, rather than through imposition of fixed beliefs and immutable facts. Perhaps the most dangerous aspect of school history is its tendency to become Official History, a sanctified version of the Truth taught by the state to captive audiences and embedded in beautiful mass-market textbooks as holy writ. When Official History is written by committees responding to political pressures, rather than by scholars synthesizing the best available research, the errors of the past are replaced by the politically fashionable errors of the present. It may be difficult to teach children that history is both important and uncertain, and that even the best historians never have all the pieces of the jigsaw puzzle, but it is necessary to do so. If state education departments permit the revision of their history courses and textbooks to become an exercise in power politics, the entire process of state-level curriculum-making becomes suspect, as does public education itself.

The question of self-esteem is extraordinarily complex, and it goes well beyond the content of the curriculum. Most of what we call self-esteem is formed in the home and in a variety of life experiences, not only in school. Nonetheless, it has been important for blacks—and for other racial groups—to learn about the history of slavery and of the civil rights movement; it has been important for blacks to know that their ancestors actively resisted enslavement and actively pursued equality; and it has been important for blacks and others to learn about black men and women who fought courageously against racism and who provide models of courage, persistence, and intellect. These are instances where the content of the curriculum reflects sound scholarship, and at the same time probably lessens racial prejudice and provides inspiration for those who are descendants of slaves. But knowing about the travails and triumphs of one's forebears does not necessarily translate into either self-esteem or personal accomplishment. For most children, self-esteem—the self-confidence that grows out of having reached a goal—comes not from hearing about the monuments of their ancestors but as a consequence of what they are able to do and accomplish through their own efforts.

As I reflected on these issues, I recalled reading an interview a few   28
years ago with a talented black runner. She said that her model is Mikhail Baryshnikov. She admires him because he is a magnificent athlete. He is not black; he is not female; he is not American-born; he is not even a runner. But he inspires her because of the way he trained and used his body. When I read this, I thought how narrow-minded it is to believe that people can be inspired *only* by those who are exactly like them in race and ethnicity.

Topics for Critical Thinking and Writing

1. How does Ravitch define ethnicity? How does it differ from race?
2. In paragraph 4 Ravitch writes of the "ethnic revival of the 1960s." To what does she refer? What is Ravitch's attitude toward the changes in schools produced by the ethnic revival?
3. What does Ravitch mean by "particularism"? How does it differ from "pluralism"?
4. In paragraph 17 Ravitch cites an example from Korean education. What point is she trying to establish through this example? How might a "particularist" dispute this point? Do you find the example relevant?
5. In paragraph 18 Ravitch argues that in the classroom "by the time that every culture gets its due there may be no time to teach the subject

itself." What is "the subject itself"? How might a "particularist" answer this argument?

6. What dangers does Ravitch ascribe to particularism? Have you been a witness to these dangers yourself? Or does your experience suggest that she exaggerates the dangers?

7. In paragraph 26, what does Ravitch imply by capitalizing "Official History" and "Truth"?

8. In the schools you attended, what history courses were offered? Were race, religion, and ethnicity prominent topics? Were the lives and works of women studied? Compare your experience of learning history with Ravitch's description of how history was taught before the "ethnic revival of the 60s." If the emphasis was what Ravitch calls "particularist" rather than "pluralistic," describe that too and try to assessss its effect on both your understanding of history and on your self-esteem.

Maya Angelou

Maya Angelou, born in St. Louis, Missouri, in 1938, grew up in Arkansas and California. She studied music, dance, and drama (she had a role in the televised version of Alex Haley's Roots)*, and she is now a professor of American studies at Wake Forest University. She has also worked as a cook, streetcar conductor, and waitress. In addition to writing books of poetry, she has written five autobiographical volumes.*

"Graduation' (editors' title) comes from her first autobiography, I Know Why the Caged Bird Sings *(1969).*

Graduation

The children in Stamps trembled visibly with anticipation. Some adults were excited too, but to be certain the whole young population had come down with graduation epidemic. Large classes were graduating from both the grammar school and the high school. Even those who were years removed from their own day of glorious release were anxious to help with preparations as a kind of dry run. The junior students who were moving into the vacating classes' chairs were tradition-bound to show their talents for leadership and management. They strutted through the school and around the campus exerting pressure on the lower grades. Their authority was so new that occasionally if they pressed a little too hard it had to be overlooked. After all, next term was coming, and it never hurt a sixth grader to have a play sister in the eighth grade, or a tenth-year student to be able to call a twelfth grader Bubba. So all was endured in a spirit of shared understanding. But the graduating classes themselves were the nobility. Like travelers with exotic destinations on their minds, the graduates were remarkably forgetful. They came to school without their books, or tablets or even pencils. Volunteers fell over themselves to secure replacements for the missing equipment. When accepted, the willing workers might or might not be thanked, and it was of no importance to the pregraduation rites. Even teachers were respectful of the now quiet and aging seniors, and tended to speak to them, if not as equals, as beings only slightly lower than themselves. After tests were returned and grades given, the student body, which acted like an extended family, knew who did well, who excelled, and what piteous ones had failed.

Unlike the white high school, Lafayette County Training School distinguished itself by having neither lawn, nor hedges, nor tennis court, nor climbing ivy. Its two buildings (main classrooms, the grade school and home economics) were set on a dirt hill with no fence to limit either its boundaries or those of bordering farms. There was a large expanse to the left of the school which was used alternately as a baseball diamond or a basketball court. Rusty hoops on the swaying poles represented the permanent recreational equipment, although bats and balls could be borrowed from the P.E. teacher if the borrower was qualified and if the diamond wasn't occupied.

Over this rocky area relieved by a few shady tall persimmon trees the graduating class walked. The girls often held hands and no longer bothered to speak to the lower students. There was a sadness about them, as if this old world was not their home and they were bound for higher ground. The boys, on the other hand, had become more friendly, more outgoing. A decided change from the closed attitude they projected while studying for finals. Now they seemed not ready to give up the old school, the familiar paths and classrooms. Only a small percentage would be continuing on to college—one of the South's A & M (agricultural and mechanical) schools, which trained Negro youths to be carpenters, farmers, handymen, masons, maids, cooks and baby nurses. Their future rode heavily on their shoulders, and blinded them to the collective joy that had pervaded the lives of the boys and girls in the grammar school graduating class.

Parents who could afford it had ordered new shoes and ready-made clothes for themselves from Sears and Roebuck or Montgomery Ward. They also engaged the best seamstresses to make the floating graduating dresses and to cut down secondhand pants which would be pressed to a military slickness for the important event.

Oh, it was important, all right. Whitefolks would attend the ceremony, and two or three would speak of God and home, and the Southern way of life, and Mrs. Parsons, the principal's wife, would play the graduation march while the lower-grade graduates paraded down the aisles and took their seats below the platform. The high school seniors would wait in empty classrooms to make their dramatic entrance.

In the Store I was the person of the moment. The birthday girl. The center. Bailey had graduated the year before, although to do so he had had to forfeit all pleasures to make up for his time lost in Baton Rouge.

My class was wearing butter-yellow piqué dresses, and Momma launched out on mine. She smocked the yoke into tiny crisscrossing puckers, then shirred the rest of the bodice. Her dark fingers ducked in and out of the lemony cloth as she embroidered raised daisies around the hem. Before she considered herself finished she had added a crocheted cuff on the puff sleeves, and a pointy crocheted collar.

I was going to be lovely. A walking model of all the various styles   8
of fine hand sewing and it didn't worry me that I was only twelve years old and merely graduating from the eighth grade. Besides, many teachers in Arkansas Negro schools had only that diploma and were licensed to impart wisdom.

The days had become longer and more noticeable. The faded beige of former times had been replaced with strong and sure colors. I began to see my classmates' clothes, their skin tones, and the dust that waved off pussy willows. Clouds that lazed across the sky were objects of great concern to me. Their shiftier shapes might have held a message that in my new happiness and with a little bit of time I'd soon decipher. During that period I looked at the arch of heaven so religiously my neck kept a steady ache. I had taken to smiling more often, and my jaws hurt from the unaccustomed activity. Between the two physical sore spots, I suppose I could have been uncomfortable, but that was not the case. As a member of the winning team (the graduating class of 1940) I had outdistanced unpleasant sensations by miles. I was headed for the freedom of open fields.

Youth and social approval allied themselves with me and we trammeled memories of slights and insults. The wind of our swift passage remodeled my features. Lost tears were pounded to mud and then to dust. Years of withdrawal were brushed aside and left behind, as hanging ropes of parasitic moss.

My work alone had awarded me a top place and I was going to be one of the first called in the graduating ceremonies. On the classroom blackboard, as well as on the bulletin board in the auditorium, there were blue stars and white stars and red stars. No absences, no tardinesses, and my academic work was among the best of the year. I could say the preamble to the Constitution even faster than Bailey. We timed ourselves often: "WethepeopleoftheUnitedStatesinordertoformamore perfectunion . . ." I had memorized the Presidents of the United States from Washington to Roosevelt in chronological as well as alphabetical order.

My hair pleased me too. Gradually the black mass had lengthened   12
and thickened, so that it kept at last to its braided pattern, and I didn't have to yank my scalp off when I tried to comb it.

Louise and I had rehearsed the exercises until we tired out ourselves. Henry Reed was class valedictorian. He was a small, very black boy with hooded eyes, a long, broad nose and an oddly shaped head. I had admired him for years because each term he and I vied for the best grades in our class. Most often he bested me, but instead of being disappointed I was pleased that we shared top places between us. Like many Southern Black children, he lived with his grandmother, who was as strict as Momma and as kind as she knew how to be. He was courteous, respectful and soft-spoken to elders, but on the playground he chose to play the roughest games. I admired him. Anyone, I reckoned, sufficiently afraid or sufficiently dull could be polite. But to be able to operate at a top level with both adults and children was admirable.

His valedictory speech was entitled "To Be or Not To Be." The rigid tenth-grade teacher had helped him to write it. He'd been working on the dramatic stresses for months.

The weeks until graduation were filled with heady activities. A group of small children were to be presented in a play about buttercups and daisies and bunny rabbits. They could be heard throughout the building practicing their hops and their little songs that sounded like silver bells. The older girls (non-graduates, of course) were assigned the task of making refreshments for the night's festivities. A tangy scent of ginger, cinnamon, nutmeg and chocolate wafted around the home economics building as the budding cooks made samples for themselves and their teachers.

In every corner of the workshop, axes and saws split fresh timber as the woodshop boys made sets and stage scenery. Only the graduates were left out of the general bustle. We were free to sit in the library at the back of the building or look in quite detachedly, naturally, on the measures being taken for our event. 16

Even the minister preached on graduation the Sunday before. His subject was, "Let your light so shine that men will see your good works and praise your Father, Who is in Heaven." Although the sermon was purported to be addressed to us, he used the occasion to speak to backsliders, gamblers, and general ne'er-do-wells. But since he had called our names at the beginning of the service we were mollified.

Among Negroes the tradition was to give presents to children going only from one grade to another. How much more important this was when the person was graduating at the top of the class. Uncle Willie and Momma had sent away for a Mickey Mouse watch like Bailey's. Louise gave me four embroidered handkerchiefs. (I gave her three crocheted doilies.) Mrs. Sneed, the minister's wife, made me an underskirt to wear for graduation, and nearly every customer gave me a nickel or maybe even a dime with the instruction "Keep on moving to higher ground," or some such encouragement.

Amazingly the great day finally dawned and I was out of bed before I knew it. I threw open the back door to see it more clearly, but Momma said, "Sister, come away from that door and put your robe on."

I hoped the memory of that morning would never leave me. Sun- 20
light was itself still young, and the day had none of the insistence maturity would bring it in a few hours. In my robe and barefoot in the back-
yard, under cover of going to see about my new beans, I gave myself up
to the gentle warmth and thanked God that no matter what evil I had
done in my life He had allowed me to live to see this day. Somewhere
in my fatalism I had expected to die, accidentally, and never have the
chance to walk up the stairs in the auditorium and gracefully receive
my hard-earned diploma. Out of God's merciful bosom I had won
reprieve.

Bailey came out in his robe and gave me a box wrapped in Christmas paper. He said he had saved his money for months to pay for it. It
felt like a box of chocolates, but I knew Bailey wouldn't save money to
buy candy when we had all we could want under our noses.

He was as proud of the gift as I. It was a soft-leather-bound copy
of a collection of poems by Edgar Allan Poe, or, as Bailey and I called
him, "Eap." I turned to "Annabel Lee" and we walked up and down
the garden rows, the cool dirt between our toes, reciting the beautifully sad lines.

Momma made a Sunday breakfast although it was only Friday.
After we finished the blessing, I opened my eyes to find the watch on
my plate. It was a dream of a day. Everything went smoothly and to my
credit. I didn't have to be reminded or scolded for anything. Near
evening I was too jittery to attend to chores, so Bailey volunteered to do
all before his bath.

Days before, we had made a sign for the Store and as we turned out 24
the lights Momma hung the cardboard over the doorknob. It read clearly: CLOSED. GRADUATION.

My dress fitted perfectly and everyone said that I looked like a sun-
beam in it. On the hill, going toward the school, Bailey walked behind
with Uncle Willie, who muttered, "Go on, Ju." He wanted him to walk
ahead with us because it embarrassed him to have to walk so slowly.
Bailey said he'd let the ladies walk together, and the men would bring
up the rear. We all laughed, nicely.

Little children dashed by out of the dark like fireflies. Their crepe-
paper dresses and butterfly wings were not made for running and we
heard more than one rip, dryly, and the regretful "uh uh" that followed.

The school blazed without gaiety. The windows seemed cold and
unfriendly from the lower hill. A sense of ill-fated timing crept over me,
and if Momma hadn't reached for my hand I would have drifted back
to Bailey and Uncle Willie, and possibly beyond. She made a few slow
jokes about my feet getting cold, and tugged me along to the now-
strange building.

Around the front steps, assurance came back. There were my fel- 28
low "greats," the graduating class. Hair brushed back, legs oiled, new
dresses and pressed pleats, fresh pocket handkerchiefs and little hand-

bags, all homesewn. Oh, we were up to snuff, all right. I joined my comrades and didn't even see my family go in to find seats in the crowded auditorium.

The school band struck up a march and all classes filed in as had been rehearsed. We stood in front of our seats, as assigned, and on a signal from the choir director, we sat. No sooner had this been accomplished than the band started to play the national anthem. We rose again and sang the song, after which we recited the pledge of allegiance. We remained standing for a brief minute before the choir director and the principal signaled to us, rather desperately I thought, to take our seats. The command was so unusual that our carefully rehearsed and smooth-running machine was thrown off. For a full minute we fumbled for our chairs and bumped into each other awkwardly. Habits change or solidify under pressure, so in our state of nervous tension we had been ready to follow our usual assembly pattern: the American National Anthem, then the pledge of allegiance, then the song every Black person I knew called the Negro National Anthem. All done in the same key, with the same passion and most often standing on the same foot.

Finding my seat at last, I was overcome with a presentiment of worse things to come. Something unrehearsed, unplanned, was going to happen, and we were going to be made to look bad. I distinctly remember being explicit in the choice of pronoun. It was "we," the graduating class, the unit, that concerned me then.

The principal welcomed "parents and friends" and asked the Baptist minister to lead us in prayer. His invocation was brief and punchy, and for a second I thought we were getting back on the high road to right action. When the principal came back to the dais, however, his voice had changed. Sounds always affected me profoundly and the principal's voice was one of my favorites. During assembly it melted and lowed weakly into the audience. It had not been in my plan to listen to him, but my curiosity was piqued and I straightened up to give him my attention.

He was talking about Booker T. Washington, our "late great 32 leader," who said we can be as close as the fingers on the hand, etc. . . . Then he said a few vague things about friendship and the friendship of kindly people to those less fortunate than themselves. With that his voice nearly faded, thin, away. Like a river diminishing to a stream and then to a trickle. But he cleared his throat and said, "Our speaker tonight, who is also our friend, came from Texarkana to deliver the commencement address, but due to the irregularity of the train schedule, he's going to, as they say, 'speak and run.'" He said that we understood and wanted the man to know that we were most grateful for the time he was able to give us and then something about how we were willing always to adjust to another's program, and without more ado— "I give you Mr. Edward Donleavy."

Not one but two white men came through the door offstage. The shorter one walked to the speaker's platform, and the tall one moved over to the center seat and sat down. But that was our principal's seat, and already occupied. The dislodged gentleman bounced around for a long breath or two before the Baptist minister gave him his chair, then with more dignity than the situation deserved, the minister walked off the stage.

Donleavy looked at the audience once (on reflection, I'm sure that he wanted only to reassure himself that we were really there), adjusted his glasses and began to read from a sheaf of papers.

He was glad "to be here and to see the work going on just as it was in the other schools."

At the first "Amen" from the audience I willed the offender to   36
immediate death by choking on the word. But Amen's and Yes, sir's began to fall around the room like rain through a ragged umbrella.

He told us of the wonderful changes we children in Stamps had in store. The Central School (naturally, the white school was Central) had already been granted improvements that would be in use in the fall. A well-known artist was coming from Little Rock to teach art to them. They were going to have the newest microscopes and chemistry equipment for their laboratory. Mr. Donleavy didn't leave us long in the dark over who made these improvements available to Central High. Nor were we to be ignored in the general betterment scheme he had in mind.

He said that he had pointed out to people at a very high level that one of the first-line football tacklers at Arkansas Agricultural and Mechanical College had graduated from good old Lafayette County Training School. Here fewer Amen's were heard. Those few that did break through lay dully in the air with the heaviness of habit.

He went on to praise us. He went on to say how he had bragged that "one of the best basketball players at Fisk sank his first ball right here at Lafayette County Training School."

The white kids were going to have a chance to become Galileos and   40
Madame Curies and Edisons and Gauguins, and our boys (the girls weren't even in on it) would try to be Jesse Owenses and Joe Louises.

Owens and the Brown Bomber were great heroes in our world, but what school official in the white-goddom of Little Rock had the right to decide that those two men must be our only heroes? Who decided that for Henry Reed to become a scientist he had to work like George Washington Carver, as a bootblack, to buy a lousy microscope? Bailey was obviously always going to be too small to be an athlete, so which concrete angel glued to what country seat had decided that if my brother wanted to become a lawyer he had to first pay penance for his skin by picking cotton and hoeing corn and studying correspondence books at night for twenty years?

The man's dead words fell like bricks around the auditorium and too many settled in my belly. Constrained by hard-learned manners I couldn't look behind me, but to my left and right the proud graduating class of 1940 had dropped their heads. Every girl in my row had found something new to do with her handkerchief. Some folded the tiny squares into love knots, some into triangles, but most were wadding them, then pressing them flat on their yellow laps.

On the dais, the ancient tragedy was being replayed. Professor Parsons sat, a sculptor's reject, rigid. His large, heavy body seemed devoid of will or willingness, and his eyes said he was no longer with us. The other teachers examined the flag (which was draped stage right) or their notes, or the windows which opened on our now-famous playing diamond.

Graduation, the hush-hush magic time of frills and gifts and congratulations and diplomas, was finished for me before my name was called. The accomplishment was nothing. The meticulous maps, drawn in three colors of ink, learning and spelling decasyllabic words, memorizing the whole of *The Rape of Lucrece*—it was nothing. Donleavy had exposed us.   44

We were maids and farmers, handymen and washerwomen, and anything higher that we aspired to was farcical and presumptuous. Then I wished that Gabriel Prosser and Nat Turner had killed all white-folks in their beds and that Abraham Lincoln had been assassinated before the signing of the Emancipation Proclamation, and that Harriet Tubman had been killed by that blow on her head and Christopher Columbus had drowned in the *Santa Maria*.

It was awful to be Negro and have no control over my life. It was brutal to be young and already trained to sit quietly and listen to charges brought against my color and no chance of defense. We should all be dead. I thought I should like to see us all dead, one on top of the other. A pyramid of flesh with the whitefolks on the bottom, as the broad base, then the Indians with their silly tomahawks and teepees and wigwams and treaties, the Negroes with their mops and recipes and cotton sacks and spirituals sticking out of their mouths. The Dutch children should all stumble in their wooden shoes and break their necks. The French should choke to death on the Louisiana Purchase (1803) while silkworms ate all the Chinese with their stupid pigtails. As a species, we were an abomination. All of us.

Donleavy was running for election, and assured our parents that if he won we could count on having the only colored paved playing field in that part of Arkansas. Also—he never looked up to acknowledge the grunts of acceptance—also, we were bound to get some new equipment for the home economics building and the workshop.

He finished, and since there was no need to give any more than the   48
most perfunctory thank-you's, he nodded to the men on the stage, and the tall white man who was never introduced joined him at the door. They left with the attitude that now they were off to something really important. (The graduation ceremonies at Lafayette County Training School had been a mere preliminary.)

The ugliness they left was palpable. An uninvited guest who wouldn't leave. The choir was summoned and sang a modern arrangement of "Onward, Christian Soldiers," with new words pertaining to graduates seeking their place in the world. But it didn't work. Elouise, the daughter of the Baptist minister, recited "Invictus," and I could have cried at the impertinence of "I am the master of my fate, I am the captain of my soul."

My name had lost its ring of familiarity and I had to be nudged to go and receive my diploma. All my preparations had fled. I neither marched up to the stage like a conquering Amazon, nor did I look in the audience for Bailey's nod of approval. Marguerite Johnson, I heard the name again, my honors were read, there were noises in the audience of appreciation, and I took my place on the stage as rehearsed.

I thought about colors I hated: ecru, puce, lavender, beige and black.

There was shuffling and rustling around me, then Henry Reed was giving his valedictory address, "To Be or Not to Be." Hadn't he heard the whitefolks? We couldn't *be,* so the question was a waste of time. Henry's voice came out clear and strong. I feared to look at him. Hadn't he got the message? There was no "nobler in the mind" for Negroes because the world didn't think we had minds, and they let us know it. "Outrageous fortune"? Now, that was a joke. When the ceremony was over I had to tell Henry Reed some things. That is, if I still cared. Not "rub," Henry, "erase." "Ah, there's the erase." Us.

Henry had been a good student in elocution. His voice rose on tides of promise and fell on waves of warnings. The English teacher had helped him to create a sermon winging through Hamlet's soliloquy. To be a man, a doer, a builder, a leader, or to be a tool, an unfunny joke, a crusher of funky toadstools. I marveled that Henry could go through with the speech as if we had a choice.

I had been listening and silently rebutting each sentence with my eyes closed; then there was a hush, which in an audience warns that something unplanned is happening. I looked up and saw Henry Reed, the conservative, the proper, the A student, turn his back to the audience and turn to us (the proud graduating class of 1940) and sing, nearly speaking,

> Lift ev'ry voice and sing
> Till earth and heaven ring
> Ring with the harmonies of Liberty . . .

It was the poem written by James Weldon Johnson. It was the music composed by J. Rosamond Johnson. It was the Negro National Anthem. Out of habit we were singing it.

Our mothers and fathers stood in the dark hall and joined the hymn of encouragement. A kindergarten teacher led the small children onto the stage and the buttercups and daisies and bunny rabbits marked time and tried to follow:

Stony the road we trod
Bitter the chastening rod
Felt in the days when hope, unborn, had died.
Yet with a steady beat
Have not our weary feet
Come to the place for which our fathers sighed?

Every child I knew had learned that song with his ABC's and along   56
with "Jesus Loves Me This I Know." But I personally had never heard it
before. Never heard the words, despite the thousands of times I had
sung them. Never thought they had anything to do with me.

On the other hand, the words of Patrick Henry had made such an
impression on me that I had been able to stretch myself tall and trembling and say, "I know not what course others may take, but as for me,
give me liberty or give me death."

And now I heard, really for the first time:

We have come over a way that with tears has been watered,
We have come, treading our path through the blood of the
slaughtered.

While echoes of the song shivered in the air, Henry Reed bowed his
head, said "Thank you," and returned to his place in the line. The tears
that slipped down many faces were not wiped away in shame.

We were on top again. As always, again. We survived. The depths   60
had been icy and dark, but now a bright sun spoke to our souls. I was
no longer simply a member of the proud graduating class of 1940; I was
a proud member of the wonderful, beautiful Negro race.

Oh, Black known and unknown poets, how often have your auc-
tioned pains sustained us? Who will compute the lonely nights made less
lonely by your songs, or the empty pots made less tragic by your tales?

If we were a people much given to revealing secrets, we might raise
monuments and sacrifice to the memories of our poets, but slavery
cured us of that weakness. It may be enough, however, to have it said
that we survive in exact relationship to the dedication of our poets
(include preachers, musicians and blues singers).

Topics for Critical Thinking and Writing

1. In paragraph 1 notice such overstatements as "glorious release," "the
   graduating classes themselves were the nobility," and "exotic destinations." Find further examples in the next few pages. What do you think
   is the function of this diction?
2. Characterize the writer as you perceive her through paragraph 28. Support your characterization with references to specific passages. Next,
   characterize her in paragraph 46, which begins "It was awful to be

Negro." Next, characterize her on the basis of the entire essay. Finally, in a sentence, try to describe the change, telling the main attitudes or moods that she goes through.

3. How would you define *poets* as Angelou uses the word in the last sentence?

Neil Postman

Neil Postman, born in New York City in 1931, has taught in elementary and secondary schools and is now a professor of communication arts and sciences at New York University.

Order in the Classroom

William O'Connor, who is unknown to me in a personal way, was once a member of the Boston School Committee, in which capacity he made the following remark: "We have no inferior education in our schools. What we have been getting is an inferior type of student."

The remark is easy to ridicule, and I have had some fun with it in the past. But there are a couple of senses in which it is perfectly sound.

In the first place, a classroom is a technique for the achievement of certain kinds of learning. It is a workable technique provided that both the teacher and the student have the skill and, particularly, the attitudes that are fundamental to it. Among these, from the student's point of view, are tolerance for delayed gratification, a certain measure of respect for and fear of authority, and a willingness to accommodate one's individual desires to the interests of group cohesion and purpose. These attitudes cannot be taught easily in school because they are a necessary component of the teaching situation itself. The problem is not unlike trying to find out how to spell a word by looking it up in the dictionary. If you do not know how a word is spelled, it is hard to look it up. In the same way, little can be taught in school unless these attitudes are present. And if they are not, to teach them is difficult.

Obviously, such attitudes must be learned during the years before a child starts school; that is, in the home. This is the real meaning of the phrase "preschool education." If a child is not made ready at home for the classroom experience, he or she usually cannot benefit from any normal school program. Just as important, the school is defenseless against such a child, who, typically, is a source of disorder in a situation that requires order. I raise this issue because education reform is impossible without order in the classroom. Without the attitudes that lead to order, the classroom is an entirely impotent technique. Therefore, one possible translation of Mr. O'Connor's remark is, "We have a useful technique for educating youth but too many of them have not been provided at home with the attitudes necessary for the technique to work."

In still another way Mr. O'Connor's remark makes plain sense. The electronic media, with their emphasis on visual imagery, immediacy, non-linearity, and fragmentation, do not give support to the attitudes that are fundamental to the classroom; that is, Mr. O'Connor's remark can be translated as, "We would not have an inferior education if it were the nineteenth century. Our problem is that we have been getting students who are products of the twentieth century." But there is nothing nonsensical about this, either. The nineteenth century had much to recommend it, and we certainly may be permitted to allow it to exert an influence on the twentieth. The classroom is a nineteenth-century invention, and we ought to prize what it has to offer. It is one of the few social organizations left to us in which sequence, social order, hierarchy, continuity, and deferred pleasure are important.

The problem of disorder in the classroom is created largely by two factors: a dissolving family structure, out of which come youngsters who are "unfit" for the presuppositions of a classroom; and a radically altered information environment, which undermines the foundation of school. The question, then, is, What should be done about the increasing tendency toward disorder in the classroom?

Liberal reformers, such as Kenneth Keniston, have answers, of a sort. Keniston argues that economic reforms should be made so that the integrity and authority of the family can be restored. He believes that poverty is the main cause of family dissolution, and that by improving the economic situation of families, we may kindle a sense of order and aspiration in the lives of children. Some of the reforms he suggests in his book *All Our Children* seem practical, although they are long-range and offer no immediate response to the problem of present disorder. Some Utopians, such as Ivan Illich, have offered other solutions; for example, dissolving the schools altogether, or so completely restructuring the school environment that its traditional assumptions are rendered irrelevant. To paraphrase Karl Kraus's epigram about psychoanalysis, these proposals are the Utopian disease of which they consider themselves the cure.

One of the best answers comes from Dr. Howard Hurwitz, who is 8 neither a liberal reformer nor a Utopian. It is a good solution, I believe, because it tries to respond to the needs not only of children who are unprepared for school because of parental failure but of children of all backgrounds who are being made strangers to the assumptions of school by the biases of the electronic media.

During the eleven years Dr. Hurwitz was principal at Long Island City High School, the average number of suspensions each year was three, while in many New York City high schools the average runs close to one hundred. Also, during his tenure, not one instance of an assault on a teacher was reported, and daily student attendance averaged better than 90 percent, which in the context of the New York City school scene represents a riot of devotion.

Although I consider some of Dr. Hurwitz's curriculum ideas uninspired and even wrong-headed, he understands a few things of overriding importance that many educators of more expansive imagination do not. The first is that educators must devote at least as much attention to the immediate consequences of disorder as to its abstract causes. Whatever the causes of disorder and alienation, the consequences are severe and, if not curbed, result in making the school impotent. At the risk of becoming a symbol of reaction, Hurwitz ran "a tight ship." He holds to the belief, for example, that a child's right to an education is terminated at the point where the child interferes with the right of other children to have one.

Dr. Hurwitz also understands that disorder expands proportionately to the tolerance for it, and that children of all kinds of home backgrounds can learn, in varying degrees, to function in situations where disorder is not tolerated at all. He does not believe that it is inevitably or only the children of the poor who are disorderly. In spite of what the "revisionist" education historians may say, poor people still regard school as an avenue of social and economic advancement for their children, and do not object in the least to its being an orderly and structured experience.

All this adds up to the common sense view that the school ought   12
not to accommodate itself to disorder, or to the biases of other communication systems. The children of the poor are likely to continue to be with us. Some parents will fail to assume competent responsibility for the preschool education of their children. The media will increase the intensity of their fragmenting influence. Educators must live with these facts. But Dr. Hurwitz believes that as a technique for learning, the classroom can work if students are oriented toward its assumptions, not the other way around. William O'Connor, wherever he is, would probably agree. And so do I. The school is not an extension of the street, the movie theater, a rock concert, or a playground. And it is certainly not an extension of the psychiatric clinic. It is a special environment that requires the enforcement of certain traditional rules of controlled group interaction. The school may be the only remaining public situation in which such rules have any meaning, and it would be a grave mistake to change those rules because some children find them hard or cannot function within them. Children who cannot ought to be removed from the environment in the interests of those who can.

Wholesale suspensions, however, are a symptom of disorder, not a cure for it. And what makes Hurwitz's school noteworthy is the small number of suspensions that have been necessary. This is not the result of his having "good" students or "bad" students. It is the result of his having created an unambiguous, rigorous, and serious attitude—a nineteenth-century attitude, if you will—toward what constitutes acceptable school behavior. In other words, Dr. Hurwitz's school turns out to be a place where children of all backgrounds—fit and unfit—can function, or can learn to function, and where the biases of our information environment are emphatically opposed.

At this point I should like to leave the particulars of Dr. Hurwitz's solution and, retaining their spirit, indicate some particulars of my own.

Let us start, for instance, with the idea of a dress code. A dress code signifies that school is a special place in which special kinds of behavior are required. The way one dresses is an indication of an attitude toward a situation. And the way one is *expected* to dress indicates what that attitude ought to be. You would not wear dungarees and a T-shirt that says "Feel Me" when attending a church wedding. That would be considered an outrage against the tone and meaning of the situation. The school has every right and reason, I believe, to expect the same sort of consideration.

Those who are inclined to think this is a superficial point are proba-   16
bly forgetting that symbols not only reflect our feelings but to some extent create them. One's kneeling in church, for example, reflects a sense of reverence but also engenders reverence. If we want school to *feel* like a special place, we can find no better way to begin than by requiring students to dress in a manner befitting the seriousness of the enterprise and the institution. I should include teachers in this requirement. I know of one high school in which the principal has put forward a dress code of sorts for teachers. (He has not, apparently, had the courage to propose one for the students.) For males the requirement is merely a jacket and tie. One of his teachers bitterly complained to me that such a regulation infringed upon his civil rights. And yet, this teacher will accept without complaint the same regulation when it is enforced by an elegant restaurant. His complaint and his acquiescence tell a great deal about how he values schools and how he values restaurants.

I do not have in mind, for students, uniforms of the type sometimes worn in parochial schools. I am referring here to some reasonable standard of dress which would mark school as a place of dignity and seriousness. And I might add that I do not believe for one moment the argument that poor people would be unable to clothe their children properly if such a code were in force. Furthermore, I do not believe that poor people have advanced that argument. It is an argument that middle-class education critics have made on behalf of the poor.

Another argument advanced in behalf of the poor and oppressed is the students' right to their own language. I have never heard this argument come from parents whose children are not competent to use Standard English. It is an argument, once again, put forward by "liberal" education critics whose children *are* competent in Standard English but who in some curious way wish to express their solidarity with and charity for those who are less capable. It is a case of pure condescension, and I do not think teachers should be taken in by it. Like the mode of dress, the mode of language in school ought to be relatively formal and exemplary, and therefore markedly different from the custom in less rigorous places. It is particularly important that teachers should avoid trying to win their students' affection by adopting the language of youth. Such teachers frequently win only the contempt of their students, who sense that the language of teachers and the language of students ought to be different; that is to say, the world of adults is different from the world of children.

In this connection, it is worth saying that the modern conception of childhood is a product of the sixteenth century, as Philippe Aries has documented in his *The Centuries of Childhood*. Prior to that century, children as young as six and seven were treated in all important respects as if they were adults. Their language, their dress, their legal status, their responsibilities, their labor, were much the same as those of adults. The concept of childhood as an identifiable stage in human growth began to develop in the sixteenth century and has continued into our own times. However, with the emergence of electronic media of communication, a reversal of this trend seems to be taking place. In a culture in which the distribution of information is almost wholly undifferentiated, age categories begin to disappear. Television, in itself, may bring an end to childhood. In truth, there is no such thing as "children's programming," at least not for children over the age of eight or nine. Everyone sees and hears the same things. We have already reached a point where crimes of youth are indistinguishable from those of adults, and we may soon reach a point where the punishments will be the same.

I raise this point because the school is one of our few remaining   20
institutions based on firm distinctions between childhood and adulthood, and on the assumption that adults have something of value to teach the young. That is why teachers must avoid emulating in dress and speech the style of the young. It is also why the school ought to be a place for what we might call "manners education": the adults in school ought to be concerned with teaching youth a standard of civilized interaction.

Again those who are inclined to regard this as superficial may be underestimating the power of media such as television and radio to teach how one is to conduct oneself in public. In a general sense, the media "unprepare" the young for behavior in groups. A young man who goes through the day with a radio affixed to his ear is learning to be indifferent to any shared sound. A young woman who can turn off a television program that does not suit her needs at the moment is learning impatience with any stimulus that is not responsive to her interests.

But school is not a radio station or a television program. It is a social situation requiring the subordination of one's own impulses and interests to those of the group. In a word, manners. As a rule, elementary school teachers will exert considerable effort in teaching manners. I believe they refer to this effort as "socializing the child." But it is astonishing how precipitously this effort is diminished at higher levels. It is certainly neglected in the high schools, and where it is not, there is usually an excessive concern for "bad habits," such as smoking, drinking, and in some nineteenth-century schools, swearing. But, as William James noted, our virtues are as habitual as our vices. Where is the attention given to the "Good morning" habit, to the "I beg your pardon" habit, to the "Please forgive the interruption" habit?

The most civilized high school class I have ever seen was one in which students and teacher said "Good morning" to each other and in which the students stood up when they had something to say. The teacher, moreover, thanked each student for any contribution made to the class, did not sit with his feet on the desk, and did not interrupt a student unless he had asked permission to do so. The students, in turn, did not interrupt each other, or chew gum, or read comic books when they were bored. To avoid being a burden to others when one is bored is the essence of civilized behavior.

Of this teacher, I might also say that he made no attempt to entertain his students or model his classroom along the lines of a TV program. He was concerned not only to teach his students manners but to teach them how to attend in a classroom, which is partly a matter of manners but also necessary to their intellectual development. One of the more serious difficulties teachers now face in the classroom results from the fact that their students suffer media-shortened attention spans and have become accustomed, also through intense media exposure, to novelty, variety, and entertainment. Some teachers have made desperate attempts to keep their students "tuned in" by fashioning their classes along the lines of *Sesame Street* or the *Tonight* show. They tell jokes. They change the pace. They show films, play records, and avoid *anything* that would take more than eight minutes. Although their motivation is understandable, this is what their students least need. However difficult it may be, the teacher must try to achieve student attention and even enthusiasm through the attraction of ideas, not razzmatazz. Those who think I am speaking here in favor of "dull" classes may themselves, through media exposure, have lost an understanding of the potential for excitement contained in an idea. The media (one prays) are not so powerful that they can obliterate in the young, particularly in the adolescent, what William James referred to as a "theoretic instinct," a need to know reasons, causes, abstract conceptions. Such an "instinct" can be seen in its earliest stages in what he calls the "sporadic metaphysical inquiries of children as to who made God, and why they have five fingers. . . ."

I trust that the reader is not misled by what I have been saying. As I see it, nothing in any of the above leads to the conclusion that I favor a classroom that is authoritarian or coldhearted, or dominated by a teacher insensitive to students and how they learn. I merely want to affirm the importance of the classroom as a special place, aloof from the biases of the media; a place in which the uses of the intellect are given prominence in a setting of elevated language, civilized manners, and respect for social symbols.

Topics for Critical Thinking and Writing

1. In paragraph 3 what does Postman mean by "tolerance for delayed gratification"? By the way, two paragraphs later Postman uses an expression that is approximately synonymous with "delayed gratification." What is this expression?

2. Postman in part blames "the electronic media," because (he says in paragraph 5) they emphasize "fragmentation." Does he give any examples in his essay? Do you think you know what he means? And do you think he is right?

3. Who is Postman's audience? High school students? Parents and teachers? Professors of education? And who is Postman—that is, putting aside the biographical note on page 244, what sort of person does the author of the essay reveal himself to be? A frustrated high school teacher? A professor of education? An intelligent layperson? Does he seem to know what he is talking about?

4. In paragraph 10 we are told, with approval, that a principal named Dr. Howard Hurwitz "ran 'a tight ship.'" First, make sure that you know what the phrase means, and then write an essay of five hundred words evaluating the degree of success of some instructor or administrator who ran a tight ship in your school. Your essay will, of course, have to give us a sense of what the instructor or administrator did, as well as your evaluation of the results of his or her teaching or administrating.

5. If you disagree with Postman on the value of a dress code, set forth your disagreement in a persuasive essay of five hundred words.

6. Write an editorial—as an alumnus or alumna—for your high school newspaper, summarizing Postman's essay in a paragraph, and then comparing your school with Postman's idea of a good school, and, finally, evaluating your school and Postman's essay. You may, for example, conclude that, thank heavens, your school was nothing like Postman's ideal school.

Merry White

Merry White is the author of The Japanese Educational Challenge *(1987). She is also the author of a book on noodles. White, who has served as an administrator of Harvard's East Asian Studies Program, now teaches sociology at Boston University. This essay was originally published in 1984, hence the average salaries specified in paragraph 19 must be adjusted upward.*

Japanese Education
How Do They Do It?

Japan has become the new reference point for the developing nations and the West, and comparisons with Japan cause increasing wonder and sometimes envy. Travel agents continue to profit from the curiosity of Americans, particularly businessmen, who take regular tours of Japan seeking the secrets of Japanese industry. They come back with photographs and full notebooks, convinced they have learned secrets that can be transplanted to their own companies.

Even the Japanese have entered the pop-sociological search for the secrets of their own success; their journalists suggest that they emphasize problem *prevention* while Americans make up for their lack of prescience and care through *remediation* (in the case of cars, recalls for flawed models). The explanation given by a European Economic Community report—that the Japanese are workaholics willing, masochistically, to live in "rabbit hutches" without complaint—was met with amused derision in Japan. But it seems that those who do not look for transportable "secrets" are nonetheless willing to believe that the source of Japanese success is genetic, and thus completely untransferable. There are alternatives to these positions, and an examination of Japanese education provides us with a backdrop for considering them.

The Social Consensus

The attention given to the decline of both American industry and American education has not yet led to an awareness here of the close relationship between the development of people and the development of society, an awareness we see everywhere in Japanese thought and institutions, and whose effects we can see in the individual achievements of Japanese children. If Americans realized how powerful the relationship is between Japanese school achievement and social and economic successes we might see the same kind of protectionist language aimed at the Japanese educational system that we see directed at their automobile industry. ("The Japanese must stop producing such able and committed students because *it isn't fair*.")

The Japanese understand how important it is to have not just a high   4
level of literacy (which they have had since well before modernization),

but also a high level of education in the whole population. It has been said that the Japanese high school graduate is as well educated as an American college graduate, and indeed it is impressive that any worker on the factory floor can be expected to understand statistical material, work from complex graphs and charts, and perform sophisticated mathematical operations. This consensus that education is important, however simple it may sound, is the single most important contributor to the success of Japanese schools. Across the population, among parents, at all institutional and bureaucratic levels, and highest on the list of national priorities, is the stress on excellence in education. This is not just rhetoric. If the consensus, societal mobilization, and personal commitment—all focused on education—are not available to Americans, the reason is not genetic, nor are we locked in an immutable cultural pattern. We simply have not mobilized around our children.

There are dear advantages to being a Japanese child: a homogeneous population focused on perpetuating its cultural identity; an occupational system where selection and promotion are based on educational credentials; a relatively equal distribution of educational opportunities; a universal core curriculum; highly trained and rewarded teachers; and families, especially mothers, devoted to enhancing the life chances of children and working cooperatively with the educational system. Finally, there are high standards for performance in every sector, and a carefully graded series of performance expectations in the school curriculum.

It is clear from these assertions that the measurable cognitive achievements of Japanese education represent only part of the picture. The American press stresses these achievements and accounts for them in terms of government expenditures, longer school years, and early use of homework. While the International Association for the Evaluation of Educational Achievement (IEA) test scores certainly indicate that Japanese children are testing higher than any children in the world (especially in math and science), and while some researchers have even claimed that Japanese children on average score 11 points more than American children on IQ tests, the social and psychological dimensions of Japanese education are similarly impressive and are primary contributors to cognitive achievement. The support given by family and teachers to the emotional and behavioral development of the child provides a base for the child's acquisition of knowledge and problem-solving skills. But beyond this, the Japanese think a major function of education is the development of a happy, engaged, and secure child, able to work hard and cooperate with others.

Inside the Japanese School

In order to understand the context of the Japanese educational system, some basic information is necessary:

1. Education is compulsory for ages six to 15, or through lower secondary school. (Age is almost always correlated with grade level, by the way, because only rarely is a child "kept back" and almost never   8

"put ahead.") Non-compulsory high school attendance (both public and private) is nearly universal, at 98 percent.

2. There is extensive "non-official" private education. Increasing numbers of children attend pre-schools. Currently, about 95 percent of the five-year olds are in kindergarten or nursery school, 70 percent of the four-year olds and 10 percent of three-year olds. Many older children attend *juku* (after school classes) as well. These are private classes in a great variety of subjects, but most enhance and reinforce the material to be learned for high school or college entrance examinations. There are also *yobiko* (cram schools) for those taking an extra year between high school and college to prepare for the exams.

3. While competition for entrance to the most prestigious universities is very stiff, nearly 40 percent of the college-age group attend college or university. (The rates are slightly higher for women, since many attend two-year junior colleges.)

4. Japanese children attend school 240 days a year, compared to 180 in the U.S. Many children spend Sundays in study or tutoring, and vacation classes are also available. Children do not necessarily see this as oppressive, and younger children often ask their parents to send them to *juku* as a way of being with their friends after school. Homework starts in first grade, and children in Japan spend more time in home study than children in any other country except Taiwan. In Japan, 8 percent of the high school seniors spend less than five hours per week on homework, compared to 65 percent of American seniors.[1]

5. Primary and lower secondary schools provide what we would call a core curriculum: a required and comprehensive course of study progressing along a logical path, with attention given to children's developmental levels. In elementary and lower secondary school, language learning dominates the school curriculum, and takes up the greatest number of classroom hours, particularly from second to fourth grade. The large number of characters to be learned requires an emphasis on memorization and drill that is not exhibited in the rest of the curriculum. Arithmetic and math are next in number of class hours, followed by social studies. The curriculum includes regular physical education and morning exercise as part of a "whole-child" program. In high school all students take Japanese, English, math, science, and social studies each year, and all students have had courses in chemistry, biology, physics, and earth sciences. All high school students take calculus.

6. Computers and other technology do not play a large role in schools. The calculator is used, but has not replaced mental calculations or, for that matter, the abacus. There is no national program to develop high technology skills in children. Americans spend much more money on science and technology in the schools; the Japanese spend more on teacher training and salaries.

[1]Thomas Rohlen, *Japan's High Schools* (Berkeley: University of California Press, 1983), p. 277.

These features should be seen in the context of a history of emphasis on education in Japan. To begin with, an interest in mass (or at least widespread) education greatly antedated the introduction of Western schools to Japan. Literacy, numeracy, and a moral education were considered important for people of all classes. When Western style universal compulsory schooling was introduced in 1872, it was after a deliberate and wide-ranging search throughout the world that resulted in a selection of features from German, French, and American educational systems that would advance Japan's modernization and complement her culture. While uniform, centralized schooling was an import, it eventually brought out Japan's already refined powers of adaptation— not the ability to adapt to a new mode as much as *the ability to adapt the foreign mode to Japanese needs and conditions.*

Also striking was the rapidity with which Japan developed a modern educational system and made it truly universal. In 1873, one year after the Education Act, there was 28 percent enrollment in primary schools, but by 1904 enrollment had already reached 98 percent—one percent less than the current rate. The rush to educate children was buttressed both by the wish to catch up with the West and by a cultural interest in schooling.

A Truly National System

Tradition, ideology, and international competition are not, however, the only motive forces in Japanese education: other factors are as significant. First, Japan has a relatively homogeneous population. Racially and economically there is little variety. Minority groups, such as Koreans and the former out-castes, exist and do suffer some discrimination, but all children have equal access to good schooling. Income is more evenly distributed in Japan than in America and most people (96 percent in a recent Prime Minister's Office poll) consider themselves middle class. There are few remaining regional differences that affect the educational system, except perhaps local accents.   16

Second, educational financing and planning are centralized. While American educational policy sees the responsibility for schooling as a local matter, Japanese planners can rely on a centralized source of funding, curriculum guidance, and textbook selection. In terms of educational spending as a percentage of total GNP, the U.S. and Japan are not so far apart: The U.S. devotes 6.8 percent of its GNP to education, and Japan devotes 8.6 percent. But in Japan about 50 percent of this is national funding, while in the U.S. the federal government provides only 8 percent of the total expenditure on education, most of which is applied to special education, not to core schooling. Moreover, in the U.S. there exist no national institutions to build a consensus on what and how our children are taught. The most significant outcome of centralization in Japan is the even distribution of resources and quality instruction across the country. National planners and policymakers can mobilize a highly qualified teaching force and offer incentives that make even the most remote areas attractive to good teachers.

Third (but perhaps most important in the comparison with the United States), teachers enjoy respect and high status, job security, and good pay. More than in any other country, teachers in Japan are highly qualified: Their mastery of their fields is the major job qualification, and all have at least a bachelor's degree in their specialty. Moreover, they have a high degree of professional involvement as teachers: 74 percent are said to belong to some professional teachers' association in which teaching methods and curriculum are actively discussed.[2]

Teachers are hired for life, at starting salaries equivalent to starting salaries for college graduates in the corporate world. Elementary and junior high school teachers earn $18,200 per year on the average, high school teachers $19,000. Compared to other Japanese public sector workers, who earn an average of $16,800, this is a high salary, but it is less than that of managers in large companies or bureaucrats in prestigious ministries. In comparison with American teachers, whose salaries average $17,600, it is an absolutely higher wage. The difference is especially striking when one considers that over all professions, salaries are lower in Japan than in the U.S. In fact, American teachers' salaries are near the bottom of the scale of jobs requiring a college degree. Relative status and prestige correlate with salary in both countries. Japanese teachers' pay increases, as elsewhere in Japan, are tied to a seniority ladder, and older "master teachers" are given extra pay as teacher supervisors in each subject.[3]

Japanese teachers see their work as permanent: Teaching is not a   20
waystation on a path to other careers. Teachers work hard at improving their skills and knowledge of their subject, and attend refresher courses and upgrading programs provided by the Ministry of Education. While there are tendencies, encouraged by the Teachers' Union, to downplay the traditional image of the "devoted, selfless teacher" (since this is seen as exploitative), and to redefine the teacher as a wage laborer with regular hours, rather than as a member of a "sacred" profession, teachers still regularly work overtime and see their job's sphere extending beyond classroom instruction. Classes are large: The average is about 40 students to one teacher. Teachers feel responsible for their students' discipline, behavior, morality, and for their general social adjustment as well as for their cognitive development. They are "on duty" after school hours and during vacations, and supervise vacation play and study.

[2]William Cummings, *Education and Equality in Japan* (Princeton: Princeton University Press, 1980), p. 159.
[3]There is a debate in Japan today concerning rewarding good teachers with higher pay: Professor Sumiko Iwao, of Keio University, reports that when quality is measured in yen, the commitment of teachers to good teaching declines.

They visit their students' families at home, and are available to parents with questions and anxieties about their children. The Teachers' Union protests strongly against this extensive role, but both teachers and parents reinforce this role, tied as it is to the high status of the teacher.

Fourth, there is strong ideological and institutional support for education because the occupational system relies on schools to select the right person for the right organization. Note that this is not the same as the "right job" or "slot": A new company recruit, almost always a recent graduate, is not expected to have a skill or special identity, but to be appropriate in general educational background and character for a company. The company then trains recruits in the skills they will need, as well as in the company style. Of course, the basic skill level of the population of high school and college graduates is extremely high. But the important fact is that the social consensus supports an educational system that creates a committed, productive labor force. And although the emphasis seems to be on educational credentials, the quality of graduates possessing these credentials is indisputably high.

Mom

The background I have presented—of national consensus, institutional centralization, and fiscal support—alone does not explain the successes of Japanese education. There are other, less tangible factors that derive from cultural conceptions of development and learning, the valued role of maternal support, and psychological factors in Japanese pedagogy, and which distinguish it from American schooling.

The role of mothers is especially important. The average Japanese mother feels her child has the potential for success: Children are believed to be born with no distinguishing abilities (or disabilities) and can be mobilized to achieve and perform at high levels. Effort and commitment are required, and, at least at the beginning, it is the mother's job to engage the child. One way of looking at Japanese child development is to look at the words and concepts related to parental goals for their children. A "good child" has the following, frequently invoked characteristics: He is *otonashii* (mild or gentle), *sunao* (compliant, obedient, and cooperative), *akarui* (bright, alert), and *genki* (energetic and spirited). *Sunao* has frequently been translated as "obedient," but it would be more appropriate to use "open minded," "nonresistant," or "authentic in intent and cooperative in spirit." The English word "obedience" implies subordination and lack of self-determination, but *sunao* assumes that what we call compliance (with a negative connotation) is really cooperation, an act of affirmation of the self. A child who is *sunao* has not yielded his personal autonomy for the sake of cooperation; cooperation does not imply giving up the self, but in fact implies that working with others is the appropriate setting for expressing and enhancing the self.

One encourages a *sunao* child through the technique, especially   24
used by mothers and elementary school teachers, of *wakaraseru*, or "getting the child to understand." The basic principle of child rearing seems to be: Never go against the child. *Wakaraseru* is often a long-term process that ultimately engages the child in the mother's goals, and makes her goals the child's own, thus producing an authentic cooperation, as in *sunao*. The distinction between external, social expectations and the child's own personal goals becomes blurred from this point on. An American might see this manipulation of the child through what we would call "indulgence" as preventing him from having a strong will of his own, but the Japanese mother sees long term benefits of self-motivated cooperation and real commitment.

Japanese mothers are active teachers as well, and have a real curriculum for their pre-school children: Games, teaching aids, ordinary activities are all focused on the child's development. There are counting games for very small babies, songs to help children learn new words, devices to focus the child's concentration. Parents buy an average of two or three new books every month for their preschoolers, and there are about 40 monthly activity magazines for preschoolers, very highly subscribed. The result is that most, at least most urban children, can read and write the phonetic syllabary before they enter school, and can do simple computations.

Maternal involvement becomes much more extensive and "serious" once she and the child enter the elementary school community. In addition to formal involvement in frequent ceremonies and school events, PTA meetings and visiting days, the mother spends much time each day helping the child with homework (sometimes to the point at which the teachers joke that they are really grading the mothers by proxy). There are classes for mothers, called *mamajuku*, that prepare mothers in subjects their children are studying. Homework is considered above all a means for developing a sense of responsibility in the child, and like much in early childhood education, it is seen as a device to train character.

The Japanese phenomenon of maternal involvement recently surfaced in Riverdale, New York, where many Japanese families have settled. School teachers and principals there noted that each Japanese family was purchasing two sets of textbooks. On inquiring, they found that the second set was for the mother, who could better coach her child if she worked during the day to keep up with his lessons. These teachers said that children entering in September with no English ability finished in June at the top of their classes in every subject.

The effort mothers put into their children's examinations has been   28
given a high profile by the press. This is called the *kyoiku mama* syndrome—the mother invested in her children's progress. In contrast to

Western theories of achievement, which emphasize individual effort and ability, the Japanese consider academic achievement to be an outgrowth of an interdependent network of cooperative effort and planning. The caricature of the mother's over-investment, however, portrays a woman who has totally identified with her child's success or failure, and who has no separate identity of her own. The press emphasizes the negative aspects of this involvement with accounts of maternal nervous breakdowns, reporting a murder by a mother of the child next-door, who made too much noise while her child was studying. But the press also feeds the mother's investment by exhorting her to prepare a good work environment for the studying child, to subscribe to special exam-preparation magazines, to hire tutors, and to prepare a nutritious and exam-appropriate diet.

High-schoolers from outlying areas taking entrance exams in Tokyo come with their mothers to stay in special rooms put aside by hotels. They are provided with special food, study rooms, counselors, and tension-release rooms, all meant to supply home-care away from home. The home study-desk bought by most parents for their smaller children symbolizes the hovering care and intensity of the mother's involvement: All models have a high front and half-sides, cutting out distractions and enclosing the workspace in womb-like protection. There is a built-in study light, shelves, a clock, electric pencil sharpener, and built-in calculator. The most popular model includes a push-button connecting to a buzzer in the kitchen to summon mother for help or for a snack.

How Do You Feel about Cubing?

Not much work has been done yet to analyze the relationship between the strongly supportive learning atmosphere and high achievement in Japan. In the home, mothers train small children in a disciplined, committed use of energy through what Takeo Doi has called the encouragement of "positive dependency"; in the schools as well there is a recognition that attention to the child's emotional relationship to his work, peers, and teachers is necessary for learning.

A look at a Japanese classroom yields some concrete examples of this. Many Westerners believe that Japanese educational successes are due to an emphasis on rote learning and memorization, that the classroom is rigidly disciplined. This is far from reality. An American teacher walking into a fourth grade science class in Japan would be horrified: children all talking at once, leaping and calling for the teacher's attention. The typical American's response is to wonder, "who's in control of this room?" But if one understands the content of the lively chatter, it is clear that all the noise and movement is focused on the work itself—children are shouting out answers, suggesting other methods, exclaiming in excitement over results, and not gossiping, teasing, or planning games for recess, As long as it is the result of this engagement, the teacher is not concerned over the noise, which may measure a teacher's success. (It has been estimated that American teachers spend about 60 percent of class time on organizing, controlling, and disciplining the class, while Japanese teachers spend only 10 percent.)

A fifth grade math class I observed reveals some elements of this pedagogy. The day I visited, the class was presented with a general statement about cubing. Before any concrete facts, formulae, or even drawings were displayed, the teacher asked the class to take out their math diaries and spend a few minutes writing down their feelings and anticipations over this new concept. It is hard for me to imagine an American math teacher beginning a lesson with an exhortation to examine one's emotional predispositions about cubing (but that may be only because my own math training was antediluvian). 32

After that, the teacher asked for conjectures from the children about the surface and volume of a cube and asked for some ideas about formulae for calculation. The teacher asked the class to cluster into its component *han* (working groups) of four or five children each, and gave out materials for measurement and construction. One group left the room with large pieces of cardboard, to construct a model of a cubic meter. The groups worked internally on solutions to problems set by the teacher and competed with each other to finish first. After a while, the cubic meter group returned, groaning under the bulk of its model, and everyone gasped over its size. (There were many comments and guesses as to how many children could fit inside.) The teacher then set the whole class a very challenging problem, well over their heads, and gave them the rest of the class time to work on it. The class ended without a solution, but the teacher made no particular effort to get or give an answer, although she exhorted them to be energetic. (It was several days before the class got the answer—there was no deadline but the excitement did not flag.)

Several characteristics of this class deserve highlighting. First, there was attention to feelings and predispositions, provision of facts, and opportunities for discovery. The teacher preferred to focus on process, engagement, commitment, and performance rather than on discipline (in our sense) and production. Second, the *han*: Assignments are made to groups, not to individuals (this is also true at the workplace) although individual progress and achievement are closely monitored. Children are supported, praised, and allowed to make mistakes through trial and error within the group. The group is also pitted against other groups, and the group's success is each person's triumph, and vice versa. Groups are made up by the teacher and are designed to include a mixture of skill levels—there is a *hancho* (leader) whose job it is to choreograph the group's work, to encourage the slower members, and to act as a reporter to the class at large.

Japanese teachers seem to recognize the emotional as well as the intellectual aspects of engagement. Japanese pedagogy (and maternal socialization) are based on the belief that effort is the most important factor in achievement, and that the teacher's job is to get the child to commit himself positively and energetically to hard work. This emphasis is most explicit in elementary school, but persists later as a prerequisite for the self-discipline and effort children exhibit in high school.

American educational rhetoric does invoke "the whole child," does   36
seek "self-expression," and does promote emotional engagement in "discovery learning." But Japanese teaching style, at least in primary schools, effectively employs an engaging, challenging teaching style that surpasses most American attempts. In the cubing class, I was struck by the spontaneity, excitement, and (to American eyes) "unruly" dedication of the children to the new idea, and impressed with the teacher's ability to create this positive mood. It could be a cultural difference: We usually separate cognition and emotional affect, and then devise artificial means of reintroducing "feeling" into learning. It is rather like the way canned fruit juices are produced—first denatured by the preserving process and then topped up with chemical vitamins to replace what was lost.

The Role of Competition

The frequent accusation that Japanese education involves children in hellish competition must also be examined. In the elementary school classroom, competition is negotiated by means of the *han*. The educational system tries to accommodate both the ideology of harmony and the interest in hierarchy and ranking. The introduction of graded, competitive Western modes of education into societies where minimizing differences between people is valued has often produced severe social and psychological dislocation (as in Africa and other parts of the Third World). In Japan, the importance of the modern educational system as a talent selector and the need to preserve harmony and homogeneity have produced complementary rather than conflicting forces. The regular classroom is a place where the individual does not stick out, but where individual needs are met and goals are set. Children are not held back nor advanced by ability: the cohesion of the age group is said to be more important. Teachers focus on pulling up the slower learners, rather than tracking the class to suit different abilities. For the most part, teachers and the school system refuse to engage in examination preparation hysteria. Part of the reason for this is pressure from the Teachers' Union, a very large and powerful labor union which consistently resists any moves away from the egalitarian and undifferentiating mode of learning. Turning teachers into drill instructors is said to be dehumanizing, and the process of cramming a poor substitute for education.

So where is the competitive selection principle served? In the *juku*. *Juku* are tough competitive classes, often with up to 500 in one lecture hall. The most prestigious are themselves very selective and there are examinations (and preparation courses for these) to enter the *juku*. Some *juku* specialize in particular universities' entrance exams, and they will boast of their rate of admission into their universities. It is estimated that one third of all primary school students and one half of all secondary school students attend *juku*, but in Tokyo the rate rises to 86 percent of junior high school students. The "king of *juku*," Furukawa Noboru, the creator of a vast chain of such classes, says that *juku* are necessary to bridge the gap of present realities in Japan. He says that public schools do not face the fact of competition, and that ignoring the reality does not help children. The Ministry of Education usually ignores this non-accredited alternative and complementary system, and permits this functional division to take the pressure off the public schools. While there is considerable grumbling by parents, and while it is clear that the *juku* introduce an inegalitarian element into the process of schooling (since they do cost money), they do, by their separation from the regular school, permit the persistence of more traditional modes of learning, while allowing for a fast track in the examinations.

It is important to note that in Japan there really is only one moment of critical importance to one's career chances—the entrance examination to college. There are few opportunities to change paths or retool. Americans' belief that one can be recreated at any time in life, that the self-made person can get ahead, simply is not possible in Japan—thus the intense focus on examinations.

The Problems—In Context

This rapid tour through the Japanese educational system cannot neglect the problems. However, two things must be kept in mind when considering these well-publicized difficulties: One is that although problems do exist, the statistical reality is that, compared to the West, Japan still looks very good indeed. The other is that the Japanese themselves tend to be quite critical, and educational problems are given attention. But this attention should be seen in context: Not that people are not truly concerned about real problems, but that the anxiety seems related to a sense of national insecurity. The Japanese focus on educational issues may emanate from a sense of the importance of intellectual development in a society where there are few other resources. Any educational problem seems to put the nation truly at risk.

Japanese parents are critical and watchful of the schools and are not complacent about their children's successes. There was a telling example of this in a recent comparative study of American and Japanese education. Mothers in Minneapolis and in Sendai, roughly comparable cities, were asked to evaluate their children's school experiences. The Minneapolis mothers consistently answered that the schools were fine and that their children were doing well, while the Sendai mothers were very critical of their schools and worried that their children were not

40

performing up to potential. Whose children were, in objective tests, doing better? The Sendai group—in fact so much better that the poorest performer in the Japanese group was well ahead of the best in the American group. Mothers in Japan and the U.S. have very different perspectives on performance: Japanese mothers attribute failure to lack of effort while American mothers explain it as lack of ability. Japanese children have an external standard of excellence to which they can aspire, while an American child normally can only say he will "do his best."

Problems have surfaced, of course. Psychotherapists report a syndrome among children related to school and examination pressure. School phobia, psychosomatic symptoms, and juvenile suicide are most frequently reported. Japan does lead the world in school-related suicides for the 15- to 19-year old age group, at about 300 per year. Recently, the "battered teacher" and "battered parent" syndromes have received much attention. There are cases where teenagers have attacked or killed parents and teachers, and these have been related to examination pressure. The numbers involved in these cases are very small—at least in comparison with American delinquency patterns and other juvenile pathologies. Dropouts, drug use, and violent juvenile crimes are almost non-existent in Japan. The crimes reported in one year among school-age children in Osaka, for example, are equal to those reported in one day in New York.

Criticism leveled at Japanese education by Western observers focuses on what they regard as a suppression of genius and individuality, and a lack of attention to the development of creativity in children. The first may indeed be a problem—for the geniuses—because there is little provision for tracking them to their best advantage. There has been discussion of introducing tracking so that individual ability can be better served, but this has not been implemented. The superbright may indeed be disadvantaged.

On the other hand, creativity and innovation *are* encouraged, but   44 their manifestations may be different from those an American observer would expect. We must look at our own assumptions, to see if they are too limited. Americans see creativity in children as a fragile blossom that is stifled by rigid educational systems or adult standards. Creativity involves a necessary break with traditional content and methods, and implies the creation of a new idea or artifact. Whether creativity is in the child or in the teaching, and how it is to be measured, are questions no one has answered satisfactorily. Why we emphasize it is another question, probably related to our theories of progress and the importance we attach to unique accomplishments that push society forward. The fact is that, if anything, our schools do less to encourage creativity than do the Japanese, especially in the arts. All children in Japan learn two instruments and how to read music in elementary school, have regular drawing and painting classes, and work in small groups to create projects they themselves devise. It is true, though, that if everyone must be a soloist or composer to be considered creative, then most Japanese are not encouraged to be creative.

It is not enough to claim that the Japanese have been successful in training children to take exams at the expense of a broader education. And it is not at all appropriate to say that they are unable to develop children's individuality and create the geniuses who make scientific breakthroughs. The first is untrue and the second remains to be shown as false by the Japanese themselves, who are now mobilizing to produce more scientists and technologists. In fact, the scales are tipped in favor of Japan, and to represent it otherwise would be a distortion.

The success of the Japanese model has led to its use in other rapidly developing countries, including South Korea, Taiwan, and Singapore. There, education is seen as the linchpin for development, and attention to children has meant the allocation of considerable resources to schools. The results are similar to those seen in Japanese schools: highly motivated, hard-working students who like school and who have achieved very high scores on international achievement tests.

Seeing Ourselves through Japanese Eyes

What *America* can learn from Japan is rather an open question. We can, to begin with, learn more *about* Japan, and in doing so, learn more about ourselves. Japanese advancements of the past 20 years were based on American principles of productivity (such as "quality control"), not on samurai management skills and zen austerities. Looking for Japanese secrets, or worse, protesting that they are inhuman or unfair, will not get us very far. They have shown they can adjust programs and policies to the needs and resources of the times; we must do the same. We need to regain the scientific literacy we lost and reacquire the concrete skills and participatory techniques we need. We should see Japan as establishing a new standard, not as a model to be emulated. To match that standard we have to aim at general excellence, develop a long-term view, and act consistently over time with regard to our children's education.

Topics for Critical Thinking and Writing

1. In paragraph 4 White contrasts Japanese commitment to education with our own. Where in our society might one look for evidence of commitment or lack of commitment to education?
2. In paragraph 5 White lists many "clear advantages to being a Japanese child." Considering your education, or any other grounds you choose, which of these "advantages" would you like to have? Are there any you would gladly do without? Can you explain why? How many of the Japanese advantages appear to be dependent on the first that White lists, "a homogeneous population"? Are you aware of advantages to growing up in a heterogeneous population? (For an explanation of Japanese homogeneity, see paragraph 16.)
3. At the end of paragraph 6 White says that "the Japanese think a major function of education is the development of a happy, engaged, and

secure child, able to work hard and cooperate with others." Complete the following sentence: "Americans think a major function of education is. . . ."

4. In paragraph 11 White discusses the amount of time Japanese students spend on homework. What were your own experiences with home- work? Did homework contribute significantly to your education? Were there assignments you now regard as counterproductive?

5. In paragraph 13 White says that computers do not play a large role in Japanese schools. If computers played a fairly large role in your educa- tion, what do you think you learned from them, aside from how to operate them?

6. In paragraph 18 White reports that Japanese teachers are highly quali- fied. Do you think that, on the whole, your high school teachers were highly qualified? If you were able to do so, what measures would you take to insure well-qualified teachers in *all* American high schools? (White's paragraph 19 may provide some ideas.)

7. In paragraph 32 White briefly describes a math class about to study cubing. Does the procedure followed in the class strike you as being of any value? Why or why not? And what about the procedure described in the next paragraph? (In thinking about this, consider also White's comments in paragraphs 34–35). Looking back at a class in which you learned a good deal, what "elements of pedagogy" (White's words, paragraph 32) made the class successful?

8. In paragraph 37 White says that children in Japanese schools are almost never held back or advanced because of ability, and there is no tracking system. What do you think of this system? (Consider also para- graphs 43 and 44.)

9. In paragraph 39 White writes of the belief of Americans that "one can be recreated at any time in life, that the self-made person can get ahead." To what extent do you share these beliefs? To what extent did the schools you attended promote them?

10. Japan has produced relatively few winners of the Nobel Prize. Did White's essay help you to understand why this might be so? Do you take the lack of Nobel Prize winners to be a significant criticism of the Japanese educational system?

11. Given the great differences between our societies, what, if anything, do you think our educational system can learn from the Japanese system? (For example, we are far less homogeneous. And the mothers in our society often hold paying jobs, whereas few Japanese mothers do. Fur- ther, two thirds of our teenagers hold part-time jobs, whereas almost no Japanese teenagers hold jobs.)

Theodore Sizer

Theodore Sizer, born in New Haven in 1937, was educated at Yale and Harvard. After serving from 1964 to 1972 as dean of the Harvard Graduate School of Education, he served as head-master of Phillips Academy, Andover. In 1981 and 1982 he visited some fifty secondary schools, preparing to write Horace's Compromise, *the book from which our selection is taken. (The title refers to an imaginary or composite teacher named Horace, who finds that he must compromise on his job.)*

Principals' Questions

As I traveled among schools, their principals pressed me with questions, many of which were practical, specific.

What's your curriculum? . . . What subjects should be offered? they asked.

I replied: Let's not start with subjects; that usually leads us into the swamp called "coverage." What counts are positive answers to three questions: Can graduates of this high school teach themselves? Are they decent people? Can they effectively use the principal ways of looking at the world, ways represented by the major and tradition academic disciplines?

What do you mean, "teach themselves"?   4

Learning how to observe and analyze a situation or problem and being able to make sense of it, use it, criticize it, reject or accept it. This is more than simple "problem-solving," since many of the enriching things in life are not, in fact, problems. "Teaching oneself" is nothing more than knowing how to inform and enrich oneself. Ideally a school would like not only to equip a student with those skills, but also to inspire him or her to use them.

How is this done?

By directly giving students the task of teaching themselves and help-ing them with it. It means providing fewer answers and insisting that stu-dents find the right (or at least defensible) answers themselves. It means that teachers must focus more on *how* kids think than on what they think.

This will take lots of time.   8

Yes, indeed. There will be far less opportunity for teachers to tell things, and, as a result, less coverage, of fewer subject areas. Of course, ultimately it means more coverage because the student is able to learn on his or her own.

Which fewer areas? Be specific.

I will, but with the clear understanding that there is no One Best Curriculum for all schools. While we all have to agree on some general outcomes that give meaning to the high school diploma, the means to these outcomes must be kept flexible. No two schools will or should have precisely the same characteristics; wise diversity is *essential* for quality. Furthermore, top-down edicts about "what" and "how" demonstrably do not work. Each school must find its own way, and in so doing gain the energy that such a search provides.

Let me give you the beginnings of one model. I would organize a   12
high school into four areas or large departments:

1. Inquiry and Expression
2. Mathematics and Science
3. Literature and the Arts
4. Philosophy and History

You will immediately note that "English," that pivotally important but often misconstrued or even unconstrued "subject," would disappear. By "expression," I mean all kinds of communication, but above all writing, the litmus paper of thought. Some of "communication" is brute skill, such as the use of a keyboard (that sine qua non for the modern citizen) and clear, if rudimentary handwriting. Visual communication is included, as are gesture and physical nuance and tone, those tools used so powerfully by such masters as Winston Churchill and Ronald Reagan. A teacher cannot ascertain a student's thought processes unless they are expressed.

Mathematics is the language of science, the language of certainties. Science, of course, is full of uncertainty, as is much of higher mathematics, but for beginners it is the certainties that dominate. Number systems work in certain ways. Axioms hold. The pituitary gland secretes certain hormones; if it fails to do so, predictable consequences ensue. The world around us has its share of certainties, and we should learn about them, learn to be masters of them. Basic arithmetic, algebra, some geometry and statistics, physics and biology, are the keys. I would merge the traditional departments of mathematics and science, thus forcing coordination of the real and abstract worlds of certainty. The fresh, modern necessity for study in computer science can be the first bit of glue in this process of collaboration; that subject nicely straddles both areas.

Human expression cuts across written and spoken languages, theater, song, and visual art. There is much common ground in these attempts of man and woman to explain their predicament, yet English, music, and art usually proceed in as much splendid isolation as do mathematics and science. This is wasteful, as aesthetic expression and learning from others' attempts to find meaning are of a piece. All need representation and benefit from an alliance.

History, if it is responsibly taught, is perhaps the most difficult subject for most high school students, because it involves the abstraction of time past. One often can engage it well first through autobiography and then through biography, proceeding finally to the "biographies" of communities, which make up most conventional history. Things were as they were for reasons, and from these incidents evolve concepts in geography, economics, and sociology. For most students at this stage, these disciplines should remain the handmaidens of history. The exception is philosophy, particularly moral and political philosophy. A political philosophy, essentially that associated with American constitutionalism, is the bedrock of enlightened democratic citizenship, and adolescence, more than any other stage of life, is filled with a search for values. The study of elementary ethics, for example, not only provides excellent opportunities for learning intellectual skills, but also powerfully engages students' interest.

Why so few subjects?   16

There are several reasons. One is to lessen the splintered view of knowledge that usually confronts high school students. Their world rarely uses the fine distinctions between academic disciplines; insisting on them confuses young scholars. A second serves teachers: strict specialization hobbles much skill training. Good coaching cuts across academic specializations. The current organization is very wasteful. A third reason: a few areas, taught in large time blocks, greatly reduce both the scheduling problems and the frenetic quality of the school day. Finally, more broadly and sensibly construed subject areas allow greater scope for teachers.

Won't students want electives?

Yes, in that they will want opportunities to study what interests them and what helps them. However, this personalization can be well accommodated *within* each broad area, rather than through a smorgasbord of unrelated courses.

This sounds deadly, very academic and removed from kids' lives.   20

It sounds deadly because it has often been taught in deadly ways. I am regularly assaulted for being an "elitist" for proposing this program, yet no critic will argue, when I press him, that any of the objectives I put forward is inappropriate for every adolescent. A teacher must start where the students are—and this may *not* be chapter one in the textbook. One works to engage each student, to get him or her to experience some aspect of an area, and to feel that experience to be successful. It takes time, ingenuity, patience. Most difficult to reach will be the demoralized youngsters, the ones who see school as a hostile place. Many of these students come from low-income families. They will need special attention and classes that use extensive coaching—not only to help them gain the skills they often lack but also to promote some fresh self-assurance in them. Vast classes heavy with lecturing must be avoided.

You've left out physical education and vocational education.

Let's start with physical education. Much of what happens in schools today under that rubric is neither education (or at best is disconnected applied biology) nor very physical (thirty minutes once a week playing volleyball does not mean much, except perhaps as a useful vent for built-up adolescent steam). Citizens should know about their bodies and be taught that the need for exercise is a good thing. These are worthy topics for a good science-mathematics area to present.

The same kind of argument can be made for vocational education.   24
Specific job training is a good thing, but not at the expense of a school's core. The best place to learn most jobs is on site. The common exception is business education, most prominently training for secretarial positions. The important points are ability to type and, beyond that, being

well informed, literate, and able to handle numbers. If typing is a schoolwide requirement, and the other skills the inevitable consequence of the student's taking the core topics, the exception is moot.

Two more points about vocational education: tomorrow's economy will be volatile and dependent on flexible workers with a high level of intellectual skills. Thus, the best vocational education will be one in general education in the use of one's mind. Second, we must remember that most of today's high school students are or wish to be in the labor market. As the age cohort shrinks, the demand for its labor in most communities will grow. Educators are not going to reverse this trend; it will be better if they seize it, and adapt schools in demanding, sensible ways to the reality of adolescent employment. Working per se can be good for adolescents.

All that may be true in the abstract. But the fact remains that you'll lose a lot of kids if you cut out voc ed and athletics.

No, not necessarily. Remember that but a small minority of high school students are significantly involved in vocational education and interscholastic athletics. Furthermore, to the extent that these activities form a bridge to the central subjects, I'm for them. Unfortunately, today in many schools they have a life of their own, at the expense of an education in mind and character.

What of foreign language?   28

The cry for its requirement in schooling is abroad in the land as a cure for American isolation and chauvinism. For many adolescents, such study has merit; for others, little sense. If you cannot master your own language, it is inefficient to start another. If you have little immediate need to use a second language, the time spent in learning it is largely wasted—unless that "foreign" language is English. An absolute requirement for study of a foreign tongue can divert from other topics time that is crucial for a particularly needy student. The issue of ethnocentrism is more important than language study and must be addressed through the history courses.

What of bilingual education?

Ideally, all Americans should enjoy it—but the real problem is that of non-English speaking students. They should be immersed in English intensively. Their nonlinguistic studies should continue—for no longer than necessary—in their mother tongues. Their self-confidence, often associated with their facility in language, should be reinforced. Empathy and patience are crucial here; rigid formulae passed down from central authorities *guarantee* inefficiency and frustration. The goal is confident youngsters, adept and effectively fluent in two languages.

I'm still skeptical about your overall plan. You can pull this off only if you   32 had none but highly motivated students in your school. What of tracking and the turned-off student?

Just as now, some kids won't hook in; I know that. If they've shown themselves competent in the minima of literacy, numeracy, and civic understanding, let them leave high school—with the promise that they can come back in the future. The community college system in many regions makes this an easy alternative.

In addition, there are the troublemakers, the kids who don't want necessarily to leave school, but want just to stay there because it's fun, where their friends are. Of course, good teachers can work with them to try to change their attitudes. However, if they disrupt, they should be expelled, with the same opportunities to return later as all dropouts have. As long as they have met the state's requirements, no one should force them into school. Ideally, too, they should have a variety of programs from which to choose. Highly personalized alternative programs have frequently worked for this sort of student.

As to tracking: there would be none and there would be a great deal. Every student would be enrolled in each subject area all the time. There would therefore be none of the current tracks, usually called honors, college preparatory, general, technical, and so forth. But within each subject area, the students would progress at their own pace. This would create multiple tracks, ones that are flexible and that put no child in any dead end.

That will be very messy.   36

Yes, it will. Learning is messy. It can be handled if the units (separate high schools, or "houses" within high schools) are kept small enough to allow a particular group of teachers to know particular students well and develop a track for each. Class patterns will vary by need, some larger for telling, some smaller for coaching and questioning. Students will be working much more on their own than they do now; there will be no strict age grading. One learns how to learn by experience, not by being told things.

Won't this add financial cost?

Some, perhaps. It need not, as long as schools retreat from the objective of "comprehensiveness" and concentrate on classroom teaching. There are models of "zero-based budgets" which demonstrate that schools, if simply organized, can have well-paid faculty and fewer than eighty students per teacher, without increasing current per-pupil expenditure.

You haven't mentioned guidance counselors.   40

Counselors today act either as administrators, arranging schedules and job and college interviews and the like, or as teachers, coaching and questioning young people about their personal concerns. Good teachers *are* good counselors, in that second sense; students turn to them for help, whether or not their titles identify them as "guidance" people. Most high school guidance departments are overloaded with obligations, many of which are contradictory—for example, serving both as a place where students can obtain confidential personal counsel and as a disciplinary arm of the school (perhaps running the "inschool suspension" program for students who have repeatedly broken rules).

A decentralized school with small academic units has less need for specialized counseling offices; improved faculty-student ratios make this possible. The administrative obligations now traditionally handled by such offices can be placed directly under the principal. Staff members who are well trained in counseling and testing skills can support the teachers in each small academic unit.

We are being asked often these days about "computer literacy" and the needs of a "new technological society." How does your plan address these areas?

Computers, like calculators, books, and other familiar products of technology, should be welcomed by schools. Well used, they might significantly extend teachers' coaching efforts as well as help students learn. While we should learn to employ the products of the new technologies, we should keep in mind two critical points: it is up to us to select the data to be put into them, and we must choose with care the uses we put them to. 44

Should public schools formally provide time for voluntary prayer?

No. There is ample time and opportunity outside school for religious observances. Furthermore, the fact that public schools would not set time aside for prayer does not imply rejection of its importance. Schools should not claim to be comprehensive, arrogating to their routines every consequential aspect of an adolescent's life. High schools are limited to helping adolescents use their minds well—and this includes becoming thoughtful and decent people.

What of standards?

The existence of final "exhibitions" by students as a condition to receiving their diplomas will give teachers a much greater control of standards than they currently have. These standards, combined with a variety of external examinations, such as the Advanced Placement Examinations of the College Board, Regents' Examinations in some states, and, it is hoped, a growing list of other instruments that a school or an individual student could adopt or take voluntarily, would give outside authorities, like regional accrediting agencies, a good sense of the quality of work being done. 48

A lot turns on those teachers. Are they good enough?

They've got to be.

Remedies like all these are neat, but abstractions, castles in the air. Seeing adolescents in classrooms reminds one that, in substantial measure, school is *their* castle, that they have to want to build it.

I arrived by car at the school at 7:15 A.M., thirty minutes before the first bell. It was a cool day, and the first arrivals to the large high school I was visiting were gathered in clots in the sun outside, around the low, meandering structures that housed their classrooms. Parking lots and hard-used lawns encircled the buildings. There were no sidewalks in this neighborhood, even though it was quite built up; the school prop- 52 erty was ringed by small houses and business establishments. Everyone came to school by bus or by private car.

I turned into one of the driveways leading toward what appeared to be the school's central building and was immediately bounced out of the seat of my rented Datsun by the first of a series of asphalt bumps in the road. These barriers, it was painfully obvious, were there to slow down the dozens of vehicles that used the driveway and were already lined up in the lots next to the school, row on row of loyal steel beasts tethered by this pedagogical water hole. I found a place and parked.

It was immediately clear from the stares I received from nearby students that I picked a student lot, not one for staff or for visitors. Since it seemed to me large enough to accommodate one more little car, I left the Datsun where it was. It was ridiculously out of place, surrounded by pickup trucks, high on their springs and mud spattered, and by jalopies, late sixties' Chevrolets, old Ford Mustangs, Plymouth Satellites, each cumbrously settled upon great oversize rear tires. While all appeared poised, snouts down, to roar purposefully off to God knows where, for the moment they simply cowered here, submissive. Their masters and mistresses leaned against them or sat on them, chatting. Many drank coffee out of paper cups. Some smoked furtively as I drew near; though unfamiliar to them, I was wearing the drab coat-tie-slacks uniform of the school administrator who might admonish them.

My first instinct was to snicker at the parking lot scene. It was an eighties' version of an *American Graffiti* strip, indeed an overdrawn one, because the dusty trucks and drag-equipped cars were grotesquely numerous. My condescension disappeared, however, when I paid more attention to the students gathered around these vehicles, kids observing the visitor who had taken a space on their turf. Their attitude was in no way menacing, but it was freighted with an absence of interest. I was an object to be observed and, if they were smoking, to be mildly reacted to. Beyond that, I might have been a bird in the vast aviary of a boring zoo; I was a piece of the scenery, glimpsed as part of hanging out before school. None of these kids was playing principal's pet by coming up and asking me whether I needed help or directions to the office, but no one hassled me, either. The human confrontation was neutral, nearly nonexistent.

These were older students, drivers. In their easy chatting among 56 themselves, in their self-absorption and nonchalance, they showed self-assurance bordering on truculence. They had their own world.

My reaction was nervousness. I tried to smile a sorry-fellas-but-I-didn't-know-where-the-visitors'-parking-lot-was message, but it did not come off. I felt the awkward outsider, at distance from these composed young people. Even as I knew that at the bell they would enter the buildings and engage in the rituals of dutiful school-going and that they would get more boisterous and engaging as the early morning mist over their spirits parted, I also knew that these were considerable people, ones who would play the game adult educators asked them to play only when and how they wanted to. The fact that many of them, for a host of reasons, chose to go along with the structures of the school did not lessen the force of the observation: they possessed the autonomous power not to.

In this sense, kids run schools. Their apparent acquiescence to what their elders want them to do is always provisional. Their ability to undermine even the illusions of certain adult authority and of an expectation of deference was admirably if benignly displayed by the students on the parking lot. A less benign challenge can be made by students in any classroom when, for whatever reason, they collectively, quietly, but assuredly decide to say no. The fact that most go along with the system masks the nascent power that students hold. Few adults outside the teaching profession understand this.

The evening before, I had met the superintendent of this school district. He was a man of great force and national reputation. His administration ran the district with efficiency and closely centralized authority. In talking of his work, we had both used the ready metaphors of schoolkeeping, most turning around an image of old folk (the teachers) passing something of self-evident importance to young folk (the students). This morning all of these metaphors seemed naïve. All assumed the young student to be a passive receptacle or, at the least, a supplicant for knowledge. The adolescents in that parking lot were neither passive nor suppliant. However much we adults may want them to be eagerly receptive and respectful of our agenda for their schooling, the choice to be that or something else—neutral, hostile, inattentive—was unequivocally theirs. If we want our well-intentioned plans to succeed, we'll have to *inspire* the adolescents to join in them—inspire even the sullen, uninterested kids one sees in parking lots at the start of a school day.

The vision of school as an uncomplicated place where teachers pass   60
along the torch of knowledge to eager students is sadly innocent.

Topics for Critical Thinking and Writing

1. Sizer's essay seems to be divided into two parts, the second part beginning with paragraph 51. What is the connection between the second part and the first? Why do you think Sizer included the second part?
2. In paragraph 5 Sizer asserts that a good high school education teaches students "to observe and analyze a situation or problem" and "to make sense of it, use it, criticize it, reject or accept it." Do you think that your high school had such goals? Did some or all of your courses seek to produce such students? If at least one course or one instructor had such goals, discuss the methods of the course or of the instructor, or both. Sizer himself gives his ideas about how these skills can be taught. Does his formula apply to your experience?

3. Sizer says in paragraph 11 that "there is no One Best Curriculum for all schools." Why can't it be argued that since all students will face the responsibility of being informed citizens, a single curriculum (for instance, so many years of American history, so many years of other history, so many years of science, or literature, and so forth) makes sense for all—for males and females, farmers and city dwellers—in short, at least for all who speak English and who are not mentally handicapped?
4. Sizer, in paragraph 12, characterizes writing as "the litmus paper of thought." What does this mean?
5. In paragraph 13 Sizer proposes merging "the traditional departments of mathematics and science, thus forcing coordination of the real and abstract worlds of certainty." Drawing on your experience of science and mathematics in high school, write an essay of 750–1000 words imagining and evaluating the results of such a merger in your high school. Or, thinking of Sizer's remark (paragraph 14) that "English, music, and art usually proceed in . . . splendid isolation," imagine and evaluate a course in which two or perhaps all three of these were combined.
6. Taking into account Sizer's remarks on history (paragraph 15), evaluate the study of history in your high school.

William Severini Kowinski

William Severini Kowinski (b. 1946), a freelance writer who lives in Greensburg, Pennsylvania, has published essays in many newspapers and magazines. We reprint an excerpt from his book, The Malling of America *(1985).*

Kids in the Mall
Growing Up Controlled

Butch heaved himself up and loomed over the group. "Like it was different for me," he piped. "My folks used to drop me off at the shopping mall every morning and leave me all day. It was like a big free baby-sitter, you know? One night they never came back for me. Maybe they moved away. Maybe there's some kind of a Bureau of Missing Parents I could check with."

—Richard Peck
Secrets of the Shopping Mall,
a novel for teenagers

From his sister at Swarthmore, I'd heard about a kid in Florida whose mother picked him up after school every day, drove him straight to the mall, and left him there until it closed—all at his insistence. I'd heard about a boy in Washington who, when his family moved from one suburb to another, pedaled his bicycle five miles every day to get back to his old mall, where he once belonged.

These stories aren't unusual. The mall is a common experience for the majority of American youth; they have probably been going there all their lives. Some ran within their first large open space, saw their first fountain, bought their first toy, and read their first book in a mall. They may have smoked their first cigarette or first joint, or turned them down, had their first kiss or lost their virginity in the mall parking lot. Teenagers in America now spend more time in the mall than anywhere else but home and school. Mostly it is their choice, but some of that mall time is put in as the result of two-paycheck and single-parent households, and the lack of other viable alternatives. But are these kids being harmed by the mall?

I wondered first of all what difference it makes for adolescents to experience so many important moments in the mall. They are, after all, at play in the fields of its little world and they learn its ways; they adapt to it and make it adapt to them. It's here that these kids get their street sense, only it's mall sense. They are learning the ways of a large-scale, artificial environment; its subtleties and flexibilities, its particular pleasures and resonances, and the attitudes it fosters.

The presence of so many teenagers for so much time was not something mall developers planned on. In fact, it came as a big surprise. But kids became a fact of mall life very easily, and the International Council of Shopping Centers found it necessary to commission a study, which they published along with a guide to mall managers on how to handle the teenage incursion.   4

The study found that "teenagers in suburban centers are bored and come to the shopping centers mainly as a place to go. Teenagers in suburban centers spent more time fighting, drinking, littering and walking than did their urban counterparts, but presented fewer overall problems." The report observed that "adolescents congregated in groups of two to four and predominantly at locations selected by them rather than management." This probably had something to do with the decision to install game arcades, which allow management to channel these restless adolescents into naturally contained areas away from major traffic points of adult shoppers.

The guide concluded that mall management should tolerate and even encourage the teenage presence because, in the words of the report. "The vast majority support the same set of values as does shopping center management." *The same set of values* means simply that mall kids are already preprogrammed to be consumers and that the mall can put the finishing touches to them as hard-core, life-long shoppers just like everybody else. That, after all, is what the mall is about. So it shouldn't be surprising that in spending a lot of time there, adolescents find little that challenges the assumption that the goal of life is to make money and buy products, or that just about everything else in life is to be used to serve those ends.

Growing up in a high-consumption society already adds inestimable pressure to kids' lives. Clothes consciousness has invaded the grade schools, and popularity is linked with having the best, newest clothes in the currently acceptable styles. Even what they read has been affected. "Miss [Nancy] Drew wasn't obsessed with her wardrobe," noted the *Wall Street Journal.* "But today the mystery in teen fiction for girls is what outfit the heroine will wear next." Shopping has become a survival skill and there is certainly no better place to learn it than the mall, where its importance is powerfully reinforced and certainly never questioned.

The mall as a university of suburban materialism, where Valley   8
Girls and Boys from coast to coast are educated in consumption, has its other lessons in this era of change in family life and sexual mores and their economic and social ramifications. The plethora of products in the mall, plus the pressure on teens to buy them, may contribute to the phenomenon that psychologist David Elkind calls "the hurried child": kids who are exposed to too much of the adult world too quickly and must respond with a sophistication that belies their still-tender emotional development. Certainly the adult products marketed for children—form-fitting designer jeans, sexy tops for preteen girls—add to the social pressure to look like an adult, along with the home-grown need to understand adult finances (why mothers must work) and adult emotions (when parents divorce).

Kids spend so much time at the mall partly because their parents allow it and even encourage it. The mall is safe, doesn't seem to harbor any unsavory activities, and there is adult supervision; it is, after all, a controlled environment. So the temptation, especially for working parents, is to let the mall be their baby-sitter. At least the kids aren't watching TV. But the mall's role as a surrogate mother may be more extensive and more profound.

Karen Lansky, a writer living in Los Angeles, has looked into the subject, and she told me some of her conclusions about the effects on its teenaged denizens of the mall's controlled and controlling environment. "Structure is the dominant idea, since true 'mall rats' lack just that in their home lives," she said, "and adolescents about to make the big leap into growing up crave more structure than our modern society cares to acknowledge." Karen pointed out some of the elements malls supply that kids used to get from their families, like warmth (Strawberry Shortcake dolls and similar cute and cuddly merchandise), old-fashioned mothering ("We do it all for you," the fast-food slogan), and even home cooking (the "homemade" treats at the food court).

The problem in all this, as Karen Lansky sees it, is that while families nurture children by encouraging growth through the assumption of responsibility and then by letting them rest in the bosom of the family from the rigors of growing up, the mall as a structural mother encourages passivity and consumption, as long as the kid doesn't make trouble. Therefore all they learn about becoming adults is how to act and how to consume.

Kids are in the mall not only in the passive role of shoppers—they   12
also work there, especially as fast-food outlets infiltrate the mall's enclosure. There they learn how to hold a job and take responsibility, but still within the same value context. When *CBS Reports* went to Oak Park Mall in suburban Kansas City, Kansas, to tape part of their hour-long consideration of malls, "After the Dream Comes True," they interviewed a teenaged girl who worked in a fast-food outlet there. In a sequence that didn't make the final program, she described the major goal of her present life, which was to perfect the curl on top of the ice-cream cones that were her store's specialty. If she could do that, she would be moved from the lowly softdrink dispenser to the more prestigious ice-cream division, the curl on top of the status ladder at her restaurant. These are the achievements that are important at the mall.

Other benefits of such jobs may also be overrated, according to Laurence D. Steinberg of the University of California at Irvine's social ecology department, who did a study on teenage employment. Their jobs, he found, are generally simple, mindlessly repetitive and boring. They don't really learn anything, and the jobs don't lead anywhere. Teenagers also work primarily with other teenagers; even their supervisors are often just a little older than they are. "Kids need to spend time with adults." Steinberg told me. "Although they get benefits from peer relationships, without parents and other adults it's one-sided socialization. They hang out with each other, have age-segregated jobs, and watch TV."

Perhaps much of this is not so terrible or even so terribly different. Now that they have so much more to contend with in their lives, adolescents probably need more time to spend with other adolescents without adult impositions, just to sort things out. Though it is more concentrated in the mall (and therefore perhaps a clearer target), the value system there is really the dominant one of the whole society. Attitudes about curiosity, initiative, self-expression, empathy, and disinterested learning aren't necessarily made in the mall; they are mirrored there, perhaps a bit more intensely—as through a glass brightly.[1]

Besides, the mall is not without its educational opportunities. There are bookstores, where there is at least a short shelf of classics at great

---

[1]**As through a glass brightly.** In the New Testament in 1 Corinthians 13.12, Paul says, speaking of life on earth before the resurrection, "For now we see through a glass, darkly."

prices, and other books from which it is possible to learn more than how to do sit-ups. There are tools, from hammers to VCRs, and products, from clothes to records, that can help the young find and express themselves. There are older people with stories, and places to be alone or to talk one-on-one with a kindred spirit. And there is always the passing show.

The mall itself may very well be an education about the future. I was struck with the realization, as early as my first forays into Greengate, that the mall is only one of a number of enclosed and controlled environments that are part of the lives of today's young. The mall is just an extension, say, of those large suburban schools—only there's Karmelkorn instead of chem lab, the ice rink instead of the gym: It's high school without the impertinence of classes.   16

Growing up, moving from home to school to the mall—from enclosure to enclosure, transported in cars—is a curiously continuous process, without much in the way of contrast or contact with unenclosed reality. Places must tend to blur into one another. But whatever differences and dangers there are in this, the skills these adolescents are learning may turn out to be useful in their later lives. For we seem to be moving inexorably into an age of preplanned and regulated environments, and this is the world they will inherit.

Still, it might be better if they had more of a choice. One teenaged girl confessed to *CBS Reports* that she sometimes felt she was missing something by hanging out at the mall so much. "But I'm here," she said, "and this is what I have."

Topics for Critical Thinking and Writing

1. In his second paragraph Kowinski says: "The mall is a common experience for the majority of American youth: They have probably been going there all their lives." Do you find that going to the mall is a common experience? If your answer is "yes," how would you answer the question at the end of the paragraph? If your answer is "I don't know," perhaps because you have only recently immigrated here, describe the place in which adolescents do spend most of their time between school and home. If you can, answer a question you adapt from the one at the end of the paragraph.

2. In his third paragraph Kowinski asserts that young people learn at the mall "the ways of a large-scale, artificial environment: its subtleties and flexibilities, its particular pleasures and resonances, and the attitudes it fosters." Scanning the article again, what are the pleasures and the attitudes the mall fosters?

3. In paragraph 9 Kowinski says: "Kids spend so much time at the mall partly because their parents allow it and even encourage it. The mall is safe, doesn't seem to harbor any unsavory activities, and there is adult supervision; it is, after all, a controlled environment." Has Kowinski here

contradicted himself? (See paragraph 2.) If not, how do you reconcile his statements?
4.   In his next-to-last paragraph Kowinski says that adolescents "moving from home to school to the mall" are learning skills that "may turn out to be useful in their later lives." Do you agree with him here? Explain why or why not.

Mary Field Belenky, Blythe McVicker Clinchy, Nancy Rule Goldberger, and Jill Mattuck Tarule

Mary Belenky is an assistant research professor at the University of Vermont, Blythe Clinchy is a professor of psychology at Wellesley College, Nancy Goldberger is a visiting scholar in psychology at New York University, and Jill Tarule is an associate professor at Lesley College Graduate School. The essay printed here is part of Chapter 9 of their book, Women's Ways of Knowing, *a study of how women's intellectual abilities develop. (The title of the extract is the editors'.)*

How Women Learn

We begin with the reminiscences of two ordinary women, each recalling an hour during her first year at college. One of them, now middle-aged, remembered the first meeting of an introductory science course. The professor marched into the lecture hall, placed upon his desk a large jar filled with dried beans, and invited the students to guess how many beans the jar contained. After listening to an enthusiastic chorus of wildly inaccurate estimates the professor smiled a thin, dry smile, revealed the correct answer, and announced, "You have just learned an important lesson about science. Never trust the evidence of your own senses."

Thirty years later, the woman could guess what the professor had in mind. He saw himself, perhaps, as inviting his students to embark upon an exciting voyage into a mysterious underworld invisible to the naked eye, accessible only through scientific method and scientific instruments. But the seventeen-year-old girl could not accept or even hear the invitation. Her sense of herself as a knower was shaky, and it was based on the belief that she could use her own firsthand experience as a source of truth. This man was saying that this belief was fallacious. He was taking away her only tool for knowing and providing her with no substitute. "I remember feeling small and scared," the woman says, "and I did the only thing I could do. I dropped the course that afternoon, and I haven't gone near science since."

The second woman, in her first year at college, told a superficially similar but profoundly different story about a philosophy class she had attended just a month or two before the interview. The teacher came into class carrying a large cardboard cube. She placed it on the desk in front of her and asked the class what it was. They said it was a cube. She asked what a cube was, and they said a cube contained six equal square sides. She asked how they knew that this object contained six equal square sides. By looking at it, they said. "But how do you know?" the teacher asked again. She pointed to the side facing her and, therefore, invisible to the students; then she lifted the cube and pointed to the side that had been face down on the desk, and, therefore, also invisible. "We can't look at all six sides of a cube at once, can we? So we can't exactly *see* a cube. And yet, you're right. You know it's a cube. But you know it not just because you have eyes but because you have intelligence. You invent the sides you cannot see. You use your intelligence to create the 'truth' about cubes."

The student said to the interviewer,   4

> It blew my mind. You'll think I'm nuts, but I ran back to the dorm and I called my boyfriend and I said, "Listen, this is just incredible," and I told him all about it. I'm not sure he could see why I was so excited. I'm not sure I understand it myself. But I really felt, for the first time, like I was really in college, like I was—I don't know—sort of *grown up*.

Both stories are about the limitations of firsthand experience as a source of knowledge—we cannot simply see the truth about either the jar of beans or the cube—but there is a difference. We can know the truth about cubes. Indeed, the students did know it. As the science professor pointed out, the students were wrong about the beans; their senses had deceived them. But, as the philosophy teacher pointed out, the students were right about the cube; their minds had served them well.

The science professor was the only person in the room who knew how many beans were in that jar. Theoretically, the knowledge was available to the students; they could have counted the beans. But faced with that tedious prospect, most would doubtless take the professor's word for it. He is authority. They had to rely upon his knowledge rather than their own. On the other hand, every member of the philosophy class knew that the cube had six sides. They were all colleagues.

The science professor exercised his authority in a benign fashion, promising the students that he would provide them with the tools they needed to excavate invisible truths. Similarly, the philosophy teacher planned to teach her students the skills of philosophical analysis, but she was at pains to assure them that they already possessed the tools to construct some powerful truths. They had built cubes on their own, using only their own powers of inference, without the aid of elaborate procedures or fancy apparatus or even a teacher. Although a teacher might have told them once that a cube contained six equal square sides, they did not have to take the teacher's word for it; they could have easily verified it for themselves.

The lesson the science professor wanted to teach is that experience   8
is a source of error. Taught in isolation, this lesson diminished the student, rendering her dumb and dependent. The philosophy teacher's lesson was that although raw experience is insufficient, by reflecting upon it the student could arrive at truth. It was a lesson that made the student feel more powerful ("sort of grown up").

No doubt it is true that, as the professor in May Sarton's novel *The Small Room* says, the "art" of being a student requires humility. But the woman we interviewed did not find the science lesson humbling; she found it humiliating. Arrogance was not then and is not now her natural habitat. Like most of the women in our sample she lacked confidence in herself as a thinker; and the kind of learning the science teacher demanded was not only painful but crippling.

In thinking about the education of women, Adrienne Rich writes, "Suppose we were to ask ourselves, simply: What does a woman need to know?" A woman, like any other human being, does need to know that the mind makes mistakes; but our interviews have convinced us that every woman, regardless of age, social class, ethnicity, and academic achievement, needs to know that she is capable of intelligent thought, and she needs to know it right away. Perhaps men learn this lesson before going to college, or perhaps they can wait until they have proved themselves to hear it; we do not know. We do know that many of the women we interviewed had not yet learned it.

Topics for Critical Thinking and Writing

1. How is the professor in the first anecdote characterized? Look particularly at the words used in paragraphs 1 and 2 to describe him. How is the student characterized? Look back at the first sentence: Why do the writers use the word *ordinary* to describe both students? Why did they not simply say, "We begin with the reminiscences of two women"?

2. In paragraph 5 the writers say, "Both stories are about the limitations of firsthand experience as a source of knowledge." What else do the stories have in common? What are the important differences? What particular difference is most relevant to the main point of the essay?

3. Look again at paragraph 6. The science teacher is described as being "authority." The students "had to rely upon his knowledge rather than their own." Is this relationship between teacher and students more likely in science courses than in philosophy or literature courses? Is it inevitable in sciences courses? If so, why?

4.   What is the main point of the concluding paragraph? Do the two anec-
     dotes support this point? To what extent does your own experience
     confirm it or not confirm it?

Fan Shen

Fan Shen came to the United States from the People's Republic of China. A translator and writer, he also teaches at Rockland Community College in Suffern, New York.

The Classroom and the Wider Culture
Identity as a Key to Learning English Composition

One day in June 1975, when I walked into the aircraft factory where I was working as an electrician, I saw many large-letter
posters on the walls and many people parading around the workshops
shouting slogans like "Down with the word 'I'!" and "Trust in masses
and the Party!" I then remembered that a new political campaign called
"Against Individualism" was scheduled to begin that day. Ten years
later, I got back my first English composition paper at the University of
Nebraska—Lincoln. The professor's first comments were: "Why did
you always use 'we' instead of 'I'?" and "Your paper would be stronger
if you eliminated some sentences in the passive voice." The clashes
between my Chinese background and the requirements of English composition had begun. At the center of this mental struggle, which has
lasted several years and is still not completely over, is the prolonged,
uphill battle to recapture "myself."

In this paper I will try to describe and explore this experience of
reconciling my Chinese identity with an English identity dictated by
the rules of English composition. I want to show how my cultural background shaped—and shapes—my approaches to my writing in English
and how writing in English redefined—and redefines—my *ideological*
and *logical* identities. By "ideological identity" I mean the system of values that I acquired (consciously and unconsciously) from my social and
cultural background. And by "logical identity" I mean the natural (or
Oriental) way I organize and express my thoughts in writing. Both had
to be modified or redefined in learning English composition. Becoming
aware of the process of redefinition of these different identities is a
mode of learning that has helped me in my efforts to write in English,
and, I hope, will be of help to teachers of English composition in this
country. In presenting my case for this view, I will use examples from

both my composition courses and literature courses, for I believe that writing papers for both kinds of courses contributed to the development of my "English identity." Although what I will describe is based on personal experience, many Chinese students whom I talked to said that they had had the same or similar experiences in their initial stages of learning to write in English.

Identity of the Self: Ideological and Cultural

Starting with the first English paper I wrote, I found that learning to compose in English is not an isolated classroom activity, but a social and cultural experience. The rules of English composition encapsulate values that are absent in, or sometimes contradictory to, the values of other societies (in my case, China). Therefore, learning the rules of English composition is, to a certain extent, learning the values of Anglo-American society. In writing classes in the United States I found that I had to reprogram my mind, to redefine some of the basic concepts and values that I had about myself, about society, and about the universe, values that had been imprinted and reinforced in my mind by my cultural background, and that had been part of me all my life.

Rule number one in English composition is: Be yourself. (More than one composition instructor has told me, "Just write what *you* think.") The values behind this rule, it seems to me, are based on the principle of protecting and promoting individuality (and private property) in this country. The instruction was probably crystal clear to students raised on these values, but, as a guideline of composition, it was not very clear or useful to me when I first heard it. First of all, the image or meaning that I attached to the word "I" or "myself" was, as I found out, different from that of my English teacher. In China, "I" is always subordinated to "We"—be it the working class, the Party, the country, or some other collective body. Both political pressure and literary tradition require that "I" be somewhat hidden or buried in writings and speeches; presenting the "self" too obviously would give people the impression of being disrespectful of the Communist Party in political writings and boastful in scholarly writings. The word "I" has often been identified with another "bad" word, "individualism," which has become a synonym for selfishness in China. For a long time the words "self" and "individualism" have had negative connotations in my mind, and the negative force of the words naturally extended to the field of literary studies. As a result, even if I had brilliant ideas, the "I" in my papers always had to show some modesty by not competing with or trying to stand above the names of ancient and modern authoritative figures. Appealing to Mao or other Marxist authorities became the required way (as well as the most "forceful" or "persuasive" way) to prove one's point in written discourse. I remember that in China I had even committed what I can call "reversed plagiarism"—here, I

4

suppose it would be called "forgery"—when I was in middle school: willfully attributing some of my thoughts to "experts" when I needed some arguments but could not find a suitable quotation from a literary or political "giant."

Now, in America, I had to learn to accept the words "I" and "self" as something glorious (as Whitman did), or at least something not to be ashamed of or embarrassed about. It was the first and probably biggest step I took into English composition and critical writing. Acting upon my professor's suggestion, I intentionally tried to show my "individuality" and to "glorify" "I" in my papers by using as many "I's" as possible—"I think," "I believe," "I see"—and deliberately cut out quotations from authorities. It was rather painful to hand in such "pompous" (I mean immodest) papers to my instructors. But to an extent it worked. After a while I became more comfortable with only "the shadow of myself." I felt more at ease to put down *my* thoughts without looking over my shoulder to worry about the attitudes of my teachers or the reactions of the Party secretaries, and to speak out as "bluntly" and "immodestly" as my American instructors demanded.

But writing many "I's" was only the beginning of the process of redefining myself. Speaking of redefining myself is, in an important sense, speaking of redefining the word "I." By such a redefinition I mean not only the change in how I envisioned myself, but also the change in how *I* perceived the world. The old "I" used to embody only one set of values, but now it had to embody multiple sets of values. To be truly "myself," which I knew was a key to my success in learning English composition, meant *not to be my Chinese self* at all. That is to say, when I write in English I have to wrestle with and abandon (at least temporarily) the whole system of ideology which previously defined me in myself. I had to forget Marxist doctrines (even though I do not see myself as a Marxist by choice) and the Party lines imprinted in my mind and familiarize myself with a system of capitalist/bourgeois values. I had to put aside an ideology of collectivism and adopt the values of individualism. In composition as well as in literature classes, I had to make a fundamental adjustment: If I used to examine society and literary materials through the microscopes of Marxist dialectical materialism and historical materialism, I now had to learn to look through the microscopes the other way around, i.e., to learn to look at and understand the world from the point of view of "idealism." (I must add here that there are American professors who use a Marxist approach in their teaching.)

The word "idealism," which affects my view of both myself and the universe, is loaded with social connotations, and can serve as a good example of how redefining a key word can be a pivotal part of redefining my ideological identity as a whole.

To me, idealism is the philosophical foundation of the dictum of English composition: "Be yourself." In order to write good English, I   8 knew that I had to be myself, which actually meant not to be my Chinese self. It meant that I had to create an English self and be *that* self. And to be that English self, I felt, I had to understand and accept idealism the way a Westerner does. That is to say, I had to accept the way a Westerner sees himself in relation to the universe and society. On the one hand, I knew a lot about idealism. But on the other hand, I knew nothing about it. I mean I knew a lot about idealism through the propaganda and objections of its opponent, Marxism, but I knew little about it from its own point of view. When I thought of the word "materialism"—which is a major part of Marxism and in China has repeatedly been "shown" to be the absolute truth—there were always positive connotations, and words like "right," "true," etc., flashed in my mind. On the other hand, the word "idealism" always came to me with the dark connotations that surround words like "absurd," "illogical," "wrong," etc. In China "idealism" is depicted as a ferocious and ridiculous enemy of Marxist philosophy. Idealism, as the simplified definition imprinted in my mind had it, is the view that the material world does not exist; that all that exists is the mind and its ideas. It is just the opposite of Marxist dialectical materialism which sees the mind as a product of the material world. It is not too difficult to see that idealism, with its idea that mind is of primary importance, provides a philosophical foundation for the Western emphasis on the value of individual human minds, and hence individual human beings. Therefore, my final acceptance of myself as of primary importance—an importance that overshadowed that of authority figures in English composition—was, I decided, dependent on an acceptance of idealism.

My struggle with idealism came mainly from my efforts to understand and to write about works such as Coleridge's *Biographia Literaria* and Emerson's "Over-Soul." For a long time I was frustrated and puzzled by the idealism expressed by Coleridge and Emerson—given their ideas, such as "I think, therefore I am" (Coleridge obviously borrowed from Descartes) and "the transparent eyeball" (Emerson's view of himself)—because in my mind, drenched as it was in dialectical materialism, there was always a little voice whispering in my ear "You are, therefore you think." I could not see how human consciousness, which is not material, could create apples and trees. My intellectual conscience refused to let me believe that the human mind is the primary world and the material world secondary. Finally, I had to imagine that I was looking at a world with my head upside down. When I imagined that I was in a new body (born with the head upside down) it was easier to forget biases imprinted in my subconsciousness about idealism, the mind, and my former self. Starting from scratch, the new inverted self—which I called my "English Self" and into which I have transformed myself—could understand and *accept*, with ease, idealism as "the truth" and "himself" (i.e., my English Self) as the "creator" of the world.

Here is how I created my new "English Self." I played a "game" similar to ones played by mental therapists. First I made a list of (simplified) features about writing associated with my old identity (the Chinese Self), both ideological and logical, and then beside the first list I added a column of features about writing associated with my new identity (the English Self). After that I pictured myself getting out of my old identity, the timid, humble, modest Chinese "I," and creeping into my new identity (often in the form of a new skin or a mask), the confident, assertive, and aggressive English "I." The new "Self" helped me to remember and accept the different rules of Chinese and English composition and the values that underpin these rules. In a sense, creating an English Self is a way of reconciling my old cultural values with the new values required by English writing, without losing the former.

An interesting structural but not material parallel to my experiences in this regard has been well described by Min-zhan Lu in her important article, "From Silence to Words: Writing as Struggle" (*College English* 49 [April 1987]: 437–48). Min-zhan Lu talks about struggles between two selves, an open self and a secret self, and between two discourses, a mainstream Marxist discourse and a bourgeois discourse her parents wanted her to learn. But her struggle was different from mine. Her Chinese self was severely constrained and suppressed by mainstream cultural discourse, but never interfused with it. Her experiences, then, were not representative of those of the majority of the younger generation who, like me, were brought up on only one discourse. I came to English composition as a Chinese person, in the fullest sense of the term, with a Chinese identity already fully formed.

Identity of the Mind: Illogical and Alogical

In learning to write in English, besides wrestling with a different ideological system, I found that I had to wrestle with a logical system very different from the blueprint of logic at the back of my mind. By "logical system" I mean two things: the Chinese way of thinking I used to approach my theme or topic in written discourse, and the Chinese critical/logical way to develop a theme or topic. By English rules, the first is illogical, for it is the opposite of the English way of approaching a topic; the second is alogical (nonlogical), for it mainly uses mental pictures instead of words as a critical vehicle. 12

The Illogical Pattern In English composition, an essential rule for the logical organization of a piece of writing is the use of a "topic sentence." In Chinese composition, "from surface to core" is an essential rule, a rule which means that one ought to reach a topic gradually and "systematically" instead of "abruptly."

The concept of a topic sentence, it seems to me, is symbolic of the values of a busy people in an industrialized society, rushing to get things done, hoping to attract and satisfy the busy reader very quickly. Thinking back, I realized that I did not fully understand the virtue of the concept until my life began to rush at the speed of everyone else's in this country. Chinese composition, on the other hand, seems to embody the values of a leisurely paced rural society whose inhabitants have the time to chew and taste a topic slowly. In Chinese composition, an introduction explaining how and why one chooses this topic is not only acceptable, but often regarded as necessary. It arouses the reader's interest in the topic little by little (and this is seen as a virtue of composition) and gives him/her a sense of refinement. The famous Robert B. Kaplan "noodles" contrasting a spiral Oriental thought process with a straight-line Western approach ("Cultural Thought Patterns in Inter-Cultural Education," *Readings on English as a Second Language,* Ed. Kenneth Croft, 2nd ed., Winthrop, 1980, 403–10) may be too simplistic to capture the preferred pattern of writing in English, but I think they still express some truth about Oriental writing. A Chinese writer often clears the surrounding bushes before attacking the real target. This bush-clearing pattern in Chinese writing goes back two thousand years to Kong Fuzi (Confucius). Before doing anything, Kong says in his *Luen Yu (Analects),* one first needs to call things by their proper names (expressed by his phrase "Zheng Ming"). In other words, before touching one's main thesis, one should first state the "conditions" of composition: how, why, and when the piece is being composed. All of this will serve as a proper foundation on which to build the "house" of the piece. In the two thousand years after Kong, this principle of composition was gradually formalized (especially through the formal essays required by imperial examinations) and became known as "Ba Gu," or the eight-legged essay. The logic of Chinese composition, exemplified by the eight-legged essay, is like the peeling of an onion: Layer after layer is removed until the reader finally arrives at the central point, the core.

Ba Gu still influences modern Chinese writing. Carolyn Matalene has an excellent discussion of this logical (or illogical) structure and its influence on her Chinese students' efforts to write in English ("Contrastive Rhetoric: An American Writing Teacher in China," *College English* 47 [November 1985]: 789–808). A recent Chinese textbook for composition lists six essential steps (factors) for writing a narrative essay, steps to be taken in this order: time, place, character, event, cause, and consequence (*Yuwen Jichu Zhishi Liushi Jiang [Sixty Lessons on the Basics of the Chinese Language],* Ed. Beijing Research Institute of Education, Beijing Publishing House, 1981, 525–609). Most Chinese students (including me) are taught to follow this sequence in composition.

The straightforward approach to composition in English seemed to me, at first, illogical. One could not jump to the topic. One had to walk step by step to reach the topic. In several of my early papers I found that the Chinese approach—the bush-clearing approach—persisted, and I

16

had considerable difficulty writing (and in fact understanding) topic sentences. In what I deemed to be topic sentences, I grudgingly gave out themes. Today, those papers look to me like Chinese papers with forced or false English openings. For example, in a narrative paper on a trip to New York, I wrote the forced/false topic sentence, "A trip to New York in winter is boring." In the next few paragraphs, I talked about the weather, the people who went with me, and so on, before I talked about what I learned from the trip. My real thesis was that one could always learn something even on a boring trip.

The Alogical Pattern In learning English composition, I found that there was yet another cultural blueprint affecting my logical thinking. I found from my early papers that very often I was unconsciously under the influence of a Chinese critical approach called the creation of "yijing," which is totally non-Western. The direct translation of the word "yijing" is: yi, "mind or consciousness," and jing, "environment." An ancient approach which has existed in China for many centuries and is still the subject of much discussion, yijing is a complicated concept that defies a universal definition. But most critics in China nowadays seem to agree on one point, that yijing is the critical approach that separates Chinese literature and criticism from Western literature and criticism. Roughly speaking, yijing is the process of creating a pictorial environment while reading a piece of literature. Many critics in China believe that yijing is a creative process of inducing oneself, while reading a piece of literature or looking at a piece of art, to create mental pictures, in order to reach a unity of nature, the author, and the reader. Therefore, it is by its very nature both creative and critical. According to the theory, this nonverbal, pictorial process leads directly to a higher ground of beauty and morality. Almost all critics in China agree that yijing is not a process of logical thinking—it is not a process of moving from the premises of an argument to its conclusion, which is the foundation of Western criticism. According to yijing, the process of criticizing a piece of art or literary work has to involve the process of creation on the reader's part. In yijing, verbal thoughts and pictorial thoughts are one. Thinking is conducted largely in pictures and then "transcribed" into words. (Ezra Pound once tried to capture the creative aspect of yijing in poems such as "In a Station of the Metro." He also tried to capture the critical aspect of it in his theory of imagism and vorticism, even though he did not know the term "yijing.") One characteristic of the yijing approach to criticism, therefore, is that it often includes a description of the created mental pictures on the part of the reader/critic and his/her mental attempt to bridge (unite) the literary work, the pictures, with ultimate beauty and peace.

In looking back at my critical papers for various classes, I discovered that I unconsciously used the approach of yijing, especially in some of my earlier papers when I seemed not yet to have been in the grip of Western logical critical approaches. I wrote, for instance, an essay entitled "Wordsworth's Sound and Imagination: The Snowdon Episode." In the major part of the essay I described the pictures that flashed in my mind while I was reading passages in Wordsworth's long poem, *The Prelude.*

> I saw three climbers (myself among them) winding up the mountain in silence "at the dead of night," absorbed in their "private thoughts." The sky was full of blocks of clouds of different colors, freely changing their shapes, like oily pigments disturbed in a bucket of water. All of a sudden, the moonlight broke the darkness "like a flash," lighting up the mountain tops. Under the "naked moon,"' the band saw a vast sea of mist and vapor, a silent ocean. Then the silence was abruptly broken, and we heard the "roaring of waters, torrents, streams/Innumerable, roaring with one voice" from a "blue chasm," a fracture in the vapor of the sea. It was a joyful revelation of divine truth to the human mind: the bright, "naked" moon sheds the light of "higher reasons" and "spiritual love" upon us; the vast ocean of mist looked like a thin curtain through which we vaguely saw the infinity of nature beyond; and the sounds of roaring waters coming out of the chasm of vapor cast us into the boundless spring of imagination from the depth of the human heart. Evoked by the divine light from above, the human spring of imagination is joined by the natural spring and becomes a sustaining source of energy, feeding "upon infinity" while transcending infinity at the same time.

Here I was describing my own experience more than Wordsworth's. The picture described by the poet is taken over and developed by the reader. The imagination of the author and the imagination of the reader are thus joined together. There was no "because" or "therefore" in the paper. There was little *logic*. And I thought it was (and it is) criticism. This seems to me a typical (but simplified) example of the yijing approach. (Incidentally, the instructor, a kind professor, found the paper interesting, though a bit "strange.")

In another paper of mine, "The Note of Life: Williams's 'The   20 Orchestra'," I found myself describing my experiences of pictures of nature while reading William Carlos Williams's poem "The Orchestra." I "painted" these fleeting pictures and described the feelings that seemed to lead me to an understanding of a harmony, a "common tone," between man and nature. A paragraph from that paper reads:

> The poem first struck me as a musical fairy tale. With rich musical sounds in my ear, I seemed to be walking in a solitary, dense forest on a spring morning. No sound from human society could be heard. I was now sitting under a giant pine tree, ready to hear the grand concert of Nature. With the sun slowly rising from the east, the cello (the creeping creek) and the clarinet (the rustling pine trees) started with a slow overture. Enthusiastically the violinists (the twittering birds) and the French horn (the mumbling cow) "interpose[d] their voices," and the bass (bears) got in at the wrong time. The orchestra did not stop, they continued to play. The musicians of Nature do not always play in harmony. "Together, unattuned," they have to seek "a common tone" as they play along. The sym-

phony of Nature is like the symphony of human life: both consist of random notes seeking a "common tone." For the symphony of life

Love is that common tone
shall raise his fiery head
and sound his note.

Again, the logical pattern of this paper, the "pictorial criticism," is illogical to Western minds but "logical" to those acquainted with yijing. (Perhaps I should not even use the words "logical" and "think" because they are so conceptually tied up with "words" and with culturally-based conceptions, and therefore very misleading if not useless in a discussion of yijing. Maybe I should simply say that yijing is neither illogical nor logical, but alogical.)

I am not saying that such a pattern of "alogical" thinking is wrong—in fact some English instructors find it interesting and acceptable—but it is very non-Western. Since I was in this country to learn the English language and English literature, I had to abandon Chinese "pictorial logic," and to learn Western "verbal logic."

If I Had to Start Again

The change is profound: Through my understanding of new meanings of words like "individualism," "idealism," and "I," I began to accept the underlying concepts and values of American writing, and by learning to use "topic sentences" I began to accept a new logic. Thus, when I write papers in English, I am able to obey all the general rules of English composition. In doing this I feel that I am writing through, with, and because of a new identity. I welcome the change, for it has added a new dimension to me and to my view of the world. I am not saying that I have entirely lost my Chinese identity. In fact I feel that I will never lose it. Any time I write in Chinese, I resume my old identity, and obey the rules of Chinese composition such as "Make the 'I' modest," and "Beat around the bush before attacking the central topic." It is necessary for me to have such a Chinese identity in order to write authentic Chinese. (I have seen people who, after learning to write in English, use English logic and sentence patterning to write Chinese. They produce very awkward Chinese texts.) But when I write in English, I imagine myself slipping into a new "skin," and I let the "I" behave much more aggressively and knock the topic right on the head. Being conscious of these different identities has helped me to reconcile different systems of values and logic, and has played a pivotal role in my learning to compose in English.

Looking back, I realize that the process of learning to write in English is in fact a process of creating and defining a new identity and balancing it with the old identity. The process of learning English composition would have been easier if I had realized this earlier and

24

consciously sought to compare the two different identities required by the two writing systems from two different cultures. It is fine and perhaps even necessary for American composition teachers to teach about topic sentences, paragraphs, the use of punctuation, documentation, and so on, but can anyone design exercises sensitive to the ideological and logical differences that students like me experience—and design them so they can be introduced at an early stage of an English composition class? As I pointed out earlier, the traditional advice "Just be yourself" is not clear and helpful to students from Korea, China, Vietnam, or India. From "Be yourself" we are likely to hear either "Forget your cultural habit of writing" or "Write as you would write in your own language." But neither of the two is what the instructor meant or what we want to do. It would be helpful if he or she pointed out the different cultural/ideological connotations of the word "I," the connotations that exist in a group-centered culture and an individual-centered culture. To sharpen the contrast, it might be useful to design papers on topics like "The Individual vs. The Group: China vs. America" or "Different 'I's' in Different Cultures."

Carolyn Matalene mentioned in her article (789) an incident concerning American businessmen who presented their Chinese hosts with gifts of cheddar cheese, not knowing that the Chinese generally do not like cheese. Liking cheddar cheese may not be essential to writing English prose, but being truly accustomed to the social norms that stand behind ideas such as the English "I" and the logical pattern of English composition—call it "compositional cheddar cheese"—is essential to writing in English. Matalene does not provide an "elixir" to help her Chinese students like English "compositional cheese," but rather recommends, as do I, that composition teachers not be afraid to give foreign students English "cheese," but to make sure to hand it out slowly, sympathetically, and fully realizing that it tastes very peculiar in the mouths of those used to a very different cuisine.

Topics for Critical Thinking and Writing

1. In his second paragraph Fan Shen says, "I will try to describe and explore this experience of reconciling my Chinese identity with an English identity." What does the article tell us is part of a "Chinese identity," and what is part of an "English identity"? How does your experience in answering this question account for the value of beginning his article with two narratives?

2. His article is based, primarily, on "personal experience." Is this part of his "English identity" or "Chinese identity"? Explain.

3. In paragraph 4 Fan Shen says that "Rule number one in English composition is: Be yourself." Whether you are from the United States or from another culture, try to explain why "being yourself" is (or is not) difficult when you enter college writing. Why did Fan Shen find it difficult?

4. Does Fan Shen's explanation (paragraphs 13–15) of the value of the topic sentence in English help to explain it to you, or do you have some other account of it? Explain.
5. In his next-to-last paragraph Fan Shen suggests topics for instructors to assign to international students. One of the two, "Different 'I's' in Different Cultures," strikes us as a good project to assign to native students as well as those from other cultures. We suggest here that you write a journal entry taking notes on the "different 'I's'" you have experienced before attending college and now. If it suits you to do this, divide your journal entry in two down the middle, taking notes on the "I" before and the "I" after.

Judith R. Shapiro

Judith R. Shapiro, born in New York City in 1942, did her undergraduate work at Brandeis University and earned a Ph.D. in anthropology from Columbia University. She taught anthropology at Bryn Mawr, where she also served as department chair, then as dean and as provost. In 1994 she was appointed president of Barnard College. We reprint an essay adapted from a lecture she gave at her installation as president.

What Women Can Teach Men

By now, the benefits of single-sex education for girls and women have been reported so often and so fully that you might think the advocates of women's institutions could snap their briefcases shut and declare the case closed.

But we can't. It isn't enough to cite the familiar statistics showing that graduates of women's colleges succeed in traditionally male fields—business, government, academia—far out of proportion to their numbers in the population. Unless we understand the reasons for the success of single-sex education for girls and women, we risk missing some important lessons about education, society and the sexes today.

What is it that women's colleges and girls' schools do that coeducation does not? All manner of research—governmental and academic—provides a clear answer: they are places where girls and women get more attention, more respect and more room to be individuals. If too many coed classrooms are places where boys will be boys and girls will be girls, all-female classrooms are places where girls stand a better chance of getting to be people.

Does this mean that we can make as compelling an argument for all-male schools? Though there are very few such institutions left, the question is more than theoretical, since the cases over admitting   4 women to the Virginia Military Institute and The Citadel remain unresolved. The answer lies in how a single-sex institution connects with the society as a whole

In a society that favors men over women, men's institutions operate to preserve privilege; women's institutions challenge privilege and attempt to expand access to the good things of life.

In addition, all-male institutions can produce a culture of male-female relations that is not everything one might wish. Certain military academies may provide particularly florid examples, with exotic degradation ceremonies in which initiates are symbolically identified with women. But generally, the link between all-male groups and misogyny is fairly robust, whether you're looking at it in the United States or in such places as lowland South America and Melanesia, as we anthropologists are in the habit of doing.

Moreover, research to date does not show that boys and men benefit academically from single-sex education in the way that girls and women do. Clearly, the rationales for women's and men's institutions are not parallel.

But even among advocates of women's institutions, we find disagreement, particularly about how they produce their beneficial effects. Some will insist that they serve women's distinctive styles of thinking and learning. This view reflects the influence of "difference feminism"—the branch of feminism that accepts and celebrates what are believed to be distinctive attributes of femaleness.   8

Now, I happen to be among those who view "difference feminism" with concern. I think it has tended to take our society's folk beliefs about the sexes and run with them, when what we need instead is some critical distance on the subject. In recent years, we have seen rather too much gender folklore in both scholarly and popular writing. Sexual stereotypes are a paradigm of what the Columbia sociologist Robert Merton long ago identified as "self-fulfilling prophecies." It is our belief in them that makes them true.

The point here is not to argue that there are no differences between men and women. Nor do I ignore the fact that men and women tend to be dealt different hands in the poker game of life.

The problem arises when discussions of gender difference turn into sweeping and ethnocentric generalizations about what men and women are basically like. Women are said to be inherently nurturing, skilled at relationships, imbued with a deep, intuitive sense of when the garbage needs to be taken out. Men, on the other hand, are predisposed toward certain aggressive pursuits, from laboratory science to rape, and they also exhibit a possibly genetically based inability to see when the garbage needs to be taken out.

We would do better to shift our focus from whether men and women   12
are the same or different (indeed, they are both) to the question of who benefits from current arrangements and how these benefits might be shared more widely in a way that better serves the society as a whole.

Women's colleges go to the heart of that issue because they exist to address inequality between the sexes and to serve the interests of women—not as places where women can think differently, or learn differently, or speak differently, but as the proverbial room of one's own. As Virginia Woolf[1] might have put it had she been from the Upper West Side, "Give a woman enough subway tokens and a college of her own, and let her tell it like it is."

People who ask questions about the purpose of women's colleges generally assume they know what "coeducation" means. But in fact this term requires some . . . deconstruction, shall we say. Coeducational institutions should be places where men and women are equally likely to study in all fields, to hold positions of responsibility and authority in extracurricular activities and to be found at all ranks of the faculty and administration. But this is not the case.

Women make up less than 30 percent of full-time faculty at four-year colleges and universities—and still less in the higher ranks of faculty. The figures are even lower at elite research universities. Although they are making progress, women continue to lag in almost every other critical category in so-called coeducational institutions.

It is best—and most accurate, I think—to look at coeducation as a project rather than as an achieved state of affairs. And it is a project in which women's colleges are pivotal players, since—paradoxically—they themselves have been pioneers of coeducation. 16

Women's colleges are places where there has long been a balance of women and men on faculties, where we don't pay much attention to whether the head of the department is a man or a woman, where we have long had both women and men in positions of major administrative responsibility. The significant contributions of women's colleges lie not only in what they do for women but also in what they do for professional and collegial relationships between women and men.

So why do we need women's colleges to move real coeducation forward? Because women have the most compelling interest in it. And women's colleges are centers of energy for mobilizing and expressing that interest. Since history, including the history of the roles men and women play in society, cannot be counted on to move progressively forward in a single line, the price of equality is eternal vigilance.

Topics for Critical Thinking and Writing

1. According to Shapiro, single-sex education for women has merit. Why does she not believe that the same merit applies to single-sex education for men?

---

[1]**Virginia Woolf** (1882–1941). British writer, and a forceful advocate of the abilities of women.

2. In her ninth paragraph Shapiro uses the first person twice. Can you justify her decision here?
3. Shapiro says that "coeducation" is a "project rather than an achieved state of affairs." Paradoxically, she claims, "women's colleges are pivotal players." How does she explain this point?
4. In her last paragraph Shapiro says that we "need women's colleges to move real coeducation forward." Do you agree with her or not? Explain.

Paul Goodman

Paul Goodman (1911–72) received his bachelor's degree from City College in New York and his Ph.D from the University of Chicago. He taught in several colleges and universities, and he was a prolific writer on literature, politics, and education. Goodman's view that students were victims of a corrupt society made him especially popular on campuses—even in the 1960s when students tended to distrust anyone over thirty. "A Proposal to Abolish Grading" (editors' title) is an extract from Compulsory Miseducation and the Community of Scholars *(1966).*

A Proposal to Abolish Grading

Let half a dozen of the prestigious Universities—Chicago, Stanford, the Ivy League—abolish grading, and use testing only and entirely for pedagogic purposes as teachers see fit.

Anyone who knows the frantic temper of the present schools will understand the transvaluation of values that would be effected by this modest innovation. For most of the students, the competitive grade has come to be the essence. The naïve teacher points to the beauty of the subject and the ingenuity of the research; the shrewd student asks if he is responsible for that on the final exam.

Let me at once dispose of an objection whose unanimity is quite fascinating. I think that the great majority of professors agree that grading hinders teaching and creates a bad spirit, going as far as cheating and plagiarizing. I have before me the collection of essays, *Examining in Harvard College,* and this is the consensus. It is uniformly asserted, however, that the grading is inevitable; for how else will the graduate schools, the foundations the corporations *know* whom to accept, reward, hire? How will the talent scouts know whom to tap?

By testing the applicants, of course, according to the specific task-requirements of the inducting institution, just as applicants for the Civil Service or for licenses in medicine, law, and architecture are tested. Why should Harvard professors do the testing *for* corporations and graduate-schools?   4

The objection is ludicrous. Dean Whitla, of the Harvard Office of Tests, points out that the scholastic-aptitude and achievement tests used for *admission* to Harvard are a super-excellent index for all-around Harvard performance, better than high-school grades or particular Harvard course-grades. Presumably, these college-entrance tests are tailored for what Harvard and similar institutions want. By the same logic, would not an employer do far better to apply his own job-aptitude test rather than to rely on the vagaries of Harvard sectionmen. Indeed, I doubt that many employers bother to look at such grades; they are more likely to be interested merely in the fact of a Harvard diploma, whatever that connotes to them. The grades have most of their weight with the graduate schools—here, as elsewhere, the system runs mainly for its own sake.

It is really necessary to remind our academics of the ancient history of Examination. In the medieval university, the whole point of the gruelling trial of the candidate was whether or not to accept him as a peer. His disputation and lecture for the Master's was just that, a masterpiece to enter the guild. It was not to make comparative evaluations. It was not to weed out and select for an extra-mural licensor or employer. It was certainly not to pit one young fellow against another in an ugly competition. My philosophic impression is that the medievals thought they knew what a good job of work was and that we are competitive because we do not know. But the more status is achieved by largely irrelevant competitive evaluation, the less will we ever know.

(Of course, our American examinations never did have this purely guild orientation, just as our faculties have rarely had absolute autonomy; the examining was to satisfy Overseers, Elders, distant Regents— and they as paternal superiors have always doted on giving grades, rather than accepting peers. But I submit that this set-up itself makes it impossible for the student to *become* a master, to *have* grown up, and to commence on his own. He will always be making A or B for some overseer. And in the present atmosphere, he will always be climbing on his friend's neck.)

Perhaps the chief objectors to abolishing grading would be the students and their parents. The parents should be simply disregarded; their anxiety has done enough damage already. For the students, it seems to me that a primary duty of the university is to deprive them of their props, their dependence on extrinsic valuation and motivation, and to force them to confront the difficult enterprise itself and finally lose themselves in it.

A miserable effect of grading is to nullify the various uses of testing. Testing, for both student and teacher, is a means of structuring, and also of finding out what is blank or wrong and what has been assimilated and can be taken for granted. Review—including high-pressure review—is a means of bringing together the fragments, so that there are flashes of synoptic insight.

There are several good reasons for testing, and kinds of test. But if the aim is to discover weakness, what is the point of down-grading and punishing it, and thereby inviting the student to conceal his weakness, by faking and bulling, if not cheating? The natural conclusion of synthesis is the insight itself, not a grade for having had it. For the important purpose of placement, if one can establish in the student the belief that one is testing *not* to grade and make invidious comparisons but for his own advantage, the student should normally seek his own level, where he is challenged and yet capable, rather than trying to get by. If the student dares to accept himself as he is, a teacher's grade is a crude instrument compared with a student's self-awareness. But it is rare in our universities that students are encouraged to notice objectively their vast confusion. Unlike Socrates, our teachers rely on power-drives rather than shame and ingenuous idealism.

Many students are lazy, so teachers try to goad or threaten them by grading. In the long run this must do more harm than good. Laziness is a character-defense. It may be a way of avoiding learning, in order to protect the conceit that one is already perfect (deeper, the despair that one *never* can). It may be a way of avoiding just the risk of failing and being down-graded. Sometimes it is a way of politely saying, "I won't." But since it is the authoritarian grown-up demands that have created such attitudes in the first place, why repeat the trauma? There comes a time when we must treat people as adult, laziness and all. It is one thing courageously to fire a do-nothing out of your class; it is quite another thing to evaluate him with a lordly F.

Most important of all, it is often obvious that balking in doing the work, especially among bright young people who get to great universities, means exactly what it says: The work does not suit me, not this subject, or not at this time, or not in this school, or not in school altogether. The student might not be bookish; he might be school-tired; perhaps his development ought now to take another direction. Yet unfortunately, if such a student is intelligent and is not sure of himself, he *can* be bullied into passing, and this obscures everything. My hunch is that I am describing a common situation. What a grim waste of young life and teacherly effort! Such a student will retain nothing of what he has "passed" in. Sometimes he must get mononucleosis to tell his story and be believed. [12]

And ironically, the converse is also probably commonly true. A student flunks and is mechanically weeded out, who is really ready and eager to learn in a scholastic setting, but he has not quite caught on. A good teacher can recognize the situation, but the computer wreaks its will.

Topics for Critical Thinking and Writing

1. In his opening paragraph Goodman limits his suggestion about grading and testing to "half a dozen of the prestigious Universities." Does he offer any reason for this limitation? Can you?

2. In paragraph 3 Goodman says that "the great majority of professors agree that grading hinders teaching." What evidence does he offer to support this claim? What arguments might be made that grading assists teaching? Should Goodman have made them?
3. As a student, have grades helped you to learn, or have grades hindered you? Explain.
4. If you have been a student in an ungraded course, describe the course and evaluate the experience.

Adrienne Rich

Adrienne Rich was born in Baltimore in 1929 and was educated at Radcliffe College. Her first book of poetry, published in the year she graduated from college, won the Yale Series of Younger Poets award, and her ninth book of poetry, Diving into the Wreck *(1973), won the National Book Award. When she accepted the award she did so not as an individual but on behalf of all women.*

The essay that we print was originally a talk delivered in 1977 at Douglass College, The Women's College of Rutgers University. It was first published in The Common Woman, *a feminist magazine.*

Claiming an Education

For this convocation, I planned to separate my remarks into two parts: some thoughts about you, the women students here, and some thoughts about us who teach in a women's college. But ultimately, those two parts are indivisible. If university education means anything beyond the processing of human beings into expected roles, through credit hours, tests, and grades (and I believe that in a women's college especially it *might* mean much more), it implies an ethical and intellectual contract between teacher and student. This contract must remain intuitive, dynamic, unwritten; but we must turn to it again and again if learning is to be reclaimed from the depersonalizing and cheapening pressures of the present-day academic scene.

The first thing I want to say to you who are students, is that you cannot afford to think of being here to *receive* an education; you will do much better to think of yourselves as being here to *claim* one. One of the dictionary definitions of the verb "to claim" is *to take as the rightful owner; to assert in the face of possible contradiction.* "To receive" is *to come into possession of; to act as receptacle or container for; to accept as authoritative or true.* The difference is that between acting and being acted-upon, and for women it can literally mean the difference between life and death.

One of the devastating weaknesses of university learning, of the store of knowledge and opinion that has been handed down through academic training, has been its almost total erasure of women's experience and thought from the curriculum, and its exclusion of women as members of the academic community. Today, with increasing numbers of women students in nearly every branch of higher learning, we still see very few women in the upper levels of faculty and administration in most institutions. Douglass College itself is a women's college in a university administered overwhelmingly by men, who in turn are answerable to the state legislature, again composed predominantly of men. But the most significant fact for you is that what you learn here, the very texts you read, the lectures you hear, the way your studies are divided into categories and fragmented one from the other—all this reflects, to a very large degree, neither objective reality, nor an accurate picture of the past, nor a group of rigorously tested observations about human behavior. What you can learn here (and I mean not only at Douglass but any college in any university) is how *men* have perceived and organized their experience, their history, their ideas of social relationships, good and evil, sickness and health, etc. When you read or hear about "great issues," "major texts," "the mainstream of Western thought," you are hearing about what men, above all white men, in their male subjectivity, have decided is important.

Black and other minority peoples have for some time recognized   4
that their racial and ethnic experience was not accounted for in the studies broadly labeled human; and that even the sciences can be racist. For many reasons, it has been more difficult for women to comprehend our exclusion, and to realize that even the sciences can be sexist. For one thing, it is only within the last hundred years that higher education has grudgingly been opened up to women at all, even to white, middle-class women. And many of us have found ourselves poring eagerly over books with titles like: *The Descent of Man; Man and His Symbols; Irrational Man; The Phenomenon of Man; The Future of Man; Man and the Machine; From Man to Man; May Man Prevail?; Man, Science and Society;* or *One-Dimensional Man*—books pretending to describe a "human" reality that does not include one-half the human species.

Less than a decade ago, with the rebirth of a feminist movement in this country, women students and teachers in a number of universities began to demand and set up women's studies courses—to *claim* a woman-directed education. And, despite the inevitable accusations of "unscholarly," "group therapy," "faddism," etc., despite backlash and budget cuts, women's studies are still growing, offering to more and more women a new intellectual grasp on their lives, new understanding of our history, a fresh vision of the human experience, and also a critical basis for evaluating what they hear and read in other courses, and in the society at large.

But my talk is not really about women's studies, much as I believe in their scholarly, scientific, and human necessity. While I think that any Douglass student has everything to gain by investigating and enrolling in women's studies courses, I want to suggest that there is a more essential experience that you owe yourselves, one which courses in women's studies can greatly enrich, but which finally depends on you, in all your interactions with yourself and your world. This is the experience of *taking responsibility toward yourselves.* Our upbringing as women has so often told us that this should come second to our relationships and responsibilities to other people. We have been offered ethical models of the self-denying wife and mother; intellectual models of the brilliant but slapdash dilettante who never commits herself to anything the whole way, or the intelligent woman who denies her intelligence in order to seem more "feminine," or who sits in passive silence even when she disagrees inwardly with everything that is being said around her.

Responsibility to yourself means refusing to let others do your thinking, talking, and naming for you; it means learning to respect and use your brains and instincts; hence, grappling with hard work. It means that you do not treat your body as a commodity with which to purchase superficial intimacy or economic security; for our bodies and minds are inseparable in this life, and when we allow our bodies to be treated as objects, our minds are in mortal danger. It means insisting that those to whom you give your friendship and love are able to respect your mind. It means being able to say, with Charlotte Brontë's *Jane Eyre:* "I have an inward treasure born with me, which can keep me alive if all the extraneous delights should be withheld or offered only at a price I cannot afford to give."

Responsibility to yourself means that you don't fall for shallow and   8
easy solutions—predigested books and ideas, weekend encounters guaranteed to change your life, taking "gut" courses instead of ones you know will challenge you, bluffing at school and life instead of doing solid work, marrying early as an escape from real decisions, getting pregnant as an evasion of already existing problems. It means that you refuse to sell your talents and aspirations short, simply to avoid conflict and confrontation. And this, in turn, means resisting the forces in society which say that women should be nice, play safe, have low professional expectations, drown in love and forget about work, live through others, and stay in the places assigned to us. It means that we insist on a life of meaningful work, insist that work be as meaningful as love and friendship in our lives. It means, therefore, the courage to be "different"; not to be continuously available to others when we need time for ourselves and our work; to be able to demand of others—parents, friends, roommates, teachers, lovers, husbands, children—that they respect our sense of purpose and our integrity as persons. Women everywhere are finding the courage to do this, more and more, and we are finding that courage both in our study of women in the past who possessed it, and in each other as we look to other women for comradeship, community, and challenge. The difference between a life lived actively, and life of passive drifting are dispersal of energies, is an immense difference. Once we begin to feel committed to our lives,

responsible to ourselves, we can never again be satisfied with the old, passive way.

Now comes the second part of the contract. I believe that in a women's college you have the right to expect your faculty to take you seriously. The education of women has been a matter of debate for centuries, and old, negative attitudes about women's role, women's ability to think and take leadership, are still rife both in and outside the university. Many male professors (and I don't mean only at Douglass) still feel that teaching in a women's college is a second-rate career. Many tend to eroticize their women students—to treat them a sexual objects—instead of demanding the best of their minds. (At Yale a legal suit [*Alexander* v. *Yale*] has been brought against the university by a group of women students demanding a stated policy against sexual advances toward female students by male professors.) Many teachers, both men and women, trained in the male-centered tradition, are still handing the ideas and texts of that tradition on to students without teaching them to criticize its antiwoman attitudes, its omission of women as part of the species. Too often, all of us fail to teach the most important thing, which is that clear thinking, active discussion, and excellent writing are all necessary for intellectual freedom, and that these require *hard work*. Sometimes, perhaps in discouragement with a culture which is both antiintellectual and antiwoman, we may resign ourselves to low expectations for our students before we have given them half a chance to become more thoughtful, expressive human beings. We need to take to heart the words of Elizabeth Barrett Browning, a poet, a thinking woman, and a feminist, who wrote in 1845 of her impatience with studies which cultivate a "passive recipiency" in the mind, and asserted that "women want to be made to *think actively*: their apprehension is quicker than that of men, but their defect lies for the most part in the logical faculty and in the higher mental activities." Note that she implies a defect which can be remedied by intellectual training; *not* an inborn lack of ability.

I have said that the contract on the student's part involves that you demand to be taken seriously so that you can also go on taking yourself seriously. This means seeking out criticism, recognizing that the most affirming thing anyone can do for you is demand that you push yourself further, show you the range of what you *can* do. It means rejecting attitudes of "take-it-easy," "why-be-so-serious," "why-worry-you'll-probably-get-married-anyway." It means assuming your share of responsibility for what happens in the classroom, because that affects the quality of your daily life here. It means that the student sees herself engaged *with* her teachers in an active, on-going struggle for a real education. But for her to do this, her teachers must be committed to the belief that women's minds and experience are intrinsically valuable and indispensable to any civilization worthy the name; that there is no more exhilarating and intellectually fertile place in the academic world today that a women's college—*if* both students and teachers in large enough numbers are trying to fulfill this contract. The contract is really a pledge of mutual seriousness about women, about language, ideas, methods, and values. It is our shared commitment toward a world in which the inborn potentialities of so many women's minds will no longer be wasted, raveled away, paralyzed, or denied.

Topics for Critical Thinking and Writing

1. In the first paragraph Rich speaks of the "processing of human beings," which, she implies, passes for but is not education. What does she mean by *processing,* and how does it become confused with education?

2. Again in paragraph 1, Rich says that university education implies an unwritten contract between students and teachers. What does the body of the essay suggest that the contract requires of both parties? Would Rich say—would *you* say—that all education implies such a contract? Or is the idea meaningful only in the context of the talk?

3. Rich was speaking to women at a women's college. To what extent, in your opinion, are her comments valid for men? Or do they now seem dated (they were delivered in 1977) for both men and women students?

4. In paragraph 9 Rich refers to sexual relationships between male professors and female students. What does she appear to assume about those relationships? (For example, who initiates them? Are they ever consensual?) What effect does she assume that they have on women's education? Do you agree?

5. Writing in the 1970s, Rich notes (in paragraph 3) that "with increasing numbers of women students in nearly every branch of higher learning, we still see very few women in the upper levels of faculty and administration in most institutions." Looking at the institution you attend in the 1990s, what changes do you see?

6. In paragraph 10 Rich says that taking yourself seriously means "seeking out criticism." Reread this paragraph and then examine and evaluate your own response to criticism. At this stage in your education, do you agree with Rich about the effect of criticism? Why or why not?

Patricia Nelson Limerick

Patricia Nelson Limerick was born in Banning, California, in 1951 and was educated at the University of California at Santa Cruz and Yale. She has taught history at Yale Harvard, and the University of Colorado (her special interests are Western history, American Indian history, and environmental history), but she is also interested in the teaching of writing and in (as this essay reveals) students. "The Phenomenon of Phantom Students" was originally published in the Harvard Gazette, *a weekly publication for the university community.*

The Phenomenon of Phantom Students
Diagnosis and Treatment

On any number of occasions, students have told me that I am the first and only professor they have spoken to. This was, at first, flattering. Then curiosity began to replace vanity. How had conversation between teacher and student become, for many students, a novelty? These students conducted themselves as if the University were a museum: the professors on display, the students at a distance, directing any questions to the museum's guides and guards—the graduate students.

The museum model is not University policy. No "guide for instructors" tells professors to cultivate aloofness and keep students in their place. No "guide for undergraduates" tells them to speak to graduate students and only approach professors on extremely solemn and serious business.

This is not University policy, and it is by no means the experience of all Harvard students. Many confidently talk to their professors; in occasional cases, introducing a measure of shyness and humility would not be altogether unfortunate. I have no notion what the actual statistics are, but it is my impression that the disengaged are no insignificant minority. Harvard has an abundance of factors creating phantoms—my term for the radically disengaged, those staying resolutely on the academic periphery, taking large lecture classes, writing survivalist papers and exams. Phantomhood—even in its milder versions—is a significant problem and deserves the University's attention.

What creates phantoms? They tell remarkably similar stories. In the [4] basic narrative, the freshman arrives with the familiar doubt: did Admissions make a mistake? Paradoxically, the doubt coexists with vanity; high school was easy, and Harvard won't be much worse for an individual of such certified achievement. Then, in the basic phantom story, a paper comes back with a devastating grade. Since a direct nerve connects the student's prose to his self-respect and dignity, and since the Expository Writing Program stands as the Ellis Island of Harvard, many of these initial injuries involve Expos.

Crucial Fork

The crucial fork in the road comes here: the paper, more than likely produced in good faith, is a disaster; the student has been judged by standards he doesn't understand. The split outcome really cannot be overdramatized: one route goes direct to defeat, resignation, and cynicism; the other offers a struggle, rewriting, and very probably, the learning of new skills.

Some of those new skills involve writing, but for this subject, the significant skill involves conversation—direct, productive—in which the grader of the paper says precisely and clearly how the paper went wrong, and how the author can make it better. (On the instructor's side, if there is any more intellectually demanding exercise in the academic world than this, I don't know what it is.) One successful round of this kind of dialogue has, I think, an immunizing effect; on the occasion of the next disastrous paper, the precedent set makes another collapse unlikely.

For the representative phantom, though, any number of things go wrong. Even if the instructor clearly explains the paper's problems, panic keeps the phantom from hearing. Conversation with instructors becomes an unhappy experience, avoided by anyone with any sense, in which papers are picked on to no particular result.

The essential groundwork completed, the phantom can become a part 8 of a community in which groups of the radically disengaged make their unfortunate academic status a matter of pride or, alternatively, the phantom can think of himself as uniquely and distinctively cut off from the University. In either case, the crucial transition is complete: from thinking, "I *may* be the fluke in Admissions," the student has moved on to certainty: "I *am* the fluke." From here on, the prospect for positive student/faculty contact meets the unpassable obstacle: the student's own fatalism.

I draw here a portrait of extreme cases—with academic underperformance part of the package. There are a substantial number of individuals doing perfectly competent academic work who still would choose a visit to the dentist over a visit to a professor. Usually, no particular unhappy event explains their shyness, and one could certainly argue that their situation is not particularly unfortunate. They are doing the reading, and writing their papers, and getting solid educations. But they are missing something. Recently, my course assistant arranged for me to have lunch with a recently graduated student who had been in my class; four years of a good academic performance, and she had never spoken to a professor. She was a remarkable person, involved over a long time in volunteer work for the homeless. I think both she and Harvard would have profited had she been comfortable talking with professors.

Student/Faculty Contact

I address myself here to the problem of student faculty contact in the case of students both with and without academic problems. Reading and writing with both ease and intensity are fundamental goals; speaking with ease and intensity should be in the package.

How are students to be persuaded to talk to professors? This encouragement should not offer false advertising. One simply cannot say that all professors are at heart accessible and friendly. Some of them are certifiably grumpy, and many of them are shy. They are still worth talking to.

With a major interest in Indian/White relations, I cannot resist   12 thinking anthropologically. White people and Indian people still confront each other through a fog of stereotypes (all Indians are noble and in touch with nature, or, alternatively, all Indians are demoralized and in touch with alcohol), and the impulse to provide a comparable analysis for student/professor relations is irresistible. Images have equal powers in both situations.

Commonly Held Student Myths about Professors

1a. *Professors Must Be Asked Specific, Better Yet, Bibliographic Questions.* Professors do not converse like ordinary people. To speak their language, you must address them in this fashion: "Professor X, I was very interested in your remarks about the unification of the Northwest Company and the Hudson's Bay Company in 1821, and I wondered if you might direct me to further reading." If you do not have a specific question like this, then you have no business troubling a professor.

1b. *Professors Only Like to Talk about Senior Theses.* This proposition was brought home to me at a Quincy House gathering. A number of students and I were speaking on a general, humane topic (sports?) when they discovered my hidden identity. The truth out, they began to tell me about their senior theses. The evening, I felt, became something of a busman's holiday.

2. *Professors Only Want to Talk with Other Elegant, Learned and Brilliant Conversationalists.* (Numbers 1 and 2 may appear to be contradictory, but they often coexist.) Living in the intellectual equivalent of Mt. McKinley or Mt. Whitney, professors do not like to descend the mountain to talk to the lowlanders. They are used to sophisticated, erudite conversation, in contrast to which normal speech sounds embarrassingly flat and pedestrian. Even if they seem to tolerate the speech of mortals, professors are inwardly thinking how stupid it sounds. They have, in their distinguished careers, heard nearly every insight there is. If a new idea seems to occur to a student in 1983, it can be assumed that the professor first heard that idea sometime in the 1950s. Having a memory built on the order of a steel trap, the professor does not need to hear it again.

3. *If I Speak to a Professor, He Will Probably (and Maybe Rightly)*   16 *Assume That I Am a Grade-grubbing Toady.* (The students, of course, use a more vivid term.) This belief actually concerns attitudes to other stu-

dents: dependent, hypocritical drudges hang around professors, asking insincere questions, and seeking recommendation letters; students with integrity keep their distance and avoid the dishonor of visibly trying to make an impression.

Countering these three assumptions does not require a debasing of professional status; respect for achievement and authority, and excessive deference and fear are two different matters. Number 1 and #2 are both extremely widespread, and #3 has, I think, the greatest power over phantoms. In the further reaches of phantomhood, these assumptions rest on considerable hostility toward the institution, a basic act of self-defense in which the individual reasons (if that's the word): "Harvard has ignored and injured me; well, Harvard is stupid anyway." We are dealing here, in other words, with wounded dignity, a condition not known for bringing out the finest in human behavior.

In the last eight years, I have seen many phantoms emerge from hiding; I have enormous faith in their potential for recovery. Nothing encouraged me more than the Committee on College Life meeting last spring. I had promised to bring expert witnesses—verifiable phantoms. Having made the promise, I began to regret it. If these individuals barely had the courage to talk to me, how would they face a panel of five professors, two deans and five students? Would any consent to appear? The first five I called said yes—without reluctance. At the committee, they spoke with frankness and energy. To be equally frank, that amazed me—I evidently expected that I would have to act as their interpreter. They were, instead, perfectly capable of speaking for themselves.

There is a fairly reliable personal solution to the problem of phantomhood for faculty to follow:

1. *Discover the phantoms* (midterm grade sheets locate the ones with academic problems; reports from course assistants and from professorial visits to sections identify the others). 20

2. *Contact them.*

3. *Get an acknowledgment of the condition of phantomhood, directly and briefly.* (Don't milk it for its misery, which is often at a pretty high level.)

4. *Engage them in a specific project—ideally, rewriting a paper.* Here, the instructor is most productive when she uses her own enthusiasm for the subject to launch a discussion of the ideas in the paper, so that the student slides, without perceiving it, into what was hitherto unimaginable—"an intellectual conversation with a professor."

5. *Keep a careful eye out for achievement on the part of the student, during the conversation, and comment on it.* This is only in part "encouragement"—the primary goal is to help the individual penetrate the mysterious standards of what constitutes "insight" or a "a solid point." 24

6. *Hold out for concrete evidence of recovery—a successfully rewritten paper, for instance.* These second drafts are almost without exception

much better papers—primarily because the student now has what was wholly lacking before—faith in a living, actual audience.

7. *Encourage a wide application of the new principles.* The student's logical next step is to say to the instructor, "I can work with you because you are different from the others." Resist this. The sports analogy is the best: you may need a coach at the start of learning a sport, but you do not need a coach at your elbow for the rest of your career in that sport. Professors, like most other individuals, like snowflakes, are all different. That, surely, is part of their charm.

Phantoms are not beyond understanding, and certainly not beyond recovery. But there is another, equally complex party to the basic transactions of student/faculty contact. We might now take up the question of the genesis of shyness, harriedness and grumpiness in professors.

How nice to lead a leisured life in a book-lined office, I used to   28 think, chatting, reading and (if *real* work meant actually teaching classes) working only a few hours a week. Cross the line into professorhood, and the plot thickens considerably. Those few minutes a week in class rest on hours of preparation. Reading exams and papers closely eats up time. Then, of course, there is "one's own work"—research and writing for promised articles and books. Add to this, participation in professional organizations and department and University committees, and one's leisured time in the book-lined office often comes down to checking the datebook to see where one is due next.

That is in part why professors can seem grumpy and aloof, even when they are genuinely committed to teaching. Phantoms, and prospective phantoms, should be advised not to take personal injury when cut short by an individual who will have to stay up most of the night revising the next day's lecture and writing recommendation letters. Schedule a meeting for a time when the universe at least gives the illusion of being a bit more in the professor's control, and try not to resent any accidental rudeness.

More important, phantoms should be encouraged to use empathy in understanding the professors. Phantoms are, after all, experts in shyness; shyness, while not universal in the professorial population, is no stranger. Consider the pattern: the individual is initially drawn to the world of books and private contemplation, communicating more often through writing than through speech. How nice, the susceptible individual thinks, that there is a profession that encourages and supports this retreat to private intellectual exertion. And that promise seems to hold for the initial years of graduate school, and then, abruptly, the treachery stands exposed. One has to walk into a classroom, cause everyone else to fall silent, and become the center of attention. It is a shy person's nightmare, and individuals evolve the best mechanisms for dealing with it that they can. Once the mechanisms are in place, the individual holds on to them. It is undeniably more dignified to seem aloof and uncaring than to seem scared and shy.

I write as a reformed phantom myself—one, happily, in the category in which academic problems did not play a part. My papers carried me through college and graduate school; I was a veritable sphinx in classes. Occupying—initially to my horror—the teacher's chair, phantomhood became a luxury I could not afford.

A few years ago, when I had just started teaching, an old professor of mine from Santa Cruz came to Yale for the year. "We're so fragmented at Santa Cruz," he said, "I am really looking forward to having hard-hitting intellectual conversations again." 32

"Hard-hitting intellectual conversations?" I didn't seem to have ever had one. It was a concept beyond the reach of an only partially recovered phantom.

Seven or eight years later, I am thoroughly addicted to the kind of conversations I thought I would never have. They provide the core of vitality for the university, the only real cement that makes such a collection of disparate individuals into a community. I want the phantoms included in the community.

Topics for Critical Thinking and Writing

1. Limerick mentions that after receiving an essay with a "devastating grade," a student finds that "conversation with instructors becomes an unhappy experience, avoided by anyone with any sense." If on some occasion your good sense deserted you and you therefore engaged in conversation with an instructor, was the conversation profitable? Why, or why not?

2. Let's assume that you find this essay interesting, and not simply because of the subject matter. *Why* is it interesting? What are some of the rhetorical devices that the author uses to engage your attention?

3. In paragraph 4 Limerick refers to the Expository Writing Program as "the Ellis Island of Harvard." Explain the metaphor. In the same paragraph she says: "A direct nerve connects the student's prose to his self-respect." Again, explain the metaphor and then try to explain why, for most of us, it rings true.

4. In paragraph 3 Limerick mentions, but does not define or explain, something she labels "survivalist papers and exams." In a paragraph invent a definition for this term, using both Limerick's essay and your own experience as sources.

5. Without naming or in any other way clearly identifying the instructor, write an essay of five hundred words in which you explain why—at least for that instructor—you are a phantom student. Or, on the other hand, write an essay explaining why you have enjoyed conversing with an instructor. *Hint*: a few bits of dialogue will probably be effective.

6. Write a dialogue of an imaginary conference between a composition teacher and a phantom. (Even though this is an exercise in writing pure fiction, you may use one of your own essays as a prop.)

E. B. White

E[lwyn] B[rooks] White (1899–1985) wrote poetry and fiction, but he is most widely known as an essayist and as the coauthor (with William Strunk, Jr.) of Elements of Style. *After a long career at* The New Yorker *he retired to Maine, but he continued to write until the year before his death at the age of 86.*

Education

I have an increasing admiration for the teacher in the country school where we have a third-grade scholar in attendance. She not only undertakes to instruct her charges in all the subjects of the first three grades, but she manages to function quietly and effectively as a guardian of their health, their clothes, their habits, their mothers, and their snowball engagements. She has been doing this sort of Augean task for twenty years, and is both kind and wise. She cooks for the children on the stove that heats the room, and she can cool their passions or warm their soup with equal competence. She conceives their costumes, cleans up their messes, and shares their confidences. My boy already regards his teacher as his great friend, and I think tells her a great deal more than he tells us.

The shift from city school to country school was something we worried about quietly all last summer. I have always rather favored public school over private school, if only because in public school you meet a greater variety of children. This bias of mine, I suspect, is partly an attempt to justify my own past (I never knew anything but public schools) and partly an involuntary defense against getting kicked in the shins by a young ceramist on his way to the kiln. My wife was unacquainted with public schools, never having been exposed (in her early life) to anything more public than the washroom of Miss Winsor's. Regardless of our backgrounds, we both knew that the change in schools was something that concerned not us but the scholar himself. We hoped it would work out all right. In New York our son went to a medium-priced private institution with semi-progressive ideas of education, and modern plumbing. He learned fast, kept well, and we were satisfied. It was an electric, colorful, regimented existence with moments of pleasurable pause and giddy incident. The day the Christmas angel fainted and had to be carried out by one of the Wise Men was educational in the highest sense of the term. Our scholar gave imitations of it around the house for weeks afterward, and I doubt if it ever goes completely out of his mind.

His days were rich in formal experience. Wearing overalls and an old sweater (the accepted uniform of the private seminary), he sallied forth at morn accompanied by a nurse or a parent and walked (or was pulled) two blocks to a corner where the school bus made a flag stop. This flashy vehicle was as punctual as death: seeing us waiting at the cold curb, it would sweep to a halt, open its mouth, suck the boy in, and spring away with an angry growl. It was a good deal like a train picking up a bag of mail. At school the scholar was worked on for six or seven hours by half a dozen teachers and a nurse, and was revived on orange juice in mid-morning. In a cinder court he played games supervised by an athletic instructor, and in a cafeteria he ate lunch worked out by a dietitian. He soon learned to read with gratifying facility and discernment and to make Indian weapons of a semi-deadly nature. Whenever one of his classmates fell low of a fever the news was put on the wires and there were breathless phone calls to physicians, discussing periods of incubation and allied magic.

In the country all one can say is that the situation is different, and somehow more casual. Dressed in corduroys, sweatshirt, and short rubber boots, and carrying a tin dinner-pail, our scholar departs at the crack of dawn for the village school, two and a half miles down the road, next to the cemetery. When the road is open and the car will start, he makes the journey by motor, courtesy of his old man. When the snow is deep or the motor is dead or both, he makes it on the hoof. In the afternoons he walks or hitches all or part of the way home in fair weather, gets transported in foul. The schoolhouse is a two-room frame building, bungalow type, shingles stained a burnt brown with weather-resistant stain. It has a chemical toilet in the basement and two teachers above the stairs. One takes the first three grades, the other the fourth, fifth, and sixth. They have little or no time for individual instruction, and no time at all for the esoteric. They teach what they know themselves, just as fast and as hard as they can manage. The pupils sit still at their desks in class, and do their milling around outdoors during recess. 4

There is no supervised play. They play cops and robbers (only they call it "Jail") and throw things at one another—snowballs in winter, rose hips in fall. It seems to satisfy them. They also construct darts, pinwheels, and "pick-up sticks" (jackstraws), and the school itself does a brisk trade in penny candy, which is for sale right in the classroom and which contains "surprises." The most highly prized surprise is a fake cigarette, made of cardboard, fiendishly lifelike.

The memory of how apprehensive we were at the beginning is still strong. The boy was nervous about the change too. The tension, on that first fair morning in September when we drove him to school, almost blew the windows out of the sedan. And when later we picked him up on the road, wandering along with his little blue lunch-pail, and got his laconic report "All right" in answer to our inquiry about how the day had gone, our relief was vast. Now, after almost a year of it, the only difference we can discover in the two school experiences is that in the country he sleeps better at night—and *that* probably is more the air than the education. When grilled on the subject of school-in-country vs. school-in-city, he replied that the chief difference is that the day seems to go so much quicker in the country. "Just like lightning," he reported.

Topics for Critical Thinking and Writing

1. Which school, public or private, does White prefer? Since White doesn't state his preference outright, from what evidence were you able to infer it?
2. In the first half of paragraph 2 White admits to a bias in favor of public schools, and he speculates, half-seriously, about the origins of his bias. If his intention here is not simply to amuse us, what is it?
3. What is White's strongest argument in favor of the school he prefers? Where in the essay do you find it?

Toni Cade Bambara

Toni Cade Bambara, born in New York City in 1939, received her B.A. from Queens College in 1959 and her M.A. from City College in 1964. Both schools are part of the City University of New York. She has studied mime and dance, has taught at Livingston College of Rutgers University, and has worked for the New York State Department of Welfare.

The Lesson

Back in the days when everyone was old and stupid or young and foolish and me and Sugar were the only ones just right, this lady moved on our block with nappy hair and proper speech and no makeup. And quite naturally we laughed at her, laughed the way we did at the junk man who went about his business like he was some big-time president and his sorry-ass horse his secretary. And we kinda hated her too, hated the way we did the winos who cluttered up our parks and pissed on our handball walls and stank up our hallways and stairs so you couldn't halfway play hide-and-seek without a goddamn gas mask. Miss Moore was her name. The only woman on the block with no first name. And she was black as hell, cept for her feet, which were fish-white and spooky. And she was always planning these boring-ass things for us to do, us being my cousin, mostly, who lived on the block cause we all moved North the same time and to the same apartment then spread out gradual to breathe. And our parents would yank our heads into some kinda shape and crisp up our clothes so we'd be presentable for travel with Miss Moore, who always looked like she was going to church, though she never did. Which is just one of the things the grownups talked about when they talked behind her back like a dog. But when she came calling with some sachet she'd sewed up or some gingerbread she'd made or some book, why then they'd all be too embarrassed to turn her down and we'd get handed over all spruced up. She'd been to college and said it was only right that she should take responsibility for the young ones' education, and she not even related by marriage or blood. So they'd go for it. Specially Aunt Gretchen. She was the main gofer in the family. You got some ole dumb shit foolishness you want somebody to go for, you send for Aunt Gretchen. She been screwed into the go-along for so long, it's a blood-deep natural thing with her. Which is how she got saddled with me and Sugar and Junior in the first place while our mothers were in a la-de-da apartment up the block having a good ole time.

So this one day Miss Moore rounds us all up at the mailbox and it's puredee hot and she's knockin herself out about arithmetic. And school suppose to let up in summer I heard, but she don't never let up. And the starch in my pinafore scratching the shit outta me and I'm really hating this nappy-head bitch and her goddamn college degree. I'd much rather go to the pool or to the show where it's cool. So me and Sugar leaning on the mailbox being surly, which is a Miss Moore word. And Flyboy checking out what everybody brought for lunch. And Fat Butt already wasting his peanut-butter-and-jelly sandwich like the pig he is. And Junebug punchin on Q.T.'s arm for potato chips. And Rosie Giraffe shifting from one hip to the other waiting for somebody to step on her foot or ask her if she from Georgia so she can kick ass, preferably Mercedes'. And Miss Moore asking us do we know what money is, like we a bunch of retards. I mean real money, she say, like it's only poker chips or monopoly papers we lay on the grocer. So right away I'm tired of this and say so. And would much rather snatch Sugar and go to the Sunset and terrorize the West Indian kids and take their hair ribbons and their money too. And Miss Moore files that remark away for next week's lesson on brotherhood, I can tell. And finally I say we oughta get to the subway cause it's cooler and besides we might meet some cute boys. Sugar done swiped her mama's lipstick, so we ready.

So we heading down the street and she's boring us silly about what things cost and what our parents make and how much goes for rent and how money ain't divided up right in this country. And then she gets to the part about we all poor and live in the slums, which I don't feature. And I'm ready to speak on that, but she steps out in the street and hails two cabs just like that. Then she hustles half the crew in with her and hands me a five-dollar bill and tells me to calculate 10 percent tip for the driver. And we're off. Me and Sugar and Junebug and Flyboy hangin out the window and hollering to everybody, putting lipstick on each other cause Flyboy a faggot anyway, and making farts with our sweaty armpits. But I'm mostly trying to figure how to spend this money. But they all fascinated with the meter ticking and Junebug starts laying bets to how much it'll read when Flyboy can't hold his breath no more. Then Sugar lays bets as to how much it'll be when we get there. So I'm stuck. Don't nobody want to go for my plan, which is to jump out at the next light and run off to the first bar-b-que we can find. Then the driver tells us to get the hell out cause we there already. And the meter reads eighty-five cents. And I'm stalling to figure out the tip and Sugar say give him a dime. And I decide he don't need it as bad as I do, so later for him. But then he tries to take off with Junebug's foot still in the door so we talk about his mama something ferocious. Then we check out that we on Fifth Avenue and everybody dressed up in stockings. One lady in a fur coat, hot as it is. White folks crazy.

"This is the place," Miss Moore say, presenting it to us in the voice   4
she uses at the museum. "Let's look in the windows before we go in."

"Can we steal?" Sugar asks very serious like she's getting the ground rules squared away before she plays. "I beg your pardon," say Miss Moore, and we fall out. So she leads us around the windows of the toy store and me and Sugar screamin, "This is mine, that's mine, I gotta have that, that was made for me, I was born for that," till Big Butt drowns us out.

"Hey, I'm goin to buy that there."

"That there? You don't even know what it is, stupid."

"I do so," he say punchin on Rosie Giraffe. "It's a microscope."   8

"Whatcha gonna do with a microscope, fool?"

"Look at things."

"Like what, Ronald?" ask Miss Moore. And Big Butt ain't got the first notion. So here go Miss Moore gabbing about the thousands of bacteria in a drop of water and the somethinorother in a speck of blood and the million and one living things in the air around us is invisible to the naked eye. And what she say that for? Junebug go to town on that "naked" and we rolling. Then Miss Moore ask what it cost. So we all jam into the window smudgin it up and the price tag say $300. So then she ask how long'd take for Big Butt and Junebug to save up their allowances. "Too long," I say. "Yeh," adds Sugar, "outgrown it by that time." And Miss Moore say no, you never outgrow learning instruments. "Why, even medical students and interns and," blah, blah, blah. And we ready to choke Big Butt for bringing it up in the first damn place.

"This here costs four hundred eighty dollars," say Rosie Giraffe. So   12
we pile up all over her to see what she pointin out. My eyes tell me it's a chunk of glass cracked with something heavy, and different-color inks dripped into the splits, then the whole thing put into a oven or something. But for $480 it don't make sense.

"That's a paperweight made of semi-precious stones fused together under tremendous pressure," she explains slowly, and her hands doing the mining and all the factory work.

"So what's a paperweight?" asks Rosie Giraffe.

"To weigh paper with, dumbbell," say Flyboy, the wise man from the East.

"Not exactly," say Miss Moore, which is what she say when you warm or way off too. "It's to weigh paper down so it won't scatter and make your desk untidy." So right away me and Sugar curtsy to each other and then to Mercedes who is more the tidy type.

"We don't keep paper on top of the desk in my class," say Junebug, figuring Miss Moore crazy or lyin one.

"At home, then," she say. "Don't you have a calendar and a pencil case and a blotter and a letter-opener on your desk at home where you do your homework?" And she know damn well what our homes look like cause she nosys around in them every chance she gets.

"I don't even have a desk," say Junebug. "Do we?"

"No. And I don't get no homework neither," says Big Butt.

"And I don't even have a home," say Flyboy like he do at school to keep the white folks off his back and sorry for him. Send this poor kid to camp posters, is his specialty.

"I do," says Mercedes. "I have a box of stationery on my desk and a picture of my cat. My godmother bought the stationery and the desk. There's a big rose on each sheet and the envelopes smell like roses."

"Who wants to know about your smelly-ass stationery," say Rosie Giraffe fore I can get my two cents in.

"It's important to have a work area all your own so that . . . "

"Will you look at this sailboat, please," say Flyboy, cuttin her off and pointin to the thing like it was his. So once again we tumble all over each other to gaze at this magnificent thing in the toy store which is just big enough to maybe sail two kittens across the pond if you strap them to the posts tight. We all start reciting the price tag like we in assembly. "Hand-crafted sailboat of fiberglass at one thousand one hundred ninety-five dollars."

"Unbelievable," I hear myself say and am really stunned. I read it again for myself just in case the group recitation put me in a trance. Same thing. For some reason this pisses me off. We look at Miss Moore and she lookin at us, waiting for I dunno what.

"Who'd pay all that when you can buy a sailboat set for a quarter at Pop's, a tube of glue for a dime, and a ball of string for eight cents? It must have a motor and a whole lot else besides," I say. "My sailboat cost me about fifty cents."

"But will it take water?" say Mercedes with her smart ass.

"Took mine to Alley Pond Park once," say Flyboy. "String broke. Lost it. Pity."

"Sailed mine in Central Park and it keeled over and sank. Had to ask my father for another dollar."

"And you got the strap," laugh Big Butt. "The jerk didn't even have a string on it. My old man wailed on his behind."

Little Q.T. was staring hard at the sailboat and you could see he   32
wanted it bad. But he too little and somebody'd just take it from him. So what the hell. "This boat for kids, Miss Moore?"

"Parents silly to buy something like that just to get all broke up," say Rosie Giraffe.

"That much money it should last forever," I figure.

"My father'd buy it for me if I wanted it."

"Your father, my ass," say Rosie Giraffe getting a chance to finally   36
push Mercedes.

"Must be rich people shop here," say Q.T.

"You are a very bright boy," say Flyboy. "What was your first clue?" And he rap him on the head with the back of his knuckles, since Q.T. the only one he could get away with. Though Q.T. liable to come up behind you years later and get his licks in when you half expect it.

"What I want to know is," I says to Miss Moore though I never talk to her, I wouldn't give the bitch that satisfaction, "is how much a real boat costs? I figure a thousand'd get you a yacht any day."

"Why don't you check that out," she says, "and report back to the   40
group?" Which really pains my ass. If you gonna mess up a perfectly good swim day least you could do is have some answers. "Let's go in," she say like she got something up her sleeve. Only she don't lead the way. So me and Sugar turn the corner to where the entrance is, but when we get there I kinda hang back. Not that I'm scared, what's there to be afraid of, just a toy store. But I feel funny, shame. But what I got to be shamed about? Got as much right to go in as anybody. But somehow I can't seem to get hold of the door, so I step away for Sugar to lead. But she hangs back too. And I look at her and she looks at me and this is ridiculous. I mean, damn, I have never ever been shy about doing nothing or going nowhere. But then Mercedes steps up and then Rosie Giraffe and Big Butt crowd in behind and shove, and next thing we all stuffed into the doorway with only Mercedes squeezing past us, smoothing out her jumper and walking right down the aisle. Then the rest of us tumble in like a glued-together jigsaw done all wrong. And people lookin at us. And it's like the time me and Sugar crashed into the Catholic church on a dare. But once we got in there and everything so hushed and holy and the candles and the bowin and the handkerchiefs on all the drooping heads, I just couldn't go through with the plan. Which was for me to run up to the altar and do a tap dance while Sugar played the nose flute and messed around in the holy water. And Sugar kept givin me the elbow. Then later teased me so bad I tied her up in the shower and turned it on and locked her in. And she'd be there till this

day if Aunt Gretchen hadn't finally figured I was lyin about the board-
er takin a shower.

Same thing in the store. We all walkin on tiptoe and hardly touchin
the games and puzzles and things. And I watched Miss Moore who is
steady watchin us like she waitin for a sign. Like Mama Drewery watches the sky and sniffs the air and takes note of just how much slant is in the
bird formation. Then me and Sugar bump smack into each other, so busy
gazing at the toys, 'specially the sailboat. But we don't laugh and go into
our fat-lady bump-stomach routine. We just stare at that price tag. Then
Sugar run a finger over the whole boat. And I'm jealous and want to hit
her. Maybe not her, but I sure want to punch somebody in the mouth.

"Whatcha bring us here for, Miss Moore?"

"You sound angry, Sylvia. Are you mad about something?" Givin
me one of them grins like she tellin a grown-up joke that never turns out
to be funny. And she's lookin very closely at me like maybe she plannin
to do my portrait from memory. I'm mad, but I won't give her that satisfaction. So I slouch around the store bein very bored and say, "Let's go."

Me and Sugar at the back of the train watchin the tracks whizzin by   44
large then small then gettin gobbled up in the dark. I'm thinkin about
this tricky toy I saw in the store. A clown that somersaults on a bar then
does chin-ups just cause you yank lightly at his leg. Cost $35. I could see
me askin my mother for a $35 birthday clown. "You wanna who that
costs what?" she'd say, cocking her head to the side to get a better view
of the hole in my head. Thirty-five dollars and the whole household
could go visit Granddaddy Nelson in the country. Thirty-five dollars
would pay for the rent and the piano bill too. Who are these people that
spend that much for performing clowns and $1000 for toy sailboats?
What kinda work they do and how they live and how come we ain't in
on it? Where we are is who we are, Miss Moore always pointin out. But
it don't necessarily have to be that way, she always adds then waits for
somebody to say that poor people have to wake up and demand their
share of the pie and don't none of us know what kind of pie she talkin
about in the first damn place. But she ain't so smart cause I still got her
four dollars from the taxi and she sure ain't gettin it. Messin up my day
with this shit. Sugar nudges me in my pocket and winks.

Miss Moore lines us up in front of the mailbox where we started
from, seem like years ago, and I got a headache for thinkin so hard. And
we lean all over each other so we can hold up under the draggy-ass lecture she always finishes us off with at the end before we thank her for
borin us to tears. But she just looks at us like she readin tea leaves.
Finally she say, "Well, what do you think of F. A. O. Schwartz?"

Rosie Giraffe mumbles, "White folks crazy."

"I'd like to go there again when I get my birthday money," says
Mercedes, and we shove her out the pack so she has to lean on the mailbox by herself.

"I'd like a shower. Tiring day," say Flyboy.   48

Then Sugar surprises me by sayin, "You know, Miss Moore, I don't think all of us here put together eat in a year what that sailboat costs." And Miss Moore lights up like somebody goosed her. "And?" she say, urging Sugar on. Only I'm standin on her foot so she don't continue.

"Imagine for a minute what kind of society, it is in which some people can spend on a toy what it would cost to feed a family of six or seven. What do you think?"

"I think," say Sugar pushing me off her feet like she never done before, cause I whip her ass in a minute, "that this is not much of a democracy if you ask me. Equal chance to pursue happiness means an equal crack at the dough, don't it?" Miss Moore is besides herself and I am disgusted with Sugar's treachery. So I stand on her foot one more time to see if she'll shove me. She shuts up, and Miss Moore looks at me, sorrowfully I'm thinkin. And somethin weird is goin on, I can feel it in my chest.

"Anybody else learn anything today?" lookin dead at me. I walk   52
away and Sugar has to run to catch up and don't even seem to notice when I shrug her arm off my shoulder.

"Well, we got four dollars anyway," she says.

"Uh hunh."

"We could go to Hascombs and get half a chocolate layer and then go to the Sunset and still have plenty money for potato chips and ice cream sodas."

"Uh hunh."   56

"Race you to Hascombs," she say.

We start down the block and she gets ahead which is O.K. by me cause I'm going to the West End and then over to the Drive to think this day through. She can run if she want to and even run faster. But ain't nobody gonna beat me at nuthin.

Topics for Critical Thinking and Writing

1. What is the point of Miss Moore's lesson? Why does Sylvia resist it?
2. Describe the relationship between Sugar and Sylvia. What is Sugar's function in the story?
3. What does the last line of the story suggest?

Wu-tsu Fa-yen

Wu-tsu Fa-yen (1025–1104) was a Chinese Zen Buddhist priest. More exactly, he was a Ch'an priest: Zen *is Japanese for the Chinese* Ch'an.

The practitioner of Zen (to use the more common name) seeks satori, *"enlightenment" or "awakening." The awakening is from a world of blind strivings (including those of reason and of morality). The awakened being, free from a sense of the self in opposition to all other things, perceives the unity of all things. Wu-tsu belonged to the branch of Zen that uses "shock therapy, the purpose of which is to jolt the student out of his analytical and conceptual way of thinking and lead him back to his natural and spontaneous faculty" (Kenneth Ch'en,* Buddhism in China *[1964, rptd. 1972], p. 359).*

The title of this story, from The Sayings of Goso Hōyen, *is the editors'.*

Zen and the Art of Burglary

If people ask me what Zen is like, I will say that it is like learning the art of burglary. The son of a burglar saw his father growing older and thought, "If he is unable to carry on his profession, who will be the breadwinner of the family, except myself? I must learn the trade." He intimated the idea to his father, who approved of it.

One night the father took the son to a big house, broke through the fence, entered the house, and, opening one of the large chests, told the son to go in and pick out the clothing. As soon as the son got into it, the father dropped the lid and securely applied the lock. The father now came out to the courtyard and loudly knocked at the door, waking up the whole family; then he quietly slipped away by the hole in the fence. The residents got excited and lighted candles, but they found that the burglar had already gone.

The son, who remained all the time securely confined in the chest, thought of his cruel father. He was greatly mortified, then a fine idea flashed upon him. He made a noise like the gnawing of a rat. The family told the maid to take a candle and examine the chest. When the lid was unlocked, out came the prisoner, who blew out the light, pushed away the maid, and fled. The people ran after him. Noticing a well by the road, he picked up a large stone and threw it into the water. The pursuers all gathered around the well trying to find the burglar drowning himself in the dark hole.

In the meantime he went safely back to his father's house. He blamed his father deeply for his narrow escape. Said the father, "Be not offended, my son. Just tell me how you got out of it." When the son told him all about his adventures, the father remarked, "There you are, you have learned the art." 4

Topics for Critical Thinking and Writing

1. What assumptions about knowledge did the father make? Can you think of any of your own experiences that substantiate these assumptions?
2. Is there anything you have studied or are studying to which Zen pedagogical methods would be applicable? If so, explain by setting forth a sample lesson.

8
WORK AND PLAY

Lettuce Cutters, Salinas Valley
Dorothea Lange, 1935

All-Americans in Training at Opa-Locka, Florida
Anonymous

Florida State Archives

Short Views

Work and play are words used to describe the same thing under differing conditions.
Mark Twain

The Battle of Waterloo was won on the playing fields of Eton.
Attributed to the Duke of Wellington

The competitive spirit goes by many names. Most simply and directly, it is called "the work ethic." As the name implies, the work ethic holds that labor is good in itself; that a man or woman at work not only makes a contribution to his fellow man, but becomes a better person by virtue of the act of working. That work ethic is ingrained in the American character. That is why most of us consider it immoral to be lazy or slothful—even if a person is well off enough not to have to work or deliberately avoids work by going on welfare.
Richard Milhous Nixon

In the laws of political economy, the alienation of the worker from his product is expressed as follows: the more the worker produces, the less he has to consume; the more value he creates, the more valueless, the more unworthy he becomes; the better formed is his product, the more deformed becomes the worker; the more civilized his product, the more brutalized becomes the worker; the mightier the work, the more powerless the worker; the more ingenious the work, the duller becomes the worker and the more he becomes nature's bondsman.

Political economy conceals the alienation inherent in labor by avoiding any mention of the evil effects of work on those who work. Thus, whereas labor produces miracles for the rich, for the worker it produces destitution. Labor produces palaces, but for the worker, hovels. It produces beauty, but it cripples the worker. It replaces labor by machines, but how does it treat the worker? By throwing some workers back into a barbarous kind of work, and by turning the rest into machines. It produces intelligence, but for the worker, stupidity and cretinism.
Karl Marx

324

My young men shall never work. Men who work cannot dream, and wisdom comes in dreams.

Smohalla, of the Nez Perce

Everyone who is prosperous or successful must have dreamed of something. It is not because he is a good worker that he is prosperous, but because he dreamed.

Lost Star, of the Maricopa

The possible quantity of play depends on the possible quantity of pay.

John Ruskin

It can't be just a job. It's not worth playing just for money. It's a way of life. When we were kids there was the release in playing, the sweetness in being able to move and control your body. This is what play is. Beating somebody is secondary. When I was a kid, to really *move* was my delight. I felt released because I could move around anybody. I was free.

Eric Nesterenko, Professional Hockey Player

Winning is not the most important thing; it's everything.

Vince Lombardi

The games don't matter to me. I have no interest in the games. The only things that interested me in sports were the issues. I was interested in Muhammad Ali, in Jackie Roosevelt Robinson, in Curtis Flood. That's the kind of thing that mattered to me. Curtis Flood's assault on baseball, the reserve clause. I remember going to see Flood, who was tending bar in a place called The Rustic Inn. . . . He told me, "There's something in my heart and in my mind that says, 'No, you can't trade me. You can't sell me. This is the United States of America, and I will not be traded as a slave.'" I was fulfilled by his attitude and his behavior. That mattered to me. I was never interested in these silly games. I can't think of anything less important in life that who wins or loses a game. There are certain causes in sports that transcend sport, that have to do with constitutional law, that have to do with the nature of society.

Howard Cosell

Serious sport has nothing to do with fair play. It is bound up with hatred, jealousy, boastfulness, disregard of all rules and sadistic pleasure in witnessing violence: in other words, it is war minus the shooting.
George Orwell

The maturity of man—that means to have reacquired the seriousness that one has as a child at play.
Friedrich Nietzsche

I see great things in baseball. It's our game—the American game. It will take our people out-of-doors, fill them with oxygen, give them a larger physical stoicism. Tend to relieve us from being a nervous, dyspeptic set. Repair these losses, and be a blessing to us.
Walt Whitman

It's great because it has no clock. You can play forever. You can't kill that clock or run a few plays up the middle as you can do in the other sports.

It's great because it is a sport of rigid, complex rules, but every field is unique. No park is the same, and no other sport can make that claim.

It's great because you can do things in foul territory; you can win a game, you can lose a game, outside the field.

It's great because it not only follows the rhythms of the seasons but it is as much about loss as it is about winning. The greatest baseball players fail seven times out of ten.

It's great because you can't go to your best player every time as you can in other sports. Even Babe Ruth came up only once every nine times.
Ken Burns

The boys throw stones at the frogs in sport, but the frogs die not in sport but in earnest.
Bion

Bertrand Russell

Bertrand Russell (1872–1970) was educated at Trinity College, Cambridge. He published his first book, The Study of German Social Democracy, *in 1896: subsequent books on mathematics and on philosophy quickly established his international reputation. His pacifist opposition to World War I cost him his appointment at Trinity College and won him a prison sentence of six months. While serving this sentence he wrote his* Introduction to Mathematical Philosophy. *In 1940 an appointment to teach at the College of the City of New York was withdrawn because of Russell's unorthodox moral views. But he was not always treated shabbily; he won numerous awards, including (in 1950) a Nobel Prize. After World War II he devoted most of his energy to warning the world about the dangers of nuclear war.*

In reading the first sentence of the essay that we reprint, you should know that the essay comes from a book called The Conquest of Happiness, *published in 1930.*

Work

Whether work should be placed among the causes of happiness or among the causes of unhappiness may perhaps be regarded as a doubtful question. There is certainly much work which is exceedingly irksome, and an excess of work is always very painful. I think, however, that, provided work is not excessive in amount, even the dullest work is to most people less painful than idleness. There are in work all grades, from mere relief of tedium up to the profoundest delights, according to the nature of the work and the abilities of the worker. Most of the work that most people have to do is not in itself interesting, but even such work has certain great advantages. To begin with, it fills a good many hours of the day without the need of deciding what one shall do. Most people, when they are left free to fill their own time according to their own choice, are at a loss to think of anything sufficiently pleasant to be worth doing. And whatever they decide on, they are troubled by the feeling that something else would have been pleasanter. To be able to fill leisure intelligently is the last product of civilization, and at present very few people have reached this level. Moreover the exercise of choice is in itself tiresome. Except to people with unusual initiative it is positively agreeable to be told what to do at each hour of the day, provided the orders are not too unpleasant. Most of the idle rich suffer unspeakable boredom as the price of their freedom from drudgery. At times, they may find relief by hunting big game in Africa, or by flying round the world, but the number of such sensations is limited, especially after youth is past. Accordingly the more intelligent rich men work nearly as hard as if they were poor, while rich women for the most part keep themselves busy with innumerable trifles of whose earth-shaking importance they are firmly persuaded.

Work therefore is desirable, first and foremost, as a preventive of boredom, for the boredom that a man feels when he is doing necessary though uninteresting work is as nothing in comparison with the boredom that he feels when he has nothing to do with his days. With this

327

advantage of work another is associated, namely that it makes holidays much more delicious when they come. Provided a man does not have to work so hard as to impair his vigor, he is likely to find far more zest in his free time than an idle man could possibly find.

The second advantage of most paid work and of some unpaid work is that it gives chances of success and opportunities for ambition. In most work success is measured by income, and while our capitalistic society continues, this is inevitable. It is only where the best work is concerned that this measure ceases to be the natural one to apply. The desire that men feel to increase their income is quite as much a desire for success as for the extra comforts that a higher income can procure. However dull work may be, it becomes bearable if it is a means of building up a reputation, whether in the world at large or only in one's own circle. Continuity of purpose is one of the most essential ingredients of happiness in the long run, and for most men this comes chiefly through their work. In this respect those women whose lives are occupied with housework are much less fortunate than men, or than women who work outside the home. The domesticated wife does not receive wages, has no means of bettering herself, is taken for granted by her husband (who sees practically nothing of what she does), and is valued by him not for her housework but for quite other qualities. Of course this does not apply to those women who are sufficiently well-to-do to make beautiful houses and beautiful gardens and become the envy of their neighbors; but such women are comparatively few, and for the great majority housework cannot bring as much satisfaction as work of other kinds brings to men and to professional women.

The satisfaction of killing time and of affording some outlet, how-   4
ever modest, for ambition, belongs to most work, and is sufficient to make even a man whose work is dull happier on the average than a man who has no work at all. But when work is interesting, it is capable of giving satisfaction of a far higher order than mere relief from tedium. The kinds of work in which there is some interest may be arranged in a hierarchy. I shall begin with those which are only mildly interesting and end with those that are worthy to absorb the whole energies of a great man.

Two chief elements make work interesting; first, the exercise of skill, and second, construction.

Every man who has acquired some unusual skill enjoys exercising it until it has become a matter of course, or until he can no longer improve himself. This motive to activity begins in early childhood: a boy who can stand on his head becomes reluctant to stand on his feet. A great deal of work gives the same pleasure that is to be derived from games of skill. The work of a lawyer or a politician must contain in a more delectable form a great deal of the same pleasure that is to be derived from playing bridge. Here of course there is not only the exercise of skill but the outwitting of a skilled opponent. Even where this competitive element is absent, however, the performance of difficult feats is agreeable. A man who can do stunts in an aeroplane finds the pleasure so great that for the sake of it he is willing to risk his life. I imagine that an able surgeon, in spite of the painful circumstances in which his work is done, derives satisfaction from the exquisite precision of his operations. The same kind of pleasure, though in a less intense form, is to be derived from a great deal of work of a humbler kind. All skilled work can be pleasurable, provided the skill required is either variable or capable of indefinite improvement. If these conditions are absent, it will cease to be interesting when a man has acquired his maximum skill. A man who runs three-mile races will cease to find pleasure in this occupation when he passes the age at which he can beat his own previous record. Fortunately there is a very considerable amount of work in which new circumstances call for new skill and a man can go on improving, at any rate until he has reached middle age. In some kinds of skilled work, such as politics, for example, it seems that men are at their best between sixty and seventy, the reason being that in such occupations a wide experience of other men is essential. For this reason successful politicians are apt to be happier at the age of seventy than any other men of equal age. Their only competitors in this respect are the men who are the heads of big businesses.

There is, however, another element possessed by the best work, which is even more important as a source of happiness than is the exercise of skill. This is the element of constructiveness. In some work, though by no means in most, something is built up which remains as a monument when the work is completed. We may distinguish construction from destruction by the following criterion. In construction the initial state of affairs is comparatively haphazard, while the final state of affairs embodies a purpose: in destruction the reverse is the case; the initial state of affairs embodies a purpose, while the final state of affairs is haphazard, that is to say, all that is intended by the destroyer is to produce a state of affairs which does not embody a certain purpose. This criterion applies in the most literal and obvious case, namely the construction and destruction of buildings. In constructing a building a previously made plan is carried out, whereas in destroying it no one decides exactly how the materials are to lie when the demolition is complete. Destruction is of course necessary very often as a preliminary to subsequent construction; in that case it is part of a whole which is constructive. But not infrequently a man will engage in activities of which the purpose is destructive without regard to any construction that may come after. Frequently he will conceal this from himself by the belief that he is only sweeping away in order to build afresh, but it is generally possible to unmask this pretense, when it is a pretense, by asking him what the subsequent construction is to be. On this subject it will be found that he will speak vaguely and without enthusiasm, whereas on the preliminary destruction he has spoken precisely and with zest. This applies to not a few revolutionaries and militarists and other apostles of violence. They are actuated, usually without their own knowledge, by hatred: the destruction of what they hate is their real purpose, and they are comparatively indifferent to the question what is to come after it. Now I cannot deny that in the work of destruction as in the work of construction there may be joy. It is a fiercer joy, perhaps at moments more intense, but it is less profoundly satisfying, since the result is one in which little satisfaction is to be found. You kill your enemy, and when he is dead your occupation is gone, and the satisfaction that you derive from victory quickly fades. The work of construction, on the other hand, when completed is delightful to contemplate, and moreover is never so fully completed that there is nothing further to do about it. The most satisfactory purposes are those that lead on indefinitely from one success to another without ever coming to a dead end; and in this respect it will be found that construction is a greater source of happiness than destruction. Perhaps it would be more correct to say that those who find satisfaction in construction find in it greater satisfaction than the lovers of destruction can find in destruction, for if once you have become filled with hate you will not easily derive from construction the pleasure which another man would derive from it.

At the same time few things are so likely to cure the habit of hatred   8
as the opportunity to do constructive work of an important kind.

The satisfaction to be derived from success in a great constructive enterprise is one of the most massive that life has to offer, although unfortunately in its highest forms it is open only to men of exceptional ability. Nothing can rob a man of the happiness of successful achievement in an important piece of work, unless it be the proof that after all his work was bad. There are many forms of such satisfaction. The man who by a scheme of irrigation has caused the wilderness to blossom like the rose enjoys it in one of its most tangible forms. The creation of an organization may be a work of supreme importance. So is the work of those few statesmen who have devoted their lives to producing order out of chaos, of whom Lenin is the supreme type in our day. The most obvious examples are artists and men of science. Shakespeare says of his verse: "So long as men can breathe, or eyes can see, so long lives this." And it cannot be doubted that the thought consoled him for misfortune. In his sonnets he maintains that the thought of his friend reconciled him to life, but I cannot help suspecting that the sonnets he wrote to his friend were even more effective for this purpose than the friend himself. Great artists and great men of science do work which is in itself delightful; while they are doing it, it secures them the respect of those whose respect is worth having, which gives them the most fundamental kind of power, namely power over men's thoughts and feelings. They have also the most solid reasons for thinking well of themselves. This combination of fortunate circumstances ought, one would think, to be enough to make any man happy. Nevertheless it is not so.

Michael Angelo, for example, was a profoundly unhappy man, and maintained (not, I am sure, with truth) that he would not have troubled to produce works of art if he had not had to pay the debts of his impecunious relations. The power to produce great art is very often, though by no means always, associated with a temperamental unhappiness, so great that but for the joy which the artist derives from his work, he would be driven to suicide. We cannot, therefore, maintain that even the greatest work must make a man happy; we can only maintain that it must make him less unhappy. Men of science, however, are far less often temperamentally unhappy than artists are, and in the main the men who do great work in science are happy men, whose happiness is derived primarily from their work.

One of the causes of unhappiness among intellectuals in the present day is that so many of them, especially those whose skill is literary, find no opportunity for the independent exercise of their talents, but have to hire themselves out to rich corporations directed by Philistines, who insist upon their producing what they themselves regard as pernicious nonsense. If you were to inquire among journalists in either England or America whether they believed in the policy of the newspaper for which they worked, you would find, I believe, that only a small minority do so; the rest, for the sake of a livelihood, prostitute their skill to purposes which they believe to be harmful. Such work cannot bring any real satisfaction, and in the course of reconciling himself to the doing of it, a man has to make himself so cynical that he can no longer derive whole-hearted satisfaction from anything whatever. I cannot condemn men who undertake work of this sort, since starvation is too serious an alternative, but I think that where it is possible to do work that is satisfactory to a man's constructive impulses without entirely starving, he will be well advised from the point of view of his own happiness if he chooses it in preference to work much more highly paid but not seeming to him worth doing on its own account. Without self-respect genuine happiness is scarcely possible. And the man who is ashamed of his work can hardly achieve self-respect.

The satisfaction of constructive work, though it may, as things are, be the privilege of a minority, can nevertheless be the privilege of a quite large minority. Any man who is his own master in his work can feel it; so can any man whose work appears to him useful and requires considerable skill. The production of satisfactory children is a difficult constructive work capable of affording profound satisfaction. Any woman who has achieved this can feel that as a result of her labor the world contains something of value which it would not otherwise contain.

Human beings differ profoundly in regard to the tendency to regard their lives as a whole. To some men it is natural to do so, and essential to happiness to be able to do so with some satisfaction. To others life is a series of detached incidents without directed movement and without unity. I think the former sort are more likely to achieve happiness than the latter, since they will gradually build up those circumstances from which they can derive contentment and self-respect, whereas the others will be blown about by the winds of circumstances now this way, now that, without ever arriving at any haven. The habit of viewing life as a whole is an essential part both of wisdom and of true morality, and is one of the things which ought to be encouraged in education. Consistent purpose is not enough to make life happy, but it is an almost indispensable condition of a happy life. And consistent purpose embodies itself mainly in work.

Topics for Critical Thinking and Writing

1. Russell says (paragraph 3): "The desire that men feel to increase their income is quite as much a desire for success as for the extra comforts that a higher income can procure." In its context, what does *success* mean? In your experience, do Russell's words ring true? Why or why not?

2. In paragraphs 7–11 Russell develops a contrast between what he calls "destructive" and "constructive" work. Is the contrast clarified by the examples he offers? What examples from your own experience or knowledge can you add?

3. In paragraph 10 Russell speaks of workers who "prostitute their skills to purposes which they believe to be harmful." What work does he use as an example here? What other examples can you offer? Imagine yourself doing work that you do not respect or that you even find "harmful." Then imagine being offered work that you do respect but at a much lower salary. How helpful would you find Russell's advice? What would you do? (Specific examples of work that you respect and work that you don't respect will help you to form a clear idea of the choice and a clear argument to support it.)

4. What new point does Russell introduce in his last paragraph? How well does this last paragraph work as a conclusion?

5. Russell is generally admired for his exceptionally clear prose. List some of the devices that make for clarity in this essay.

6. Through most of his essay, Russell writes as if only men were engaged in work. What references to women working do you find? From these references and from the predominant references to men, would you describe Russell as sexist? Why or why not?

7. Compare Russell with Steinem (page 360) on the value of work.

W. H. Auden

W[ystan] H[ugh] Auden (1907–73) was born and educated in England. In 1939 he came to the United States and became an American citizen, but in 1972 he returned to England to live. Although Auden established his reputation chiefly with his poetry, he also wrote excellent plays, libretti, and essays.

One of Auden's most unusual works, A Certain World: A Commonplace Book, is an anthology of some of his favorite passages from other people's books, along with brief reflections on his reading. The passage we print here begins with a reference to Hannah Arendt's The Human Condition.

Work, Labor, and Play

So far as I know, Miss Hannah Arendt was the first person to define the essential difference between work and labor. To be happy, a man must feel, firstly, free and, secondly, important. He cannot be really happy if he is compelled by society to do what he does not enjoy doing, or if what he enjoys doing is ignored by society as of no value or importance. In a society where slavery in the strict sense has been abolished, the sign that what a man does is of social value is that he is paid money to do it, but a laborer today can rightly be called a wage slave. A man is a laborer if the job society offers him is of no interest to himself but he is compelled to take it by the necessity of earning a living and supporting his family.

The antithesis to labor is play. When we play a game, we enjoy what we are doing, otherwise we should not play it, but it is a purely private activity; society could not care less whether we play it or not.

Between labor and play stands work. A man is a worker if he is personally interested in the job which society pays him to do; what from the point of view of society is necessary labor is from his own point of view voluntary play. Whether a job is to be classified as labor or work depends, not on the job itself, but on the tastes of the individual who undertakes it. The difference does not, for example, coincide with the difference between a manual and a mental job; a gardener or a cobbler may be a worker, a bank clerk a laborer. Which a man is can be seen from his attitude toward leisure. To a worker, leisure means simply the hours he needs to relax and rest in order to work efficiently. He is therefore more likely to take too little leisure than too much; workers die of coronaries and forget their wives' birthdays. To the laborer, on the other hand, leisure means freedom from compulsion, so that it is natural for him to imagine that the fewer hours he has to spend laboring, and the more hours he is free to play, the better.

What percentage of the population in a modern technological society are, like myself, in the fortunate position of being workers? At a guess I would say sixteen per cent, and I do not think that figure is likely to get bigger in the future.

Technology and the division of labor have done two things: by eliminating in many fields the need for special strength or skill; they

333

have made a very large number of paid occupations which formerly were enjoyable work into boring labor, and by increasing productivity they have reduced the number of necessary laboring hours. It is already possible to imagine a society in which the majority of the population, that is to say, its laborers, will have almost as much leisure as in earlier times was enjoyed by the aristocracy. When one recalls how aristocracies in the past actually behaved, the prospect is not cheerful. Indeed, the problem of dealing with boredom may be even more difficult for such a future mass society than it was for aristocracies. The latter, for example, ritualized their time; there was a season to shoot grouse, a season to spend in town, etc. The masses are more likely to replace an unchanging ritual by fashion which it will be in the economic interest of certain people to change as often as possible. Again, the masses cannot go in for hunting, for very soon there would be no animals left to hunt. For other aristocratic amusements like gambling, dueling, and warfare, it may be only too easy to find equivalents in dangerous driving, drug-taking, and senseless acts of violence. Workers seldom commit acts of violence, because they can put their aggression into their work, be it physical like the work of a smith, or mental like the work of a scientist or an artist. The role of aggression in mental work is aptly expressed by the phrase "getting one's teeth into a problem."

Topics for Critical Thinking and Writing

1. Some readers have had trouble following Auden in his first three paragraphs, although by the end of the third paragraph the difficulties have disappeared. Can you summarize the first paragraph in a sentence? If you think that the development of the idea in these first three paragraphs could be clearer, insert the necessary phrases or sentences, or indicate with arrows the places to which sentences should be moved.

2. Compare Auden with Russell (page 327) on the relationship between work and happiness.

Malcolm X, born Malcolm Little in Nebraska in 1925, was the son of a Baptist minister. He completed the eighth grade, but then he got into trouble and was sent to a reformatory. After his release he became a thief, dope peddler, and pimp. In 1944 he was sent to jail, where he spent six and a half years. During his years in jail he became a convert to the Black Muslim faith. Paroled in 1950, he served as a minister and founded Muslim temples throughout the United States. In 1964, however, he broke with Elijah Muhammad, leader of the Black Muslims and a powerful advocate of separation of whites and blacks. Malcolm X formed a new group, the Organization of Afro-American Unity, but a year later he was assassinated in New York. His Autobiography, *written with Alex Haley, was published in 1964. Haley (1921–92) is also the author of* Roots, *a study tracing a black family back through seven generations.*

"The Shoeshine Boy" (editors' title) is from The Autobiography of Malcolm X, chapter 3.

The Shoeshine Boy

When I got home, Ella said there had been a telephone call from somebody named Shorty. He had left a message that over at the Roseland State Ballroom, the shoeshine boy was quitting that night, and Shorty had told him to hold the job for me.

"Malcolm, you haven't had any experience shining shoes," Ella said. Her expression and tone of voice told me she wasn't happy about my taking that job. I didn't particularly care, because I was already speechless thinking about being somewhere close to the greatest bands in the world. I didn't even wait to eat any dinner.

The ballroom was all lighted when I got there. A man at the front door was letting in members of Benny Goodman's band. I told him I wanted to see the shoeshine boy, Freddie.

"You're going to be the new one?" he asked. I said I thought I was, and he laughed, "Well, maybe you'll hit the numbers and get a Cadillac, too." He told me that I'd find Freddie upstairs in the men's room on the second floor.   4

But downstairs before I went up, I stepped over and snatched a glimpse inside the ballroom. I just couldn't believe the size of that waxed floor! At the far end, under the soft, rose-colored lights, was the bandstand with the Benny Goodman musicians moving around, laughing and talking, arranging their horns and stands.

A wiry, brown-skinned, conked fellow upstairs in the men's room greeted me. "You Shorty's homeboy?" I said I was, and he said he was Freddie. "Good old boy," he said. "He called me, he just heard I hit the big number, and he figured right I'd be quitting." I told Freddie what the man at the front door had said about a Cadillac. He laughed and said, "Burns them white cats up when you get yourself something. Yeah, I told them I was going to get me one—just to bug them."

Freddie then said for me to pay close attention, that he was going to be busy and for me to watch but not get in the way, and he'd try to get me ready to take over at the next dance, a couple of nights later.

As Freddie busied himself setting up the shoeshine stand, he told   8
me, "Get here early . . . your shoeshine rags and brushes by this footstand
. . . your polish bottles, paste wax, suede brushes over here . . . everything
in place, you get rushed, you never need to waste motion . . . "

While you shined shoes, I learned, you also kept watch on customers inside, leaving the urinals. You darted over and offered a small
white hand towel. "A lot of cats who ain't planning to wash their
hands, sometimes you can run up with a towel and shame them. Your
towels are really your best hustle in here. Cost you a penny apiece to
launder—you always get at least a nickel tip."

The shoeshine customers, and any from the inside rest room who
took a towel, you whiskbroomed a couple of licks. "A nickel or a dime
tip, just give 'em that," Freddie said. "But for two bits, Uncle Tom a little—white cats especially like that. I've had them to come back two,
three times a dance."

From down below, the sound of the music had begun floating up. I
guess I stood transfixed. "You never seen a big dance?" asked Freddie.
"Run on awhile, and watch."

There were a few couples already dancing under the rose-covered   12
lights. But even more exciting to me was the crowd thronging in. The
most glamorous-looking white women I'd ever seen—young ones, old
ones, white cats buying tickets at the window, sticking big wads of
green bills back into their pockets, checking the women's coats, and
taking their arms and squiring them inside.

Freddie had some early customers when I got back upstairs.
Between the shoeshine stand and thrusting towels to me just as they
approached the wash basin, Freddie seemed to be doing four things at
once. "Here, you can take over the whiskbroom," he said, "just two or
three licks—but let 'em feel it."

When things slowed a little, he said, "You ain't seen nothing
tonight. You wait until you see a spooks' dance! Man, our own people
carry *on!*" Whenever he had a moment, he kept schooling me.
"Shoelaces, this drawer here. You just starting out, I'm going to make
these to you as a present. Buy them for a nickel a pair, tell cats they need
laces if they do, and charge two bits."

Every Benny Goodman record I'd ever heard in my life, it seemed,
was filtering faintly into where we were. During another customer lull,
Freddie let me slip back outside again to listen. Peggy Lee was at the
mike singing. Beautiful! She had just joined the band and she was from
North Dakota and had been singing with a group in Chicago when Mrs.
Benny Goodman discovered her, we had heard some customers say. She
finished the song and the crowd burst into applause. She was a big hit.

"It knocked me out, too, when I first broke in here," Freddie said,   16
grinning, when I went back in there. "But, look, you ever shined any
shoes?" He laughed when I said I hadn't, excepting my own. "Well,
let's get to work. I never had neither." Freddie got on the stand and
went to work on his own shoes. Brush, liquid polish, brush, paste wax,

shine rag, lacquer sole dressing . . . step by step, Freddie showed me what to do.

"But you got to get a whole lot faster. You can't waste time!" Freddie showed me how fast on my own shoes. Then, because business was tapering off, he had time to give me a demonstration of how to make the shine rag pop like a firecracker. "Dig the action?" he asked. He did it in slow motion. I got down and tried it on his shoes. I had the principle of it. "Just got to do it faster," Freddie said. "It's a jive noise, that's all. Cats tip better, they figure you're knocking yourself out!"

Topics for Critical Thinking and Writing

1. In this selection Malcolm X is more concerned with Benny Goodman than with learning about shining shoes. Freddie is concerned with teaching Malcolm the trade. What are we concerned with in this selection?
2. How would you characterize Freddie's attitude toward his job? Compare it with Maggie Holmes's attitude (pages 353–59) toward her job.
3. In paragraph 17 Freddie demonstrates a "jive noise." Using evidence from this selection, the library, mother wit, or what you will, define *jive.*
4. On what date did Malcolm begin his apprenticeship as a shoeshine boy? How did you arrive at that date?

Studs Terkel

Studs Terkel was born Louis Terkel in New York City in 1912. He was brought up in Chicago and graduated from the University of Chicago. Terkel has been an actor, playwright, columnist, and disc jockey, but he is best known as the man who makes books out of tape recordings of people he gets to talk. Among these oral histories are Division Street America *(1966),* Hard Times *(1970), and* Working *(1974).*

"Three Workers" (editors' title) is from the last of these books.

Three Workers

I. Terry Mason, Airline Stewardess

She has been an airline stewardess for six years. She is twenty-six-years old, recently married. "The majority of airline stewardesses are from small towns. I myself am from Nebraska. It's supposed to be one of the nicest professions for a woman—if she can't be a model or in the movies. All the great benefits: flying around the world, meeting all those people. It is a nice status symbol.

"I have five older sisters and they were all married before they were twenty. The minute they got out of high school, they would end up getting married. That was the thing everybody did, was get married. When I told my parents I was going to the airlines, they got excited. They were so happy that one of the girls could go out and see the world and spend some time being single. I didn't get married until I was almost twenty-five. My mother especially thought it would be great that I could have the ambition, the nerve to go to the big city on my own and try to accomplish being a stewardess."

When people ask you what you're doing and you say stewardess, you're really proud, you think it's great. It's like a stepping stone. The first two months I started flying I had already been to London, Paris, and Rome. And me from Broken Bow, Nebraska. But after you start working, it's not as glamorous as you thought it was going to be.

They like girls that have a nice personality and that are pleasant to   4
look at. If a woman has a problem with blemishes, they take her off. Until the appearance counselor thinks she's ready to go back on. One day this girl showed up, she had a very slight black eye. They took her off. Little things like that.

We had to go to stew school for five weeks. We'd go through a whole week of makeup and poise. I didn't like this. They make you feel like you've never been out in public. They showed you how to smoke a cigarette, when to smoke a cigarette, how to look at a man's eyes. Our teacher, she had this idea we had to be sexy. One day in class she was showing us how to accept a light for a cigarette from a man and never blow it out. When he lights it, just look in his eyes. It was really funny, all the girls laughed.

It's never proper for a woman to light her own cigarette. You hold it up and of course you're out with a guy who knows the right way to light the cigarette. You look into their eyes as they're lighting your cigarette and you're cupping his hand, but holding it just very light, so that he can feel your touch and your warmth. (Laughs.) You do not blow the match out. It used to be really great for a woman to blow the match out when she looked in his eyes, but she said now the man blows the match out.

The idea is not to be too obvious about it. They don't want you to look too forward. That's the whole thing, being a lady but still giving out that womanly appeal, like the body movement and the lips and the eyes. The guy's supposed to look in your eyes. You could be a real mean woman. You're a lady and doing all these evil things with your eyes.

She did try to promote people smoking. She said smoking can be   8
part of your conversation. If you don't know what to say, you can always pull out a cigarette. She says it makes you more comfortable. I started smoking when I was on the airlines.

Our airline picks the girl-next-door type. At one time they wouldn't let us wear false eyelashes and false fingernails. Now it's required that you wear false eyelashes, and if you do not have the right length nails, you wear false nails. Everything is supposed to be becoming to the passenger.

That's the whole thing: meeting all these great men that either have great business backgrounds or are good looking or different. You do meet a lot of movie stars and a lot of political people, but you don't get to really visit with them that much. You never really get to go out with these men. Stewardesses are impressed only by name people. But a normal millionaire that you don't know you're not impressed about. The only thing that really thrills a stewardess is a passenger like Kennedy or movie stars or somebody political. Celebrities.

I think our average age is twenty-six. But our supervisors tell us what kind of make-up to wear, what kind of lipstick to wear, if our hair is not the right style for us, if we're not smiling enough. They even tell us how to act when you're on a pass. Like last night I met my husband. I was in plain clothes. I wanted to kiss him. But I'm not supposed to kiss anybody at the terminal. You're not supposed to walk off with a passenger, hand in hand. After you get out of the terminal, that's all yours.

The majority of passengers do make passes. The ones that do make passes are married and are business people. When I tell them I'm married, they say, "I'm married and you're married and you're away from home and so am I and nobody's gonna find out." The majority of those who make passes at you, you wouldn't accept a date if they were friends of yours at home.

After I was a stewardess for a year, and I was single, I came down to the near North Side of Chicago, which is the swinging place for singles. Stewardess, that was a dirty name. In a big city, it's an easy woman. I didn't like this at all. All these books—*Coffee, Tea and Me.*

I lived in an apartment complex where the majority there were stewardesses.[1] The other women were secretaries and teachers. They would go to our parties and they would end up being among the worst. They never had stories about these secretaries and nurses, but they sure had good ones about stewardesses.

I meet a lot of other wives or single women. The first minute they start talking to me, they're really cold. They think the majority of stewardesses are snobs or they may be jealous. These women think we have a great time, that we are playgirls, that we have the advantage to go out with every type of man we want. So when they first meet us, they really turn off on us.

When you first start flying, the majority of girls do live in apartment complexes by the airport. The men they meet are airport employees: ramp rats, cleaning airplanes and things like that, mechanics, and young pilots, not married, ones just coming in fresh.

After a year we get tired of that, so we move into the city to get involved with men that are usually young executives, like at Xerox or something. Young businessmen in the early thirties and late twenties, they really think stewardesses are the gals to go out with if they want to get so far. They wear their hats and their suits and in the winter their black gloves. The women are getting older, they're getting twenty-four, twenty-five. They get involved with bartenders too. Stewardesses and bartenders are a pair. (Laughs.)

One time I went down into the area of swinging bars with two other girls. We just didn't want anybody to know that we were stewardesses,

---

[1]"In New York, stewardesses live five or six girls to one apartment. They think they can get by because they're in and out so much. But there's gonna be a few nights they're all gonna be home at once and a couple of 'em will have to sleep on the floor."

so we had this story made up that we were going to a women's college in Colorado. That went over. We had people that were talking to us, being nice to us, being polite. Down there, they wouldn't even be polite. They'd buy you drinks but then they'd steal your stool if you got up to go to the restroom. But when they knew you weren't stewardesses, just young ladies that were going to a women's college, they were really nice to us.

They say you can spot a stewardess by the way she wears her makeup. At that time we all had short hair and everybody had it cut in stew school exactly alike. If there's two blondes they have their hair cut very short, wearing the same shade of makeup, and they get into uniform, people say, "Oh, you look like sisters." Wonder why? (Laughs.)

The majority of us were against it because they wouldn't let you   20
say how *you'd* like your hair cut, they wouldn't let you have your own personality, *your* makeup, *your* clothes. They'd tell you what length skirts to wear. At one time they told us we couldn't wear anything one inch above the knees. And no pants at that time. It's different now.

Wigs used to be forbidden. Now it's the style. Now it's permissible for nice women to wear wigs, eyelashes, and false fingernails. Before it was the harder looking women that wore them. Women showing up in pants, it wasn't ladylike. Hot pants are in now. Most airlines change styles every year.

> She describes stewardess schools in the past as being like college dorms: it was forbidden to go out during the week; signing in and out on Friday and Saturday nights. "They've cut down stewardess school quite a bit. Cut down on how-to-serve meal classes and paperwork. A lot of girls get on aircraft these days and don't know where a magazine is, where the tray tables are for passengers. . . . Every day we used to have an examination. If you missed over two questions, that was a failure. They'd ask us ten questions. If you failed two tests out of the whole five weeks, you would have to leave. Now they don't have any exams at all. Usually we get a raise every year. We haven't been getting that lately."

We have long duty hours. We can be on duty for thirteen hours. But we're not supposed to fly over eight hours. This is in a twenty-four-hour period. During the eight hours, you could be flying from Chicago to Flint, to Moline, short runs. You stop twenty minutes. So you get to New York finally, after five stops, let's say. You have an hour on your own. But you have to be on the plane thirty minutes before departure time. How many restaurants can serve you food in thirty minutes? So you've gone thirteen hours, off and on duty, having half-hours and no time to eat. This is the normal thing. If we have only thirty minutes and we don't have time to eat, it's our hard luck.

Pilots have the same thing too. They end up grabbing a sandwich   24
and eating in the cockpit. When I first started flying we were not supposed to eat at all on the aircraft, even though there was an extra meal left over. Now we can eat in the buffet. We have to stand there with all those dirty dishes and eat our meals—if there's one left over. We cannot eat in the public eye. We cannot bring it out if there's an extra seat. You can smoke in the cockpit, in the restrooms, but not in the public's eye.

"We have a union. It's a division of the pilot's union. It helps us out on duty time and working privileges. It makes sure that if we're in Cleveland and stuck because of weather and thirteen hours have gone by, we can go to bed. Before we had a union the stew office would call and say, 'You're working another seven.' I worked one time thirty-six hours straight."

The other day I had fifty-five minutes to serve 101 coach passengers, a cocktail and full-meal service. You do it fast and terrible. You're very rude. You don't mean to be rude, you just don't have time to answer questions. You smile and you just ignore it. You get three drink orders in a hurry. There's been many times when you miss the glass, pouring, and you pour it in the man's lap. You just don't say I'm sorry. You give him a cloth and you keep going. That's the bad part of the job.

Sometimes I get tired of working first class. These people think they're great, paying for more, and want more. Also I get tired of coach passengers asking for something that he thinks he's a first-class passenger. We get this attitude of difference from our airlines. They're just dividing the class of people. If we're on a first-class pass, the women are to wear a dress or a nice pants suit that has a matching jacket, and the men are to dress with suit jacket and tie and white shirt. And yet so many types of first-class passengers: some have grubby clothes, jeans and moccasins and everything. They can afford to dress the way they feel. . . .

If I want to fly first class, I pay the five dollars difference. I like the idea of getting free drinks, free champagne, free wine. In a coach, you don't. A coach passenger might say, "Could I have a pillow?" So you give him a pillow. Then he'll say, "Could you bring me a glass of water?" A step behind him there's the water fountain. In first class, if the guy says, "I want a glass of water," even if the water fountain is right by his arm, you'd bring it for him. We give him all this extra because he's first class. Which isn't fair. . . .   28

When you're in a coach, you feel like there's just heads and heads and heads of people. That's all you can see. In first class, being less people, you're more relaxed, you have more time. When you get on a 727, we have one coatroom. Our airline tells us you hang up first class coats only. When a coach passenger says, "Could you hang up my coat?" most of the time I'll hang it up. Why should I hang up first class and not coach?

One girl is for first class only and there's two girls for coach. The senior girl will be first class. That first-class girl gets used to working first class. If she happens to walk through the coach, if someone asks her for something, she'll make the other girls do it. The first stew always stays at the door and welcomes everybody aboard and says good-by to everybody when they leave. That's why a lot of girls don't like to be first class.

There's an old story on the airline. The stewardess asks if he'd like something to drink, him and his wife. He says, "I'd like a martini." The stewardess asks the wife, "Would you like a drink?" She doesn't say anything, and the husband says, "I'm sorry, she's not used to talking to the help." (Laughs.) When I started flying, that was the first story I heard.

I've never had the nerve to speak up to anybody that's pinched me   32
or said something dirty. Because I've always been afraid of these onion

letters. These are bad letters. If you get a certain amount of bad letters, you're fired. When you get a bad letter you have to go in and talk to the supervisor. Other girls now, there are many of 'em that are coming around and telling them what they feel. The passenger reacts: She's telling me off! He doesn't believe it. Sometimes the passenger needs it.

One guy got his steak and he said, "This is too medium, I want mine rarer." The girl said, "I'm sorry, I don't cook the food, it's pre-cooked." He picked up the meal and threw it on the floor. She says, "If you don't pick the meal up right now, I'll make sure the crew members come back here and make you pick it up." (With awe) She's talking right back at him and loud, right in front of everybody. He really didn't think she would yell at him. Man, he picked up the meal. . . . The younger girls don't take that guff any more, like we used to. When the passenger is giving you a bad time, you talk back to him.

It's always: the passenger is right. When a passenger says something mean, we're supposed to smile and say, "I understand." We're supposed to *really* smile because stewardesses' supervisors have been getting reports that the girls have been back-talking passengers. Even when they pinch us or say dirty things, we're supposed to smile at them. That's one thing they taught us at stew school. Like he's rubbing your body somewhere, you're supposed to just put his hand down and not say anything and smile at him. That's the main thing, smile.

When I first went to class, they told me I had a crooked smile. She showed me how to smile. She said, "Kinda press a little smile on"—which I did. "Oh, that's great," she said, "that's a *good* smile." But I couldn't do it. I didn't feel like I was doing it on my own. Even if we're sad, we're supposed to have a smile on our face.

I came in after a flight one day, my grandfather had died. Usually they call you up or meet you at the flight and say, "We have some bad news for you." I pick up this piece of paper in my mailbox and it says, "Mother called in. Your grandfather died today." It was written like, say, two cups of sugar. Was I mad! They wouldn't give me time off for the funeral. You can only have time off for your parents or somebody you have lived with. I have never lived with my grandparents. I went anyway.

A lot of our girls are teachers, nurses, everything. They do this part-time, 'cause you have enough time off for another kind of job. I personally work for conventions. I work electronic and auto shows. Companies hire me to stay in their booth and talk about products. I have this speech to tell. At others, all I do is pass out matches or candy. Nowadays every booth has a young girl in it.

People just love to drink on airplanes. They feel adventurous. So you're serving drinks and meals and there's very few times that you can sit down. If she does sit down, she's forgotten how to sit down and talk to passengers. I used to play bridge with passengers. But that doesn't happen any more. We're not supposed to be sitting down, or have a magazine or read a newspaper. If it's a flight from Boston to Los Ange-

36

les, you're supposed to have a half an hour talking to passengers. But the only time we can sit down is when we go to the cockpit. You're not supposed to spend any more than five minutes up there for a cigarette.

We could be sitting down on our jump seat and if you had a supervisor on board, she would write you up—for not mixing with the crowd. We're supposed to be told when she walks on board. Many times you don't know. They do have personnel that ride the flights that don't give their names—checking, and they don't tell you about it. Sometimes a girl gets caught smoking in the cabin. Say it's a long flight, maybe a night flight. You're playing cards with a passenger and you say, "Would it bother you if I smoke?" And he says no. She would write you up and get you fired for smoking in the airplane.

They have a limit on how far you can mix. They want you to be   40
sociable, but if he offers you a cigarette, not to take it. When you're outside, they encourage you to take cigarettes.

You give your time to everybody, you share it, not too much with one passenger. Everybody else may be snoring away and there's three guys, maybe military, and they're awake 'cause they're going home and excited. So you're playing cards with 'em. If you have a supervisor on, that would be a no-no. They call a lot of things no-no's.

They call us professional people but they talk to us as very young, childishly. They check us all the time on appearance. They check our weight every month. Even though you've been flying twenty years, they check you and say that's a no-no. If you're not spreading yourself around passengers enough, that's a no-no. Not hanging up first-class passenger's coats, that's a no-no, even though there's no room in the coatroom. You're supposed to somehow make room. If you're a pound over, they can take you off flight until you get under.

Accidents? I've never yet been so scared that I didn't want to get in the airplane. But there've been times at take-offs, there's been something funny. Here I am thinking, What if I die today? I've got too much to do. I can't die today. I use it as a joke.

I've had emergencies where I've had to evacuate the aircraft. I was   44
coming back from Las Vegas and being a lively stewardess I stayed up all night, gambled. We had a load full of passengers. The captain tells me we're going to have an emergency landing in Chicago because we lost a pin out of the nose gear. When we land, the nose gear is gonna collapse. He wants me to prepare the whole cabin for the landing, but not for two more hours. And not to tell the other stewardesses, because they were new girls and would get all excited. So I had to keep this in me for two more hours, wondering, Am I gonna die today? And this is Easter Sunday. And I was serving the passengers drinks and food and this guy got mad at me because his omelet was too cold. And I was gonna say, "You just wait, buddy, you're not gonna worry about that omelet." But I was nice about it, because I didn't want to have trouble with a passenger, especially when I have to prepare him for an emergency.

I told the passengers over the intercom: "The captain says it's just a precaution, there's nothing to worry about." I'm just gonna explain how to get out of the airplane fast, how to be in a braced position. They can't wear glasses or high heels, purses, things out of aisles, under the seats. And make sure everybody's pretty quiet. We had a blind woman on with a dog. We had to get people to help her off and all this stuff.

They were fantastic. Nobody screamed, cried, or hollered. When we got on the ground, everything was fine. The captain landed perfect. But there was a little jolt, and the passengers started screaming and hollering: They held it all back and all of a sudden we got on the ground, blah.

I was great. (Laughs.) That's what was funny. I thought, I have a husband now. I don't know how he would take it, my dying on an airplane. So I thought, I can't die. When I got on the intercom, I was so calm. Also we're supposed to keep a smile on our face. Even during an emergency, you're supposed to walk through the cabin and make everybody feel comfortable with a smile. When you're on the jump seat everybody's looking at you. You're supposed to sit there, holding your ankles, in a position to get out of that airplane fast with a big fat smile on your face.

Doctors tell stewardesses two bad things about them. They're gonna 48 get wrinkles all over their face because they smile with their mouth and their eyes. And also with the pressurization on the airplane, we're not supposed to get up while we're climbing because it causes varicose veins in our legs. So they say being a stewardess ruins your looks.

A lot of stewardesses wanted to be models. The Tanya girl used to be a stewardess on our airline. A stewardess is what they could get and a model is what they couldn't get. They weren't the type of person, they weren't that beautiful, they weren't that thin. So their second choice would be stewardess.

What did you want to be? I wanted to get out of Broken Bow, Nebraska. (Laughs.)

POSTSCRIPT: *"Everytime I go home, they all meet me at the airplane. Not one of my sisters has been on an airplane. All their children think that Terry is just fantastic, because their mom and dad—my sisters and their husbands—feel so stupid. 'Look at us. I wish I could have done that.' I know they feel bad, that they never had the chance. But they're happy I can come home and tell them about things. I send them things from Europe. They get to tell all their friends that their sister's a stewardess. They get real excited about that. The first thing they come out and say, 'One of my sisters is a stewardess.'*

"My father got a promotion with his company and they wrote in their busi- 52 *ness news that he had a family of seven, six girls and a boy, and one girl is a stewardess in Chicago. And went on to say what I did, and didn't say a word about anything else."*[2]

---

[2]Questions on this selection appear on page 359.

II. Roberta Victor, Hooker

She had been a prostitute, starting at the age of fifteen. During the first five or six years, she worked as a high-priced call girl in Manhattan. Later she was a streetwalker. . . .

You never used your own name in hustling. I used a different name practically every week. If you got busted, it was more difficult for them to find out who you really were. The role one plays when hustling had nothing to do with who you are. It's only fitting and proper you take another name.

There were certain names that were in great demand. Every second hustler had the name Kim or Tracy or Stacy and a couple others that were in vogue. These were all young women from seventeen to twenty-five, and we picked these very non-ethnic-oriented WASP names, rich names.

A hustler is any woman in American society. I was the kind of hustler who received money for favors granted rather than the type of hustler who signs a lifetime contract for her trick. Or the kind of hustler who carefully reads women's magazines and learns what it is proper to give for each date, depending on how much money her date or trick spends on her.

The favors I granted were not always sexual. When I was a call girl, men were not paying for sex. They were paying for something else. They were either paying to act out a fantasy or they were paying for companionship or they were paying to be seen with a well-dressed young woman. Or they were paying for somebody to listen to them. They were paying for a *lot* of things. Some men were paying for sex that *they* felt was deviant. They were paying so that nobody would accuse them of being perverted or dirty or nasty. A large proportion of these guys asked things that were not at all deviant. Many of them wanted oral sex. They felt they couldn't ask their wives or girl friends because they'd be repulsed. Many of them wanted somebody to talk dirty to them. Every good call girl in New York used to share her book and we all knew the same tricks.

We know a guy who used to lie in a coffin in the middle of his bedroom and he would see the girl only once. He got his kicks when the door would be open, the lights would be out, and there would be candles in the living room, and all you could see was his coffin on wheels. As you walked into the living room, he'd suddenly sit up. Of course, you screamed. He got his kicks when you screamed. Or the guy who set a table like the Last Supper and sat in a robe and sandals and wanted you to play Mary Magdalene. (Laughs.)

I was about fifteen, going on sixteen. I was sitting in a coffee shop in the Village, and a friend of mine came by. She said: "I've got a cab waiting. Hurry up. You can make fifty dollars in twenty minutes."

56

Looking back, I wonder why I was so willing to run out of the coffee shop, get in a cab, and turn a trick. It wasn't traumatic because my training had been in how to be a hustler anyway.

I learned it from the society around me, just as a woman. We're 60 taught how to hustle, how to attract, hold a man, and give sexual favors in return. The language that you hear all the time, "Don't sell yourself cheap." "Hold out for the highest bidder." "Is it proper to kiss a man good night on the first date?" The implication is it may not be proper on the first date, but if he takes you out to dinner on the second date, it's proper. If he brings you a bottle of perfume on the third date, you should let him touch you above the waist. And go on from here. It's a market place transaction.

Somehow I managed to absorb that when I was quite young. So it wasn't even a moment of truth when this woman came into the coffee shop and said; "Come on." I was back in twenty-five minutes and I felt no guilt.

She was a virgin until she was fourteen. A jazz musician, with whom she had fallen in love, avoided her. "So I went out to have sex with somebody to present him with an accomplished fact. I found it nonpleasurable. I did a lot of sleeping around before I ever took money."

A precocious child, she was already attending a high school of demanding academic standards. "I was very lonely. I didn't experience myself as being attractive. I had always felt I was too big, too fat, too awkward, didn't look like a Pepsi-Cola ad, was not anywhere near the American Dream. Guys were mostly scared of me. I was athletic, I was bright, and I didn't know how to keep my mouth shut. I didn't know how to play the games right.

"I understood very clearly they were not attracted to me for what I was, but 64 *as a sexual object. I was attractive. The year before I started hustling there were a lot of guys that wanted to go to bed with me. They didn't want to get involved emotionally, but they did want to ball. For a while I was willing to accept that. It was feeling intimacy, feeling close, feeling warm.*

"The time spent in bed wasn't unpleasant. It just wasn't terribly pleasant. It was a way of feeling somebody cared about me, at least for a moment. And it mattered that I was there, that I was important. I discovered that in bed it was possible. It was one skill that I had and I was proud of my reputation as an amateur.

"I viewed all girls as being threats. That's what we were all taught. You can't be friends with another woman, she might take your man. If you tell her anything about how you really feel, she'll use it against you. You smile at other girls and you spend time with them when there's nothing better to do, but you'd leave any girl sitting anywhere if you had an opportunity to go somewhere with a man. Because the most important thing in life is the way men feel about you."

How could you forget your first trick? (Laughs.) We took a cab to midtown Manhattan, we went to a penthouse. The guy up there was quite well known. What he really wanted to do was watch two women make love, and then he wanted to have sex with me. It was barely sex. He was almost finished by the time we started. He barely touched me and we were finished.

Of course, we faked it, the woman and me. The ethic was: You 68
don't participate in a sexual act with another woman if a trick is watching. You always fake it. You're putting something over on him and he's
paying for something he didn't really get. That's the only way you can
keep any sense of self-respect.

The call girl ethic is very strong. You were the lowest of the low if
you allowed yourself to feel anything with a trick. The bed puts you on
their level. The way you maintain your integrity is by acting all the way
through. It's not too far removed from what most American women
do—which is to put on a big smile and act.

It was a tremendous kick. Here I was doing absolutely nothing, *feeling* nothing, and in twenty minutes I was going to walk out with fifty
dollars in my pocket. That just made me feel absolutely marvelous. I
came downtown. I can't believe this! I'm not changed, I'm the same as
I was twenty minutes ago, except that now I have fifty dollars in my
pocket. It really was tremendous status. How many people could make
fifty dollars for twenty minutes' work? Folks work for eighty dollars
take-home pay. I worked twenty minutes for fifty dollars clear, no taxes,
nothing! I was still in school, I was smoking grass, I was shooting heroin, I wasn't hooked yet, and I had money. It was terrific.

After that, I made it my business to let my friend know that I was
available for more of these situations. (Laughs.) She had good connections. Very shortly I linked up with a couple of others who had a good
call book.

Books of phone numbers are passed around from call girl to call 72
girl. They're numbers of folks who are quite respectable and with
whom there is little risk. They're not liable to pull a knife on you,
they're not going to cheat you out of money. Businessmen and society
figures. There's three or four groups. The wealthy executive, who
makes periodic trips into the city and is known to several girls. There's
the social figure, whose name appears quite regularly in the society
pages and who's a regular once-a-week John. Or there's the quiet, independently wealthy type. Nobody knows how they got their money. I
know one of them made his money off munitions in World War II. Then
there's the entertainer. There's another crowd that runs around the
night spots, the 21 Club. . . .

These were the people whose names you saw in the paper almost
every day. But I knew what they were really like. Any John who was
obnoxious or aggressive was just crossed out of your book. You passed
the word around that this person was not somebody other people
should call.

We used to share numbers—standard procedure. The book I had I
got from a guy who got it from a very good call girl. We kept a copy of
that book in a safe deposit box. The standard procedure was that somebody new gave half of what they got the first time for each number.
You'd tell them: "Call so-and-so, that's a fifty-dollar trick." They would

give you twenty-five dollars. Then the number was theirs. My first book, I paid half of each trick to the person who gave it to me. After that, it was my book.

The book had the name and phone number coded, the price, what the person wants, and the contact name. For four years I didn't turn a trick for less than fifty dollars. They were all fifty to one hundred dollars and up for twenty minutes, an hour. The understanding is: it doesn't get conducted as a business transaction. The myth is that it's a social occasion.

You're expected to be well dressed, well made up, appear glad to   76
see the man. I would get a book from somebody and I would call and say, "I'm a friend of so-and-so's, and she thought it would be nice if we got together." The next move was his. Invariably he'd say, "Why don't we do that? Tonight or tomorrow night. Why don't you come over for a drink?" I would get very carefully dressed and made up. . . .

There's a given way of dressing in that league—that's to dress well but not ostentatiously. You have to pass doormen, cabdrivers. You have to look as if you belong in those buildings on Park Avenue or Central Park West. You're expected not to look cheap, not to look hard. Youth is the premium. I was quite young, but I looked older, so I had to work very hard at looking my age. Most men want girls who are eighteen. They really want girls who are younger, but they're afraid of trouble.

Preparations are very elaborate. It has to do with beauty parlors and shopping for clothes and taking long baths and spending money on preserving the kind of front that gives you a respectable address and telephone and being seen at the right clubs and drinking at the right bars. And being able to read the newspapers faithfully, so that not only can you talk about current events, you can talk about the society columns as well.

It's a social ritual. Being able to talk about what is happening and learn from this great master, and be properly respectful and know the names that he mentions. They always drop names of their friends, their contacts, and their clients. You should recognize these. Playing a role. . . .

At the beginning I was very excited. But in order to continue I had to   80
turn myself off. I had to disassociate who I was from what I was doing.

It's a process of numbing yourself. I couldn't associate with people who were not in the life—either the drug life or the hustling life. I found I couldn't turn myself back on when I finished working. When I turned myself off, I was numb—emotionally, sexually numb.

At first I felt like I was putting one over on all the other poor slobs that would go to work at eight-thirty in the morning and come home at five. I was coming home at four in the morning and I could sleep all day. I really thought a lot of people would change places with me because of the romantic image: being able to spend two hours out, riding cabs, and coming home with a hundred dollars. I could spend my mornings doing my nails, going to the beauty parlor, taking long baths, going shopping. . . .

It was usually two tricks a night. That was easily a hundred, a hundred and a quarter. I always had money in my pocket. I didn't know what the inside of a subway smelled like. Nobody traveled any other way except by cab. I ate in all the best restaurants and I drank in all the best clubs. A lot of people wanted you to go out to dinner with them. All you had to do was be an ornament.

Almost all the call girls I knew were involved in drugs. The fast life, the night hours. At after-hours clubs, if you're not a big drinker, you usually find somebody who has cocaine, 'cause that's the big drug in those places. You wake up at noon, there's not very much to do till nine or ten that night. Everybody else is at work, so you shoot heroin. After a while the work became a means of supplying drugs, rather than drugs being something we took when we were bored.

The work becomes boring because you're not part of the life. You're the part that's always hidden. The doormen smirk when you come in, 'cause they know what's going on. The cabdriver, when you give him a certain address—he knows exactly where you're going when you're riding up Park Avenue at ten o'clock at night, for Christ sake. You leave there and go back to what? Really, to what? To an emptiness. You've got all this money in your pocket and nobody you care about.

When I was a call girl I looked down on streetwalkers. I couldn't understand why anybody would put themselves in that position. It seemed to me to be hard work and very dangerous. What I was doing was basically riskless. You never had to worry about disease. These were folks who you know took care of themselves and saw the doctor regularly. Their apartments were always immaculate and the liquor was always good. They were always polite. You didn't have to ask them for money first. It was always implicit: when you were ready to leave, there would be an envelope under the lamp or there'd be something in your pocketbook. It never had to be discussed.

I had to work an awful lot harder for the same money when I was a streetwalker. I remember having knives pulled on me, broken bottles held over my head, being raped, having my money stolen back from me, having to jump out of a second-story window, having a gun pointed at me.

As a call girl, I had lunch at the same places society women had lunch. There was no way of telling me apart from anybody else in the upper tax bracket. I made my own hours, no more than three or so hours of work an evening. I didn't have to accept calls. All I had to do was play a role.

As a streetwalker, I didn't have to act. I let myself show the contempt I felt for the tricks. They weren't paying enough to make it worth performing for them. As a call girl, I pretended I enjoyed it sexually.

You have to act as if you had an orgasm. As a streetwalker, I didn't. I used to lie there with my hands behind my head and do mathematics equations in my head or memorize the keyboard typewriter.

It was strictly a transaction. No conversation, no acting, no myth around it, no romanticism. It was purely a business transaction. You always asked for your money in front. If you could get away without undressing totally, you did that.

It's not too different than the distinction between an executive secretary and somebody in the typing pool. As an executive secretary you really identify with your boss. When you're part of the typing pool, you're a body, you're hired labor, a set of hands on the typewriter. You have nothing to do with whoever is passing the work down to you. You do it as quickly as you can.

What led you to the streets?   92

My drug habit. It got a lot larger. I started looking bad. All my money was going for drugs. I didn't have any money to spend on keeping myself up and going to beauty parlors and having a decent address and telephone.

If you can't keep yourself up, you can't call on your old tricks. You drop out of circulation. As a call girl, you have to maintain a whole image. The trick wants to know he can call you at a certain number and you have to have a stable address. You must look presentable, not like death on a soda cracker.

I looked terrible. When I hit the streets, I tried to stick to at least twenty dollars and folks would laugh. I needed a hundred dollars a night to maintain a drug habit and keep a room somewhere. It meant turning seven or eight tricks a night. I was out on the street from nine o'clock at night till four in the morning. I was taking subways and eating in hamburger stands.

For the first time I ran the risk of being busted. I was never arrest-   96
ed as a call girl. Every once in a while a cop would get hold of some-body's book. They would call one of the girls and say, "I'm a friend of so-and-so's." They would try to trap them. I never took calls from peo-ple I didn't know. But on the streets, how do you know who you're gonna pick up?

As a call girl, some of my tricks were upper echelon cops, not patrolmen. Priests, financiers, garment industry folks, bigtimers. On the street, they ranged from *junior* executive types, blue-collar workers, upwardly striving postal workers, college kids, suburban white collars who were in the city for the big night, restaurant workers. . . .

You walk a certain area, usually five or six blocks. It has a couple of restaurants, a couple of bars. There's the step in-between: hanging out in a given bar, where people come to you. I did that briefly.

You'd walk very slowly, you'd stop and look in the window. Some-body would come up to you. There was a ritual here too. The law says in order to arrest a woman for prostitution, she has to mention money and she has to tell you what she'll do for the money. We would keep within the letter of the law, even though the cops never did.

Somebody would come up and say, "It's a nice night, isn't it?"   100
"Yes." They'd say, "Are you busy?" I'd say, "Not particularly." "Would you like to come with me and have a drink?" You start walking and they say, "I have fifteen dollars or twelve dollars and I'm very lonely." Something to preserve the myth. Then they want you to spell out exactly what you're willing to do for the money.

I never approached anybody on the street. That was the ultimate risk. Even if he weren't a cop, he could be some kind of supersquare, who would call a cop. I was trapped by cops several times.

The first one didn't even trap me as a trick. It was three in the morning. I was in Chinatown. I ran into a trick I knew. We made contact in a restaurant. He went home and I followed him a few minutes later. I knew the address. I remember passing a banana truck. It didn't dawn on me that it was strange for somebody to be selling bananas at three in the morning. I spent about twenty minutes with my friend. He paid me. I put the money in my shoe. I opened the door and got thrown back against the wall. The banana salesman was a vice squad cop. He'd stood on the garbage can to peer in the window. I got three years for that one.

I was under age. I was four months short of twenty-one. They sent me to what was then called Girls' Term Court. They wouldn't allow me a lawyer because I wasn't an adult, so it wasn't really a criminal charge. The judge said I was rehabilitable. Instead of giving me thirty days, he gave me three years in the reformatory. It was very friendly of him. I was out on parole a couple of times before I'd get caught and sent back.

I once really got trapped. It was about midnight and a guy came   104
down the street. He said he was a postal worker who just got off the shift. He told me how much money he had and what he wanted. I took him to my room. The cop isn't supposed to undress. If you can describe the color of his shorts, it's an invalid arrest. Not only did he show me the color of his shorts, he went to bed with me. Then he pulled a badge and a gun and busted me.

He lied to me. He told me he was a narc and didn't want to bust me for hustling. If I would tell him who was dealing in the neighborhood, he'd cut me loose. I lied to him, but he won. He got me to walk out of the building past all my friends and when we got to the car, he threw me in. (Laughs.) It was great fun. I did time for that—close to four years.

What's the status of the streetwalker in prison?

It's fine. Everybody there has been hustling. It's status in reverse. Anybody who comes in saying things like they could never hustle is looked down on as being somewhat crazy.

She speaks of a profound love she had for a woman who she's met in prison; of her   108
nursing her lover after the woman had become blind.

"I was out of the country for a couple of years. I worked a house in Mexico. It had heavy velour curtains—a Mexican version of a French whorehouse. There was a reception area, where the men would come and we'd parade in front of them.

"The Mexicans wanted American girls. The Americans wanted Mexican girls. So I didn't get any American tricks. I had to give a certain amount to the house for each trick I turned and anything I negotiated over that amount was mine. It was far less than anything I had taken in the States.

"I was in great demand even though I wasn't a blonde. A girl friend of mine worked there two nights. She was Norwegian and very blonde. Every trick who came in wanted her. Her head couldn't handle it all. She quit after two nights. So I was the only American.

"That was really hard work. The Mexicans would play macho. American   112 tricks will come as quickly as they can. Mexicans will hold back and make me work for my money. I swear to God they were doing multiplication tables in their heads to keep from having an orgasm. I would use every trick I knew to get them to finish. It was crazy!

"I was teaching school at the same time. I used Alice in Wonderland as the text in my English class. During the day I tutored English for fifth- and sixth-grade kids. In the evening, I worked in the call house.

"The junk down there was quite cheap and quite good. My habit was quite large. I loved dope more than anything else around. After a while I couldn't differentiate between working and not working. All men were tricks, all relationships were acting. I was completely turned off."

She quit shooting dope the moment she was slugged, brutally beaten by a dealer who wanted her. This was her revelatory experience. "It was the final indignity. I'd had tricks pulling broken bottles on me, I'd been in razor fights, but nobody had ever hit me." *It was a threat to her status.* "I was strong. I could handle myself. A tough broad. This was threatened, so . . . "

I can't talk for women who were involved with pimps. That was   116 where I always drew the line. I always thought pimps were lower than pregnant cockroaches. I didn't want anything to do with them. I was involved from time to time with some men. They were either selling dope or stealing, but they were not depending on my income. Nor were they telling me to get my ass out on the street. I never supported a man.

As a call girl I got satisfaction, an unbelievable joy—perhaps perverted—in knowing what these reputable folks were really like. Being able to open a newspaper every morning, read about this pillar of society, and know what a pig he really was. The tremendous kick in knowing that I didn't feel anything, that I was acting and they weren't. It's sick, but no sicker than what every woman is taught, all right?

I was in *control* with every one of those relationships. You're vulnerable if you allow yourself to be involved sexually. I wasn't. They were. I called it. Being able to manipulate somebody sexually, I could determine when I wanted that particular transaction to end. 'Cause I could make the guy come. I could play all kinds of games. See? It was a tremendous sense of power.

What I did was no different from what ninety-nine percent of American women are taught to do. I took the money from under the lamp instead of in Arpege. What would I do with 150 bottles of Arpege a week?

You become your job. I became what I did. I became a hustler. I   120
became cold, I became hard, I became turned off, I became numb. Even when I wasn't hustling, I was a hustler. I don't think it's terribly differ-ent from somebody who works on the assembly line forty hours a week and comes home cut off, numb, dehumanized. People aren't built to switch on and off like water faucets.

What was really horrifying about jail is that it really isn't horrify-ing. You adjust very easily. The same thing with hustling. It became my life. It was too much of an effort to try to make contact with another human being, to force myself to care, to feel.

I didn't care about me. It didn't matter whether I got up or didn't get up. I got high as soon as I awoke. The first thing I'd reach for, with my eyes half-closed, was my dope. I didn't like my work. It was messy. That was the biggest feeling about it. Here's all these guys slobbering over you all night long. I'm lying there, doing math or conjugations or Spanish poetry in my head. (Laughs.) And they're slobbering. God! God! What enabled me to do it was being high—high and numb.

The overt hustling society is the microcosm of the rest of the soci-ety. The power relationships are the same and the games are the same. Only this one I was in control of. The greater one I wasn't. In the out-side society, if I tried to be me, I wasn't in control of anything. As a bright, assertive woman, I had no power. As a cold, manipulative hus-tler, I had a lot. I knew I was playing a role. Most women are taught to become what they act. All I did was act out the reality of American womanhood.[3]

III. Maggie Holmes, Domestic

What bugs me now, since I'm on welfare, is people saying they give you   124
the money for nothin'. When I think back what we had to come through, up from the South, comin' here. The hard work we had to do. It really gets me, when I hear people . . . It do somethin' to me. I think violence.

I think what we had to work for. I used to work for $1.50 a week. This is five days a week, sometimes six. If you live in the servant quar-ter, your time is never off, because if they decide to have a party at night, you gotta come out. My grandmother, I remember when she used to work, we'd get milk and a pound of butter. I mean this was pay. I'm thinkin' about what my poor parents worked for, gettin' nothing.

[3]Questions on this selection appear on page 359.

What do the white think about when they think? Do they ever think about what *they* would do?

> *She had worked as a domestic, hotel chambermaid, and as "kitchen help in cafés" for the past twenty-five years, up North and down South. She lives with her four children.*

When it come to housework, I can't do it now. I can't stand it, cause it do somethin' to my mind. They want you to clean the house, want you to wash, even the windows, want you to iron. You not supposed to wash no dishes. You ain't supposed to make no beds up. Lots of 'em try to sneak it in on you, think you don't know that. So the doorbell rings and I didn't answer to. The bell's ringin' and I'm still doin' my work. She ask me why I don't answer the bell, I say; "Do I come here to be a butler?" And I don't see myself to be no doormaid. I came to do some work, and I'm gonna do my work. When you end up, you's nursemaid, you's cook. They puts all this on you. If you want a job to cleanin', you ask for just cleanin'. She wants you to do in one day what she hasn't did all year.

Now this bug me: the first thing she gonna do is pull out this damn   128
rubber thing—just fittin' for your knees. Knee pads—like you're workin' in the fields, like people pickin' cotton. No mop or nothin'. That's why you find so many black women here got rheumatism in their legs, knees. When you get on that cold floor, I don't care how warm the house is, you can feel the cold on the floor, the water and stuff. I never see nobody on their knees until I come North. In the South, they had mops. Most times, if they had real heavy work, they always had a man to come in. Washin' windows, that's a man's job. They don't think nothin' about askin' you to do that here. They don't have no feeling that that's what bothers you. I think to myself; My God, if I had somebody come and do my floors, clean up for me, I'd appreciate it. They don't say nothin' about it. Act like you haven't even done anything. They has no feelin's.

I worked for one old hen on Lake Shore Drive. You remember that big snow they had there?[4] Remember when you couldn't get there? When I gets to work she says: "Call the office." She complained to the lady where I got the job, said I was late to work. So I called. So I said, in the phone (Shouts), *What do you want with me?* I got home four black, beautiful kids. Before I go to anybody's job in the morning I see that my kids are at school. I gonna see that they have warm clothes on and they fed." I'm lookin' right at the woman I'm workin' for. (Laughs.) When I get through the phone I tell this employer: "That goes for you too. The only thing I live for is my kids. There's nothin', you and nobody else." The expression on her face: What is this? (Laughs.) She thought I was

---

[4]It was the week of Chicago's Big Snow-In, beginning January 25, 1967. Traffic was hopelessly snarled. Scores of thousands couldn't get to work.

gonna be like (mimics "Aunt Jemima"): "Yes ma'am, I'll try to get here a little early." But it wasn't like that. (Laughs.)

When I come in the door that day she told me pull my shoes off. I said, "For what? I can wipe my feet at the door here, but I'm not gettin' out of my shoes, it's cold." She look at me like she said: Oh my God, what I got here? (Laughs.) I'm knowin' I ain't gonna make no eight hours here. I can't take it.

She had everything in there snow white. And that means work, believe me. In the dining room she had a blue set, she had sky-blue chairs. They had a bedroom with pink and blue. I look and say, "I know what this means." It means sho' 'nough-knees. I said, "I'm gonna try and make it today, *if* I can make it." Usually when they're so bad, you have to leave.

I ask her where the mop is. She say she don't have no mop. I said, "Don't tell me you mop the floor on your knees. I know you don't." They usually hid these mops in the clothes closet. I go out behind all these clothes and get the mop out. (Laughs.) They don't get on their knees, but they don't think nothin' about askin' a black woman. She says, "All you—you girls . . ." She stop. I say, "All you *niggers,* is that what you want to say?" She give me this stupid look. I say, "I'm glad you tellin' me that there's more like me." (Laughs.) I told her, "You better give me my money and let me go, 'cause I'm gettin' angry. So I made her give me my carfare and what I had worked that day. 132

Most when you find decent work is when you find one that work themselves. They know what it's like to get up in the morning and go to work. In the suburbs they ain't got nothin' to do. They has nothin' else to think about. Their mind's just about blowed.

It's just like they're talkin' about mental health. Poor people's mental health is different than the rich white. Mine could come from a job or not havin' enough money for my kids. Mine is from me being poor. That don't mean you're sick. His sickness is from money, graftin' where he want more. I don't have *any.* You live like that day to day, penny to penny.

I worked for a woman, her husband's a judge. I cleaned the whole house. When it was time for me to go home, she decided she wants some ironing. She goes in the basement, she turn on the air conditioner. She said, "I think you can go down in the basement and finish your day out. It's air conditioned." I said, "I don't care what you got down there, I'm not ironing. You look at that slip, it says cleanin'. Don't say no ironin'. She wanted me to wash the walls in the bathroom. I said, "If you look at that telephone book they got all kinds of ads there under house cleanin'." She said the same thing as the other one, "All you girls—" I said same thing I said to the other one; "You mean niggers." (Laughs.)

They ever call you by your last name?   136

Oh God, they wouldn't do that. (Laughs.)

Do you call her by her last name?

Most time I don't call her, period. I don't say anything to her. I don't talk nasty to nobody, but when I go to work I don't talk to people. Most time they don't like what you're gonna say. So I keeps quiet.

Most of her jobs were "way out in the suburbs. You get a bus and you ride til you   140
get a subway. After you gets to Howard,[5] you gets the El. If you get to the end of the line and there's no bus, they pick you up. I don't like to work in the city, 'cause they don't pay you nothin'. And these old buildings are so nasty. It takes so much time to clean 'em. They are not kept up so good, like suburbs. Most of the new homes out there, it's easier to clean."

A commonly observed phenomenon: during the early evening hour, trains, crowded, predominantly by young white men carrying attaché cases, pass trains headed in the opposite direction, crowded, predominantly by middle-aged black women carrying brown paper bags. Neither group, it appears, glances at the other.

"We spend most of the time ridin'. You get caught goin' out from the suburbs at nighttime, man, you're really sittin' there for hours. There's nothin' movin'. You got a certain hour to meet trains. You get a transfer, you have to get that train. It's a shuffle to get in and out of the job. If you miss that train at five o'clock, what time you gonna get out that end? Sometime you don't get home till eight o'clock. . . ."

You don't feel like washin' your own window when you come from out there, scrubbin'. If you work in one of them houses eight hours, you gotta come home do the same thing over . . . you don't feel like . . . (sighs softly) . . . tired. You gotta come home, take care of your kids, you gotta cook, you gotta wash. Most of the time, you gotta wash for the kids for somethin' to wear to school. You gotta clean up, 'cause you didn't have time in the morning. You gotta wash and iron and whatever you do, nights. You be so tired, until you don't feel like even doin' nothin'.

You get up at six, you fix breakfast for the kids, you get them ready   144
to go on to school. Leave home about eight. Most of the time I make biscuits for my kids, cornbread you gotta make. I don't mean the canned kind. This I don't call cookin', when you go in that refrigerator and get some beans and drop 'em in a pot. And TV dinners, they go stick 'em in the stove and she say she cooked. This is not cookin'.

And *she's* tired. Tired from doin' what? You got a washing dryer, you got an electric sweeper, anything at fingertips. All she gotta do is unfroze 'em, dump 'em in the pot, and she's tired! I go to the store, I get my vegetables, greens, I wash 'em. I gotta pick 'em first. I don't eat none of that stuff, like in the cans. She don't do that, and she says she's tired.

When you work for them, when you get in that house in the morning, boy, they got one arm in their coat and a scarf on their head. And when you open that door, she shoots by you, she's gone. Know what I mean? They want you to come there and keep the kids and let them get out. What she think about how am I gonna do? Like I gets tired of my

---

[5]The boundary line separating Chicago from the North Shore suburb, Evanston.

kids too. I'd like to go out too. It bugs you to think that they don't have no feelin's about that.

Most of the time I work for them and they be out. I don't like to work for 'em when they be in the house so much. They don't have no work to do. All they do is get on the telephone and talk about one another. Make you sick. I'll go and close the door. They're all the same, everybody's house is the same. You think they rehearse it. . . .

When I work, only thing I be worryin' about is my kids. I just don't like to leave 'em too long. When they get out of school, you wonder if they out on the street. The only thing I worry is if they had a place to play in easy. I always call two, three times. When she don't like you to call, I'm in a hurry to get out of there. (Laughs.) My mind is gettin' home, what are you gonna find to cook before the stores close.

This Nixon was sayin' he don't see nothin' wrong with people doin' scrubbin'. For generations that's all we done. He should know we wants to be doctors and teachers and lawyers like him. I don't want my kids to come up and do domestic work. It's degrading. You can't see no tomorrow there. We done this for generation and generation cooks and butlers all your life. They want their kids to be lawyers, doctors, and things. You don't want 'em in no cafes workin'.. . .

When they say about the neighborhood we live in is dirty, why do they ask me to come and clean their house? We, the people in the slums, the same nasty women they have come to their house in the suburbs every day. If these women are so filthy, why you want them to clean for you? They don't go and clean for us. We go and clean for them.

I worked one day where this white person did some housework. I'm lookin' at the difference how she with me and her. She had a guilt feeling towards that lady. They feel they shouldn't ask them to do this type of work, but they don't mind askin' me.

They want you to get in a uniform. You take me and my mother, she work in what she wear. She tells you, "If that place so dirty where I can't wear my dress, I won't do the job." You can't go to work dressed like they do, 'cause they think you're not working—like you should get dirty, at least. They don't say what kind of uniform, just say uniform. This is in case anybody come in, the black be workin'. They don't want you walkin' around dressed up, lookin' like them. They asks you some-times, "Don't you have somethin' else to put on?" I say, "No, 'cause I'm not gettin' on my knees."

They move with caution now, believe me. They want to know, "What should I call you?" I say, "Don't call me a Negro, I'm black." So they say, "Okay, I don't want to make you angry with me." (Laughs.) The old-timers, a lot of 'em was real religious. "Lord'll make a way." I say, "I'm makin' my own way." I'm not anti-Bible or anti-God, but I just let 'em know I don't think thataway.

The younger women, they don't pay you too much attention. Most of 'em work. The older women, they behind you, wiping. I don't like nobody checkin' behind me. When you go to work, they want to show you how to clean. That really gets me, somebody showin' me how to clean. I been doin' it all my life. They come and get the rag and show you how to do it. (Laughs.) I stand there, look at 'em. Lotta times I ask her, "You finished?" I say, "If there's anything you gotta go and do, I wish you'd go." I don't need nobody to show me how to clean.

I had them put money down and pretend they can't find it and have me look for it. I worked for one, she had dropped ten dollars on the floor, and I was sweepin' and I'm glad I seen it, because if I had put that sweeper on it, she coulda said I got it. I had to push the couch back and the ten dollars was there. Oh, I had 'em, when you go to dust, they put something . . . to test you.

I worked at a hotel. A hotel's the same thing. You makin' beds,   156
scrubbin' toilets, and things. You gotta put in linens and towels. You still cleanin'. When people come in the room—that's what bugs me—they give you that look: You just a maid. It do somethin' to me. It really gets into me.

Some of the guests are nice. The only thing you try to do is to hurry up and get this bed made and get outa here, 'cause they'll get you to do somethin' else. If they take that room, they want everything they paid for. (Laughs.) They get so many towels, they can't use 'em all. But you gotta put up all those towels. They want that pillow, they want that blanket. You gotta be trottin' back and forth and gettin' all those things.

In the meantime, when they have the hotel full, we put in extra beds—the little foldin' things. They say they didn't order the bed. They stand and look at you like you crazy. Now you gotta take this bed back all the way from the twelfth floor to the second. The guy at the desk, he got the wrong room. He don't say, "I made a mistake." You take the blame.

And you get some guys . . . you can't work with afightin' 'em. He'll call down and say he wants some towels. When you knock, he says, "Come in." He's standing there without a stitch of clothes on, buck naked. You're not goin' in there. You only throw those towels and go back. Most of the time you wait till he got out of there.

When somethin's missin', it's always the maid took it. If we find   160
one of those type people, we tell the house lady, "You have to go in there and clean it yourself." If I crack that door, and nobody's in, I wouldn't go in there. If a girl had been in there, they would call and tell you, "Did you see something?" They won't say you got it. It's the same thing. You say no. They say, "It *musta* been in there."

Last summer I worked at a place and she missed a purse. I didn't work on that floor that day. She called the office, "Did you see that lady's purse?" I said, "No, I haven't been in the room." He asked me again, Did I . . . ? I had to stay till twelve o'clock. She found it. It was under some papers. I quit, 'cause they end up sayin' you stole somethin'.

You know what I wanted to do all my life? I wanted to play piano. And I'd want to write songs and things, that's what I really wanted to do. If I could just get myself enough to buy a piano. . . . And I'd like to write about my life, if I could sit long enough: How I growed up in the South and my grandparents and my father—I'd like to do that. I would like to dig up more of black history, too. I would love to for my kids.

Lotta times I'm tellin' 'em about things, they'll be sayin', "Mom, that's olden days." (Laughs.) They don't understand, because it's so far from what happening now. Mighty few young black women are doin' domestic work. And I'm glad. That's why I want my kids to go to school. This one lady told me, "All you people are gettin' like that." I said, "I'm glad." There's no more gettin' on their knees.

Topics for Critical Thinking and Writing

Terry Mason, Airline Stewardess

1. How satisfied is Terry Mason with her job? What are the sources of her satisfactions? Her dissatisfactions? Try to sketch her values, and to characterize her.
2. Using Mason's remarks as evidence, evaluate the training program for stewardesses (now called *flight attendants*). Is it intelligent? Is it immoral? Do you think that after stew school the airlines deal fairly with the stewardesses?
3. Has this selection changed your idea of the job of a flight attendant? If so, in what ways?

Roberta Victor, Hooker

1. In paragraph 55 Victor lists some desirable ("very non-ethnic-oriented WASP") names: Kim, Tracy, Stacy. Why are such names considered desirable?
2. In the first paragraph of her interview Victor says: "The role one plays when hustling had nothing to do with who you are." Judging from the interview as a whole, is she deceiving herself? In paragraph 56 she says that all women in America are hustlers, and she returns to this notion, especially in the final paragraph. Again, is she deceiving herself, or has she put her finger on a truth, or at least a partial truth? Terkel tells us (paragraph 63) that she was a bright child. During the interview does Victor say anything that strikes you as especially perceptive? Does her language occasionally show unusual vitality? Are there touches of wit?

Maggie Holmes, Domestic

1. How do you account for the difference in treatment (paragraph 128) of domestic help in the North and the South?

2.   What evidence is there that Holmes is witty? resourceful? insightful?
3.   How would you describe Holmes's attitude toward suburban house-
     wives? Does it make sense?

Gloria Steinem

Gloria Steinem was born in Toledo in 1934 and educated at Smith College. An active figure in politics, civil rights affairs, and feminist issues, she was a cofounder of the Women's Action Alliance and a co-founder and editor of Ms. *magazine. We reprint an essay from one of her books,* Outrageous Acts and Everyday Rebellions *(1983).*

The Importance of Work

Toward the end of the 1970s, *The Wall Street Journal* devoted an eight-part, front-page series to "the working woman"—that is, the influx of women into the paid-labor force—as the greatest change in American life since the Industrial Revolution.

Many women readers greeted both the news and the definition with cynicism. After all, women have always worked. If all the productive work of human maintenance that women do in the home were valued at its replacement cost, the gross national product of the United States would go up by 26 percent. It's just that we are now more likely than ever before to leave our poorly rewarded, low-security, high-risk job of homemaking (though we're still trying to explain that it's a perfectly good one and that the problem is male society's refusal both to do it and to give it an economic value) for more secure, independent, and better-paid jobs outside the home.

Obviously, the real work revolution won't come until all productive work is rewarded—including child rearing and other jobs done in the home—and men are integrated into so-called women's work as well as vice versa. But the radical change being touted by the *Journal* and other media is one part of that long integration process: the unprecedented flood of women into salaried jobs, that is, into the labor force as it has been male-defined and previously occupied by men. We are already more than 41 percent of it—the highest proportion in history. Given the fact that women also make up a whopping 69 percent of the "discouraged labor force" (that is, people who need jobs but don't get counted in the unemployment statistics because they've given up looking), plus an official female unemployment rate that is substantially higher than men's, it's clear that we could expand to become fully half of the national work force by 1990.

Faced with this determination of women to find a little independence and to be paid and honored for our work, experts have rushed to   4 ask: "Why?" It's a question rarely directed at male workers. Their basic motivations of survival and personal satisfaction are taken for granted. Indeed, men are regarded as "odd" and therefore subjects for sociological study and journalistic reports only when they *don't* have work, even if they are rich and don't need jobs or are poor and can't find them. Nonetheless, pollsters and sociologists have gone to great expense to prove that women work outside the home because of dire financial need, or if we persist despite the presence of a wage-earning male, out of some desire to buy "little extras" for our families, or even out of good old-fashioned penis envy.

Job interviewers and even our own families may still ask salaried women the big "Why?" If we have small children at home or are in some job regarded as "men's work," the incidence of such questions increases. Condescending or accusatory versions of "What's a nice girl like you doing in a place like this?" have not disappeared from the workplace.

How do we answer these assumptions that we are "working" out of some pressing or peculiar need? Do we feel okay about arguing that it's as natural for us to have salaried jobs as for our husbands—whether or not we have young children at home? Can we enjoy strong career ambitions without worrying about being thought "unfeminine"? When we confront men's growing resentment of women competing in the work force (often in the form of such guilt-producing accusations as "You're taking men's jobs away" or "You're damaging your children"), do we simply state that a decent job is a basic human right for everybody?

I'm afraid the answer is often no. As individuals and as a movement, we tend to retreat into some version of a tactically questionable defense: "Womenworkbecausewehaveto." The phrase has become one word, one key on the typewriter—an economic form of the socially "feminine" stance of passivity and self-sacrifice. Under attack, we still tend to present ourselves as creatures of economic necessity and familial devotion. "Womenworkbecausewehaveto" has become the easiest thing to say.

Like most truisms, this one is easy to prove with statistics. Economic need *is* the most consistent work motive—for women as well as men. In 1976, for instance, 43 percent of all women in the paid-labor force were single, widowed, separated, or divorced, and working to support themselves and their dependents. An additional 21 percent were married to men who had earned less than ten thousand dollars in the previous year, the minimum then required to support a family of four. In fact, if you take men's pensions, stocks, real estate, and various forms of accumulated wealth into account, a good statistical case can be made that there are more women who "have" to work (that is, who have neither the accumulated wealth, nor husbands whose work or wealth can support them for the rest of their lives) than there are men with the same need. If we were going to ask one group "Do you really need this job?" we should ask men.

But the first weakness of the whole "have to work" defense is its deceptiveness. Anyone who has ever experienced dehumanized life on welfare or any other confidence-shaking dependency knows that a paid job may be preferable to the dole, even when the hand-out is coming from a family member. Yet the will and self-confidence to work on one's own can diminish as dependency and fear increase. That may explain why—contrary to the "have to" rationale—wives of men who earn less than three thousand dollars a year are actually *less* likely to be employed than wives whose husbands make ten thousand dollars a year or more.

Furthermore, the greatest proportion of employed wives is found among families with a total household income of twenty-five to fifty thousand dollars a year. This is the statistical underpinning used by some sociologists to prove that women's work is mainly important for boosting families into the middle or upper middle class. Thus, women's incomes are largely used for buying "luxuries" and "little extras": a neat double-whammy that renders us secondary within our families, and makes our jobs expendable in hard times. We may even go along with this interpretation (at least, up to the point of getting fired so a male can have our job). It preserves a husbandly ego-need to be seen as the primary breadwinner, and still allows us a safe "feminine" excuse for working.

But there are often rewards that we're not confessing. As noted in *The Two-Career Couple,* by Francine and Douglas Hall: "Women who hold jobs by choice, even blue-collar routine jobs, are more satisfied with their lives than are the full-time housewives."

In addition to personal satisfaction, there is also society's need for all its members' talents. Suppose that jobs were given out on only a "have to work" basis to both women and men—one job per household. It would be unthinkable to lose the unique abilities of, for instance, Eleanor Holmes Norton, the distinguished chair of the Equal Employment Opportunity Commission. But would we then be forced to question the important work of her husband, Edward Norton, who is also a distinguished lawyer? Since men earn more than twice as much as women on the average, the wife in most households would be more likely to give up her job. Does that mean the nation could do as well without millions of its nurses, teachers, and secretaries? Or that the rare man who earns less than his wife should give up his job?

It was this kind of waste of human talents on a society-wide scale that traumatized millions of unemployed or underemployed Americans during the Depression. Then, a one-job-per-household rule seemed somewhat justified, yet the concept was used to displace women workers only, create intolerable dependencies, and waste female talent that the country needed. That Depression experience, plus the energy and example of women who were finally allowed to work during the manpower shortage created by World War II, led Congress to reinterpret the meaning of the country's full-employment goal in its Economic Act of 1946. Full employment was officially defined as "the employment of those who want to work, without regard to whether their employment is, by some definition, necessary. This goal applies equally to men and to women." Since bad economic times are again creating a resentment of employed women—as well as creating more need for women to be employed—we need such a goal more than ever. Women are again being caught in a tragic double bind: We are required to be strong and then punished for our strength.

Clearly, anything less than government and popular commitment to this 1946 definition of full employment will leave the less powerful groups, whoever they may be, in danger. Almost as important as the financial penalty paid by the powerless is the suffering that comes from being shut out of paid and recognized work. Without it, we lose much of our self-respect and our ability to prove that we are alive by making some difference in the world. That's just as true for the suburban woman as it is for the unemployed steel worker.

But it won't be easy to give up the passive defense of "weworkbe-causewehaveto."

When a woman who is struggling to support her children and 16 grandchildren on welfare sees her neighbor working as a waitress, even though that neighbor's husband has a job, she may feel resentful; and the waitress (of course, not the waitress's husband) may feel guilty. Yet unless we establish the obligation to provide a job for everyone who is willing and able to work, that welfare woman may herself be penalized by policies that give out only one public-service job per household. She and her daughter will have to make a painful and divisive decision about which of them gets that precious job, and the whole household will have to survive on only one salary.

A job as a human right is a principle that applies to men as well as women. But women have more cause to fight for it. The phenomenon of the "working woman" has been held responsible for everything from an increase in male impotence (which turned out, incidentally, to be attributable to medication for high blood pressure) to the rising cost of steak (which was due to high energy costs and beef import restrictions, not women's refusal to prepare the cheaper, slower-cooking cuts). Unless we see a job as part of every citizen's right to autonomy and personal fulfillment, we will continue to be vulnerable to someone else's idea of what "need" is, and whose "need" counts the most.

In many ways, women who do not have to work for simple survival, but who choose to do so nonetheless, are on the frontier of asserting this right for all women. Those with well-to-do husbands are dangerously easy for us to resent and put down. It's easier still to resent women from families of inherited wealth, even though men generally control and benefit from that wealth. (There is no Rockefeller Sisters Fund, no J. P. Morgan & Daughters, and sons-in-law may be the ones who really sleep their way to power.) But to prevent a woman whose husband or father is wealthy from earning her own living, and from gaining the self-confidence that comes with that ability, is to keep her needful of that unearned power and less willing to disperse it. Moreover, it is to lose forever her unique talents.

Perhaps modern feminists have been guilty of a kind of reverse snobbism that keeps us from reaching out to the wives and daughters of wealthy men; yet it was exactly such women who refused the restrictions of class and financed the first wave of feminist revolution.

For most of us, however, "womenworkbecausewehaveto" is just   20
true enough to be seductive as a personal defense.

If we use it without also staking out the larger human right to a job, however, we will never achieve that right. And we will always be subject to the false argument that independence for women is a luxury affordable only in good economic times. Alternatives to layoffs will not be explored, acceptable unemployment will always be used to frighten those with jobs into accepting low wages, and we will never remedy the real cost, both to families and to the country, of dependent women and a massive loss of talent.

Worst of all, we may never learn to find productive, honored work as a natural part of ourselves and as one of life's basic pleasures.

Topics for Critical Thinking and Writing

1. In paragraph 2 Steinem characterizes homemaking as a "poorly rewarded, low-security, high-risk job." How might she justify each of these descriptions of homemaking? Do you agree that homemaking is rightly classified as a job? If so, do you agree with her description of it?
2. Restate in your own words Steinem's explanation (paragraph 9) of why "wives of men who earn *less* than three thousand dollars a year are actually *less* likely to be employed than wives whose husbands make ten thousand dollars a year or more." The salary figures are, of course, out of date. Is the point nevertheless still valid? Explain.
3. To whom does Steinem appear to address her remarks? Cite evidence for your answer. In your opinion, is this audience likely to find her argument persuasive? Would a different audience find it more or less persuasive? Explain.
4. In addition to arguments, what persuasive devices does Steinem use? How, for example, does she persuade you that she speaks with authority? What other authorities does she cite? How would you characterize her diction and tone, for instance in paragraph 18? (On diction, and tone, see pages 20–21.)
5. Steinem suggests two reasons for working: "personal satisfaction" and "society's need for all its members' talents." Suppose that you had no financial need to work. Do you imagine that you would choose to work in order to gain "personal satisfaction"? Or, again if you had no need to work, would you assume that you are morally obligated to contribute to society by engaging in paid work?

6. Summarize, in a paragraph of about 100–150 words, Steinem's argument that it is entirely proper for wealthy women to work for pay. In the course of your paragraph, you may quote briefly from the essay.
7. Compare Steinem with Russell (page 327) on the value of work.

Barbara Ehrenreich

Barbara Ehrenreich, born in Butte, Montana, in 1941, and educated at Reed College and Rockefeller University, has taught at the State University of New York in Old Westbury. The author of several books, since 1982 she has been a fellow of the Institute of Policy Studies in Washington, D.C. This essay was originally published in Ms.

A Step Back to the Workhouse?

The commentators are calling it a "remarkable consensus." Workfare, as programs to force welfare recipients to work are known, was once abhorred by liberals as a step back toward the 17th-century workhouse or—worse—slavery. But today no political candidate dares step outdoors without some plan for curing "welfare dependency" by putting its hapless victims to work—if necessary, at the nearest Burger King. It is as if the men who run things, or who aspire to run things (and we are, unfortunately, talking mostly about men when we talk about candidates), had gone off and caucused for a while and decided on the one constituency that could be safely sacrificed in the name of political expediency and "new ideas," and that constituency is poor women.

Most of the arguments for workfare are simply the same indestructible stereotypes that have been around, in one form or another, since the first public relief program in England 400 years ago: that the poor are poor because they are lazy and dissolute, and that they are lazy and dissolute because they are suffering from "welfare dependency." Add a touch of modern race and gender stereotypes and you have the image that haunts the workfare advocates: a slovenly, overweight, black woman who produces a baby a year in order to augment her welfare checks.

But there is a new twist to this season's spurt of welfare-bashing: workfare is being presented as a kind of *feminist* alternative to welfare. As Senator Daniel Patrick Moynihan (D.-N.Y.) has put it, "A program that was designed to pay mothers to stay at home with their children [i.e., welfare, or Aid to Families with Dependent Children] cannot succeed when we now observe most mothers going out to work." Never mind the startling illogic of this argument, which is on a par with saying that no woman should stay home with her children because other women do not, or that a laid-off male worker should not receive unemployment compensation because most men have been observed holding jobs. We are being asked to believe that pushing destitute mothers into the work force (in some versions of workfare, for no other compensation than the welfare payments they would have received anyway) is consistent with women's strivings toward self-determination.

Now I will acknowledge that most women on welfare—like most   4
unemployed women in general—would rather have jobs. And I will further acknowledge that many of the proponents of workfare, possibly including Senator Moynihan and the Democratic Presidential candidates, have mounted the bandwagon with the best of intentions. Welfare surely needs reform. But workfare is not the solution, because "dependency"—with all its implications of laziness and depravity—is not the problem. The problem is poverty, which most women enter in a uniquely devastating way—with their children in tow.

Let me introduce a real person, if only because real people, as opposed to imaginative stereotypes, never seem to make an appearance in the current rhetoric on welfare. "Lynn," as I will call her, is a friend and onetime neighbor who has been on welfare for two years. She is also about as unlike the stereotypical "welfare mother" as one can get—which is to say that she is a fairly typical welfare recipient. She has only one child, which puts her among the 74 percent of welfare recipients who have only one or two children. She is white (not that that should matter), as are almost half of welfare recipients. Like most welfare recipients, she is not herself the daughter of a welfare recipient, and hence not part of anything that could be called an "intergenerational cycle of dependency." And like every woman on welfare I have ever talked to, she resents the bureaucratic hassles that are the psychic price of welfare. But, for now, there are no alternatives.

When I first met Lynn, she seemed withdrawn and disoriented. She had just taken the biggest step of her 25 years; she had left an abusive husband and she was scared: scared about whether she could survive on her own and scared of her estranged husband. He owned a small restaurant; she was a high school dropout who had been a waitress when she met him. During their three years of marriage he had beaten her repeatedly. Only after he threw her down a flight of stairs had she realized that her life was in danger and moved out. I don't think I fully grasped the terror she had lived in until one summer day when he chased Lynn to the door of my house with a drawn gun.

Gradually Lynn began to put her life together. She got a divorce and went on welfare; she found a pediatrician who would accept Medicaid and a supermarket that would take food stamps. She fixed up her apartment with second-hand furniture and flea market curtains. She was, by my admittedly low standards, a compulsive housekeeper and an overprotective mother; and when she wasn't waxing her floors or ironing her two-year-old's playsuits, she was studying the help-wanted ads. She spent a lot of her time struggling with details that most of us barely notice—the price of cigarettes, mittens, or of a bus ticket to the welfare office—yet, somehow, she regained her sense of humor. In fact, most of the time we spent together was probably spent laughing—over the foibles of the neighbors, the conceits of men, and the snares of welfare and the rest of "the system."

Yet for all its inadequacies, Lynn was grateful for welfare. Maybe if she had been more intellectually inclined she would have found out that she was suffering from "welfare dependency," a condition that is supposed to sap the will and demolish the work ethic. But "dependency" is not an issue when it is a choice between an abusive husband and an impersonal government. Welfare had given Lynn a brief shelter in a hostile world, and as far as she was concerned, it was her ticket to *independence.* 8

Suppose there had been no welfare at the time when Lynn finally summoned the courage to leave her husband. Suppose she had gone for help and been told she would have to "work off" her benefits in some menial government job (restocking the toilet paper in rest rooms is one such "job" assigned to New York women in a current workfare program). Or suppose, as in some versions of workfare, she had been told she would have to take the first available private sector job, which (for a non-high school graduate like Lynn) would have paid near the minimum wage, or $3.35 an hour. How would she have been able to afford child care? What would she have done for health insurance (as a welfare recipient she had Medicaid, but most low-paying jobs offer little or no coverage)? Would she have ever made the decision to leave her husband in the first place?

As Ruth Sidel points out in *Women and Children Last* (Viking), most women who are or have been on welfare have stories like Lynn's. They go onto welfare in response to a crisis—divorce, illness, loss of a job, the birth of an additional child to feed—and they remain on welfare for two years or less. They are not victims of any "welfare culture," but of a society that increasingly expects women to both raise and support children—and often on wages that would barely support a woman alone. In fact, even some of the most vociferous advocates of replacing welfare with workfare admit that, in their own estimation, only about 15 percent of welfare recipients fit the stereotype associated with "welfare dependency": demoralization, long-term welfare use, lack of drive, and so on.

But workfare will not help anyone, not even the presumed 15 percent of "bad apples" for whose sake the majority will be penalized. First, it will not help because it does not solve the problem that drives most women into poverty in the first place: how to hold a job *and* care for children. Child care in a licensed, professionally run center can easily cost as much as $100 a week per child—more than most states now pay in welfare benefits and (for two children) more than most welfare recipients could expect to earn in the work force. Any serious effort to get welfare recipients into the work force would require childcare provisions at a price that would probably end up higher than the current budget for AFDC. But none of the workfare advocates are proposing that sort of massive public commitment to child care.

Then there is the problem of jobs. So far, studies show that existing   12
state workfare programs have had virtually no success in improving their participants' incomes or employment rates. Small wonder: nearly half the new jobs generated in recent years pay poverty-level wages; and most welfare recipients will enter jobs that pay near the minimum wage, which is $6,900 a year—26 percent less than the poverty level for a family of three. A menial, low-wage job may be character-building (from a middle-class vantage point), but it will not lift anyone out of poverty.

Some of my feminist activist friends argue that it is too late to stop the workfare juggernaut. The best we can do, they say, is to try to defeat the more pernicious proposals: those that are over-coercive, that do not offer funds for child care, or that would relegate workfare clients to a "subemployee" status unprotected by federal labor and civil rights legislation. Our goal, the pragmatists argue, should be to harness the current enthusiasm for workfare to push for services welfare recipients genuinely need, such as child care and job training and counseling.

I wish the pragmatists well, but for me, it would be a betrayal of women like Lynn to encourage the workfare bandwagon in any way. Most women, like Lynn, do not take up welfare as a career, but as an emergency measure in a time of personal trauma and dire need. At such times, the last thing they need is to be hustled into a low-wage job, and left to piece together child care, health insurance, transportation, and all the other ingredients of survival. In fact, the main effect of workfare may be to discourage needy women from seeking any help at all—a disastrous result in a nation already suffering from a child poverty rate of nearly 25 percent. Public policy should be aimed at giving impoverished mothers (and, I would add, fathers) the help they so urgently need—not only in the form of job opportunities, but sufficient income support to live on until a job worth taking comes along.

Besides, there is an ancient feminist principle at stake. The premise of all the workfare proposals—the more humane as well as the nasty—is that single mothers on welfare are *not working*. But, to quote the old feminist bumper sticker, EVERY MOTHER IS A WORKING MOTHER. And those who labor to raise their children in poverty—to feed and clothe them on meager budgets and to nurture them in an uncaring world—are working the hardest. The feminist position has never been that all women must pack off their children and enter the work force, but that all women's work—in the home or on the job—should be valued and respected.

Barbara Ehrenreich's essay stimulated a lively response from Ms. readers. The following letters were published in the February 1988 issue.

I was absolutely thrilled when I read Barbara Ehrenreich's article on work- 16
fare ("A Step Back to the Workhouse?" November 1987). As a single mother who received welfare for several years (with no child support) I'm
against everything that workfare stands for. I belong to an organization
called Women, Work, and Welfare, a group of current and former welfare
recipients trying to empower ourselves and become a part of the decisions
that affect our lives as poor women. It seems as if everybody but the welfare recipient herself has a hand in the decisions that are made.

Cheri Honkala
Minneapolis, Minn.

I arrived in Chicago in 1952 with a husband and two children from a camp
in Europe. I had another child in 1953, lost a newborn in 1954, had a miscarriage, a hysterectomy, and a divorce in 1955. I *never* received child support. My ex-husband was remarried within two months.

I *never* received welfare. I worked in another culture, while in very bad
health. I found a two-room flat, had no furniture and slept for years on the
floor. I even went back to school at night and had to contend with companies like Gulf Oil Corp., which did not believe in promoting women. But I
just slugged on.

By the end of the sixties, I had two daughters in college, and I had
bought a house. My total earnings for 1970 from three jobs came to a whopping $8,000.

A full-time minimum wage job *can* support one adult and one child. 20
One just has to learn how to do it.

Ursula Schramm
Hurley, Wis.

I found myself agreeing with the problems that Barbara Ehrenreich outlines in the present workfare program.

Yet deep inside a protesting rumbling exploded when I read that
impoverished mothers should receive sufficient income support to live on
"until a job worth taking comes along." *Bullshit!* Sure, we all should have
the right to only work a job we love, but how many of us can afford to wait
for it? That we are often forced to work at jobs that are not fulfilling says a
lot about our society in which more needs to be changed than just the welfare system!

My mother was forced to go to work when I was nine years old. Our
family was in dire financial straits and at the age of 50 she took a job in a
factory. Was that job "worth taking"? Did it utilize her unique talents? *No!*
Did it bring her personal fulfillment? *No!* Did it prevent the bank from
foreclosing on our home? *Yes!* Did it give my mother the power to overcome our financial crisis and maintain her autonomy? *Yes!* You tell me if it
was "worth taking." That depends on what your self-respect is worth to
you.

Gail Frei
Newtown Square, Pa.

Barbara Ehrenreich omitted a major element in her discussion of the vic- 24
timization of welfare families: the inability or unwillingness of the legal

system to award *and enforce* realistic child support. Until it stops being easier to abandon your children than to default on that car loan, women and those who depend on them will be welfare/workfare victims.

Susan Martin Rynard
Durham, N.C.

I went on welfare when my daughter was three, when I left my husband. I had a high school education, but had always wanted to go to college. I was 25.

So, with the help of the government, I got my B.S. in nursing. I worked for several years as an R.N. and then returned to school for my master's degree. For graduate school, I lived on savings, loans, and grants. The loans ($19,000 for undergrad and graduate in all) will be paid off in less than a year, in time for my daughter to begin college!

Kathryn Reid
Silverado, Calif.

Although I share Barbara Ehrenreich's concerns about workfare and the plight of her friend Lynn, the conclusions she draws strike me as misguided. We live in a society where the myths of the work ethic and self-help are deeply embedded in the popular culture; where resort to the dole is frowned upon unless the need is temporary or arises from disability; where the middle-class majority feels inequitably taxed, as compared to the wealthy, to support a system that directly benefits few of its members.

Feminists and other liberals should acknowledge the swelling demand for welfare reform. Our support should be conditional upon the incorporation in any welfare reform plan of provision for *quality* childcare facilities; upon the minimization of coercion; and upon further efforts to compel ex-spouses to pay their fair share of support. Nothing in this approach rules out our going ahead simultaneously with other, parallel efforts to question the mystique of work or to expose the links between welfare and poverty, on the one hand, and capitalism and the subordination of women, on the other. 28

David G. Becker
Hanover, N.H.

California *is* serious about workfare, but we call it GAIN (Greater Avenues for Independence). It offers welfare recipients vocational counseling, up to two years of vocational training, and workshops in how to get and hold a job.

GAIN also pays for child care and transportation. No job need be accepted by the recipient unless she/he will net at least as much as their AFCD grant, *including* child care, transportation, and medical insurance. And even then, they will receive funds to cover these costs for three months after they begin working to help them make the transition to the work force.

Jane Kirchman
Guerneville, Calif.

Topics for Critical Thinking and Writing

1. List the objections Ehrenreich makes to workfare, and pose an answer for each. Your answers may attempt to rebut her objections, on grounds either of their logic or of information she neglects to consider (for example, provisions in workfare programs you know of). Where her objections seem reasonable, propose improvements to workfare that you would like to see embodied in a program in your community. The letters answering Ehrenreich may provide some assistance. If so, quote, summarize, or paraphrase useful parts of the letters, giving appropriate acknowledgment to the writers.

2. Gloria Steinem in "The Importance of Work" (page 360) does not address the issue of welfare versus workfare, but a careful reading of her essay will suggest ideas and arguments on both sides of the question. Read her essay and report on the two or three ideas that struck you as interesting contributions to a discussion of workfare.

Henry Louis Gates, Jr.

Henry Louis Gates, Jr., born in West Virginia in 1950, holds degrees from Yale University and Clare College in Cambridge, England. Returning to the United States, Gates quickly established a reputation as a leading scholar of African-American literature. He is now chair of Harvard's program in African-American Studies, and he is also the director of the W. E. B. Du Bois Institute.

We reprint an essay that originally appeared in Sports Illustrated.

Delusions of Grandeur

Standing at the bar of an all-black VFW post in my hometown of Piedmont, W.Va., I offered five dollars to anyone who could tell me how many African-American professional athletes were at work today. There are 35 million African-Americans, I said.

"Ten million!" yelled one intrepid soul, too far into his cups.

"No way . . . more like 500,000," said another.

"You mean *all* professional sports," someone interjected, "including golf and tennis, but not counting the brothers from Puerto Rico?" Everyone laughed.   4

"Fifty thousand, minimum," was another guess.

Here are the facts:

There are 1,200 black professional athletes in the U.S.

There are 12 times more black lawyers than black athletes.   8

There are 2 1/2 times more black dentists than black athletes.

There are 15 times more black doctors than black athletes.

Nobody in my local VFW believed these statistics; in fact, few people would believe them if they weren't reading them in the pages of *Sports Illustrated.* In spite of these statistics, too many African-American youngsters still believe that they have a much better chance of becoming another Magic Johnson or Michael Jordan than they do of matching the achievements of Baltimore Mayor Kurt Schmoke or neurosurgeon Dr. Benjamin Carson, both of whom, like Johnson and Jordan, are black.

In reality, an African-American youngster has about as much   12 chance of becoming a professional athlete as he or she does of winning the lottery. The tragedy for our people, however, is that few of us accept that truth.

Let me confess that I love sports. Like most black people of my generation—I'm 40—I was raised to revere the great black athletic heroes, and I never tired of listening to the stories of triumph and defeat that, for blacks, amount to a collective epic much like those of the ancient Greeks: Joe Louis's demolition of Max Schmeling; Satchel Paige's dazzling repertoire of pitches; Jesse Owens's in-your-face performance in Hitler's 1936 Olympics; Willie Mays's over-the-shoulder basket catch; Jackie Robinson's quiet strength when assaulted by racist taunts; and a thousand other grand tales.

Nevertheless, the blind pursuit of attainment in sports is having a devastating effect on our people. Imbued with a belief that our principal avenue to fame and profit is through sport, and seduced by a win-at-any-cost system that corrupts even elementary school students, far too many black kids treat basketball courts and football fields as if they were classrooms in an alternative school system. "O.K., I flunked English," a young athlete will say. "But I got an A plus in slam-dunking ."

The failure of our public schools to educate athletes is part and parcel of the schools' failure to educate almost everyone. A recent survey of the Philadelphia school system, for example, stated that "more than half of all students in the third, fifth and eighth grades cannot perform minimum math and language tasks." One in four middle school students in that city fails to pass to the next grade each year. It is a sad truth that such statistics are repeated in cities throughout the nation. Young athletes—particularly young black athletes—are especially ill-served. Many of them are functionally illiterate, yet they are passed along from year to year for the greater glory of good old Hometown High. We should not be surprised to learn, then, that only 26.6% of black athletes at the collegiate level earn their degrees. For every successful educated black professional athlete, there are thousands of dead and wounded. Yet young blacks continue to aspire to careers as athletes, and it's no wonder why; when the University of North Carolina recently commissioned a sculptor to create archetypes of its student body, guess which ethnic group was selected to represent athletes?

Those relatively few black athletes who do make it in the profes-   16
sional ranks must be prevailed upon to play a significant role in the
education of all of our young people, athlete and nonathlete alike.
While some have done so, many others have shirked their social obligations: to earmark small percentages of their incomes for the United
Negro College Fund; to appear on television for educational purposes
rather than merely to sell sneakers; to let children know the message
that becoming a lawyer, a teacher or a doctor does more good for our
people than winning the Super Bowl; and to form productive liaisons
with educators to help forge solutions to the many ills that beset the
black community. These are merely a few modest proposals.

A similar burden falls upon successful blacks in all walks of life.
Each of us must strive to make our young people understand the realities. Tell them to cheer Bo Jackson but to emulate novelist Toni Morri-
son or businessman Reginald Lewis or historian John Hope Franklin or
Spelman College president Johnetta Cole—the list is long.

Of course, society as a whole bears responsibility as well. Until colleges stop using young blacks as cannon fodder in the big-business
wars of so-called nonprofessional sports, until training a young black's
mind becomes as important as training his or her body, we will continue to perpetuate a system akin to that of the Roman gladiators, sacrificing a class of people for the entertainment of the mob.

Topics for Critical Thinking and Writing

1. Strictly speaking, the first five paragraphs are not necessary to Gates's
   argument. Why do you suppose he included them? Evaluate his strategy for opening the essay.
2. In his next-to-last paragraph Gates says that "successful blacks in all
   walks of life" have a special obligation. In his last paragraph he widens
   his vision, saying that "society as a whole bears responsibility as well."
   Two questions: (a) In what ways is society responsible? (b) How effective do you think the final paragraph is, and why? (Consider especially
   the comparison to gladiatorial games.)
3. In paragraph 9 Gates mentions Joe Louis, Satchel Paige, Jesse Owens,
   Willie Mays, and Jackie Robinson. Do a little research on one of these
   men and write a short paragraph explaining Gates's reference to him.
   For instance, *when* did Joe Louis defeat Max Schmeling (and who *was*
   Schmeling)—in what year, in what round, and with what sort of
   punches?
4. In paragraph 9 Gates says the he "never tired of listening to the stories
   of triumph and defeat that, for blacks, amount to a collective epic much
   like those of the ancient Greeks. . . ." The appeal of stories of triumph is
   evident, but what is the appeal of stories of defeat? If you are familiar
   with stories of defeat that concern your heritage, analyze the sources of
   their appeal.

Sir Thomas More

Sir Thomas More (1478–1535) was an extremely able English administrator and diplomat who rose to high rank in the government of King Henry VIII, but when he opposed the King's break with Roman Catholicism (Henry demanded that his subjects recognize him as Supreme Head of the Church), More was beheaded. Four hundred years later, in 1935, he was canonized.

More wrote Utopia in Latin (the international language of the Renaissance) in 1516. The word is Greek for no place, *but the Greek-sounding names for officials in this imaginary land—a* syphogrant *is elected by a group of thirty households, and a* tranibor *governs a group of ten syphogrants—have no meaning. Though the book is fictional, setting forth a playful vision of an ideal society, there is no story; it is not a novel but a sort of essay.*

"Work and Play" (editors' title) represents about one-tenth of the book.

Work and Play in Utopia

Their Occupations

Agriculture is the one occupation at which everyone works, men and women alike, with no exceptions. They are trained in it from childhood, partly in the schools where they learn theory, and partly through field trips to nearby farms, which make something like a game of practical instruction. On these trips they not only watch the work being done, but frequently pitch in and get a workout by doing the jobs themselves.

Besides farm work (which, as I said, everybody performs), each person is taught a particular trade of his own, such as wool-working, linen-making, masonry, metal-work, or carpentry. There is no other craft that is practiced by any considerable number of them. Throughout the island people wear, and down through the centuries they have always worn, the same style of clothing, except for the distinction between the sexes, and between married and unmarried persons. Their clothing is attractive, does not hamper bodily movement, and serves for warm as well as cold weather; what is more, each household can make its own.

Every person (and this includes women as well as men) learns a second trade, besides agriculture. As the weaker sex, women practice the lighter crafts, such as working in wool or linen; the heavier crafts are assigned to the men. As a rule, the son is trained to his father's craft; for which most feel a natural inclination. But if anyone is attracted to another occupation, he is transferred by adoption into a family practicing the trade he prefers. When anyone makes such a change, both his father and the authorities make sure that he is assigned to a grave and responsible householder. After a man has learned one trade, if he wants to learn another, he gets the same permission. When he has learned both, he pursues whichever he likes better, unless the city needs one more than the other.

The chief and almost the only business of the syphogrants is to   4
manage matters so that no one sits around in idleness, and assure that
everyone works hard at his trade. But no one has to exhaust himself
with endless toil from early morning to late at night, as if he were a
beast of burden. Such wretchedness, really worse than slavery, is the
common lot of workmen in all countries, except Utopia. Of the day's
twenty-four hours, the Utopians devote only six to work. They work
three hours before noon, when they go to dinner. After dinner they rest
for a couple of hours, then go to work for another three hours. Then
they have supper, and at eight o'clock (counting the first hour after
noon as one), they go to bed and sleep eight hours.

The other hours of the day, when they are not working, eating, or
sleeping, are left to each man's individual discretion, provided he does
not waste them in roistering or sloth, but uses them busily in some
occupation that pleases him. Generally these periods are devoted to
intellectual activity. For they have an established custom of giving public lectures before daybreak; attendance at these lectures is required
only of those who have been specially chosen to devote themselves to
learning, but a great many other people, both men and women, choose
voluntarily to attend. Depending on their interests, some go to one lecture, some to another. But if anyone would rather devote his spare time
to his trade, as many do who don't care for the intellectual life, this is
not discouraged; in fact, such persons are commended as especially
useful to the commonwealth.

After supper, they devote an hour to recreation, in their gardens
when the weather is fine, or during winter weather in the common
halls where they have their meals. There they either play music or
amuse themselves with conversation. They know nothing about gambling with dice, or other such foolish and ruinous games. They do play
two games not unlike our own chess. One is a battle of numbers, in
which one number captures another. The other is a game in which the
vices fight a battle against the virtues. The game is set up to show how
the vices oppose one another, yet readily combine against the virtues;
then, what vices oppose what virtues, how they try to assault them
openly or undermine them in secret; how the virtues can break the
strength of the vices or turn their purposes to good; and finally, by what
means one side or the other gains the victory.

But in all this, you may get a wrong impression, if we don't go back
and consider one point more carefully. Because they allot only six hours
to work, you might think the necessities of life would be in scant supply. This is far from the case. Their working hours are ample to provide
not only enough but more than enough of the necessities and even the
conveniences of life. You will easily appreciate this if you consider how
large a part of the population in other countries exists without doing
any work at all. In the first place, hardly any of the women, who are a

full half of the population, work; or, if they do, then as a rule their husbands lie snoring in the bed. Then there is a great lazy gang of priests and so-called religious men. Add to them all the rich, especially the landlords, who are commonly called gentlemen and nobility. Include with them their retainers, that mob of swaggering bullies. Finally, reckon in with these the sturdy and lusty beggars, who go about feigning some disease as an excuse for their idleness. You will certainly find that the things which satisfy our needs are produced by far fewer hands than you had supposed.

And now consider how few of those who do work are doing really 8
essential things. For where money is the standard of everything, many superfluous trades are bound to be carried on simply to satisfy luxury and licentiousness. Suppose the multitude of those who now work were limited to a few trades, and set to producing more and more of those conveniences and commodities that nature really requires. They would be bound to produce so much that the prices would drop, and the workmen would be unable to gain a living. But suppose again that all the workers in useless trades were put to useful ones, and that all the idlers (who now guzzle twice as much as the workingmen who make what they consume) were assigned to productive tasks—well, you can easily see how little time each man would have to spend working, in order to produce all the goods that human needs and conveniences require—yes, and human pleasure too, as long as it's true and natural pleasure.

The experience of Utopia makes this perfectly apparent. In each city and its surrounding countryside barely five hundred of those men and women whose age and strength make them fit for work are exempted from it. Among these are the syphogrants, who by law are free not to work; yet they don't take advantage of the privilege, preferring to set a good example to their fellow-citizens. Some others are permanently exempted from work so that they may devote themselves to study, but only on the recommendation of the priests and through a secret vote of the syphogrants. If any of these scholars disappoints their hopes, he becomes a workman again. On the other hand, it happens from time to time that a craftsman devotes his leisure so earnestly to study, and makes such progress as a result, that he is relieved of manual labor, and promoted to the class of learned men. From this class of scholars are chosen ambassadors, priests, tranibors, and the prince himself, who used to be called Barzanes, but in their modern tongue is known as Ademus. Since all the rest of the population is neither idle nor occupied in useless trades, it is easy to see why they produce so much in so short a working day.

Apart from all this, in several of the necessary crafts their way of life requires less total labor than does that of people elsewhere. In other countries, building and repairing houses requires the constant work of

many men, because what a father has built, his thriftless heirs lets fall
into ruin; and then his successor has to repair, at great expense, what
could easily have been maintained at a very small charge. Further, even
when a man has built a splendid house at large cost, someone else may
think he has finer taste, let the first house fall to ruin, and then build
another one somewhere else for just as much money. But among the
Utopians, where everything has been established, and the commonwealth is carefully regulated, building a brand-new home on a new site
is a rare event. They are not only quick to repair damage, but foresight-
ed in preventing it. The result is that their buildings last for a very long
time with minimum repairs; and the carpenters and masons sometimes
have so little to do, that they are set to hewing timber and cutting stone
in case some future need for it should arise.

Consider, too, how little labor their clothing requires. Their work
clothes are loose garments made of leather which last as long as seven
years. When they go out in public, they cover these rough working-
clothes with a cloak. Throughout the entire island, everyone wears the
same colored cloak, which is the color of natural wool. As a result, they
not only need less wool than people in other countries, but what they
do need is less expensive. They use linen cloth most, because it requires
least labor. They like linen cloth to be white and wool cloth to be clean;
but they put no price on fineness of texture. Elsewhere a man is not satisfied with four or five woolen cloaks of different colors and as many
silk shirts, or if he's a show-off, even ten of each are not enough. But a
Utopian is content with a single cloak, and generally wears it for two
seasons. There is no reason at all why he should want any others, for if
he had them, he would not be better protected against the cold, nor
would he appear in any way better dressed.

When there is an abundance of everything, as a result of everyone
working at useful trades, and nobody consuming to excess, then great
numbers of the people often go out to work on the roads, if any of them
need repairing. And when there is no need even for this sort of public
work, then the officials very often proclaim a short work day, since they
never force their citizens to perform useless labor. The chief aim of their
constitution and government is that, whenever public needs permit, all
citizens should be free, so far as possible, to withdraw their time and
energy from the service of the body, and devote themselves to the freedom and culture of the mind. For that, they think, is the real happiness
of life. . . .

Their Moral Philosophy

They conclude, after carefully considering and weighing the matter,
that all our actions and the virtues exercised within them look toward
pleasure and happiness at their ultimate end.

By pleasure they understand every state or movement of body or mind in which man naturally finds delight. They are right in considering man's appetites natural. By simply following his senses and his right reason a man may discover what is pleasant by nature—it is a delight which does not injure others, which does not preclude a greater pleasure, and which is not followed by pain. But a pleasure which is against nature, and which men call "delightful" only by the emptiest of fictions (as if one could change the real nature of things just by changing their names), does not really make for happiness; in fact they say, it destroys happiness. And the reason is that men whose minds are filled with false ideas of pleasure have no room left for true and genuine delight. As a matter of fact, there are a great many things which have no sweetness in them, but are mainly or entirely bitter—yet which through the perverse enticements of evil lusts are considered very great pleasures, and even the supreme goals of life.

Among those who pursue this false pleasure the Utopians include those whom I mentioned before, the men who think themselves finer fellows because they wear finer clothes. These people are twice mistaken: first in thinking their clothes better than anyone else's, and then in thinking themselves better because of their clothes. As far as a coat's usefulness goes, what does it matter if it was woven of thin thread or thick? Yet they act as if they were set apart by nature herself, rather than their own fantasies; they strut about, and put on airs. Because they have a fancy suit, they think themselves entitled to honors they would never have expected if they were poorly dressed, and they get very angry if someone passes them by without showing special respect.

It is the same kind of absurdity to be pleased by empty, ceremonial honors. What true and natural pleasure can you get from someone's bent knee or bared head? Will the creaks in your own knees be eased thereby, or the madness in your head? The phantom of false pleasure is illustrated by other men who run mad with delight over their own blue blood, plume themselves on their nobility, and applaud themselves for all their rich ancestors (the only ancestors worth having nowadays), and all their ancient family estates. Even if they don't have the shred of an estate themselves, or if they've squandered every penny of their inheritance, they don't consider themselves a bit less noble.

In the same class the Utopians put those people I described before, who are mad for jewelry and gems, and think themselves divinely happy if they find a good specimen, especially of the sort which happens to be fashionable in their country at the time—for stones vary in value from one market to another. The collector will not make an offer for the stone till it's taken out of its setting, and even then he will not buy unless the dealer guarantees and gives security that it is a true and genuine stone. What he fears is that his eyes will be deceived by a counterfeit. But if you consider the matter, why should a counterfeit give any less pleasure when your eyes cannot distinguish it from a real gem?

Both should be of equal value to you, as they would be, in fact, to a blind man.

Speaking of false pleasure, what about those who pile up money, not because they want to do anything with the heap, but so they can sit and look at it? Is that true pleasure they experience, or aren't they simply cheated by a show of pleasure? Or what of those with the opposite vice, the men who hide away money they will never use and perhaps never even see again? In their anxiety to hold onto their money, they actually lose it. For what else happens when you deprive yourself, and perhaps other people too, of a chance to use money, by burying it in the ground? And yet when the miser has hidden his treasure, he exults over it as if his mind were now free to rejoice. Suppose someone stole it, and the miser died ten years later, knowing nothing of the theft. During all those ten years, what did it matter whether the money was stolen or not? In either case, it was equally useless to the owner.

To these false and foolish pleasures they add gambling, which they have heard about, though they've never tried it, as well as hunting and hawking. What pleasure can there be, they wonder, in throwing dice on a table? If there were any pleasure in the action, wouldn't doing it over and over again quickly make one tired of it? What pleasure can there be in listening to the barking and yelping of dogs—isn't that rather a disgusting noise? Is there any more real pleasure when a dog chases a rabbit than there is when a dog chases a dog? If what you like is fast running, there's plenty of that in both cases; they're just about the same. But if what you really want is slaughter, if you want to see a living creature torn apart under your eyes, then the whole thing is wrong. You ought to feel nothing but pity when you see the hare fleeing from the hound, the weak creature tormented by the stronger, the fearful and timid beast brutalized by the savage one, the harmless hare killed by the cruel dog. The Utopians, who regard this whole activity of hunting as unworthy of free men, have assigned it, accordingly, to their butchers, who as I said before, are all slaves. In their eyes, hunting is the lowest thing even butchers can do. In the slaughterhouse, their work is more useful and honest—besides which, they kill animals only from necessity; but in hunting they seek merely their own pleasure from the killing and mutilating of some poor little creature. Taking such relish in the sight of death, even if it's only beasts, reveals, in the opinion of the Utopians, a cruel disposition. Or if he isn't cruel to start with, the hunter quickly becomes so through the constant practice of such brutal pleasures.

Most men consider these activities, and countless others like them, to be pleasures; but the Utopians say flatly they have nothing at all to do with real pleasure since there's nothing naturally pleasant about them. They often please the senses, and in this they are like pleasure, but that does not alter their basic nature. The enjoyment doesn't arise

20

from the experience itself, but only from the perverse mind of the individual, as a result of which he mistakes the bitter for the sweet, just as pregnant women, whose taste has been turned awry, sometimes think pitch and tallow taste sweeter than honey. A man's taste may be similarly depraved, by disease or by custom, but that does not change the nature of pleasure, or of anything else.

Topics for Critical Thinking and Writing

1. What does More assume are the only functions of clothing? Do you agree with More, or do you find other important reasons why people wear the clothes that they wear?
2. The "work ethic" assumes that labor is good in itself—that there is some sort of virtue in work. (See Nixon's remark on page 324.) Further, many people assume that work, at least certain kinds of work done under certain conditions, affords happiness to the worker. What does More's attitude seem to be on these two related points?
3. What is More's opinion of hunting? What arguments in support of hunting are commonly offered? In your opinion, does More successfully counter those arguments?
4. In approximately five hundred words set forth More's assumptions about the sources of happiness.
5. More says that each Utopian is free to do what he wishes with leisure hours, "provided he does not waste them in roistering or sloth." (By the way, since the Utopians work six hours a day, if they sleep eight hours they have ten hours of free time.) In five hundred words develop an argument for or against this proviso concerning the pursuit of happiness. (You may want to recall that our own government to some degree regulates our pleasure, for instance by outlawing bullfights.)
6. Note the passage (paragraph 6) in which More describes two games enjoyed by Utopians. Imitating More's style in describing the second game, write a paragraph describing a video game as a Utopian or anti-Utopian recreation.

Marie Winn

Marie Winn, born in Czechoslovakia in 1936, came to New York when she was still a child. She later graduated from Radcliffe College and then did further academic work at Columbia University. Our selection comes from Childhood without Children *(1983), a book based in part on interviews with hundreds of children and parents.*

The End of Play

Of all the changes that have altered the topography of childhood, the most dramatic has been the disappearance of childhood play. Whereas a decade or two ago children were easily distinguished from the adult world by the very nature of their play, today children's occupations do not differ greatly from adult diversions.

Infants and toddlers, to be sure, continue to follow certain timeless patterns of manipulation and exploration; adolescents, too, have not changed their free-time habits so very much, turning as they ever have towards adult pastimes and amusements in their drive for autonomy, self-mastery, and sexual discovery. It is among the ranks of school-age children, those six-to-twelve-year-olds who once avidly filled their free moments with childhood play, that the greatest change is evident. In the place of traditional, sometimes ancient childhood games that were still popular a generation ago, in the place of fantasy and make-believe play—"You be the mommy and I'll be the daddy"—doll play or toy-soldier play, jump-rope play, ball-bouncing play, today's children have substituted television viewing and, most recently, video games.

Many parents have misgivings about the influence of television. They sense that a steady and time-consuming exposure to passive entertainment might damage the ability to play imaginatively and resourcefully, or prevent this ability from developing in the first place. A mother of two school-age children recalls: "When I was growing up, we used to go out into the vacant lots and make up week-long dramas and sagas. This was during third, fourth, fifth grades. But my own kids have never done that sort of thing, and somehow it bothers me. I wish we had cut down on the TV years ago, and maybe the kids would have learned how to play."

The testimony of parents who eliminate television for periods of time strengthens the connection between children's television watching and changed play patterns. Many parents discover that when their children don't have television to fill their free time, they resort to the old kinds of imaginative, traditional "children's play." Moreover, these parents often observe that under such circumstances "they begin to seem more like children" or "they act more childlike." Clearly, a part of the definition of childhood, in adults' minds, resides in the nature of children's play.

Children themselves sometimes recognize the link between play and their own special definition as children. In an interview about children's books with four ten-year-old girls, one of them said: "I read this story about a girl my age growing up twenty years ago—you know, in 1960 or so,—and she seemed so much younger than me in her behavior. Like she might be playing with dolls, or playing all sorts of children's games, or jump-roping or something." The other girls all agreed that they had noticed a similar discrepancy between themselves and fictional children in books of the past: those children seemed more like children. "So what do *you* do in your spare time, if you don't play with dolls or play make-believe games or jump rope or do things kids did twenty years ago?" they were asked. They laughed and answered, "We watch TV."

4

But perhaps other societal factors have caused children to give up play. Children's greater exposure to adult realities, their knowledge of adult sexuality, for instance, might make them more sophisticated, less likely to play like children. Evidence from the counterculture communes of the sixties and seventies adds weight to the argument that it is television above all that has eliminated children's play. Studies of children raised in a variety of such communes, all television-free, showed the little communards continuing to fill their time with those forms of play that have all but vanished from the lives of conventionally reared American children. And yet these counterculture kids were casually exposed to all sorts of adult matters—drug taking, sexual intercourse. Indeed, they sometimes incorporated these matters into their play: "We're mating," a pair of six-year-olds told a reporter to explain their curious bumps and grinds. Nevertheless, to all observers the commune children preserved a distinctly childlike and even innocent demeanor, an impression that was produced mainly by the fact that they spent most of their time playing. Their play defined them as belonging to a special world of childhood.

Not all children have lost the desire to engage in the old-style childhood play. But so long as the most popular, most dominant members of the peer group, who are often the most socially precocious, are "beyond" playing, then a common desire to conform makes it harder for those children who still have the drive to play to go ahead and do so. Parents often report that their children seem ashamed of previously common forms of play and hide their involvement with such play from their peers. "My fifth-grader still plays with dolls," a mother tells," but she keeps them hidden in the basement where nobody will see them." This social check on the play instinct serves to hasten the end of childhood for even the least advanced children.

What seems to have replaced play in the lives of great numbers of   8
preadolescents these days, starting as early as fourth grade, is a burgeoning interest in boy-girl interactions—"going out" or "going together." These activities do not necessarily involve going anywhere or doing anything sexual, but nevertheless are the first stage of a sexual process that used to commence at puberty or even later. Those more sophisticated children who are already involved in such manifestly unchildlike interest make plain their low opinion of their peers who still *play*. "Some of the kids in the class are real weird," a fifth-grade boy states. "They're not interested in going out, just in trucks and stuff, or games pretending they're monsters. Some of them don't even *try* to be cool."

Video Games versus Marbles

Is there really any great difference, one might ask, between that gang of kids playing video games by the hour at their local candy store these days and those small fry who used to hang around together spending equal amounts of time playing marbles? It is easy to see a similarity between the two activities: each requires a certain amount of manual dexterity, each is almost as much fun to watch as to play, each is simple and yet challenging enough for that middle-childhood age group for whom time can be so oppressive if unfilled.

One significant difference between the modern pre-teen fad of video games and the once popular but now almost extinct pastime of marbles is economic: playing video games costs twenty-five cents for approximately three minutes of play; playing marbles, after a small initial investment, is free. The children who frequent video-game machines require a considerable outlay of quarters to subsidize their fun; two, three, or four dollars is not an unusual expenditure for an eight-or nine-year-old spending an hour or two with his friends playing Asteroids or Pac-Man or Space Invaders. For most of the children the money comes from their weekly allowance. Some augment this amount by enterprising commercial ventures—trading and selling comic books, or doing chores around the house for extra money.

But what difference does it make *where* the money comes from? Why should that make video games any less satisfactory as an amusement for children? In fact, having to pay for the entertainment, whatever the source of the money, and having its duration limited by one's financial resources changes the nature of the game, in a subtle way diminishing the satisfactions it offers. Money and time become intertwined, as they so often are in the adult world and as, in the past, they almost never were in the child's world. For the child playing marbles, meanwhile, time has a far more carefree quality, bounded only by the requirements to be home by suppertime or by dark.

But the video-game-playing child has an additional burden—a 12 burden of choice, of knowing that the money used for playing Pac-Man could have been saved for Christmas, could have been used to buy something tangible, perhaps something "worthwhile," as his parents might say, rather than being "wasted" on video games. There is a certain sense of adultness that spending money imparts, a feeling of being a consumer, which distinguishes a game with a price from its counterparts among the traditional childhood games children once played at no cost.

There are other differences as well. Unlike child-initiated and child-organized games such as marbles, video games are adult-created mechanisms not entirely within the child's control, and thus less likely to impart a sense of mastery and fulfillment: the coin may get jammed, the machine may go haywire, the little blobs may stop eating the funny little dots. Then the child must go to the storekeeper to complain, to get his money back. He may be "ripped off" and simply lose his quarter, much as his parents are when they buy a faulty appliance. This possibility of disaster gives the child's play a certain weight that marbles never imposed on its light-hearted players.

Even if a child has a video game at home requiring no coin outlay, the play it provides is less than optimal. The noise level of the machine is high—too high, usually, for the child to conduct a conversation easily with another child. And yet, according to its enthusiasts, this very noisiness is a part of the game's attraction. The loud whizzes, crashes, and whirrs of the video-game machine "blow the mind" and create an excitement that is quite apart from the excitement generated simply by trying to win a game. A traditional childhood game such as marbles, on the other hand, has little built-in stimulation; the excitement of playing is generated entirely by the players' own actions. And while the pace of a game of marbles is close to the child's natural physiological rhythms, the frenzied activities of video games serve to "rev up" the child in an artificial way, almost in the way a stimulant or an amphetamine might. Meanwhile the perceptual impact of a video game is similar to that of watching television—the action, after all, takes place on a television screen—causing the eye to defocus slightly and creating a certain alteration in the child's natural state of consciousness.

Parents' instinctive reaction to their children's involvement with video games provides another clue to the difference between this contemporary form of play and the more traditional pastimes such as marbles. While parents, indeed most adults, derive open pleasure from watching children at play, most parents today are not delighted to watch their kids flicking away at the Pac-Man machine. This does not seem to them to be real play. As a mother of two school-age children anxiously explains, "We used to do real childhood sorts of things when I was a kid. We'd build forts and put on crazy plays and make up new languages, and just generally we *played*. But today my kids don't play that way at all. They like video games and of course they still go in for sports outdoors. They go roller skating and ice skating and skiing and all. But they don't seem to really *play*."

Some of this feeling may represent a certain nostalgia for the past 16 and the old generation's resistance to the different ways of the new. But it is more likely that most adults have an instinctive understanding of the importance of play in their own childhood. This feeling stokes their fears that their children are being deprived of something irreplaceable when they flip the levers on the video machines to manipulate the electronic images rather than flick their fingers to send a marble shooting towards another marble.

Play Deprivation

In addition to television's influence, some parents and teachers ascribe children's diminished drive to play to recent changes in the school curriculum, especially in the early grades.

"Kindergarten, traditionally a playful port of entry into formal school, is becoming more academic, with children being taught specific skills, taking tests, and occasionally even having homework," begins a report on new directions in early childhood education. Since 1970, according to the United States census, the proportion of three- and four-year-olds enrolled in school has risen dramatically, from 20.5 percent to 36.7 percent in 1980, and these nursery schools have largely joined the push towards academic acceleration in the early grades. Moreover, middle-class nursery schools in recent years have introduced substantial doses of academic material into their daily programs, often using those particular devices originally intended to help culturally deprived preschoolers in compensatory programs such as Headstart to catch up with their middle-class peers. Indeed, some of the increased focus on academic skills in nursery schools and kindergartens is related to the widespread popularity among young children and their parents of *Sesame Street,* a program originally intended to help deprived children attain academic skills, but universally watched by middle-class toddlers as well.

Parents of the *Sesame Street* generation often demand a "serious," skill-centered program for their preschoolers in school, afraid that the old-fashioned, play-centered curriculum will bore their alphabet-spouting, number-chanting four- and five-year-olds. A few parents, especially those whose children have not attended television classes or nursery school, complain of the high-powered pace of kindergarten these days. A father whose five-year-old daughter attends a public kindergarten declares: "There's a lot more pressure put on little kids these days than when we were kids, that's for sure. My daughter never went to nursery school and never watched *Sesame,* and she had a lot of trouble when she entered kindergarten this fall. By October, just a month and a half into the program, she was already flunking. The teacher told us our daughter couldn't keep up with the other kids. And believe me, she's a bright kid! All the other kids were getting gold stars and smiley faces for their work, and every day Emily would come home in tears because she didn't get a gold star. Remember when we were in kindergarten? We were *children* then. We were allowed just to play!"

A kindergarten teacher confirms the trend towards early academic 20
pressure. "We're expected by the dictates of the school system to push a lot of curriculum," she explains. "Kids in our kindergarten can't sit around playing with blocks any more. We've just managed to squeeze in one hour of free play a week, on Fridays."

The diminished emphasis on fantasy and play and imaginative activities in early childhood education and the increased focus on early academic-skill acquisition have helped to change childhood from a play-centered time of life to one more closely resembling the style of adulthood: purposeful, success-centered, competitive. The likelihood is that these preschool "workers" will not metamorphose back into players when they move on to grade school. This decline in play is surely one of the reasons why so many teachers today comment that their third- or fourth-graders act like tired businessmen instead of like children.

What might be the consequences of this change in children's play? Children's propensity to engage in that extraordinary series of behaviors characterized as "play" is perhaps the single great dividing line between childhood and adulthood, and has probably been so throughout history. The make-believe games anthropologists have recorded of children in primitive societies around the world attest to the universality of play and to the uniqueness of this activity to the immature members of each society. But in those societies, and probably in Western society before the middle or late eighteenth century, there was always a certain similarity between children's play and adult work. The child's imaginative play took the form of imitation of various aspects of adult life, culminating in the gradual transformation of the child's play from make-believe work to *real* work. At this point, in primitive societies or in our own society of the past, the child took her or his place in the adult work world and the distinctions between adulthood and childhood virtually vanished. But in today's technologically advanced society there is no place for the child in the adult work world. There are not enough jobs, even of the most menial kind, to go around for adults, much less for children. The child must continue to be dependent on adults for many years while gaining the knowledge and skills necessary to become a working member of society.

This is not a new situation for children. For centuries children have endured a prolonged period of dependence long after the helplessness of early childhood is over. But until recent years children remained childlike and playful far longer than they do today. Kept isolated from the adult world as a result of deliberate secrecy and protectiveness, they continued to find pleasure in socially sanctioned childish activities until the imperatives of adolescence led them to strike out for independence and self-sufficiency.

Today, however, with children's inclusion in the adult world both   24
through the instrument of television and as a result of a deliberately preparatory, integrative style of child rearing, the old forms of play no longer seem to provide children with enough excitement and stimulation. What then are these so-called children to do for fulfillment if their desire to play has been vitiated and yet their entry into the working world of adulthood must be delayed for many years? The answer is precisely to get involved in those areas that cause contemporary parents so much distress: addictive television viewing during the school years followed, in adolescence or even before, by a search for similar oblivion via alcohol and drugs; exploration of the world of sensuality and sexuality before achieving the emotional maturity necessary for altruistic relationships.

Psychiatrists have observed among children in recent years a marked increase in the occurrence of depression, a state long considered antithetical to the nature of childhood. Perhaps this phenomenon is at least somewhat connected with the current sense of uselessness and alienation that children feel, a sense that play may once upon a time have kept in abeyance.

Topics for Critical Thinking and Writing

1. In a sentence or two sum up Winn's thesis.
2. When you were a child, what did you do in your "spare time"? Judging from your own experience, is Winn's first paragraph true, or at least roughly true?
3. Assuming that children today do indeed spend many hours watching television and playing video games, is it true that these activities "do not differ greatly from adult diversions"? To test Winn's assertion, list the diversions of adults and of children that you know of from your own experience. Are the two lists indeed strikingly similar? Or do the lists reveal important differences? Explain.
4. Winn's argument is largely composed of a series of comparisons between the play of children before access to TV and after; between traditional and contemporary kindergarten; between childhood in "primitive" (and our own preindustrial) society and in technologically advanced societies. List the points she makes to develop each of these comparisons. How well does each comparison support her thesis?
5. Winn obviously prefers that children play by making up stories rather than watching television. What reasons can be given to prefer making up stories, or reading stories in a book, to watching stories on television? Winn does not mention being read to by an adult as an activity of childhood, Draw your own comparison between traditional bedtime story-reading and nighttime TV-watching. Would such a comparison have strengthened or weakened Winn's argument?
6. Speaking of video games (paragraph 11), Winn argues that "having to pay for the entertainment . . . changes the nature of the game, in a subtle way diminishing the satisfactions it offers." Can one reply that having to pay helps a child to appreciate the value of money? In short, can it be argued that paying for one's pleasure is a way of becoming mature?

Doris Kearns Goodwin

Doris Kearns Goodwin was born in Rockville Centre, New York, in 1943, and educated at Colby College (BA) and Harvard University (Ph.D). As an undergraduate she served in Washington as a State Department intern, and between college and graduate school she served as a House of Representatives intern. In 1968, the year she received her Ph.D., she served as special assistant to President Lyndon Johnson—a rather remarkable appointment, since Johnson offered it to her knowing that in 1967 she had published an article urging the Democrats not to renominate him for the 1968 election.

One product of her work with Johnson was a highly acclaimed biography (which she published under the name of Doris Helen Kearns), Lyndon Johnson and the American Dream *(1976). She has also written two more books which are widely regarded as major works:* The Fitzgeralds and the Kennedys: An American Saga *(1987) and* No Ordinary Time: Franklin and Eleanor Roosevelt *(1994).*

Fan

My continuing love of baseball is inseparably linked to memories of my father. On summer nights, when he came home from work, the two of us would sit together on our porch, reliving that day's Brooklyn Dodger game, which I had permanently preserved in the large red scorebook he'd given me for my seventh birthday.

I can still remember how proud I was when I first mastered all the miniature symbols that allowed me to record every movement, play by play, of our favorite players, Jackie Robinson and Duke Snider. Pee Wee Reese and Gil Hodges. With the scorebook spread between us, my dad would ask me questions about different plays, whether a strikeout was called or swinging, and if I'd been careful in my scoring, I would know the answers. At such moments, when he smiled at me, I could not help but smile, too, for he had one of those contagious smiles that started in his eyes and traveled across his face, leaving laugh lines on either side of his mouth.

Sometimes a particular play would trigger in my dad a memory of a similar situation framed forever in his mind, and suddenly we were back in time recalling the Dodgers of his childhood—Casey Stengel, Zack Wheat, and Jimmy Johnston. Mingling together the present and the past, our conversations nurtured within me an irresistible fascination with history, which has remained to this day.

It fell to me to be the family scorekeeper not only because I was   4
the third daughter and youngest child, but because my idea of a perfect afternoon was lying in front of our ten-inch-screen television, watching baseball. What is more, there was real power in being the one to keep score. For all through my early childhood, my father kept from me the knowledge that the daily papers printed daily box scores, permitting me to imagine that without my symbolic renderings of all the games he had missed while he was at work, he would never have been able to follow the Dodgers in the only proper way a team should be followed, day by day, inning by inning. In other words, without me, his love for baseball would be forever unrequited.

In our neighborhood in Rockville Centre, New York, allegiance was equally divided among Dodger, Yankee, and Giant fans. As families emigrated from different parts of the city to the suburbs of Long Island, the old loyalties remained intact, creating rival enclaves on every street. Born and bred in Brooklyn, my father would always love the Dodgers, fear the Giants, and hate the abominable Yankees.

The butcher shop in our neighborhood was owned by a father and son, Old Joe and Young Joe Schmidt. They were both rabid Giant fans, as was Max, the man in charge of the vegetables. Knowing how much I loved baseball, they all took great delight in teasing me. They called me Ragmop, in honor of my unruly hair, and they constantly made fun of my Dodgers. I'd pretend to be angry, but the truth was that I loved going into their shop; I loved the sawdust on the floor, the sides of beef hanging from the ceiling, the enormous walk-in freezer behind the counter. And most of all, I loved the attention I received.

During the glorious summer of 1951, when I was eight years old and the Dodgers seemed invincible, I visited my friends in the butcher shop every day. Jackie Robinson was awesome that year, hitting .338; Roy Campanella was the MVP; Gil Hodges hit 40 homers. It seemed that no one could beat us. But then, in the third week of August, the Giants began an astonishing stretch that whittled the Dodger lead away until the season ended in a tie.

When the deciding play-off began, I was so nervous I couldn't sit by the television. Each time the Giants came to bat in the early innings, I left the room, returning only when I knew they were out and the Dodgers were up. I began to relax slightly as the Dodgers pulled ahead 4–1, but when the Giants came to bat in the last of the ninth, I could hear the beating of my heart. Then, as Bobby Thomson stepped to the plate, with one run in and two men on base, my sister Charlotte predicted that he would hit a home run and win the game for the Giants. When Thomson did precisely that, crushing Ralph Branca's pitch into the left field stand, I thought for a moment my sister had made it happen and I hated her with all my heart.

In the days that followed, I refused to go into the butcher shop, unable to face the mocking laughter that I imagined would accompany my first steps into the store. I was wrong. After a week's absence, a bouquet of flowers arrived at my door. "Ragmop, come back," the card read. "We miss you. Your friends at Bryn Mawr Meat Market."

"Wait till next year," my father consoled, repeating a refrain that would become all too familiar in the years ahead. But at eight years of age, it was easy to gamble in expectation, to believe that as soon as winter gave way to spring, a splendid new season would begin.

This indomitable belief in the future was vitally important to me when I was a child, for my mother's life was slowly ebbing away. The rheumatic fever she had when she was young had left her heart permanently damaged; every year, it seemed, she suffered another heart attack, which sent her to the hospital for days or weeks at a time. I was never made privy to the full extent of her illness; on the contrary, I took great comfort from the ritual of knowing that each time she went away, she came back. It's only a matter of time. I kept telling myself, as the ambulance carried her away, until she'll walk through the door again and everything will be all right.

In my prayers, the Dodgers figured prominently. Every night I said two sets of Hail Marys and Our Fathers. Believing that each prayer was worth a certain number of days off my inevitable sentence to purgatory, I dedicated the first set of prayers to my account in heaven. At the end of the week I would add up my nightly prayers and fold the total into a note. "Dear God. I have said 935 days worth of prayers this week. Please put this to my account. I live at 125 Southard Avenue." My second set of prayers was directed toward more earthly desires, chief among them the wish for the Dodgers to win the World Series at least once before I died.

It took tens of thousands of Hail Marys and Our Fathers, but finally on October 4, 1955, the Dodgers won their first-ever world championship. It was one of the happiest moments of my life, made all the more special because this time, I predicted the outcome. In the sixth inning, Sandy Amoros made a spectacular catch in left field of a wicked fly ball that would have tied the score with two Yankee runs. I knew then that the Dodgers would win, just as, on other occasions, a failed sacrifice or a double play signaled an inevitable loss.

Everything happened quickly after that until, stunningly, it was the bottom of the ninth with the Dodgers up 2–0. And this time there was no Bobby Thomson to destroy the cherished dreams of delirious Brooklyn fans. When my father came home that night, we celebrated by re-creating the entire game, play by play, and there was more. When the newspaper arrived on our lawn the next morning with the fabulous headline THIS *IS* NEXT YEAR, we relished every word as if we were hearing about the game for the first time.

Things fell apart all too quickly after that magical summer. When I first heard the rumor that Brooklyn owner Walter O'Malley was contemplating taking the Dodgers to Los Angeles, I refused to believe it, assuming he was simply jockeying for a new stadium. I hated all the talk about the need for a new stadium. When they said Ebbets Field was too small, too dilapidated, I took it as a personal insult. I couldn't imagine a more beautiful place.

I dreamed one night I was being ushered into O'Malley's office to make the case for Brooklyn. He was standing behind his desk, a diabolic look on his race that chilled my heart. But as I started to talk, his face softened and when I finished, he threw his arms around me and promised to stay at Ebbets Field. I had saved the Dodgers for Brooklyn! 16

In reality, of course, neither I nor anyone else could prevent the unforgivable O'Malley from completing his invidious act of betrayal. When the move was officially announced in the fall of 1957, I felt as if I, too, were being uprooted. Never again to sit in the stands at Ebbets Field, never again to watch the papers for the first news out of spring training, it was impossible to imagine.

My sense of being uprooted was real. As the 1958 season got under way, a weird, empty season with neither the Dodgers nor the Giants in New York, my mother suffered another heart attack. As before, she was taken away, but this time she didn't return. Six months later, we sold our house and moved to an apartment. My father couldn't bear sleeping in his bedroom without my mother.

Suddenly, my feelings for baseball seemed an aspect of my departing youth, to be discarded along with my childhood freckles and my collection of *Archie* comics. I didn't entirely forget about baseball during those last years in high school, but without a team to root for, my emotions became detached; my heart wasn't in it anymore.

Then, one September day, having settled in Massachusetts while   20
getting my Ph.D. at Harvard, I agreed, half reluctantly, to go to Fenway Park. There it was again: the cozy ball field scaled to human dimensions so that every word of encouragement and every scornful yell could be heard on the field; the fervent crowd that could, with equal passion, curse a player for today's failures after cheering his heroics the day before; the team that always seemed to break your heart in the last weeks of the season. It was love at first sight as I found myself directing all my old intensities toward my new team—the Boston Red Sox.

By this time, my dad had become a Mets fan so there was no need to feel guilty about my new love. Indeed, my return to baseball reinforced the old link between my father and me: providing endlessly absorbing topics for conversation. Once again our talks produced a sequence of mental images, vivid recollections of similar plays from the past; once again, we were united by an easy affection.

In the summer of 1972, while I was still single and teaching at Harvard, my father died. He had just settled down in his favorite chair to watch the Mets when he suffered a fatal heart attack. I remember the inconsolable feeling that the children I hoped to have someday would never know this extraordinary man, who had given me such steadfast love for so many years.

When I got married and had children my passion for the Sox assumed a strange urgency: at times I felt almost as if I were circling back to my childhood, as I found myself following the same rituals with my sons that I had practiced with my father. At Fenway Park, there are a number of ramps one can take to get from the crowded concession stands selling hot dogs, Cokes, tacos, and beer to the interior of the park itself. Ramp 33 is "my" ramp—with a curious attachment to a ritual my father followed by entering Ebbets Field at the same angle each time, I find myself walking up exactly the same ramp every game so that my first sight of the field comes at the same angle.

Indeed, sometimes when I close my eyes against the sun as I sit   24
with my boys at Fenway, I am suddenly back at Ebbets Field, a young girl once more in the presence of my father, watching the players of my youth on the grassy field below. There is magic in these moments, for when I open my eyes and see my sons in the place where my father once sat, I feel an invisible bond among our three generations, an anchor of loyalty linking my sons to the grandfather whose face they have never seen, but whose person they have come to know through this most timeless of all sports.

When the Sox won the pennant in 1986, my boys were absolutely certain they would win the World Series. I, of course, was less sure, having been at the edge of victory so many times before only to see my hopes dashed at the final moment. Yet by the sixth game, with the Sox leading 3 games to 2 over the Mets and ahead 5–3 in the bottom of the tenth, I told my husband to break out the champagne. Then, of course, in an agonizing replay of the Bobby Thomson fiasco, Boston first baseman Bill Buckner let a routine grounder slip through his legs and the Mets came back to win both the game and the World Series.

I tried to control my emotions but I couldn't. "Mom, it's all right," my boys consoled me. "They'll win next year. Don't worry."

Oh, my God, I thought. These kids don't know yet that the Sox haven't won since 1918, that this may be as close as they will ever come in any of our lifetimes. Suddenly I felt possessed of a terrible wisdom that I did not ever want to impart to my children.

"Right," I said. "Wait till next year."   28

Topics for Critical Thinking and Writing

1. In paragraph 17 Goodwin says "neither I nor anyone else could prevent the unforgivable O'Malley from completing his invidious act of betrayal." What was O'Malley's "act of betrayal"? And how would you characterize Goodwin's style here?
2. In paragraph 20 how does Goodwin characterize baseball? What does she *leave out* of her characterization? In a paragraph try to create an impression of a game, focusing on a particular angle to highlight.
3. In her next-to-last paragraph Goodwin writes of a "terrible wisdom" but does not define it. What was the wisdom?
4. If you ever have been a fan of baseball or some other sport, write a narrative essay explaining how you came to be a fan and whether or not your enthusiasm continues.

Black Elk

Black Elk, a wichasha wakon (holy man) of the Oglala Sioux, as a small boy witnessed the battle of the Little Bighorn (1876). He lived to see his people all but annihilated and his hopes for them extinguished. In 1931, toward the end of his life, he told his life story to the poet and scholar John G. Neihardt to preserve a sacred vision given him.

"War Games" (editors' title) is from Black Elk Speaks.

War Games

When it was summer again we were camping on the Rosebud, and I did not feel so much afraid, because the Wasichus seemed farther away and there was peace there in the valley and there was plenty of meat. But all the boys from five or six years up were playing war. The little boys would gather together from the different bands of the tribe and fight each other with mud balls that they threw with willow sticks. And the big boys played the game called Throwing-Them-Off-Their-Horses, which is a battle all but the killing; and sometimes they got hurt. The horsebacks from the different bands would line up and charge upon each other, yelling; and when the ponies came together on the run, they would rear and flounder and scream in a big dust, and the riders would seize each other, wrestling until one side had lost all its men, for those who fell upon the ground were counted dead.

When I was older, I, too, often played this game. We were always naked when we played it, just as warriors are when they go into battle if it is not too cold, because they are swifter without clothes. Once I fell off on my back right in the middle of a bed of prickly pears, and it took my mother a long while to pick all the stickers out of me. I was still too little to play war that summer, but I can remember watching the other boys, and I thought that when we all grew up and were big together, maybe we could kill all the Wasichus or drive them far away from our country. . . .

There was a war game that we little boys played after a big hunt. We went out a little way from the village and built some grass tepees, playing we were enemies and this was our village. We had an adviser, and when it got dark he would order us to go and steal some dried meat from the big people. He would hold a stick up to us and we had to bite off a piece of it. If we bit a big piece we had to get a big piece of meat, and if we bit a little piece, we did not have to get so much. Then we started for the big people's village, crawling on our bellies, and when we got back without getting caught, we would have a big feast and a dance and make kill talks, telling of our brave deeds like warriors. Once, I remember, I had no brave deed to tell. I crawled up to a leaning tree beside a tepee and there was meat hanging on the limbs. I wanted a tongue I saw up there in the moonlight, so I climbed up. But just as I was about to reach it, the man in the tepee yelled "Ye-a-a!" He was saying this to his dog, who was stealing some meat too, but I thought the man had seen me, and I was so scared I fell out of the tree and ran away crying.

Then we used to have what we called a chapped breast dance. Our adviser would look us over to see whose breast was burned most from not having it covered with the robe we wore; and the boy chosen would lead the dance while we all sang like this:

> I have a chapped breast.
> My breast is red.
> My breast is yellow.

And we practiced endurance too. Our adviser would put dry sunflower seeds on our wrists. These were lit at the top, and we had to let them burn clear down to the skin. They hurt and made sores, but if we knocked them off or cried Owh!, we would be called women.

Topics for Critical Thinking and Writing

1. Notice the subjective passages in Black Elk's descriptions of the games he played as a child. What do they reveal about Black Elk as a child and as an adult? How appropriate are these revelations to his topic?
2. The Duke of Wellington is reported to have said that the battle of Waterloo was won on the playing fields of Eton. Try to describe a game that is a small version of an adult activity and that teaches adult habits—good or bad. As an experiment, write the description as objectively as you can. Then rewrite it, allowing your description to reveal your attitudes—as a child and now—to the game, to other children, and to the adult world.

Joseph Epstein

Joseph Epstein was born in Chicago in 1937. He is the author of several books on American culture, the editor of American Scholar *(a quarterly review published by Phi Beta Kappa), and an occasional teacher of English at Northwestern University. This essay first appeared in* Harper's *Magazine.*

Obsessed with Sport

I cannot remember when I was not surrounded by sports, when talk of sports was not in the air, when I did not care passionately about sports. As a boy in Chicago in the late Forties, I lived in the same building as the sister and brother-in-law of Barney Ross, the welterweight champion. Half a block away, down near the lake, the Sullivan High School football team worked out in the spring and autumn. Summers the same field was given over to baseball and men's softball on Sundays. A few blocks to the north was the Touhy Avenue Fieldhouse, where basketball was played, and lifeguards trained, and behind which, in a softball field frozen over in winter, crack-the-whip, hockey, and speed skating took over. To the west, a block or so up Morse Avenue, was the Morse Avenue "L" Recreations, a combined pool hall and bowling alley. Life, in short, was games.

My father had no interest in sports. He had grown up, one of the ten children of Russian Jewish immigrant parents, on tough Notre Dame

Street in Montreal, where the major sports were craps, poker, and petty larceny. He left Montreal at seventeen to come to Chicago, where he worked hard and successfully so that his sons might play. Two of his boyhood friends from Notre Dame Street, who had the comic-book names of Sammy and Danny Spunt, had also come to Chicago, where they bought the Ringside Gym on Dearborn Street in the Loop. All the big names worked out at Ringside for their Chicago fights: Willie Pep, Tony Zale, Joe Louis. At eight or nine I would take the El downtown to the Ringside, be introduced around by Danny Spunt ("Tony Zale, I'd like you to meet the son of an old friend of mine. Kid, I'd like you to meet the middleweight champion of the world"), and return home with an envelope filled with autographed 8-by-10 glossies of Gus Lesnevich, Tammy Maurielo, Kid Gavilan, and the wondrous Sugar Ray.

I lived on, off, and in sports. *Sport* magazine had recently begun publication, and I gobbled up its issues cover to cover, soon becoming knowledgeable not only about the major sports—baseball, football, and basketball—but about golf, hockey, tennis, and horse racing, so that I scored reputably on the Sport Quiz, a regular department at the front of the magazine. Another regular department was the Sport Classic, which featured longish profiles of the legendary figures in the history of sports: Ty Cobb, Jim Thorpe, Bobby Jones, Big Bill Tilden, Red Grange, Man o' War. I next moved on to the sports novels of John R. Tunis—*All-American, The Iron Duke, The Kid from Tomkinsville, The Kid Comes Back, World Series*, the lot—which I read with as much excitement as any books I have read since.

The time was, as is now apparent, a splendid era in sports. Ted　4 Williams, Joe DiMaggio, and Stan Musial were afield; first Jack Kramer, then Pancho Gonzales, dominated tennis; George Mikan led the Minneapolis Lakers, and the Harlem Globetrotters could still be taken seriously; Doc Blanchard and Glen Davis, Mr. Inside and Mr. Outside, were playing for Army, Johnny Lujack was at Notre Dame; in the pros Sammy Baugh, Bob Waterfield, and Sid Luckman were the major T-formation quarterbacks; Joe Louis and Sugar Ray Robinson fought frequently; the two Willies, Mosconi and Hoppe, put in regular appearances at Bensinger's in the Loop; Eddie Arcaro seemed to ride three, four winners a day. Giants, it truly seemed, walked the earth.

All learning of craft—which sport, like writing, most assuredly is—involves imitation, especially in the early stages; and I was an excellent mimic. By the time I was ten years old I had mastery over all the big-time moves: the spit in the mitt, the fluid infield chatter, the knocking of dirt from the spikes; the rhythmic barking out of signals, hands high under the center's crotch to take the ball; the three bounces and deep breath before shooting the free throw (on this last, I regretted not being a Catholic, so that I might be able to make the sign of the cross before shooting, as was then the fashion among Catholic high-school and college players). I went in for athletic haberdashery in a big way, often going beyond mimicry to the point of flat-out phoniness—wearing, for example, a knee pad while playing basketball, though my knees were always, exasperatingly, intact.

I always looked good, which was important, because form is intrinsic to sports; but in my case it was doubly important, because the truth is that I wasn't really very good. Or at any rate not good enough. Two factors accounted for this. The first was that, without being shy about body contact, I lacked a certain indispensable aggressiveness; the second, connected closely to the first, was that, when it came right down to it, I did not care enough about winning. I would rather lose a point attempting a slashing cross-court backhand than play for an easier winner down the side; the long jump shot always had more allure for me than the safer drive to the basket. Given a choice between the two vanities of winning and looking good, I almost always preferred looking good.

I shall never forget the afternoon, sometime along about my thirteenth year, when, shooting baskets alone, I came upon the technique for shooting the hook. Although today it has nowhere near the consequence of the jump shot—an innovation that has been to basketball what the jet has been to air travel—the hook is still the single most beautiful shot in the game. The rhythm and grace of it, the sway of the body off the pivot, the release of the ball behind the head and off the fingertips, the touch and instinct involved in its execution, make the hook altogether a balletic thing, and to achieve it is to feel one of the most delectable sensations in sports. That afternoon, on a deserted side street, shooting on a rickety wooden backboard and a black rim without a net, I felt it and grew nearly drunk on the feeling. Rain came down, dirt washed in the gutters, flecks of it spattering my clothes and arms and face, but, soaked and cold though I was, I do not think I would have left that basket on that afternoon for anything. I threw up hook after hook, from every angle, from farther and farther out, off the board, without the board, and hook after hook went in. Only pitch darkness drove me home.

I do not say that not to have shot the hook is never to have lived, [8] but only that, once having done so, the pleasure it gives is not so easily forgotten. Every sport offers similar pleasures, the pleasures taken differing by temperament: the canter into the end zone to meet a floating touchdown pass, or the clean, crisp feel of a perfect block or tackle; the long straight drive or the precisely played approach shot to the green; the solid overhead; the pickup on the tricky short hop or the long ball down one of the power alleys. Different sports, different pleasures. But so keen are these pleasures—pleasures of execution, of craft completed—that, along with being unforgettable, they are also worth recapturing in any available way, and the most available way, when reflexes have slowed, when muscle no longer responds so readily to brain, is from the grandstand or, perhaps more often nowadays, from the chair before the television.

Pleasures of the Spectator

I have put in days on the bench but years in my chair before the television set. Recently it has occurred to me that over the years I have heard more hours of talk from the announcer Curt Gowdy than from my own father, who is not a reticent man. I have been thoroughly Schenkeled, Mussbergered, Summeralled, Cosselled, DeRogotissed, and Garagiolaed. How many hundreds—thousands—of hours have I spent watching sports of all sorts, either at parks or stadiums or over television? I am glad I shall never have a precise answer. Yet neither apparently can I get enough. What is the fascination? Why is it that, with the prospect of a game to watch in the evening or on the weekend, the day seems lighter and brighter? What do I get out of it?

What I get out of it, according to one fairly prominent view, is an outlet for my violent emotions. Knee-wrenching, rib-cracking, head-busting, this view has it, is what sports are really about, with sports fans being essentially sadists, and cowardly sadists at that, for they take their violence not at firsthand but at second remove. Enthusiasm for sports among Americans is little more than a reflection of the national penchant for violence. Military men talk about game plans; the long touchdown pass is called the bomb. The average pro-football fan, seeing a quarterback writhing on the ground at midfield as a result of the ministrations of Joe Green, Carl Eller, or Lyle Alzado, twitters with glee, finds his ultimate reward, and declares a little holiday in the blackest corner of his heart.

But this is a criticism that comes at sports by way of politics. To believe it one has to believe that the history of the United States is chiefly one of rape, expropriation, and aggressive imperialism. To dismiss it, however, one need only know something about sports. Violence is indubitably a part of some sports; in some—hockey is an example—it sometimes comes close to being featured. But in no sport—not even boxing, that most rudimentary of sports—is it the main item, and in many other sports it plays no part at all. A distinction worth insisting on is that between violence and roughness. Roughness, a willingness to mix it up, to take if need be an elbow in the jaw, is part of rebounding in basketball, yet violence is not. Even in pro football, most maligned of modern American sports, more of roughness than of violence is involved. Roughness raises the stakes, provides the pressure, behind execution. A splendid because true phrase has come about in pro football to cover the situation in which a pass receiver, certain that he will be tackled upon the instant he makes his reception, drops a ball he should otherwise have caught easily—the phrase, best delivered in a

Southern accent such as Don Meredith's, is "He heard footsteps on that one, Howard." Although a part of the attraction, it is not so much those footsteps that fill the stands and the den chairs on Sunday afternoons as it is those men who elude them: the Lynn Swanns, the Fran Tarkentons, the O. J. Simpsons. The American love of violence theory really will not wash. Dick Butkus did not get us into Vietnam.

Many who would not argue that sports reflect American violence   12
nevertheless claim that they imbue one with the competitive spirit. In some who are already amply endowed with it, sports doubtless do tend to refine (or possibly brutalize) the desire to win. Yet sports also teach a serious respect for craft. Competition, though it flourishes as always, is in bad odor nowadays; but craft, officially respected, does not flourish greatly outside the boutique.

If the love of violence or the competitive urge does not put me in my chair for the countless games I watch, is it, then, nostalgia, a yearning to regain the more glowing moments of adolescence? Many argue that this is precisely so, that American men exist in a state of perpetual immaturity, suspended between boy- and manhood. "The difference between men and boys," says Liberace, "is the price of their toys." (I have paid more than $300 for two half-season tickets to the Chicago Bulls games, parking fees not included.) Such unending enthusiasm for games may have something to do with adolescence, but little, I suspect, with regaining anything whatever. Instead, it has more to do with watching men do regularly and surpassingly what, as an adolescent, one did often bumblingly though with an occasional flash of genius. To have played these games oneself as a boy or a young man helps immeasurably the appreciation that in watching a sport played at professional caliber one is witnessing the extraordinary made to look ordinary. That a game may have no consequence outside itself—no effect on history, on one's own life, on anything really—does not make it trivial but only makes the enjoyment of it all the purer.

The notion that men watch sports to regain their adolescence pictures them sitting in the stands or at home watching a game and, within their psyches, muttering, "There, but for the lack of grace of God, go I." And it is true that a number of contemporary authors who are taken seriously have indeed written about sports with a strong overlay of yearning. In the men's softball games described in the fiction of Philip Roth, center field is a place akin to Arcady. Arcadian, too, is the outfield in Willie Morris's memoir of growing up in the South, *North Toward Home*. In the first half of *Rabbit Run* John Updike takes up the life of a man whose days are downhill all the way after hitting his peak as a high-school basketball star—and in the writing Updike himself evinces a nice soft touch of undisguised longing. In *A Fan's Notes*, a book combining yearning and self-disgust in roughly equal measure, Frederick Exley makes plain that he would much prefer to have been born into the skin of Frank Gifford rather than into his own.

But most men who are enraptured by sports do not think any such thing. I should like to have Kareem Abdul-Jabbar's sky hook, but not, especially for civilian life, the excessive height that is necessary to its execution. I should like to have Jimmy Connors's ground strokes, but no part of his mind. These are men born with certain gifts, gifts honed by practice and determination, that I, and millions along with me, enjoy seeing on display. But the reality principle is too deeply ingrained, at least in a man of my years, for me to even imagine exchanging places with them. One might as well imagine oneself in the winner's circle at Churchill Downs as the horse.

Fantasy is an element in sports when they are played in adolescence—an alley basket becomes the glass backboard at Madison Square Garden, a concrete park district tennis court with grass creeping out of the service line becomes center court at Wimbledon—but fantasy of this kind is hard to come by. Part of this has to do with age; but as large a part has to do with the age in which we live. Sport has always been a business but never more so than currently, and nothing lends itself less to fantasy than business. Reading the sports section has become rather like reading the business section—mergers, trades, salary negotiations, contract disputes, options, and strikes fill the columns. Along with the details of business, those of the psychological and social problems of athletes have come to the fore. The old *Sport* magazine concentrated on play on the field, with only an occasional digressive reference to personal life. ("Yogi likes plenty of pizza in the off-season and spends a lot of his time at his teammate Phil Rizzuto's bowling alley" is a rough facsimile of a sentence from its pages that I recall.) But the magazine in its current version, as well as the now more popular *Sports Illustrated*, expends much space on the private lives of athletes—their divorces, hang-ups, race relations, need for approval, concern for security, potted philosophies—with the result that the grand is made to seem small.

On the other side of the ledger, there is a view that finds a shimmering significance in everything having to do with sports. Literary men in general are notoriously to be distrusted on the subject. They dig around everywhere, and can be depended upon to find much treasure where none is buried. Norman Mailer mining metaphysical ore in every jab of Muhammad Ali, an existential nugget in each of his various and profuse utterances, is a particularly horrendous example. Even the sensible William Carlos Williams was not above this sort of temptation. In a poem entitled "At the Ball Game," we find the lines "It is the Inquisition, the Revolution." Dr. Williams could not have been much fun at the ball park.

The Real Thing

If enthusiasm for sports has little to do with providing an outlet for violent emotions, regaining adolescence, discovering metaphysical truths, the Inquisition or the Revolution, then what, I ask myself, am I doing past midnight, when I have to be up at 5:30 the next morning, watching on television what will turn out to be a seventeen-inning game between the New York Mets and the St. Louis Cardinals? The conversation coming out of my television set is of a very low grade, even for sports announcing. But even the dreary talk cannot put me off—the rehash of statistics, the advice to youngsters to keep their gloves low when in the field, the thin jokes. Neither the Mets nor the Cards figure to be contenders this year. The only possible effect that this game can have on my life is to make me dog-tired the next day. Yet I cannot pull myself away. I want to know how it is going to end. True, the score will be available in the morning paper. But that is not the same thing. What is going on here?

One thing that is going on is the practice of craft of a very high order, which is intrinsically interesting. But something as important is involved, something rarer in contemporary life, the spectacle of which gives enormous satisfaction. To define this satisfaction negatively, it is the absence of fraudulence and fakery. No small item, this, when one stops to think that in nearly every realm of contemporary life fraud and fakery have an established—some would say a preponderant—place. Advertising, politics, business, and journalism are only the most obvious examples. Fraud seems similarly pervasive in modern art: in painters whose reputations rest on press agentry; in writers who write one way and live quite another; in composers who are taken seriously but whose work cannot be seriously listened to. At a time when *image* is one of the most frequently used words in American speech and writing, one does not too often come upon the real thing.

Sport may be the toy department of life, but one of its abiding compensations is that, at least on the field, it is the real thing. Much has been done in recent years in the attempt to ruin sport—the ruthlessness of owners, the greed of players, the general exploitation of fans. But even all this cannot destroy it. On the court, down on the field, sport is fraud-free and fakeproof. With a full count, two men on, his team down by one run in the last of the eighth, a batter (as well as a pitcher) is beyond the aid of public relations. At match point at Forest Hills a player's press clippings are of no help. Last year's earnings will not sink a twelve-foot putt on the eighteenth at Augusta. Alan Page, galloping up along a quarterback's blind side, figures to be neglectful of that quarterback's image as a swinger. In all these situation, and hundreds of others, a man either comes through or he doesn't. He is alone out there, naked but for his ability, which counts for everything. Something there is that is elemental about this, and something greatly satisfying.

Another part of the satisfaction to be got from sports—from playing them, but also from watching them being played—derives from their special clarity. Sports offer clarity of a kind sufficient to engage the most serious minds. That the Cambridge mathematician G. H. Hardy closely followed cricket and avidly read cricket scores is not altogether surprising. Numbers in sports are ubiquitous. Scores, standings, averages, times, records—comfort is found in such numbers. ERA, RBI,

20

FGP, pass completions, turnovers, category upon category of statistics are kept for nearly every aspect of athletic activity. (Why, I recently heard someone ask, are records not kept for catchers throwing out runners attempting to steal? Because, the answer is, often runners steal on pitchers, and so it would be unfair to charge these stolen bases against catchers.) As perhaps in no other sphere, numbers in sports tell one where things stand. No loopholes here, where figures, for once, do not lie. Nowhere else is such specificity of result available.

Clarity about character is also available in sports. "You Americans hold to the proposition that it is self-evident that all men are created equal," I not long ago heard an Englishman say, adding, "it had better be self-evident, for no other evidence for it exists." Sport coldly demonstrates physical inequalities—there are the larger, the faster, the stronger, the more graceful athletes—but it also throws up human types who have devised ways to redress these inequalities. One such type is the hustler. In every realm but that of sports the word *hustle* is pejorative, whereas in sports it is approbative. Two of the hustler breed, Pete Rose of the Cincinnati Reds and Jerry Sloan of the Chicago Bulls, are men who supplement reasonably high levels of ability with unreasonably high levels of courage and desire. Other athletes—Joe Morgan and Oscar Robertson come to mind—bring superior athletic intelligence to bear upon their play. And Bill Russell, late of the Boston Celtics, who if the truth be known was not an inherently superior athlete, blended hustle and intelligence with what abilities he did have and through force of character established supremacy.

Whence do hustle, intelligence, and character in sports derive, especially since they apparently do not necessarily carry over into life? Joe DiMaggio and Sugar Ray Robinson, two of the most instinctively intelligent and physically elegant athletes, brought little of either of these qualities over into their business or personal activities. Some athletes can do all but one important thing well: Wilt Chamberlain at the free-throw line, for those who recall his misery there, leaves a permanent picture of a mental block in action. Other athletes—Connie Hawkins, Ilie Nastase, Dick Allen—have all the physical gifts in superabundance, yet, because of some insufficiency of character, some searing flaw, never come near to fulfilling their promise. Coaches supply yet another gallery of human types, from the fanatical Vince Lombardi to the comical Casey Stengel to the measured and aptly named John Wooden. The cast of characters in sport, the variety of situations, the complexity of behavior it puts on display, the overall human exhibit it offers—together these supply an enjoyment akin to that once provided by reading interminably long but inexhaustibly rich nineteenth-century novels.

In a wider sense, sport is culture. For many American men it represents a common background, a shared interest. It has a binding power that transcends social class and education. Some years ago I found myself working in the South among men with whom I shared nothing 24 in the way of region, religion, education, politics, or general views; we shared nothing, in fact, but sports, which was enough for us to get along and grow to become friends, in the process showing how superficial all the things that might have kept us apart in fact were. More recently, in Chicago, at a time when race relations were in a particularly jagged state, I recall emerging from an NBA game, in which the Chicago Bulls in overtime beat the Milwaukee Bucks, into a snowy night and an aura of common good feeling that, for a time, submerged the enmity between races; laughing, throwing snowballs, exuberant generally, the crowd leaving the Chicago Stadium that night was not divided by being black and white but unified by being Bull fans. Last year's Boston-Cincinnati World Series, one of the most gratifying in memory, coming hard upon a year of extreme political divisiveness, performed, however briefly, something of the same function. How much better it felt to agree about the mastery of Luis Tiant than to argue about the wretchedness of Richard Nixon.

In sports as in life, character does not much change. I have recently begun to play a game called racquet ball, and I find I would still rather look good than win, which is what I usually do: look good and lose. I beat the rum-dums but go down before quality players. I get compliments in defeat. Men who beat me admire the whip of my strokes, my wrist action, my anticipation, the power I get behind the ball. When this occurs I feel like a woman who is complimented for the shape of her bottom when it is her mind she craves admiration for, though of course she will take what praise she can get.

R. H. Tawney, the great historian of religion and capitalism, once remarked that the only progress he could note during the course of his lifetime was in the deportment of dogs. For myself, I would say that the chief progress in the course of my lifetime has been in the quality and variety of athletic gear. Racquets made of metal, aluminum, wood, and fiberglass, balls of different colors, sneakers of all materials and designs, posh warm-up suits, tube socks, sweat-bands for the head and wrist in various colors and pipings; only the athletic supporter, the old jockstrap, remains unornamented, but perhaps even now Vera or Peter Max is at the drawing board. In any event, with all this elegant plumage available, it is a nice time to be playing ball again.

Sports can be impervious to age. My father-in-law, a man of style, seriousness, and great good humor who died a year ago in his late sixties, was born in South Bend, Indiana, and in his early manhood left the Catholic Church—two facts that conjoined to give him an intense interest in the fortunes of the teams from Notre Dame. He loved to see them lose. The torch has been passed on. I now love to see Notre Dame lose, and when it does I think of him and remember his smile.

When I was a boy I had a neighbor, a man who, after retirement, 28 had a number of strokes. An old man and a young boy, we had in common a love of sports, which, when we met on the street, was our only topic of conversation. He once inspected a new glove of mine, and instructed me to rub it down with neat's-foot-oil, place a ball firmly in the pocket, wrap string tightly around the glove, and leave it like that for the winter. I did, and it worked. After his last stroke but one, he seldom left his house. Afternoons he spent in a chair in his bedroom, a blanket over his lap, listening to Cub games over the radio. It was while listening to a ball game that he quietly died. I cannot imagine a better way.

Topics for Critical Thinking and Writing

1. In his first two paragraphs Epstein writes of the opportunities he had when growing up in Chicago in the 1940s to live "on, off, and in sports." Compare or contrast those opportunities with your own. How do you account for the differences? (Were there some similarities?)

2. In paragraph 4 Epstein writes of the 1940s: "The time was, as is now apparent, a splendid era in sports." Looking back at the decade in your life (which can be the current decade) in which you have been most engaged as a sports fan, would you characterize it also as "a splendid era"? If not, how would you characterize it—disillusioning, mediocre, uneven? Try to support your characterization concretely, as Epstein does in paragraph 4.

3. In paragraph 5 Epstein writes: "All learning of craft—which sport, like writing, most assuredly is—involves imitation, especially in the early stages." Did you learn sports by imitation? Explain. Did you also learn writing by imitation? Why or why not?

4. In paragraph 13 Epstein points out that having played a game as a boy or young man (presumably also as a girl or young woman) helps one to appreciate the performance of professionals. Do you think the same principle holds true for literature, music, dance, art? Should all children have a chance to learn to play musical instruments, to paint, and to write—not in the expectation that they will all practice those arts as adults, but to enhance their later enjoyment and support of concerts, museums, books, and theater?

5. What makes spectator sports appealing? After dismissing violence and the spectator's nostalgia for adolescence as the source of their appeal, Epstein cites three or four reasons why spectator sports appeal to him. Why does your favorite spectator sport appeal to you?

6. If you are not a sports fan, is there an area of your experience in which you feel close to being obsessed? Music? food? clothes? dogs? sex? If you were to write about this obsession, how might outlining Epstein's essay help you to find ideas?

Pete Hamill

Pete Hamill, born in Brooklyn in 1935, attended Pratt Institute and Mexico City College, worked as a reporter in Vietnam in the 1960s, and now works as a freelance writer. His essays have appeared in such magazines as Cosmopolitan, Playboy, *and (the source of the piece that we reprint)* Gentlemen's Quarterly.

Winning Isn't Everything

One of the more widely accepted maxims of modern American life was uttered on a frozen winter afternoon during the early sixties. The late Vince Lombardi, who coached the Green Bay Packers when they were the greatest team in football, said it. "Winning isn't everything," he declared, "It's the only thing."

Vince Lombardi's notion was immediately appropriated by an extraordinary variety of American males: presidents and lesser politicians, generals, broadcasters, political columnists, Little League coaches, heads of corporations, and probably millions of others. In fact, it sometimes seems that Lombardi's words have had greater impact than any sentence uttered by an American since Stephen Decatur's "our country, right or wrong."

That's surprising on many levels, beginning with the obvious: It's a deceptively simple premise. Winning *isn't* "the only thing." Such an idea muddles the idea of competition, not simply in sports, but in all aspects of our lives. We've learned the hard way in this century that the world is a complex place; it's certainly not the National Football League. Winning isn't the only thing in love, art, marriage, commerce, or politics; it's not even the only thing in sports.

In sports, as in so many other areas of our national life, we've always cherished gallant losers. I remember one afternoon in the fall of 1956 when Sal Maglie was pitching for the Brooklyn Dodgers against the hated Yankees. Maglie was an old man that year, as age is measured in sports. But this was the World Series, and he hauled his thirty-nine-year-old body to the mound, inning after inning, gave everything he had, held the Yankees to a few scattered hits and two runs—and lost. That day Don Larsen pitched his perfect game: no runs, no hits, no errors. Yet, to me, the afternoon belonged to Maglie—tough, gallant, and a loser. 4

There was an evening in Manila when Joe Frazier went up against Muhammad Ali for the third and final time. That night, Frazier brought his workman's skills into combat against the magic of the artist, called on his vast reservoir of courage and will, and came up empty, at the end of fourteen rounds. Frazier was the loser, but that evening, nobody really lost. Because of that fight, Joe Frazier can always boast with honor that he made Muhammad Ali a great fighter. He was the test, the implacable force who made Ali summon all of his own considerable reserves of skill, heart, and endurance for a final effort. The contest consumed them both. Neither was ever again a good fighter. But during their violent confrontation, winning or losing was, in the end, a marginal concern; that all-consuming effort was everything.

There are hundreds of similar examples of losers who showed us how to be more human, and their performances make the wide acceptance of Lombardi's notions even more mystifying. Lombardi's thesis, in fact, represented something of a shift in the nation's popular thought. Americans had been the people who remembered the Alamo or Pearl Harbor; we blew taps over the graves of those who lost at the Battle of the Bulge or Anzio or the Yalu Basin. Those soldiers had all been defeated, but we honored them for their display of a critical human quality: courage.

Ernest Hemingway once defined courage as grace under pressure, and that's always struck me as an eminently useful definition. The best professional athletes not only possess that kind of courage but, more important, are willing to display it to strangers. Baseball's Reggie Jackson or Richard ("Goose") Gossage, for instance, function most completely as athletes and as men when appearing before gigantic crowds under pressure: bases loaded, late innings, a big game. They come to their tasks with gladness and absolute focus, neither whimpering, complaining, nor shirking when doing their job; they just try their best to get that job done. And, of course, sometimes they fail. Gossage gives up a single and his team loses. Jackson strikes out. No matter. The important thing is that such men keep their appointments with confidence and grace. Courage has become so deep a part of their character that they don't even think about it. (They certainly *want* to win. Sometimes they absolutely lust for victory. But they know that winning isn't everything. All a man can do is his best.)

Competition isn't really a problem for Americans. All sports, in one way or another, are competitive. But an individual's primary competition is with himself and all his attendant weaknesses. That's obviously true of boxing, where fear must be dominated and made to work to the fighter's benefit. Yet it's also true for team sports, as well as such solitary endeavors as golf, where a player must learn control before anything else. The problem isn't competition, which is a part of life; it's in the notion of the necessity of triumph. A man can lose but still win. And the point of competition in sports is an old and not very fashionable one: It builds character.

That's especially true of prizefighters, the athletes I've known best. Outside the ring, almost all fighters are the gentlest of men. They carry themselves with the dignity of those who have little to prove, either to others or themselves. They're not bullies, rarely use their dangerous skills against ordinary citizens and avoid pointless confrontations. When a fighter hears that a colleague has been involved in a bar brawl or a swingout with a cop, he dismisses that fighter as a cowardly bum. Most of the boxers I know are honest, generous, funny. Yet they also know that as good as they are, there might be someone down the line who has their number. Again, they would prefer to be winners. But they're aware that losing, if a courageous effort is made, is never a disgrace. The highest compliment one fighter can pay another is to say that he has "heart."

There are lessons to be learned from such athletes that can be applied to how we live our lives. In the long run, we'll all come up losers because there's no greater loss than death. And since primitive man first began to think, we humans have devised strategies to deal with dying. Religion is the most obvious one, usually demanding that we adhere to a moral code on earth in exchange for a serene existence after death. Ideologies offer secular versions of the same instinct, insisting that we sacrifice now, directing our lives toward the ideal of a better future, with each man becoming an architect of his own utopia. Patriotism and nationalism carry some of the same fearful baggage.

An athlete's goals are less cosmic, his field of struggle less grandiose and therefore more applicable to ordinary citizens. Great athletes teach us that life is a series of struggles, not one giant effort. Just when we appear to have triumphed, we must stop like Sisyphus and again begin rolling the boulder up that mountain. The true athlete teaches us that winning isn't everything, but struggle is—the struggle to simply get up in the morning or to see hope through the minefields of despair.

Viewed that way, a marriage, or any relationship with another   12
human being, is an ongoing struggle. The mastering of a skill or craft doesn't end with the granting of a diploma; it goes on for life. The relationship between parents and children doesn't end when the children turn eighteen. The running of a corporation isn't a one-shot affair, measured by a single year's statements of profits and losses; it's a continuing process, accomplished by human beings who learn from mistakes, plunge fearlessly into the struggle, take risks and prepare for the future.

It's probably no accident that American capitalism, with its often permanently infantile male executives, experienced a decline that coincided with the period when Vince Lombardi's values received their widest acceptance. The results are visible everywhere. Sit on a plane with American businessmen and they'll be chattering about the Pittsburgh Steelers. Join a group of Japanese businessmen and they'll be discussing twenty-first-century technology. One group is trapped in a philosophy that demands winning as its goal; the other cares more about patient, long-term growth—and for the moment at least, the latter is winning.

Another great maxim of the years of America's triumphs also came from the sports page via the writer Grantland Rice: "It matters not who won or lost," declared the esteemed chronicler of the prewar years, "but how they played the game." By the time Vince Lombardi came along, such sentiments were sneered at. We had then become a superpower, capable of blowing up the world. The man of grace, courage, endurance, and compassion was replaced in the public imagination by the swaggering macho blowhard; Humphrey Bogart gave way to John Wayne. With such attitudes dominating the landscape, we were certain to get into trouble, and we did. Vietnam and Watergate underscored the idea of winning at all costs. Yet today we seem incapable of admitting that an obsession with winning often leads to the most squalid of defeats.

Solid marriages are often built upon the experience of disastrous one. Politicians who lose elections become tempered for the contests that follow, sometimes going on to solid, useful careers. Painters, playwrights, novelists, and other artists often learn as much from their failures as they do from those rare moments when vision, craft, and ambition come together to produce masterpieces. It's also that way in sports.

I remember a night when my friend José Torres, then a middle-   16
weight, was boxing Florentino Fernandez in Puerto Rico. I couldn't go to the fight, so I spent the night tuning in and out of the all-news radio stations, anxious about the result because Florentino was a great puncher. About three in the morning, Torres called.

"Oh, Pete," he said, close to tears. "I'm so sorry."

"What happened?"

"I got knocked out," Torres replies, his voice brimming with emotion, since he'd never lost as a professional. We started discussing what had happened. Emotions cooled; the talk became technical. Torres explained that he had learned some things about himself, about boxing. He now understood some of his flaws, and thought he could correct them. We talked for an hour. Then I asked what he was going to do next.

"Go to the gym," he said. "I'm going to be champion of the world."   20

Two years later, Torres *was* the world's light-heavyweight champion. He didn't quit after his first defeat. That night in San Juan he didn't say winning was the only thing, that it was time to pack it in. He had learned something from defeat, and knew that one violent night, somewhere down the line, he would show the world what he had learned. And that was precisely what he did. But he was aware of something else too: Sooner or later, someone might come along who was better than he was, for at least one evening. After all, even champions are human. Even champions eventually lose. That happened to José Torres as well. But then it didn't really matter. José Torres, like the rest of us, had learned that winning wasn't everything. Living was all, and in life, defeat and victory are inseparable brothers.

Topics for Critical Thinking and Writing

1. In paragraph 6 Hamill finds "The wide acceptance of Lombardi's notions . . . mystifying." Do you find it mystifying? If not, why not?
2. Hamill thinks (paragraph 6) that Lombardi's view represents "something of a shift in the nation's popular thought," and he gives some evidence. How convincing do you find this evidence? Why?
3. In paragraph 8 Hamill says that competition "builds character." Drawing on your experience—what you have witnessed as well as what you have actually undergone—can you offer evidence that supports or rebuts this assertion?

4. In paragraph 11 Hamill says that "great athletes teach us that life is a series of struggles, not one giant step." Had you ever thought that great athletes teach this lesson? In any case, now that Hamill has said it, do you think there is something to his claim? If so, try to provide an example; think of athletes whom you admire, and try to formulate the lessons they teach. Conversely, if there is an athlete whom you despise, what message is conveyed by his or her life or game?

5. On the basis of Hamill's essay and Epstein's (page 394), which writer would you invite to accompany you to a ball game, and why?

John Updike

John Updike was born in 1932 in Shillington, Pennsylvania. After graduating from college he studied art for a year in England, but he then returned to the United States and began work-ing as a staff reporter for the New Yorker. *He soon published stories in the magazine and continues to do so. He has also written novels (including* Rabbit. Run *and* The Witches of Eastwick*), essays, and light verse. The story we print here, "A & P," was published in 1961, but many readers find that except for the prices mentioned there is nothing dated about it.*

A & P

In walks these three girls in nothing but bathing suits. I'm in the third checkout slot, with my back to the door, so I don't see them until they're over by the bread. The one that caught my eye first was the one in the plaid green two-piece. She was a chunky kid, with a good tan and a sweet broad soft-looking can with those two crescents of white just under it, where the sun never seems to hit, at the top of the backs of her legs. I stood there with my hand on a box of HiHo crackers trying to remember if I rang it up or not. I ring it up again and the customer starts giving me hell. She's one of these cash-register-watchers, a witch about fifty with rouge on her cheekbones and no eyebrows, and I know it made her day to trip me up. She'd been watching cash registers for fifty years and probably never seen a mistake before.

By the time I got her feathers smoothed and her goodies into a bag—she gives me a little snort in passing, if she'd been born at the right time they would have burned her over in Salem—by the time I get her on her way the girls had circled around the bread and were coming back, without a pushcart, back my way along the counters, in the aisle between the checkouts and the Special bins. They didn't even have shoes on. There was this chunky one, with the two-piece—it was bright green and the seams on the bra were still sharp and her belly was still pretty pale so I guessed she just got it (the suit)—there was this one, with one of those chubby berry-faces, the lips all bunched together under her nose, this one, and a tall one, with black hair that hadn't quite

frizzed right, and one of these sunburns right across under the eyes,
and a chin that was too long—you know, the kind of girl other girls
think is very "striking" and "attractive" but never quite makes it, as
they very well know, which is why they like her so much—and then the
third one, that wasn't quite so tall. She was the queen. She kind of led
them, the other two peeking around and making their shoulders round.
She didn't look around, not this queen, she just walked straight on
slowly, on these long white prima-donna legs. She came down a little
hard on her heels, as if she didn't walk in her bare feet that much,
putting down her heels and then letting the weight move along to her
toes as if she was testing the floor with every step, putting a little deliberate extra action into it. You never know for sure how girls' minds
work (do they really think it's a mind in there or just a little buzz like a
bee in a glass jar?) but you got the idea she had talked the other two into
coming in here with her, and now she was showing them how to do it,
walk slow and hold yourself straight.

She had on a kind of dirty pink—beige maybe, I don't know—
bathing suit with a little nubble all over it and, what got me, the straps
were down. They were off her shoulders looped loose around the cool
tops of her arms, and I guess as a result the suit had slipped on her, so
all around the top of the cloth there was this shining rim. If it hadn't
been there you wouldn't have known there could have been anything
whiter than those shoulders. With the straps pushed off, there was
nothing between the top of the suit and the top of her head except just
her, this clean bare plane of the top of her chest down from the shoulder
bones like a dented sheet of metal tilted in the light. I mean, it was more
than pretty.

She had sort of oaky hair that the sun and salt had bleached, done   4
up in a bun that was unravelling, and a kind of prim face. Walking into
the A & P with your straps down, I suppose it's the only kind of face
you *can* have. She held her head so high her neck, coming up out of
those white shoulders, looked kind of stretched, but I didn't mind. The
longer her neck was, the more of her there was.

She must have felt in the corner of her eye me and over my shoulder Stokesie in the second slot watching, but she didn't tip. Not this
queen. She kept her eyes moving across the racks, and stopped, and
turned so slow it made my stomach rub the inside of my apron, and
buzzed to the other two, who kind of huddled against her for relief,
and then they all three of them went up the cat and dog food-breakfast
cereal-macaroni-rice-raisins-seasonings-spreads-spaghetti-soft drinks-
crackers-and-cookies aisle. From the third slot I look straight up this
aisle to the meat counter, and I watched them all the way. The fat one
with the tan sort of fumbled with the cookies, but on second thought
she put the package back. The sheep pushing their carts down the
aisle—the girls were walking against the usual traffic (not that we have
one-way signs or anything)—were pretty hilarious. You could see

them, when Queenie's white shoulders dawned on them, kind of jerk, or hop, or hiccup, but their eyes snapped back to their own baskets and on they pushed. I bet you could set off dynamite in the A & P and the people would by and large keep reaching and checking oatmeal off their lists and muttering "Let me see, there was a third thing, began with A, asparagus, no, ah, yes, applesauce!" or whatever it is they do mutter. But there was no doubt, this jiggled them. A few house slaves in pin curlers even look around after pushing their carts past to make sure what they had seen was correct.

You know, it's one thing to have a girl in a bathing suit down on the beach, where what with the glare nobody can look at each other much anyway, and another thing in the cool of the A & P, under the fluorescent lights, against all those stacked packages, with her feet paddling along naked over our checker-board green-and-cream rubber-tile floor.

"Oh, Daddy," Stokesie said beside me. "I feel so faint."

"Darling," I said. "Hold me tight." Stokesie's married, with two   8
babies chalked up on his fuselage already, but as far as I can tell that's the only difference. He's twenty-two, and I was nineteen this April.

"Is it done?" he asks, the responsible married man finding his voice. I forgot to say he thinks he's going to be a manager some sunny day, maybe in 1990 when it's called the Great Alexandrov and Petrooshki Tea Company or something.

What he meant was, our town is five miles from a beach, with a big summer colony out on the Point, but we're right in the middle of town, and the women generally put on a shirt or shorts or something before they get out of the car into the street. And anyway these are usually women with six children and varicose veins mapping their legs and nobody, including them, could care less. As I say, we're right in the middle of town, and if you stand at our front doors you can see two banks and the Congregational church and the newspaper store and three real estate offices and about twenty-seven old freeloaders tearing up Central Street because the sewer broke again. It's not as if we're on the Cape; we're north of Boston and there's people in this town haven't seen the ocean for twenty years.

The girls had reached the meat counter and were asking McMahon something. He pointed, they pointed, and they shuffled out of sight behind a pyramid of Diet Delight peaches. All that was left for us to see was old McMahon patting his mouth and looking after them sizing up their joints. Poor kids, I began to feel sorry for them, they couldn't help it.

Now here comes the sad part of the story, at least my family says   12
it's sad, but I don't think it's so sad myself. The store's pretty empty, it being Thursday afternoon, so there was nothing much to do except lean on the register and wait for the girls to show up again. The whole store was like a pinball machine and I didn't know which tunnel they'd come out of. After a while they come around out of the far aisle, around the light bulbs, records at discount of the Caribbean Six or Tony Martin

Sings or some such gunk you wonder they waste the wax on, sixpacks of candy bars, and plastic toys done up in cellophane that fall apart when a kid looks at them anyway. Around they come, Queenie still leading the way, and holding a little gray jar in her hand. Slots Three through Seven are unmanned and I could see her wondering between Stokes and me, but Stokesie with his usual luck draws an old party in baggy gray pants who stumbles up with four giant cans of pineapple juice (what do these bums *do* with all that pineapple juice? I've often asked myself) so the girls come to me. Queenie puts down the jar and I take it into my fingers icy cold. Kingfish Fancy Herring Snacks in Pure Sour Cream: 49¢. Now her hands are empty, not a ring or a bracelet, bare as God made them, and I wonder where the money's coming from. Still with the prim look she lifts a folded dollar bill out of the hollow at the center of her nubbled pink top. The jar went heavy in my hand. Really, I thought that was so cute.

Then everybody's luck begins to run out. Lengel comes in from haggling with a truck full of cabbages on the lot and is about to scuttle into the door marked MANAGER behind which he hides all day when the girls touch his eye. Lengel's pretty dreary, teaches Sunday school and the rest, but he doesn't miss that much. He comes over and says, "Girls, this isn't the beach."

Queenie blushes, though maybe it's just a brush of sunburn I was noticing for the first time, now that she was so close. "My mother asked me to pick up a jar of herring snacks." Her voice kind of startled me, the way voices do when you see the people first, coming out so flat and dumb yet kind of tony, too, the way it ticked over "pick up" and "snacks." All of a sudden I slid right down her voice into her living room. Her father and the other men were standing around in ice-cream coats and bow ties and the women were in sandals picking up herring snacks on toothpicks off a big glass plate and they were all holding drinks the color of water with olives and sprigs of mint in them. When my parents have somebody over they get lemonade and if it's a real racy affair Schlitz in tall glasses with "They'll Do It Every Time" cartoons stencilled on.

"That's all right," Lengel said. "But this isn't the beach." His repeating this struck me as funny, as if it had just occurred to him, and he had been thinking all these years the A & P was a great big dune and he was the head lifeguard. He didn't like my smiling—as I say he doesn't miss much—but he concentrates on giving the girls that sad Sunday-school-superintendent stare.

Queenie's blush was no sunburn now, and the plump one in plaid, that I liked better from the back—a really sweet can—pipes up, "We weren't doing any shopping. We just came in for the one thing." 16

"That makes no difference," Lengel tells her, and I could see from the way his eyes went that he hadn't noticed she was wearing a two-piece before. "We want you decently dressed when you come in here."

"We *are* decent," Queenie says suddenly, her lower lip pushing, getting sore now that she remembers her place, a place from which the crowd that runs the A & P must look pretty crummy. Fancy Herring Snacks flashed in her very blue eyes.

"Girls, I don't want to argue with you. After this come in here with your shoulders covered. It's our policy." He turns his back. That's policy for you. Policy is what the kingpins want. What the others want is juvenile delinquency.

All this while, the customers had been showing up with their carts 20 but, you know, sheep, seeing a scene, they had all bunched up on Stokesie, who shook open a paper bag as gently as peeling a peach, not wanting to miss a word. I could feel in the silence everybody getting nervous, most of all Lengel, who asks me, "Sammy, have you rung up this purchase?"

I thought and said "No" but it wasn't about that I was thinking. I go through the punches, 4, 9, GROC, TOT—it's more complicated than you think and after you do it often enough, it begins to make a little song, that you hear words to, in my case "Hello (*bing*) there, you (*gung*) happy *pee*pul (*splat*)!"—the *splat* being the drawer flying out. I uncrease the bill, tenderly as you may imagine, it just having come from between the two smoothest scoops of vanilla I had ever known were there, and pass a half and a penny into her narrow pink palm and nestle the herrings in a bag and twist its neck and hand it over, all the time thinking.

The girls, and who'd blame them, are in a hurry to get out, so I say "I quit" to Lengel quick enough for them to hear, hoping they'll stop and watch me, their unsuspected hero. They keep right on going, into the electric eye; the door flies open and they flicker across the lot to their car, Queenie and Plaid and Big Tall Goony-Goony (not that as raw material she was so bad), leaving me with Lengel and a kink in his eyebrow.

"Did you say something, Sammy?"

"I said I quit."   24

"I thought you did."

"You didn't have to embarrass them."

"It was they who were embarrassing us."

I started to say something that came out "Fiddle-de-doo." It's a say-   28
ing of my grandmother's, and I know she would have been pleased.

"I don't think you know what you're saying," Lengel said.

"I know you don't," I said. "But I do." I pull the bow at the back of my apron and start shrugging it off my shoulders. A couple customers that had been heading for my slot begin to knock against each other, like scared pigs in a chute.

Lengel sighs and begins to look very patient and old and gray. He's been a friend of my parents for years. "Sammy, you don't want to do this to your Mom and Dad," he tells me. It's true, I don't. But it seems to me that once you begin a gesture it's fatal not to go through with it. I fold the apron, "Sammy" stitched in red on the pocket, and put it on the counter, and drop the bow tie on top of it. The bow tie is theirs, if you've ever wondered. "You'll feel this for the rest of your life," Lengel says, and I know that's true, too, but remembering how he made that pretty girl blush makes me so scrunchy inside I punch the No Sale tab and the machine whirs "peepul" and the drawer splats out. One advantage to this scene taking place in summer, I can follow this up with a clean exit, there's no fumbling around getting your coat and galoshes, I just saunter into the electric eye in my white shirt that my mother ironed the night before, and the door heaves itself open, and outside the sunshine is skating around on the asphalt.

I look around for my girls, but they're gone, of course. There was-   32
n't anybody but some young married screaming with her children about some candy they didn't get by the door of a powder-blue Falcon station wagon. Looking back in the big windows, over the bags of peat moss and aluminum lawn furniture stacked on the pavement, I could see Lengel in my place in the slot, checking the sheep through. His face was dark gray and his back stiff, as if he'd just had an injection of iron, and my stomach kind of fell as I felt how hard the world was going to be to me hereafter.

Topics for Critical Thinking and Writing

1. Have you ever quit a job on a matter of principle? If so, explain the circumstances, and the short- and long-term consequences.
2. If you have ever thought of quitting a job on a matter of principle but then did not do so, explain the circumstances and your present analysis of your behavior.
3. Some students regard Sammy as a sexist, and say that the failure of the girls to notice his gesture is a fitting punishment for his sexism. Evaluate this view.

Robert Francis

Robert Francis (1901–87) was born in Upland, Pennsylvania, and was educated at Harvard. He taught occasionally, a term here or there or in the summer, but for the most part he devoted himself to reading and writing.

Pitcher

His art is eccentricity, his aim
How not to hit the mark he seems to aim at,

His passion how to avoid the obvious,   4
His technique how to vary the avoidance.

The others throw to be comprehended. He
Throws to be a moment misunderstood.

Yet not too much. Not errant, arrant, wild,   8
But every seeming aberration willed.

Not to, yet still, still to communicate
Making the batter understand too late.

Topics for Discussion and Writing

1.   Why is the pitcher's art "eccentricity"? Consult a dictionary for the origin
     (etymology) of *eccentricity*. How is the origin of the word *eccentricity* apt
     for the meaning here? How is the origin of *errant* (and *arrant* and *aber-*
     ration) appropriate?
2.   The first four stanzas do not rhyme, though the fourth uses a device
     close to rhyme (*wild, willed*). The last stanza, however, rhymes exactly.
     Why?
3.   It has been said that pitching is "the art of instilling fear." Francis says
     that the pitcher's "art is eccentricity." Which view of pitching seems more
     accurate? Can the two views be reconciled? Who are some pitchers who
     instill fear? Who are some who practice the art of "eccentricity"?

9
OPEN FOR BUSINESS

Wellington Museum, by courtesy of the Victoria & Albert Museum

A Graveyard and a Steel Mill in Bethlehem, Pennsylvania
Walker Evans, 1935

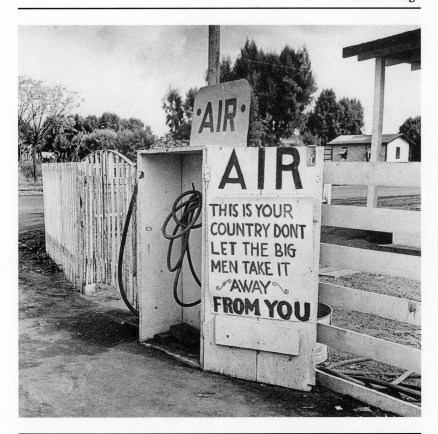

Short Views

The chief business of the American people is business.
Calvin Coolidge

The business of business is business.
Anonymous

Business underlies everything in our national life, including our spiritual life. Witness the fact that in the Lord's Prayer the first petition is for daily bread. No one can worship God or love his neighbor on an empty stomach.
Woodrow Wilson

We demand that big business give the people a square deal; in return we must insist that when anyone engaged in big business honestly endeavors to do right he shall himself be given a square deal.
Theodore Roosevelt

Entrepreneurial profit . . . is the expression of the value of what the entrepreneur contributes to production in exactly the same sense that wages are the value expression of what the worker "produces." It is not a profit of exploitation any more than are wages.
Joseph Alois Schumpeter

Every individual necessarily labors to render the annual revenue of the society as great as he can. He generally indeed neither intends to promote the public interest, nor knows how much he is promoting it. . . . He intends only his own gain, and he is in this, as in many other cases, led by an invisible hand to promote an end which was no part of his intention. . . . By pursuing his own interest he frequently pro-

motes that of the society more effectually than when he really intends to promote it. I have never known much good done by those who affected to trade for the public good.
Adam Smith

It's every man for herself.
Diane Sawyer

Don't gamble. Take all your savings and buy some good stock and hold it till it goes up. If it don't go up, don't buy it.
Will Rogers

Men of business must not break their word twice.
Thomas Fuller

A corporation cannot blush.
Attributed to Howel Walsh

All business sagacity reduces itself in the last analysis to a judicious use of sabotage.
Thorstein Veblen

Benjamin Franklin

Benjamin Franklin (1706–90), born in Boston, left school at the age of ten to help his father, a soapmaker, and then was apprenticed to his half-brother, a printer. They did not get along, and in 1723 Franklin went to Philadelphia to work as a printer. In time he acquired a part-ownership of The Pennsylvania Gazette, *for which he wrote regularly, and he went on to other publishing adventures, including* Poor Richard's Almanack *(1732–57). By 1748—the year of the essay we reprint—he had acquired enough wealth to devote himself largely to careers as a statesman and as an inventor. He continued to write, however, working (from 1771 to 1789) especially on his autobiography.*

Advice to a Young Tradesman, Written by an Old One. To My Friend A. B.

As *you have desired it of me, I write the following Hints, which have been of Service to me, and may, if observed, be so to you.*

Remember that TIME is Money. He that can earn Ten Shillings[1] a Day by his Labour, and goes abroad, or sits idle one half of that Day, tho' he spends but Sixpence during his Diversion or Idleness, ought not to reckon That the only Expence; he has really spent or rather thrown away Five Shillings besides.

Remember that CREDIT is Money. If a Man lets his Money lie in my Hands after it is due, he give me the Interest, or so much as I can make of it during that Time. This amounts to a considerable Sum where a Man has good and large Credit, and makes good Use of it.

Remember that Money is of a prolific generating Nature. Money can beget Money, and its Offspring can beget more, and so on. Five Shillings turn'd, is *Six*: Turn'd again, 'tis Seven and Three Pence; and so on 'til it becomes an Hundred Pound. The more there is of it, the more it produces every Turning, so that the Profits Use quicker and quicker. He that kills a breeding Sow, destroys all her Offspring to the thousandth Generation. He that murders a Crown, destroys all it might have produc'd, even Scores of Pounds.

Remember that Six Pounds a Year is but a Groat a Day. For this lit-   4 tle Sum (which may be daily wasted either in Time or Expence unperceiv'd) a Man of Credit may on his own Security have the constant Pos-

---

[1]**Ten Shillings:** A shilling is a monetary unit. Later in the essay Franklin speaks also of other units—pounds, crowns, pennies, and groats. A pound was worth 20 shillings; a crown was worth five shillings; a shilling was worth 12 pennies; a groat (fourpence) was virtually worthless.

session and Use of an Hundred Pounds. So much in Stock briskly turn'd by an industrious Man, produces great advantage.

Remember this Saying, *That the good Paymaster is Lord of another Man's Purse.* He that is known to pay punctually and exactly to the Time he promises, may at any Time, and on any Occasion, raise all the Money his Friends can spare. This is sometimes of great Use: Therefore never keep borrow'd Money an Hour beyond the Time you promis'd, lest a Disappointment shuts up your Friends Purse forever.

The most trifling Actions that affect a Man's Credit, are to be regarded. The Sound of your Hammer at Five in the Morning or Nine at Night, heard by a Creditor, makes him easy Six Months longer. But if he sees you at a Billiard Table, or hears your Voice in a Tavern, when you should be at Work, he sends for his Money the next Day. Finer Cloaths than he or his Wife wears, or greater Expence in any particular than he affords himself, shocks his Pride, and he duns you to humble you. Creditors are a kind of People, that have the sharpest Eyes and Ears, as well as the best Memories of any in the World.

Good-natur'd Creditors (and such one would always chuse to deal with if one could) feel Pain when they are oblig'd to ask for Money. Spare 'em that Pain, and they will love you. When you receive a Sum of Money, divide it among 'em in Proportion to your Debts. Don't be asham'd of paying a small Sum because you owe a greater. Money, more or less, is always welcome; and your Creditor had rather be at the Trouble of receiving Ten Pounds voluntarily brought him, tho' at ten different Times or Payments, than be oblig'd to go ten Times to demand it before he can receive it in a Lump. It shews, besides, that you are mindful of what you owe; it makes you appear a careful as well as an honest Man; and that still encreases your Credit.

Beware of thinking all your own that you possess, and of living accordingly. 'Tis a Mistake that many People who have Credit fall into. To prevent this, keep an exact Account for some Time of both your Expences and your Incomes. If you take the Pains at first to mention Particulars, it will have this good Effect; you will discover how wonderfully small trifling Expences mount up to large Sums, and will discern what might have been, and may for the future be saved, without occasioning any great Inconvenience.

In short, the Way to Wealth, if you desire it, is as plain as the Way to Market. It depends chiefly on two Words, INDUSTRY and FRUGALITY; i.e. Waste neither Time nor Money, but make the best Use of both. He that gets all he can honestly, and saves all he gets (necessary Expences excepted) will certainly become RICH; If that Being who governs the World, to whom all should look for a Blessing on their honest Endeavours, doth not in his wise Providence otherwise determine.

Topics for Critical Thinking and Writing

1. Look at the first sentence of each of the first five paragraphs. Describe the pattern you find, and then describe the effect.
2. Look at the pattern of paragraph 6. What does the first sentence do? Describe the succeeding sentences.
3. What does Franklin mean in paragraph 3 by the words *turn'd* and *Turning*? What is his point in this paragraph? Paraphrase the last sentence. (See *paraphrase* in the glossary, page 799.)
4. If one or two of Franklin's maxims strike you as particularly sound or particularly repellent, specify which they are and explain why you admire or abhor them.
5. Would you agree that Franklin's advice is suitable only for a maniac whose life is devoted exclusively to making money? Or do you think that it has value for all of us?
6. What do you make of Franklin's last sentence?

Ellen Goodman

Ellen Goodman, born in Boston in 1941, was educated at Radcliffe College. After graduating she worked as a reporter for Newsweek, *a feature writer for the* Detroit Free Press, *and (from 1967) a feature writer and columnist for* The Boston Globe. *Her column is now syndicated in some four hundred newspapers. In 1980 she was awarded a Pulitzer Prize.*

The Company Man

He worked himself to death, finally and precisely, at 3:00 A.M. Sunday morning.

The obituary didn't say that, of course. It said that he died of a coronary thrombosis—I think that was it—but everyone among his friends and acquaintances knew it instantly. He was a perfect Type A, a workaholic, a classic, they said to each other and shook their heads—and thought for five or ten minutes about the way they lived.

This man who worked himself to death finally and precisely at 3:00 A.M. Sunday morning—on his day off—was fifty-one years old and a vice-president. He was, however, one of six vice-presidents, and one of three who might conceivably—if the president died or retired soon enough—have moved to the top spot. Phil knew that.

He worked six days a week, five of them until eight or nine at night,   4
during a time when his own company had begun the four-day week for everyone but the executives. He worked like the Important People. He had no outside "extracurricular interests," unless, of course, you think about a monthly golf game that way. To Phil, it was work. He always ate egg salad sandwiches at his desk. He was, of course, overweight, by 20 or 25 pounds. He thought it was okay, though, because he didn't smoke.

On Saturdays, Phil wore a sports jacket to the office instead of a suit, because it was the weekend.

He had a lot of people working for him, maybe sixty, and most of them liked him most of the time. Three of them will be seriously considered for his job. The obituary didn't mention that.

But it did list his "survivors" quite accurately. He is survived by his wife, Helen, forty-eight years old, a good woman of no particular marketable skills, who worked in an office before marrying and mothering. She had, according to her daughter, given up trying to compete with his work years ago, when the children were small. A company friend said, "I know how much you will miss him." And she answered, "I already have."

"Missing him all these years," she must have given up part of herself which had cared too much for the man. She would be "well taken care of." 8

His "dearly beloved" eldest of the "dearly beloved" children is a hard-working executive in a manufacturing firm down South. In the day and a half before the funeral, he went around the neighborhood researching his father, asking the neighbors what he was like. They were embarrassed.

His second child is a girl, who is twenty-four and newly married. She lives near her mother and they are close, but whenever she was alone with her father, in a car driving somewhere, they had nothing to say to each other.

The youngest is twenty, a boy, a high-school graduate who has spent the last couple of years, like a lot of his friends, doing enough odd jobs to stay in grass and food. He was the one who tried to grab at his father, and tried to mean enough to him to keep the man at home. He was his father's favorite. Over the last two years, Phil stayed up nights worrying about the boy.

The boy once said, "My father and I only board here." 12

At the funeral, the sixty-year-old company president told the forty-eight-year-old widow that the fifty-one-year-old deceased had meant much to the company and would be missed and would be hard to replace. The widow didn't look him in the eye. She was afraid he would read her bitterness and, after all, she would need him to straighten out the finances—the stock options and all that.

Phil was overweight and nervous and worked too hard. If he wasn't at the office, he was worried about it. Phil was a Type A, a heart-attack natural. You could have picked him out in a minute from a lineup.

So when he finally worked himself to death, at precisely 3:00 A.M. Sunday morning, no one was really surprised.

By 5:00 P.M. the afternoon of the funeral, the company president had begun, discreetly of course, with care and taste, to make inquiries about his replacement. One of three men. He asked around: "Who's been working the hardest?" 16

Topics for Critical Thinking and Writing

1. Do you assume that the man Goodman is writing about is a fairly typical business man? Or a highly exceptional exception? Or a caricature?
2. What would you say Goodman's attitude toward the man is? Pity? Contempt? (Of course you don't have to settle for a single word.) How would you support your view of what you take to be her attitude?
3. Would you agree that Goodman is trying to teach a lesson? If so, what is the lesson? And do you agree with it?
4. Compare and contrast Goodman's "Company Man" with Auden's "Unknown Citizen" (page 470).

Felice N. Schwartz

Felice N. Schwartz is founder and president of Catalyst, a not-for-profit organization that works with corporations to foster the career development of women.

In 1989 Schwartz published in the Harvard Business Review *an article that was widely interpreted as advising women to limit their expectations of advancement if they entered the business world. The controversy was reported in the newspapers, and Schwartz took the opportunity to reach a mass audience by writing an essay—printed below—for* The New York Times.

The "Mommy Track" Isn't Anti-Woman

"The cost of employing women in business is greater than the cost of employing men."

This sentence, the first of my recent article in the *Harvard Business Review*, has provoked an extraordinary debate, now labeled by others "the Mommy track." The purpose of the article was to urge employers to create policies that help mothers balance career and family responsibilities, and to eliminate barriers to female productivity and advancement.

But two fears have emerged in the debate. One is that, by raising the issue that it costs more to employ women, we will not be hired and promoted. The other is the fear that if working mothers are offered a variety of career paths, including a part-time option, all women will be left with the primary responsibility for child care.

Acknowledging that there are costs associated with employing   4 women will not lead companies to put women in dead-end jobs. Time taken from work for childbearing, recovery and child care, as well the counterproductive attitudes and practices women face in a male-dominated workplace, do take their toll on women's productivity. But in our competitive marketplace, the costs of employing women pale beside the payoffs.

Current "baby-bust" demographics compel companies to employ women at every level, no matter what the cost. Why? Women comprise half the talent and competence in the country. The idea that companies are looking for excuses to send women home again is untrue. Companies are looking for solutions, not excuses.

Over and over, corporate leaders tell me that their most pressing concern is not why but *how* to respond cost-effectively to the needs of women. Some take bold steps to provide women with the flexibility and family supports they need; others implement ground-breaking programs to remove barriers to women's leadership. The farsighted do both.

Their programs address the needs of women as individuals. There can be no one career "track" to which women, or men, can be expected to adhere throughout their lives. Few can know from the start to what degree they will be committed to career or to family. Raising the issue of the costs of employing women motivates companies to find solutions that work for individuals with diverse and sometimes changing goals and needs.

The second fear voiced in this debate is that making alternative   8
career paths available to women may freeze them in the role of primary caretakers of children.

Today, men are more involved in their children's upbringing, from fixing breakfast to picking up kids at school—enriching our children's lives. But despite increased sharing of parental responsibilities, women remain at the center of family life. According to a recent study, 54 percent of married women who work full-time said child care was their responsibility—contrasted with two percent of surveyed men.

The danger of charting our direction on the basis of wishful thinking is clear. Whether or not men play a greater role in child rearing, companies must reduce the family-related stresses on working women. The flexibility companies provide for women now will be a model in the very near future for men—thus women will not be forced to continue to take primary responsibility for child care. Giving men flexibility will benefit companies in many ways, including greater women's productivity.

What I advocate is that companies create options that allow employees to set their own pace, strive for the top, find satisfaction at the midlevel or cut back for a period of time—not to be penalized for wanting to make a substantial commitment to family. Achievement should not be a function of whether an employee has children. Success is the reward of talent, hard work and commitment.

What benefits women benefits companies. In reducing the cost of   12
employing women—by clearing obstacles to their advancement and providing family benefits—companies create an environment in which all can succeed. But employers will not be motivated to reduce the costs if it remains taboo to discuss them. Only by putting the facts on the table will employers and women—and men—be able to form a partnership in addressing the issues.

Felice N. Schwartz's short essay stimulated responses. The following let-ters were published in The New York Times, *on 2 April 1989.*

To the Editor:

Felice N. Schwartz might have had the best of intentions when she wrote "Management Women and the New Facts of Life" for the *Harvard Business Review* and reiterated her thesis in "The 'Mommy Track' Isn't Anti-Woman" (Op-Ed, March 22). Her arguments, however, are hardly supported by her scholarship, which relies on unidentified studies at unnamed corporations about undefined "turnover" rates, assertions that begin with phrases like "we know" and "what we know to be true," and an undocumented assumption that women in business cost more.

The linchpin of Ms. Schwartz's thesis is an unidentified study at a sin-gle multinational corporation where the turnover rate for female managers was allegedly two and a half times that for male managers. Ms. Schwartz does not say whether the actual rates were an insignificant 1 percent for men and 2.5 percent for women, a significant 40 percent for men and 100 percent for women or something between. Moreover, she fails to explore the reasons for the difference. These might include poor personnel policies, like rigid relocation demands or a lack of parental leave, better job oppor-tunities at other corporations or downturns in the company's fortunes that prompted more recently hired female managers to seek greener pastures.

Ms. Schwartz cites a second unidentified study (apparently of all female employees, not just managers) at another unnamed company, where "half of the women who take maternity leave return to their jobs late or not at all." That is, half returned as scheduled, and an unspecified number did not return, but for unexplained reasons.

Singling out turnover rates among female employees, whether clerks   16
or managers, is a dubious approach. The days of an employee's spending 50 years with a single employer and retiring with a gold watch and a handshake are over. (Indeed, thanks to the buyout, merger and acquisi-tion mania of the 1980s, the days of a company's lasting even a few years under the same ownership, management or even the same name, are diminishing.)

A January 1983 Bureau of Labor Statistics job-tenure survey that rep-resented 54 million male and 42 million female workers reported that fewer that 10 percent of workers of either sex had been with their current employers 25 years or more. Of the 14 million male and 9.5 million female managers and executives covered by the survey, the median tenure was 6.6 years for males and 4.7 years for females.

The survey also showed that 60 percent of the male managers and executives and 74 percent of their female counterparts had the same employer for 9 years or less. Only 11 percent of the males and 3 percent of the females had the same employer for 25 years or more.

In short, few men or women remain with one employer for their entire careers, and women's somewhat lower managerial tenures might be explained partly by women's having only recently entered the executive ranks in significant numbers.

If Ms. Schwartz's scholarship is suspect, her two-track career model   20
(future mommies in this corner, future nonmommies in that corner) is

quaint—indeed Victorian—in view of what businesses are doing for men and women.

Impelled by the changing American work force and striving to remain competitive, corporations like U S West, I.B.M., A.T.&T., Time Inc., Corning Glass, Quaker Oats and Merck have concluded that productivity and family obligations are not mutually exclusive, that the almighty dollar and the family are not enemies. To accommodate these new realities companies have instituted such employment practices as parental leave, flexible and part-time schedules, sabbaticals, child care, telecommuting and job sharing.

But workers are not the only beneficiaries of these new practices. Employers are finding that meeting the needs of employees makes companies more productive and more competitive.

Pat Schroeder
Member of Congress, 1st Dist., Colo.
Washington, March 27, 1989

To the Editor:

Corporations may welcome Felice Schwartz's discovery of the "career and family" woman and "her willingness to accept lower pay and little advancement in return for a flexible schedule" (news story, March 8), but such women should consider the recent history of divorce laws before agreeing to this definition.

Although the law says marriage is an economic partnership that values child rearing and other domestic contributions as well as earning power, the reality is that when a marriage ends, women are not adequately compensated for having devoted themselves to their families at the expense of pursuing their career development.

If young women are going to be doubly penalized this way for choosing "the mommy track," they would do well to look closely at the experience of a generation of middle-aged women who have been left divorced and financially derailed by that choice.

Lois Brenner
New York, March 19, 1989

The writer of the following letter heads the family law department of a law firm and is co-author of not-yet-published book on divorce for women.

To the Editor:

Felice N. Schwartz, in her attempt to persuade us that "The 'Mommy Track' Isn't Anti-Woman" (Op-Ed, March 22), cites an intriguing statistic. According to a recent study, she says, 54 percent of married women working full-time regard child care as their responsibility, whereas only 2 percent of men say the same.

Does this mean that 46 percent of women in these circumstances see child care as a shared responsibility—presumably because men are sharing in the work? While not a majority, such a figure would be a significant enough minority to lend force to the argument for the importance of making businesses more responsive to the needs of both mothers and fathers—and, perhaps more compellingly, to the needs of the nation's children.

While Ms. Schwartz's assurance that "current 'baby-bust' demo- 28
graphics compel companies to employ women at every level" may be true,
it is also true that few mothers have reached the top.

The idea of tracks has always had its limitations—whether in junior
high school or in the corporate world. But if we must have such tracks in
business, the chances of discrimination are surely much less for a "parent
track" than for a "mommy track." Corporations may or may not believe
that they can get along without mothers in high places, but they must realize that they cannot function without parents.

Hope Dellon
New York, March 24, 1989

To the Editor:

Another problem with Felice Schwartz's proposal to track working
women according to the likelihood they will want to raise children is that
it is impossible to tell ahead of time which women are which.

In interviewing highly successful career women in predominantly
male fields, I found that some women who as late as age 34 said adamantly that they did not want children had, by 40, had them. One executive
who had had her tubes tied at 29, with the idea that she wanted a career
and no children was, at 35, about to be married; she wanted desperately to
have the ligation reversed and was seriously contemplating a completely
different line of work.

Women who in their 20's had expected to quit work to have families 32
found themselves in their 30's still single or divorced and enjoying their
careers. Most women, married or single, with or without children,
expressed ambivalence both about children and about their careers.

The problem is not that women don't know what they want, but that
women, like men, grow and change along the life cycle. Stereotyping
women early on into mothers and nonmothers would hamper their ability
to develop fully both as individuals and as productive employees.

Even worse, it would perpetuate a cycle in which generations of
women have been depreciated, divided and weakened through a paradoxical message that says women are inferior if they—and unless they—compete in terms that are set by and for men.

Anita M. Harris
Cambridge, Mass., March 13, 1989

*The writer of the following letter, an assistant professor of communications at
Simmons College in Boston, is completing a book on professional women.*

To the Editor:

While I mostly agree with your response to "Management Women
and the New Facts of Life" (editorial, March 13), your perspective does not
include or explore the profoundly different attitudes men and women
have toward money, which is, after all, why people work. There has been a
spate of surveys highlighting these different attitudes.

Men see money as a means to power, heightening their visibility for 36
selection for leadership within society. Looked at this way, the insatiable
appetite for money, frequently bordering on greed, makes sense, albeit an
insane sense. Capital accumulation is seen as primarily a male activity.

Women, on the other hand, see money as a means of power to purchase. Money purchases food, clothing, shelter or the means of nurturing. This idea too has its insane side, giving rise to gross materialism. Excessive spending is seen as a female trait.

Both these traits cross gender, but a greater number fall within a male-female perspective.

Women cannot satisfy their primary need, nurturing family and society, with the same single-minded directness that men can bring to their primary need of territory (capital accumulation). The marketplace, a male invention, reflects this bias, presenting women with unnatural choices, creating for them a practical as well as psychological disadvantage.

We must force the news media to include differing economic attitudes in covering the brave woman who daily deals with the multifaceted pressures of family life and living up to her potential as described by others.   40

Peg McAuley Byrd
Madison, N.J., March 20, 1989

Topics for Critical Thinking and Writing

1. In paragraph 5 Schwartz says that "'baby-bust' demographics compel companies to employ women at every level, no matter what the cost." Exactly what does she mean?
2. In paragraph 9 Schwartz says that "Today, men are more involved in their children's upbringing. . . ." One often hears comparable statements, but are they true? How would one verify such a statement? In any case, if *you* have any reason to agree or disagree with the statement, express the grounds. To what extent do you think men *ought* to be involved in child-rearing?
3. Schwartz begins her final paragraph by asserting, "What benefits women benefits companies." What evidence or arguments does she offer to support this claim? Or do you think the point is self-evident and needs no support?
4. List the three most cogent arguments the letter-writers make against Schwartz's position.
5. Imagine that you are Schwartz. Write a letter to *The New York Times* in which you reply to one of the letters.

Alexandra Armstrong

Alexandra Armstrong, president of an independent financial planning firm, has appeared on such television programs as Good Morning America *and* Wall Street Week. *In 1987* Money *magazine called her one of the "most qualified Financial Planners in the U.S." The essay reprinted here appeared in* Ms. *magazine.*

Starting a Business

Marian Strong, a 33-year-old married woman with two children, ages six and eight, worked at a bank until her first child was born. Her husband, Edward, has worked for the same corporation for the past 10 years. Paid $50,000 annually, he feels that his job is stable. Their expenses are moderate, both the mortgage on their home and the car loan payments are low. Although they live on Edward's salary, three years ago Marian went to work for H & R Block preparing tax returns. While there, she managed to save $5,000 of her earnings.

In addition to enjoying the work, Marian discovered that many of the company's clients needed to know how to set up and maintain financial records. A number were willing to pay a fee to have this done and some even wanted her to pay their monthly bills. As a result, Marian, who recently inherited $5,000 from an aunt, would like to use this windfall to start her own home-based business to organize and maintain financial records for clients.

I recommended Marian prepare a business plan describing the nature of her business, and why she believes there's a need for it. Estimates of her start-up costs, as well as projected expenses and income for the first year, must also be included. I also reminded her that people in home-based offices often find excuses not to work, and that a wise move would be to have a separate room devoted exclusively to business.

Having decided to give one room totally to her work, Marian need- 4 ed a computer, a copying machine, some furniture and stationery. Her savings, which she estimates at $5,000, will cover these expenses. I told her not to expect to be profitable in the first year, but to plan for the worst case. Marian has her inheritance to fall back on, as well as an untapped $5,000 line of credit that she shares with her husband.

Marian wasn't sure whether her business should be a sole proprietorship, partnership, or a corporation. As a rule one should achieve $100,000 in revenues before incorporation is worthwhile. I recommended a sole proprietorship until her revenues become substantial, because it is less encumbering than a partnership.

We then discussed her marketing strategy. She needs to make sure that people find out about her business, while keeping her costs minimal. I suggested that she write letters introducing herself to estate planners and CPAs who don't want to be involved in record keeping; use personal contacts for referrals, like her former colleagues at H & R Block; and also make contact with organizations that cater to women over the age of 60, since they usually have little experience handling their own financial affairs.

It is important that Marian regularly review her situation to see how her sales and profits are progressing in line with projections and whether more marketing should be done or cost reduction techniques be employed.

Last, but not least, I stressed the importance when starting a business 8 of getting good advisers: a lawyer to help determine potential liabilities that might be involved; an insurance agent to make sure of sufficient liability coverage; and a tax adviser who specializes in small businesses. This is not an area where one should try to save money, but on the other hand, one good initial conversation with a business lawyer or consultant at an hourly rate is often sufficient, and the same holds true for a tax adviser. Then one can continue to consult on a need-to-know basis.

There are also a number of organizations that Marian can turn to for advice and valuable information. The National Association of Women Business Owners, 600 South Federal Street, Suite 400, Chicago, Illinois 60605, is an excellent resource for women in sole proprietorships and has many local chapters. The National Alliance of Home-based Businesswomen, P. O. Box 306, Midland Park, New Jersey 07432, and the Small Business Administration are also useful.

Topics for Critical Thinking and Writing

1. This essay is fundamentally an essay on a process—in this case, how to start a business. Reread it, and see whether (within the severe limitations of the space allowed) it covers all the main points. And does it waste space on irrelevant matters?
2. Do you think the essay is well organized? What *is* the organization?
3. What do you think of Marian Strong's idea for a business, and why?

Bill Totten

Bill Totten, an American, runs a company in Tokyo. His essay appeared in American newspapers as part of a paid advertising supplement about doing business in Japan.

Eigyoman

I am an "Eigyo-man"—a Salesman. My company, K.K. Ashisuto, neither creates nor manufactures, but sells computer software packages. I started Ashisuto with only $5,000 when I arrived from America in 1969. The company now boasts over 600 employees and more than $100 million in annual revenues. I owe my success in large measure to an understanding of the critical differences between Japanese "Eigyo" and American "Sales."

Ashisuto has only three goals. For our customers—to be the best supplier of software products. For creators of software—to be the best distributor of their products. For employees—to be the best employer of people who want to sell software products. Our customers come first, our suppliers second, and we, the employees, third. Our stockholders are all employees and are rewarded as employees, not as stockholders.

Does all this sound strange? Not to Japanese ears. This is how most Japanese companies operate. The most important Japanese business value is to serve customers, not to enrich stockholders or executives. Revenue, profit, and return-on-investment goals are measures of how well a company is doing for its stockholders, not for its customers.

Ashisuto and other Japanese companies are not against making a 4
profit. To the contrary. But we do not want profits that come at the expense of our customers. We believe that serving our customers best encourages our customers to continue buying from us and recommending us to their friends. As in baseball or tennis, the player who wants the higher score must concentrate on the ball, not the scoreboard.

Our salespersons do not have quotas—the hallmark of American sales—nor are they rewarded on how much they sell over short periods. We believe that such quotas merely stimulate to sell as much to each customer as fast as possible, and encourage practices that produce sales and revenues at the expense of customers.

"Eigyo" versus "Sales"

At Ashisuto, we expect each of our salespersons to visit fifteen customers per week and to visit each customer at least once a month. We measure how many sales calls our salespersons make rather than the business they bring in. Why? Because the salespersons who visit their customers frequently, without being pressed to close sales quickly, build personal friendships, discover ways to satisfy customers' problems and needs. Over the long term, they bring in a lot of business, because most customers prefer to buy from people they know, and like, and trust.

Providing the best service to existing customers makes then excellent prospects for additional products. Seventy-five percent of our business is repeat business. Moreover, building a reputation for providing the best service to customers is the best way to convert new prospects into customers. The circle continues—prospect, customer, repeat customer, recommender, repeat customer. The key to this "Eigyo" approach is that it works best over the long term. Unlike Americans, Japanese are more interested in the long-term health of their businesses than in short-term profits.

Our second priority is to be the best distributor for the creators and 8
manufacturers of computer software products. Just as customers buy

from us because we put them first, creators of software distribute through us because we put their needs above our own.

In Ashisuto as in most Japanese companies, employees are given higher priority than stockholders or executives. Executives, in fact, are merely the highest ranking employees. Their power and compensation are on the same scale as all other employees'. Although I am the president and majority stockholder of Ashisuto, my total income last year, after taxes, was only nine times that of a new employee and only six times that of our average employee. This ratio is typical of Japanese company presidents and much lower than in the United States where the average CEO makes ninety-three times as much as the average factory worker.

Trust Is a Product

Stockholders matter even less. Japanese companies sacrifice profits to maintain employment. They do not lay off employees to maintain profits. Only employees can produce high productivity and quality—the only impact executives have is through employees. So Japanese companies make sure that the benefits of prosperity go first to employees, then to executive as employees, and lastly to stockholders. Since employees know that they are the first to benefit from high productivity and higher quality, they are motivated to produce both. And they do!

The most important thing I have learned as an Eigyo-man is that trust is a product. Customers are looking for salespersons they can trust. Life is easy for a salesperson who earns a reputation for serving customers, for putting their interests first and ensuring they get the value they expect.

I am tempted to say I learned this in Japan, but I really learned it   12 from my father while growing up in the United States in the 1940s and '50s. It seems that the "Japanese secret" for success is that they have adopted the values that made America great at the same time we have abandoned them.

Topics for Critical Thinking and Writing

1. How (and where) does Totten describe his job with K.K. Ashisuto? How would his job be described in the United States? In addition to providing information, what point is Totten making with his description?
2. Consider paragraphs 2–7, on relations with customers. Do you assume that Americans should use this approach, or do you assume that the approach would work only in Japan? Explain why you hold your view.
3. Totten says (paragraph 11) that he has learned that "trust is a product." What does he mean, and how is this idea important to his argument?

4. In so far as the essay explains Japanese ways of doing business, it is an expository essay. Is there also a thesis? If so, what is the thesis?
5. Do you think Benjamin Franklin (page 422) would invest in Bill Totten's company? Explain.

Robert W. Keidel

Robert W. Keidel, a graduate of Williams College and the Wharton School of the University of Pennsylvania, directs a consulting firm. He is the author of Game Plans: Sports Strategies for Business *(1985) and* Corporate Players: Designs for Working and Winning Together *(1988).*

A New Game for Managers to Play

As the football season gradually gives way to basketball, corporate managers would do well to consider the differences between these games. For just as football mirrors industrial structures of the past, basketball points the way to the corporate structure of the future.

It's the difference between the former chief executive officer of I. T. T., Harold Geneen, the master football coach who dictates his players' roles and actions, and Donald Burr, the People Express Airlines chief executive officer, who puts his players on the floor and lets them manage themselves.

Football is, metaphorically, a way of life in work today—the corporate sport. This is reflected in the language many managers use:

"It's taken my staff and me a sizable chunk of time, but we now have a solid game plan for the XYZ job. Jack, I want you to quarterback this thing all the way into the end zone. Of course, a lot of it will be making the proper assignments—getting the right people to run interference and the right ones to run with the ball. But my main concern is that we avoid mistakes. No fumbles, no interceptions, no sacks, no penalties. I don't want us to have to play catch-up; no two-minute drills at the end. I want the game plan executed exactly the way it's drawn. When we're done we want to look back with pride at a win—and not have to Monday-morning-quarterback a loss."

Does this football language represent more than just a convenient shorthand? Almost certainly it does, because the metaphors we use routinely are the means by which we structure experience. Thus, football metaphors may well reflect—and reinforce—underlying organizational dynamics. But football, despite its pervasiveness, is the wrong model for most corporations.

Consider the scenario above. Planning has been neatly separated from implementation; those expected to carry out the game plan had no part in creating it. Also, the communication flow is one-way: from the head coach (speaker) to the quarterback (Jack)—and, presumably, from the quarterback to the other players. And the thrust of the message is risk-averse; the real name of the game is control—minimizing mistakes. But perhaps most significant is the assumption of stability—that nothing will change to invalidate the corporate game plan. "No surprises!" as Mr. Geneen likes to say.

Stability is a realistic assumption in football, even given the sport's enormous complexity, because of the time available to coaches—between games and between plays. A pro football game can very nearly be programmed. Carl Peterson, formerly with the Philadelphia Eagles and now president of the United States Football League's champions, the Baltimore Stars, has estimated that managing a game is 75 percent preparation and only 25 percent adjustment.

Thus, football truly is the realm of the coach—the head coach, he   8
who calls the shots. (Most pro quarterbacks do not call their own plays.) As Bum Phillips has said in tribute to the head coach of the Miami Dolphins, Don Shula, "He can take his'n and beat your'n, or he can take your'n and beat his'n."

But football is not an appropriate model for most businesses precisely because instability is an overwhelming fact of life. Market competition grows ever more spastic, product life-cycles shrink unimaginably and technology courses on paths of its own.

In this milieu, corporate "players" simply cannot perform effectively if they must wait for each play to be called for them, and remain in fixed positions—or in narrowly defined roles—like football players; increasingly, they need to deploy themselves flexibly, in novel combinations.

Thirty years ago it may have been possible to regard core business functions—R&D, manufacturing and marketing as separate worlds, with little need for interaction. R&D would design the product and then lob it over the wall to manufacturing; manufacturing would make the product and lob it over another wall to the customer.

No need to worry about problems that do not fit neatly into the   12
standard departments; these are inconsequential and infrequent. And when they do arise, they are simply bumped up the hierarchy to senior management—the head coach and his staff.

In effect, performance is roughly the sum of the functions—just as a football team's performance is the sum of the performances of its platoons—offense, defense and special teams. Clearly, this view of the corporation is anachronistic. Yet it remains all too common.

Business's "season" is changing, and a new metaphor is needed. While football will continue to be a useful model for pursuing machine-like efficiency and consistency—that is, for minimizing redundancies, bottlenecks and errors—this design favors stability at the expense of change. Since now more than ever businesses must continuously innovate and adapt, a more promising model is basketball.

To begin with, basketball is too dynamic a sport to permit the rigid separation of planning and execution that characterizes football. Unlike football teams, basketball teams do not pause and regroup after each play. As the former star player and coach Bill Russell has noted, "Your game plan may be wiped out by what happens in the first minute of play." Success in basketball depends on the ability of the coach and players to plan and adjust while in motion. Such behavior requires all-around communication—just as basketball demands all-around passing, as opposed to football's linear sequence of "forward," one-way passing.

Basketball also puts a premium on generalist skills. Although different players will assume somewhat different roles on the court, all must be able to dribble, pass, shoot, rebound and play defense. Everyone handles the ball—a far cry from what happens on the grid-iron. Indeed, basketball is much more player-oriented than football—a sport in which players tend to be viewed as interchangeable parts.   16

If football is a risk-averse game, basketball is risk-accepting. In basketball, change is seen as normal, not exceptional; hence, change is regarded more as the source of opportunities than of threats. Mr. Geneen has claimed that "Ninety-nine percent of all surprises in business are negative."

Mr. Geneen's perspective is classic football and is tenable in stable, "controllable" environments. But such environments are becoming rare. The future increasingly belongs to managers like Mr. Burr or James Treybig, the founder of Tandem Computers, who thrive on change rather than flee from it.

We need fewer head coaches and more player-coaches, less scripted teamwork and more spontaneous teamwork. We need to integrate planning and doing—managing and working—far more than we have to date. Are you playing yesterday's game—or tomorrow's?

Topics for Critical and Writing

1. In his first paragraph Keidel lays that "football mirrors industrial structures of the past" whereas "basketball points the way to the corporate structure of the future." He several times makes similar assertions—for instance, in paragraph 5 he says "football . . . is the wrong model for most corporations." Does he support his view with evidence? If so, call attention to the evidence he offers. Are you convinced by his argument? Why, or why not?

2. Keidel says (paragraph 5) that "the metaphors we use routinely are the means by which we structure experience." Consider metaphors drawn from the world of business but used in the context of education. An administrator, for instance, may say, "Last year we *produced* 1,000 majors in business administration; next year we hope to *turn out* twelve hundred; the *bottom line* is, the *supply still falls short of the demand*." What do such metaphors tell us about the ways in which the speaker sees

education (or, to use Keidel's words, the ways in which he or she "structure[s] experience")?

3. As the preceding question indicates, business itself can provide metaphors, such as "producing" or "turning out" students. In the next few days jot down examples that you encounter in newspapers, television ads, political speeches, or whatever and analyze their implications. (You may even find businesses that use metaphors drawn from business.)

4. In paragraph 2 Keidel refers to People Express Airlines. What point does he hope to make? Is People Express still in business? (If you don't know, how would you go about finding out?) Does the current status of People Express affect the status of his argument?

Warren Bennis

Warren Bennis, born in New York City in 1925, was educated at Antioch College and the Massachusetts Institute of Technology. From 1971 to 1977 he served as the president of the University of Cincinnati. The author of several important books on management, he now teaches in the School of Business of the University of Southern California.

Time to Hang Up the Old Sports Clichés

Americans are, on the whole, simple and direct people. We do not incline toward nuances or subtleties, in either our lives or our work. We opt inevitably for the concrete over the abstract. We are also extremely competitive, relishing opponents' losses as we boast of our own victories. For these reasons, sports are not only our favorite form of entertainment but the principal model and metaphor for our own lives.

At home and at work, we talk often of winning and losing, scoring touchdowns, carrying the ball, close calls, going down to the wire, batting a thousand, hitting paydirt and going into extra innings, and while we may like movie, TV and music stars, we admire sports stars. Every father wants his sons to shine on the playing fields, which is why Little League games frequently have all the carefree air of the London blitz.

Preachers and politicians, among others, see this national obsession as healthy, portray us as good people interested in good, clean fun. Universities, including mine, celebrate and reward their athletes as heroes. When the Super Bowl rolls around, the country focuses on The Game.

I am admittedly as obsessed as anyone. I seem to remember forever great plays, great players and even the scores of great games, though I sometimes cannot recall whom I sat next to at dinner three nights ago. But I am also convinced that it is time to find a new model. 4

Life is not a baseball game. It's never called on account of darkness, much less canceled because of inclement weather. And while major sports are big business now, business is not a sport, and never was. Indeed, thinking of business as a kind of game or sport was always simplistic. Now it's downright dangerous.

Games are of limited duration, take place on or in fixed and finite sites and are governed by openly promulgated rules that are enforced on the spot by neutral professionals. Moreover, they are performed by relatively evenly matched teams that are counseled and led through every move by seasoned hands. Scores are kept, and at the end of the game, a winner is declared.

Business is usually a little different. In fact, if there is anyone out there who can say that his business is of limited duration, takes place on a fixed site, is governed by openly promulgated rules that are enforced on the spot by neutral professionals, competes only on relatively even terms and performs in a way that can be measured in runs or points, then he is either extraordinarily lucky or seriously deluded.

The risks in thinking of business in sports terms are numerous.   8
First, to measure a business on the basis of wins and losses is to misunderstand both the purposes of a specific business and the nature of business itself. No business—whether it sells insurance or manufactures cars—can or should be designed to win. Rather, it should be designed to grow, both quantitatively and qualitatively. In this sense, it vies more with itself than with its competition. This is not to say there are never winners or losers—in head-to-head contests, as when two ad agencies are competing for the same account, someone will win and someone will lose. It is to say, to paraphrase Vince Lombardi's legendary dictum, winning isn't everything, it's one of many things a business must accomplish.

Thus, a company designed merely to win will probably lose in the long run. For example, the John Doe Insurance Company could win the auto market overnight by offering comprehensive coverage for $100 a year. However, the company would fail when the claims began coming in.

Second, it is perilous to think of limits, rules and absolutes in business. Athletes compete for a given number of hours in a given number of games over a given period of weeks or months. Businesses are in the arena for decades, sometimes centuries. Though the action may rise and subside, it never stops. It does not offer any timeouts, much less neatly defined beginnings and endings.

American business has traditionally been schizophrenic about rules. When it is flourishing, it wants no rules or regulations. When it failing, it wants a plethora of rules. For example, Detroit saw Washington as its nemesis until foreign cars flooded the market. Then, Chrysler went to the Feds for a loan, and now Detroit begs Washington to regulate imports while lobbying against Federal safety and quality controls.

Athletes perform in a static environment—the size of the field, the   12
length of the contest, even the wardrobes of the players remain the same, day after month after year. Businesses function in a volatile universe, which changes from moment to moment, and hardly ever repeats. It is affected by droughts half a world away, a new gizmo down the street, consumer attitudes and needs, a million things. Given this mercurial context, any business that is not at least as dynamic and flexible as the world in which it functions will soon be out of step or out of business.

Clearly, then, there are far more differences between sports and business than similarities. But the danger is that many people will continue to imagine that success in business is like success in sports—flat-out, total victory; a world championship. But the best-run and most successful companies in America do not think in terms of victories and defeats, coming from behind, last-minute saves or shining moments, and they do not count on regulations or referees. Instead, they think in terms of staying power, dedication to quality, and an endless effort to do better than they have done. They see change as the only constant, and they try to adapt to the world rather than expect the world to adapt to them. Indeed, it is a business's ability to adapt to an everchanging world that is the basis for both its success and progress.

I should emphasize that I am not criticizing the management of professional sports teams, which are themselves businesses. Some teams are poorly run, but others, like the Boston Celtics or Los Angeles Lakers, operate on the same principles that other successful businesses do. They change, they plan for the long-term, and they strive ceaselessly for quality. What I object to is comparing the playing field to the marketplace.

The truth is that there is no workable or appropriate metaphor for business except business itself, and that should be sufficient. Like a well-played game, a well-run business is something to see, but, unlike a well-played game, it is not a diversion. Rather, it is life itself—complex, difficult, susceptible to both success and failure, sometimes unruly, always challenging, and often joyful.

So let's leave the home runs to the Phillies' Mike Schmidt and the   16
touchdowns to the Bears' Walter Payton, and get down to business.

Topics for Critical Thinking and Writing

1. In paragraph 5 Bennis suggests that "it's downright dangerous" to see business in terms of metaphors drawn from the world of sports. On the other hand, presumably those who use metaphors believe that the metaphors help them see things freshly and clearly. If you have read Robert Keidel's essay (page 436), do you think that Keidel's use of

metaphor clarifies your understanding of business or, on the contrary, does it lead to dangerous misapprehensions? Be as specific as possible.

2. In paragraph 8, when Bennis says that a business "should be designed to grow," he is using a metaphor, for he is comparing a business to a living organism. And in paragraph 11, when he says that American business is "schizophrenic," he uses a metaphor from psychiatry. Reread his essay closely and jot down a list of the metaphors he uses. Do you think his metaphors are useful, or are they (to quote paragraph 5) "dangerous"?

3. Evaluate Bennis's final paragraph as a final paragraph. What makes it effective or ineffective? Now look at Bennis's opening paragraph. Does his description of Americans largely exclude some groups? Are there readers his opening paragraph might unintentionally "exclude" or turn away?

Milton Friedman

Milton Friedman, born in Brooklyn in 1912, is a graduate of Rutgers University, the University of Chicago, and Columbia University. A leading conservative economist, Friedman has had considerable influence on economic thought in America through his popular writings (he wrote a regular column in Newsweek*) his numerous scholarly writings and his presence on national committees.*

The Social Responsibility of Business Is to Increase Its Profits

When I hear businessmen speak eloquently about the "social responsibilities of business in a free-enterprise system," I am reminded of the wonderful line about the Frenchman who discovered at the age of 70 that he had been speaking prose all his life. The businessmen believe that they are defending free enterprise when they declaim that business is not concerned "merely" with profit but also with promoting desirable "social" ends; that business has a "social conscience" and takes seriously its responsibilities for providing employment, eliminating discrimination, avoiding pollution and whatever else may be the catchwords of the contemporary crop of reformers. In fact they are—or would be if they or anyone else took them seriously—preaching pure and unadulterated socialism. Businessmen who talk this way are unwitting puppets of the intellectual forces that have been undermining the basis of a free society these past decades.

The discussions of the "social responsibilities of business" are notable for their analytical looseness and lack of rigor. What does it mean to say that "business" has responsibilities? Only people can have responsibilities. A corporation is an artificial person and in this sense may have artificial responsibilities, but "business" as a whole cannot be said to have responsibilities, even in this vague sense. The first step toward clarity in examining the doctrine of the social responsibility of business is to ask precisely what it implies for whom.

Presumably, the individuals who are to be responsible are businessmen, which means individual proprietors or corporate executives. Most of the discussion of social responsibility is directed at corporations, so in what follows I shall mostly neglect the individual proprietors and speak of corporate executives.

In a free-enterprise, private-property system, a corporate executive   4
is an employee of the owners of the business. He has direct responsibility to his employers. That responsibility is to conduct the business in accordance with their desires, which generally will be to make as much money as possible while conforming to the basic rules of the society, both those embodied in law and those embodied in ethical custom. Of course, in some cases his employers may have a different objective. A group of persons might establish a corporation for an eleemosynary purpose—for example, a hospital or a school. The manager of such a corporation will not have money profit as his objectives but the rendering of certain services.

In either case, the key point is that, in his capacity as a corporate executive, the manager is the agent of the individuals who own the corporation or establish the eleemosynary institution, and his primary responsibility is to them.

Needless to say, this does not mean that it is easy to judge how well he is performing his task. But at least the criterion of performance is straightforward, and the persons among whom a voluntary contractual arrangement exists are clearly defined.

Of course, the corporate executive is also a person in his own right. As a person, he may have many other responsibilities that he recognizes or assumes voluntarily—to his family, his conscience, his feelings of charity, his church, his clubs, his city, his country. He may feel impelled by these responsibilities to devote part of his income to causes he regards as worthy, to refuse to work for particular corporations, even to leave his job, for example, to join his country's armed forces. If we wish, we may refer to some of these responsibilities as "social responsibilities." But in these respects he is acting as a principal, not an agent; he is spending his own money or time or energy, not the money of his employers or the time or energy he has contracted to devote to their purposes. If these are "social responsibilities," they are the social responsibilities of individuals, not of business.

What does it mean to say that the corporate executive has a "social   8
responsibility" in his capacity as businessman? If this statement is not pure rhetoric, it must mean that he is to act in some way that is not in

the interest of his employers. For example, that he is to refrain from increasing the price of the product in order to contribute to the social objective of preventing inflation, even though a price increase would be in the best interests of the corporation. Or that he is to make expenditures on reducing pollution beyond the amount that is in the best interests of the corporation or that is required by law in order to contribute to the social objective of improving the environment. Or that, at the expense of corporate profits, he is to hire "hardcore" unemployed instead of better qualified available workmen to contribute to the social objective of reducing poverty.

In each of these cases, the corporate executive would be spending someone else's money for a general social interest. Insofar as his actions in accord with his "social responsibility" reduce returns to stockholders, he is spending their money. Insofar as his actions raise the price to customers, he is spending the customers' money. Insofar as his actions lower the wages of some employees, he is spending their money.

The stockholders or the customers or the employees could separately spend their own money on the particular action if they wished to do so. The executive is exercising a distinct "social responsibility," rather than serving as an agent of the stockholders or the customers or the employees, only if he spends the money in a different way than they would have spent it.

But if he does this, he is in effect imposing taxes, on the one hand, and deciding how the tax proceeds shall be spent, on the other.

This process raises political questions on two levels: principle and consequences. On the level of political principle, the imposition of taxes and the expenditure of tax proceeds are governmental functions. We have established elaborate constitutional, parliamentary and judicial provisions to control these functions, to assure that taxes are imposed so far as possible in accordance with the preferences and desires of the public—after all, "taxation without representation" was one of the battle cries of the American Revolution. We have a system of checks and balances to separate the legislative function of imposing taxes and enacting expenditures from the executive function of collecting taxes and administering expenditure programs and from the judicial function of mediating disputes and interpreting the law.

Here the businessman—self-selected or appointed directly or indirectly by stockholders—is to be simultaneously legislator, executive and jurist. He is to decide whom to tax by how much and for what purpose, and he is to spend the proceeds—all this guided only by general exhortations from on high to restrain inflation, improve the environment, fight poverty and so on and on.

The whole justification for permitting the corporate executive to be selected by the stockholders is that the executive is an agent serving the interests of his principal. This justification disappears when the corporate executive imposes taxes and spends the proceeds for "social" purposes. He becomes in effect a public employee, a civil servant, even though he remains in name an employee of a private enterprise. On grounds of political principle, it is intolerable that such civil servants—insofar as their actions in the name of social responsibility are real and not just window-dressing,—should be selected as they are now. If they are to be civil servants, then they must be elected through a political process. If they are to impose taxes and make expenditures to foster "social" objectives, then political machinery must be set up to make the assessment of taxes and to determine through a political process the objectives to be served.

This is the basic reason why the doctrine of "social responsibility" involves the acceptance of the socialist view that political mechanisms, not market mechanisms, are the appropriate way to determine the allocation of scarce resources to alternative uses.

On the grounds of consequences, can the corporate executive in fact discharge his alleged "social responsibilities"? On the other hand, suppose he could get away with spending the stockholders' or customers' or employees' money. How is he to know how to spend it? He is told that he must contribute to fighting inflation. How is he to know what action of his will contribute to that end? He is presumably an expert in running his company—in producing a product or selling it or financing it. But nothing about his selection makes him an expert on inflation. Will his holding down the price of his product reduce inflationary pressure? Or, by leaving more spending power in the hands of his customers, simply divert it elsewhere? Or, by forcing him to produce less because of the lower price, will it simply contribute to shortages? Even if he could answer these questions, how much cost is he justified in imposing on his stockholders, customers and employees for this social purpose? What is his appropriate share and what is the appropriate share of others? 16

And, whether he wants to or not, can he get away with spending his stockholders', customers' or employees' money? Will not the stockholders fire him? (Either the present ones or those who take over when his actions in the name of social responsibility have reduced the corporation's profits and the price of its stock.) His customers and his employees can desert him for other producers and employers less scrupulous in exercising their social responsibilities.

This facet of "social responsibility" doctrine is brought into sharp relief when the doctrine is used to justify wage restraint by trade unions. The conflict of interest is naked and clear when union officials are asked to subordinate the interest of their members to some more general purpose. If the union officials try to enforce wage restraint, the consequence is likely to be wildcat strikes, rank-and-file revolts and the emergence of strong competitors for their jobs. We thus have the ironic phenomenon that union leaders—at least in the U.S.—have objected to Government interference with the market far more consistently and courageously than have business leaders.

The difficulty of exercising "social responsibility" illustrates, of course, the great virtue of private competitive enterprise—it forces people to be responsible for their own actions and makes it difficult for them to "exploit" other people for either selfish or unselfish purposes. They can do good—but only at their own expense.

Many a reader who has followed the argument this far may be   20
tempted to remonstrate that it is all well and good to speak of Government's having the responsibility to impose taxes and determine expenditures for such "social" purposes as controlling pollution or training the hard-core unemployed, but that the problems are too urgent to wait on the slow course of political processes, that the exercise of social responsibility by businessmen is a quicker and surer way to solve pressing current problems.

Aside from the question of fact—I share Adam Smith's skepticism about the benefits that can be expected from "those who affected to trade for the public good"—this argument must be rejected on grounds of principle. What it amounts to is an assertion that those who favor the taxes and expenditures in question have failed to persuade a majority of their fellow citizens to be of like mind and that they are seeking to attain by undemocratic procedures what they cannot attain by democratic procedures. In a free society, it is hard for "evil" people to do "evil," especially since one man's good is another's evil.

I have, for simplicity, concentrated on the special case of the corporate executive, except only for the brief digression on trade unions. But precisely the same argument applies to the newer phenomenon of calling upon stockholders to require corporations to exercise social responsibility (the recent G.M. crusade for example). In most of these cases, what is in effect involved is some stockholders trying to get other stockholders (or customers or employees) to contribute against their will to "social" causes favored by the activists. Insofar as they succeed, they are again imposing taxes and spending the proceeds.

The situation of the individual proprietor is somewhat different. If he acts to reduce the returns of his enterprise in order to exercise his "social responsibility," he is spending his own money, not someone else's. If he wishes to spend his money on such purposes, that is his right, and I cannot see that there is any objection to his doing so. In the process, he, too, may impose costs on employees and customers. However, because he is far less likely than a large corporation or union to have monopolistic power, any such side effects will tend to be minor.

Of course, in practice the doctrine of social responsibility is fre-   24
quently a cloak for actions that are justified on other grounds rather than a reason for those actions.

To illustrate, it may well be in the long-run interest of a corporation that is a major employer in a small community to devote resources to providing amenities to that community or to improving its government. That may make it easier to attract desirable employees, it may reduce the wage bill or lessen losses from pilferage and sabotage or have other worthwhile effects. Or it may be that, given the laws about the deductibility of corporate charitable contributions, the stockholders can contribute more to charities they favor by having the corporation make the gift than by doing it themselves, since they can in that way contribute an amount that would otherwise have been paid as corporate taxes.

In each of these—and many similar—cases, there is a strong temptation to rationalize these actions as an exercise of "social responsibility." In the present climate of opinion, with its widepread aversion to "capitalism," "profits," the "soulless corporation" and so on, this is one way for a corporation to generate goodwill as a byproduct of expenditures that are entirely justified in its own self-interest.

It would be inconsistent of me to call on corporate executives to refrain from this hypocritical window-dressing because it harms the foundations of a free society. That would be to call on them to exercise a "social responsibility"! If our institutions and the attitudes of the public make it in their self-interest to cloak their actions in this way, I cannot summon much indignation to denounce them. At the same time, I can express admiration for those individual proprietors or owners of closely held corporations or stockholders of more broadly held corporations who disdain such tactics as approaching fraud.

Whether blameworthy or not, the use of the cloak of social responsibility, and the nonsense spoken in its name by influential and prestigious businessmen, does clearly harm the foundations of a free society. I have been impressed time and again by the schizophrenic character of many businessmen. They are capable of being extremely far-sighted and clear-headed in matters that are internal to their businesses. They are incredibly short-sighted and muddle-headed in matters that are outside their businesses but affect the possible survival of business in general. This short-sightedness is strikingly exemplified in the calls from many businessmen for wage and price guidelines or controls or income policies. There is nothing that could do more in a brief period to destroy a market system and replace it by a centrally controlled system than effective governmental control of prices and wages.

The short-sightedness is also exemplified in speeches by businessmen on social responsibility. This may gain them kudos in the short run. But it helps to strengthen the already too prevalent view that the pursuit of profits is wicked and immoral and must be curbed and controlled by external forces. Once this view is adopted, the external forces that curb the market will not be the social consciences, however highly

28

developed, of the pontificating executives; it will be the iron fist of Government bureaucrats. Here, as with price and wage controls, businessmen seem to me to reveal a suicidal impulse.

The political principle that underlies the market mechanism is unanimity. In an ideal free market resting on private property, no individual can coerce any other, all cooperation is voluntary, all parties to such cooperation benefit or they need not participate. There are no values, no "social" responsibilities in any sense other than the shared values and responsibilities of individuals. Society is a collection of individuals and of the various groups they voluntarily form.

The political principle that underlies the political mechanism is conformity. The individual must serve a more general social interest—whether that be determined by a church or a dictator or a majority. The individual may have a vote and say in what is to be done, but if he is overruled, he must conform. It is appropriate for some to require others to contribute to a general social purpose whether they wish to or not.

Unfortunately, unanimity is not always feasible. There are some respects in which conformity appears unavoidable, so I do not see how one can avoid the use of the political mechanism altogether.   32

But the doctrine of "social responsibility" taken seriously would extend the scope of the political mechanism to every human activity. It does not differ in philosophy from the most explicitly collectivist doctrine. It differs only by professing to believe that collectivist ends can be attained without collectivist means. That is why, in my book "Capitalism and Freedom," I have called it a "fundamentally subversive doctrine" in a free society, and have said that in such a society, "there is one and only one social responsibility of business—to use its resources and engage in activities designed to increase its profits so long as it stays within the rules of the game, which is to say, engages in open and free competition without deception or fraud."

Topics for Critical Thinking and Writing

1. Friedman says that corporate executives who spend the corporation's money "for a general social interest" are "in effect imposing taxes . . . and deciding how the tax proceeds shall be spent . . . " (paragraphs 9 and 11). Is the use of the word *tax* effective? Is it fair? (Notice that paragraphs 12, 13, and 14, as well as some later paragraphs, also speak of taxes.)

2. "The socialist view," Friedman says in paragraph 15, is "that political mechanisms, not market mechanisms, are the appropriate way to determine the allocation of scarce resources to alternative uses." Suppose a fellow student told you that he or she found this passage puzzling. How would you clarify it?

3. Some persons in business have replied to Friedman by arguing that because the owners of today's corporations are rarely involved in running them, the corporations can properly be viewed not as private

property but as social institutions able to formulate goals of their own. These people argue that the managers of a corporation are public trustees of a multipurpose organization, and their job is to use their power to promote the interests not only of stockholders but of employees and of the general public. What do you think are the strengths and the weaknesses of this reply?
4. Does Friedman argue that corporations have no responsibilities?
5. In *Religion and the Rise of Capitalism*, R. H. Tawney said that "economic organization must allow for the fact that, unless industry is to be paralyzed by recurrent revolts on the part of outraged human nature, it must satisfy criteria which are not purely economic." Do you think Friedman would agree? Why, or why not?

Barbara Ehrenreich and Annette Fuentes

Barbara Ehrenreich writes regularly for the New York Times and for Ms. magazine. Annette Fuentes, the editor of Sisterhood Is Global, has also written for Ms., where this article originally appeared.

Life on the Global Assembly Line

In Ciudad Juárez, Mexico, Anna M. rises at 5 A.M. to feed her son before starting on the two-hour bus trip to the maquiladora (factory). He will spend the day along with four other children in a neighbor's one-room home. Anna's husband, frustrated by being unable to find work for himself, left for the United States six months ago. She wonders, as she carefully applies her new lip gloss, whether she ought to consider herself still married. It might be good to take a night course, become a secretary. But she seldom gets home before eight at night, and the factory, where she stitches brassieres that will be sold in the United States through J. C. Penney, pays only $48 a week.

In Penang, Malaysia, Julie K. is up before the three other young women with whom she shares a room, and starts heating the leftover rice from last night's supper. She looks good in the company's green-trimmed uniform, and she's proud to work in a modern, American-owned factory. Only not quite so proud as when she started working three years ago—she thinks as she squints out the door at a passing group of women. Her job involves peering all day through a microscope, bonding hair-thin gold wires to a silicon chip destined to end up inside a pocket calculator, and at 21, she is afraid she can no longer see very clearly.

Every morning, between four and seven, thousands of women like Anna and Julie head out for the day shift. In Ciudad Juárez, they crowd into *ruteras* (rundown vans) for the trip from the slum neighborhoods to the industrial parks on the outskirts of the city. In Penang they squeeze, 60 or more at a time, into buses for the trip from the village to the low, modern factory buildings of the Bayan Lepas free trade zone.

In Taiwan, they walk from the dormitories—where the night shift is already asleep in the still-warm beds—through the checkpoints in the high fence surrounding the factory zone.

This is the world's new industrial proletariat: young, female, Third   4 World. Viewed from the "first world," they are still faceless, genderless "cheap labor," signaling their existence only through a label or tiny imprint,—"made in Hong Kong," or Taiwan, Korea, the Dominican Republic, Mexico, the Philippines. But they may be one of the most strategic blocs of womanpower in the world of the 1980s. Conservatively, there are 2 million Third World female industrial workers employed now, millions more looking for work, and their numbers are rising every year. Anyone whose image of Third World women features picturesque peasants with babies slung on their backs should be prepared to update it. Just in the last decade, Third World women have become a critical element in the global economy and a key "resource" for expanding multinational corporations.

It doesn't take more than second-grade arithmetic to understand what's happening. In the United States, an assembly-line worker is likely to earn, depending on her length of employment, between $3.10 and $5 an hour. In many Third World countries, a woman doing the same work will earn $3 to $5 a *day*. According to the magazine *Business Asia*, in 1976 the average hourly wage for unskilled work (male or female) was 55 cents in Hong Kong, 52 cents in South Korea, 32 cents in the Philippines, and 17 cents in Indonesia. The logic of the situation is compelling: why pay someone in Massachusetts $5 an hour to do what someone in Manila will do for $2.50 a day? Or, as a corollary, why pay a male worker anywhere to do what a female worker will do for 40 to 60 percent less?

And so, almost everything that can be packed up is being moved out to the Third World; not heavy industry, but just about anything light enough to travel—garment manufacture, textiles, toys, footwear, pharmaceuticals, wigs, appliance parts, tape decks, computer components, plastic goods. In some industries, like garment and textile, American jobs are lost in the process, and the biggest losers are women, often black and Hispanic. But what's going on is much more than a matter of runaway shops. Economists are talking about a "new international division of labor," in which the process of production is broken down and the fragments are dispersed to different parts of the world. In general, the low-skilled jobs are farmed out to the Third World, where labor costs are minuscule, while control over the overall process and technology remains safely at company headquarters in "first world" countries like the United States and Japan.

The American electronics industry provides a classic example: circuits are printed on silicon wafers and tested in California; then the wafers are shipped to Asia for the labor-intensive process by which they are cut into tiny chips and bonded to circuit boards; final assembly into products such as calculators or military equipment usually takes place in the United States. Garment manufacture too is often broken into geographically separated steps, with the most repetitive, labor-intensive jobs going to the poor countries of the southern hemisphere. Most Third World countries welcome whatever jobs come their way in the new division of labor, and the major international development agencies—like the World Bank and the United States Agency for International Development (AID)—encourage them to take what they can get.

So much any economist could tell you. What is less often noted is the *gender* breakdown of the emerging international division of labor. Eighty to 90 percent of the low-skilled assembly jobs that go to the Third World are performed by women—in a remarkable switch from earlier patterns of foreign-dominated industrialization. Until now, "development" under the aegis of foreign corporations has usually meant more jobs for men and—compared to traditional agricultural society—a diminished economic status for women. But multinational corporations and Third World governments alike consider assembly-line work—whether the product is Barbie dolls or missile parts—to be "women's work." 8

One reason is that women can, in many countries, still be legally paid less than men. But the sheer tedium of the jobs adds to the multinationals' preference for women workers—a preference made clear, for example, by this ad from a Mexican newspaper: *We need female workers; older than 17, younger than 30; single and without children; minimum education primary school, maximum education one year of preparatory school [high school]: available for all shifts.*

It's an article of faith with management that only women can do, or will do, the monotonous, painstaking work that American business is exporting to the Third World. Bill Mitchell, whose job is to attract United States businesses to the Bermudez Industrial Park in Ciudad Juárez told us with a certain macho pride: "A man just won't stay in this tedious kind of work. He'd walk out in a couple of hours." The personnel manager of a light assembly plant in Taiwan told anthropologist Linda Gail Arrigo: "Young male workers are too restless and impatient to do monotonous work with no career value. If displeased, they sabotage the machines and even threaten the foreman. But girls? At most, they cry a little."

In fact, the American businessmen we talked to claimed that Third World women genuinely enjoy doing the very things that would drive a man to assault and sabotage. "You should watch these kids going into work" Bill Mitchell told us. "You don't have any sullenness here. They smile." A top-level management consultant who specializes in advising American companies on where to relocate their factories gave us this global generalization: "The [factory] girls genuinely enjoy themselves. They're away from their families. They have spending money. They can buy motorbikes, whatever. Of course it's a regulated experience too—with dormitories to live in—so it's a healthful experience."

What is the real experience of the women in the emerging Third   12
World industrial work force? The conventional Western stereotypes leap
to mind: You can't really compare, the standards are so different. . . .
Everything's easier in warm countries. . . . They really don't have any
alternatives. . . . Commenting on the low wages his company pays its
women workers in Singapore, a Hewlett-Packard vice-president said,
"They live much differently here than we do. . . ." But the differences are
ultimately very simple. To start with, they have less money.

The great majority of the women in the new Third World work
force live at or near the subsistence level for one person, whether they
work for a multinational corporation or a locally owned factory. In the
Philippines, for example, starting wages in U.S.-owned electronics
plants are between $34 to $46 a month, compared to a cost of living of
$37 a month; in Indonesia the starting wages are actually about $7 a
month less than the cost of living. "Living," in these cases, should be
interpreted minimally: a diet of rice, dried fish, and water—a Coke
might cost a half-day's wages—lodging in a room occupied by four or
more other people. Rachael Grossman, a researcher with the Southeast
Asia Resource Center, found women employees of U.S. multinational
firms in Malaysia and the Philippines living four to eight in a room in
boardinghouses, or squeezing into tiny extensions built onto squatter
huts near the factory. Where companies do provide dormitories for
their employees, they are not of the "healthful," collegiate variety
implied by our corporate informant. Staff from the American Friends
Service Committee report that dormitory space is "likely to be crowded, with bed rotation paralleling shift rotation—while one shift works,
another sleeps, as many as twenty to a room." In one case in Thailand,
they found the dormitory "filthy," with workers forced to find their
own place to sleep among "splintered floorboards, rusting sheets of
metal, and scraps of dirty cloth."

Wages do increase with seniority, but the money does not go to pay
for studio apartments or, very likely, motorbikes. A 1970 study of young
women factory workers in Hong Kong found that 88 percent of them
were turning more than half their earnings over to their parents. In
areas that are still largely agricultural (such as parts of the Philippines
and Malaysia), or places where male unemployment runs high (such as
northern Mexico), a woman factory worker may be the sole source of
cash income for an entire extended family.

But wages on a par with what an 11-year-old American could earn
on a paper route, and living conditions resembling what Engels found
in nineteenth-century Manchester are only part of the story. The rest
begins at the factory gate. The work that multinational corporations
export to the Third World is not only the most tedious, but often the
most hazardous part of the production process. The countries they go
to are, for the most part, those that will guarantee no interference from

health and safety inspectors, trade unions, or even free-lance reformers. As a result, most Third World factory women work under conditions that already have broken or will break their health—or their nerves— within a few years, and often before they've worked long enough to earn any more than a subsistence wage.

Consider first the electronics industry, which is generally thought to be the safest and cleanest of the exported industries. The factory buildings are low and modern, like those one might find in a suburban American industrial park. Inside, rows of young women, neatly dressed in the company uniform or T-shirt, work quietly at their stations. There is air conditioning (not for the women's comfort, but to protect the delicate semiconductor parts they work with), and high-volume piped-in Bee Gees hits (not so much for entertainment, as to prevent talking).

For many Third World women, electronics is a prestige occupation, at least compared to other kinds of factory work. They are unlikely to know that in the United States the National Institute on Occupational Safety and Health (NIOSH) has placed electronics on its select list of "high health-risk industries using the greatest number of toxic substances." If electronics assembly work is risky here, it is doubly so in countries where there is no equivalent of NIOSH to even issue warnings. In many plants toxic chemicals and solvents sit in open containers, filling the work area with fumes that can literally knock you out. "We have been told of cases where ten to twelve women passed out at once," an AFSC field worker in northern Mexico told us, "and the newspapers report this as 'mass hysteria.'"

In one stage of the electronics assembly process, the workers have to dip the circuits into open vats of acid. According to Irene Johnson and Carol Bragg, who toured the National Semiconductor plant in Penang, Malaysia, the women who do the dipping "wear rubber gloves and boots, but these sometimes leak, and burns are common." Occasionally, whole fingers are lost. More commonly, what electronics workers lose is the 20/20 vision they are required to have when they are hired. Most electronics workers spend seven to nine hours a day peering through microscopes, straining to meet their quotas. One study in South Korea found that most electronics assembly workers developed severe eye problems after only one year of employment: 88 percent had chronic conjunctivitis; 44 percent became nearsighted; and 19 percent developed astigmatism. A manager for Hewlett-Packard's Malaysia plant, in an interview with Rachael Grossman, denied that there were any eye problems: "These girls are used to working with 'scopes.' We've found no eye problems. But it sure makes me dizzy to look through those things."

Electronics, recall, is the "cleanest" of the exported industries. Conditions in the garment and textile industry rival those of any nineteenth-century sweatshop. The firms, generally local subcontractors to

¹⁶ appears in the right margin beside the second paragraph.

large American chains such as J. C. Penney and Sears, as well as smaller manufacturers, are usually even more indifferent to the health of their employees than the multinationals. Some of the worst conditions have been documented in South Korea, where the garment and textile industries have helped spark that country's "economic miracle." Workers are packed into poorly lit rooms, where summer temperatures rise above 100 degrees. Textile dust, which can cause permanent lung damage, fills the air. When there are rush orders, management may require forced overtime of as much as 48 hours at a stretch, and if that seems to go beyond the limits of human endurance, pep pills and amphetamine injections are thoughtfully provided. In her diary (originally published in a magazine now banned by the South Korean government) Min Chong Suk, 30, a sewing-machine operator, wrote of working from 7 A.M. to 11:30 P.M. in a garment factory: "When [the apprentices] shake the waste threads from the clothes, the whole room fills with dust, and it is hard to breathe. Since we've been working in such dusty air, there have been increasing numbers of people getting tuberculosis, bronchitis, and eye diseases. Since we are women, it makes us so sad when we have pale, unhealthy, wrinkled faces like dried-up spinach. . . . It seems to me that no one knows our blood dissolves into the threads and seams, with sighs and sorrow."

In all the exported industries, the most invidious, inescapable [20] health hazard is stress. On their home ground United States corporations are not likely to sacrifice productivity for human comfort. On someone else's home ground, however, anything goes. Lunch breaks may be barely long enough for a woman to stand in line at the canteen or hawkers' stalls. Visits to the bathroom are treated as privilege; in some cases, workers must raise their hands for permission to use the toilet, and waits up to a half hour are common. Rotating shifts—the day shift one week, the night shift the next—wreak havoc with sleep patterns. Because inaccuracies or failure to meet production quotas can mean substantial pay losses, the pressures are quickly internalized; stomach ailments and nervous problems are not unusual in the multinationals' Third World female work force. In some situations, good work is as likely to be punished as slow or shoddy work. Correspondent Michael Flannery, writing for the AFL-CIO's *American Federationist*, tells the story of 23-year-old Basilia Altagracia, a seamstress who stitched collars onto ladies' blouses in the La Romana (Dominican Republic) free trade zone (a heavily guarded industrial zone owned by Gulf & Western Industries, Inc.):

"A nimble veteran seamstress, Miss Altagracia eventually began to earn as much as $5.75 a day. . . . 'I was exceeding my piecework quota by a lot.' . . . But then, Altagracia said, her plant supervisor, a Cuban emigré, called her into his office. 'He said I was doing a fine job, but that I and some other of the women were making too much money, and he was being forced to lower what we earned for each piece we sewed.' On the best days, she now can clear barely $3, she said. 'I was earning less, so I started working six and seven days a week. But I was tired and I could not work as fast as before.'" Within a few months, she was too ill to work at all.

As if poor health and the stress of factory life weren't enough to drive women into early retirement, management actually encourages a high turnover in many industries. "As you know, when seniority rises, wages rise," the management consultant to U.S. multinationals told us. He explained that it's cheaper to train a fresh supply of teenagers than to pay experienced women higher wages. "Older" women, aged 23 or 24, are likely to be laid off and not rehired.

We estimate, based on fragmentary data from several sources, that the multinational corporations may already have used up (cast off) as many as 6 million Third World workers—women who are too ill, too old (30 is over the hill in most industries), or too exhausted to be useful any more. Few "retire" with any transferable skills or savings. The lucky ones find husbands.

The unlucky ones find themselves at the margins of society—as bar girls, "hostesses," or prostitutes.   24

> At 21, Julie's greatest fear is that she will never be able to find a husband. She knows that just being a "factory girl" is enough to give anyone a bad reputation. When she first started working at the electronics company, her father refused to speak to her for three months. Now every time she leaves Penang to go back to visit her home village she has to put up with a lecture on morality from her older brother—not to mention a barrage of lewd remarks from men outside her family. If they knew that she had actually gone out on a few dates, that she had been to a discotheque, that she had once kissed a young man who said he was a student. . . . Julie's stomach tightens as she imagines her family's reaction. She tries to concentrate on the kind of man she would like to marry: an engineer or technician of some sort, someone who had been to California, where the company headquarters are located and where even the grandmothers wear tight pants and lipstick—someone who had a good attitude about women. But if she ends up having to wear glasses, like her cousin who worked three years at the "scopes," she might as well forget about finding anyone to marry her.

One of the most serious occupational hazards that Julie and millions of women like her may face is the lifelong stigma of having been a "factory girl." Most of the cultures favored by multinational corporations in their search for cheap labor are patriarchal in the grand old style: any young woman who is not under the wing of a father, husband, or older brother must be "loose." High levels of unemployment among men, as in Mexico, contribute to male resentment of working women. (Ironically, in some places the multinationals have increased male unemployment—for example, by paving over fishing and farming villages to make way for industrial parks.) Add to all this the fact that certain companies—American electronics firms are in the lead—actively promote Western-style sexual objectification as a means of insuring employee loyalty: there are company-sponsored cosmetics classes, "guess whose legs these are" contests, and swim-suit-style beauty contests where the prize might be a free night *for two* in a fancy hotel. Corporate-promoted Westernization only heightens the hostility many men feel toward any independent working women—having a job is bad enough, wearing jeans and mascara to work is going too far.

Anthropologist Patricia Fernandez, who has worked in a *maquiladora* herself, believes that the stigmatization of working women serves, indirectly, to keep them in line. "You have to think of the kind of socialization that girls experience in a very Catholic—or, for that matter, Muslim—society. The fear of having a 'reputation' is enough to make a lot of women bend over backward to be 'respectable' and ladylike, which is just what management wants." She points out that in northern Mexico, the tabloids delight in playing up stories of alleged vice in the *maquiladoras*—indiscriminate sex on the job, epidemics of venereal disease, fetuses found in factory rest rooms. "I worry about this because there are those who treat you differently as soon as they know you have a job at a *maquiladora*," one woman told Fernandez. "Maybe they think that if you have to work, there is a chance you're a whore."

And there is always a chance you'll wind up as one. Probably only   28
a small minority of Third World factory workers turn to prostitution when their working days come to an end. But it is, as for women everywhere, the employment of last resort, the only thing to do when the factories don't need you and traditional society won't—or, for economic reasons, can't—take you back. In the Philippines, the brothel business is expanding as fast as the factory system. If they can't use you one way, they can use you another.

Topics for Critical Thinking and Writing

1. Consider the title of the essay. When you first saw it, what connotations did "global assembly line" immediately suggest? Now that you have finished reading the essay, evaluate the title.
2. Before you read this essay, what was your image of the multinational corporation? Was it mostly positive, or negative, or neutral? To what extent has the article affected the way you think about multinational corporations? If, for example, you were offered a managerial job in a multinational, would you be inclined to ask questions about their employment practices abroad that you might not have asked before reading this article?
3. Paragraph 1, which gives us a quick portrait of Anna, tells us that "Anna's husband, frustrated by being unable to find work for himself, left for the United States six months ago." Why do the authors bother to include this detail? Is it in any way relevant to their thesis, or is it simply for human interest?
4. According to paragraph 10, management believes "that only women can do, or will do, the monotonous, painstaking work that American busi-

ness is exporting to the Third World." Do the authors of the essay believe this? Do you believe that women by nature,—or by training—are more suited than men "to do monotonous work with no career value"?

5. Paragraph 11 reports some statements businessman offer as reasons why Third World women supposedly enjoy their jobs. Do you think these reasons (or some of them) have any merit? Do paragraphs 12–14 and 17–21 adequately refute these reasons?

6. In paragraph 14 we learn that 88 percent of the young female workers in Hong Kong turned more than half of their wages over to their parents. What conclusions can one reasonably draw from this assertion?

7. Why do you suppose that Julie (paragraphs 2 and 26) works in a factory?

8. In paragraph 27 the author tells us that "high levels of unemployment among men, as in Mexico, contribute to male resentment of working women." Does this analysis strike you as probably true? If so, what do you think American business can do about the Mexican economy?

9. What is the effect of using the second person pronoun (*you*) in the final paragraph?

10. Given what you have read about the working conditions of women in Third World countries, when you buy your next sweater (or tennis racquet or calculator or whatever) will you reject products made in Third World countries?

John S. Fielden

John S. Fielden, formerly an associate editor of the Harvard Business Review*—the journal in which this essay first appeared—is now University Professor of Management at the University of Alabama.*

"What Do You Mean You Don't Like My Style"

In large corporations all over the country, people are playing a game of paddleball—with drafts of letters instead of balls. Volley after volley goes back and forth between those who sign the letters and those who actually write them. It's a game nobody likes, but it continues, and we pay for it. The workday has no extra time for such unproductiveness. What causes this round robin of revision?

Typos? Factual misstatements? Poor format? No. *Style* does. Ask yourself how often you hear statements like these:

"It takes new assistants about a year to learn my style. Until they do, I have no choice but to bounce letters back for revision. I won't sign a letter if it doesn't sound like me."

"I find it difficult, almost impossible, to write letters for my boss's signature. The boss's style is different from mine."

In companies where managers primarily write their own letters, confusion about style also reigns. Someone sends out a letter and hears later that the reaction was not at all the one desired. It is reported that the reader doesn't like the writer's "tone." A colleague looks over a copy of the letter and says, "No wonder the reader doesn't like this letter. You shouldn't have said things the way you did. You used the wrong style for a letter like this." "Style?" the writer says. "What's wrong with my style?" "I don't know" is the response. "I just don't like the way you said things."

Everybody talks about style, but almost nobody understands the meaning of the word in the business environment. And this lack of understanding hurts both those who write letters for another's signature and those who write for themselves. Neither knows where to turn for help. Strunk and White's marvelous book *The Elements of Style* devotes only a few pages to a discussion of style, and that concerns only literary style.[2] Books like the Chicago *Manual of Style*[3] seem to define style as all the technical points they cover, from abbreviations and capitalizations to footnotes and bibliographies. And dictionary definitions are usually too vague to be helpful.

Even such a general definition as this offers scant help, although perhaps it comes closest to how business people use the word:

> Style is "the way something is said or done, as distinguished from its substance."[4]

Managers signing drafts written by subordinates, and the subordinates themselves, already know that they have trouble agreeing on "the way things should be said." What, for instance, is meant by "way"? In trying to find that way, both managers and subordinates are chasing a will-o'-the-wisp. There is no magical way, no perfect, universal way of writing things that will fend off criticism of style. There *is* no one style of writing in business that is appropriate in all situations and for all readers, even though managers and subordinates usually talk and behave as if there were.

But why all the confusion? Isn't style really the way we say things? Certainly it is. Then writing style must be made up of the particular words we select to express our ideas and the types of sentences and paragraphs we put together to convey those ideas. What else could it be? Writing has no tone of voice or body gesture to impart additional meanings. In written communication, tone comes from what a reader reads into the words and sentences used.

---

[2]William Strunk, Jr., and E. B. White, *The Elements of Style* (New York: Macmillan, 1979).
[3]*A Manual of Style* (Chicago: University of Chicago Press, 1969).
[4]*The American Heritage Dictionary of the English Language* (Boston: American Heritage and Houghton Mifflin, 1969).

Words express more than *denotations*, the definitions found in dictionaries. They also carry *connotations*. In the feelings and images associated with each word lies the capacity a writing style has for producing an emotional reaction in a reader. And in that capacity lies the tone of a piece of writing. Style is largely a matter of tone. The writer uses a style; the reader infers a communication's tone. Tone comes from what a reader reads into the words and sentences a writer uses.

In the business environment, tone is especially important. Business writing is not literary writing. Literary artists use unique styles to "express" themselves to a general audience. Business people write to particular persons in particular situations, not so much to express themselves as to accomplish particular purposes, "to get a job done." If a reader doesn't like a novelist's tone, nothing much can happen to the writer short of failing to sell some books. In the business situation, however, an offensive style may not only prevent a sale but may also turn away a customer, work against a promotion, or even cost you a job.

While style can be distinguished from substance, it cannot be divorced from substance. In business writing, style cannot be divorced from the circumstances under which something is written or from the likes, dislikes, position, and power of the reader.

A workable definition of style in business writing would be something like this:

> Style is that choice of words, sentences, and paragraph format which by virtue of being appropriate to the situation and to the power positions of both writer and reader produces the desired reaction and result.

Let's take a case and see what we can learn from it. Assume that you are an executive in a very large information-processing company. You receive the following letter:

Mr. (Ms.) Leslie J. Cash
XYZ Corporation
Main Street
Anytown, U.S.A.

Dear Leslie:

As you know, I respect your professional opinion highly. The advice your people have given us at ABC Corporation as we have moved into a comprehensive information system over the past three years has been very helpful. I'm writing to you now, however, in my role as chairman of the executive committee of the trustees of our hospital. We at Community General Hospital have decided to establish a skilled volunteer data processing evaluation team to assess proposals to automate our hospital's information flow.

I have suggested your name to my committee. I know you could get real satisfaction from helping your community as a member of this evaluation team. Please say yes. I look forward to being able to count on your advice. Let me hear from you soon.

Frank J. Scalpel
Chairman
Executive Committee
Community General Hospital
Anytown, U.S.A.

If you accepted the appointment mentioned in this letter, you would have a conflict of interest. You are an executive at XYZ, Inc. You know that XYZ will submit a proposal to install a comprehensive information system for the hospital. Mr. Scalpel is the vice president of finance at ABC Corp., a very good customer of yours. You know him well since you have worked with him on community programs as well as in the business world.

I can think of four typical responses to Scalpel's letter. Each says essentially the same thing, but each is written in a different business style:

Response 1
Mr. Frank J. Scalpel
Chairman, Executive Committee
Community General Hospital
Anytown, U.S.A.

Dear Frank,

As you realize, this litigious age often makes it necessary for large companies to take stringent measures not only to avoid conflicts of interest on the part of their employees but also to preclude even the very suggestion of conflict. And, since my company intends to submit a proposal with reference to automating the hospital's information flow, it would not appear seemly for me to be part of an evaluation team assessing competitors' proposals. Even if I were to excuse myself from consideration of the XYZ proposal, I would still be vulnerable to charges that I gave short shrift to competitors' offerings.

   If there is any other way that I can serve the committee that will not raise this conflict-of-interest specter, you know that I would find it pleasurable to be of service, as always.

Sincerely,

Response 2

Dear Frank,

Your comments relative to your respect for my professional opinion are most appreciated. Moreover, your invitation to serve on the hospital's data processing evaluation team is received with gratitude, albeit with some concern.

The evaluation team must be composed of persons free of alliance with any of the vendors submitting proposals. For that reason, it is felt that my services on the team could be construed as a conflict of interest.

Perhaps help can be given in some other way. Again, please be assured that your invitation has been appreciated.

Sincerely,

Response 3

Dear Frank,

Thank you for suggesting my name as a possible member of your data processing evaluation team. I wish I could serve, but I cannot.

XYZ intends, naturally, to submit a proposal to automate the hospital's information flow. You can see the position of conflict I would be in if I were on the evaluation team.

Just let me know of any other way I can be of help. You know I would be more than willing. Thanks again for the invitation.

Cordially,

Response 4

Dear Frank,

Thanks for the kind words and the invitation. Sure wish I could say yes. Can't, though.

XYZ intends to submit a sure-fire proposal on automating the hospital's information. Shouldn't be judge and advocate at the same time!

Any other way I can help, Frank—just ask. Thanks again.

Cordially,

What Do You Think of These Letters?

Which letter has the style you like best? Check off the response you prefer.

Response   1   2   3   4
                  ☐   ☐   ☐   ☐

Which letter has the style resembling the one you customarily use? 16
Again, check off your choice.

Response   1   2   3   4
                  ☐   ☐   ☐   ☐

Which terms best describe the style of each letter? Check the appropriate boxes.

Response	☐ Colorful	☐ Passive	☐ Personal
1	☐ Dull	☐ Forceful	☐ Impersonal
Response	☐ Colorful	☐ Passive	☐ Personal
2	☐ Dull	☐ Forceful	☐ Impersonal

Response 3	☐ Colorful ☐ Dull	☐ Passive ☐ Forceful	☐ Personal ☐ Impersonal
Response 4	☐ Colorful ☐ Dull	☐ Passive ☐ Forceful	☐ Personal ☐ Impersonal

Let's Compare Reactions

Now that you've given your reactions, let's compare them with some of mine.

Response 1 seems cold, impersonal, complex. Most business people would, I think, react somewhat negatively to this style because it seems to push the reader away from the writer. Its word choice has a cerebral quality that, while flattering to the reader's intelligence, also parades the writer's.

Response 2 is fairly cool, quite impersonal, and somewhat complex. Readers' reactions will probably be neither strongly positive nor strongly negative. This style of writing is "blah" because it is heavily passive. Instead of saying "I appreciate your comments," it says "Your comments are most appreciated"; instead of "I think that my service could be construed as a conflict of interest," it says "It is felt that my service could be construed. . . ." The use of the passive voice subordinates writers modestly to the back of sentences or causes them to disappear.

This is the impersonal, passive style of writing that many with engineering, mathematics, or scientific backgrounds feel most comfortable using. It is harmless, but it is certainly not colorful; nor is it forceful or interesting.

Response 3 illustrates the style of writing that most high-level executives use. It is simple; it is personal; it is warm without being syrupy; it is forceful, like a firm handshake. Almost everybody in business likes this style, although lower-level managers often find themselves afraid to write so forthrightly (and, as a result, often find themselves retreating into the styles of responses 1 and 2—the style of 1 to make themselves look "smart" to superiors and the style of 2 to appear unbossy and fairly impersonal). Persons who find response 2 congenial may feel a bit dubious about the appropriateness of response 3. (Although I have no way of proving this judgment, I would guess that more readers in high positions—perhaps more owner-managers—would like response 3 than would readers who are still in lower positions.)

Response 4 goes beyond being forceful; it is annoyingly self-confident and breezy. It is colorful and conversational to an extreme, and it is so intensely personal and warm that many business people would be offended, even if they were very close acquaintances of Frank Scalpel's. "It sounds like an advertising person's chitchat," some would probably say.

As you compared your responses with mine, did you say, "What difference does it make which style *I* like or which most resembles *my* customary style? What matters is which style will go over best with Mr. Scalpel in this situation"? If you did, we're getting somewhere.

Earlier, when we defined business writing style, some may have wanted to add, "And that style should sound like me." This was left out for a good reason. Circumstances not only alter cases; they alter the "you" that it is wise for your style to project. Sometimes it's wise to be forceful; at other times it's suicidal. Sometimes being sprightly and colorful is appropriate; at other times it's ludicrous. There are times to be personal and times to be impersonal.

Not understanding this matter of style and tone is why the big corporation game of paddleball between managers and subordinates goes on and on. The subordinate tries to imitate the boss's style, but in actuality—unless the boss is extremely insensitive—he or she has no single style for all circumstances and for all readers. What usually happens is that after several tries, the subordinate writes a letter that the boss signs. "Aha!" the subordinate says. "So that's what the boss wants!" And then the subordinate tries to use that style for all situations and readers. Later, the superior begins rejecting drafts written in the very style he or she professed liking before. Both parties throw up their hands.

This volleying is foolish and wasteful. Both superior and subordinate have to recognize that in business writing, style cannot be considered apart from the given situation or from the person to whom the writing is directed. Expert writers select the style that fits a particular reader and the type of writing situation with which they are faced. In business, people often face the following writing situations:

Positive situations.
Saying yes or conveying good news.

Situations where some action is asked of the reader.
Giving orders or persuading someone to do as requested.

Information-conveying situations.
Giving the price of ten widgets, for example.

Negative situations.
Saying no or relaying bad news.

In each of these situations, the choice of style is of strategic importance.

In positive situations, a writer can relax on all fronts. Readers are usually so pleased to hear the good news that they pay little attention to anything else. Yet it is possible for someone to communicate good news in such a cold, impersonal, roundabout, and almost begrudging way that the reader becomes upset.

Action-request situations involve a form of bargaining. In a situation where the writer holds all the power, he or she can use a forceful commanding style. When the writer holds no power over the reader, though, actions have to be asked for and the reader persuaded, not ordered. In such cases, a forceful style will not be suitable at all.

In information-conveying situations, getting the message across forcefully and straightforwardly is best. Such situations are not usually charged emotionally.

In negative situations, diplomacy becomes very important. The 32 right style depends on the relative positions of the person saying no and the person being told no.

For instance, if you were Leslie Cash, the person in the example at the beginning of the article whom Frank Scalpel was inviting to serve on a hospital's evaluation team, you would be in a situation of having to say no to a very important customer of your company. You would also be in a doubly sensitive situation because it is unlikely that Mr. Scalpel would fail to recognize that he is asking you to enter a conflict-of-interest situation. He is probably asking you *anyway*. Therefore, you would not only have to tell him no, but you would have to avoid telling him that he has asked you to do something that is highly unethical. In this instance, you would be faced with communicating two negative messages at once or else not giving Scalpel any sensible reason for refusing to serve.

Now that we've thought about the strategic implications of style, let's go back to look at each of the responses to Scalpel's request and ask ourselves which is best.

Do we *want* to be personal and warm? Usually yes. But in this situation? Do we want to communicate clearly and directly and forcefully? Usually yes. But here? Do we want to appear as if we're brushing aside the conflict, as the third response does? Or do we want to approach that issue long-windedly, as in the first response, or passively, as in the second? What is the strategically appropriate style?

In the abstract, we have no way of knowing which of these respons- 36 es will go over best with Mr. Scalpel. The choice is a matter of judgment in a concrete situation. Judging the situation accurately is what separates successful from unsuccessful executive communicators.

Looking at the situation with strategy in mind, we note that in the first response, the writer draws back from being close, knowing that it is necessary to reject not only one but two of the reader's requests. By using legalistic phraseology and Latinate vocabulary, the writer lowers the personal nature of the communication and transforms it into a formal statement. It gives an abstract, textbook-like response that removes the tone of personal rejection.

The very fact that response 1 is difficult to read and dull in impact may be a strategic asset in this type of negative situation. But if in this situation a subordinate presented response 1 to you for your signature, would it be appropriate for you to reject it because it is not written in the style *you* happen to *like* best in the abstract—say, the style of response 3?

Now let's look at response 2. Again, we see that a lack of personal warmth may be quite appropriate to the situation at hand. Almost immediately, the letter draws back into impersonality. And by using the passive constantly, the writer avoids the need to say "I must say no." Furthermore, the term *construed* reinforces the passive in the second paragraph. This term is a very weak but possibly a strategically wise way of implying that *some* persons (*other* people, not the writer) could interpret Scalpel's request as an invitation to participate in an improper action. Now we can see that, instead of seeming dull and lacking in personal warmth as it did in the abstract, response 2 may be the type of letter we would be wise to send out, that is, when we have taken the whole situation into careful consideration and not just our personal likes and dislikes.

The third response, and to even greater extent the fourth, have 40
styles that are strategically inappropriate for this situation. In fact, Scalpel might well regard the colorful style of the fourth response as highly offensive. Both responses directly and forcefully point out the obvious conflict, but by being so direct each runs the risk of subtly offending him. (The third response is "you can see the position of conflict I'd be in if I were on the evaluation team," and the fourth is "Shouldn't be judge and advocate at the same time!") We could make a pretty strong argument that the direct, forceful, candid style of the third response and the breezy, warm, colorful, intensely personal "advertising" style of the fourth response may both prove ineffectual in a delicate, negative situation such as this.

At this point, readers may say, "All right. I'm convinced. I need to adjust my style to what is appropriate in each situation. And I also need to give directions to others to let them know how to adjust their styles. But I haven't the foggiest notion of how to do either!" Some suggestions for varying your writing style follow. I am not implying that a communication must be written in one style only. A letter to be read aloud at a colleague's retirement party, for instance, may call not only for a warm, personal style but for colorfulness as well. A long analytic report may require a passive, impersonal style, but the persuasive cover letter may call for recommendations being presented in a very forceful style.

For a Forceful Style

This style is usually appropriate only in situations where the writer has the power, such as in action requests in the form of orders or when you are saying no firmly but politely to a subordinate.

Use the active voice. Have your sentences do something to people and to objects, not just lie there having things done to them;

have them give orders: "Correct this error immediately" (you-understood is the subject) instead of "A correction should be made" (which leaves the reader wondering, made by whom).

Step up front and be counted: "I have decided not to recommend you for promotion" instead of "Unfortunately, a positive recommendation for your promotion is not forthcoming."

Do not beat around the bush or act like a politician. If something needs to be said, say it directly.

Write most of your sentences in subject-verb-object order. Do not weaken them by putting namby-pamby phrases before the subject: "I have decided to fund your project" instead of "After much deliberation and weighing of the pros and cons, I have decided to fund your project."

Do not weaken sentences by relegating the point or the action to a subordinate clause: If your point is that your company has won a contract, say "Acme won the contract, although the bidding was intense and highly competitive," not "Although Acme won the contract, the bidding was intense and highly competitive."

Adopt a tone of confidence and surety about what you say by avoiding weasel words like: "Possibly," "maybe," "perhaps," "It could be concluded that . . . " "Some might conclude that . . . "

For a Passive Style

This style is often appropriate in negative situations and in situations where the writer is in a lower position than the reader.

Avoid the imperative—never give an order: Say "A more effective and time-conserving presentation of ideas should be devised before our next meeting" as opposed to "Do a better job of presenting your ideas at our next meeting. Respect my time and get right to the point."

Use the passive voice heavily because it subordinates the subject to the end of the sentence or buries the subject entirely. The passive is especially handy when you are in a low-power position and need to convey negative information to a reader who is in a higher position (an important customer, for instance): Say "Valuable resources are being wasted" instead of "Valuable resources are being wasted by your company" or, even worse, "You are wasting valuable resources."

Avoid taking responsibility for negative statements by attributing them to faceless, impersonal "others": Say "It is more than possible that several objections to your proposed plans might be raised by some observers" or "Several objections might be raised by those hostile to your plans" instead of "I have several objections to your plans."

Use weasel words, especially if the reader is in a high-power position and will not like what you are saying.

Use long sentences and heavy paragraphs to slow down the reader's comprehension of sensitive or negative information.

For a Personal Style

This style is usually appropriate in good-news and persuasive action-request situations.

Use the active voice, which puts you, as the writer, at the front of sentences: "Thank you very much for your comments" or "I appreciated your comments" instead of "Your comments were very much appreciated by me" or the even more impersonal "Your comments were very much appreciated."

Use persons' names (first names, when appropriate) instead of referring to them by title: "Bill James attended the meeting" instead of "Acme's director attended the meeting."

Use personal pronouns—especially "you" and "I"—when you are saying positive things: "I so much appreciate the work you've done" as opposed to "The work you've done is appreciated."

Use short sentences that capture the rhythm of ordinary conversation: "I discussed your proposal with Frank. He's all for it!" as opposed to "This is to inform you that your proposal was taken up at Friday's meeting and that it was regarded with favor."

Use contractions ("can't," "won't," "shouldn't") to sound informal and conversational.

Direct questions to the reader: "Just ask yourself, how would your company like to save $10,000?"

Interject positive personal thoughts and references that will make the reader know that this letter is really to him or her and not some type of form letter sent to just anyone.

For an Impersonal Style

This style is usually appropriate in negative and information-conveying situations. It's always appropriate in technical and scientific writing and usually when you are writing to technical readers.

Avoid using persons' names, especially first names. Refer to people, if at all, by title or job description: "I would like to know what you think of this plan" instead of "What do you think of this, Herb?" "Our vice president of finance" or "the finance department," not "Ms. Jones."

Avoid using personal pronouns, especially "you" and "I" ("we" may be all right because the corporate we is faceless and impersonal): "The logistics are difficult, and the idea may not work" instead of "I think you have planned things so that the logistics are difficult and your idea may not work." "We wonder if the idea will work" rather than "I don't think the idea will work."

Use the passive voice to make yourself conveniently disappear when desirable: "An error in the calculations has been made" instead of "I think your calculations are wrong."

Make some of your sentences complex and some paragraphs long; avoid the brisk, direct, simple-sentence style of conversation.

For a Colorful Style

Sometimes a lively style is appropriate in good-news situations. It is most commonly found in the highly persuasive writing of advertisements and sales letters.

Insert some adjectives and adverbs: Instead of "This proposal will save corporate resources," write "This (hard-hitting) (productivity-building) (money-saving) proposal will (easily) (surely) (quickly) (immediately) save our (hard-earned) (increasingly scarce) (carefully guarded) corporate resources."

If appropriate, use a metaphor (A is B) or a simile (A is like B) to make a point: "Truly this program is a miracle of logical design." "Our solution strikes at the very root of Acme's problems." "This program is like magic in its ability to. . . ."

For a Less Colorful Style

By avoiding adjectives, adverbs, metaphors, and figures of speech, you can make your style less colorful. Such a style is appropriate for ordinary business writing and also results from:

Blending the impersonal style with the passive style.

Employing words that remove any semblance of wit, liveliness, and vigor from the writing.

Please bear in mind that these six styles are not mutually exclusive. 48
There is some overlap. A passive style is usually far more impersonal than personal and also not very colorful. A forceful style is likely to be

more personal than impersonal, and a colorful style is likely to be fairly forceful. Nevertheless, these styles are distinct enough to justify talking about them. If we fail to make such distinctions, style becomes a catchall term that means nothing specific. Even if not precise, these distinctions enable us to talk about style and its elements and to learn to write appropriately for each situation.

What conclusions can we draw from this discussion? Simply that, whether you write your own letters or have to manage the writing of subordinates, to be an effective communicator, you must realize that:

1. Each style has an impact on the reader.
2. Style communicates to readers almost as much as the content of a message.
3. Style cannot be isolated from a situation.
4. Generalizing about which style is the best in all situations is impossible.
5. Style must be altered to suit the circumstances.
6. Style must be discussed sensibly in the work situation.

These conclusions will be of obvious help to managers who write their own letters. But what help will these conclusions be to managers who direct assistants in the writing of letters? In many instances, writing assignments go directly to subordinates for handling. Often, manager and assistant have no chance to discuss style strategy together. In such cases, rather than merely submitting a response for a signature, the subordinate would be wise to append a note: e.g., "This is a very sensitive situation, I think. Therefore, I deliberately drew back into a largely impersonal and passive style." At least, the boss will not jump to the conclusion that the assistant has written a letter of low impact by accident.

When they do route writing assignments to assistants, superiors could save much valuable time and prevent mutual distress if they told the subordinates what style seemed strategically wise in each situation. Playing guessing games also wastes money.

And if, as is often the case, neither superior nor subordinate has a clear sense of what style is best, the two can agree to draft a response in one style first, and if that doesn't sound right, to adjust the style appropriately. 52

Those who write their own letters can try drafting several responses to tough but important situations, each in a different style. It's wise to sleep on them and then decide which sounds best.

Whether you write for yourself or for someone else, it is extremely unlikely that in difficult situations a first draft will be signed by you or anyone else. Only the amateur expects writing perfection on the first try. By learning to control your style and to engineer the tone of your communications, you can make your writing effective.

Topics for Critical Thinking and Writing

1. Characterize the style of Fielden's first two paragraphs. (His essay, of course, says much about style, but for a brief additional discussion of style you may wish to consult page 801 in the glossary.)
2. In paragraph 11 Fielden offers what he calls a "workable definition of style in business writing." Do you find this definition workable for other forms of writing as well—for example, term papers, editorials in the school newspaper, love letters? Why, or why not?
3. If you disagree with Fielden's analysis of any of the four letters Leslie Cash drafts to send to Frank Scalpel, explain the basis of your disagreement.
4. Many textbooks urge students to avoid using the passive voice, but in paragraph 43 Fielden says that the passive "is often appropriate in negative situations and in situations where the writer is in a lower position than the reader." Look at his examples and then evaluate his advice.
5. This essay appeared in the *Harvard Business Review* and has been one of its most popular reprints. Explain why, in your opinion, it has been popular, or why you find its popularity surprising.
6. Let's assume that Cash sent Scalpel the third letter. You are Scalpel; write a letter to Cash acknowledging receipt of Cash's letter. In fact, write two letters, one a poor letter and one a good letter.
7. In discussing "strategy," Fielden writes in paragraph 25: "Sometimes it's wise to be forceful; at other times it's suicidal. Sometimes being sprightly and colorful is appropriate; at other times it's ludicrous. There are times to be personal and times to be impersonal." Try to recall examples from your own experience (whether writing or speaking) that illustrate one or more of these circumstances. Then write a paragraph combining Fielden's sentence (which you should feel free to modify) with your illustration of it.

W. H. Auden

W[ystan] H[ugh] Auden (1907–73) was born and educated in England. In 1939 he came to the United States and later became an American citizen; but in 1972 he returned to England to live. Auden established his reputation chiefly with his poetry, but he also wrote plays, libretti, and essays (we include two of his essays in this book), all bearing the stamp of his highly original mind.

The Unknown Citizen
(To JS/O7/M/378 This Marble Monument Is Erected by the State)

He was found by the Bureau of Statistics to be
One against whom there was no official complaint,
And all the reports on his conduct agree
That, in the modern sense of an old-fashioned word, he was a saint,   4

For in everything he did he served the Greater Community.
Except for the War till the day he retired
He worked in a factory and never got fired,
But satisfied his employers, Fudge Motors Inc.   8
Yet he wasn't a scab or odd in his views,
For his Union reports that he paid his dues,
(Our report on his Union shows it was sound)
And our Social Psychology workers found   12
That he was popular with his mates and liked a drink.
The press are convinced that he bought a paper every day
And that his reactions to advertisements were normal in every way.
Policies taken out in his name prove that he was fully insured,   16
And his Health-card shows he was once in hospital but left it cured.
Both Producers Research and High-Grade Living declare
He was fully sensible to the advantages of the Installment Plan
And had everything necessary to the Modern Man,   20
A phonograph, radio, a car and a frigidaire.
Our researchers into Public Opinion are content
That he held the proper opinions for the time of year;
When there was peace, he was for peace; when there was war, he   24
    went.
He was married and added five children to the population,
Which our Eugenist says was the right number for a parent of his
    generation,
And our teachers report that he never interfered with their educa-
    tion.
Was he free? Was he happy? The question is absurd: 28
Had anything been wrong, we should certainly have heard.

Topics for Critical Thinking and Writing

1. Who is the speaker, and on what occasion is he supposed to be
    speaking?
2. What do the words "The Unknown Citizen" suggest to you?
3. How does Auden suggest that he doesn't share the attitudes of the
    speaker and is, in fact, satirizing them? What else does he satirize?
4. If Auden were writing the poem today, what might he substitute for
    "Installment Plan" in line 19 and the items listed in line 21?
5. Explicate the last two lines.
6. Write a tribute to The Unknown Student or The Unknown Professor or
    Politician or Professional Athlete or some other object of your well-
    deserved scorn.

10
MESSAGES

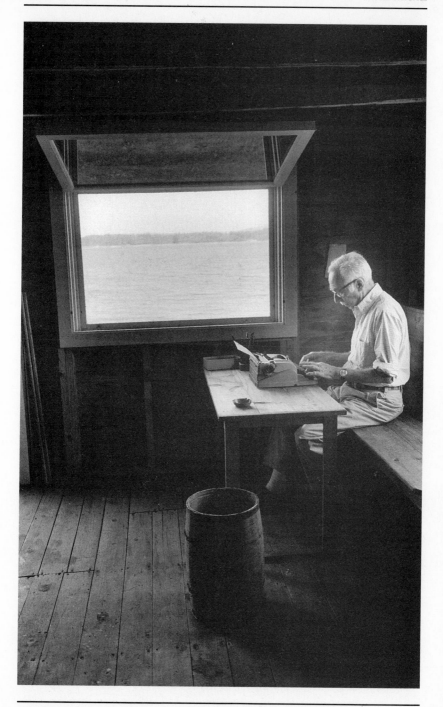

Photograph © 1976 by Jill Krementz

Washoe Makes the Sign for "Drink"
T. J. Kaminski

Courtesy R. A. and B. T. Gardner

Just what is it that makes today's homes so different, so appealing?
Richard Hamilton, 1956

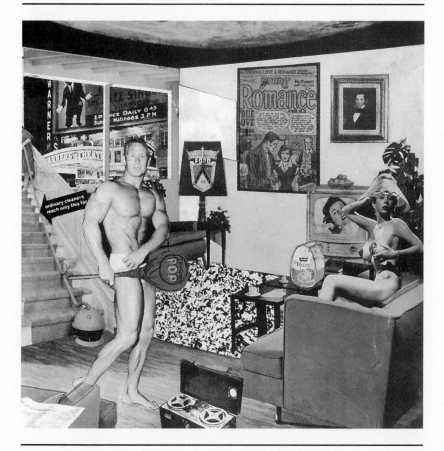

Courtesy of Kunsthalle Tubingen, Germany. Collection of Prof. Dr. Georg Zundel

Short Views

Men . . . employ speech only to conceal their thoughts.
Voltaire

We must be as clear as our natural reticence allows us to be.
Marianne Moore

To change your language you must change your life.
Derek Walcott

If you saw a bullet hit a bird, and he told you he wasn't shot, you might weep at his courtesy, but you would certainly doubt his word.
Emily Dickinson

Language is political. That's why you and me, my Brother and Sister, that's why we sposed to choke our natural self into the weird, lying, barbarous, unreal, white speech and writing habits that the schools lay down like holy law. Because, in other words, the powerful don't play; they mean to keep that power, and those who are the powerless (you and me) better shape up—mimic/ape/suck—in the very image of the powerful, or the powerful will destroy you—you and our children.
June Jordan

While I am thinking about metaphor, a flock of purple finches arrives on the lawn. Since I haven't seen these birds for some years, I am only fairly sure of their being in fact purple finches, so I get down Peterson's *Field Guide* and read his description: "Male: About size of House Sparrow, rosy-red, brightest on head and rump." That checks quite well, but his next remark—"a sparrow dipped in raspberry juice," is decisive: it fits. I look out the window again, and now I know that I am seeing purple finches.
Howard Nemerov

We will understand the world, and preserve ourselves and our values in it, only insofar as we have a language that is alert and responsive to it, and careful of it. I mean that literally. When we give our plows such brand names as "Sod Blaster," we are imposing on their use conceptual limits which raise the likelihood that they will be used destructively. When we speak of man's "war against nature," or of a "peace offensive," we are accepting the limitations of a metaphor that suggests, and even proposes, violent solutions. When students ask for the right of "participatory input" at the meetings of a faculty organization, they are thinking of democratic process, but they are *speaking* of a convocation of robots, and are thus devaluing the very traditions that they invoke.

Wendell Berry

Sticks and stones will break my bones, but words will never hurt me.

Anonymous

Language both reflects and shapes society. The textbook on American government that consistently uses male pronouns for the president, even when not referring to a specific individual (e.g., "a president may cast his veto"), reflects the fact that all our presidents have so far been men. But it also shapes a society in which the idea of a female president somehow "doesn't sound right."

Rosalie Maggio

I keep six honest serving men
(They taught me all I knew);
Their names are What and Why and When
And How and Where and Who.

Rudyard Kipling

The search is for the just word, the happy phrase, that will give expression to the thought, but somehow the thought itself is transfigured by the phrase when found.

Benjamin Cardozo

"Wild and Free." An American dream-phrase loosing images: a long-maned stallion racing across the grasslands, a V of Canada Geese high and honking, a squirrel chattering and leaping limb to limb overhead in an oak. It also sounds like an ad for a Harley-Davidson. Both words, profoundly political and sensitive as they are, have become consumer baubles.

Gary Snyder

The current flows fast and furious. It issues in a spate of words from the loudspeakers and the politicians. Every day they tell us that we are a free people fighting to defend freedom. That is the current that has whirled the young airman up into the sky and keeps him circulating there among the clouds. Down here, with a roof to cover us and a gasmask handy, it is our business to punctuate gasbags and discover the seeds of truth.

Virginia Woolf (writing in 1940)

Abraham Lincoln

Abraham Lincoln (1809–65), sixteenth president of the United States, is not usually thought of as a writer, but his published speeches and writings comprise about 1,078,000 words, the equivalent of about four thousand pages of double-spaced typing. They were all composed without the assistance of a speech writer.

The Gettysburg campaign—a series of battles fought near Gettysburg in southeastern Pennsylvania—took place in June and July of 1863. Each side lost something like twenty-three thousand men. The battle is regarded as a turning point in the war, but the Confederate army escaped and the war continued until April, 1865.

On November 19, 1863, Lincoln delivered a short speech (printed below) at the dedication of a national cemetery on the battlefield at Gettysburg.

Address at the Dedication of the Gettysburg National Cemetery

Four score and seven years ago our fathers brought forth on this continent, a new nation, conceived in Liberty, and dedicated to the proposition that all men are created equal.

Now we are engaged in a great civil war; testing whether that nation, or any nation so conceived and so dedicated, can long endure. We are met on a great battlefield of that war. We have come to dedicate a portion of that field as a final resting-place for those who here gave their lives that that nation might live. It is altogether fitting and proper that we should do this.

But, in a larger sense, we cannot dedicate—we cannot consecrate—we cannot hallow—this ground. The brave men, living and dead, who struggled here have consecrated it, far above our poor power to add or detract. The world will little note, nor long remember, what we say here, but it can never forget what they did here. It is for us the living, rather, to be dedicated here to the unfinished work which they who fought here have thus far so nobly advanced. It is rather for us to be here dedicated to the great task remaining before us—that from these honored dead we take increased devotion to that cause for which they gave the last full measure of devotion; that we here highly resolve that these dead shall not have died in vain; that this nation, under God, shall have a new birth of freedom; and that government of the people, by the people, for the people, shall not perish from the earth.

Gilbert Highet

Gilbert Highet (1906–78) was born in Glasgow, Scotland, and was educated at Glasgow University and at Oxford University. In 1937 he came to the United States, and in 1951 he was naturalized. Until his retirement in 1972 he taught Latin, Greek, and comparative literature at Columbia University. In addition to writing scholarly studies of classical authors, he wrote several general and more popular books.

The Gettysburg Address

Fourscore and seven years ago. . . .

These five words stand at the entrance to the best-known monument of American prose, one of the finest utterances in the entire language, and surely one of the greatest speeches in all history. Greatness is like granite: it is molded in fire, and it lasts for many centuries.

Fourscore and seven years ago. . . . It is strange to think that President Lincoln was looking back to the 4th of July 1776, and that he and his speech are now further removed from us than he himself was from George Washington and the Declaration of Independence. Fourscore and seven years before the Gettysburg Address, a small group of patriots signed the Declaration. Fourscore and seven years after the Gettysburg Address, it was the year 1950, and that date is already receding rapidly into our troubled, adventurous, and valiant past.

Inadequately prepared and at first scarcely realized in its full importance, the dedication of the graveyard at Gettysburg was one of the supreme moments of American history. The battle itself had been a turning point of the war. On the 4th of July 1863, General Meade repelled Lee's invasion of Pennsylvania. Although he did not follow up his victory, he had broken one of the most formidable aggressive enterprises of the Confederate armies. Losses were heavy on both sides. Thousands of dead were left on the field, and thousands of wounded died in the hot days following the battle. At first, their burial was more or less haphazard; but thoughtful men gradually came to feel that an adequate burying place and memorial were required. These were established by an interstate commission that autumn, and the finest speaker in the North was invited to dedicate them. This was the scholar and statesman Edward Everett of Harvard. He made a good speech—which is still extant: not at all academic, it is full of close strategic analysis and deep historical understanding.

Lincoln was not invited to speak, at first. Although people knew him as an effective debater, they were not sure whether he was capable of making a serious speech on such a solemn occasion. But one of the impressive things about Lincoln's career is that he constantly strove to *grow.* He was anxious to appear on that occasion and to say something worthy of it. (Also, it has been suggested, he was anxious to remove the impression that he did not know how to behave properly—an impression which had been strengthened by a shocking story about his clowning on the battlefield of Antietam the previous year.) Therefore when he was invited he took considerable care with his speech. He drafted rather more than half of it in the White House before leaving, finished it in the hotel at Gettysburg the night before the ceremony (not in the train, as sometimes reported), and wrote a fair copy next morning.

There are many accounts of the day itself, 19 November 1863. There are many descriptions of Lincoln, all showing the same curious blend of grandeur and awkwardness, or lack of dignity, or—it would be best to call it humility. In the procession he rode horseback: a tall lean man in a high plug hat, straddling a short horse, with his feet too near the ground. He arrived before the chief speaker, and had to wait patiently for half an hour or more. His own speech came right at the end of a long and exhausting ceremony, lasted less than three minutes, and made little impression on the audience. In part this was because they were tired, in part because (as eyewitnesses said) he ended almost before they knew he had begun, and in part because he did not speak the Address, but read it, very slowly, in a thin high voice, with a marked Kentucky accent, pronouncing "to" as "toe" and dropping his final R's.

Some people of course were alert enough to be impressed. Everett congratulated him at once. But most of the newspapers paid little attention to the speech, and some sneered at it. The *Patriot and Union* of Harrisburg wrote, "We pass over the silly remarks of the President; for the credit of the nation we are willing . . . that they shall no more be repeated or thought of"; and the London *Times* said, "The ceremony was rendered ludicrous by some of the sallies of that poor President Lincoln," calling his remarks "dull and commonplace." The first commendation of the Address came in a single sentence of the Chicago *Tribune,* and the first discriminating and detailed praise of it appeared in the Springfield *Republican,* the Providence *Journal,* and the Philadelphia *Bulletin.* However, three weeks after the ceremony and then again the following spring, the editor of *Harper's Weekly* published a sincere and thorough eulogy of the Address, and soon it was attaining recognition as a masterpiece.

At the time, Lincoln could not care much about the reception of his   8
words. He was exhausted and ill. In the train back to Washington, he
lay down with a wet towel on his head. He had caught smallpox. At
that moment he was incubating it, and he was stricken down soon after
he re-entered the White House. Fortunately it was a mild attack, and it
evoked one of his best jokes: he told his visitors, "At last I have something I can give to everybody."

He had more than that to give to everybody. He was a unique person, far greater than most people realize until they read his life with
care. The wisdom of his policy, the sources of his statesmanship—these
were things too complex to be discussed in a brief essay. But we can say
something about the Gettysburg Address as a work of art.[1]

A work of art. Yes: for Lincoln was a literary artist, trained both by
others and by himself. The textbooks he used as a boy were full of difficult exercises and skillful devices in formal rhetoric, stressing the
qualities he practiced in his own speaking: antithesis, parallelism, and
verbal harmony. Then he read and reread many admirable models of
thought and expression: the King James Bible, the essays of Bacon, the
best plays of Shakespeare. His favorites were *Hamlet, Lear, Macbeth,
Richard III,* and *Henry VIII,* which he had read dozens of times. He
loved reading aloud, too, and spent hours reading poetry to his friends.
(He told his partner Herndon that he preferred getting the sense of any
document by reading it aloud.) Therefore his serious speeches are
important parts of the long and noble classical tradition of oratory
which begins in Greece, runs through Rome to the modern world, and
is still capable (if we do not neglect it) of producing masterpieces.

The first proof of this is that the Gettysburg Address is full of quotations—or rather of adaptations—which give it strength. It is partly
religious, partly (in the highest sense) political: therefore it is interwoven with memories of the Bible and memories of American history. The
first and the last words are Biblical cadences. Normally Lincoln did not
say "fourscore" when he meant eighty; but on this solemn occasion he
recalled the important dates in the Bible—such as the age of Abraham
when his first son was born to him, and he was "fourscore and six years
old." Similarly, he did not say there was a chance that democracy might
die out: he recalled the somber phrasing in the Book of Job—where Bil-
dad speaks of the destruction of one who shall vanish without a trace,
and says that "his branch shall be cut off; his remembrance shall perish
from the earth." Then again, the famous description of our State as
"government of the people, by the people, for the people" was adum-
brated by Daniel Webster in 1830 (he spoke of "the people's government, made for the people, made by the people, and answerable to the

[1]For further reference, see W. E. Barton, *Lincoln at Gettysburg* (Indianapolis: Bobbs-Merrill,
1930); R. P. Basler, "Abraham Lincoln's Rhetoric," *American Literature* 11 (1939–40),
167–82; and L. E. Robinson, *Abraham Lincoln as a Man of Letters* (Chicago, 1918).

people") and then elaborated in 1854 by the abolitionist Theodore Parker (as "government of all the people, by all the people, for all the people"). There is good reason to think that Lincoln took the important phrase "under God" (which he interpolated at the last moment) from Weems, the biographer of Washington; and we know that it had been used at least once by Washington himself.

Analyzing the Address further, we find that it is based on a highly   12
imaginative theme, or group of themes. The subject is—how can we put it so as not to disfigure it?—the subject is the kinship of life and death, that mysterious linkage which we see sometimes as the physical succession of birth and death in our world, sometimes as the contrast, which is perhaps a unity, between death and immortality. The first sentence is concerned with birth:

> Our *fathers brought forth a new* nation, *conceived* in liberty.

The final phrase but one expresses the hope that

> this nation, under God, shall have a *new birth* of freedom.

And that last phrase of all speaks of continuing life as the triumph over death. Again and again throughout the speech, this mystical contrast and kinship reappear: "those who *gave their lives* that that nation might *live*," "the brave men *living* and *dead*," and so in the central assertion that the dead have already consecrated their own burial place, while "it is for us, the *living*, rather to be dedicated . . . to the great task remaining." The Gettysburg Address is a prose poem; it belongs to the same world as the great elegies, and the adagios of Beethoven.

Its structure, however, is that of a skillfully contrived speech. The oratorical pattern is perfectly clear. Lincoln describes the occasion, dedicates the ground, and then draws a larger conclusion by calling on his hearers to dedicate themselves to the preservation of the Union. But within that, we can trace his constant use of at least two important rhetorical devices.

The first of these is *antithesis:* opposition, contrast. The speech is full of it. Listen:

The world will little	*note*		
nor long	*remember*	what	*we say* here
but it can never	*forget*	what	*they did* here

And so in nearly every sentence: "brave men, *living* and *dead*"; "to *add* or *detract*." There is the antithesis of the Founding Fathers and men of Lincoln's own time:

> Our *fathers brought forth* a new nation . . .
> now *we* are testing whether that nation . . . can *long endure.*

And there is the more terrible antithesis of those who have already died and those who still live to do their duty. Now, antithesis is the figure of contrast and conflict. Lincoln was speaking in the midst of a great civil war.

The other important pattern is different. It is technically called *tricolon*—the division of an idea into three harmonious parts, usually of increasing power. The most famous phrase of the Address is a tricolon:

> government of the people
> >   by the people
> >   for the people.

The most solemn sentence is a tricolon:

> we cannot dedicate
>
> we cannot consecrate
>
> we cannot hallow   this ground.

And above all, the last sentence (which has sometimes been criticized as too complex) is essentially two parallel phrases, with a tricolon growing out of the second and then producing another tricolon: a trunk, three branches, and a cluster of flowers. Lincoln says that it is for his hearers to be dedicated to the great task remaining before them. Then he goes on.

> that from these honored dead

—apparently he means "in such a way that from these honored dead"—

> we take increased devotion to that cause.

Next, he restates this more briefly:

> that we here highly resolve. . . .

And now the actual resolution follows, in three parts of growing intensity:

> that these dead shall not have died in vain
>
> that this nation, under God, shall have a new birth
> >   of freedom

and that (one more tricolon)

> government of the people
> >   by the people
> >   for the people

shall not perish from the earth.

Now, the tricolon is the figure which, through division, emphasizes basic harmony and unity. Lincoln used antithesis because he was speaking to a people at war. He used the tricolon because he was hoping, planning, praying for peace.

No one thinks that when he was drafting the Gettysburg Address,   16
Lincoln deliberately looked up these quotations and consciously chose these particular patterns of thought. No, he chose the theme. From its development and from the emotional tone of the entire occasion, all the rest followed, or grew—by that marvelous process of choice and rejection which is essential to artistic creation. It does not spoil such a work of art to analyze it as closely as we have done; it is altogether fitting and proper that we should do this: for it helps us to penetrate more deeply into the rich meaning of the Gettysburg Address, and it allows us the very rare privilege of watching the workings of a great man's mind.

Topics for Critical Thinking and Writing

1. At the start of his essay, after quoting the opening words of Lincoln's speech, Highet uses a metaphor and a simile: he says that the words "stand at the entrance to the best-known monument," and that "greatness is like granite: it is molded in fire, and it lasts for many centuries." Are these figures of speech effective? Why or why not? How are the two figures related to each other?
2. Analyze the structure of Highet's essay.
3. This essay was a talk given on the radio, presumably to a large general public. Find passages in the essay that suggest oral delivery to an unspecialized audience. How would you describe Highet's tone?
4. It has been suggested that "government of the people, by the people" is redundant; a government *of* the people, it is argued, must be the same as a government *by* the people. Did Lincoln repeat himself merely to get a triad: "of the people, by the people, for the people"? If so, is this a fault? Or can it be argued that "government of the people" really means "government over the people"? If so, what does the entire expression mean?
5. Highet claims that Lincoln was not only a great statesman but also a literary artist. According to Highet, what was Lincoln's training as a literary artist? Highet implies that such training is still available. To what extent has it been available to you? Traditionally, studying "admirable models of thought and expession," including poetry, was an important part of writing instruction, but it is less common now. Should such study be included in writing courses? Why, or why not?
6. In paragraph 11 Highet points out that "the Gettysburg Address is full of quotations—or rather of adaptations," and he analyzes several examples of Lincoln's adaptations of sources. How is such adaptation different from plagiarism? Or is it?

George Orwell

George Orwell (1903–50) was the pen name adopted by Eric Blair, an Englishman born in India. Orwell was educated at Eton, in England, but in 1921 he went back to the East and served for five years as a police officer in Burma. He then returned to Europe, doing odd jobs while writing novels and stories. In 1936 he fought in the Spanish Civil War on the side of the Republicans, an experience reported in Homage to Catalonia *(1938). His last years were spent writing in England.*

Politics and the English Language

Most people who bother with the matter at all would admit that the English language is in a bad way, but it is generally assumed that we cannot by conscious action do anything about it. Our civilization is decadent and our language—so the argument runs—must inevitably share in the general collapse. It follows that any struggle against the abuse of language is a sentimental archaism, like preferring candles to electric light or hansom cabs to aeroplanes. Underneath this lies the half-conscious belief that language is a natural growth and not an instrument which we shape for our own purposes.

Now, it is clear that the decline of a language must ultimately have political and economic causes: it is not due simply to the bad influence of this or that individual writer. But an effect can become a cause, reinforcing the original cause and producing the same effect in an intensified form, and so on indefinitely. A man may take to drink because he feels himself to be a failure, and then fail all the more completely because he drinks. It is rather the same thing that is happening to the English language. It becomes ugly and inaccurate because our thoughts are foolish, but the slovenliness of our language makes it easier for us to have foolish thoughts. The point is that the process is reversible. Modern English, especially written English, is full of bad habits which spread by imitation and which can be avoided if one is willing to take the necessary trouble. If one gets rid of these habits one can think more clearly, and to think clearly is a necessary first step towards political regeneration: so that the fight against bad English is not frivolous and is not the exclusive concern of professional writers. I will come back to this presently, and I hope that by that time the meaning of what I have said here will have become clearer. Meanwhile, here are five specimens of the English language as it is now habitually written.

These five passages have not been picked out because they are especially bad—I could have quoted far worse if I had chosen—but because they illustrate various of the mental vices from which we now suffer. They are a little below the average, but are fairly representative samples. I number them so that I can refer back to them when necessary:

1. I am not, indeed, sure whether it is not true to say that the Milton who once seemed not unlike a seventeenth-century Shelley had not become,

487

out of an experience ever more bitter in each year, more alien [*sic*] to the founder of that Jesuit sect which nothing could induce him to tolerate.

Professor Harold Laski (Essay in *Freedom of Expression*)

2. Above all, we cannot play ducks and drakes with a native battery of idioms which prescribes such egregious collocations of vocables as the Basic *put up with* for *tolerate* or *put at a loss* for *bewilder*.

Professor Lancelot Hogben (*Interglossa*)

3. On the one side we have the free personality: by definition it is not neurotic, for it has neither conflict nor dream. Its desires, such as they are, are transparent, for they are just what institutional approval keeps in the forefront of consciousness; another institutional pattern would alter their number and intensity; there is little in them that is natural, irreducible, or culturally dangerous. But *on the other side,* the social bond itself is noticing but the mutual reflection of these self-secure integrities. Recall the definition of love. Is not this the very picture of a small academic? Where is there a place in this hall of mirrors for either personality or fraternity?

Essay on Psychology in *Politics* (New York)

4. All the "best people" from the gentlemen's clubs, and all the frantic fascist captains, united in common hatred of Socialism and bestial horror of the rising tide of the mass revolutionary movement, have turned to acts of provocation, to foul incendiarism, to medieval legends of poisoned wells, to legalize their own destruction of proletarian organizations, and rouse the agitated petty, bourgeoisie to chauvinistic fervor on behalf of the fight against the revolutionary way out of the crisis.

Communist Pamphlet

5. If a new spirit *is* to be infused into this old country, there is one thorny and contentious reform which must be tackled, and that is the humanization and galvanization of the B.B.C. Timidity here will bespeak canker and atrophy of the soul. The heart of Britain may be sound and of strong beat, for instance, but the British lion's roar at present is like that of Bottom in Shakespeare's *Midsummer Night's Dream*—as gentle as any sucking dove. A virile new Britain cannot continue indefinitely to be traduced in the eyes, or rather ears, of the world by the effete languors of Langham Place, brazenly masquerading as "standard English." When the voice of Britain is heard at nine o'clock, better far and infinitely less ludicrous to hear aitches honestly dropped than the present priggish, inflated, inhibited, school-ma'amish arch braying of blameless bashful mewing maidens!

Letter in *Tribune*

Each of these passages has faults of its own, but, quite apart from avoidable ugliness, two qualities are common to all of them. The first is staleness of imagery; the other is lack of precision. The writer either has a meaning and cannot express it, or he inadvertently says something else, or he is almost indifferent as to whether his words mean anything or not. This mixture of vagueness and sheer incompetence is the most marked characteristic of modern English prose, and especially of any kind of political writing. As soon as certain topics are raised, the concrete melts into the abstract and no one seems able to think of turns of speech that are not hackneyed: prose consists less and less of *words* chosen for the sake of their meaning, and more and more of *phrases* tacked together like the sections of a prefabricated henhouse. I list below, with notes and examples, various of the tricks by means of which the work of prose-construction is habitually dodged:

Dying Metaphors

A newly invented metaphor assists thought by evoking a visual image, while on the other hand a metaphor which is technically "dead" (e.g., *iron resolution*) has in effect reverted to being an ordinary word and can generally be used without loss of vividness. But in between these two classes there is a huge dump of worn-out metaphors which have lost all evocative power and are merely used because they save people the trouble of inventing phrases for themselves. Examples are: *Ring the changes on, take up the cudgels for, toe the line, ride roughshod over, stand shoulder to shoulder with, play into the hands of, no axe to grind, grist to the mill, fishing in troubled waters, on the order of the day, Achilles' heel, swan song, hotbed.* Many of these are used without knowledge of their meaning (what is a "rift," for instance?), and incompatible metaphors are frequently mixed, a sure sign that the writer is not interested in what he is saying. Some metaphors now current have been twisted out of their original meaning without those who use them even being aware of the fact. For example, *toe the line* is sometimes written *tow the line*. Another example is the *hammer and the anvil,* now always used with the implication that the anvil gets the worst of it. In real life it is always the anvil that breaks the hammer, never the other way about: a writer who stopped to think what he was saying would be aware of this, and would avoid perverting the original phrase.

Operators or Verbal False Limbs

These save the trouble of picking out appropriate verbs and nouns, and at the same time pad each sentence with extra syllables which give it an appearance of symmetry. Characteristic phrases are *render inoperative, militate against, make contact with, be subjected to, give rise to, give grounds for, have the effect of, play a leading part (role) in, make itself felt, take effect, exhibit a tendency to, serve the purpose of, etc., etc.* The keynote is the elimination of simple verbs. Instead of being a single word, such as *break, stop, spoil, mend, kill,* a verb becomes *a phrase,* made up of a noun or adjective tacked on to some general-purpose verb such as *prove, serve, form, play, render.* In addition, the passive voice is wherever possible used in preference to the active, and noun constructions are used instead of gerunds (*by examination of* instead of *by examining*). The range of verbs is further cut down by means of the *-ize* and *de-* formations, and the banal statements are given an appearance of profundity by means of the *not un-* formation. Simple conjunctions and prepositions are replaced by such phrases as *with respect to, having regard to, the fact that, by dint of, in view of, in the interests of, on the hypothesis that;* and the ends of sentences are saved from anticlimax by such resounding com-mon-places as *greatly to be desired, cannot be left out of account, a develop-ment to be expected in the near future, deserving of serious consideration, brought to a satisfactory conclusion,* and so on and so forth.

Pretentious Diction

Words like *phenomenon, element, individual* (as noun), *objective, categori-cal, effective, virtual, basic, primary, promote, constitute, exhibit, exploit, uti-lize, eliminate, liquidate,* are used to dress up simple statements and give an air of scientific impartiality to biased judgments. Adjectives like *epoch-making, epic, historic, unforgettable, triumphant, age-old, inevitable, inexorable, veritable,* are used to dignify the sordid processes of interna-tional politics, while writing that aims at glorifying war usually takes on an archaic color, its characteristic words being: *realm, throne, chariot, mailed fist, trident, sword, shield, buckler, banner, jackboot, clarion.* Foreign words and expressions such as *cul de sac, ancien regime, deus ex machina, mutatis mutandis, status quo, gleichschaltung, weltanschauung,* are used to give an air of culture and elegance. Except for the useful abbreviations *i.e., e.g.,* and *etc.,* there is no real need for any of the hundreds of foreign phrases now current in English. Bad writers, and especially scientific, political and sociological writers, are nearly always haunted by the notion that Latin or Greek words are grander than Saxon ones, and unnecessary words like *expedite, ameliorate, predict, extraneous, deracinat-ed, clandestine, subaqueous* and hundreds of others constantly gain ground from their Anglo-Saxon opposite numbers.[2] The jargon peculiar to Marxist writing (*hyena, hangman, cannibal, petty bourgeois, these gentry, lacquey, flunkey, mad dog, White Guard,* etc.) consists largely of words and phrases translated from Russian, German or French; but the normal way of coining a new word is to use a Latin or Greek root with the appropriate affix and, where necessary, the *-ize* formation. It is often

---

[2]An interesting illustration of this is the way in which the English flower names which were in use till very recently are being ousted by Greek ones, *snapdragon* becoming *antir-rhinum, forget-me-not* becoming *myosotis,* etc. It is hard to see any practical reason for this change of fashion: it is probably due to an instinctive turning-away from the more home-ly word and a vague feeling that the Greek word is scientific.

easier to make up words of this kind (*deregionalize, impermissible, extra-marital, nonfragmentary* and so forth) than to think up the English words that will cover one's meaning. The result, in general, is an increase in slovenliness and vagueness.

Meaningless Words

In certain kinds of writing, particularly in art criticism and literary criticism, it is normal to come across long passages which are almost completely lacking in meaning.[3] Words like *romantic, plastic, values, human, dead, sentimental, natural, vitality,* as used in art criticism, are strictly meaningless, in the sense that they not only do not point to any discoverable object, but are hardly ever expected to do so by the reader. When one critic writes, "The outstanding feature of Mr. *X*'s work is its living quality," while another writes, "the immediately striking thing about Mr. *X*'s work is its peculiar deadness," the reader accepts this as a simple difference of opinion. If words like *black* and *white* were involved, instead of the jargon words *dead* and *living,* he would see at once that language was being used in an improper way. Many political words are similarly abused. The word *Fascism* has now no meaning except in so far as it signifies "something not desirable." The words *democracy, socialism, freedom, patriotic, realistic, justice,* have each of them several different meanings which cannot be reconciled with one another. In the case of a word like *democracy,* not only is there no agreed definition, but the attempt to make one is resisted from all sides. It is almost universally felt that when we call a country democratic we are praising it: consequently the defenders of every kind of régime claim that it is a democracy, and fear that they might have to stop using the word if it were tied down to any one meaning. Words of this kind are often used in a consciously dishonest way. That is, the person who uses them has his own private definition, but allows his hearer to think he means something quite different. Statements like *Marshal Pétain was a true patriot, The Soviet Press is the freest in the world, The Catholic Church is opposed to persecution,* are almost always made with intent to deceive. Other words used in variable meanings, in most cases more or less dishonestly, are: *class, totalitarian, science, progressive, reactionary, bourgeois, equality.*

Now that I have made this catalogue of swindles and perversions, let me give another example of the kind of writing that they lead to.

---

[3]*Example*: "Comfort's catholicity of perception and image, strangely Whitmanesque in range, almost the exact opposite in aesthetic compulsion, continues to evoke that trembling atmospheric accumulative hinting at a cruel, an inexorably serene timelessness. . . . Wrey Gardiner scores by aiming at simple bull's-eyes with precision. Only they are not simple, and through this contented sadness runs more than the surface bitter-sweet of resignation." (*Poetry Quarterly*)

This time it must of its nature be an imaginary one. I am going to translate a passage of good English into modern English of the worst sort. Here is a well-known verse from *Ecclesiastes:*

> I returned and saw under the sun, that the race is not to the swift, nor the battle to the strong, neither yet bread to the wise, nor yet riches to men of understanding, nor yet favour to men of skill; but time and chance happeneth to them all.

Here it is in modern English:

> Objective consideration of contemporary phenomena compels the conclusion that success or failure in competitive activities exhibits no tendency to be commensurate with innate capacity, but that a considerable element of the unpredictable must invariably be taken into account.

This is a parody, but not a very gross one. Exhibit (3), above, for instance, contains several patches of the same kind of English. It will be seen that I have not made a full translation. The beginning and ending of the sentence follow the original meaning fairly closely, but in the middle the concrete illustrations—race, battle, bread—dissolve into the vague phrase "success or failure in competitive activities." This had to be so, because no modern writer of the kind I am discussing—no one capable of using phrases like "objective consideration of contemporary phenomena"—would ever tabulate his thoughts in that precise and detailed way. The whole tendency of modern prose is away from concreteness. Now analyze these two sentences a little more closely. The first contains forty-nine words but only sixty syllables, and all its words are those of everyday life. The second contains thirty-eight words of ninety syllables: eighteen of its words are from Latin roots, and one from Greek. The first sentence contains six vivid images, and only one phrase ("time and chance") that could be called vague. The second contains not a single fresh, arresting phrase, and in spite of its ninety syllables it gives only a shortened version of the meaning contained in the first. Yet without a doubt it is the second kind of sentence that is gaining ground in modern English. I do not want to exaggerate. This kind of writing is not yet universal, and outcrops of simplicity will occur here and there in the worst-written page. Still, if you or I were told to write a few lines on the uncertainty of human fortunes, we should probably come much nearer to my imaginary sentence than to the one from *Ecclesiastes.*

As I have tried to show, modern writing at its worst does not consist in picking out words for the sake of their meaning and inventing images in order to make the meaning clearer. It consists in gumming together long strips of words which have already been set in order by someone else, and making the results presentable by sheer humbug. The attraction of this way of writing is that it is easy. It is easier—even quicker, once you have the habit—to say *In my opinion it is not an unjustifiable assumption that* than to say *I think*. If you use ready-made phrases, you not only don't have to hunt about for words; you also don't have to bother with the rhythms of your sentences, since these phrases are generally so arranged as to be more or less euphonious. When you are composing in a hurry—when you are dictating to a stenographer, for instance, or making a public speech—it is natural to fall into a pretentious, Latinized style. Tags like *a consideration which we should do well to bear in mind* or *a conclusion to which all of us would readily assent* will save many a sentence from coming down with a bump. By using stale metaphors, similes and idioms, you save much mental effort, at the cost of leaving your meaning vague, not only for your reader but for yourself. This is the significance of mixed metaphors. The sole aim of a metaphor is to call up a visual image. When these images clash—as in *The Fascist octopus has sung its swan song, the jackboot is thrown into the melting pot*—it can be taken as certain that the writer is not seeing a mental image of the objects he is naming; in other words he is not really thinking. Look again at the examples I gave at the beginning of this essay. Professor Laski (1) uses five negatives in fifty-three words. One of these is superfluous, making nonsense of the whole passage, and in addition there is the slip *alien* for *akin*, making further nonsense, and several avoidable pieces of clumsiness which increase the general vagueness. Professor Hogben (2) plays ducks and drakes with a battery which is able to write prescriptions, and while, disapproving of the everyday phrase *put up with*, is unwilling to look *egregious* up in the dictionary and see what it means; (3), if one takes an uncharitable attitude towards it, is simply meaningless: probably one could work out its intended meaning by reading the whole of the article in which it occurs. In (4), the writer knows more or less what he wants to say, but an accumulation of stale phrases chokes him like tea leaves blocking a sink. In (5), words and meaning have almost parted company. People who write in this manner usually have a general emotional meaning—they dislike one thing and want to express solidarity with another—but they are not interested in the detail of what they are saying. A scrupulous writer, in every sentence that he writes, will ask himself at least four questions, thus: What am I trying to say? What words will express it? What image or idiom will make it clearer? Is this image fresh enough to have an effect? And he will probably ask himself two more: Could I put it more shortly? Have I said anything that is avoidably ugly? But you are not obliged to go to all this trouble. You can shirk it by simply throwing your mind open and letting the ready-made phrases come crowding in. They will construct your sentences for you—even think your thoughts for you, to a certain extent—and at need they will perform the important service of partially concealing your meaning even from yourself. It is at this point that the special connection between politics and the debasement of language becomes clear.

In our time it is broadly true that political writing is bad writing.   12
Where it is not true, it will generally be found that the writer is some

kind of rebel, expressing his private opinions and not a "party line." Orthodoxy, of whatever color, seems to demand a lifeless, imitative style. The political dialects to be found in pamphlets, leading articles, manifestos, White Papers and the speeches of undersecretaries do, of course, vary from party to party, but they are all alike in that one almost never finds in them a fresh, vivid, homemade turn of speech. When one watches some tired hack on the platform mechanically repeating the familiar phrases—*bestial atrocities, iron heel, bloodstained tyranny, free peoples of the world, stand shoulder to shoulder*—one often has a curious feeling that one is not watching a live human being but some kind of dummy: a feeling which suddenly becomes stronger at moments when the light catches the speaker's spectacles and turns them into blank discs which seem to have no eyes behind them. And this is not altogether fanciful. A speaker who uses that kind of phraseology has gone some distance towards turning himself into a machine. The appropriate noises are coming out of his larynx, but his brain is not involved as it would be if he were choosing his words for himself. If the speech he is making is one that he is accustomed to make over and over again, he may be almost unconscious of what he is saying, as one is when one utters the responses in church. And this reduced state of consciousness, if not indispensable, is at any rate favorable to political conformity.

In our time, political speech and writing are largely the defense of the indefensible. Things like the continuance of British rule in India, the Russian purges and deportations, the dropping of the atom bombs on Japan, can indeed be defended, but only by arguments which are too brutal for most people to face, and which do not square with the professed aims of political parties. Thus political language has to consist largely of euphemism, question-begging and sheer cloudy vagueness. Defenseless villages are bombarded from the air, the inhabitants driven out into the countryside, the cattle machine-gunned, the huts set on fire with incendiary bullets: this is called *pacification*. Millions of peasants are robbed of their farms and sent trudging along the roads with no more than they can carry: this is called *transfer of population* or *rectification of frontiers*. People are imprisoned for years without trial, or shot in the back of the neck or sent to die of scurvy in Arctic lumber camps: this is called *elimination of unreliable elements*. Such phraseology is needed if one wants to name things without calling up mental pictures of them. Consider for instance some comfortable English professor defending Russian totalitarianism. He cannot say outright, "I believe in killing off your opponents when you can get good results by doing so." Probably, therefore, he will say something like this:

> While freely conceding that the Soviet regime exhibits certain features which the humanitarian may be inclined to deplore, we must, I think, agree that a certain curtailment of the right to political opposition is an unavoidable concomitant of transitional periods, and that the rigors which

the Russian people have been called upon to undergo have been amply justified in the sphere of concrete achievement.

The inflated style is itself a kind of euphemism. A mass of Latin words falls upon the facts like soft snow, blurring the outlines and covering up all the details. The great enemy of clear language is insincerity. When there is a gap between one's real and one's declared aims, one turns as it were instinctively to long words and exhausted idioms, like a cuttlefish squirting out ink. In our age there is no such thing as "keeping out of politics." All issues are political issues, and politics itself is a mass of lies, evasions, folly, hatred and schizophrenia. When the general atmosphere is bad, language must suffer. I should expect to find— this is a guess which I have not sufficient knowledge to verify—that the German, Russian and Italian languages have all deteriorated in the last ten to fifteen years, as a result of dictatorship.

But if thought corrupts language, language can also corrupt thought. A bad usage can spread by tradition and imitation, even among people who should and do know better. The debased language that I have been discussing is in some ways very convenient. Phrases like *a not unjustifiable assumption, leaves much to be desired, would serve no good purpose, a consideration which we should do well to bear in mind,* are a continuous temptation, a packet of aspirins always at one's elbow. Look back through this essay, and for certain you will find that I have again and again committed the very faults I am protesting against. By this morning's post I have received a pamphlet dealing with conditions in Germany. The author tells me that he "felt impelled" to write it. I open it at random, and here is almost the first sentence that I see: "[The Allies] have an opportunity not only of achieving a radical transformation of Germany's social and political structure in such a way as to avoid a nationalistic reaction in Germany itself, but at the same time of laying the foundations of cooperative and unified Europe." You see, he "feels impelled" to write—feels, presumably, that he has something new to say—and yet his words, like cavalry horses answering the bugle, group themselves automatically into the familiar dreary pattern. This invasion of one's mind by ready-made phrases (*lay the foundations, achieve a radical transformation*) can only be prevented if one is constantly on guard against them, and every such phrase anaesthetizes a portion of one's brain.

I said earlier that the decadence of our language is probably curable. Those who deny this would argue, if they produced an argument at all, that language merely reflects existing social conditions, and that we cannot influence its development by any direct tinkering with words and constructions. So far as the general tone or spirit of a language goes, this may be true, but it is not true in detail. Silly words and expressions have often disappeared, not through any evolutionary process but owing to the conscious action of a minority. Two recent

16

examples were *explore every avenue* and *leave no stone unturned,* which were killed by the jeers of a few journalists. There is a long list of fly-blown metaphors which could similarly be got rid of if enough people would interest themselves in the job; and it should also be possible to laugh the *not un-* formation out of existence,[4] to reduce the amount of Latin and Greek in the average sentence, to drive out foreign phrases and strayed scientific words, and, in general, to make pretentiousness unfashionable. But all these are minor points. The defense of the English language implies more than this, and perhaps it is best to start by saying what it does *not* imply.

To begin with it has nothing to do with archaism, with the salvaging of obsolete words and turns of speech, or with the setting up of a "standard English" which must never be departed from. On the contrary, it is especially concerned with the scrapping of every word or idiom which has outworn its usefulness. It has nothing to do with correct grammar and syntax, which are of no importance so long as one makes one's meaning clear, or with the avoidance of Americanisms, or with having what is called a "good prose style." On the other hand it is not concerned with fake simplicity and the attempt to make written English colloquial. Nor does it even imply in every case preferring the Saxon word to the Latin one, though it does imply using the fewest and shortest words that will cover one's meaning. What is above all needed is to let the meaning choose the word, and not the other way about. In prose, the worst thing one can do with words is to surrender to them. When you think of a concrete object, you think wordlessly, and then, if you want to describe the thing you have been visualizing you probably hunt about till you find the exact words that seem to fit in. When you think of something abstract you are more inclined to use words from the start, and unless you make a conscious effort to prevent it, the existing dialect will come rushing in and do the job for you, at the expense of blurring or even changing your meaning. Probably it is better to put off using words as long as possible and get one's meaning as clear as one can through pictures or sensations. Afterwards one can choose—not simply accept—the phrases that will best cover the meaning, and then switch round and decide what impression one's words are likely to make on another person. This last effort of the mind cuts out all stale or mixed images, all prefabricated phrases, needless repetitions, and humbug and vagueness generally. But one can often be in doubt about the effect of a word or a phrase, and one needs rules that one can rely on when instinct fails. I think the following rules will cover most cases:

1. Never use a metaphor, simile or other figure of speech which you are used to seeing in print.

---

[4]One can cure oneself of the *not un-* formation by memorizing this sentence: *A not unblack dog was chasing a not unsmall rabbit across a not ungreen field.*

2. Never use a long word where a short one will do.
3. If it is possible to cut a word out, always cut it out.
4. Never use the passive where you can use the active.
5. Never use a foreign phrase, a scientific word or a jargon word if you can think of an everyday English equivalent.
6. Break any of these rules sooner than say anything outright barbarous.

These rules sound elementary, and so they are, but they demand a deep change of attitude in anyone who has grown used to writing in the style now fashionable. One could keep all of them and still write bad English, but one could not write the kind of stuff that I quoted in those five specimens at the beginning of this article.

I have not here been considering the literary use of language, but merely language as an instrument for expressing and not for concealing or preventing thought. Stuart Chase and others have come near to claiming that all abstract words are meaningless, and have used this as a pretext for advocating a kind of political quietism. Since you don't know what Fascism is, how can you struggle against Fascism? One need not swallow such absurdities as this, but one ought to recognize that the present political chaos is connected with the decay of language, and that one can probably bring about some improvement by starting at the verbal end. If you simplify your English, you are freed from the worst follies of orthodoxy. You cannot speak any of the necessary dialects, and when you make a stupid remark its stupidity will be obvious, even to yourself. Political language—and with variations this is true of all political parties, from Conservatives to Anarchists—is designed to make lies sound truthful and murder respectable, and to give an appearance of solidity to pure wind. One cannot change this all in a moment, but one can at least change one's own habits, and from time to time, one can even, if one jeers loudly enough, send some worn-out and useless phrase—some *jackboot, Achilles' heel, hotbed, melting pot, acid test, veritable inferno* or other lump of verbal refuse—into the dustbin where it belongs.

Topics for Critical Thinking and Writing

1. Revise one or two of Orwell's examples of bad writing.
2. Examine Orwell's metaphors. Do they fulfill his requirements for good writing?
3. Look again Orwell's grotesque revision (paragraph 10) of a passage from the Bible. Write a similar version of another passage from the Bible.
4. Can you recall any occasion when you have used words, in writing or speaking, in a consciously dishonest way? If so, can you explain why, or go further and justify your behavior?

5. In paragraph 2 Orwell says, "Written English is full of bad habits which spread by imitation." Are you aware of having acquired any bad writing habits by imitation? If so, imitation of what or whom?

Casey Miller and Kate Swift

Casey Miller (b. 1914), educated at Smith College and Yale University, and Kate Swift (b. 1923), educated at Connecticut College, the University of North Carolina, and New York University, worked as freelance editors. They became especially interested in the effect of language on women and wrote several books about sexism in language, including Words and Women *(1977) and* The Handbook of Nonsexist Writing for Writers, Editors and Speakers, *2nd ed. (1988). We reprint an earlier study, which was first published in 1972 in* The New York Times Magazine. *Now, after more than two decades, it remains a major statement.*

One Small Step for Genkind

A riddle is making the rounds that goes like this: A man and his young son were in an automobile accident. The father was killed and the son, who was critically injured, was rushed to a hospital. As attendants wheeled the unconscious boy into the emergency room, the doctor on duty looked down at him and said, "My God, it's my son!" What was the relationship of the doctor to the injured boy?

If the answer doesn't jump to your mind, another riddle that has been around a lot longer might help: The blind beggar had a brother. The blind beggar's brother died. The brother who died had no brother. What relation was the blind beggar to the blind beggar's brother?

As with all riddles, the answers are obvious once you see them: The doctor was the boy's mother and the beggar was her brother's sister. Then why doesn't everyone solve them immediately? Mainly because our language, like the culture it reflects, is male oriented. To say that a woman in medicine is an exception is simply to confirm that statement. Thousands of doctors are women, but in order to be seen in the mind's eye, they must be called women doctors.

Except for words that refer to females by definition (mother, actress, congresswoman), and words for occupations traditionally held by females (nurse, secretary, prostitute), the English language defines everyone as male. The hypothetical person ("If a man can walk 10 miles in two hours . . . "), the average person ("the man in the street") and the active person ("the man on the move") are male. The assumption is that unless otherwise identified, people in general—including doctors and beggars—are men. It is a semantic mechanism that operates to keep women invisible: *man* and *mankind* represent everyone; *he* in generalized use refers to either sex; the "land where our fathers died" is also

4

the land of our mothers—although they go unsung. As the beetle-browed and mustachioed man in a Steig cartoon says to his two male drinking companions, "When I speak of mankind, one thing I *don't* mean is womankind."

Semantically speaking, woman is not one with the species of man, but a distinct subspecies. "Man," says the 1971 edition of the *Britannica Junior Encyclopedia,* "is the highest form of life on earth. His superior intelligence, combined with certain physical characteristics, have enabled man to achieve things that are impossible for other animals." (The prose style has something in common with the report of a research team describing its studies on "the development of the uterus in rats, guinea pigs and men.") As though quoting the Steig character, still speaking to his friends in McSorley's, the *Junior Encyclopedia* continues: "Man must invent most of his behavior, because he lacks the instincts of lower animals. . . . Most of the things he learns have been handed down from his ancestors by language and symbols rather than by biological inheritance."

Considering that for the last 5,000 years society has been patriarchal, that statement explains a lot. It explains why Eve was made from Adam's rib instead of the other way around, and who invented all those Adam-rib words like *fe*male and *wo*man in the first place. It also explains why, when it is necessary to mention woman, the language makes her a lower caste, a class separate from the rest of man; why it works to "keep her in her place."

This inheritance through language and other symbols begins in the home (also called a man's castle) where man and wife (not husband and wife, or man and woman) live for a while with their children. It is reinforced by religious training, the educational system, the press, government, commerce and the law. As Andrew Greeley wrote not long ago in his magazine, "Man is a symbol-creating animal. He orders and interprets his reality by his symbols, and he uses the symbols to reconstruct that reality."

Consider some of the reconstructed realities of American history. 8 When school children learn from their textbooks that the early colonists gained valuable experience in governing themselves, they are not told that the early colonists who were women were denied the privilege of self-government; when they learn that in the 18th century the average man had to manufacture many of the things he and his family needed, they are not told that this "average man" was often a woman who manufactured much of what she and her family needed. Young people learn that intrepid pioneers crossed the country in covered wagons with their wives, children and cattle; they do not learn that women themselves were intrepid pioneers rather than part of the baggage.

In a paper published this year in Los Angeles as a guide for authors and editors of social-studies textbooks, Elizabeth Burr, Susan Dunn and Norma Farquhar document unintentional skewings of this kind that occur either because women are not specifically mentioned as affecting or being affected by historical events, or because they are discussed in terms of outdated assumptions. "One never sees a picture of women captioned simply 'farmers' or 'pioneers,'" they point out. The sub-species nomenclature that requires a caption to read "women farmers" or "women pioneers" is extended to impose certain jobs on women by definition. The textbook guide gives as an example the word *housewife*, which it says not only "suggests that domestic chores are the exclusive burden of females," but gives "female students the idea that they were born to keep house and teaches male students that they are automatically entitled to laundry, cooking and housecleaning services from the women in their families."

Sexist language is any language that expresses such stereotyped attitudes and expectations, or that assumes the inherent superiority of one sex over the other. When a woman says of her husband, who has drawn up plans for a new bedroom wing and left out closets, "Just like a man," her language is as sexist as the man's who says, after his wife has changed her mind about needing the new wing after all, "Just like a woman."

Male and female are not sexist words, but masculine and feminine almost always are. Male and female can be applied objectively to individual people and animals and, by extension, to things. When electricians and plumbers talk about male and female couplings, everyone knows or can figure out what they mean. The terms are graphic and culture free.

Masculine and feminine, however, are as sexist as any words can be, since it is almost impossible to use them without invoking cultural stereotypes. When people construct lists of "masculine" and "feminine" traits they almost always end up making assumptions that have nothing to do with innate differences between the sexes. We have a friend who happens to be going through the process of pinning down this very phenomenon. He is 7 years old and his question concerns why his coats and shirts button left over right while his sister's button the other way. He assumes it must have something to do with the differences between boys and girls, but he can't see how.   12

What our friend has yet to grasp is that the way you button your coat, like most sex-differentiated customs, has nothing to do with real differences but much to do with what society wants you to feel about yourself as a male or female person. Society decrees that it is appropriate for girls to dress differently from boys, to act differently, and to think differently. Boys must be masculine, whatever that means, and girls must be feminine.

Unabridged dictionaries are a good source for finding out what society decrees to be appropriate, though less by definition than by their choice of associations and illustrations. Words associated with males—*manly, virile* and *masculine*, for example—are defined through a broad range of positive attributes like strength, courage, directness and independence, and they are illustrated through such examples of contemporary usage as "a manly determination to face what comes," "a virile literary style," "a masculine love of sports." Corresponding words associated with females are defined with fewer attributes (though weakness is often one of them) and the examples given are generally negative if not clearly pejorative: "feminine wiles," "womanish tears," "a womanlike lack of promptness," "convinced that drawing was a waste of time, if not downright womanly."

Male-associated words are frequently applied to females to describe something that is either incongruous ("a mannish voice") or presumably commendable ("a masculine mind," "she took it like a man"), but female-associated words are unreservedly derogatory when applied to males, and are sometimes abusive to females as well. The opposite of "masculine" is "effeminate," although the opposite of "feminine" is simply "unfeminine."

One dictionary, after defining the word *womanish* as "suitable to or 16 resembling a woman," further defines it as "unsuitable to a man or to a strong character of either sex." Words derived from "sister" and "brother" provide another apt example, for whereas "sissy," applied either to a male or female, conveys the message that sisters are expected to be timid and cowardly, "buddy" makes clear that brothers are friends.

The subtle disparagement of females and corresponding approbation of males wrapped up in many English words is painfully illustrated by "tomboy." Here is an instance where a girl who likes sports and the out-of-doors, who is curious about how things work, who is adventurous and bold instead of passive, is defined in terms of something she is not—a boy. By denying that she can be the person she is and still be a girl, the word surreptitiously undermines her sense of identity: it says she is unnatural. A "tomboy," as defined by one dictionary, is a "girl, especially a young girl, who behaves like a spirited boy." But who makes the judgment that she is acting like a spirited boy, not a spirited girl? Can it be a coincidence that in the case of the dictionary just quoted the editor, executive editor, managing editor, general manager, all six members of the Board of Linguists, the usage editor, science editor, all six general editors of definitions, and 94 out of the 104 distinguished experts consulted on usage—are men?

It isn't enough to say that any invidious comparisons and stereotypes lexicographers perpetuate are already present in the culture. There are ways to define words like womanly and tomboy that don't put women down, though the tradition has been otherwise. Samuel Johnson, the lexicographer, was the same Dr. Johnson who said, "A woman preaching is like a dog's walking on his hind legs. It is not done well; but you are surprised to find it done at all."

Possibly because of the negative images associated with womanish and womanlike, and with expressions like "woman driver" and "woman of the street," the word woman dropped out of fashion for a time. The women at the office and the women on the assembly line and the women one first knew in school all became ladies or girls or gals. Now a countermovement, supported by the very term women's liberation, is putting back into words like woman and sister and sisterhood the meaning they were losing by default. It is as though, in the nick of time, women had seen that the language itself could destroy them.

Some long-standing conventions of the news media add insult to injury. When a woman or girl makes news, her sex is identified at the   20 beginning of a story, if possible in the headline or its equivalent. The assumption, apparently, is that whatever event or action is being reported, a woman's involvement is less common and therefore more newsworthy than a man's. If the story is about achievement, the implication is: "pretty good for a woman." And because people are assumed to be male unless otherwise identified, the media have developed a special and extensive vocabulary to avoid the constant repetition of "woman." The results, "Grandmother Wins Nobel Prize," "Blonde Hijacks Airliner," "Housewife to Run for Congress," convey the kind of information that would be ludicrous in comparable headlines if the subjects were men. Why, if "Unsalaried Husband to Run for Congress" is unacceptable to editors, do women have to keep explaining that to describe them through external or superficial concerns reflects a sexist view of women as decorative objects, breeding machines and extensions of men, not real people?

Members of the Chicago chapter of the National Organization for Women recently studied the newspapers in their area and drew up a set of guidelines for the press. These include cutting out descriptions of the "clothes, physical features, dating life and marital status of women where such references would be considered inappropriate if about men"; using language in such a way as to include women in copy that refers to homeowners, scientists and business people where "newspaper descriptions often convey the idea that all such persons are male"; and displaying the same discretion in printing generalizations about women as would be shown toward racial, religious and ethnic groups. "Our concern with what we are called may seem trivial to some people," the women said, "but we regard the old usages as symbolic of women's position within this society."

The assumption that an adult woman is flattered by being called a girl is matched by the notion that a woman in a menial or poorly paid job finds compensation in being called a lady. Ethel Strainchamps has pointed out that since lady is used as an adjective with nouns designating both high and low occupations (lady wrestler, lady barber, lady doctor, lady judge), some writers assume they can use the noun form without betraying value judgments. Not so, Strainchamps says, rolling the issue into a spitball: "You may write, 'He addressed the Republican ladies,' or 'The Democratic ladies convened'. . . but I have never seen 'the Communist ladies' or 'the Black Panther ladies' in print."

Thoughtful writers and editors have begun to repudiate some of the old usages. "Divorcée," "grandmother" and "blonde," along with "vivacious," "pert," "dimpled" and "cute," were dumped by the Washington Post in the spring of 1970 by the executive editor, Benjamin Bradlee. In a memo to his staff, Bradlee wrote, "The meaningful equality and dignity of women is properly under scrutiny today . . . because this equality has been less than meaningful and the dignity not always free of stereotype and condescension."

What women have been called in the press—or at least the part that 24 operates above ground—is only a fraction of the infinite variety of alternatives to "women" used in the subcultures of the English-speaking world. Beyond "chicks," "dolls," "dames," "babes," "skirts" and "broads" are the words and phrases in which women are reduced to their sexuality and nothing more. It would be hard to think of another area of language in which the human mind has been so fertile in devising and borrowing abusive terms. In *The Female Eunuch,* Germaine Greer devotes four pages to anatomical terms and words for animals, vegetables, fruits, baked goods, implements and receptacles, all of which are used to dehumanize the female person. Jean Faust, in an article aptly called "Words That Oppress," suggests that the effort to diminish women through language is rooted in a male fear of sexual inadequacy. "Woman is made to feel guilty for and akin to natural disasters," she writes; "hurricanes and typhoons are named after her. Any negative or threatening force is given a feminine name. If a man runs into bad luck climbing up the ladder of success (a male-invented game), he refers to the 'bitch goddess' success."

The sexual overtones in the ancient and no doubt honorable custom of calling ships "she" have become more explicit and less honorable in an age of air travel: "I'm Karen. Fly me." Attitudes of ridicule, contempt and disgust toward female sexuality have spawned a rich glossary of insults and epithets not found in dictionaries. And the usage in which four-letter words meaning copulate are interchangeable with cheat, attack and destroy can scarcely be unrelated to the savagery of rape.

In her updating of Ibsen's *A Doll's House,* Clare Booth Luce has Nora tell her husband she is pregnant—"In the way only men are supposed to get pregnant." "Men, pregnant?" he says, and she nods; "With ideas. Pregnancies there [*she taps his head*] are masculine. And a very superior form of labor. Pregnancies here [*taps her tummy*] are feminine—a very inferior form of labor."

Public outcry followed a revised translation of the New Testament describing Mary as "pregnant" instead of "great with child." The objections were made in part on esthetic grounds: there is no attractive adjective in modern English for a woman who is about to give birth. A less obvious reason was that replacing the euphemism with a biological term undermined religious teaching. The initiative and generative power in the conception of Jesus are understood to be God's; Mary, the mother, was a vessel only.

Whether influenced by this teaching or not, the language of human   28
reproduction lags several centuries behind scientific understanding. The male's contribution to procreation is still described as though it were the entire seed from which a new life grows: the initiative and generative power involved in the process are thought of as masculine, receptivity and nurturance as feminine. "Seminal" remains a synonym for "highly original," and there is no comparable word to describe the female's equivalent contribution.

An entire mythology has grown from this biological misunderstanding and its semantic legacy; its embodiment in laws that for centuries made women nonpersons was a key target of the 19th-century feminist movement. Today, more than 50 years after women finally won the basic democratic right to vote, the word "liberation" itself, when applied to women, means something less than when used of other groups of people. An advertisement for the N.B.C. news department listed Women's Liberation along with crime in the streets and the Vietnam war as "bad news." Asked for his views on Women's Liberation, a highly placed politician was quoted as saying, "Let me make one thing perfectly clear. I wouldn't want to wake up next to a lady pipe-fitter."

One of the most surprising challenges to our male-dominated culture is coming from within organized religion, where the issues are being stated, in part, by confronting the implications of traditional language. What a growing number of theologians and scholars are saying is that the myths of the Judeo-Christian tradition, being the products of patriarchy, must be reexamined, and that the concept of an exclusively male ministry and the image of a male god have become idolatrous.

Women are naturally in the forefront of this movement, both in their efforts to gain ordination and full equality and through their contributions to theological reform, although both these efforts are often subtly diminished. When the Rev. Barbara Anderson was ordained by the American Lutheran Church, one newspaper printed her picture over a caption headed "Happy Girl." Newsweek's report of a protest staged last December by women divinity students at Harvard was jocular ("another tilt at the windmill") and sarcastic: "Every time anyone in the room lapsed into what [the students] regarded as male chauvinism—such as using the word 'mankind' to describe the human race in general—the outraged women . . . drowned out the offender with earpiercing blasts from party-favor kazoos. . . . What annoyed the women most was the universal custom of referring to God as 'He.'"

The tone of the report was not merely unfunny; it missed the con-   32
nection between increasingly outmoded theological language and the accelerating number of women (and men) who are dropping out of

organized religion, both Jewish and Christian. For language, including pronouns, can be used to construct a reality that simply mirrors society's assumptions. To women who are committed to the reality of religious faith, the effect is doubly painful. Professor Harvey Cox, in whose classroom the protest took place, stated the issue directly: The women, he said, were raising the "basic theological question of whether God is more adequately thought of in personal or suprapersonal terms."

Toward the end of Don McLean's remarkable ballad "American Pie," a song filled with the imagery of abandonment and disillusion, there is a stanza that must strike many women to the quick. The church bells are broken, the music has died; then:

And the three men I admire most,
The Father, Son and the Holy Ghost,
They caught the last train for the Coast—
The day the music died.

Three men I admired most. There they go, briefcases in hand and topcoats buttoned left over right, walking down the long cold platform under the city, past the baggage wagons and the hissing steam onto the Pullman. Bye, bye God—all three of you—made in the image of male supremacy. Maybe out there in L.A. where the weather is warmer, someone can believe in you again.

The Roman Catholic theologian Elizabeth Farians says "the bad theology of an overmasculinized church continues to be one of the root causes of women's oppression." The definition of oppression is "to crush or burden by abuse of power or authority; burden spiritually or mentally as if by pressure."

When language oppresses, it does so by any means that disparage 36 and belittle. Until well into the 20th century, one of the ways English was manipulated to disparage women was through the addition of feminine endings to nonsexual words. Thus a woman who aspired to be a poet was excluded from the company of real poets by the label poetess, and a woman who piloted an airplane was denied full status as an aviator by being called an aviatrix. At about the time poetess, aviatrix, and similar Adam-ribbisms were dropping out of use, H. W. Fowler was urging that they be revived. "With the coming expansion of women's vocations," he wrote in the first edition (1926) of "Modern English Usage," "feminines for vocation-words are a special need of the future." There can be no doubt he subconsciously recognized the relative status implied in the -ess designations. His criticism of a woman who wished to be known as an author rather than an authoress was that she had no need "to raise herself to the level of the male author by asserting her right to his name."

Who has the prior right to a name? The question has an interesting bearing on words that were once applied to men alone, or to both men and women, but now, having acquired abusive associations, are assigned to women exclusively. Spinster is a gentle case in point. Prostitute and many of its synonyms illustrate the phenomenon better. If Fowler had chosen to record the changing usage of harlot from hired man (in Chaucer's time) through rascal and entertainer to its present definition, would he have maintained that the female harlot is trying to raise herself to the level of the male harlot by asserting her right to his name? Or would he have plugged for harlotress?

The demise of most -ess endings came about before the start of the new feminist movement. In the second edition of "Modern English Usage," published in 1965, Sir Ernest Gowers frankly admitted what his predecessors had been up to. "Feminine designations," he wrote, "seem now to be falling into disuse. Perhaps the explanation of this paradox is that it symbolizes the victory of women in their struggle for equal rights; it reflects the abandonment by men of those ideas about women in the professions that moved Dr. Johnson to his rude remark about women preachers."

If Sir Ernest's optimism can be justified, why is there a movement back to feminine endings in such words as chairwoman, councilwoman and congresswoman? Betty Hudson, of Madison, Conn., is campaigning for the adoption of "selectwoman" as the legal title for a female member of that town's executive body. To have to address a woman as "Selectman," she maintains, "is not only bad grammar and bad biology, but it implies that politics is still, or should be, a man's business." A valid argument, and one that was, predictably, countered by ridicule, the surefire weapon for undercutting achievement. When the head of the Federal Maritime Commission, Helen D. Bentley, was named "Man of the Year" by an association of shipping interests, she wisely refused to be drawn into light-hearted debate with interviewers who wanted to make the award's name a humorous issue. Some women, of course, have yet to learn they are invisible. An 8-year-old who visited the American Museum of Natural History with her Brownie scout troop went through the impressive exhibit on pollution and overpopulation called "Can Man Survive?" Asked afterward, "Well, can he?" she answered, "I don't know about him, but we're working on it in Brownies."

Nowhere are women rendered more invisible by language than in politics. The United States Constitution, in describing the qualifications for Representative, Senator and President, refers to each as *he*. No wonder Shirley Chisholm, the first woman since 1888 to make a try for the Presidential nomination of a major party, has found it difficult to be taken seriously.

The observation by Andrew Greeley already quoted—that "man" uses "his symbols" to reconstruct "his reality"—was not made in reference to the symbols of language but to the symbolic impact the "nomination of a black man for the Vice-Presidency" would have on race relations in the United States. Did the author assume the generic term

40

"man" would of course be construed to include "woman"? Or did he deliberately use a semantic device to exclude Shirley Chisholm without having to be explicit?

Either way, his words construct a reality in which women are ignored. As much as any other factor in our language, the ambiguous meaning of *man* serves to deny women recognition as people. In a recent magazine article, we discussed the similar effect on women of the generic pronoun *he,* which we proposed to replace by a new common gender pronoun *tey.* We were immediately told, by a number of authorities, that we were dabbling in the serious business of linguistics, and the message that reached us from these scholars was loud and clear: It-is-absolutely-impossible-for-anyone-to-introduce-a-new-word-into-the-language-just-because-there-is-a-need-for-it,-so-stop-wasting-your-time.

When words are suggested like "herstory" (for history), "sportsoneship" (for sportsmanship) and "mistresspiece" (for the work of a Virginia Woolf) one suspects a not-too-subtle attempt to make the whole language problem look silly. But unless Alexander Pope, when he wrote "The proper study of mankind is man," meant that women should be relegated to the footnotes (or, as George Orwell might have put it, "All men are equal, but men are more equal than women"), viable new words will surely someday supersede the old.

Without apologies to Freud, the great majority of women do not wish in their hearts that they were men. If having grown up with a language that tells them they are at the same time men and not men raises psychic doubts for women, the doubts are not of their sexual identity but of their human identity. Perhaps the present unrest surfacing in the Women's Movement is part of an evolutionary change in our particular form of life—the one form of all in the animal and plant kingdoms that orders and interprets its reality by symbols. The achievements of the species called man have brought us to the brink of self-destruction. If the species survives into the next century with the expectation of going on, it may only be because we have become part of what Harlow Shapley calls the psychozoic kingdom, where brain overshadows brawn and rationality has replaced superstition.

Searching the roots of Western civilization for a word to call this new species of man and woman, someone might come up with *gen,* as in genesis and generic. With such a word, *man* could be used exclusively for males as *woman* is used for females, for gen would include both sexes. Like the words deer and bison, gen would be both plural and singular. Like progenitor, progeny, and generation, it would convey continuity. Gen would express the warmth and generalized sexuality of generous, gentle, and genuine; the specific sexuality of genital and genetic. In the new family of gen, girls and boy would grow to genhood, and to speak of genkind would be to include all the people of the earth.

Topics for Critical Thinking and Writing

1. In the third paragraph Casey Miller and Kate Swift say "Thousands of doctors are women, but in order to be seen in the mind's eye, they must be called women doctors." Keeping in mind "in the mind's eye," do you find this sentence still true? Or has it changed over the past twenty or more years? What about the "reconstructed realities of American history" in paragraphs 8 and 9? Are they also still valid? And has the word *housewife* undergone any change?

2. In paragraph 17 the authors, referring to their current dictionary, note that the editor, managing editor, and so on—down to the list of "distinguished experts"—are almost all men. Check your own dictionary (or one in the library) to see if this is still true of a dictionary compiled in the 1990s. Compare your notes with those of others in your class. Once again, have things changed or not?

3. The authors raise the point, in paragraphs 30–35, that both Jewish and Christian religious institutions continue to oppress women by outmoded theological language and practice. Has this been true in the church you know? Is it true in religions other than Judaism and Christianity? What defense, if any, can you offer for the language and practice?

4. A mini-research topic: Read Barbara Lawrence's "Four-Letter Words Can Hurt You" (page 514), and Katha Pollitt's "Checkbook Maternity: When Is a Mother Not a Mother" (page 66), and Swift and Miller's "One Small Step for Genkind, and devise an essay on "Gender and Language." Your essay should not simply summarize these essays but have a point—an argument to make. Do you, for example, find the use of words for and about women increasing, decreasing, or remaining about the same in their tendency to denigrate women? How do you explain what you have found?

Robin Lakoff

Robin Lakoff was born in 1943 and educated at Radcliffe College and Harvard University. A professor of linguistics at the University of California at Berkeley, she has been especially interested in the language that women use. The essay that we give here was first published in Ms. *magazine in 1974.*

You Are What You Say

Women's language is that pleasant (dainty?), euphemistic never-aggressive way of talking we learned as little girls. Cultural bias was built into the language we were allowed to speak, the subjects we were allowed to speak about, and the ways we were spoken of. Having learned our linguistic lesson well, we go out in the world, only to discover that we are communicative cripples—damned if we do, and damned if we don't.

If we refuse to talk "like a lady," we are ridiculed and criticized for being unfeminine. ("She thinks like a man" is, at best, a left-handed compliment.) If we do learn all the fuzzy-headed, unassertive language of our sex, we are ridiculed for being unable to think clearly, unable to take part in a serious discussion, and therefore unfit to hold a position of power.

It doesn't take much of this for a woman to begin feeling she deserves such treatment because of inadequacies in her own intelligence and education.

"Women's language" shows up in all levels of English. For example,   4
women are encouraged and allowed to make far more precise discriminations in naming colors than men do. Words like *mauve, beige, ecru, aquamarine, lavender,* and so on, are unremarkable in a woman's active vocabulary, but largely absent from that of most men. I know of no evidence suggesting that women actually *see* a wider range of colors than men do. It is simply that fine discriminations of this sort are relevant to women's vocabularies, but not to men's; to men, who control most of the interesting affairs of the world, such distinctions are trivial—irrelevant.

In the area of syntax, we find similar gender-related peculiarities of speech. There is one construction, in particular, that women use conversationally far more than men: the tag question. A tag is midway between an outright statement and a yes-no question; it is less assertive than the former, but more confident than the latter.

A *flat statement* indicates confidence in the speaker's knowledge and is fairly certain to be believed; a *question* indicates a lack of knowledge on some point and implies that the gap in the speaker's knowledge can and will be remedied by an answer. For example, if, at a Little League game, I have had my glasses off, I can legitimately ask someone else: "Was the player out at third?" A *tag question,* being intermediate between statement and question, is used when the speaker is stating a claim, but lacks full confidence in the truth of that claim. So if I say, "Is Joan here?" I will probably not be surprised if my respondent answers "no"; but if I say, "Joan is here, isn't she?" instead, chances are I am already biased in favor of a positive answer, wanting only confirmation. I still want a response, but I have enough knowledge (or think I have) to predict that response. A tag question, then, might be thought of as a statement that doesn't demand to be believed by anyone but the speaker, a way of giving leeway, of not forcing the addressee to go along with the views of the speaker.

Another common use of the tag question is in small talk when the speaker is trying to elicit conversation: "Sure is hot here, isn't it?"

But in discussing personal feelings or opinions, only the speaker   8
normally has any way of knowing the correct answer. Sentences such as "I have a headache, don't I?" are clearly ridiculous. But there are other examples where it is the speaker's opinions, rather than perceptions, for which corroboration is sought, as in "The situation in Southeast Asia is terrible, isn't it?"

While there are, of course, other possible interpretations of a sentence like this, one possibility is that the speaker has a particular answer in mind "yes" or "no"—but is reluctant to state it baldly. This sort of tag question is much more apt to be used by women than by men in conversation. Why is this the case?

The tag question allows a speaker to avoid commitment, and thereby avoid conflict with the addressee. The problem is that, by so doing, speakers may also give the impression of not really being sure of themselves, or looking to the addressee for confirmation of their views. This uncertainty is reinforced in more subliminal ways, too. There is a peculiar sentence-intonation pattern, used almost exclusively by women, as far as I know, which changes a declarative answer into a question. The effect of using the rising inflection typical of a yes-no question is to imply that the speaker is seeking confirmation, even though the speaker is clearly the only one who has the requisite information, which is why the question was put to her in the first place:

(Q) When will dinner be ready?
(A) Oh . . . around six o'clock . . . ?

It is as though the second speaker was saying, "Six o'clock—if that's okay with you, if you agree." The person being addressed is put in the position of having to provide confirmation. One likely consequence of this sort of speech pattern in a woman is that, often unbeknownst to herself, the speaker builds a reputation of tentativeness, and others will refrain from taking her seriously or trusting her with any real responsibilities, since she "can't make up her mind," and "isn't sure of herself."

Such idiosyncrasies may explain why women's language sounds much more "polite" than men's. It is polite to leave a decision open, not impose your mind, or views, or claims, or anyone else. So a tag question is a kind of polite statement, in that it does not force agreement or belief on the addressee. In the same way a request is a polite command, in that it does not force obedience on the addressee, but rather suggests something be done as a favor to the speaker. A clearly stated order implies a threat of certain consequences if it is not followed, and—even more impolite—implies that the speaker is in a superior position and able to enforce the order. By couching wishes in the form of a request, on the other hand, a speaker implies that if the request is not carried out, only the speaker will suffer; noncompliance cannot harm the addressee. So the decision is really left up to the addressee. The distinction becomes clear in these examples:

Close the door.

Please close the door.

Will you close the door?

Will you please close the door?

Won't you close the door?

In the same ways as words and speech patterns used *by* women   12
undermine her image, those used to *describe* women make matters even
worse. Often a word may be used of both men and women (and perhaps of things as well); but when it is applied to women, it assumes a
special meaning that, by implication rather than outright assertion, is
derogatory to women as a group.

The use of euphemisms has this effect. A euphemism is a substitute
for a word that has acquired a bad connotation by association with
something unpleasant or embarrassing. But almost as soon as the new
word comes into common usage, it takes on the same old bad connotations, since feelings about the things or people referred to are not altered
by a change of name; thus new euphemisms must be constantly found.

There is one euphemism for *woman* still very much alive. The word,
of course, is *lady. Lady* has a masculine counterpart, namely *gentleman,*
occasionally shortened to *gent.* But for some reason *lady* is very much
commoner than *gent(leman).*

The decision to use *lady* rather than *woman,* or vice versa, may considerably alter the sense of a sentence, as the following examples show:

a.   A woman (lady) I know is a dean at Berkeley.
b.   A woman (lady) I know makes amazing things out of shoelaces
     and old boxes.

The use of *lady* in (a) imparts a frivolous, or nonserious, tone to the   16
sentence: the matter under discussion is not one of great moment. Similarly, in (b), using *lady* here would suggest that the speaker considered
the "amazing things" not to be serious art, but merely a hobby or an
aberration. If *woman* is used, she might be a serious sculptor. To say *lady
doctor* is very condescending, since no one ever says *gentleman doctor* or
even *man doctor.* For example, mention in the San Francisco *Chronicle* of
January 31, 1972, of Madalyn Murray O'Hair as the *lady atheist* reduces
her position to that of scatterbrained eccentric. Even *woman atheist* is
scarcely defensible: sex is irrelevant to her philosophical position.

Many women argue that, on the other hand, *lady* carries with it
overtones recalling the age of chivalry: conferring exalted stature on the
person so referred to. This makes the term seem polite at first, but we
must also remember that these implications are perilous: they suggest
that a "lady" is helpless, and cannot do things by herself.

Lady can also be used to infer frivolousness, as in titles of organizations. Those that have a serious purpose (not merely that of enabling
"the ladies" to spend time with one another) cannot use the word *lady*
in their titles, but less serious ones may. Compare the *Ladies' Auxiliary* of
a men's group, or the *Thursday Evening Ladies' Browning and Garden
Society* with *Ladies' Liberation* or *Ladies' Strike for Peace.*

What is curious about this split is that *lady* is in origin a euphemism—a substitute that puts a better face on something people find uncomfortable—for *woman*. What kind of euphemism is it that subtly denigrates the people to whom it refers? Perhaps *lady* functions as a euphemism for *woman* because it does not contain the sexual implications present in *woman*: it is not "embarrassing" in that way. If this is so, we may expect that, in the future, *lady* will replace woman as the primary word for the human female, since *woman* will have become too blatantly sexual. That this distinction is already made in some contexts at least is shown in the following examples, where you can try replacing *woman* with *lady:*

a.   She's only twelve, but she's already a woman.
b.   After ten years in jail, Harry wanted to find a woman.
c.   She's my woman, see, so don't mess around with her.

Another common substitute for *woman* is *girl*. One seldom hears a   20
man past the age of adolescence referred to as a boy, save in expressions like "going out with the boys," which are meant to suggest an air of adolescent frivolity and irresponsibility. But women of all ages are "girls": one can have a man—not a boy—Friday, but only a girl—never a woman or even a lady—Friday; women have girlfriends, but men do not—in a nonsexual sense—have boyfriends. It may be that this use of *girl* is euphemistic in the same way the use of *lady* is: in stressing the idea of immaturity, it removes the sexual connotations lurking in *woman. Girl* brings to mind irresponsibility: you don't send a girl to do a woman's errand (or even, for that matter, a boy's errand). She is a person who is both too immature and too far from real life to be entrusted with responsibilities or with decisions of any serious or important nature.

Now let's take a pair of words which, in terms of the possible relationships in an earlier society, were simple male-female equivalents, analogous to *bull: cow.* Suppose we find that, for independent reasons, society has changed in such a way that the original meanings now are irrelevant. Yet the words have not been discarded, but have acquired new meanings, metaphorically related to their original senses. But suppose these new metaphorical uses are no longer parallel to each other. By seeing where the parallelism breaks down, we discover something about the different roles played by men and women in this culture. One good example of such a divergence through time is found in the pair, *master: mistress.* Once used with reference to one's power over servants, these words have become unusable today in their original master-servant sense as the relationship has become less prevalent in our society. But the words are still common.

Unless used with reference to animals, *master* now generally refers to a man who has acquired consummate ability in some field, normally nonsexual. But its feminine counterpart cannot be used this way. It is practically restricted to its sexual sense of "paramour." We start out with two terms, both roughly paraphrasable as "one who has power over another." But the masculine form, once one person is no longer able to have absolute power over another, becomes usable metaphorically in the sense of "having power over *something.*" *Master* requires as its object only the name of some activity, something inanimate and abstract. But *mistress* requires a masculine noun in the possessive to precede it. One cannot say: "Rhonda is a mistress." One must be *someone's* mistress. A man is defined by what he does, a woman by her sexuality, that is, in terms of one particular aspect of her relationship to men. It is one thing to be an *old master* like Hans Holbein,[1] and another to be an *old mistress.*

The same is true of the words *spinster* and *bachelor*—gender words for "one who is not married." The resemblance ends with the definition. While *bachelor* is a neuter term, often used as a compliment, *spinster* normally is used pejoratively, with connotations of prissiness, fussiness, and so on. To be a bachelor implies that one has a choice of marrying or not, and this is what makes the idea of a bachelor existence attractive, in the popular literature. He has been pursued and has successfully eluded his pursuers. But a spinster is one who has not been pursued, or at least not seriously. She is old, unwanted goods. The metaphorical connotations of *bachelor* generally suggest sexual freedom; of *spinster*, puritanism or celibacy.

These examples could be multiplied. It is generally considered a   24
faux pas, in society, to congratulate a woman on her engagement, while it is correct to congratulate her fiancé. Why is this? The reason seems to be that it is impolite to remind people of things that may be uncomfortable to them. To congratulate a woman on her engagement is really to say, "Thank goodness! You had a close call!" For the man, on the other hand, there was no such danger. His choosing to marry is viewed as a good thing, but not something essential.

The linguistic double standards holds throughout the life of the relationship. After marriage, bachelor and spinster become man and wife, not man and woman. The woman whose husband dies remains "John's widow"; John, however, is never "Mary's widower."

Finally, why is it that salesclerks and others are so quick to call women customers "dear," "honey," and other terms of endearment they really have no business using? A male customer would never put up with it. But women, like children, are supposed to enjoy these endearments, rather than being offended by them.

In more ways than one, it's time to speak up.

Topics for Critical Thinking and Writing

1. Lakoff's first example of "women's language" (paragraph 4) has to do with colors. She says that women are more likely than men to use such words as *mauve, beige,* and *lavender* not because women see a wider

---

[1]German painter of the sixteenth century.

range of colors but because men, "who control most of the interesting affairs of the world," regard distinctions of color as trivial and presumably leave them to the women. How adequate does this explanation seem to you?

2. For a day or so, try to notice if Lakoff's suggestion is correct that women are more inclined than men to use "tag questions" and to use a "rising inflection" with a declarative sentence. Jot down examples you hear, and write an essay of about five hundred words, either supporting or refuting Lakoff.

3. While you are eavesdropping, you might notice, too, whether or not in mixed company women talk more than men. Many men assume that "women talk a lot," but is it true? If, for instance, you spend an evening with an adult couple, try to form an impression about which of the two does more of the talking. Of course this is too small a sample to allow for a generalization; still, it is worth thinking about. If you are at a meeting—perhaps a meeting of a committee with men and women—again try to see whether the males or the females do most of the talking. Try also to see whether one sex interrupts the other more often than the other way around. And try to make some sense out of your findings.

4. In paragraph 11 Lakoff says, "Women's language sounds much more 'polite' than men's," and she implies that this politeness is a way of seeming weak. Do you associate politeness with weakness?

5. The essay originally appeared in *Ms.*, a feminist magazine, rather than in an academic journal devoted to language or to sociology. Why do you suppose she chose *Ms.*? What would you say Lakoff's purpose was in writing and publishing the essay?

6. This essay was first published in 1974. Do you think it is dated? You might begin by asking yourself if women today use "women's language."

Barbara Lawrence

Barbara Lawrence was born in Hanover, New Hampshire, and educated at Connecticut College and New York University. She teaches at the State University of New York, at Old Westbury. This essay first appeared in The New York Times.

Four-letter Words Can Hurt You

Why should any words be called obscene? Don't they all describe natural human functions? Am I trying to tell them, my students demand, that the "strong, earthy, gut-honest"—or, if they are fans of Norman Mailer, the "rich, liberating, existential"—language they use to describe sexual activity isn't preferable to "phony-sounding, middle-class words like 'intercourse' and 'copulate'?" "Cop You Late!" they say with fancy inflections and gagging grimaces. "Now, what is *that* supposed to mean?"

Well, what is it supposed to mean? And why indeed should one group of words describing human functions and human organs be acceptable in ordinary conversation and another, describing presumably the same organs and functions, be tabooed—so much so, in fact, that some of these words still cannot appear in print in many parts of the English-speaking world?

The argument that these taboos exist only because of "sexual hangups" (middle-class, middle-age, feminist), or even that they are a result of class oppression (the contempt of the Norman conquerors for the language of their Anglo-Saxon serfs), ignores a much more likely explanation, it seems to me, and that is the sources and functions of the words themselves.

The best known of the tabooed sexual verbs, for example, comes   4
from the German *ficken,* meaning "to strike"; combined, according to Partridge's etymological dictionary *Origins,* with the Latin sexual verb *futuere;* associated in turn with the Latin *fustis,* "a staff or cudgel"; the Celtic *buc,* "a point, hence to pierce"; the Irish *bot,* "the male member"; the Latin *battuere,* "to beat"; the Gaelic *batair,* "a cudgeller"; the Early Irish *bualaim,* "I strike"; and so forth. It is one of what etymologists sometimes call "the sadistic group of words for the man's part in copulation."

The brutality of this word, then, and its equivalents ("screw," "bang," etc.), is not an illusion of the middle class or a crotchet of Women's Liberation. In their origins and imagery these words carry undeniably painful, if not sadistic, implications, the object of which is almost always female. Consider, for example, what a "screw" actually does to the wood it penetrates; what a painful, even mutilating, activity this kind of analogy suggests. "Screw" is particularly interesting in this context, since the noun, according to Partridge, comes from words meaning "groove," "nut," "ditch," "breeding sow," "scrofula" and "swelling," while the verb, besides its explicit imagery, has antecedent associations to "write on," "scratch," "scarify," and so forth—a revealing fusion of a mechanical or painful action with an obviously denigrated object.

Not all obscene words, of course, are as implicitly sadistic or denigrating to women as these, but all that I know seem to serve a similar purpose: to reduce the human organism (especially the female organism) and human functions (especially sexual and procreative) to their least organic, most mechanical dimension; to substitute a trivializing or deforming resemblance for the complex human reality of what is being described.

Tabooed male descriptives, when they are not openly denigrating to women, often serve to divorce a male organ or function from any significant interaction with the female. Take the word "testes," for example, suggesting "witnesses" (from the Latin *testis*) to the sexual and procreative strengths of the male organ; and the obscene counterpart of this word, which suggests little more than a mechanical shape. Or compare almost any of the "rich," "liberating" sexual verbs, so fashionable today among male writers, with that much-derided Latin word "copulate" ("to bind or join together") or even that AngloSaxon phrase (which seems to have had no trouble surviving the Norman Conquest) "make love."

How arrogantly self-involved the tabooed words seem in comparison to either of the other terms, and how contemptuous of the female partner. Understandably so, of course, if she is only a "skirt," a "broad," a "chick," a "pussycat" or a "piece." If she is, in other words, no more than her skirt, or what her skirt conceals; no more than a breeder, or the broadest part of her; no more than a piece of a human being or a "piece of tail."

The most severely tabooed of all the female descriptives, incidentally, are those like a "piece of tail," which suggest (either explicitly or through antecedents) that there is no significant difference between the female channel through which we are all conceived and born and the anal outlet common to both sexes—a distinction that pornographers have always enjoyed obscuring.

This effort to deny women their biological identity, their individuality, their humanness, is such an important aspect of obscene language that one can only marvel at how seldom, in an era preoccupied with definitions of obscenity, this fact is brought to our attention. One problem, of course, is that many of the people in the best position to do this (critics, teachers, writers) are so reluctant today to admit that they are angered or shocked by obscenity. Bored, maybe, unimpressed, aesthetically, displeased, but—no matter how brutal or denigrating the material—never angered, never shocked.

And yet how eloquently angered, how piously shocked many of these same people become if denigrating language is used about any minority group other than women; if the obscenities are racial or ethnic, that is, rather than sexual. Words like "coon," "kike," "spic," "wop," after all, deform identity, deny individuality and humanness in almost exactly the same way that sexual vulgarisms and obscenities do.

No one that I know, least of all my students, would fail to question the values of a society whose literature and entertainment rested heavily on racial or ethnic pejoratives. Are the values of a society whose literature and entertainment rest as heavily as ours on sexual pejoratives any less questionable?

Topics for Critical Thinking and Writing

1. In addition to giving evidence to support her view, what persuasive devices (such as irony, analogy) does Lawrence use? (On irony, see page 798; on analogy, see page 793.)

2. Examine your own use or nonuse of four-letter words. How and when did you learn to use them or to avoid using them? If you have reasons to avoid them other than the ones Lawrence provides, what are they? If you do use such words, under what circumstances are you likely to use them? Will Lawrance's analysis persuade you to avoid them altogether? Why or why not?

Edward T. Hall

Edward T. Hall, born in Missouri in 1914, was for many years a professor of anthropology at Northwestern University.

Hall is especially concerned with "proxemics," a word derived from the Latin proximus, *"nearest." Proxemics is the study of people's responses to spatial relationships—for example, their ways of marking out their territory in public places and their responses to what they consider to be crowding. In these pages from his book,* The Hidden Dimension *(1966), Hall suggests that Arabs and Westerners must understand the proxemic customs of each others culture; without such understanding, other communications between them are likely to be misunderstood.*

Proxemics in the Arab World

In spite of over two thousand years of contact, Westerners and Arabs still do not understand each other. Proxemic research reveals some insights into this difficulty. Americans in the Middle East are immediately struck by two conflicting sensations. In public they are compressed and overwhelmed by smells, crowding, and high noise levels; in Arab homes Americans are apt to rattle around, feeling exposed and often somewhat inadequate because of too much space! (The Arab houses and apartments of the middle and upper classes which Americans stationed abroad commonly occupy are much larger than the dwellings such Americans usually inhabit.) Both the high sensory stimulation which is experienced in public places and the basic insecurity which comes from being in a dwelling that is too large provide Americans with an introduction to the sensory world of the Arab.

Behavior in Public

Pushing and shoving in public places is characteristic of Middle Eastern culture. Yet it is not entirely what Americans think it is (being pushy and rude) but stems from a different set of assumptions concerning not only the relations between people but how one experiences the body as well. Paradoxically, Arabs consider northern Europeans and Americans pushy, too. This was very puzzling to me when I started investigating these two views. How could Americans who stand aside and avoid touching be considered pushy? I used to ask Arabs to explain this paradox. None of my subjects was able to tell me specifically what particulars of American behavior were responsible, yet they all agreed that the impression was widespread among Arabs. After repeated unsuccessful attempts to gain insight into the cognitive world of the Arab on this particular point, I filed it away as a question that only time would answer. When the answer came, it was because of a seemingly inconsequential annoyance.

While waiting for a friend in a Washington, D.C. hotel lobby and wanting to be both visible and alone, I had seated myself in a solitary chair outside the normal stream of traffic. In such a setting most Americans follow a rule, which is all the more binding because we seldom think about it, that can be stated as follows: as soon as a person stops or is seated in a public place, there balloons around him a small sphere of privacy which is considered inviolate. The size of the sphere varies with the degree of crowding, the age, sex, and the importance of the person, as well as the general surroundings. Anyone who enters this zone and stays there is intruding. In fact, a stranger who intrudes, even for a specific purpose, acknowledges the fact that he has intruded by beginning his request with "Pardon me, but can you tell me . . . ?"

To continue, as I waited in the deserted lobby, a stranger walked up 4 to where I was sitting and stood close enough so that not only could I easily touch him but I could even hear him breathing. In addition, the dark mass of his body filled the peripheral field of vision on my left side. If the lobby had been crowded with people, I would have understood his behavior, but in an empty lobby his presence made me exceedingly uncomfortable. Feeling annoyed by this intrusion, I moved my body in such a way as to communicate annoyance. Strangely enough, instead of moving away, my actions seemed only to encourage him, because he moved even closer. In spite of the temptation to escape the annoyance, I put aside thoughts of abandoning my post, thinking, "To hell with it. Why should I move? I was here first and I'm not going to let this fellow drive me out even if he is a boor." Fortunately, a group of people soon arrived whom my tormentor immediately joined. Their mannerisms explained his behavior, for I knew from both speech and gestures that they were Arabs. I had not been able to make this crucial identification by looking at my subject when he was alone because he wasn't talking and he was wearing American clothes.

In describing the scene later to an Arab colleague, two contrasting patterns emerged. My concept and my feelings about my own circle of privacy in a "public" place immediately struck my Arab friend as strange and puzzling. He said, "After all, it's a public place, isn't it?" Pursuing this line of inquiry, I found that an Arab thought I had no rights whatsoever by virtue of occupying a given spot; neither my place nor my body was inviolate! For the Arab, there is no such thing as an intrusion in public. Public means public. With this insight, a great range of Arab behavior that had been puzzling, annoying, and sometimes even frightening began to make sense. I learned, for example, that if *A* is standing on a street corner and *B* wants his spot, *B* is within his rights if he does what he can to make *A* uncomfortable enough to move. In Beirut only the hardy sit in the last row in a movie theater, because there are usually standees who want seats and who push and shove and make such a nuisance that most people give up and leave. Seen in this light, the Arab who "intruded" on my space in the hotel lobby had apparently selected it for the very reason I had: it was a good place to watch two doors and the elevator. My show of annoyance, instead of driving him away, had only encouraged him. He thought he was about to get me to move.

Another silent source of friction between Americans and Arabs is in an area that Americans treat very informally—the manners and rights of the road. In general, in the United States we tend to defer to the vehicle that is bigger, more powerful, faster, and heavily laden. While a pedestrian walking along a road may feel annoyed he will not think it unusual to step aside for a fast-moving automobile. He knows that because he is moving he does not have the right to the space around him that he has when he is standing still (as I was in the hotel lobby). It appears that the reverse is true with the Arabs who apparently *take on rights to space as they move.* For someone else to move into a space an Arab is also moving into is a violation of his rights. It is infuriating to an Arab to have someone else cut in front of him on the highway. It is the American's cavalier treatment of moving space that makes the Arab call him aggressive and pushy.

Concepts of Privacy

The experience described above and many others suggested to me that Arabs might actually have a wholly contrasting set of assumptions concerning the body and the rights associated with it. Certainly the Arab tendency to shove and push each other in public and to feel and pinch women in public conveyances would not be tolerated by Westerners. It appeared to me that they must not have any concept of a private zone outside the body. This proved to be precisely the case.

In the Western world, the person is synonymous with an individual inside a skin. And in northern Europe generally, the skin and even the clothes may be inviolate. You need permission to touch either if you are a stranger. This rule applies in some parts of France, where the mere touching of another person during an argument used to be legally defined as assault. For the Arab the location of the person in relation to the body is quite different. The person exists somewhere down inside the body. The ego is not completely hidden, however, because it can be reached very easily with an insult. It is protected from touch but not from words. The dissociation of the body and the ego may explain why the public amputation of a thief's hand is tolerated as standard punishment in Saudi Arabia. It also sheds light on why an Arab employer living in a modern apartment can provide his servant with a room that is a box-like cubicle approximately 5 by 10 by 4 feet in size that is not only hung from the ceiling to conserve floor space but has an opening so that the servant can be spied on.

As one might suspect, deep orientations toward the self such as the one just described are also reflected in the language. This was brought to my attention one afternoon when an Arab colleague who is the author of an Arab-English dictionary arrived in my office and threw himself into a chair in a state of obvious exhaustion. When I asked him what had been going on, he said: "I have spent the entire afternoon trying to find the Arab equivalent of the English word 'rape.' There is no such word in Arabic. All my sources, both written and spoken, can come up with no more than an approximation, such as 'He took her against her will.' There is nothing in Arabic approaching your meaning as it is expressed in that one word."

Differing concepts of the placement of the ego in relation to the body are not easily grasped. Once an idea like this is accepted, however, it is possible to understand many other facets of Arab life that would otherwise be difficult to explain. One of these is the high population density of Arab cities like Cairo, Beirut, and Damascus. According to the animal studies described [elsewhere], the Arabs should be living in a perpetual behavioral sink. While it is probable that Arabs are suffering from population pressures, it is also just as possible that continued pressure from the desert has resulted in a cultural adaptation to high density which takes the form described above. Tucking the ego down inside the body shell not only would permit higher population densities but would explain why it is that Arab communications are stepped up as much as they are when compared to northern European communication patterns. Not only is the sheer noise level much higher, but the piercing look of the eyes, the touch of the hands, and the mutual bathing in the warm moist breath during conversation represent stepped-up sensory inputs to a level which many Europeans find unbearably intense.

The Arab dream is for lots of space in the home, which unfortunately many Arabs cannot afford. Yet when he has space, it is very different from what one finds in most American homes. Arab spaces inside their upper middle-class homes are tremendous by our standards. They avoid partitions because Arabs *do not like to be alone*. The form of the home is such as to hold the family together inside a single protective shell, because Arabs are deeply involved with each other. Their personalities are intermingled and take nourishment from each other like the roots and soil. If one is not with people and actively involved in some way, one is deprived of life. An old Arab saying reflects this value: "Paradise without people should not be entered because it is Hell." Therefore, Arabs in the United States often feel socially and sensorially deprived and long to be back where there is human warmth and contact.

Since there is no physical privacy as we know it in the Arab family, not even a word for privacy, one could expect that the Arabs might use some other means to be alone. Their way to be alone is to stop talking. Like the English, an Arab who shuts himself off in this way is not indicating that anything is wrong or that he is withdrawing, only that he wants to be alone with his own thoughts or does not want to be intruded upon. One subject said that her father would come and go for days at a time without saying a word, and no one in the family thought anything of it. Yet for this very reason, an Arab exchange student visiting a Kansas farm failed to pick up the cue that his American hosts were mad at him when they gave him the "silent treatment." He only discovered something was wrong when they took him to town and tried forcibly to put him on a bus to Washington, D.C., the headquarters of the exchange program responsible for his presence in the U.S.

Arab Personal Distances

Like everyone else in the world, Arabs are unable to formulate specific rules for their informal behavior patterns. In fact, they often deny that there are any rules, and they are made anxious by suggestions that such is the case. Therefore, in order to determine how the Arab sets distances, I investigated the use of each sense separately. Gradually, definite and distinctive behavioral patterns began to emerge.

Olfaction occupies a prominent place in the Arab life. Not only is it one of the distance-setting mechanisms, but it is a vital part of a complex system of behavior. Arabs consistently breathe on people when they talk. However, this habit is more than a matter of different manners. To the Arab good smells are pleasing and a way of being involved with each other. To smell one's friend is not only nice but desirable, for to deny him your breath is to act ashamed. Americans, on the other hand, trained as they are not to breathe in people's faces, automatically communicate shame in trying to be polite. Who would expect that when our highest diplomats are putting on their best manners they are also communicating shame? Yet this is what occurs constantly, because diplomacy is not only "eyeball to eyeball" but breath to breath.

By stressing olfaction, Arabs do not try to eliminate all the body's odors, only to enhance them and use them in building human relationships. Nor are they self-conscious about telling others when they don't like the way they smell. A man leaving his house in the morning may be told by his uncle, "Habib, your stomach is sour and your breath doesn't smell too good. Better not talk too close to people today." Smell is even considered in the choice of a mate. When couples are being matched for marriage, the man's go-between will sometimes ask to smell the girl, who may be turned down if she doesn't "smell nice." Arabs recognize that smell and disposition may be linked.

In a word, the olfactory boundary performs two roles in Arab life. 16 It enfolds those who want to relate and separates those who don't. The Arab finds it essential to stay inside the olfactory zone as a means of keeping tab on changes in emotion. What is more, he may feel crowded as soon as he smells something unpleasant. While not much is known about "olfactory crowding," this may prove to be as significant as any other variable in the crowding complex because it is tied directly to the body chemistry and hence to the state of health and emotions. It is not surprising, therefore, that the olfactory boundary constitutes for the Arabs an informal distance-setting mechanism in contrast to the visual mechanisms of the Westerner.

Facing and Not Facing

One of my earliest discoveries in the field of intercultural communication was that the position of the bodies of people in conversation varies with the culture. Even so, it is used to puzzle me that a special Arab friend seemed unable to walk and talk at the same time. After years in the United States, he could not bring himself to stroll along, facing forward while talking. Our progress would be arrested while he edged ahead, cutting slightly in front of me and turning sideways so we could see each other. Once in this position, he would stop. His behavior was explained when I learned that for the Arabs to view the other person peripherally is regarded as impolite, and to sit or stand back-to-back is considered very rude. You must be involved when interacting with Arabs who are friends.

One mistaken American notion is that Arabs conduct all conversations at close distances. This is not the case at all. On social occasions, they may sit on opposite sides of the room and talk across the room to each other. They are, however, apt to take offense when Americans use what are to them ambiguous distances, such as the four- to seven-foot social-consultative distance. They frequently complain that Americans are cold or aloof or "don't care." This was what an elderly Arab diplomat in an American hospital thought when the American nurses used "professional" distance. He had the feeling that he was being ignored, that they might not take good care of him. Another Arab subject remarked, referring to American behavior, "What's the matter? Do I smell bad? Or are they afraid of me?"

Arabs who interact with Americans report experiencing a certain flatness traceable in part to a very different use of the eyes in private and in public as well as between friends and strangers. Even though it is rude for a guest to walk around the Arab home eying things, Arabs look at each other in ways which seem hostile or challenging to the American. One Arab informant said that he was in constant hot water with Americans because of the way he looked at them without the slightest intention of offending. In fact, he had on several occasions barely avoided fights with American men who apparently thought their masculinity was being challenged because of the way he was looking at them. As noted earlier, Arabs look each other in the eye when talking with an intensity that makes most Americans highly uncomfortable.

Involvement

As the reader must gather by now, Arabs are involved with each other on many different levels simultaneously. Privacy in a public place is foreign to them. Business transactions in the bazaar, for example, are not just between buyer and seller, but are participated in by everyone. Anyone who is standing around may join in. If a grownup sees a boy breaking a window, he must stop him even if he doesn't know him. Involvement and participation are expressed in other ways as well. If two men are fighting, the crowd must intervene. On the political level, *to fail to intervene* when trouble is brewing is to take sides, which is what our State Department always seems to be doing. Given the fact that few people in the world today are even remotely aware of the cultural mold that forms their thoughts, it is normal for Arabs to view *our* behavior as though it stemmed from *their* own hidden set of assumptions.

Feelings about Enclosed Spaces

In the course of my interviews with Arabs the term "tomb" kept cropping up in conjunction with enclosed space. In a word, Arabs don't mind being crowded by people but hate to be hemmed in by walls. They show a much greater overt sensitivity to architectural crowding than we do. Enclosed space must meet at least three requirements that I know of if it is to satisfy the Arabs: there must be plenty of unobstructed space in which to move around (possibly as much as a thousand square feet); very high ceilings—so high in fact that they do not normally impinge on the visual field; and, in addition, there must be an unobstructed view. It was spaces such as these in which the Americans referred to earlier felt so uncomfortable. One sees the Arab's need for a view expressed in many ways, even negatively, for to cut off a neighbor's view is one of the most effective ways of spiting him. In Beirut one can see what is known locally as the "spite house." It is nothing more than a thick, four-story wall, built at the end of a long fight between neighbors, on a narrow strip of land, for the express purpose of denying a view of the Mediterranean to any house built on the land behind. According to one of my informants, there is also a house on a small plot of land between Beirut and Damascus which is completely surrounded by a neighbor's wall built high enough to cut off the view from all windows!

Boundaries

Proxemic patterns tell us other things about Arab culture. For example, the whole concept of the boundary as an abstraction is almost impossible to pin down. In one sense, there are no boundaries. "Edges" of towns, yes, but permanent boundaries out in the country (hidden lines), no. In the course of my work with Arab subjects I had a difficult time translating our concept of a boundary into terms which could be equated with theirs. In order to clarify the distinctions between the two very different definitions, I thought it might be helpful to pinpoint acts which constituted trespass. To date, I have been unable to discover anything even remotely resembling our own legal concept of trespass.

Arab behavior in regard to their own real estate is apparently an extension of, and therefore consistent with, their approach to the body. My subjects simply failed to respond whenever trespass was mentioned. They didn't seem to understand what I meant by this term. This may be explained by the fact that they organize relationships with each other according to closed social systems rather than spatially. For thousands of years Moslems, Marinites, Druses, and Jews have lived in their own villages, each with strong kin affiliations. Their hierarchy of loyalties is: first to one's self, then to kinsman, townsman, or tribesman, co-religionist and/or countryman. Anyone not in these categories is a stranger. Strangers and enemies are very closely linked, if not synonymous, in Arab thought. Trespass in this context is a matter of who you are, rather than a piece of land or a space with a boundary that can be denied to anyone and everyone, friend and foe alike.

In summary, proxemic patterns differ. By examining them it is possible to reveal hidden cultural frames that determine the structure of a given people's perceptual world. Perceiving the world differently leads to differential definitions of what constitutes crowded living, different interpersonal relations, and a different approach to both local and international politics.   24

Topics for Critical Thinking and Writing

1. According to Hall, why do Arabs think Americans are pushy? And, again according to Hall, why do Arabs not consider themselves pushy?
2. Explain what Hall means by "cognitive world" (paragraph 2); by "ego" (paragraph 10); by "behavioral sink" (in the same paragraph). Then explain, for the benefit of someone who does not understand the terms, how you know what Hall means by each.
3. In paragraph 9 Hall points out that there is no Arabic equivalent of the English word *rape*. Can you provide an example of a similar gap in English or in another language? Does a cultural difference account for the linguistic difference?

4. In paragraph 3 Hall says of a rule that it "is all the more binding because we seldom think about it." Is this generally true of rules? What examples or counterexamples support your view?

Deborah Tannen

Deborah Tannen holds a Ph.D. in linguistics from the University of California, Berkeley, and is an associate professor of linguistics at Georgetown University. She is the author of scholarly articles and books as well as of popular articles in such magazines as New York *and* Vogue. *We reprint a chapter from one of her books,* That's Not What I Meant!

The Workings of Conversational Style

The Meaning Is the Metamessage

You're sitting at a bar—or in a coffee shop or at a party—and suddenly you feel lonely. You wonder, "What do all these people find to talk about that's so important?" Usually the answer is, Nothing. Nothing that's so important. But people don't wait until they have something important to say in order to talk.

Very little of what is said is important for the information expressed in the words. But that doesn't mean that the talk isn't important. It's crucially important, as a way of showing that we are involved with each other, and how we feel about being involved. Our talk is saying something about our relationship.

Information conveyed by the meanings of words is the message. What is communicated about relationships—attitudes toward each other, the occasion, and what we are saying—is the metamessage. And it's metamessages that we react to most strongly. If someone says, "I'm not angry," and his jaw is set hard and his words seem to be squeezed out in a hiss, you won't believe the message that he's not angry; you'll believe the metamessage conveyed by the way he said it—that he is. Comments like "It's not what you said but the way you said it" or "Why did you say it like that?" or "Obviously it's not nothing; something's wrong" are responses to metamessages of talk.

Many of us dismiss talk that does not convey important informa- 4
tion as worthless—meaningless small talk if it's a social setting or "empty rhetoric" if it's public. Such admonitions as "Skip the small talk," "Get to the point," or "Why don't you say what you mean?" may seem to be reasonable. But they are reasonable only if information is all that counts. This attitude toward talk ignores the fact that people are

emotionally involved with each other and that talking is the major way we establish, maintain, monitor, and adjust our relationships.

Whereas words convey information, how we speak those words—how loud, how fast, with what intonation and emphasis—communicates what we think we're doing when we speak: teasing, flirting, explaining, or chastising; whether we're feeling friendly, angry, or quizzical; whether we want to get closer or back off. In other words, how we say what we say communicates social meanings.

Although we continually respond to social meaning in conversation, we have a hard time talking about it because it does not reside in the dictionary definitions of words, and most of us have unwavering faith in the gospel according to the dictionary. It is always difficult to talk about—even to see or think about—forces and processes for which we have no names, even if we feel their impact. Linguistics provides terms that describe the processes of communication and therefore make it possible to see, talk, and think about them.

This chapter introduces some of the linguistic terms that give names to concepts that are crucial for understanding communication—and therefore relationships. In addition to the concept of metamessages—underlying it, in a sense—there are universal human needs that motivate communication: the needs to be connected to others and to be left alone. Trying to honor these conflicting needs puts us in a double bind. The linguistic concept of politeness accounts for the way we serve these needs and react to the double bind—through metamessages in our talk.

Involvement and Independence

The philosopher Schopenhauer gave an often-quoted example of por-   8
cupines trying to get through a cold winter. They huddle together for warmth, but their sharp quills prick each other, so they pull away. But then they get cold. They have to keep adjusting their closeness and distance to keep from freezing and from getting pricked by their fellow porcupines—the source of both comfort and pain.

We need to get close to each other to have a sense of community, to feel we're not alone in the world. But we need to keep our distance from each other to preserve our independence, so others don't impose on or engulf us. This duality reflects the human condition. We are individual and social creatures. We need other people to survive, but we want to survive as individuals.

Another way to look at this duality is that we are all the same—and all different. There is comfort in being understood and pain in the impossibility of being understood completely. But there is also comfort in being different—special and unique—and pain in being the same as everyone else, just another cog on the wheel.

Valuing Involvement and Independence

We all keep balancing the needs for involvement and independence, but individuals as well as cultures place different relative values on these needs and have different ways of expressing those values. America as a nation has glorified individuality, especially for men. This is in stark contrast to people in many parts of the world outside Western Europe, who more often glorify involvement in family and clan, for women and men.

The independent pioneers—and later our image of them—have served us well. The glorification of independence served the general progress of the nation as (traditionally male) individuals have been willing to leave their hometowns—the comfort of the familiar and familial—to find opportunity, get the best education, travel, work wherever they could find the best jobs or wherever their jobs sent them. The yearning for involvement enticed (traditionally female) individuals to join them.

The values of the group are reflected in personal values. Many Americans, especially (but not only) American men, place more emphasis on their need for independence and less on their need for social involvement. This often entails paying less attention to the metamessage level of talk—the level that comments on relationships—focusing instead on the information level. The attitude may go as far as the conviction that only the information level really counts—or is really there. It is then a logical conclusion that talk not rich in information should be dispensed with. Thus, many daughters and sons of all ages, calling their parents, find that their fathers want to exchange whatever information is needed and then hang up, but their mothers want to chat, to "keep in touch."

American men's information-focused approach to talk has shaped the American way of doing business. Most Americans think it's best to "get down to brass tacks" as soon as possible, and not "waste time" in small talk (social talk) or "beating around the bush." But this doesn't work very well in business dealings with Greek, Japanese, or Arab counterparts for whom "small talk" is necessary to establish the social relationship that must provide the foundation for conducting business.

Another expression of this difference—one that costs American tourists huge amounts of money—is our inability to understand the logic behind bargaining. If the African, Indian, Arab, South American, or Mediterranean seller wants to sell a product, and the tourist wants to buy it, why not set a fair price and let the sale proceed? Because the sale is only one part of the interaction. Just as important, if not more so, is the interaction that goes on during the bargaining: an artful way for buyer and seller to reaffirm their recognition that they're dealing with—and that they are—humans, not machines.

Believing that only the information level of communication is important and real also lets men down when it comes to maintaining

12

16

personal relationships. From day to day, there often isn't any significant news to talk about. Women are negatively stereotyped as frivolously talking at length without conveying significant information. Yet their ability to keep talking to each other makes it possible for them to maintain close friendships. *Washington Post* columnist Richard Cohen observed that he and the other men he knows don't really have friends in the sense that women have them. This may be at least partly because they don't talk to each other if they can't think of some substantive topic to talk about. As a result, many men find themselves without personal contacts when they retire.

The Double Bind

No matter what relative value we place on involvement and independence, and how we express these values, people, like porcupines, are always balancing the conflicting needs for both. But the porcupine metapor is a little misleading because it suggests a sequence: alternately drawing close and pulling back. Our needs for involvement and independence—to be connected and to be separate—are not sequential but simultaneous. We must serve both needs at once in all we say.

And that is why we find ourselves in a double bind. Anything we say to show we're involved with others is in itself a threat to our (and their) individuality. And anything we say to show we're keeping our distance from others is in itself a threat to our (and their) need for involvement. It's not just a conflict—feeling torn between two alternatives—or ambivalence—feeling two ways about one thing. It's a double bind because whatever we do to serve one need necessarily violates the other. And we can't step out of the circle. If we try to withdraw by not communicating, we hit the force field of our need for involvement and are hurled back in.

Because of this double bind, communication will never be perfect; we cannot reach stasis. We have no choice but to keep trying to balance independence and involvement, freedom and safety, the familiar and the strange—continually making adjustments as we list to one side or the other. The way we make these adjustments in our talk can be understood as politeness phenomena.

Information and Politeness in Talk

A language philosopher, H. P. Grice, codified the rules by which conversation would be constructed if information were its only point: 20

Say as much as necessary and no more.
Tell the truth.

Be relevant.

Be clear.

These make perfect sense—until we start to listen to and think about real conversations. For one thing, all the seeming absolutes underlying these injunctions are really relative. How much is necessary? Which truth? What is relevant? What is clear?

But even if we could agree on these values, we wouldn't want simply to blurt out what we mean, because we're juggling the needs for involvement and independence. If what we mean shows involvement, we want to temper it to show we're not imposing. If what we mean shows distance, we want to temper it with involvement to show we're not rejecting. If we state what we want to believe, others may not agree or may not want the same thing, so our statement could introduce disharmony; therefore we prefer to get an idea of what others want or think, or how they feel about what we want or think, before we commit ourselves to—maybe even before we make up our minds about—what we mean.

This broad concept of the social goals we serve when we talk is called "politeness" by linguists and anthropologists—not the pinky-in-the-air idea of politeness, but a deeper sense of trying to take into account the effect of what we say on other people.

Linguist Robin Lakoff devised another set of rules that describe the motivations behind politeness—that is, how we adjust what we say to take into account its effects on others. Here they are as Lakoff presents them:

1. Don't impose; keep your distance.
2. Give options; let the other person have a say.
3. Be friendly; maintain camaraderie.

Following Rule 3, Be friendly, makes others comfortable by serving their need for involvement. Following Rule 1, Don't impose, makes others comfortable by serving their need for independence. Rule 2, Give options, falls between Rules 1 and 3. People differ with respect to which rules they tend to apply, and when, and how.

To see how these rules work, let's consider a fairly trivial but common conversation. If you offer me something to drink, I may say, "No, thanks," even though I am thirsty. In some societies this is expected; you insist, and I give in after about the third offer. This is polite in the sense of Rule 1, Don't impose. If you expect this form of politeness and I accept on the first offer, you will think I'm too forward—or dying of thirst. If you don't expect this form of politeness, and I use it, you will take my refusal at face value—and I might indeed die of thirst while waiting for you to ask again.

I may also say, in response to your offer, "I'll have whatever you're having." This is polite in the sense of Rule 2, Give options: I'm letting you decide what to give me. If I do this, but you expect me to refuse the first offer, you may still think I'm pushy. But if you expect Rule 3, Be friendly, you may think me wishy-washy. Don't I know what I want?

Exercising Rule 3-style politeness, Be friendly, I might respond to your offer of something to drink by saying, "Yes, thanks, some apple juice, please." In fact, if this is my style of politeness. I might not wait for you to offer at all, but ask right off, "Have you got anything to drink?," or even head straight for your kitchen, throw open the refrigerator door, and call out, "Got any juice?"

If you and I both feel this is appropriate, my doing it will reinforce our rapport because we both subscribe to the rule of breaking rules; not having to follow the more formal rule sends a metamessage: "We are such good friends, we don't have to stand on ceremony." But if you don't subscribe to this brand of politeness, or don't want to get that chummy with me, you will be offended by my way of being friendly. If we have only recently met, that could be the beginning of the end of our friendship.

Of course, these aren't actually rules, but senses we have of the "natural" way to speak. We don't think of ourselves as following rules, or even (except in formal situations) of being polite. We simply talk in ways that seem obviously appropriate at the time they pop out of our mouths—seemingly self-evident ways of being a good person.   28

Yet our use of these "rules" is not unconscious. If asked about why we said one thing or another in this way or that, we are likely to explain that we spoke the way we did "to be nice" or "friendly" or "considerate." These are commonsense terms for what linguists refer to, collectively, as politeness—ways of taking into account the effect on others of what we say.

The rules, or senses, of politeness are not mutually exclusive. We don't choose one and ignore the others. Rather we balance them all to be appropriately friendly without imposing, to keep appropriate distance without appearing aloof.

Negotiating the offer of a drink is a fairly trivial matter, though the importance of such fleeting conversations should not be underestimated. The way we talk in countless such daily encounters is part of what constitutes our image of ourselves, and it is on the basis of such encounters that we form our impressions of each other. They have a powerful cumulative effect on our personal and interactive lives.

Furthermore, the process of balancing these conflicting senses of politeness—serving involvement and independence—is the basis for   32 the most consequential of interactions as well as the most trivial. Let's consider the linguistic means we have of serving these needs—and their inherent indeterminacy, which means they can easily let us down.

The Two-Edged Sword of Politeness

Sue was planning to visit Amy in a distant city, but shortly before she was supposed to arrive, Sue called and canceled. Although Amy felt disappointed, she tried to be understanding. Being polite by not imposing, and respecting Sue's need for independence, Amy said it was really okay if Sue didn't come. Sue was very depressed at that time, and she got more depressed. She took Amy's considerateness—a sign of caring, respecting Sue's independence—as indifference—not caring at all, a lack of involvement. Amy later felt partly responsible for Sue's depression because she hadn't insisted that Sue visit. This confusion was easy to fall into and hard to climb out of because ways of showing caring and indifference are inherently ambiguous.

You can be nice to some one either by showing your involvement or by not imposing. And you can be mean by refusing to show involvement—cutting her off—or by imposing—being "inconsiderate." You can show someone you're angry by shouting at her—imposing—or refusing to talk to her at all: the silent activity called snubbing.

You can be kind by saying something or by saying nothing. For example, if someone has suffered a misfortune—failed an exam, lost a job, or contracted a disease—you may show sympathy by expressing your concern in words or by deliberately not mentioning it to avoid causing pain by bringing it up. If everyone takes the latter approach, silence becomes a chamber in which the ill, the bereaved, and the unemployed are isolated.

If you choose to avoid mentioning a misfortune, you run the risk of seeming to have forgotten, or of not caring. You may try to circumvent that interpretation by casting a knowing glance, making an indirect reference, or softening the impact with euphemisms ("your situation"), hedges and hesitations ("your . . . um . . . well . . . er . . . you know"), or apologies ("I hope you don't mind my mentioning this"). But meaningful glances and verbal hedging can themselves offend by sending the metamessage "This is too terrible to mention" or "Your condition is shameful." A person thus shielded may feel like shouting, "Why don't you just say it!?"

An American couple visited the husband's brother in Germany, where he was living with a German girlfriend. One evening during dinner, the girlfriend asked the brother where he had taken his American guests that day. Upon hearing that we had taken them to the concentration camp at Dachau, she exclaimed in revulsion that that was an awful place to take them; why would he do such a stupid thing?

The brother cut off her exclamations by whispering to her while glancing at the American woman. His girlfriend immediately stopped complaining and nodded in understanding, also casting glances at the American, who was not appreciative of their discretion. Instead, she was offended by the assumption that being Jewish is cause for whispering and furtive glances.

Any attempt to soften the impact of what is said can have the opposite effect. For example, a writer recalled the impression that a colleague had written something extremely critical about the manuscript of her book. Preparing to revise the manuscript, she returned to his comments and was surprised to see that the criticism was very mild indeed. The guilty word was the one that preceded the comment, not the comment itself. By beginning the sentence with "Frankly," her colleague sent a metamessage: "Steel yourself. This is going to hurt a lot."

Such layers of meaning are always at work in conversation; anything you say or don't say sends metamessages that become part of the meaning of the conversation.

Mixed Metamessages at Home

Parental love puts relative emphasis on involvement, but as children grow up, most parents give more and more signs of love by respecting their independence. Usually this comes too late for the children's tastes. The teenager who resents being told to put on a sweater or eat breakfast interprets the parent's sign of involvement as an imposition. Although this isn't in the message, the teenager hears a metamessage to the effect "You're still a child who needs to be told how to take care of yourself."   40

Partners in intimate relationships often differ about how they balance involvement and independence. There are those who show love by making sure the other eats right, dresses warmly, or doesn't drive alone at night. There are others who feel this is imposing and treating them like children. And there are those who feel that their partners don't care about them because they aren't concerned with what they eat, wear, or do. What may be meant as a show of respect for their independence is taken as lack of involvement—which it also might be.

Maxwell wants to be left alone, and Samantha wants attention. So she gives him attention, and he leaves her alone. The adage "Do unto others as you would have others do unto you" may be the source of a lot of anguish and misunderstanding if the doer and the done unto have different styles.

Samantha and Maxwell might feel differently if the other acted differently. He may want to be left alone precisely because she gives him so much attention, and she may want attention precisely because he leaves her alone. With a doting spouse she might find herself craving to be left alone, and with an independent spouse, he might find himself craving attention. It's important to remember that others' ways of talking to you are partly a reaction to your style, just as your style with them is partly a reaction to their style—with you.

The ways we show our involvement and considerateness in talk   44
seem self-evidently appropriate. And in interpreting what others say, we assume they mean what we would mean if we said the same thing in the same way. If we don't think about differences in conversational style, we see no reason to question this. Nor do we question whether what we perceive as considerate or inconsiderate, loving or not, was *intended* to be so.

In trying to come to an understanding with someone who has mis-interpreted our intentions, we often end up in a deadlock, reduced to childlike insistence:

"You said so."

"I said no such thing!"

"You did! I heard you!"

"Don't tell me what I said ."

In fact, both parties may be sincere—and both may be right. He recalls what he meant, and she recalls what she heard. But what he intended was not what she understood—which was what she would have meant if she had said what he said in the way he said it.

These paradoxical metamessages are recursive and potentially con-fusing in all conversations. In a series of conversations between the same people, each encounter bears the burdens as well as the fruits of earlier ones. The fruits of ongoing relationships are an ever-increasing sense of understanding based on less and less talk. This is one of the great joys of intimate conversations. But the burdens include the incre-mental confusion and disappointment of past misunderstandings, and hardening conviction of the other's irrationality or ill will.

The benefits of repeated communication need no explanation; all our conventional wisdom about "getting to know each other," "working it out," and "speaking the same language" gives us ways to talk about and understand that happy situation. But we need some help—and some terms and concepts—to understand why communicating over time doesn't always result in understanding each other better, and why some times it begins to seem that one or the other is speaking in tongues.

Mixed Metamessages across Cultures

The danger of misinterpretation is greatest, of course, among speakers   48
who actually speak different native tongues, or come from different cultural backgrounds, because cultural difference necessarily implies different assumptions about natural and obvious ways to be polite.

Anthropologist Thomas Kochman gives the example of a white office worker who appeared with a bandaged arm and felt rejected because her black fellow worker didn't mention it. The (doubly) wounded worker assumed that her silent colleague didn't notice or didn't care. But the co-worker was purposely not calling attention to something her colleague might not want to talk about. She let her decide whether or not to mention it: being considerate by not imposing. Kochman says, based on his research, that these differences reflect recognizable black and white styles.

An American woman visiting England was repeatedly offended—even, on bad days, enraged—when Britishers ignored her in settings in which she thought they should pay attention. For example, she was sitting at a booth in a railroad-station cafeteria. A couple began to settle into the opposite seat in the same booth. They unloaded their luggage; they laid their coats on the seat; he asked what she would like to eat and went off to get it; she slid into the booth facing the American. And throughout all this, they showed no sign of having noticed that someone was already sitting in the booth.

When the British woman lit up a cigarette, the American had a concrete object for her anger. She began ostentatiously looking around for another table to move to. Of course there was none; that's why the British couple had sat in her booth in the first place. The smoker immediately crushed out her cigarette and apologized. This showed that she had noticed that someone else was sitting in the booth, and that she was not inclined to disturb her. But then she went back to pretending the American wasn't there, a ruse in which her husband collaborated when he returned with their food and they ate it.

To the American, politeness requires talk between strangers forced to share a booth in a cafeteria, if only a fleeting "Do you mind if I sit down?" or a conventional "Is anyone sitting here?" even if it's obvious no one is. The omission of such talk seemed to her like dreadful rudeness. The American couldn't see that another system of politeness was at work. (She could see nothing but red.) By not acknowledging her presence, the British couple freed her from the obligation to acknowledge theirs. The American expected a show of involvement; they were being polite by not imposing.   52

An American man who had lived for years in Japan explained a similar politeness ethic. He lived, as many Japanese do, in frightfully close quarters—a tiny room separated from neighboring rooms by paper-thin walls. In this case the walls were literally made of paper. In order to preserve privacy in this most unprivate situation, his Japanese neighbors simply acted as if no one else lived there. They never showed signs of having overheard conversations, and if, while walking down the hall, they caught a neighbor with the door open, they steadfastly glued their gaze ahead as if they were alone in a desert. The American confessed to feeling what I believe most Americans would feel if a next-door neighbor passed within a few feet without acknowledging their presence—snubbed. But he realized that the intention was not rudeness by omitting to show involvement, but politeness by not imposing.

The fate of the earth depends on cross-cultural communication. Nations must reach agreements, and agreements are made by individual representatives of nations sitting down and talking to each other—public analogues of private conversations. The processes are the same, and so are the pitfalls. Only the possible consequences are more extreme.

We Need the Eggs

Despite the fact that talking to each other frequently fails to yield the understanding we seek, we keep at it, just as nations keep trying to negotiate and reach agreement. Woody Allen knows why, and tells, in his film *Annie Hall*, which ends with a joke that is heard voice over:

> This guy goes to a psychiatrist and says, "Doc my brother's crazy. He thinks he's a chicken." And the doctor says, "Well, why don't you turn him in?" And the guy says, "I would, but I need the eggs." Well, I guess that's pretty much how I feel about relationships.

Even though intimate as well as fleeting conversations don't yield the perfect communication we crave—and we can see from past experience and from the analysis presented here that they can't—we still keep hoping and trying because we need the eggs of involvement and independence. The communication chicken can't give us these golden eggs because of the double bind: Closeness threatens our lives as individuals, and our real differences as individuals threaten our needs to be connected to other people.

But because we can't step out of the situation—the human situation—we keep trying to balance these needs. We do it by not saying exactly what we mean in our messages, while at the same time negotiating what we mean in metamessages. Metamessages depend for their meaning on subtle linguistic signals and devices.

Notes

[The page references have been changed to accord with pages in *The Little, Brown Reader*, 7th ed., and the bibliographic citations have been amplified where necessary.]

pp. 525, 528. The terms *metamessage* and *double bind* are found in Gregory Bateson, *Steps to an Ecology of Mind* (1972). For Bateson, a double bind entailed contradictory orders at different levels: the message and metamessage conflict. I use the term, as do other linguists (for example, Scollon, "The Rythmic Integration of Ordinary Talk," in *Analyzing Discourse: Text and Talk,* Deborah Tannen, ed. [1981]), simply to describe the state of receiving contradictory orders without being able to step out of the situation.

p. 528. I am grateful to Pamela Gerloff for bringing to my attention Bettelheim's reference (in *Surviving* [1979]) to Schopenhauer's porcupine metaphor.

p. 528. Mary Catherine Bateson, *With a Daughters Eye: A Memoir of Margaret Mead and Gregory Bateson* (1984), discusses G. Bateson's idea that living systems (biological processes as well as human interaction) never achieve a static state of balance, but achieve balance only as a series of adjustments within a range.

p. 528. For his conversational maxims see H. P. Grice, "Logic and Conservation," rptd. in *Syntax and Semantics,* vol. 3, *Speech Acts,* eds. Peter Cole and Jerry Morgan (1975).

p. 528. Lakoff's original statement of the rules of politeness is in Lakoff, "The Logic of Politeness, or Minding Your P's and Q's," *Papers from the Ninth Regional Meeting of the Chicago Linguistics Society* (1973). She also presents this system in the context of discussing male/female differences (Lakoff, *Language and Woman's Place* [1975]). Penelope Brown and Stephen Levinson, "Universals in Language Usage: Politeness Phenomena," in *Questions and Politeness,* ed. Esther Goody (1978), provide an extended and formalized discussion of politeness phenomena.

p. 534. Thomas Kochman presents an extended analysis of *Black and White Styles in Conflict* (1981).

p. 535. The quotation from *Annie Hall* is taken from the screenplay by Woody Allen and Marshall Brickman in *Four Films of Woody Allen* (NY: Random House, 1982).

Topics for Critical Thinking and Writing

1. Tannen begins this chapter using the second person ("You're sitting at a bar—or in a coffee shop or at a party—and suddenly you feel lonely. You wonder . . . "), a usage often prohibited in high school English classes and textbooks. How well do you think it works here? Try to make the same point without using the second person. *Have* you made the same point? What has been left out?

2. How does Tannen define *metamessages?* The word will not appear in most dictionaries, but we can probably guess what it means, even without Tannen's explanation. What does *meta* usually mean as a prefix to a word? (Most dictionaries do define *meta* as a prefix.)

3. Why, according to Tannen, has the word *metamessages* been invented? What other linguistic terms does she introduce, and what do they mean?

4. What is the example of porcupines introduced to explain? Why do you suppose it is easier to remember the example than to remember what it explains?

5. In paragraph 11, Tannen says "individuals as well as cultures place different relative values" on the "needs for involvement and independence." In the same paragraph and in the next several paragraphs, she says that Americans glorify independence and she offers an historical explanation of the glorification of independence and other values that flow from it. What does she assume here about "Americans," American culture, and American history?

6. In paragraph 16, Tannen contrasts women talking to women and men talking to men. What does she *assume* here, in addition to what she says, about the differences? On the whole, do you agree with her about women's talk and men's talk?

7. In paragraphs 47–53 Tannen talks about misinterpretations between persons of different cultural backgrounds. If possible, provide an example from your own experience.

8. Write an essay or a journal entry analyzing an encounter which illustrates the "double bind," a "politeness phenomenon," or "mixed metamessages," as Tannen defines these terms and situations. Or summarize this chapter in 750 words.

Steven Pinker

Steven Pinker, professor of brain and cognitive sciences at the Massachusetts Institute of Technology, is the author of The Language Instinct *(1994). We reprint an essay that originally appeared in* The New York Times, *5 April 1994.*

The Game of the Name

The *Los Angeles Times's* new "Guidelines on Racial and Ethnic Identification," for its writers and editors, bans or restricts some 150 words and phrases such as "birth defect," "Chinese fire drill," "crazy," "dark continent," "stepchild," "WASP" and "to welsh."

Defying such politically correct sensibilities, *The Economist* allows the use of variants of "he" for both sexes (as in "everyone should watch his language"), and "crippled" for disabled people.

One side says that language insidiously shapes attitudes and that vigilance against subtle offense is necessary to eliminate prejudice. The other bristles at legislating language, seeing a corrosion of clarity and expressiveness at best, and thought control at worst, changing the way reporters render events and opinions.

Both arguments make assumptions about language and how it   4
relates to thoughts and attitudes—a connection first made in 1946 by

George Orwell in his essay "Politics and the English Language," which suggested that euphemisms, clichés and vague writing could be used to reinforce orthodoxy and defend the indefensible. We understand language and thought better than we did in Orwell's time, and our discoveries offer insights about the P.C. controversy.

First, words are not thoughts. Despite the appeal of the theory that language determines thought, no cognitive scientist believes it. People coin new words, grapple for *le mot juste*[6], translate from other languages and ridicule or defend P.C. terms. None of this would be possible if the ideas expressed by words were identical to the words themselves. This should alleviate anxiety on both sides, reminding us that we are talking about style manuals, not brain programming.

Second, words are arbitrary. The word "duck" does not look, walk or quack like a duck, but we all know it means duck because we have memorized an arbitrary association between a sound and a meaning.

Some words can be built out of smaller pieces and their meanings can be discerned by examining how the pieces are arranged (a dishwasher washes dishes), but even complex words turn opaque, and people become oblivious to the logic of their derivation, memorizing them as arbitrary symbols. (Who last thought of "breakfast" as "breaking a fast"?)

The Los Angeles Times style manual seems to assume that readers are reflexive etymologists; for it bans "invalid" (literally "not valid" and thus an offensive reference to a disabled person), "New World" (ignores the indigenous cultures that preceded Columbus's voyage) and "Dutch treat" (offensive, presumably, to Netherlanders). But I doubt if Americans associate the dozen-odd idioms in which Dutch means "ersatz" ("Dutch uncle," "Dutch oven") with the Dutch; presumably, the sting has worn off in the three centuries since the English coined such terms to tweak their naval rivals.

The bewildering feature of political correctness is the mandated replacement of formerly unexceptionable terms by new ones: "Negro" by "black" by "African-American"; "Spanish-American" by "Hispanic" by "Latino"; "slum" by "ghetto" by "inner city" by, according to *The Los Angeles Times,* "slum" again.

How should a thoughtful person react to this carousel? Respect means treating people as they wish to be treated, beginning with names. That is why there is a clear need for guidelines. One wonders, though, why *The Los Angeles Times*'s style panel apparently did not consult those it defends. Many deaf people insist on being called "deaf," not "individuals who cannot hear," and as one who was taught to revere the Wailing Wall, I was surprised to learn that the term is "highly offensive" rather than merely obsolete.

---

[6]*Le mot juste,* the most suitable word.

But if users of new ethnic terms have responsibilities, so do those who promulgate the terms. What are their motives? What are the effects?

Occasionally, neologisms are defended with some semantic ratio- **12** nale: "black" emphasized parity with the corresponding "white." "Native American" reminds us of who was here first and eschews the inaccurate European label "Indian." But when new terms replace ones that had been justified in their own day with equal moral force and when offensive and sanctioned terms are near-synonyms—"colored people," "people of color"; "Afro-American," "African-American"; Negro (Spanish for "black"), "black"—something else must be driving the process.

To a linguist, the phenomenon is familiar: the euphemism treadmill. People invent new "polite" words to refer to emotionally laden or distasteful things, but the euphemism becomes tainted by association and the new one that must be found acquires its own negative connotations.

"Water closet" becomes "toilet" (originally a term for any body care, as in "toilet kit"), which becomes "bathroom," which becomes "rest room," which becomes "lavatory." "Garbage collection" turns into "sanitation," which turns into "environmental services."

The euphemism treadmill shows that concepts, not words, are in charge: give a concept a new name, and the name becomes colored by the concept; the concept does not become freshened by the name. (We will know we have achieved equality and mutual respect when names for minorities stay put.)

People learn a word by witnessing other people using it, so when **16** they use a word, they provide a history of their reading and listening. Using the latest term for a minority often shows not sensitivity but subscribing to the right magazines or going to the right cocktail parties.

Shifts in terms have an unfortunate side effect. Many people who don't have a drop of malice or prejudice but happen to be older or distant from university, media and government spheres find themselves tainted as bigots for innocently using passé terms like "Oriental" or "crippled." Arbiters of the changing linguistic fashions must ask themselves whether this stigmatization is really what they set out to accomplish.

Topics for Critical Thinking and Discussion

1. In paragraph 8 Pinker expresses the opinion that because three centuries have passed since the English used the term *Dutch* to refer to something that is not quite the real thing, the term is no longer offensive. Do you suppose that an American of Dutch ancestry is bothered by such a term as *Dutch oven* (a heavy pot with a cover)? In any case, does the length of time since a phrase was originated have anything to do with whether the phrase is offensive today? Explain.

2. If you have heard a word or phrase that is deeply offensive to you, indicate the circumstances under which it was spoken. Who said it, and with what intention? As you now reflect on the experience, do you think you were overly sensitive, or was the speaker insensitive? How would *you* have worded the sentence?

3. If you have ever innocently used a term that offended someone, describe the incident and the hearer's reaction. (Possibly the hearer did not react visibly, but you now realize that the term must have been offensive.)

4. In his final paragraph Pinker mentions that *Oriental* is now out of favor. Explain why. If you don't know why, begin by looking in a good dictionary to see what the etymology of the word is, and think about why a word with this origin might offend a person from East Asia.

5. Now that you know (having responded to Question 4) why *Oriental* is out of favor, do you think the reason is valid? Or do you think that objection to the word is trivial? If the latter, are you nevertheless willing to agree that if persons who used to be called *Oriental* do not like the term—even though their reasons strike you as trivial—other people should not use the word?

Sven Birkerts

Sven Birkerts, born in 1951 in Pontiac, Michigan, is a graduate of the University of Michigan. He is the author of several books of essays on writers and on reading, the most recent of which is The Gutenberg Elegies: The Fate of Reading in an Electronic Age *(1994). Birkerts is also a teacher of writing, and the author of a textbook on literature.*

Objections Noted: Word Processing

People ask me why I refuse to use a word processor. I tell them because it feels like a typewriter with a condom over it. The very sight of one of those sculpted plastic instruments with its pert ticket-counter "everything's under control" screen depresses me beyond measure. It makes me feel how close the final victory of technology over spirit really is. Hell, it *is* the victory of technology over spirit.

Neither can I bear the chirping good humor with which owners talk about their disks and programs.

The word-processor argument. Most people, I'm sure, maintain that there *is* no word-processor argument. Indeed, I hardly ever meet anyone who writes who isn't using one—a few poets, maybe . . . Louis Simpson[1]. . .

Lemmings!   4

Literature has got lightweight and modular enough without writers all shifting their idly fluffed-together paragraphs around. If you can't organize it in your head, it's not ready to be organized.

The WP is a death-ray directed at the last remnants of the prophetic soul.

The word processor is just a tool, they say. Just a tool. Just a tool. Never mind that it's an ugly tool, utterly alien from anything relating to spirit. (Would you paint with a steel-handled brush?) Never mind that the machine you work on changes the compositional process, changes you. It's just a tool.

Like any tool, the WP came into being to meet a need. Writers were   8 tired of wadding up sheets of paper, of playing cut and paste with paragraphs, of drawing lines to bridge one part of a text to another. The technology was there to bring the material/production side of writing in line with the rest of the twentieth century. The quasi-"intelligence" of the computer was put into the service of the infinitely complex intellectual/psychological operation of writing.

Given that so many writers profess themselves to be iconoclasts, sturdy individualists, etc., the rate of defection from paper and metal to plastic and electricity is nothing short of astonishing.

These are the same people who love the old game of baseball and scream at any move to modernize or streamline its immemorial rituals.

But the lemmings did line up to leap. Why?

They say it's because the user can *quickly* make changes, correc-   12 tions, erasures, rearrangements. Because he can try things out and then get rid of them. Because he has more access to his text, more control, a sense of mastery. Because the WP vanquishes fear, eliminates the block-inducing threat that the white page seems to hold.

I've heard it said that now *everyone* can become a writer.

Hot dog.

I think the real reason for the rash to molded plastic, the deep-down unacknowledged reason, is that the apparatus confers a feeling of power, of being plugged in to something. For we all know, in that same deep-down place, that the writer, the thinker, the person who would speak up for spirit, has never had less power. Ever. Has never been such a zero. Why not a humming bright unit that allows the user to say, "I, too, belong to the modern world. You can see screens just like this at the airport, on Wall Street, in the offices on Madison Avenue."

---

[1]**Louis Simpson,** poet and teacher, born in the British West Indies in 1923.

The word processor has, among other things, made the word more   16
susceptible to the directives of the will. The ruling paradigm is now
one of change, of changeability. The writer says, with Valéry,[2] that the
work is never finished. Clearly demarcated draft stages have been
superseded by a single stage—the unstable, open, "in-process" stage.
Writing is closer to becoming that unfixed play of signifiers[3] celebrated by French literary theoreticians. Literary morticians. Indeed: writing has been brought many steps closer to resembling the mutability of
thought itself—which never rests, except in the crystallizations of written language.

The stability of the word—epitomized by the independent, fixed,
printed sign—has been correspondingly undermined.

Writing on the word processor: It's like eating those force-fed new
chickens that have never seen sunlight. Like eating fish bred in indoor
pools.

Word "processing": In the sixties the word "processed" was a term
of fierce derision. Blacks called a brother "processed" when they wanted to mark him as a "Tom."

The shift from manual writing to the typewriter to the word proces-   20
sor roughly corresponds to the shift from walking to riding in a carriage
to riding in a car. In both cases, the progression is toward ease and facil-
itation. But, we might ask, what has become of our ancient relationship
to land, to sky, to time itself.?

A flat, opaque two-sided sheet of paper is replaced by an electronic
screen of indeterminate depth. Where a black mark was conspicuously
imposed upon the white surface, we now find a green mark elicited from
the humming green screen. The broken-up left-to-right linearity is
replaced, for the writer, by what *feels* like an unbroken continuity (the
apparatus does the lineation). The static character of the typed sign
gives way to the fluid, provisional character of the processed sign. The
composition blocks—sentences, paragraphs—are no less fluid.

If the movement from speech to writing was, in part, an attempt
to impose fixity upon the fleeting, then might we not in some sense be
moving back toward the laxity of the impromptu—at least on the
level of conception, where everything exists under the aspect of
replaceability?

---

[2]**Valéry,** Paul Valéry (1871–1945), French poet.
[3]**signifiers:** The French-speaking Swiss student of linguistics, Ferdinand de Saussure
(1857–1913), used the term *signifier* to refer to the sound or written squiggles of a word, in
distinction from the *signified,* which is the idea called to mind when the signifier is heard
or seen.

Writing on a word processor: the principle of Don Juanism project-ed upon the sentence. The writer is more likely to be haunted by the thought that there is a better word than this, a better sentence, a more interesting ordering of paragraphs.

Writing by hand, even typewriter, inevitably results in visible cor-   24
rections, in drafts. These are, in effect, the record of the evolution of the thought and its expression. The WP handily eliminates every trace. The writer never has to look over his shoulder and see what a botch he's made of things. Less conscience, less sense of consequence.

As Louis Simpson wrote: "If I think I can easily change the next word and there's nothing final about what I'm writing, then the nature of my writing changes."
How would you live if you knew you could live forever?
The ideal of *le mot juste*[4] is vaporized; the new ideals are of plurali-ty and provisionality.

I've noticed that I read a word-processed page differently—more   28
casually—than a typewritten page. Could the mode of writing signifi-cantly influence the mode of reading? Maybe. When everybody becomes a writer, no one will read.
The difference between seeing your words drawn forth from the depths of a screen versus seeing them planted on the page through the mechanical action of a key is enormous. The screen, with its electrical "live" humming and its impatiently pulsing cursor, represents (much like TV) a quasi-consciousness. Does the writer feel just the slightest bit less responsible?

Speaking for myself: writing is very much a matter of drafts, *distinct* written drafts. I believe that prose is produced as much by the body, the rhythmic sense, as it is by intellect and verbal imagination. It wants to build up a certain musculature on the page. The instant correctability afforded by the WP allows for cosmetic alterations that are often quite adequate. But *merely* adequate. My experience has shown me that the best writing comes when I am forced to type over something that I've already deemed to be finished. My impatience—not to mention the new rhythmic state I'm in—forces me to push the language further. In the process of retyping the text, I reach more deeply into it. Later, the words give me the impression of having been handled, worn smooth.
Even simple mistakes can be read as signs, parapraxias signaling the incompleteness of an expression. When a page of prose is done, I no longer make typos.

---

[4]***Le mot juste,*** the most suitable word (French).

Already it's getting hard to find ribbons. The people who used to   32
repair typewriters are retiring, dying off. The day will come—soon—
when journals will accept only disk submissions.

There . . . I've succeeded in depressing myself. All of a sudden my
desk looks like a museum: the beautiful pencil, the sharpener, the pens,
the stack of paper like a street of dreams. The Olivetti clattering as I
type this: sad hoofbeats of a retreating army. . . .

Topics for Critical Thinking and Writing

1. Analyze and then evaluate Birkerts's opening paragraph as an opening paragraph. That is, examine the parts of the paragraph to see how
   they function and then give your opinion on the effectiveness of the
   paragraph.
2. Similarly analyze and evaluate the concluding paragraph.
3. In paragraph 7 Birkerts says that "the machine you work on changes
   the compositional process, changes you." Perhaps you began with a
   pencil, moved up to a pen, then to a typewriter or a word processor. Or
   perhaps you still use a pencil. In any case, examine the influence on
   your writing—and on you—of the tool(s) you use(d).
4. In a paragraph or two, characterize Birkerts's persona. In thinking
   about this matter, of course, you will take account of the whole essay,
   but be sure to consider the one-word paragraph 4 ("Lemmings!") and
   the two-word paragraph 14 ("Hot dog.")

Richard A. Hawley

*Richard Hawley was born in Chicago in 1945 and was educated at Middlebury College, Cam-
bridge University, and Case Western Reserve University. Since 1968 he has taught at University School, Hunting Valley, Ohio, where he is now the headmaster. In addition to writing
books on adolescence and issues in teaching, Hawley has written a half-dozen works of fiction and nonfiction, two volumes of poetry, and an opera libretto.*

Television and Adolescents
A Teacher's View

Ever since its novelty wore off in the fifties, we have all
known, really, that television in its commercial form wasn't up to much
good. This isn't to say that millions of people don't still depend on it,
but dependency is hardly a sign of virtue. Except for Marshall
McLuhan's grab-bag theoretics, few claims have been advanced for the
improving effects of television. In fact, recently there has been a flurry
of publishing activity, most notably Marie Winn's *The Plug-in Drug,*

about television as a cause of downright mental erosion. But what I think Marie Winn and others need is a concrete, closely observed, and intensely felt illustration of the larger thesis. That's what I offer here.

Television has a way of intruding into our lives, and last year it intruded into my life and into the life of the school where I work in a way that many of us there will never forget. We had all taken our seats for morning assembly. The usual announcements were read, after which the morning's senior speaker was introduced. Like many independent schools, ours requires each senior to address the student body in some manner before he graduates. Since public speaking is not a widely distributed gift these days, the senior speeches are infrequently a source of much interest or intentional amusement.

As the curtains parted, we could see that the speaker had opted for a skit. On the stage were a covered table and a number of cooking implements. Out stepped the speaker wearing an apron and chef's hat, which very quickly established that he was going to satirize one of my colleagues who has a national reputation as a gourmet chef. Since this colleague is also a man who can take a joke, the prospects for the skit seemed bright. But not for long.

At first, I think almost all of us pretended that we didn't hear, that   4
we were making too much of certain, possibly accidental, double entendres. But then came the direct statements and a few blatant physical gestures. Then it was clear! This boy was standing before five hundred of us making fun of what he suggested at some length was the deviant sexual nature of one of his teachers. The response to this was at first stupefaction, then some outbursts of laughter (the groaning kind of laughter that says, "I don't believe you said that"), then a quieting, as the speech progressed, to periodic oohs (the kind that say, "You *did* say that, and you're in for it").

When he had finished, there was a nearly nauseating level of tension afloat. As the students filed off to class, I made my way backstage to find the speaker. It had by now dawned on him that he had done something wrong, even seriously wrong. We met in my office.

He expressed remorse at having offended a teacher whom he said he particularly liked. (Before the conference I had checked briefly with the teacher and found him badly flustered and deeply hurt.) The remorse was, I felt, genuine. But something was decidedly missing in the boy's explanation of how he came to think that such a presentation might, under any circumstances, have been appropriate. He hadn't, he admitted, really thought about it, and some of his friends thought the idea was funny, and, well, he didn't know. When it occurred to him that serious school action was in the offing, he protested that in no way had he intended the sexual references to be taken seriously—they were, you know, a joke.

I pointed out to him that the objects of such jokes have no way to respond: To ignore the insinuation might affirm its validity; on the other hand, to object vigorously would draw additional attention to the offense and sustain the embarrassment connected with it. I pointed out further that sometimes innocent parties *never* regain their stature after being offended in this manner, and that the injured party was, at the very least, in for a terrible day of school.

The boy became reflective and said, "Was it *that* bad? You can see worse on 'Saturday Night Live'." I told him I doubted this, but if it were true, and were I in a position to judge, I would be in favor of expelling "Saturday Night Live" from the air. He left the office, and subsequently endured the appropriate consequences.   8

For my part, I resolved to turn on "Saturday Night Live," and when I did, I realized the student had spoken truly. The show's quick-succession, absurdist comedy spots depended for their appeal on establishing an almost dangerous sense of inappropriateness: exactly that sense created by our senior speaker. To me, for some years a lapsed viewer, it seemed that both the variety and specificity of sexual innuendo had developed considerably since, say, the once daring Smothers Brothers show of the sixties. What struck me more, however, was how many punch lines and visual gags depended on suddenly introducing the idea of injury or violent death.

I happened to tune in the night a funny caption was put over the documentary shot of Middle Eastern political partisans being dragged to death behind an automobile. Was this funny? I asked my students. They said it was "sick" and laughed. Does this kind of fun trivialize crisis? Trivialize cruelty? Inure us to both? Or is it, you know, a joke?

The right things were said, I think, to our students about the boy's speech. But I can't say the situation improved. Not more than a couple of weeks later, a speaker garbed in a woman's tennis dress took the podium and began to talk humorously about the transsexual tennis player Renee Richards. I can't think of a subject harder for an adolescent to discuss before an adolescent audience. Rarely noted for their confidence and breadth of vision in matters of human sexuality, adolescents are unlikely to be objective, sympathetic, or (let me tell you) funny about so disturbing a phenomenon as sex change. This particular boy, whose inflection is very flat and whose normal countenance is especially stony, managed to convey almost a sense of bitterness in making his string of insulting and, in his reference to genitals and to menstruation, awfully tasteless cracks.

So there it was again: the inappropriateness, the tension. This time the injured party was remote from our particular world, so the hastily arranged conference with the boy turned on general considerations of taste and judgment. This time, however, the speaker was recalcitrant: We could disapprove of his speech and discipline him if we chose, but we ought to know that we could hear the same thing on television.   12

At that moment something clicked for me. Not only did my brief exposure to "Saturday Night Live" convince me that, yes, I would hear the same thing on television, but I was suddenly struck with the realization that he was using television as an arbiter of taste—that is, *as an arbiter of good taste.* I began to see in this premise a common ground upon which he and I could at least argue. Both of us were in agreement that what is broadcast over television ought to be acceptable; our point of disagreement was his feeling that broadcasting something over television *made* it acceptable. Alarming as such a feeling is to me, it is not hard to see how it has developed over the past few decades.

Until the middle sixties, with the exception of the very earthiest plays and novels, the values of home and school and the values of the popular culture were fairly continuous; if anything, radio, television, and motion pictures were more staid than real life. Of course, all this would change very quickly—not because change was requested or even consented to, but because it wasn't, perhaps couldn't be, resisted. And suddenly there it all was at once: the most embarrassing expletives as common speech; every imaginable kind of sexual coupling depicted in ever-increasing candor; obsessively specific wounds, mutilations.

These formerly unacceptable kinds of stimulation made their way more easily into the relatively insulated world of print and film than they did into the more communal world of the television set. Television is typically viewed in homes, and what is communally seen and heard must be communally integrated, or there will be friction. Since American households—set-holds?—share this communal experience for an estimated two to seven hours per day, the potential for friction is considerable. This is why, on grounds of taste, criticism of television programming tends to be more bitter and more relentless than criticism of books and films.

Television foes and partisans alike continue to advise, with some reason, that those who object to certain programs ought not to watch them. But given the impossibility of monitoring the set at all hours, control over the amount and quality of viewing is difficult to maintain even in principled, surveillant households. Too, some viewers will insist on being their brother's keeper. Not everyone who is convinced that what is beaming over the national airwaves is inhumane, unscrupulous, or scurrilous is going to fight to the death for the networks' right to be so.

For many people, television is no longer on the polite side of real life. This is an obvious observation about a novel development, one whose consequences are only just dawning on us. A realist or an existentialist may argue that the unflappably suburban world of "Father Knows Best" revealed none of the complex, ambivalent, and often irrational forces at work in real families: But it is hard to argue that "Father Knows Best" in any way *contributed* to those dark forces. On the contrary, it is possible to argue—although one hesitates to carry it too far—that the theme of Father Knowing Best serves as a psychologically soothing backdrop to the prickly dynamics of real family life. And

16

while today's most highly rated shows suggest that the prevailing seventies' theme is Nobody Knows Anything, there are still apparently enough viewers who like Father Knowing Best to support series like "The Waltons" and "Little House on the Prairie."

Sometimes the theme is compromised in a typical seventies' manner, of which "James at 16" provides a good example: The parents are cast very much in the Robert Young-Jane Wyatt mold, but their son James is, to borrow a phrase, kind of now. By far the most interesting thing he did was to lose his virginity on prime time. The fifteen-going-on-sixteen-year-old boys I work with, many of them at least as sophisticated as James, typically hold on to their virginity a bit longer, until the disposition of their sexual feelings is under surer control. The best clinical evidence maintains that the process of bringing newly emergent sexuality under control is *inherently* delicate and troublesome. James' television plunge planted the anxiety-provoking notion in the mind of the adolescent viewer that he was sexually lagging behind not only the precocious kid down the block, but the Average American Boy character of James. (One was allowed to be less anxious when Father Knew Best.)

Why shouldn't television make people anxious? say the producers of programs that make people anxious. After all, the *world* is anxious. (An awfully self-serving position: Programs that arouse anxiety are relevant; those that don't are enjoyable.) Before long, this line of argument begins to lay claim that programs which bring up irritating subjects in an irritating manner are performing a valuable social mission. Norman Lear, the producer of comedies such as "All in the Family" and "Maude," makes such a claim. According to the Lear formula, a controversial topic will be raised, tossed around for laughs, then either discarded or resolved. Resolution occurs when one of the characters tolerates or forgives the controversial person or practice, while some other character, usually a combination of lovable old coot and ass, does not.

As many critics have pointed out, this is only apparent resolution.   20
Nothing much really happens to a racial or sexual conflict when it is laughed at (a device that is supposed to soften outright slurring and stereotyping), discarded, tolerated, or forgiven. The idea that "if we can joke about it this way, we have taken a humanitarian stride" is mistaken. There is plenty of evidence, particularly among the student population, that, for one thing, race relations are more strained today than they were a decade ago. No one would want to claim that racism among youth disappeared during the politically active sixties; however, a claim can be made that when a student was confronted then with having made a racial slur, he seemed to be aware of having violated a standard.

Who is to say that Archie Bunker hath no sting? More and more television comedians, in the manner of Don Rickles, seek *only* to sting. It is really an empirical question, not a matter of taste, whether or not it is harmless, much less healing, to denigrate everybody, including oneself. A hit song by Randy Newman insults small people: this is no parody of unkindness or bigotry, but the real thing. My students understand it perfectly and parrot it enthusiastically. Rebuked, they grimace in exasperation. Nothing in their youthful experience tells them that bigotry is a sign of cultural regression ("It isn't bigotry; it's, you know, a joke"). They prefer to see whatever wicked delights crop up in the media as a progressive casting off of prudish inhibitions. According to such a view, progress is whatever happens next.

Toleration of the intolerable is always worrying, but it is especially so when it takes place among the young, in whom we want to invest so much hope. Tolerating the intolerable is part of a dynamic, not a static, process; the intolerable, when it is nurtured, grows.

Which brings me back to the senior speeches. Two so thoroughly inappropriate presentations in a single year represented a high count for us, so we were not ready, at least I wasn't, for the third.

This time the talk was about a summer spent working on a ranch, 24 and the format was that of a commentary with slides. No apparent harm in this, but there were a number of factors working against the speech's success. The first was that the speaker was renowned for being a card, a reputation the welcoming ovation insisted he live up to. Second, he had not adequately rehearsed the projection of the slides, so that they tended to appear out of order and askew, the effect of which was to provide a subtextual comedy of visual non sequiturs. Third, he chose to capitalize on the audience's nearly unrestrained hilarity by playing up certain questionable references.

The speaker made a fairly good, not too inappropriate crack about a slide which depicted a bull mounting a cow—"Sometimes the corrals get so crowded we have to stack the cattle on top of one another." But he chose to exploit his references to the gelding of bulls. There were, in all, four jokey and brutal evocations of this process which served to keep the image of bull genitalia before our minds for quite a few minutes. Since laughter had already been spent, the castration jokes were met with a kind of nervous applause. Bolstered by this, the speaker closed with a coda to the effect that he would be available after assembly to anybody who wanted tips on "cutting meat."

Since I happened to be in charge that day, I sent him home. It seemed to me, in light of the various reprisals and forewarnings connected with the previous speeches, that this particular performance, though perhaps less offensive in its specific references than the other two, ought to be the last straw. The speaker had clearly exceeded anything required by either schoolboy or cowboy saltiness. He had created an anything-goes atmosphere, and then he had let it go—for which he was applauded. "That was great!" said the boy next to me on the way out of the auditorium.

That morning and afterward scores of students, most, but not all, of them civil, hastened to let me know that they felt it was unfair to have sent the speaker home. Not one of them failed to remind me that I could see worse on television. Had I never seen "Saturday Night Live"? That afternoon an opinion poll went up requesting signatures from those who disapproved of the action I had taken and, in an opposing column, those who approved. Within the hour, hundreds expressed disapproval, only one approved.

For a day or two at school there was an animated atmosphere of   28
martyrdom (the speaker's, not mine), but it dissipated rapidly, possibly because the right to make castration jokes from the stage was not, as a cause, very catalytic. The banished speaker, a very likable boy, returned, was received warmly, and apologized not at all cringingly.

In the calm that has followed, my colleagues and I have taken pains to stress to our students, especially at the commencement of the new school year, that whenever somebody addresses an assembly, it is a special occasion. Speakers are expected to observe definite standards when they speak or perform; audiences are expected to be courteous and restrained. Humor at someone else's expense is out, unless it is prearranged with the party lampooned, and even then it ought not to be inhumane. Excretory and copulatory humor is out; it's too easy. Preparation is important. Being persuasive is important. Being controversial is important. Being funny is a delight to all, though it is harder than it looks.

Perhaps these expectations are high. However, schools, especially parochial and independent schools, are gloriously unencumbered in setting such standards: Schools are often *chosen* for the standards they set, the difference they represent. One of the things schools have an opportunity to be different from is television, for although we are all wired into it and it feels public, like the law, it is actually private, like a door-to-door salesman. We don't have to buy the goods.

Since children who watch a fair amount of television will quite naturally assume they are being told and shown the truth, it seems to me crucial that they are exposed to models who view it selectively and critically, who judge it by criteria other than its potential to engage. My own experience has been that students are surprised, but not hostile, when television programming is harshly judged. I think they may even come to like the idea that they themselves, at their discriminating best, are in the process of becoming people television ought to measure up to.

Topics for Critical Thinking and Writing

1. In paragraph 10 Hawley refers to a "comedy spot" on *Saturday Night Live,* which his students labeled "sick" humor. He then asks "Does this kind of fun trivialize crisis? Trivialize cruelty? Inure us to both?" Reread the paragraph and explain how you might respond to Hawley's questions. If you can think of a recent example of similar humor, explain your response to it as well.

2. In paragraph 14 Hawley refers to a sudden change in what became acceptable on television and film. All at once, he says, there were "the most embarrassing expletives as common speech; every imaginable kind of sexual coupling depicted in ever-increasing candor; obsessively specific wounds, mutilations." Are these forms of "unacceptable kinds of stimulation" (paragraph 15) available in the films and television shows of the nineties? If so, how do you feel about them? Are there actions (including speech) that you also find unacceptable?

3. Why, according to Hawley, is criticism of television programming "more bitter and more relentless than criticism of books and films"? Try to recall the last public controversy over taste. Was it over a television show, or some other form of popular entertainment?

4. In paragraph 16, what does Hawley seem to suggest that viewers can do about objectionable television programs? What does he mean by "some viewers will insist on being their brother's keeper"?

5. In paragraph 17 Hawley comments on the family values represented in shows popular in the sixties and seventies, such as "Father Knows Best," "The Waltons," and "Little House on the Prairie." What generalizations can you make about families in shows of the nineties? If you have seen reruns of the earlier shows, have you bean struck by any differences in representations of family life then and now?

6. In paragraphs 20–22, Hawley implies that popular culture (his examples include a popular singer, a television show, and a comedian seen primarily on television) promotes the "toleration of the intolerable," particularly of racial and sexual bigotry. Using some current examples in which racial and sexual conflicts are represented, would you argue that they tend to reinforce bigotry, reduce it, or leave the audience's biases unaffected?

7. Hawley argues for restrictions in students' behavior and speech. How does he defend such restrictions on freedom? How would you feel about attending a school with such restrictions? How does the school you currently attend deal with speech or behavior containing racial, ethnic, or sexual slurs? What is your attitude toward current policy?

8. Hawley reveals that his school is "independent." What else can we infer about the school, its student body, teachers, parents, administration? How do these inferences affect your willingness to accept Hawley's argument?

Marya Mannes

Marya Mannes served as an editor for Vogue *and* Mademoiselle, *and wrote for many magazines, including* TV Guide *and* The New Republic. *The essay that we reprint originally appeared in* The Saturday Review, *a magazine devoted to the arts and to social issues.*

Television Advertising
The Splitting Image

A bride who looks scarcely fourteen whispers, "Oh, Mom, I'm so *happy!*" while a doting family adjust her gown and veil and a male voice croons softly, "A woman is a harder thing to be than a man. She has more feelings to feel." The mitigation of these excesses, it appears, is a feminine deodorant called Secret, which allows our bride to approach the altar with security as well as emotion.

Eddie Albert, a successful actor turned pitchman, bestows his attention on a lady with two suitcases, which prompt him to ask her whether she has been on a journey. "No," she says, or words to that effect, as she opens the suitcases. "My two boys bring back their soiled clothes every weekend from college for me to wash." And she goes into the familiar litany of grease, chocolate, mud, coffee, and fruitjuice stains, which presumably record the life of the average American male from two to fifty. Mr. Albert compliments her on this happy device to bring her boys home every week and hands her a box of Biz, because "Biz *is* better."

Two women with stony faces meet cart to cart in a supermarket as one takes a jar of peanut butter off a shelf. When the other asks her in a voice of nitric acid why she takes that brand, the first snaps, "Because I'm choosy for my family!" The two then break into delighted smiles as Number Two makes Number One taste Jif for "mothers who are choosy."

If you have not come across these dramatic interludes, it is because 4 you are not home during the day and do not watch daytime television. It also means that your intestinal tract is spared from severe assaults, your credibility unstrained. Or, for that matter, you may look at commercials like these every day and manage either to ignore them or find nothing—given the fact of advertising—wrong with them. In that case, you are either so brainwashed or so innocent that you remain unaware of what this daily infusion may have done and is doing to an entire people as the long-accepted adjunct of free enterprise and support of "free" television.

"Given the fact" and "long-accepted" are the key words here. Only socialists, communists, idealists (or the BBC) fail to realize that a mass television system cannot exist without the support of sponsors, that the massive cost of maintaining it as a free service cannot be met without the massive income from selling products. You have only to read of the unending struggle to provide financial support for public, noncommercial television for further evidence.

Besides, aren't commercials in the public interest? Don't they help you choose what to buy? Don't they provide needed breaks from programming? Aren't many of them brilliantly done, and some of them funny? And now, with the new sexual freedom, all those gorgeous chicks with their shining hair and gleaming smiles? And if you didn't have commercials taking up a good part of each hour, how on earth would you find enough program material to fill the endless space/time void?

Tick off the yesses and what have you left? You have, I venture to submit, these intangible but possibly high costs: the diminution of human worth, the infusion and hardening of social attitudes no longer valid or desirable, pervasive discontent, and psychic fragmentation.

Should anyone wonder why deception is not an included detri- 8
ment, I suggest that our public is so conditioned to promotion as a way of life, whether in art or politics or products, that elements of exaggeration or distortion are taken for granted. Nobody really believes that a certain shampoo will get a certain swain, or that an unclogged sinus can make a man a swinger. People are merely prepared to hope it will.

But the diminution of human worth is much more subtle and just as pervasive. In the guise of what they consider comedy, the producers of television commercials have created a loathsome gallery of men and women patterned, presumably, on Mr. and Mrs. America. Women liberationists have a major target in the commercial image of woman flashed hourly and daily to the vast majority. There are, indeed, only four kinds of females in this relentless sales procession: the gorgeous teen-age swinger with bouncing locks; the young mother teaching her baby girl the right soap for skin care; the middle-aged housewife with a voice like a power saw; and the old lady with dentures and irregularity. All these women, to be sure, exist. But between the swinging sex object and the constipated granny there are millions of females never shown in commercials. These are—married or single—intelligent, sensitive women who bring charm to their homes, who work at jobs as well as lend grace to their marriage, who support themselves, who have talents or hobbies or commitments, or who are skilled at their professions.

To my knowledge, as a frequent if reluctant observer, I know of only one woman on a commercial who has a job; a comic plumber pushing Comet. Funny, heh? Think of a dame with a plunger.

With this one representative of our labor force, which is well over thirty million women, we are left with nothing but the full-time housewife in all her whining glory: obsessed with whiter wash, moister cakes, shinier floors, cleaner children, softer diapers, and greaseless fried chicken. In the rare instances when these ladies are not in the kitchen, at the washing machine, or waiting on hubby, they are buying beauty soaps (fantasy, see?) to take home so that their hair will have more body. Or out at the supermarket being choosy.

If they were attractive in their obsessions, they might be bearable. 12
But they are not. They are pushy, loud-mouthed, stupid, and—of all

things now—bereft of sexuality. Presumably, the argument in the tenets of advertising is that once a woman marries she changes overnight from plaything to floor-waxer.

To be fair, men make an equivalent transition in commercials. The swinging male with the mod hair and the beautiful chick turns inevitably into the paunchy slob who chokes on his wife's cake. You will notice, however, that the voice urging the viewer to buy the product is nearly always male: gentle, wise, helpful, seductive. And the visible presence telling the housewife how to get shinier floors and whiter wash and lovelier hair is almost invariably a man: the Svengali in modern dress, the Trilby (if only she were!), his willing object.[1]

Woman, in short, is consumer first and human being fourth. A wife and mother who stays home all day buys a lot more than a woman who lives alone or who—married or single—has a job. The young girl hellbent on marriage is the next most susceptible consumer. It is entirely understandable, then, that the potential buyers of detergents, foods, polishes, toothpastes, pills, and housewares are the housewives, and that the sex object spends more of *her* money on cosmetics, hair lotions, soaps, mouthwashes, and soft drinks.

Here we come, of course, to the youngest class of consumers, the swinging teen-agers so beloved by advertisers keen on telling them (and us) that they've "got a lot to live, and Pepsi's got a lot to give." This affords a chance to show a squirming, leaping, jiggling group of beautiful kids having a very loud high on rock and—of all things—soda pop. One of commercial TV's most dubious achievements, in fact, is the reinforcement of the self-adulation characteristic of the young as a group.

As for the aging female citizen, the less shown of her the better. She is   16
useful for ailments, but since she buys very little of anything, not having a husband or any children to feed or house to keep, nor—of course—sex appeal to burnish, society and commercials have little place for her. The same is true, to be sure, of older men, who are handy for Bosses with Bad Breath or Doctors with Remedies. Yet, on the whole, men hold up better than women at any age—in life or on television. Lines on their faces are marks of distinction, while on women they are signatures of decay.

There is no question, in any case, that television commercials (and many of the entertainment programs, notably the soap serials that are part of the selling package) reinforce, like an insistent drill, the assumption that a woman's only valid function is that of wife, mother, and servant of men: the inevitable sequel to her earlier function as sex object and swinger.

At a time when more and more women are at long last learning to reject these assumptions as archaic and demeaning, and to grow into individual human beings with a wide option of lives to live, the sellers of the nation are bent upon reinforcing the ancient pattern. They know

[1]In George Du Maurier's novel, *Trilby* (1894), Svengali mesmerizes Trilby and causes her to become a famous singer; when Svengali dies, Trilby loses her voice, dwindles, and soon dies. (Editors' note)

only too well that by beaming their message to the Consumer Queen they can justify her existence as the house-bound Mrs. America: dumber than dumb, whiter than white.

The conditioning starts very early: with the girl child who wants the skin Ivory soap has reputedly given her mother, with the nine-year-old who brings back a cake of Camay instead of the male deodorant her father wanted. (When she confesses that she bought it so she could be "feminine," her father hugs her, and, with the voice of a child-molester, whispers, "My little girl is growing up on me, huh.") And then, before long, comes the teen-aged bride who "has feelings to feel." It is the little boys who dream of wings, in an airplane commercial; who grow up (with fewer cavities) into the doers. Their little sisters turn into *Cosmopolitan* girls, who in turn become housewives furious that their neighbors' wash is cleaner than theirs.

There is good reason to suspect that this manic obsession with 20 cleanliness, fostered, quite naturally, by the giant soap and detergent interests, may bear some responsibility for the cultivated sloppiness of so many of the young in their clothing as well as in their chosen hide-outs. The compulsive housewife who spends more time washing and vacuuming and polishing her possessions than communicating to, or stimulating her children creates a kind of sterility that the young would instinctively reject. The impeccably tidy home, the impeccably tidy lawn are—in a very real sense—unnatural and confining. Yet the commercials confront us with broods of happy children, some of whom—believe it or not—notice the new fresh smell their clean, white sweat-shirts exhale thanks to Mom's new "softener."

Some major advertisers, for that matter, can even cast a benign eye on the population explosion. In another Biz commercial, the genial Eddie Albert surveys with surprise a long row of dirty clothes heaped before him by a young matron. She answers his natural query by telling him gaily they are the products of her brood of eleven "with one more to come!" she adds as the twelfth turns up. "That's great!" says Mr. Albert, curdling the soul of Planned Parenthood and the future of this planet.

Who are, one cannot help but ask, the writers who manage to combine the sales of products with the selling-out of human dreams and dignity? Who people this cosmos of commercials with dolts and fools and shrews and narcissists? Who know so much about quirks and mannerisms and ailments and so little about life? So much about presumed wants and so little about crying needs?

Can women advertisers so demean their own sex? Or are there no women in positions of decision high enough to see that their real selves stand up? Do they not know, these extremely clever creators of commercials, what they could do for their audience even while they exploit and entertain them? How they could raise the levels of manners and attitudes while they sell their wares? Or do they really share the worm's-eye view of mass communication that sees, and addresses, only the lowest common denominator?

It can be argued that commercials are taken too seriously, that their   24
function is merely to amuse, engage, and sell, and that they do this brilliantly. If that were all to this wheedling of millions, well and good. But
it is not. There are two more fallouts from this chronic sales explosion
that cannot be measured but that at least can be expected. One has to do
with the continual celebration of youth at the expense of maturity. In
commercials only the young have access to beauty, sex, and joy in life.
What do older women feel, day after day, when love is the exclusive
possession of a teen-age girl with a bobbing mantle of hair? What older
man would not covet her in restless impotence?

The constant reminder of what is inaccessible must inevitably produce a subterranean but real discontent, just as the continual sight of
things and places beyond reach has eaten deeply into the ghetto soul. If
we are constantly presented with what we are not or cannot have, the dislocation deepens, contentment vanishes, and frustration reigns. Even for
the substantially secure, there is always a better thing, a better way, to buy.
That none of these things makes a better life may be consciously acknowledged, but still the desire lodges in the spirit, nagging and pulling.

This kind of fragmentation works in potent ways above and beyond
the mere fact of program interruption, which is much of the time more
of a blessing than a curse, especially in those rare instances when the
commercial is deft and funny: the soft and subtle sell. Its overall curse,
due to the large number of commercials in each hour, is that it reduces
the attention span of a people already so conditioned to constant change
and distraction that they cannot tolerate continuity in print or on the air.

Specifically, commercial interruption is most damaging during that 10
per cent of programing (a charitable estimate) most important to the mind
and spirit of a people: news and public affairs, and drama. To many (and
among these are network news producers), commercials have no place or
business during the vital process of informing the public. There is something obscene about a newscaster pausing to introduce a deodorant or
shampoo commercial between an airplane crash and a body count. It is
more than an interruption; it tends to reduce news to a form of running
entertainment, to smudge the edges of reality by treating death or disaster
or diplomacy on the same level as household appliances or a new gasoline.

The answer to this would presumably be to lump the commercials   28
before and after the news or public affairs broadcasts—an answer
unpalatable, needless to say, to the sponsors who support them.

The same is doubly true of that most unprofitable sector of television, the original play. Essential to any creative composition, whether
drama, music or dance, are mood and continuity, both inseparable from
form and meaning. They are shattered by the periodic intrusion of commercials, which have become intolerable to the serious artists who have
deserted commercial television in droves because the system allows
them no real freedom or autonomy. The selling comes first, the creation
must accommodate itself. It is the rare and admirable sponsor who

restricts or fashions his commercials so as to provide a minimum of intrusion or damaging inappropriateness.

If all these assumptions and imponderables are true, as many suspect, what is the answer or alleviation?

One is in the course of difficult emergence: the establishment of a public television system sufficiently funded so that it can give a maximum number of people an alternate diet of pleasure, enlightenment, and stimulation free from commercial fragmentation. So far, for lack of funds to buy talent and equipment, this effort has been in terms of public attention a distinctly minor operation. Even if public television should greatly increase its scope and impact, it cannot in the nature of things and through long public conditioning equal the impact and reach the size of audience now tuned to commercial television.

Enormous amounts of time, money, and talent go into commercials. 32 Technically they are often brilliant and innovative—the product not only of the new skills and devices but of imaginative minds. A few of them are both funny and endearing. Who, for instance, will forget the miserable young man with the appalling cold, or the kids taught to use—as an initiation into manhood—a fork instead of a spoon with a certain spaghetti? Among the enlightened sponsors, moreover, are some who manage to combine an image of their corporation and their products with accuracy and restraint.

What has to happen to mass medium advertisers as a whole, and especially on TV, is a totally new approach to their function not only as sellers but as social influencers. They have the same obligation as the broadcast medium itself: not only to entertain but to reflect, not only to reflect but to enlarge public consciousness and human stature.

This may be a tall order, but it is a vital one at a time when Americans have ceased to know who they are and where they are going, and when all the multiple forces acting upon them are daily diminishing their sense of their own value and purpose in life, when social upheaval and social fragmentation have destroyed old patterns, and when survival depends on new ones.

If we continue to see ourselves as the advertisers see us, we have no place to go. Nor, I might add, has commercial broadcasting itself.

Topics for Critical Thinking and Writing

1. What does "The Splitting Image" in the title mean? How does it begin to communicate Mannes's attitude toward television ads?
2. In the first three paragraphs, Mannes describes three commercials. How does she indicate her contempt for them?
3. In paragraph 9 Mannes lists "four kinds of females" pictured in daytime television commercials. She wrote the essay in 1970. If you tune in on daytime television today, what kinds of females do you see depicted? Are there still four kinds? The same four?

4. Mannes says (paragraph 17) that advertisements assume that "a woman's only valid function is that of wife, mother, and servant of men." What do television advertisers assume about a man's "valid function"?

5. In paragraph 20 Mannes suggests: "There is good reason to suspect that this manic obsession with cleanliness, fostered, quite naturally, by the giant soap and detergent interests, may bear some responsibility for the cultivated sloppiness of so many of the young in their clothing as well as in their chosen hideouts." Is there really good reason to suspect this connection? Does Mannes sometimes make doubtful assumptions? If so, point them out.

6. Examine some of Mannes's metaphors, such as "There are two more fallouts from this chronic sales explosion" (paragraph 24), and evaluate them. Are they effective or strained?

7. Mannes writes about daytime television commercials; Richard Hawley (page 544) is primarily concerned with evening television shows. What concerns do they share about the effects of television?

Dolores Hayden

Dolores Hayden was born in New York City in 1945. She did her undergraduate work at Mount Holyoke, and she earned a master's degree in architecture at Harvard. Hayden has taught architecture at the University of California (Berkeley) and at Massachusetts Institute of Technology. She is especially concerned with the political and social implications of public spaces.

Advertisements, Pornography, and Public Space

Americans need to look more consciously at the ways in which the public domain is misused for spatial displays of gender stereotypes: These appear in outdoor advertising, and to a lesser extent in commercial displays, architectural decoration, and public sculpture. While the commercial tone and violence of the American city is often criticized, there is little analysis of the routine way that crude stereotypes appear in public, urban spaces as the staple themes of commercial art. Most Americans are accustomed to seeing giant females in various states of undress smiling and carressing products such as whiskey, food, and records. Male models also sell goods, but they are usually active and clothed—recent ad campaigns aimed at gay men seem to be the first major exception. Several geographers have established that men are most often shown doing active things, posed in the great outdoors; women are shown in reflective postures responding to male demands in interior spaces. As the nineteenth-century sexual double standard is preserved by the urban advertising, many twentieth-century urban men behave as if good women are at home while bad ones adorn the billboards and travel on their own in urban space; at the same time, many urban women are encouraged to think of emotionlessness, war-mongering, and sexual inexhaustibility as natural to the Marlboro cowboy, war heroes' statues, and every other male adult.

This double standard is the result of advertising practices, graphic design, and urban design. Sanctioned by the zoning laws, billboards are approved by the same urban planning boards who will not permit child care centers or mother-in-law apartments in many residential districts. But the problem with billboards is not only aesthetic degradation. By presenting gender stereotypes in the form of nonverbal body language, fifty feet long and thirty feet high, billboards turn the public space of the city into a stage set for a drama starring enticing women and stern men.

Let us observe outdoor advertising and other urban design phenomena with similar effects, as they are experienced by two women on an urban commuting trip along the Sunset Strip in Los Angeles in June 1981. Standing on a street corner, the two women are waiting for a bus to go to work. The bus arrives, bearing a placard on the side advertising a local night club. It shows strippers doing their act, their headless bodies naked from neck to crotch except for a few blue sequins. The two women get on the bus and find seats for the ride along Sunset Boulevard. They look out the windows. As the bus pulls away, their heads appear incongruously above the voluptuous cardboard female bodies displayed on the side. They ride through a district of record company headquarters and film offices, one of the most prosperous in L.A.

Their first views reveal rows of billboards. Silent Marlboro man   4 rides the range; husky, khaki-clad Camel man stares at green hills; gigantic, uniformed professional athletes catch passes and hit home runs on behalf of booze. These are the male images. Then, on a billboard for whiskey, a horizontal blonde in a backless black velvet dress, slit to the thigh, invites men to "Try on a little Black Velvet." Next, a billboard shows a well-known actress, reclining with legs spread, who notes that avocadoes are only sixteen calories a slice. "Would this body lie to you?" she asks coyly, emphasizing that the body language which communicates blatant sexual availability is only meant to bring attention to her thin figure. Bo Derek offers a pastoral contrast garbed in nothing but a few bits of fur and leather, as she swings on a vine of green leaves, promoting *Tarzan, the Ape Man*.

Next the bus riders pass a club called the Body Shop that advertises "live, nude girls." Two reclining, realistic nudes, one in blue tones in front of a moonlight cityscape, one in orange sunshine tones, stretch their thirty-foot bodies along the sidewalk. This is the same neighborhood where a billboard advertising a Rolling Stones' record album called "Black and Blue" made news ten years ago. A manacled, spread-legged woman with torn clothes proclaimed "I'm Black and Blue from the Rolling Stones—and I love it!" Members of a group called Women Against Violence Against Women (WAVAW) arrived with cans of spray paint and climbed the scaffolding to make small, uneven letters of protest: "This is a crime against women." Demonstrations and boycotts eventually succeeded in achieving the removal of that image, but not in eliminating the graphic design problem. "Black and Blue" has been replaced by James Bond in a tuxedo, pistol in hand, viewed through the spread legs and buttocks of a giant woman in a bathing suit and improbably high heels, captioned "For Your Eyes Only."

When the two women get off the bus in Hollywood, they experience more gender stereotypes as pedestrians. First, they walk past a department store. In the windows mannequins suggest the prevailing ideals of sartorial elegance. The male torsos lean forward, as if they are about to clinch a deal. The female torsos, pin-headed, tip backward and sideways, at odd angles, as if they are about to be pushed over onto a bed. The themes of gender advertisements are trumpeted here in the mannequins' body language as well as on billboards. Next, the women pass an apartment building. Two neoclassical caryatids support the entablature over the front door. Their breasts are bared, their heads carry the load. They recall the architecture of the Erechtheum on the Acropolis in Athens, dating from the 5th century B.C., where the sculptured stone forms of female slaves were used as support for a porch in place of traditional columns and capitals. This is an ancient image of servitude.

After the neo-classical apartment house, the commuters approach a construction site. Here they are subject to an activity traditionally called "running the gauntlet," but referred to as "girl watching" by urban sociologist William H. Whyte. Twelve workers stop whatever they are doing, whistle, and yell: "Hey, baby!" The women put their heads down, and walk faster, tense with anger. The construction workers take delight in causing exactly this response: "You're cute when you're mad!" Whyte regards this type of behavior as charming, pedestrian fun in "Street Life," where he even takes pleasure in tracing its historic antecedents, but he has never been whistled at, hooted at, and had the dimensions of his body parts analyzed out loud on a public street.[1]

Finally, these women get to the office building where they work. It has two statues out front of women. Their bronze breasts culminate in erect nipples. After they pass this last erotic public display of women's flesh, sanctioned as fine art, they walk in the door to begin the day's work. Their journey has taken them through an urban landscape filled

8

---

[1]William H. Whyte, "Street Life," *Urban Open Spaces* (Summer 1980), 2. For a more detailed critique of hassling: Lindsy Van Gelder. "The International Language of Street Hassling," *Ms.* 9 (May 1981), 15–20, and letters about this article, *Ms.* (Sept. 1981); and Cheryl Benard and Edith Schlaffer, "The Man in the Street: Why He Harasses," *Ms.* 9 (May 1981), 18–19.

with images of men as sexual aggressors and women as submissive sexual objects.

The transient quality of male and female interaction in public streets makes the behavior provoked by billboards and their public design images particularly difficult to attack. Psychologist Erving Goffman has analyzed both print ads and billboards as *Gender Advertisements* because art directors use exaggerated body language to suggest that consumers buy not products but images of masculinity or femininity.[2] If passers-by are driving at fifty miles per hour, these gender cues cannot be subtle. In *Ways of Seeing,* art historian John Berger describes the cumulative problem that gender stereotypes in advertising create for woman as "split consciousness."[3] While many women guard themselves, some men assume that ogling is part of normal public life. Women are always wary, watching men watch them, and wondering if and when something is going to happen to them.

Urban residents also encounter even more explicit sexual images in urban space. Tawdry strip clubs, X-rated films, "adult" bookstores and sex shops are not uncommon sights. Pornographic video arcades are the next wave to come. Pornography is a bigger, more profitable industry in the United States than all legitimate film and record business combined.[4] It spills over into soft-porn, quasi-porn, and tasteless public imagery everywhere. In the midst of this sex-exploitation, if one sees a real prostitute, there is mild surprise. Yet soliciting is still a crime. Of course, the male customer of an adult prostitute is almost never arrested, but the graphic designer, the urban designer, and the urban planner never come under suspicion for their contributions to a commercial public landscape that preserves the sexual double standard in a brutal and vulgar way.

Feminist Laura Shapiro calls our society a "rape culture."[5] Adrienne Rich has written of "a world masculinity made unfit for women or men."[6] But surely most Americans do not consciously, deliberately accept public space given over to commercial exploitation, violence and harassment of women. Indeed, the success of the "Moral Majority" displays how a few activists were able to tap public concern effectively about commercialized sexuality, albeit in a narrow, antihumanist way. In contrast, the example of the Women's Christian Temperance Union

[2]Erving Goffman, *Gender Advertisements* (New York: Harper Colphon, 1976), 24–27; Nancy Henley, *Body Politics: Power, Sex, and Nonverbal Communication* (Englewood Cliffs, N.J.: Prentice-Hall, 1977), 30, Marianne Wex, *Let's Take Back Our Space* (Berlin: Movimento Druck, 1979).

[3]John Berger, et al., *Ways of Seeing* (Harmondsworth, England: BBC and Penguin, 1972), 45–64.

[4]Tom Hayden, *The American Future: New Visitors Beyond Old Frontiers* (Boston: South End Press, 1980), 15.

[5]Laura Shapiro, "Violence: The Most Obscene Fantasy," in Freeman, ed., *Women: A Feminist Perspective,* 469–73.

[6]*Ibid.,* 469.

under Frances Willard's leadership, and the parks movement under Olmsted's,[7] show religious idealism, love of nature, and concern for female safety can be activated into dynamic urban reform movements that enlarge domestic values into urban values, instead of diminishing them into domestic pieties.

Topics for Critical Thinking and Writing

1. How does Hayden organize her material? Note, in particular, the narrative of two women traveling to work. What does this device add to the essay?
2. How does Hayden suggest that displays of gender stereotypes contribute to violence against women? What evidence supports this assumption?
3. In a paragraph or two, describe and analyze a magazine advertisement that promotes gender stereotypes or one that is aimed at gay men (see Hayden's first paragraph).
4. If you are familiar with a sculpture of a female figure in a public space in your neighborhood (perhaps in a plaza or in a public building), in a paragraph set forth what the image "says." Or, compare two sculptures—one of a female and one of a male—and explain what each says.
5. In an essay of two or three pages, describe and analyze two billboards, one featuring a man and one featuring a woman. How do they present the "gender stereotypes" that Hayden talks about? Your essay should respond to this question with a clearly formulated thesis sentence (see page 802).

Stevie Smith

Stevie Smith (1902–71) was born Florence Margaret Smith in England. Her first book was a novel, published in 1936, but she is best known for her several volumes of poetry.

Not Waving but Drowning

Nobody heard him, the dead man,
But still he lay moaning:
I was much further out than you thought
And not waving but drowning.

Poor chap, he always loved larking
And now he's dead
It must have been too cold for him his heart gave way,

---

[7]Frederick Law Olmsted (1822–1903) was an American landscape architect. Among his noble works are Central Park in Manhattan and Prospect Park in Brooklyn.

They said

Oh, no no no, it was too cold always
(Still the dead one lay moaning)
I was much too far out all my life
And not waving but drowning.

Topics for Critical Thinking and Writing

1. The first line, "Nobody heard him, the dead man," is, of course, literally true. Dead men do not speak. In what other ways is it true?
2. Who are "they" whose voices we hear in the second stanza? What does the punctuation—or lack of it—in line 7 tell us of their feelings for the dead man? What effect is produced by the brevity of line 6? of line 8?
3. In the last stanza, does the man reproach himself, or others, or simply bemoan his fate? What was the cause of his death?

11
ART AND LIFE

the Checkered House is old,
this as it looked in 1853.
   It was the Headquarters of
General Baum in the revolution
war, and afterwards He used
it as a Hospital,
   then it was a stoping place
for the stage,
   where they changed Horses every
two miles,
   oh we traveled <u>fast</u> in those
   days,

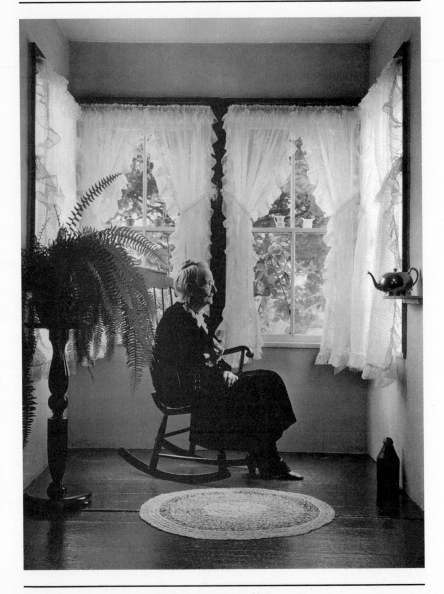

Grandma Moses, Eagle Bridge, New York, 1949 © 1974, Arnold Newman

Place de l'Europe, Paris, 1932
Henri Cartier-Bresson

Henri Cartier-Bresson/Magnum Photos

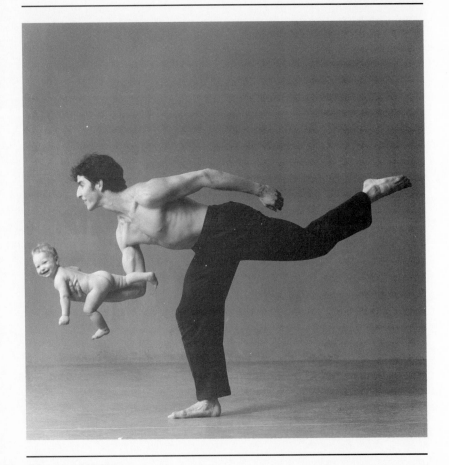

Short Views

Art for art's sake.
Théophile Gautier

What is art, that it should have a sake?
Samuel Butler

Art for art's sake is an empty phrase. Art for the sake of the true, art for the sake of the good and the beautiful, that is the faith I am searching for.
George Sand (Amandine Aurore Lucie Dupin)

The end of reading is not more books but more life.
Holbrook Jackson

The storyteller's own experience of people and things, whether for good or ill—not only what he has passed through himself, but even events which he has only witnessed or been told of—has moved the writer to an emotion so passionate that he can no longer keep it shut up in his heart. Again and again something in his own life or in that around him will seem to the writer so important that he cannot bear to let it pass into oblivion. There must never come a time, he feels, when people do not know about it.
Lady Murasaki, *The Tale of Genji*

If I had to give young writers advice, I'd say don't listen to writers talking about writing.
Lillian Hellman

Artistic growth is, more than anything else, a refining of the sense of truthfulness. The stupid believe that to be truthful is easy; only the artist, the great artist, knows how difficult it is.
Willa Cather

Art, it seems to me, should simplify. That, indeed, is very nearly the whole of the higher artistic process; finding what conventions of form and what detail one can do without and yet preserve the spirit of the whole—so that all that one has suppressed and cut away is there to the reader's consciousness as much as if it were in type on the page.

    Willa Cather

I think art, literature, fiction, poetry, what it is, makes justice in the world. That's why it almost always has to be on the side of the underdog.

    Grace Paley

Literature is news that stays news.

    Ezra Pound

The two worst sins of bad taste in fiction are pornography and sentimentality. One is too much sex and the other is too much sentiment.

    Flannery O'Connor

It is easier to understand a nation by listening to its music than by learning its language.

    Anonymous

What's swinging in words? If a guy makes you pat your foot and if you feel it down your back, you don't have to ask anybody if that's good music or not. You can always feel it.

    Miles Davis

It started with the moans and groans of the people in the cotton fields. Before it got the name of soul, men were sellin' watermelons and vegetables on a wagon drawn by a mule, hollerin' "watermelon!" with a cry in their voices. And the man on the railroad track layin' crossties—every time they hit the hammer it was with a sad feelin', but with a beat. And the Baptist preacher—he the one who had the soul—he give out the meter, a long and short meter, and the old mothers of the church would reply. This musical thing has been here since America been here. This is trial and tribulation music.

    Mahalia Jackson

You don't take a photograph, you make it.
      Ansel Adams

A good painter is to paint two main things, namely, man and the working of man's mind. The first is easy, the second difficult, for it is to be represented through the gestures and movements of the limbs.
      Leonardo da Vinci

I like pretty things the best, what's the use of painting a picture if it isn't something nice? So I think real hard till I think of something real pretty, and then I paint it. I like to paint old timey things, historical landmarks of long ago, bridges, mills and hostelries, those old time homes, there are a few left, and they are going fast. I do them all from memory, most of them are day dreams, as it were.
      Grandma Moses

The truest expression of a people is in its dances and its music. Bodies never lie.
      Agnes de Mille

Dancing is like bank robbery, it takes split-second timing.
      Twyla Tharpe

Pablo Picasso

Pablo Picasso (1881–1973) was born in Spain, but after 1900 he lived most of his life in Paris. Although he is known chiefly as a painter, he also produced drawings, sculptures, ceramics, and stage designs. He is widely regarded as the most important artist of the twentieth century.

Although Picasso made only a few formal statements about art, he often spoke about art to friends and interviewers. We reproduce some of his comments, and reports of his comments. Although by art *he usually means painting or sculpture, the word can, of course, also refer to works of literature, music, dance, and so on.*

Talking about Art

[Art and Truth]

We all know that Art is not truth. Art is a lie that makes us realize truth, at least the truth that is given us to understand. The artist must know the manner whereby to convince others of the truthfulness of his lies. If he only shows in his work that he has searched, and researched, for the way to put over lies, he would never accomplish anything.

[A Work of Art Changes]

A picture is not thought out and settled beforehand. While it is being done it changes as one's thoughts change. And when it is finished, it still goes on changing, according to the state of mind of whoever is looking at it. A picture lives a life like a living creature, undergoing the changes imposed on us by our life from day to day. This is natural enough, as the picture lives only through the man who is looking at it.

[On Understanding Art, and Explaining It]

Everyone wants to understand art. Why not try to understand the songs of a bird? Why does one love the night, flowers, everything around one, without trying to understand them? But in the case of a painting people have to *understand*. If only they would realize above all that an artist works of necessity, that he himself is only a trifling bit of the world, and that no more importance should be attached to him than to plenty of other things which please us in the world, though we can't explain them. People who try to explain pictures are usually barking up the wrong tree. Gertrude Stein joyfully announced to me the other day that she had at last understood what my picture of the three musicians was meant to be. It was a still life!

[Art as Discovery]

We just left Don Pablo. He was doing a large charcoal drawing of a terrifi-
cally dramatic rooster. "Roosters—" he said, "we always have roosters, but

4

like everything else in life we must discover them. Just as Corot discovered the morning and Renoir discovered little girls. Everything must be discovered—this box—a piece of paper. You must always leave the door open, always open—and the main thing is never to turn back once you pass through that door. Never to dismay and never to compromise. Roosters have always been seen but seldom so well as in American weather vanes."

[The Artist's Subject Matter]

Picasso: "Actually, it's through one's work that one is understood. One must work, work." Then he talks of the difficulties he has in inventing—even in inventing a new subject. "There are, basically, very few subjects. Everybody is repeating them. Venus and Love become the Virgin and Child, then—maternity, but it's always the same subject. It's magnificent to invent new subjects. Take Van Gogh: Potatoes, those shapeless things! To have painted that, or a pair of old shoes! That's really something!"

[Originality]

The individual who insists on being original wastes his time and deceives himself; if he attains something it is but an imitation of what he likes, and if he goes farther it may be that what he does not even resemble him. One day I told Angel Ortiz: to make a circle without a compass, try to trace a line always equidistant from the center, but do not think about other forms or about the many people who have traced circles before you. If you kill yourself, you will not make it perfectly round; and in the discrepancy between perfect roundness and your closest approximation to it, you will find your personal expression. If you work in good faith you will try to make it perfect, but each of your circles, in spite of your improved dexterity in drawing them will always suffer from the same defect. Every one of them will bear your mark.

* * *

"What does it mean," says Picasso, "for a painter to paint in the manner of So-and-So or to actually imitate someone else? What's wrong with that? On the contrary, it's a good idea. You should constantly try to paint like someone else. But the thing is, you can't! You would like to. You try. But it turns out to be a botch. . . .

"And it's at the very moment you make a botch of it that you're yourself." 8

* * *

"Freedom," says Picasso, "one must be very careful with that. In painting as in everything else. Whatever you do, you find yourself once more in chains. Freedom not to do one thing requires that you do another, imperatively. And there you have it, chains. That reminds me of a story of Jarry about the anarchist soldiers at drill. They are told:

right face. And immediately, since they are anarchists, they all face left.
. . . Painting is like that. You take freedom and you shut yourself up
with your idea, just that particular one and no other. And there you are
again, in chains."

[Realism and Pure Form]

When you start with a portrait and search for a pure form, a clear volume, through successive eliminations, you arrive inevitably at the egg.
Likewise, starting with the egg and following the same process in
reverse, one finishes with the portrait. But art, I believe, escapes these
simplistic exercises which consist in going from one extreme to the
other. It's necessary to know when to stop.

Topics for Critical Thinking and Writing

1. Picasso says, in the first paragraph, that "Art is a lie that makes us real-
    ize truth." Does this make sense? If you think it does, draw on your
    own experience either as a creator of art or as a consumer of art—for
    instance, as a reader of a novel, a visitor to a museum, or a member of
    the audience at a concert—and clarify the point by giving at least two
    concrete examples.
2. In the third paragraph Picasso suggests that there is little or no point in
    trying to "understand art." Drawing on your own experience, perhaps in
    a literature, art, or music course, consider whether an attempt to under-
    stand a work of art led to increased understanding and pleasure.
3. Take any one of Picasso's comments (other than the two just men-
    tioned) and test it against your own experience.

W. E. B. Du Bois

W. E. B. Du Bois (1868–1963) was born in Massachusetts, where he seems to have had a rel-
atively happy early childhood—though in grade school he was shocked to learn that his
classmates considered him different because of his color. In 1885 he went to Fisk University
in Nashville, Tennessee; and then, for doctoral work, he studied history at Harvard University
and sociology at the University of Berlin. His doctoral dissertation, The Suppression of the
Slave Trade in the United States of America, *was published in* Harvard Historical Studies *in 1896.*

Although Du Bois had embarked on a scholarly career, he became increasingly con-
cerned with the injustices of contemporary society, and his writings were now directed at a
general public. In 1903 he published The Souls of Black Folk, *a book challenging Booker T.*
Washington's more resigned position. From 1910 to the mid–1930s he edited The Crisis, *the*
journal of the National Association for the Advancement of Colored People. Although he
energetically solicited the writings of other people, he wrote so many essays for the journal
that he can almost be said to be its author as well as its editor. Eventually Du Bois joined the
Communist party, and in 1963 he left the United States for Ghana, where he died.

We reprint part of chapter 14 from The Souls of Black Folk.

Of the Sorrow Songs

I walk through the churchyard
To lay this body down;
I know moon-rise, I know star-rise;
I walk in the moonlight, I walk in the starlight;
I'll lie in the grave and stretch out my arms,
I'll go to judgment in the evening of the day,
And my soul and thy soul shall meet that day,
When I lay this body down.

Negro Song

They that walked in darkness sang songs in the olden days—Sorrow Songs—for they were weary at heart. And so before each thought that I have written in this book I have set a phrase, a haunting echo of these weird old songs in which the soul of the black slave spoke to men. Ever since I was a child these songs have stirred me strangely. They came out of the South unknown to me, one by one, and yet at once I knew them as of me and of mine. Then in after years when I came to Nashville I saw the great temple builded of these songs towering over the pale city. To me Jubilee Hall seemed ever made of the songs themselves, and its bricks were red with the blood and dust of toil. Out of them rose for me morning, noon, and night, bursts of wonderful melody, full of the voices of my brothers and sisters, full of the voices of the past.

Little of beauty has America given the world save the rude grandeur God himself stamped on her bosom; the human spirit in this new world has expressed itself in vigor and ingenuity rather than in beauty. And so by fateful chance the Negro folk-song—the rhythmic cry of the slave—stands to-day not simply as the sole American music, but as the most beautiful expression of human experience born this side the seas. It has been neglected, it has been, and is, half despised, and above all it has been persistently mistaken and misunderstood; but notwithstanding, it still remains as the singular spiritual heritage of the nation and the greatest gift of the Negro people.

Away back in the thirties the melody of these slave songs stirred the nation, but the songs were soon half forgotten. Some, like "Near the lake where drooped the willow," passed into current airs and their source was forgotten; others were caricatured on the "minstrel" stage and their memory died away. Then in war-time came the singular Port Royal experiment after the capture of Hilton Head, and perhaps for the first time the North met the Southern slave face to face and heart to heart with no third witness. The Sea Islands of the Carolinas, where they met, were filled with a black folk of primitive type, touched and moulded less by the world about them than any others outside the Black Belt. Their appearance was uncouth, their language funny, but their hearts were human and their singing stirred men with a mighty power. Thomas Wentworth Higginson hastened to tell of these songs, and Miss McKim and others urged upon the world their rare beauty. But the world listened only half credulously until the Fisk Jubilee Singers sang the slave songs so deeply into the world's heart that it can never wholly forget them again.

There was once a blacksmith's son born at Cadiz, New York, who in the changes of time taught school in Ohio and helped defend Cincinnati from Kirby Smith. Then he fought at Chancellorsville and Gettysburg and finally served in the Freedman's Bureau at Nashville. Here he formed a Sunday-school class of black children in 1866, and sang with them and taught them to sing. And then they taught him to sing, and when once the glory of the Jubilee songs passed into the soul of George L. White, he knew his life-work was to let those Negroes sing to the world as they had sung to him. So in 1871 the pilgrimage of the Fisk Jubilee Singers began. North to Cincinnati they rode,—four half-clothed black boys and five girl-women,—led by a man with a cause and a purpose. They stopped at Wilberforce, the oldest of Negro schools, where a black bishop blessed them. Then they went, fighting cold and starvation, shut out of hotels, and cheerfully sneered at, ever northward; and ever the magic of their song kept thrilling hearts, until a burst of applause in the Congregational Council at Oberlin revealed them to the world. They came to New York and Henry Ward Beecher dared to welcome them, even though the metropolitan dailies sneered at his "Nigger Minstrels." So their songs conquered till they sang across the land and across the sea, before Queen and Kaiser, in Scotland and

Ireland, Holland and Switzerland. Seven years they sang, and brought back a hundred and fifty thousand dollars to found Fisk University.

* * *

The words that are left to us are not without interest, and, cleared of evident dross, they conceal much of real poetry and meaning beneath conventional theology and unmeaning rhapsody. Like all primitive folk, the slave stood near to Nature's heart. Life was a "rough and rolling sea" like the brown Atlantic of the Sea Islands; the "Wilderness" was the home of God, and the "lonesome valley" led to the way of life. "Winter'll soon be over," was the picture of life and death to a tropical imagination. The sudden wild thunder-storms of the South awed and impressed the Negroes,—at times the rumbling seemed to them "mournful," at times imperious:

> "My Lord calls me,
> He calls me by the thunder,
> The trumpet sounds it in my soul."

The monotonous toil and exposure is painted in many words. One sees the ploughmen in the hot, moist furrow, singing:

> "Dere's no rain to wet you,
> Dere's no sun to burn you,
> Oh, push along, believer,
> I want to go home."

The bowed and bent old man cries, with thrice-repeated wail:

> "O Lord, keep me from sinking down,"

and he rebukes the devil of doubt who can whisper:

> "Jesus is dead and God's gone away."

Yet the soul-hunger is there, the restlessness of the savage, the wail of the wanderer, and the plaint is put in one little phrase:
My soul wants something that's new, that's new.

* * *

Of death the Negro showed little fear, but talked of it familiarly and even fondly as simply a crossing of the waters, perhaps—who knows?—back to his ancient forests again. Later days transfigured his fatalism, and amid the dust and dirt the toiler sang:

> "Dust, dust and ashes, fly over my grave,
> But the Lord shall bear my spirit home."

The things evidently borrowed from the surrounding world undergo characteristic change when they enter the mouth of the slave. Especially is this true of Bible phrases. "Weep, O captive daughter of Zion," is quaintly turned into "Zion, weep-a-low," and the wheels of Ezekiel are turned every way in the mystic dreaming of the slave, till he says:

> "There's a little wheel a-turnin' in-a-my heart."

As in olden time, the words of these hymns were improvised by some leading minstrel of the religious band. The circumstances of the gathering, however, the rhythm of the songs, and the limitations of allowable thought, confined the poetry for the most part to single or double lines, and they seldom were expanded to quatrains or longer tales, although there are some few examples of sustained efforts, chiefly paraphrases of the Bible. Three short series of verses have always attracted me,—the one that heads this chapter, of one line of which Thomas Wentworth Higginson has fittingly said, "Never, it seems to me, since man first lived and suffered was his infinite longing for peace uttered more plaintively." The second and third are descriptions of the Last Judgment,—the one a late improvisation, with some traces of outside influence:

> "Oh, the stars in the elements are falling,
> And the moon drips away into blood,
> And the ransomed of the Lord are returning unto God,
> Blessed be the name of the Lord."

And the other earlier and homelier picture from the low coast lands:

> "Michael, haul the boat ashore,
> Then you'll hear the horn they blow,
> Then you'll hear the trumpet sound,
> Trumpet sound the world around,
> Trumpet sound for rich and poor,
> Trumpet sound for Jubilee,
> Trumpet sound for you and me."

Through all the sorrow of the Sorrow Songs there breathes a hope—a faith in the ultimate justice of things. The minor cadences of despair change often to triumph and calm confidence. Sometimes it is faith in life, sometimes a faith in death, sometimes assurance of boundless justice in some fair world beyond. But whichever it is, the meaning is always clear: that sometime, somewhere, men will judge men by their souls and not by their skins. Is such a hope justified? Do the Sorrow Songs sing true?

The silently growing assumption of this age is that the probation of races is past, and that the backward races of to-day are of proven inefficiency and not worth the saving. Such an assumption is the arrogance of peoples irreverent toward Time and ignorant of the deeds of men. A 12
thousand years ago such an assumption, easily possible, would have made it difficult for the Teuton to prove his right to life. Two thousand years ago such dogmatism, readily welcome, would have scouted the idea of blond races ever leading civilization. So wofully unorganized is sociological knowledge that the meaning of progress, the meaning of "swift" and "slow" in human doing, and the limits of human perfectability, are veiled, unanswered sphinxes on the shores of science. Why should Æschylus have sung two thousand years before Shakespeare was born? Why has civilization flourished in Europe, and flickered, flamed, and died in Africa? So long as the world stands meekly dumb before such questions, shall this nation proclaim its ignorance and unhallowed prejudices by denying freedom of opportunity to those who brought the Sorrow Songs to the Seats of the Mighty?

Your country? How came it yours? Before the Pilgrims landed we were here. Here we have brought our three gifts and mingled them with yours: a gift of story and song—soft, stirring melody in an ill-harmonized and unmelodious land; the gift of sweat and brawn to beat back the wilderness, conquer the soil, and lay the foundations of this vast economic empire two hundred years earlier than your weak hands could have done it; the third, a gift of the Spirit. Around us the history of the land has centred for thrice a hundred years; out of the nation's heart we have called all that was best to throttle and subdue all that was worst; fire and blood, prayer and sacrifice, have billowed over this people, and they have found peace only in the altars of the God of Right. Nor has our gift of the Spirit been merely passive. Actively we have woven ourselves with the very warp and woof of this nation,—we fought their battles, shared their sorrow, mingled our blood with theirs, and generation after generation have pleaded with a headstrong, careless people to despise not Justice, Mercy, and Truth, lest the nation be smitten with a curse. Our song, our toil, our cheer, and warning have been given to this nation in blood-brotherhood. Are not these gifts worth the giving? Is not this work and striving? Would America have been America without her Negro people?

Even so is the hope that sang in the songs of my fathers well sung. If somewhere in this whirl and chaos of things there dwells Eternal Good, pitiful yet masterful, then anon in His good time America shall rend the Veil and the prisoned shall be free. Free, free as the sunshine trickling down the morning into these high windows of mine, free as yonder fresh young voices welling up to me from the caverns of brick and mortar below—welling with song, instinct with life, tremulous treble and darkening bass. My children, my little children, are singing to the sunshine, and thus they sing:

Let us cheer the weary traveller,
Cheer the weary traveller,
Let us cheer the weary traveller
Along the heavenly way.

And the traveller girds himself, and sets his face toward the Morning, and goes his way.
[1903]

Topics for Critical Thinking and Writing

1. Du Bois uses some terms that may disconcert a reader, such as *primitive* and *backward races.* Look especially closely at the passages in which these terms occur and then summarize Du Bois's view of the African Americans of his time. Look closely, too, at passages in which he discusses white attitudes toward African Americans, and summarize his views of these whites also.
2. Read the three spirituals quoted below—or, better, hear a performance of spirituals. To what extent has Du Bois helped you (if he has) to understand and enjoy these works?
3. Alain Locke (1886–1954), African-American educator and literary critic and historian, in *The Negro and His Music,* says of the spirituals,

   Over-emphasize the melodic elements of a spiritual, and you get a sentimental ballad a la Stephen Foster. Stress the harmony and you get a cloying glee or "barber-shop" chorus. Over-emphasize, on the other hand, the rhythmic idiom and instantly you secularize the product and it becomes a syncopated shout, with the religious tone and mood completely evaporated.

   If you are familiar with performances of spirituals, test the performances against Locke's words—or test Locke's words against the performances.

Anonymous

Three Spirituals

A Note on Spirituals

Spirituals, or Sorrow Songs, by slaves in the United States, seem to have been created chiefly in the first half of the nineteenth century. Their origins are still a matter of some dispute, but probably most students of the subject agree that the songs represent a distinctive fusion of African rhythms with white hymns; and, of course, many of the texts derive ultimately from Biblical sources. One of the chief themes is the desire for release, sometimes presented with imagery drawn from ancient

Israel. Examples include references to crossing the River Jordan (a river that runs from north of the Sea of Galilee to the Dead Sea), the release of the Israelites from slavery in Egypt (Exodus), Jonah's release from the whale (Book of Jonah), and Daniel's deliverance from a fiery furnace and from the lions' den (Book of Daniel, chapters 3 and 6).

The texts were collected and published especially in the 1860s, for instance in *Slave Songs of the United States* (1867). These books usually sought to reproduce the singers' pronunciation, and we have followed the early texts here.

Deep River

Deep river, my home is over Jordan, Deep river,
Lord, I want to cross over into campground,
Lord, I want to cross over into campground,
Lord, I want to cross over into campground.	4
Oh, chillun, Oh, don't you want to go to that gospel feast,
That promised land, that land, where all is peace?
Walk into heaven, and take my seat,
And cast my crown at Jesus feet,	8
Lord, I want to cross over into campground,
Lord, I want to cross over into campground,
Lord, I want to cross over into campground.
Deep river, my home is over Jordan, Deep river	12
Lord, I want to cross over into campground,
Lord, I want to cross over into campground,
Lord, I want to cross over into campground, Lord!

Go Down, Moses

When Israel was in Egypt's land,
    Let my people go;
Oppressed so hard they could not stand,
    Let my people go.	4

Chorus:
Go down, Moses, way down in Egypt's land;
Tell old Pharoah, to let my people go.
Thus saith the Lord, bold Moses said,
    Let my people go;	8
If not I'll smite your first born dead,
    Let my people go.
No more shall they in bondage toil,
    Let my people go;	12
Let them come out with Egypt's spoil,
    Let my people go.

O 'twas a dark and dismal night,
　Let my people go;
When Moses led the Israelites,
　Let my people go.
16

The Lord told Moses what to do,
　Let my people go;
To lead the children of Israel through,
　Let my people go.
20

O come along, Moses, you won't get lost,
　Let my people go;
Stretch our your rod and come across,
　Let my people go.
24

As Israel stood by the water side,
　Let my people go;
At the command of God it did divide,
　Let my people go.
28

And when they reached the other side,
　Let my people go;
They sang a song of triumph o'er,
　Let my people go.
32

You won't get lost in the wilderness,
　Let my people go;
With a lighted candle in your breast,
　Let my people go.
36

O let us all from bondage flee,
　Let my people go;
And let us all in Christ be free,
　Let my people go.
40

We need not always weep and moan,
　Let my people go;
And wear these slavery chains forlorn,
　Let my people go.
44

What a beautiful morning that will be,
　Let my people go;
When time breaks up in eternity,
　Let my people go.
48

Didn't My Lord Deliver Daniel

Didn't my Lord deliver Daniel, deliver Daniel, deliver Daniel,
Didn't my Lord deliver Daniel,
　An' why not every man.
He delivered Daniel from de lion's den,
4

Jonah from de belly of de whale,
An' de Hebrew chillun from de fiery furnace,
An' why not every man.   8
   Didn't my Lord deliver Daniel, deliver Daniel, deliver Daniel,
   Didn't my Lord deliver Daniel,
   An' why not every man.
De moon run down in a purple stream,   12
De sun forbear to shine,
An' every star disappear,
King Jesus shall-a be mine.
   (Refrain)   16
De win' blows eas' an' de win' blows wes',
It blows like de judgament day,
An' every po' soul dat never did pray
'll be glad to pray dat day.   20
   (Refrain)
I set my foot on de Gospel ship,
An de ship begin to sail,
It landed me over on Canaan's shore,[1]   24
An' I'll never come back no mo'.
   (Refrain)

Topic for Critical Thinking and Writing

As we mention in our introductory note, we give the texts of the songs as they were printed in the second half of the nineteenth century, when an effort to indicate pronunciation was made (e.g., *chillun* for *children*). If you were printing the songs, would you retain these attempts to indicate pronunciation. What, if anything, is gained by keeping them? What, if any, unintentional side effects are produced?

Lena Williams

Lena Williams, who describes herself here as "a 40-something black woman," published the essay in The New York Times *in 1994.*

A Black Fan of Country Music Finally Tells All

I heard that Reba McEntire's new album, "Read My Mind," shot to No. 5 on the Billboard chart the first weekend of its release.

---

[1]**Canaan's shore,** *Canaan* is the ancient name of a territory that included part of what is now Israel.

Well, she got my $11.95.

I'm a 40-something black woman who spent her youth in Washington, lip-syncing to the Supremes and slow dancing to the Temptations. Now I often come home to my Manhattan apartment and put on Vince Gill, Randy Travis or Reba. Consider me a fan of country music. So there. Deal with it.

For most of my adult life, I was a closet country music fan. I'd hide   4
my Waylon Jennings and Willie Nelson albums between the dusty, pyschedelic rock. I'd listen to Dolly Parton on my earphones, singing along softly, afraid my neighbors might mistake my imitation twang for a cry for help. I'd enter a music store, looking over my shoulder in search of familiar faces and flip through the rhythm-and-blues section for about five minutes before sneaking off to the country aisle where I'd surreptitiously grab a Travis Tritt tape off the rack and make a beeline for the shortest cashier's line.

Just when I'd reached for my American Express card, I'd spot a tall, dark, handsome type in an Armani suit standing behind me with a puzzled look. What's he going to think? "The sister seems down, but what's she doing with that Dwight Yoakum CD?"

So now I'm publicly coming out of the closet and proclaiming my affection for country perennials like Ms. McEntire.

When I told a friend I was preparing this confessional, he offered a word of caution: "No self-respecting black person would ever admit to that in public."

I thought about his comment. As a child growing up in the 1950's, in   8
a predominantly black community, I wasn't allowed to play country-and-western music in my house. Blacks weren't supposed to like country—or classical for that matter—but that's another story. Blacks' contribution to American music was in jazz, blues and funk. Country music was dismissed as poor white folks' blues and associated with regions of the nation that symbolized prejudice and racial bigotry. Even mainstream white America viewed country as lower class and less desirable, often poking fun at its twangy chords and bellyaching sentiments.

But I was always a cowgirl at heart. I liked country's wild side; its down-home, aw-shucks musicians with the yodel in their voices and the angst in their lyrics. I saw an honesty in country and its universal tales of love lost and found. Besides, the South didn't have a monopoly on racial hatred, and country artists, like everybody else, were stealing black music, so why should I hold it against country?

And while snickering at country, white America also demonstrated a similar cultural backwardness toward black music, be it gospel, ragtime or the blues. So I allowed country to enter my heart and my mind, in spite of its faults. Indeed, when prodded, some blacks who rejected country conceded that there was a spirituality that resounded in the music and that in its heartfelt sentiment, country was a lot like blues. Yet they could never bring themselves to spend hard-earned dollars on Hank Williams Jr.

The 1980's saw country (western was dropped, much to my chagrin) become mainstream. Suddenly there was country at the Copa and at Town Hall. WYNY-FM radio in New York now claims the largest audience of any country station, with more than one million listeners. Dolly Parton and Kenny Rogers became movie stars. Garth Brooks became an American phenomenon.

Wall Street investment bankers bought cowboy boots and hats and   12
learned to do the two-step. And black and white artists like Patti La Belle and Lyle Lovett and Natalie Cole and Ms. McEntire now sing duets and clearly admire one another's music.

Perhaps the nation's acceptance of country has something to do with an evolutionary change in the music. Country has got edge. It has acquired an attitude. Womens' voices have been given strength. Oh, the hardship and misery is still there. But the stuff about "standing by your man" has changed to a more assertive posture.

In "I Won't Stand in Line," a song on Ms. McEntire's new album, she makes it clear to a skirt-chasing lover that "I'd do almost anything just to make you mine, but I won't stand in line." That line alone makes me think of Aretha Franklin's "Respect."

One other thing: I don't like sad songs. I've cried enough for a lifetime. Country makes me laugh, always has. Maybe because it never took itself so seriously. Think about it. "Drop-Kick Me, Jesus, Through the Goal Posts of Life." "A Boy Named Sue."

Ms. McEntire serves up a humorous touch in "Why Haven't I   16
Heard From You." "That thing they call the telephone/Now there's one on every corner, in the back of every bar/You can get one in your briefcase, on a plane or in your car/So tell me why haven't I heard from you, darlin', honey, what is your excuse?" Call it Everywoman's lament.

Well, it's off my chest, and it feels good.

I will no longer make excuses for my musical tastes. Not when millions are being made by performers exhorting listeners to "put your hands in the air and wave 'em like you just don't care."

Compare that with the haunting refrain of Ms. McEntire's "I Think His Name Was John," a song about a woman, a one-night stand and AIDS: "She lays all alone and cries herself to sleep/'Cause she let a stranger kill her hopes and her dreams/And in the end when she was barely hanging on/All she could say is she thinks his name was John."

Topics for Critical Thinking and Writing

1. In her eighth paragraph Williams briefly explains why "Blacks weren't supposed to like country," and why "mainstream white America viewed country as lower class." If you are familiar with country music, amplify (by means of specific details) these two points, and then evaluate them. That is, are there good reasons for African Americans and for "mainstream white America" to hold a low opinion of country music?

2. Argue on behalf of some form of any art—for instance, comic strips or soap operas—that you like but that many people regard as less than respectable.

Camille Paglia

Camille Paglia, born in Endicott, New York, in 1947 and educated at the State University of New York at Binghamton and Yale University, teaches humanities at the University of the Arts, in Philadelphia. Paglia achieved fame in 1990 with the publication of her book, Sexual Personae, *a study of pornographic, voyeuristic, and sadistic elements in literature. She considers herself a feminist, but she has sharply criticized many other feminists, and in turn has been sharply criticized. As she said in the preface to* Sexual Personae, *"My stress on the truth in sexual stereotypes and on the biologic basis of sex difference is sure to cause controversy." We reprint an essay first printed in* The New York Times *in 1990, which has been reprinted in a collection of Paglia's essays,* Sex, Art, and American Culture.

Madonna I: Animality and Artifice

Madonna, don't preach.

Defending her controversial new video, "Justify My Love," on *Nightline* last week, Madonna stumbled, rambled, and ended up seeming far less intelligent than she really is.

Madonna, 'fess up.

The video is pornographic. It's decadent. And it's fabulous. MTV   4
was right to ban it, a corporate resolve long overdue. Parents cannot possibly control television, with its titanic omnipresence.

Prodded by correspondent Forrest Sawyer for evidence of her responsibility as an artist, Madonna hotly proclaimed her love of children, her social activism, and her condom endorsements. Wrong answer. As Baudelaire and Oscar Wilde knew, neither art nor the artist has a moral responsibility to liberal social causes.

"Justify My Love" is truly avant-garde, at a time when that word has lost its meaning in the flabby art world. It represents a sophisticated European sexuality of a kind we have not seen since the great foreign films of the 1950s and 1960s. But it does not belong on a mainstream music channel watched around the clock by children.

On *Nightline*, Madonna bizarrely called the video a "celebration of sex." She imagined happy educational scenes where curious children would ask their parents about the video. Oh, sure! Picture it: "Mommy, please tell me about the tired, tied-up man in the leather harness and the mean, bare-chested lady in the Nazi cap." Okay, dear, right after the milk and cookies.

Sawyer asked for Madonna's reaction to feminist charges that, in   8
the neck manacle and floor-crawling of an earlier video, "Express Yourself," she condoned the "degradation" and "humiliation" of women.
Madonna waffled: "But I chained myself! I'm in charge." Well, no.
Madonna the producer may have chosen the chain, but Madonna the
sexual persona in the video is alternately a cross-dressing dominatrix
and a slave of male desire.

But who cares what the feminists say anyhow? They have been out-
rageously negative about Madonna from the start. In 1985, *Ms.* magazine pointedly feted quirky, cuddly singer Cyndi Lauper as its woman
of the year. Great judgment: gimmicky Lauper went nowhere, while
Madonna grew, flourished, metamorphosed, and became an international star of staggering dimensions. She is also a shrewd business
tycoon, a modern new woman of all-around talent.

Madonna is the true feminist. She exposes the puritanism and suffocating ideology of American feminism, which is stuck in an adolescent whining mode. Madonna has taught young women to be fully
female and sexual while still exercising control over their lives. She
shows girls how to be attractive, sensual, energetic, ambitious, aggressive, and funny—all at the same time.

American feminism has a man problem. The beaming Betty Crock-
ers, hangdog dowdies, and parochial prudes who call themselves feminists want men to be like women. They fear and despise the masculine.
The academic feminists think their nerdy bookworm husbands are the
ideal model of human manhood.

But Madonna loves real men. She sees the beauty of masculinity, in   12
all its rough vigor and sweaty athletic perfection. She also admires the
men who are actually like women: transsexuals and flamboyant drag
queens, the heroes of the 1969 Stonewall rebellion, which started the
gay liberation movement.

"Justify My Love" is an eerie, sultry tableau of jaded androgynous
creatures, trapped in a decadent sexual underground. Its hypnotic
images are drawn from such sadomasochistic films as Liliana Cavani's
The Night Porter and Luchino Visconti's *The Damned.* It's the perverse
and knowing world of the photographers Helmut Newton and Robert
Mapplethorpe.

Contemporary American feminism, which began by rejecting Freud
because of his alleged sexism, has shut itself off from his ideas of ambiguity, contradiction, conflict, ambivalence. Its simplistic psychology is
illustrated by the new cliché of the date-rape furor: "'No' always means
'no.'" Will we ever graduate from the Girl Scouts? "No" has always
been, and always will be, part of the dangerous, alluring courtship ritual of sex and seduction, observable even in the animal kingdom.

Madonna has a far profounder vision of sex than do the feminists.
She sees both the animality and the artifice. Changing her costume style
and hair color virtually every month, Madonna embodies the eternal

values of beauty and pleasure. Feminism says, "No more masks." Madonna says we are nothing but masks.

Through her enormous impact on young women around the world, Madonna is the future of feminism.   16

[1990]

Topics for Critical Thinking and Writing

1. In paragraph 5 Paglia says that art and artists do not have "a moral responsibility to liberal social causes." In your opinion, do they have a responsibility to *any* kinds of causes? To anything at all? If so, why? If not, why not?
2. In paragraph 10 Paglia sums up what she takes to be Madonna's contribution. If you are familiar with Madonna's work, evaluate Paglia's appraisal.
3. As the headnote mentions, this essay originally appeared in *The New York Times.* Write a letter to the newspaper (250 words), expressing your approval or disapproval. Consider the essay as a whole but call attention to certain passages that you find particularly offensive or particularly praiseworthy and explain why.

John Simon

John Simon, born in Yugoslavia in 1925, received his higher education in the United States. He has written criticism of plays, books, and films for several magazines, as well as a book on Ingmar Bergman. We reprint an article from New York magazine—a periodical aimed not only at New Yorkers but at all middle-class, general-interest readers.

Triumph over Death

Why is dance enjoying such all-but-unprecedented popularity in our time? At least partly, I think, because of the withdrawal of the word from our culture—or, more precisely, our withdrawal from the word. Whether in or out of school, Dick and Jane write, read, and express themselves orally with increasing difficulty. One of the consequences is that, among the arts, the wholly or largely nonverbal ones become favored—especially dance, where the body has it all over the mind. In the fine arts and in serious music, the mind seems to make greater demands than in dance, whose only appreciable competition comes from the movies, where the word appears to be undemanding and the visuals are seemingly all that matters. Highly kinetic, then, is what dance and film are: forms, as it were, of body language, which may yet become our lingua franca.

In the domain of dance, ballet is unquestioned king, because it is the least earthbound, the most death-defying, form of dance: it appears to defeat the laws of gravity, defy death itself. The danseur noble[1] at the height of an entrechat or jeté, the ballerina carried aloft but looking more airborne than handheld, are no longer a little lower than the angels, but fully of their company. Even a simple pas de bourrée, perfectly executed, conveys a skimming along the surface of the earth rather than a walk or run upon it; it is perhaps a water bird skittering along the mirror of a lake. And dancers are always young and beautiful. Just as at a university only the sedentary faculty ages, watching students who are always twentyish come and go, at the ballet only the audience grows old. The faces and bodies may not belong to the same dancers—although, in another way, they do, for the perfectly stylized steps, highly dramatic makeup, and formalized costumes bestow their own uniformity and continuity—but those privileged beings up there are forever beautiful and young.

So our two greatest limitations are overcome before our eyes: we become like unto the angels who need not touch ground, and do not have to die. I think it is no accident that three of the greatest, ever-popular story ballets deal with the triumph over death. In *Swan Lake,* the wicked enchanter and the demanding parent are both bested as the lovers float off into shared immortality. In *Giselle,* the beloved remains faithful to her deceitful lover beyond death, rises from her tomb to save his life, and thus binds him to herself forever. In *The Sleeping Beauty,* Prince Charming awakens the heroine from a sleep perilously resembling death. Even the fourth hardy perennial, *The Nutcracker,* takes us back to the ageless world of childhood, whose animated toys, benign fairies, and transfigured children mortality cannot touch.

It is easier to project ourselves into dancers than into actors.   4
Dancers, especially in ballet, are abstract: they symbolize rather than express, they are mythic rather than specific. The particular words of Shakespeare's Ophelia may leave some audiences cold, but an Ophelia balletically transmuted into a symbol of unfulfilled yearning is an image for everybody. Louis MacNeice's poem, "Les Sylphides," begins, significantly, "Life in a day: he took his girl to the ballet"; stanza three runs: "Now, he thought, we are floating—ageless, oarless—/Now there is no separation, from now on/You will be wearing white/Satin and a real sash/Under the waltzing trees." It seems noteworthy how many extremely obese people there are among balletomanes; they, more than

---

[1]**Danseur noble**, leading male dancer in a ballet company; an **entrechat** is a leap during which the dancer crosses his feet a number of times, a **jeté** is a leap from one foot to the other.

anyone, want to think themselves disembodied sylphs. But all of us, regardless of weight, size, and age, would like to soar, be lighter than air, than care.

Topics for Critical Thinking and Writing

1. Simon offers no evidence that dance is "enjoying . . . all but unprecedented popularity." Should he have? Explain.
2. In his first paragraph Simon makes a distinction between verbal and nonverbal arts. What are some examples of verbal arts? What are some nonverbal arts other than those he mentions?
3. What contrasts does Simon find between ballet and other forms of dance, and between dance and other theatrical forms?
4. In the first paragraph Simon speaks of "our withdrawal from the word." What does he mean? In the last paragraph he quotes from a poem. How can this apparent inconsistency be explained?
5. How would you characterize the readers Simon addresses in this essay? On what evidence do you base your characterization?

Perri Klass

Perri Klass, a physician and a writer of fiction and nonfiction, was born in Trinidad in 1958 and educated in the United States. In the essay that we reprint, from The New York Times, *Klass considers the view that Disney's* The Lion King, *with its themes of patricide and guilt, may be too upsetting for small children.*

King of the Jungle

Last summer, people worried about whether the dinosaurs in *Jurassic Park* were too frightening for children. This summer, some may look at, *The Lion King* and wonder if the death of the father lion is too traumatic. In the first case, the worry was that brilliant special effects would leave children frightened of animals they know do not really walk the earth; in the second, that a well-told story would have children identifying with an animated lion cub and his grief and guilt over the loss of his father.

In *The Lion King,* which opened on Wednesday, Mufasa, the king of beasts, is trampled in a wildebeest stampede as he saves his little cub, Simba. Mufasa's evil brother, Scar, who provoked the stampede to kill has brother and take over the lion kingdom, convinces Simba that he killed his father. The distraught cub leaves home, nearly dies and wanders the veldt until he grows up enough to return and challenge his usurping uncle.

Many reviewers have specifically noted the potentially frightening aspects of the movie. Janet Maslin, writing in *The New York Times*, referred to "Mufasa's disturbing on-screen death" and wondered if the film "really warranted a G rating." Terrence Rafferty, writing in *The New Yorker*, said the film dredged up "deep-seated insecurities and terrors." Richard Corliss, in *Time* magazine, said, "Get ready to explain to the kids why a good father should die violently and why a child should have to witness the death." And *Variety* pointed to "scenes of truly terrifying animal-kingdom violence that should cause parents to think twice before bringing along the 'Little Mermaid' set."

Hamlet with fur. An animated movie with the potential to move its   4
audience, adults and children, to make them wonder and worry and cheer and, yes, cry. Isn't that what stories are supposed to do, on the page, on the stage or on the screen?

If children's entertainment is purged of the powerful, we risk homogenization, predictability and boredom, and we deprive children of any real understanding of the cathartic and emotional potentials of narrative. As Marie Antoinette once remarked, "Let them watch Barney."

So this is a Disney cartoon about animals in which a loving parent dies. Surely we've had this discussion before, at some point in our collective cultural pageant. In fact, the world is full of adults who think that the death of Bambi's mother is too upsetting for small children. Too sad. Too scary. There will be parents who feel that *The Lion King* may be too upsetting for children, too; a movie about lions is a little, well, redder in tooth and claw than a movie about a deer. As Timon the meerkat says—and there is no way to convey how much exasperation Nathan Lane gets into his voice—Carnivores!"

I myself tend to worry more about human villains, both in real life and at the movies. By my standards, *Snow White* is the much more upsetting movie. There is nothing in *The Lion King* that can compare to a wicked queen who wants to kill her stepdaughter for being too beautiful or to a huntsman ordered to kill the girl and cut her heart out. And for that matter, are two lions fighting for control as scary as Cruella De Vil, who, in *101 Dalmatians*, wants to kill the puppies and make them into coats?

Do we really want to protect our children from being saddened or   8
scared or even upset by movies—or by books? Do we want to eliminate surprise, reversal, tragedy, conflict and leave children with stories in which they can be smugly confident that the good will always be rewarded and the bad always punished? Children don't have to sit through "Friday the 13th" at a tender age, but neither do they need an unending diet of wholesomely bland entertainment. A child who is worried, truly worried, about the outcome of a book is a child who is learning to understand what pulls someone into literature, and in fact it is a triumph that in an age of special effects and interactive videos, words on a page still have the power to move children.

Similarly, in an age when cartoons and live action films are full of bang'-em-on-the-head violence that has no true dramatic impact, this is a movie in which a noble character dies and is truly mourned. And when we talk about children made sad by a movie, we are talking about children being moved by things that are not really happening to real people, and that is what art and drama and literature are all about. Those children are recognizing a character and feeling for that character, and that is a giant step toward empathy.

Maria Tatar, professor of German studies at Harvard and the author of *Off With Their Heads! Fairy Tales and the Culture of Childhood,* points out that stories and folk tales have always offered children a way to consider and even control death and other difficult and forbidden topics. "Kids can handle almost anything if they're authorized to see it, talk about it," she says. "They're much smarter than we give them credit for."

Barry Zuckerman, chairman of the department of pediatrics at Boston City Hospital and an expert on child development, agrees that these stories offer children an opportunity to master troubling issues. "It's not bad for children to be exposed to stressful things. They can cope by having a parent available, so they can cuddle up to a parent who provides safety and security."

And if a child responds to *The Lion King* on some level that is deeper and more intense than a pow-pow Saturday morning cartoon, that is because the people who made this movie are trying for something more complex here, and children know it. 12

What there is in *The Lion King,* along with sometimes breathtaking animation and well-cast voices, is an interesting mix of *Hamlet, Bambi* and *The Jungle Book,* all shot through with some contemporary sensibility about men who can't grow up. Is this just a late-20th-century take on *Hamlet* imbued with self-help books and actualization therapy? Instead of a young man who could not make up his mind, we have a young man who cannot share his feelings and has trouble with commitment. Still, when the ghost of the dead king appears to the young lion and charges him to depose his treacherous uncle to reclaim the kingdom, you can't help looking around for Rosencrantz and Guildenstern (played here by a wart hog and a meerkat).

Yes, the father dies. And there is a stampede, which is some kind of heroic triumph of animation. But the stampede is not so much scary as it is inexorable, an animal-world event, even if it is provoked by the evil uncle and his hyena henchmen.

Yes, the cub is tortured by guilt, thinking that he started the wildebeests running and is therefore responsible for his father's death. But even small children will have no trouble identifying whose fault it really is; Jeremy Irons gives the evil uncle, Scar, a personality worthy of the long and distinguished line of Disney cartoon villains. And cartoon villains have always had a certain license to be evil, just because they are not real people, and children can see that they are not.

In *The Lion King,* they aren't people at all. It's always a little tricky   16
to know how children absorb animal stories. *Born Free* was the great lion movie of my childhood, another movie about a lion cub who loses a parent, and I can dimly recall discussions of whether the hunting (and eating) scenes were too strong for children. In addition to the loss of Bambi's mother, there is Babar's mother, killed by a wicked hunter on the third page of *The Story of Babar;* within two pages, Babar is consoling himself by buying new clothes. In my experience, children are interested in the death of Babar's mother, and then quickly curious about Babar's new clothes.

I cried when Bambi's mother shot, but my son, who was then 4, did not; he was interested in what would happen next. Parents are terrified of dying and leaving their child unprotected. For children, the issues are often different.

Note it was Bambi's and Babar's *mothers* who were killed off. Most Disney cartoon features have not included mothers at all; the title character in *The Little Mermaid* has only a father, as do Princess Jasmine in *Aladdin* and Belle in *Beauty and the Beast.* Snow White and Cinderella, of course, have evil stepmothers. Bambi has a mother, but she dies; Dumbo's mother spends most of the movie locked up.

In *The Lion King,* it is the father who dies. Though this may be dictated by the plot structure of *Hamlet,* it is connected to the movie's 90's-style celebration of the involved dad. Bambi's father, after all, was the archetypal distant father of the 1940's, the kind of stag who would stay out of sight and let his son take the hard knocks, and only show up the end to point the way to manhood. But Mufasa in *The Lion King* is there romping with his cub, offering sensitive advice about what it means to be the King of Beasts: "I'm only brave when I have to be," he tells his admiring son.

Will children see the deeper themes—Disney describes the movie   20
as "allegorical"—or will they simply be entertained by the surface story? Will they understand the central moral, that Simba has to confess the guilt he has been hiding, and has to give up his carefree bachelorhood and accept the responsibilities of leadership? Well, some children will understand some of it. And some of this New-Age-tinged message is there for adults, as are the numerous and clever animated references, from the Busby Berkeley animal acrobatics to the Leni Riefenstahl Nuremberg rally scene in which Scar reviews his hyena troops. You don't have to understand these associations to appreciate the scenes, and, similarly, most of the worrying about Oedipal overtones, guilt and responsibility will be done by parents.

It all comes down to what is real and what is not-real, which can admittedly be a complex question for children. A few months ago my 4-year-old daughter, Josephine, was going to her first opera. Her opera-loving but perhaps overambitious father prepared her as carefully as possible, playing his favorite recording of *La Traviata,* a little each day, explaining the story, showing her a photograph of Maria Callas, and teaching Josephine to listen for her voice of voices. Toward the end of the week, I came into the living room to find Josephine sobbing hysterically on the couch, with the music blaring and her father looking flummoxed.

Why was she crying? "Because Maria Callas is dying!" she wailed. And it was hard to know exactly how to comfort her; when her father told her that no, Callas was just playing the part of a woman who was dying, Josephine promptly asked, "So Maria Callas did not die?" Then, of course, he had to explain that as a matter of fact she was dead—and Josephine was in tears again.

She was eventually comforted, and went on to enjoy the opera tremendously, probably because Maria Callas did not die in our local production.

Children do, in general, understand the difference between real   24
people and cartoon characters. And they understand the difference between people and animals. And these differences give movie makers a certain latitude to explore themes and scenes that they couldn't really touch in a live action movie for children.

Are there some children, maybe children trader 4, who could be too upset by this movie? Probably.

Will I take Josephine, my own 4-year-old? Certainly, and I would have taken her a year ago. The bad guys get it most satisfactorily in the end, and none of the sweet, cute, funny little fellows get hurt—the bird Zazu is actually endowed with cartoon invulnerability and can emerge unscathed from a lion's mouth or a boiling pot. Children may be made sad by the film, as their parents certainly will be, and they may find the villains scary, but they will also be interested and amused and involved, and that, after all, is the point of art.

Some children may make it through the death of Mufasa, and then fall apart at the final apocalyptic battle between lions and hyenas, which goes on a little too long for the just-keep-your-eyes-closed crowd (the ones who were traumatized by the wolves in *Beauty and the Beast*). I myself did not go to see *Jaws* as an adult, since I was a fairly timid ocean swimmer who did not want to watch images that would make me even more wary. On the other hand, I had no problem sending my 9-year-old to *Jurassic Park* last summer; I wouldn't really mind if he ended up very scared of live dinosaurs.

But let us, for heaven's sake, not start worrying that it's a problem   28
if children respond to art with sadness or dismay or even fear, as long

as these emotions can be discussed, as long as the sad can be comforted and the frightened reassured.

And if you do have a child who identifies too completely with Bambi or Simba, you can practice some reassurances, just to see how they feel. Then decide which you would be more comfortable saying: "Darling, I promise, there are no bad men with guns," or "Darling, I promise, there won't be a wildebeest stampede."

Topics for Critical Thinking and Writing

1. In her fourth paragraph Klass says that literature is "supposed" to make audiences "wonder and worry and cheer and, yes, cry." Much of Klass's essay is in effect addressed to someone whose position might be summarized as saying, "Perhaps *adult* literature is supposed to do these things, but not children's literature." List Klass's arguments. Which is the strongest? The weakest? Why?
2. Think back to your childhood and recall a book or film (or perhaps even an event at a circus or fair) that in some ways distressed you. Do you now feel that you should not have been put through this experience, or that an adult should in some way have helped you to cope with it? Explain.
3. Evaluate Klass's final paragraph as a concluding paragraph.

Eudora Welty

Eudora Welty was born in Jackson, Mississippi, in 1909. Although she earned a bachelor's degree at the University of Wisconsin and spent a year studying advertising in New York City at the Columbia University Graduate School of Business, she has lived almost all of her life in Jackson.

In the preface to her Collected Stories *she says,*

I have been told, both in approval and in accusation, that I seem to love all my characters. What I do in writing of any character is to try to enter into the mind, heart and skin of a human being who is not myself. Whether this happens to be a man or a woman, old or young, with skin black or white, the primary challenge lies in making the jump itself. It is the act of a writer's imagination that I set most high.

In addition to writing stories and novels, Welty has written a book about fiction, The Eye of the Story *(1977), and a memoir,* One Writer's Beginnings *(1984). Here is one of her stories, "A Worn Path," followed by her discussion of the work, in* The Eye of the Story.

A Worn Path

It was December—a bright frozen day in the early morning. Far out in the country there was an old Negro woman with her head tied in a red rag, coming along a path through the pinewoods. Her name was Phoenix Jackson. She was very old and small and she walked slowly in the dark pine shadows, moving a little from side to side in her steps, with the balanced heaviness and lightness of a pendulum in a grandfather clock. She carried a thin, small cane made from an umbrella, and with this she kept tapping the frozen earth in front of her. This made a grave and persistent noise in the still air, that seemed meditative like the chirping of a solitary little bird.

She wore a dark striped dress reaching down to her shoe tops, and an equally long apron of bleached sugar sacks, with a full pocket: all neat and tidy, but every time she took a step she might have fallen over her shoe-laces, which dragged from her unlaced shoes. She looked straight ahead. Her eyes were blue with age. Her skin had a pattern all its own of numberless branching wrinkles and as though a whole little tree stood in the middle of her forehead, but a golden color ran underneath, and the two knobs of her cheeks were illuminated by a yellow burning under the dark. Under the red rag her hair came down on her neck in the frailest of ringlets, still black, and with an odor like copper.

Now and then there was a quivering in the thicket. Old Phoenix said, "Out of my way, all you foxes, owls, beetles, jack rabbits, coons, and wild animals! . . . Keep out from under these feet, little bob-whites. . . . Keep the big wild hogs out of my path. Don't let none of those come running my direction. I got a long way." Under her small black-freckled hand her cane, limber as a buggy whip, would switch at the brush as if to rouse up any hiding things.

On she went. The woods were deep and still. The sun made the pine needles almost too bright to look at, up where the wind rocked. The cones dropped as light as feathers. Down in the hollow was the mourning dove—it was not too late for him. 4

The path ran up a hill. "Seem like there is chains about my feet, time I get this far," she said, in the voice of argument old people keep to use with themselves. "Something always take a hold of me on this hill—pleads I should stay."

After she got to the top she turned and gave a full, severe look behind her where she had come. "Up through pines," she said at length. "Now down through oaks."

Her eyes opened their widest, and she started down gently. But before she got to the bottom of the hill a bush caught her dress.

Her fingers were busy and intent, but her skirts were full and long, so that before she could pull them free in one place they were caught in another. It was not possible to allow the dress to tear. "I in the thorny bush," she said. "Thorns, you doing your appointed work. Never want to let folks pass—no sir. Old eyes thought you was a pretty little *green* bush." 8

Finally, trembling all over, she stood free, and after a moment dared to stoop for her cane.

"Sun so high!" she cried, leaning back and looking, while the thick tears went over her eyes. "The time getting all gone here."

At the foot of this hill was a place where a log was laid across the creek.

"Now comes the trial," said Phoenix.   12

Putting her right foot out, she mounted the log and shut her eyes. Lifting her skirt, levelling her cane fiercely before her, like a festival figure in some parade, she began to march across. Then she opened her eyes and she was safe on the other side.

"I wasn't as old as I thought," she said.

But she sat down to rest. She spread her skirts on the bank around her and folded her hands over her knees. Up above her was a tree in a pearly cloud of mistletoe. She did not dare to close her eyes, and when a little boy brought her a little plate with a slice of marble-cake on it she spoke to him. "That would be acceptable," she said. But when she went to take it there was just her own hand in the air.

So she left that tree, and had to go through a barbed-wire fence.   16 There she had to creep and crawl, spreading her knees and stretching her fingers like a baby trying to climb the steps. But she talked loudly to herself: she could not let her dress be torn now, so late in the day, and she could not pay for having her arm or leg sawed off if she got caught fast where she was.

At last she was safe through the fence and risen up out in the clearing. Big dead trees, like black men with one arm, were standing in the purple stalks of the withered cotton field. There sat a buzzard.

"Who you watching?"

In the furrow she made her way along.

"Glad this not the season for bulls," she said, looking sideways,   20 "and the good Lord made his snakes to curl up and sleep in the winter. A pleasure I don't see no two-headed snake coming around that tree, where it come once. It took a while to get by him, back in the summer."

She passed through the old cotton and went into a field of dead corn. It whispered and shook and was taller than her head. "Through the maze now," she said, for there was no path.

Then there was something tall, black, and skinny there, moving before her.

At first she took it for a man. It could have been a man dancing in the field. But she stood still and listened, and it did not make a sound. It was as silent as a ghost.

"Ghost," she said sharply, "who be you the ghost of? For I have   24 heard of nary death close by."

But there was no answer—only the ragged dancing in the wind.

She shut her eyes, reached out her hand, and touched a sleeve. She found a coat and inside that an emptiness, cold as ice.

"You scarecrow," she said. Her face lighted. "I ought to be shut up for good," she said with laughter. "My senses is gone, I too old. I the oldest people I ever know. Dance, old scarecrow," she said, "while I dancing with you."

She kicked her foot over the furrow, and with mouth drawn down, 28 shook her head once or twice in a little strutting way. Some husks blew down and whirled in streamers about her skirts.

Then she went on, parting her way from side to side with the cane, through the whispering field. At last she came to the end, to a wagon truck where the silver grass blew between the red ruts. The quail were walking around like pullets, seeming all dainty and unseen.

"Walk pretty," she said. "This the easy place. This the easy going."

She followed the track, swaying through the quiet bare fields, through the little strings of trees silver in their dead leaves, past cabins silver from weather, with the doors and windows boarded shut, all like old women under a spell sitting there. "I walking in their sleep," she said, nodding her head vigorously.

In a ravine she went where a spring was silently flowing through a 32 hollow log. Old Phoenix bent and drank. "Sweet-gum makes the water sweet," she said, and drank more. "Nobody know who made this well, for it was here when I was born."

The track crossed a swampy part where the moss hung as white as lace from every limb. "Sleep on, alligators, and blow your bubbles." Then the track went into the road.

Deep, deep the road went down between the high green-colored banks. Overhead the live-oaks met, and it was as dark as a cave.

A black dog with a lolling tongue came up out of the weeds by the ditch. She was meditating, and not ready, and when he came at her she only hit him a little with her cane. Over she went in the ditch, like a little puff of milk-weed.

Down there, her senses drifted away. A dream visited her, and she 36 reached her hand up, but nothing reached down and gave her a pull. So she lay there and presently went to talking. "Old woman," she said to herself, "that black dog come up out of the weeds to stall you off, and now there he sitting on his fine tail, smiling at you."

A white man finally came along and found her—a hunter, a young man, with his dog on a chain.

"Well, Granny!" he laughed, "what are you doing there?"

"Lying on my back like a June-bug waiting to be turned over, mister," she said, reaching up her hand.

He lifted her up, gave her a swing in the air, and set her down. 40 "Anything broken, Granny?"

"No sir, them old dead weeds is springy enough," said Phoenix, when she had got her breath. "I thank you for your trouble."

"Where do you live, Granny?" he asked, while the two dogs were growling at each other.

"Away back yonder, sir, behind the ridge. You can't even see it from here."

"On your way home?"   44

"No, sir, I going to town."

"Why, that's too far! That's as far as I walk when I come out myself, and I get something for my trouble." He patted the stuffed bag he carried, and there hung down a little closed claw. It was one of the bobwhites, with its beak hooked bitterly to show it was dead. "Now you go on home, Granny!"

"I bound to go to town, mister," said Phoenix. "The time come around."

He gave another laugh, filling the whole landscape. "I know you   48
old colored people! Wouldn't miss going to town to see Santa Claus!"

But something held Old Phoenix very still. The deep lines in her face went into a fierce and different radiation. Without warning, she had seen with her own eyes a flashing nickel fall out of the man's pocket onto the ground.

"How old are you, Granny?" he was saying.

"There is no telling, mister," she said, "no telling."

Then she gave a little cry and clapped her hands and said, "Git on   52
away from here, dog! Look! Look at that dog!" She laughed as if in admiration. "He ain't scared of nobody. He a big black dog." She whispered, "Sic him!"

"Watch me get rid of that cur," said the man. "Sic him, Pete! Sic him!"

Phoenix heard the dogs fighting, and heard the man running and throwing sticks. She even heard a gunshot. But she was slowly bending forward by that time, further and further forward, the lids stretched down over her eyes, as if she were doing this in her sleep. Her chin was lowered almost to her knees. The yellow palm of her hand came out from the fold of her apron. Her fingers slid down and along the ground under the piece of money with the grace and care they would have in lifting an egg from under a sitting hen. Then she slowly straightened up, she stood erect, and the nickel was in her apron pocket. A bird flew by. Her lips moved. "God watching me the whole time, I come to stealing."

The man came back, and his own dog panted about them. "Well, I scared him off that time," he said, and then he laughed and lifted his gun and pointed it at Phoenix.

She stood straight and faced him.   56

"Doesn't the gun scare you?" he said, still pointing it.

"No, sir. I seen plenty go off closer by, in my day, and for less than what I done," she said, holding utterly still.

He smiled, and shouldered the gun. "Well, Granny," he said, "You must be a hundred years old, and scared of nothing. I'd give you a dime if I had any money with me. But you take my advice and stay home, and nothing will happen to you."

"I bound to go on my way, mister," said Phoenix. She inclined her   60
head in the red rag. Then they went in different directions, but she could hear the gun shooting again and again over the hill.

She walked on. The shadows hung from the oak trees to the road like curtains. Then she smelled wood-smoke, and smelled the river, and she saw a steeple and the cabins on their steep steps. Dozens of little black children whirled around her. There ahead was Natchez shining. Bells were ringing. She walked on.

In the paved city it was Christmas time. There were red and green electric lights strung and crisscrossed everywhere, and all turned on in the daytime. Old Phoenix would have been lost if she had not distrusted her eyesight and depended on her feet to know where to take her.

She paused quietly on the sidewalk where people were passing by. A lady came along in the crowd, carrying an armful of red-, green-, and silver-wrapped presents; she gave off perfume like the red roses in hot summer, and Phoenix stopped her.

"Please, missy, will you lace up my shoe?" She held up her foot.   64

"What do you want, Grandma?"

"See my shoe," said Phoenix. "Do all right for out in the country, but wouldn't look right to go in a big building."

"Stand still then, Grandma," said the lady. She put her packages down on the sidewalk beside her and laced and tied both shoes tightly.

"Can't lace 'em with a cane," said Phoenix. "Thank you, missy. I   68 doesn't mind asking a nice lady to tie up my shoe, when I gets out on the street."

Moving slowly and from side to side, she went into the big building and into a tower of steps, where she walked up and around and around until her feet knew to stop.

She entered a door, and there she saw nailed up on the wall the document that had been stamped with the gold seal and framed in the gold frame, which matched the dream that was hung up in her head.

"Here I be," she said. There was a fixed and ceremonial stiffness over her body.

"A charity case, I suppose," said an attendant who sat at the desk   72 before her.

But Phoenix only looked above her head. There was sweat on her face, the wrinkles in her skin shone like a bright net.

"Speak up, Grandma," the woman said. "What's your name? We must have your history, you know. Have you been here before? What seems to be the trouble with you?"

Old Phoenix only gave a twitch to her face as if a fly were bothering her.

"Are you deaf?" cried the attendant.   76

But then the nurse came in.

"Oh, that's just old Aunt Phoenix," she said. "She doesn't come for herself—she has a little grandson. She makes these trips just as regular as clockwork. She lives away back off the old Natchez Trace." She bent down. "Well, Aunt Phoenix, why don't you just take a seat? We won't keep you standing after your long trip." She pointed.

The old woman sat down, bolt upright in the chair.

"Now, how is the boy?" asked the nurse.   80

Old Phoenix did not speak.

"I said, how is the boy?"

But Phoenix only waited and stared straight ahead, her face very solemn and withdrawn into the rigidity.

"Is his throat any better?" asked the nurse. "Aunt Phoenix, don't   84
you hear me? Is your grandson's throat any better since the last time you came for the medicine?"

With her hands on her knees, the old woman waited, silent, erect and motionless, just as if she were in armor.

"You mustn't take up our time this way, Aunt Phoenix," the nurse said. "Tell us quickly about your grandson, and get it over. He isn't dead, is he?"

At last there came a flicker and then a flame of comprehension across her face, and she spoke.

"My grandson. It was my memory had left me. There I sat and for-   88
got why I made my long trip."

"Forgot?" The nurse frowned. "After you came so far?"

Then Phoenix was like an old woman begging a dignified forgive-ness for waking up frightened in the night. "I never did go to school. I was too old at the Surrender," she said in a soft voice. "I'm an old woman without an education. It was my memory fail me. My little grandson, he is just the same, and I forgot it in the coming."

"Throat never heals, does it?" said the nurse, speaking in a loud, sure voice to Old Phoenix. By now she had a card with something writ-ten on it, a little list. "Yes. Swallowed lye. When was it—January—two-three years ago—"

Phoenix spoke unasked now. "No, missy, he not dead, he just the   92
same. Every little while his throat begin to close up again, and he not able to swallow. He not get his breath. He not able to help himself. So the time come around, and I go on another trip for the soothing medicine."

"All right. The doctor said as long as you came to get it, you could have it," said the nurse. "But it's an obstinate case."

"My little grandson, he sit up there in the house all wrapped up, waiting by himself," Phoenix went on. "We is the only two left in the world. He suffer and it don't seem to put him back at all. He got a sweet look. He going to last. He wear a little patch quilt and peep out holding his mouth open like a little bird. I remembers so plain now. I not going to forget him again, no, the whole enduring time. I could tell him from all the others in creation."

"All right." The nurse was trying to hush her now. She brought her a bottle of medicine. "Charity," she said, making a check mark in a book.

Old Phoenix held the bottle close to her eyes and then carefully put   96
it into her pocket.

"I thank you," she said.

"It's Christmas time, Grandma," said the attendant. "Could I give you a few pennies out of my purse?"

"Five pennies is a nickel," said Phoenix stiffly.

"Here's a nickel," said the attendant. 100

Phoenix rose carefully and held out her hand. She received the nickel and then fished the other nickel out of her pocket and laid it beside the new one. She stared at her palm closely, with her head on one side.

Then she gave a tap with her cane on the floor.

"This is what come to me to do," she said. "I going to the store and buy my child a little windmill they sells, made out of paper. He going to find it hard to believe there such a thing in the world. I'll march myself back where he waiting, holding it straight up in this hand."

She lifted her free hand, gave a little nod, turned round, and 104 walked out of the doctor's office. Then her slow step began on the stairs, going down.

Topics for Critical Thinking and Writing

1. If you do not know the legend of the phoenix, look it up in a dictionary or, better, in an encyclopedia. Then carefully reread the story to learn whether the story in any way connects with the legend.
2. Characterize the hunter.
3. What would be lost if the episode (with all of its dialogue) of Phoenix falling into the ditch and being helped out of it by the hunter were omitted?
4. Is Christmas a particularly appropriate time in which to set the story? Why or why not?
5. What do you make of the title?

Eudora Welty

Is Phoenix Jackson's Grandson Really Dead?

A story writer is more than happy to be read by students; the fact that these serious readers think and feel something in response to his work he finds life-giving. At the same time he may not always be able to reply to their specific questions in kind. I wondered if it might clarify something, for both the questioners and myself, if I set down a general reply to the question that comes to me most often in the mail, from both students and their teachers, after some classroom discussion. The unrivaled favorite is this: "Is Phoenix Jackson's grandson really *dead?*"

It refers to a short story I wrote years ago called "A Worn Path," which tells of a day's journey an old woman makes on foot from deep in the country into town and into a doctor's office on behalf of her little grandson; he is at home, periodically ill, and periodically she comes for his medicine; they give it to her as usual, she receives it and starts the journey back.

I had not meant to mystify readers by withholding any fact; it is not a writer's business to tease. The story is told through Phoenix's mind as she undertakes her errand. As the author at one with the character as I tell it, I must assume that the boy is alive. As the reader, you are free to think as you like, of course: The story invites you to believe that no matter what happens, Phoenix for as long as she is able to walk and can hold to her purpose will make her journey. The *possibility* that she would keep on even if he were dead is there in her devotion and its single-minded, single-track errand. Certainly the *artistic* truth, which should be good enough for the fact, lies in Phoenix's own answer to that question. When the nurse asks, "He isn't dead, is he?" she speaks for herself: "He still the same. He going to last."

The grandchild is the incentive. But it is the journey, the going of the errand, that is the story, and the question is not whether the grandchild is in reality alive or dead. It doesn't affect the outcome of the story or its meaning from start to finish. But it is not the question itself that has struck me as much as the idea, almost without exception implied in the asking, that for Phoenix's grandson to be dead would somehow make the story "better." 4

It's *all right*, I want to say to the students who write to me, for things to be what they appear to be, and for words to mean what they say. It's all right, too, for words and appearances to mean more than one thing—ambiguity is a fact of life. A fiction writer's responsibility covers not only what he presents as the facts of a given story but what he chooses to stir up as their implications; in the end, these implications, too, become facts, in the larger, fictional sense. But it is not all right, not in good faith, for things *not* to mean what they say.

The grandson's plight was real and it made the truth of the story, which is the story of an errand of love carried out. If the child no longer lived, the truth would persist in the "wornness" of the path. But his being dead can't increase the truth of the story, can't affect it one way or the other. I think I signal this, because the end of the story has been reached before Old Phoenix gets home again: she simply starts back. To the question "Is the grandson really dead?" I could reply that it doesn't make any difference. I could also say that I did not make him up in order to let him play a trick on Phoenix. But my best answer would be: "*Phoenix* is alive."

The origin of a story is sometimes a trustworthy clue to the author—or can provide him with the clue—to its key image; maybe in this case it will do the same for the reader. One day I saw a solitary old woman like Phoenix. She was walking; I saw her, at middle distance, in a winter country landscape, and watched her slowly make her way across my line of vision. That sight of her made me write the story. I invented an errand for her, but that only seemed a living part of the figure she was herself: What errand other than for someone else could be making her go? And her going was the first thing, her persisting in her landscape was the real thing, and the first and the real were what I wanted and worked to keep. I brought her up close enough, by imagination, to describe her face, make her present to the eyes, but the full-length figure moving across the winter fields was the indelible one and the image to keep, and the perspective extending into the vanishing distance the true one to hold in mind.

I invented for my character, as I wrote, some passing adventures— 8
some dreams and harassments and a small triumph or two, some jolts to her pride, some flights of fancy to console her, one or two encounters to scare her, a moment that gave her cause to feel ashamed, a moment to dance and preen—for it had to be a *journey,* and all these things belonged to that, parts of life's uncertainty.

A narrative line is in its deeper sense, of course, the tracing out of a meaning, and the real continuity of a story lies in this probing forward. The real dramatic force of a story depends on the strength of the emotion that has set it going. The emotional value is the measure of the reach of the story. What gives any such content to "A Worn Path" is not its circumstances but its *subject:* the deep-grained habit of love.

What I hoped would come clear was that in the whole surround of this story, the world it threads through, the only certain thing at all is the worn path. The habit of love cuts through confusion and stumbles or contrives its way out of difficulty, it remembers the way even when it forgets, for a dumfounded moment, its reason for being. The path is the thing that matters.

Her victory—old Phoenix's—is when she sees the diploma in the doctor's office, when she finds "nailed up on the wall the document that had been stamped with the gold seal and framed in the gold frame, which matched the dream that was hung up in her head." The return with the medicine is just a matter of retracing her own footsteps. It is the part of the journey, and of the story, that can now go without saying.

In the matter of function, old Phoenix's way might even do as a sort 12
of parallel to your way of work if you are a writer of stories. The way to get there is the all-important, all-absorbing problem, and this problem is your reason for undertaking the story. Your only guide, too, is your

sureness about your subject, about what this subject is. Like Phoenix, you work all your life to find your way, through all the obstructions and the false appearances and the upsets you may have brought on yourself, to reach a meaning—using inventions of your imagination, perhaps helped out by your dreams and bits of good luck. And finally too, like Phoenix, you have to assume that what you are working in aid of is life, not death.

But you would make the trip anyway—wouldn't you?—just on hope.

Topics for Critical Thinking and Writing

1. In paragraph 4 Welty suggests that those who ask the question about the grandson imply "that for Phoenix's grandson to be dead would somehow make the story 'better.'" Why might anyone think this? And *would* the story be better if the grandson were dead? Explain your answer.

2. Did Welty's comment increase your enjoyment and your understanding of her story? If so, offer specific details.

3. Although it seems natural to want to hear what authors have to say about their work, consider the possibility that authors may consciously or unconsciously misrepresent their work. (The painter Claes Oldenburg said that anyone who pays attention to what artists write about their pictures ought to have his eyes examined.) Do you think, therefore, that we should ignore what writers say about their works? Explain.

Patrick Buchanan

Patrick Buchanan, a nationally syndicated columnist and cohost of the television program Crossfire, *in 1991–92 unsuccessfully sought the Republican nomination for president of the United States. The following essay appeared in* Washington Times, *May 22, 1989.*

The background of the essay is as follows. On May 18, 1989, Senator Alfonse D'Amato held up a photograph of a plastic image of Christ on the Cross, tinged with gold and set against a golden background. D'Amato angrily tore the picture to pieces, saying that "This so-called piece of art is a deplorable, despicable display of vulgarity." The photograph was by Andres Serrano, an artist who had received a grant from the National Endowment for the Arts. Serrano, born a Roman Catholic, says that he left the Church at the age of thirteen but that he remains a believer. Earlier, he had created a work called Blood Cross, *a cross-shaped plexiglass container holding blood, symbolizing, he said "what the crucifixion and Christianity are all about—sacrifice." Later he created a companion piece,* Milk Cross, *presumably alluding to the maternal aspect of the church.*

Serrano continued to experiment by creating works using body fluids. The image that Senator D'Amato displayed and destroyed probably would have aroused no anger if it had not been titled Piss Christ, *and indeed the photo showed a crucified Christ submerged in a container of the artist's urine. Senator D'Amato's anger was matched by others in Washington and elsewhere, and something of a national debate ensued. Is the work blasphemous, or is it a powerful (though admittedly odd) way of emphasizing Jesus' immersion in this material world? If it is blasphemous, must it be tolerated? Should it be tolerated but not subsidized by taxpayers? Or should the government subsidize artists and ask no questions?*

We give three responses–Buchanan's, Senator John Danforth's, and Arthur Danto's. (Danto, an art critic, was also, at the time, a professor of philosophy.)

Losing the War for America's Culture?

As altarpiece of his exhibit, Andres Serrano has a photograph of a crucifix, a replica of Christ dying on the cross. The unusual feature of Mr. Serrano's exhibit, however, is that his crucifix is submerged in a vat of urine, his own. Lest one miss the point, it is titled *Piss Christ;* others are *Piss God* and *Piss Pope.*

Mr. Serrano's pièce de résistance apparently captivated judges of The Awards in the Visual Arts program of the Southeastern Center for Contemporary Art of Winston-Salem, N.C., who chose it for display and tour.

According to James Cooper, art critic of *The New York City Tribune,* AVA is funded by the National Endowment for the Arts, which, in 1985, gave Mr. Serrano its own grant of $15,000 for "creating art works composed from human body parts and decapitated heads of animals exhibited in glass vats." Your tax dollars at work.

The downhill slide of American culture gathers momentum. In a 4 year, we have seen Martin Scorsese's *The Last Temptation of Christ*—portraying Jesus as an adulterous wimp—nominated for an Academy Award, and a modern art exhibit in Chicago where patrons were invited to walk on an American flag.

Rising above New York's West Side Highway, for a late summer unveiling, is a 75-foot-high mural celebrating Marx, Lenin, Trotsky, Mao, Castro and Che, a six-story shrine to communism, a Marxist Mount Rushmore in Greenwich Village. Funding for the *Pathfinder Mural* comes in part from Managua's Ministry of Culture.

"[F]or those who create the popular culture ... patriotism is no longer in style," President Ronald Reagan warned in his farewell address. It was a dramatic understatement; America's art and culture are, more and more, openly anti-Christian, anti-American, nihilistic.

About last year's "Committed to Print" exhibit at the New York Museum of Modern Art, Mr. Cooper writes:

> The visitor is bombarded with picture after picture, gallery after gallery, of supposed crimes that the United States has inflicted. . . . President Reagan is portrayed . . . as a bloodthirsty vampire urging a rabid fanged dog to kill innocent Latin American peasants. Another picture portrays an ocean of skulls filling the mall in front of the United States Capital. . . . Pictures of Lt. William Calley, blackened skulls, dead babies, all serve to inculcate in the mind of the viewer one continuous unending image of America's past and present "sins." Nowhere is there any evidence of the achievements of American capitalism or democracy. Instead, posters of heroic Red Chinese soldiers . . . and Malcolm X are offered to remind us of the glorious political alternatives available by embracing socialism, communism, or worse.

While the right has been busy winning primaries and elections, cutting taxes and funding anti-communist guerrillas abroad, the left has been quietly seizing all the commanding heights of American art and culture. Mr. Cooper, who edits the excellent little magazine *American Arts Quarterly,* is direct in his blame, scathing in his commentary:

> Conservatives have not even made the attempt of creating their own culture program during the last 100 years. Nor has the religious community, despite a tradition of glorious art that has produced Gothic cathedrals, the Sistine Chapel, the music of Johann Sebastian Bach and the art of Raphael, Durer and Rembrandt.
>
> American churches, business corporations, and government and educational institutions have . . . meekly embraced without protest a nihilist, existential, relativist, secular humanist culture they profess to abhor. Later, they wonder why films are made that are as sacrilegious as *The Last Temptation of Christ* . . . or why art shows that are blatantly pro-communist can . . . be seen at such locations as the Museum of Modern Art.
>
> The reason for all of this is simple. Those who believe in absolute values such as God and beauty do nothing, and those who believe in existential humanism have captured the culture. Businessmen, political leaders and bankers have failed to recognize the importance of culture as a force for good and a force for evil. . . .
>
> Political leaders in Washington believe that the battle against communism is being fought in the jungles of Asia and Central America, while fail-

8

12

ing to realize the war is also raging on the battlefield of the arts within our own borders.

The United States spends $5 billion a year on the arts, but no one questions the nihilist values this art disseminates to the American public. The conservatives simply bury their heads in the sand and do nothing.

Is he wrong? So, what is to be done?

Conservatives and the religious community that comprise the vast middle-American population should actively support those artists that advocate the same values and ideas as they do. They should also choose to withdraw support and funding from the modernist culture they profess to despise. In short, they should do what the liberals did long ago—"capture the culture."

Surely the place to begin is with the National Endowment of the Arts, whose new chairman is to be selected, soon, by president George Bush.   16

A nation absorbs its values through its art. A corrupt culture will produce a corrupt people, and vice versa; between rotten art, films, plays and books—and rotten behavior—the correlation is absolute. The hour is late; America needs a cultural revolution in the '90s as sweeping as its political revolution in the '80s.

End of sermon. Amen.

Topics for Critical Thinking and Writing

In paragraph 15, Buchanan quotes a writer who urges his readers "to withdraw support and funding" from a culture they disapprove of. In the context, this means that they should write to their representatives in Washington, urging Congress to impose restrictions on the National Endowment for the Arts. Do you believe our government should fund the arts? If so, should there be restrictions? What sorts of restrictions?

John Danforth

John Danforth, born in St. Louis in 1936, was ordained an Episcopalian priest in 1964. From 1976 to 1994 he served as a Republican senator from Missouri. We reprint a statement that he made on the floor of the Senate on September 29, 1989.

Statement to the Senate

Mr. President, I have unfortunately had the opportunity to look very briefly at the exhibits that the Senator from North Carolina has brought to the floor and everything that has been said about them is true. These are gross. These are terrible. These are totally indefensible. I do not think they are art.

Mr. President, however I do not believe that the issue before us tonight is whether we like or do not like these pictures. I do not like them and my guess is that not a single resident of my State would like them. They would not like the idea of the Government paying for them. I am sorry Government did pay for them.

That is not the issue before us. The issue is very simple: The Senator from Texas used the expression, and I think it was very well chosen, the question is: What is suitable art? And the issue before the Senate is very simple, and it is whether we in the U.S. Senate should attempt to make definitions of what we consider to be suitable art.

Maybe there should not be any National Endowment for the Arts.   4
Maybe the Government should never be in the business of making judgments of taste, because that is what the NEA does. I think that is an arguable position. But the question is not whether the NEA should do it or not do it. We have already decided that the NEA is in that business.

The question is whether we in the Congress of the United States should try to establish some criteria by which we define what is or is not suitable art. That is what the Senator from North Carolina does by his amendment. His amendment does not say that the Mapplethorpe exhibition[1] is pornography and it should not be funded. He does not say that. He goes much more broadly than that. He does not say that Mr. Serrano should or should not be funded by the NEA.

He goes much more broadly than that in the terms of his amendment, and I want to read a couple paragraphs because we have been focusing on obscenity and I think everybody knows that obscenity has been a problem for the Supreme Court of the United States. But he also says in paragraph 2 that the amendment covers material which denigrates the object or beliefs of the adherents of a particular religion or nonreligion.

Mr. President, consider what that means: Material which denigrates the object or beliefs of the adherents of a particular religion or nonreligion.

Does it denigrate the object of a religion to portray Christ as a   8
clown? Well, the musical *Godspell* did just that. It portrayed Christ as a clown. Could it be found by some administrator that the portrayal of Christ as a clown denigrates the object of somebody's religion? Of course it could.

Godspell probably would be covered by the breadth of this amendment. How about a portrayal of Christ as a wild animal? Would that

---

[1]**The Mapplethorpe exhibition:** In June 1989, the Corcoran Gallery of Art, in Washington, D.C., cancelled a forthcoming exhibition of photographs by Robert Mapplethorpe. The exhibition, which was to have included some sexually explicit homosexual pictures, was funded partly by a grant from the National Endowment for the Arts.

portrayal denigrate a person's religion? Well, C.S. Lewis did that in *The Lion, the Witch and the Wardrobe*. It was a book about Christianity and the Christ figure was a lion and some administrator, some bureaucrat could have said that denigrates a person's religion. C.S. Lewis spent his academic and literary life describing his religious beliefs which were very, very profound beliefs.

How about in the world of music? Could it be said that the beliefs of the Quaker faith are denigrated by "Onward Christian Soldiers Marching as to War"?

And then how about the question of race. I remember from my own part the country, *Tom Sawyer* and *Huckleberry Finn*. There have been those throughout the last number of decades who have tried for one reason or another to get *Tom Sawyer* and *Huckleberry Finn* off of the shelves of our schools.

This amendment would say that *Tom Sawyer* would not have qual-   12
ified for an NEA grant and *Huckleberry Finn* because it could be argued that they denigrated an individual, namely Nigger Jim, as he was called according to his race.

Or how about creed? Can we think of anything in the annals of literature that denigrates an individual because of his religion? How about the *Merchant of Venice?* How about William Shakespeare himself? Would that be covered by this amendment? I think it would be. This amendment is not just about Mapplethorpe. It is also about Shakespeare.

And in our own time in American literature Alice Walker's great little book, *The Color Purple* made into a movie, clearly denigrates men. And this amendment says that material that denigrates or reviles a person on the basis of sex falls within the parameters. I take it that *The Color Purple* would not have qualified for an NEA grant.

How about age? I do not remember the name of the book, but I do remember that Bill Cosby, the famous comedian, wrote a book about kids. It is a spoof of children, and his television programs are always doing that. And I take it that those programs and that book denigrate people on the basis of age.

Then there is national origin which is also covered material that   16
denigrates or reviles on the basis of national origin. Perhaps *The Godfather*. The head of Paramount Theaters was visiting with me recently. I said. "What is the greatest movie you ever made?" He said, "The two Godfather movies taken together, absolutely the essence of American art" and it would be covered by this amendment.

I am not for Mapplethorpe. I am sick that a dollar of taxpayer money went to pay for this kind of junk. I am sick about it. I could just see the faces of the people of Sedalia, or Cabool, or Mountain Grove, MO, if they were told that they had to pay for this. It truly is outlandish. That is not the issue.

The issue is: How good are we at defining whether something is suitable art or not-suitable art and how do we draw those definitions?

And should we really write definitions on the floor of the Senate which cover *Godspell,* and *Tom Sawyer,* and the *Merchant of Venice,* and *The Color Purple,* and *The Godfather?* Mr. President, I think the answer is no.

Topics for Critical Thinking and Writing

1. Evaluate Danforth's final paragraph as a concluding paragraph to his essay.
2. What are your answers to the three questions Danforth asks in his final paragraph? Explain your position.

Arthur Danto

Arthur Danto, a professor emeritus of philosophy at Columbia University, is the author of many books, some on philosophy and some on art. He is also the art critic for The Nation, *where the following piece appeared on August 21/28, 1989.*

Art and Taxpayers

The Corcoran Gallery's pre-emptive decision in June to cancel a planned exhibition of Robert Mapplethorpe's photographs in order to forestall Congressional indignation at their content brought far greater notoriety to the now-famous images than showing them would have. Many of the same photographs of men who engage in the sexual domination of other willing men were presented at the Whitney Museum in New York City last year to no greater stir than some isolated tongue-clucking and wonderment as to what the museum thought it was doing. Indeed, *The Nation* was nearly alone in drawing attention to the homoerotic content of those explicit images in a show whose works conveyed a homoerotic sensibility whatever the subject, even when flowers or faces [see Danto, "Art," *The Nation,* September 26, 1988]. The issue that had to be raised was how to respond to such charged representations in works of the highest photographic beauty. Mapplethorpe was still alive, although his sickness with AIDS was common knowledge in the art world, and that gave a certain solemn urgency to the showing of those sexually unsettling pictures. It was Mapplethorpe's wish that they be shown, as if he regarded them as an artistic testament.

The position of many neoconservatives is that this is not the kind of art taxpayers want to support. Hilton Kramer advanced this view in *The New York Times* recently. And this is now the position of the United States Senate—as a result of the July 26 passage of Jesse Helms' amendment banning Federal support for "obscene or indecent" art. But the issue could not be more obscurely framed. It is imperative to distinguish taxpayers from individuals who pay taxes, as we distinguish the uniform from the individual who wears it. As individuals, we have divergent aesthetic preferences. Kramer has little interest in supporting art that others find of great interest. But aesthetic preference does not enter into the concept of the taxpayer, which is a civic category. What does enter into it is freedom. It is very much in the interest of every taxpayer that freedom be supported, even—or especially—in its most extreme expressions. However divided individuals are on matters of taste, freedom is in the interest of every citizen. The taxpayer does not support one form of art and withhold support from another as a taxpayer, except in the special case of public art. The taxpayer supports the freedom to make and show art, even when it is art of a kind this or that *individual* finds repugnant.

Mapplethorpe did not make these photographs to test his freedoms. They are disturbing images for many, exciting images for some, but were not intended to strike a blow for artistic liberty (though perhaps for sexual liberty). They very much belong to an intersection of the art world and a certain erotic underground, and they have never been easy to view. The Whitney demonstrated that they could be shown to a wide audience without inducing riots.

Although there may never come a time when one can look at their subjects as commonplace, like female nudes or landscapes or still lifes, these works contrast completely with the now-also-notorious photograph by Andres Serrano of a plastic Jesus in a pool of pee. They contrast as well with the recent gesture, by a senior at the School of the Art Institute of Chicago, of laying a U.S. flag on the floor in a student exhibition so that visitors found it necessary to walk on it. Both works were intended to offend, and did offend. People responded indignantly and directly, by confrontations, demonstrations, protest. It would have been absurd to argue that they ought not to have done this on the ground that the objects were art. Art has the privileges of freedom only because it is a form of expression. And to be seriously interested in making an expression is to be seriously prepared to endure the consequences of making it. It is also not an offense to counter outrage with outrage. On the contrary, it is taking art seriously to do so. One cannot distance the flag and think of it as an arresting composition of stars and bars. One cannot distance one of the powerful religious symbols of the West and view a derogatory photograph of it merely as a formal composition.

It is healthy for art to vacate the position of pure aestheticism in which conservative critics seek to imprison it, and to try to affect the way viewers respond to the most meaningful matters of their lives. It is healthy for the museum to play a role in the life of its time rather than to stand outside as a cloister for aesthetic delectations. Art has been primarily aesthetic only throughout a very brief interval of its history of political, moral and religious engagement. As taxpayers our interest is solely in everyone's freedom to participate in the thought of the age.

Whatever grave reservations regarding Congress may have motivated the directors of the Corcoran, they weakened the entire social fabric by yielding their freedom. Their decision should have been to show the work, whose merit they must have believed in to have scheduled the exhibition. Since then individual members of Congress have revealed themselves as enemies of freedom by letting their aesthetic attitudes corrupt their political integrity as custodians of the deepest values of a democratic society.

Topics for Critical Thinking and Writing

1. In his second paragraph Danto argues that by supporting art—even art that offends the individual—the taxpayer is supporting freedom, and "freedom is in the interest of every citizen." Do you agree? Or do you think that although artists should be free to express themselves, taxpayers should not support some kinds of artistic expression? Explain your position.

2. Suppose someone said to you that he or she did not understand the first sentence of paragraph 5. How would you explain it? And do you agree with it? Why?

3. Later in paragraph 5 Danto says that a museum "should play a role in the life of its time rather than . . . stand outside as a cloister for aesthetic delectations." Think of an art museum in your community. Has it played a role "in the life of its time," or is it merely "a cloister for aesthetic delectations"? *Should* it play a role of the sort Danto advocates? Why?

12
LAW AND ORDER

Flower Power
Bernie Boston, 1967

Washington Evening Star, photo by Bernie Boston

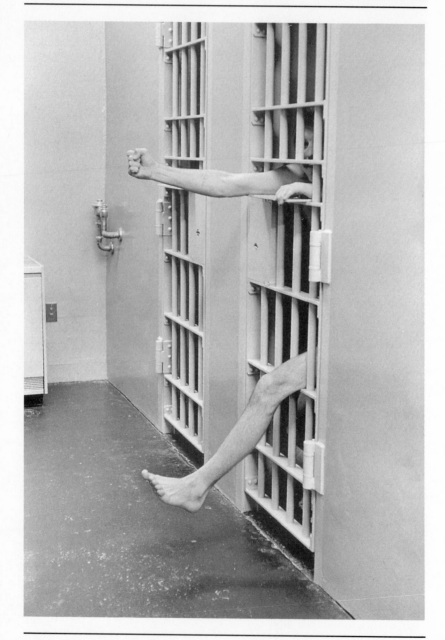

The Problem We All Live With
Norman Rockwell, 1964

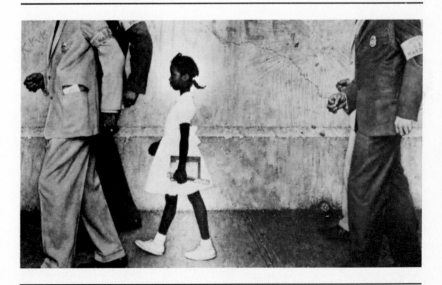

Short Views

The trouble for the thief is not how to steal the bugle, but where to blow it.

African proverb

Whether there was ever a significant increase in crime and when it might have occurred is puzzling, since the phrase, "the land is full of bloody crimes and the city full of violence," did not appear in a recent Chicago newspaper but in a report on a crime wave in the promised land about 600 B.C. as recorded in Ezekiel VII:23. The logical possibility of an ever-increasing crime wave becomes more doubtful when we consider the biblical origin of humankind: Adam, Eve and Cain committed the worst offenses possible and after Abel was killed, all survivors—or 75 percent of the first four human beings—had criminal records. In spite of all righteous claims to the opposite, this crime wave seems to have subsided, never to reach its biblical heights again. It is simpler and more correct to state that crime has always existed but statistics have not.

Kurt Weis and Michael F. Milakovich

Whoever desires to found a state and give it laws, must start with assuming that all men are bad and ever ready to display their vicious nature, whenever they may find occasion for it.

Niccolò Machiavelli

It is questionable whether, when we break a murderer on the wheel, we aren't lapsing into precisely the mistake of the child who hits the chair he bumps into.

G. C. Lichtenberg

If a man were permitted to make all the ballads, he need not care who should make the laws of a nation.

Andrew Fletcher

Nature has given women so much power that the law has very wisely given them very little.
Samuel Johnson

I asked him whether, as a moralist, he did not think that the practice of the law, in some degree, hurt the nice feeling of honesty. JOHNSON. "Why no, Sir, if you act properly. You are not to deceive your clients with false representations of your opinion: you are not to tell lies to a judge." BOSWELL. "But what do you think of supporting a cause which you know to be bad?" JOHNSON. "Sir, you do not know it to be good or bad till the Judge determines it. I have said that you are to state facts fairly; so that your thinking, or what you call knowing, a cause to be bad, must be from reasoning, must be from your supposing your arguments to be weak and inconclusive. But, Sir, that is not enough. An argument which does not convince yourself, may convince the Judge to whom you urge it; and if it does convince him, why, then, Sir, you are wrong, and he is right. It is his business to judge; and you are not to be confident in your own opinion that a cause is bad, but to say all you can for your client, and then hear the Judge's opinion." BOSWELL. "But, Sir, does not affecting a warmth when you have no warmth, and appearing to be clearly of one opinion when you are in reality of another opinion, does not such dissimulation impair one's honesty? Is there not some danger that a lawyer may put on the same mask in common life, in the intercourse with his friends?" JOHNSON. "Why no, Sir. Everybody knows you are paid for affecting warmth for your client; and it is, therefore, properly no dissimulation: the moment you come from the bar you resume your usual behaviour. Sir, a man will no more carry the artifice of the bar into the common intercourse of society, than a man who is paid for tumbling upon his hands will continue to tumble upon his hands when he should walk on his feet."
James Boswell

One law for the ox and the ass is oppression.
William Blake

The law, in its majestic equality, forbids the rich as well as the poor to sleep under bridges, to beg in the streets, and to steal bread.
Anatole France

Decency, security and liberty alike demand that government officials shall be subjected to the same rules of conduct that are commands to the citizen. In a government of laws, existence of the government will be imperilled if it fails to observe the law scrupulously. Our Government is the potent, the omnipresent teacher. For good or for ill, it teaches the whole people by its example. Crime is contagious. If the Government becomes a lawbreaker, it breeds contempt for law; it invites every man to become a law unto himself; it invites anarchy. To declare that in the administration of the criminal law the end justifies the means—to declare that the Government may commit crimes in order to secure the conviction of a private criminal—would bring terrible retribution. Against that pernicious doctrine this Court should resolutely set its face.

Louis D. Brandeis

The trouble about fighting for human freedom is that you have to spend much of your life defending sons of bitches; for oppressive laws are always aimed at them originally, and oppression must be stopped in the beginning if it is to be stopped at all.

H. L. Mencken

Censorship upholds the dignity of the profession, know what I mean?

Mae West

Thomas Jefferson

Thomas Jefferson (1743–1826), governor of Virginia and the third president of the United States, devoted most of his adult life, until his retirement, to the service of Virginia and of the nation. The spirit and the wording of the Declaration are almost entirely Jefferson's.

The Declaration of Independence

In CONGRESS, July 4, 1776.
The Unanimous Declaration of the Thirteen United States of America.

When in the Course of human events, it becomes necessary for one people to dissolve the political bands which have connected them with another, and to assume among the powers of the earth, the separate and equal station to which the Laws of Nature and of Nature's God entitle them, a decent respect to the opinions of mankind requires that they should declare the causes which impel them to the separation.

We hold these truths to be self-evident, that all men are created equal, that they are endowed by their Creator with certain unalienable Rights, that among these are Life, Liberty and the pursuit of Happiness.

That to secure these rights, Governments are instituted among Men, deriving their just powers from the consent of the governed.

That whenever any Form of Government becomes destructive of these ends, it is the Right of the People to alter or to abolish it, and to institute new Government, laying its foundation on such principles and organizing its powers in such form, as to them shall seem most likely to effect their Safety and Happiness. Prudence, indeed, will dictate that Governments long established should not be changed for light and transient causes; and accordingly all experience hath shewn, that mankind are more disposed to suffer, while evils are sufferable, than to right themselves by abolishing the forms to which they are accustomed. But when a long train of abuses and usurpations, pursuing invariably the same Object evinces a design to reduce them under absolute Despotism, it is their right, it is their duty, to throw off such Government, and to provide new Guards for their future security.

Such has been the patient sufferance of these Colonies; and such is now the necessity which constrains them to alter their former Systems of Government. The history of the present King of Great Britain is a history of repeated injuries and usurpations, all having in direct object the establishment of an absolute Tyranny over these States. To prove this, let Facts be submitted to a candid world.

He has refused his Assent to Laws, the most wholesome and necessary for the public good.

He has forbidden his Governors to pass Laws of immediate and pressing importance, unless suspended in their operation till his Assent should be obtained; and when so suspended, he has utterly neglected to attend to them.

He has refused to pass other Laws for the accommodation of large   8
districts of people, unless those people would relinquish the right of Representation in the Legislature, a right inestimable to them and formidable to tyrants only.

He has called together legislative bodies at places unusual, uncomfortable, and distant from the depository of their public Records, for the sole purpose of fatiguing them into compliance with his measures.

He has dissolved Representative Houses repeatedly, for opposing with manly firmness his invasions on the rights of people.

He has refused for a long time, after such dissolutions, to cause others to be elected; whereby the Legislative powers, incapable of Annihilation, have returned to the People at large for their exercise; the State remaining in the mean time exposed to all the dangers of invasion from without, and convulsions within.

He has endeavoured to prevent the population of these States; for   12
that purpose obstructing the Laws for Naturalization of Foreigners; refusing to pass others to encourage their migrations hither, and raising the conditions of new Appropriations of Lands.

He has obstructed the Administration of Justice, by refusing his Assent to Laws for establishing Judiciary powers.

He has made Judges dependent on his Will alone, for the tenure of their offices, and the amount and payment of their salaries.

He has erected a multitude of New Offices, and sent hither swarms of Officers to harass our people, and eat out their substance.

He has kept among us, in times of peace, Standing Armies without   16
the Consent of our legislatures.

He has affected to render the Military independent of and superior to the Civil power.

He has combined with others to subject us to a jurisdiction foreign to our constitution, and unacknowledged by our laws; giving his Assent to their Acts of pretended Legislation:

For Quartering large bodies of armed troops among us:

For Protecting them, by a mock Trial, from punishment for any   20
Murders which they should commit on the Inhabitants of these States:

For cutting off our Trade with all parts of the world:

For imposing Taxes on us without our Consent:

For depriving us in many cases, of the benefits of Trial by Jury:

For transporting us beyond Seas to be tried for pretended offences: 24

For abolishing the free System of English Laws in a neighbouring Province, establishing therein an Arbitrary government, and enlarging its Boundaries so as to render it at once an example and fit instrument for introducing the same absolute rule into these Colonies:

For taking away our Charters, abolishing our most valuable Laws, and altering fundamentally the Forms of our Governments:

For suspending our own Legislatures, and declaring themselves invested with power to legislate for us in all cases whatsoever.

He has abdicated Government here, by declaring us out of his Protection and waging War against us: 28

He has plundered our seas, ravaged our Coasts, burnt our towns, and destroyed the lives of our people.

He is at this time transporting large Armies of foreign Mercenaries to compleat the works of death, desolation and tyranny, already begun with circumstances of Cruelty & perfidy scarcely paralleled in the most barbarous ages, and totally unworthy the Head of a civilized nation.

He has constrained our fellow Citizens taken Captive on the high Seas to bear Arms against their Country, to become the executioners of their friends and Brethren, or to fall themselves by their Hands.

He has excited domestic insurrections amongst us, and has endeavoured to bring on the inhabitants of our frontiers, the merciless Indian Savages, whose known rule of warfare, is an undistinguished destruction of all ages, sexes and conditions. In every stage of these Oppressions We have Petitioned for Redress in the most humble terms: Our repeated Petitions have been answered only by repeated injury. A Prince, whose character is thus marked by every act which may define a Tyrant, is unfit to be the ruler of a free people. Nor have We been wanting in attentions to our British brethren. We have warned them from time to time of attempts by their legislature to extend an unwarrantable jurisdiction over us. We have reminded them of the circumstances of our emigration and settlement here. We have appealed to their native justice and magnanimity, and we have conjured them by the ties of our common kindred to disavow these usurpations, which, would inevitably interrupt our connections and correspondence. They too have been deaf to the voice of justice and of consanguinity. We must, therefore, acquiesce in the necessity, which denounces our Separation, and hold them, as we hold the rest of mankind, Enemies in War, in Peace Friends.   32

We, THEREFORE, the Representatives of the UNITED STATES OF AMERICA, in General Congress Assembled, appealing to the Supreme Judge of the world for the rectitude of our intentions, do, in the Name and by Authority of the good People of these Colonies, solemnly publish and declare, That these United Colonies are, and of Right ought to be FREE AND INDEPENDENT STATES; that they are Absolved from all Allegiance to the British Crown, and that all political connection between them and the State of Great Britain, is and ought to be totally dissolved; and that as Free and Independent States, they have full Power to levy War, conclude Peace, contract Alliances, establish Commerce, and to do all other Acts and Things which Independent States may of right do.

And for the support of this Declaration, with a firm reliance on the protection of divine Providence, we mutually pledge to each other our Lives, our Fortunes and our sacred Honor.

Topics for Critical Thinking and Writing

1. What audience is being addressed in the Declaration of Independence? Cite passages in the text that support your answer.

2. The Library of Congress has the original manuscript of the rough draft of the Declaration. This manuscript itself includes revisions that are indicated below, but it was later further revised. We print the first part of the second paragraph of the draft and, after it, the corresponding part of the final version. Try to account for the changes within the draft, and from the revised draft to the final version.

> We hold these truths to be *~~sacred & undeniable~~*, *self evident* that all men are created equal *~~& independent,~~* that *~~from that equal creation they derive equal~~* *they are endowed by their creator* *with*
>
> *~~rights some of which are~~* *~~in rights~~*
>
> inherent & inalienable, *rights; that* among *~~which~~ ~~are~~ these ~~the preservation of~~* life, liberty, & the pursuit of happiness.

> We hold these Truths to be self-evident, that all Men are created equal, that they are endowed by their Creator with certain unalienable Rights, that among these are Life, Liberty, and the Pursuit of Happiness

In a paragraph evaluate the changes. Try to put yourself into Jefferson's mind and see if you can sense why Jefferson made the changes.

3. In a paragraph define *happiness,* and then in a second paragraph explain why, in your opinion, Jefferson spoke of "the pursuit of happiness" rather than of "happiness."

4. In "We Have No 'Right to Happiness'" (page 24) C. S. Lewis discusses the meaning of "the pursuit of happiness" in the Declaration and a current misinterpretation of the phrase. How does he explain and define the phrase? How does his interpretation differ from what he considers an erroneous interpretation?

5. What assumptions lie behind the numerous specific reasons that are given to justify the rebellion? Set forth the gist of the argument of the Declaration using the form of reasoning known as a *syllogism,* which consists of a major premise (such as "All men are mortal"), a minor premise ("Socrates is a man"), and a conclusion ("Therefore, Socrates is mortal"). For a brief discussion of syllogisms, see pages 794–95 (deduction).

6. In a paragraph argue that the assertion that "all Men are created equal" is nonsense, or, on the other hand, that it makes sense.

7. If every person has an unalienable right to life, how can capital punishment be reconciled with the Declaration of Independence? You need not in fact be a supporter of capital punishment; simply offer the best defense you can think of, in an effort to make it harmonious with the Declaration.

Martin Luther King, Jr.

Martin Luther King, Jr. (1929–68), clergyman and civil rights leader, achieved national fame in 1955–56 when he led the boycott against segregated bus lines in Montgomery, Alabama. His policy of passive resistance succeeded in Montgomery, and King then organized the Southern Christian Leadership Conference in order to extend his efforts. In 1964 he was awarded the Nobel Peace Prize, but he continued to encounter strong opposition. On April 4, 1968, while in Memphis to support striking sanitation workers, he was shot and killed.

Nonviolent Resistance

Oppressed people deal with their oppression in three characteristic ways. One way is acquiescence: the oppressed resign themselves to their doom. They tacitly adjust themselves to oppression, and thereby become conditioned to it. In every movement toward freedom some of the oppressed prefer to remain oppressed. Almost 2800 years ago Moses set out to lead the children of Israel from the slavery of Egypt to the freedom of the promised land. He soon discovered that slaves do not always welcome their deliverers. They become accustomed to being slaves. They would rather bear those ills they have, as Shakespeare pointed out, than flee to others that they know not of. They prefer the "fleshpots of Egypt" to the ordeals of emancipation.

There is such a thing as the freedom of exhaustion. Some people are so worn down by the yoke of oppression that they give up. A few years ago in the slum areas of Atlanta, a Negro guitarist used to sing almost daily: "Ben down so long that down don't bother me." This is the type of negative freedom and resignation that often engulfs the life of the oppressed.

But this is not the way out. To accept passively an unjust system is to cooperate with that system; thereby the oppressed become as evil as the oppressor. Noncooperation with evil is as much a moral obligation as is cooperation with good. The oppressed must never allow the conscience of the oppressor to slumber. Religion reminds every man that he is his brother's keeper. To accept injustice or segregation passively is to say to the oppressor that his actions are morally right. It is a way of allowing his conscience to fall asleep. At this moment the oppressed fails to be his brother's keeper. So acquiescence—while often the easier way—is not the moral way. It is the way of the coward. The Negro cannot win the respect of his oppressor by acquiescing; he merely increases the oppressor's arrogance and contempt. Acquiescence is interpreted as proof of the Negro's inferiority. The Negro cannot win the respect of the white people of the South or the peoples of the world if he is willing to sell the future of his children for his personal and immediate comfort and safety.

A second way that oppressed people sometimes deal with oppres- 4
sion is to resort to physical violence and corroding hatred. Violence

often brings about momentary results. Nations have frequently won their independence in battle. But in spite of temporary victories, violence never brings permanent peace. It solves no social problem; it merely creates new and more complicated ones.

Violence as a way of achieving racial justice is both impractical and immoral. It is impractical because it is a descending spiral ending in destruction for all. The old law of an eye for an eye leaves everybody blind. It is immoral because it seeks to humiliate the opponent rather than win his understanding; it seeks to annihilate rather than to convert. Violence is immoral because it thrives on hatred rather than love. It destroys community and makes brotherhood impossible. It leaves society in monologue rather than dialogue. Violence ends by defeating itself. It creates bitterness in the survivors and brutality in the destroyers. A voice echoes through time saying to every potential Peter, "Put up your sword." History is cluttered with the wreckage of nations that failed to follow his command.

If the American Negro and other victims of oppression succumb to the temptation of using violence in the struggle for freedom, future generations will be the recipients of a desolate night of bitterness, and our chief legacy to them will be an endless reign of meaningless chaos. Violence is not the way.

The third way open to oppressed people in their quest for freedom is the way of nonviolent resistance. Like the synthesis in Hegelian philosophy, the principle of nonviolent resistance seeks to reconcile the truths of two opposites—acquiescence and violence—while avoiding the extremes and immoralities of both. The nonviolent resister agrees with the person who acquiesces that one should not be physically aggressive toward his opponent; but he balances the equation by agreeing with the person of violence that evil must be resisted. He avoids the nonresistance of the former and the violent resistance of the latter. With nonviolent resistance, no individual or group need submit to any wrong, nor need anyone resort to violence in order to right a wrong.

It seems to me that this is the method that must guide the actions of   8
the Negro in the present crisis in race relations. Through nonviolent resistance the Negro will be able to rise to the noble height of opposing the unjust system while loving the perpetrators of the system. The Negro must work passionately and unrelentingly for full stature as a citizen, but he must not use inferior methods to gain it. He must never come to terms with falsehood, malice, hate, or destruction.

Nonviolent resistance makes it possible for the Negro to remain in the South and struggle for his rights. The Negro's problem will not be solved by running away. He cannot listen to the glib suggestion of those who would urge him to migrate en masse to other sections of the country. By grasping his great opportunity in the South he can make a lasting contribution to the moral strength of the nation and set a sublime example of courage for generations yet unborn.

By nonviolent resistance, the Negro can also enlist all men of good will in his struggle for equality. The problem is not a purely racial one, with Negroes set against whites. In the end, it is not a struggle between people at all, but a tension between justice and injustice. Nonviolent resistance is not aimed against oppressors but against oppression. Under its banner consciences, not racial groups, are enlisted.

If the Negro is to achieve the goal of integration, he must organize himself into a militant and nonviolent mass movement. All three elements are indispensable. The movement for equality and justice can only be a success if it has both a mass and militant character; the barriers to be overcome require both. Nonviolence is an imperative in order to bring about ultimate community.

A mass movement of militant quality that is not at the same time   12
committed to nonviolence tends to generate conflict, which in turn breeds anarchy. The support of the participants and the sympathy of the uncommitted are both inhibited by the threat that bloodshed will engulf the community. This reaction in turn encourages the opposition to threaten and resort to force. When, however, the mass movement repudiates violence while moving resolutely toward its goal, its opponents are revealed as the instigators and practitioners of violence if it occurs. Then public support is magnetically attracted to the advocates of nonviolence, while those who employ violence are literally disarmed by overwhelming sentiment against their stand.

Only through a nonviolent approach can the fears of the white community be mitigated. A guilt-ridden white minority lives in fear that if the Negro should ever attain power, he would act without restraint or pity to revenge the injustices and brutality of the years. It is something like a parent who continually mistreats a son. One day that parent raises his hand to strike the son, only to discover that the son is now as tall as he is. The parent is suddenly afraid—fearful that the son will use his new physical power to repay his parent for all the blows of the past.

The Negro, once a helpless child, has now grown up politically, culturally, and economically. Many white men fear retaliation. The job of the Negro is to show them that they have nothing to fear, that the Negro understands and forgives and is ready to forget the past. He must convince the white man that all he seeks is justice, *for both himself and the white man*. A mass movement exercising nonviolence is an object lesson in power under discipline, a demonstration to the white community that if such a movement attained a degree of strength, it would use its power creatively and not vengefully.

Nonviolence can touch men where the law cannot reach them. When the law regulates behavior it plays an indirect part in molding public sentiment. The enforcement of the law is itself a form of peaceful persuasion. But the law needs help. The courts can order desegregation of the public schools. But what can be done to mitigate the fears, to disperse the hatred, violence, and irrationality gathered around school integration, to take the initiative out of the hands of racial demagogues, to release respect for the law? In the end, for laws to be obeyed, men must believe they are right.

Here nonviolence comes in as the ultimate form of persuasion. It is   16
the method which seeks to implement the just law by appealing to the conscience of the great decent majority who through blindness, fear, pride, or irrationality have allowed their consciences to sleep.

The nonviolent resisters can summarize their message in the following simple terms: We will take direct action against injustice without waiting for other agencies to act. We will not obey unjust laws or submit to unjust practices. We will do this peacefully, openly, cheerfully because our aim is to persuade. We adopt the means of nonviolence because our end is a community at peace with itself. We will try to persuade with our words, but if our words fail, we will try to persuade with our acts. We will always be willing to talk and seek fair compromise, but we are ready to suffer when necessary and even risk our lives to become witnesses to the truth as we see it.

The way of nonviolence means a willingness to suffer and sacrifice. It may mean going to jail. If such is the case the resister must be willing to fill the jail houses of the South. It may even mean physical death. But if physical death is the price that a man must pay to free his children and his white brethren from a permanent death of the spirit, then nothing could be more redemptive.

Topics for Critical Thinking and Writing

1. In the first paragraph, the passage about Moses and the children of Israel is not strictly necessary; the essential idea of the paragraph is stated in the previous sentence. Why, then, does King add this material? And why the quotation from Shakespeare?

2. Pick out two or three sentences that seem to you to be especially effective and analyze the sources of their power. You can choose either isolated sentences or (because King often effectively links sentences with repetition of words or of constructions) consecutive ones.

3. In a paragraph set forth your understanding of what nonviolent resistance is. Use whatever examples from your own experience or reading you find useful. In a second paragraph, explain how Maya Angelou's "Graduation" (page 234) offers an example of nonviolent resistance.

Linda M. Hasselstrom

Linda M. Hasselstrom, a South Dakota rancher, writer, and environmentalist, has wielded a gun as a last resort, but she has never used it. Her essay first appeared in High Country News *and later appeared in a somewhat longer form in a collection of her essays,* Land Circle: Writings Collected from the Land *(Golden, Col.: Fulcrum, 1991).*

Ms. Hasselstrom has asked us to indicate that her choices for self-defense are based on a particular set of circumstances, that she does not advocate handgun ownership, and that she is not a member of any group that advocates handgun use.

A Peaceful Woman Explains Why She Carries a Gun

I am a peace-loving woman. But several events in the past 10 years have convinced me I'm safer when I carry a pistol. This was a personal decision, but because handgun possession is a controversial subject, perhaps my reasoning will interest others.

I live in western South Dakota on a ranch 25 miles from the nearest large town: for several years I spent winters alone here. As a free-lance writer, I travel alone a lot—more than 100,000 miles by car in the last four years. With women freer than ever before to travel alone, the odds of our encountering trouble seem to have risen. And help, in the West, can be hours away. Distances are great, roads are deserted, and the terrain is often too exposed to offer hiding places.

A woman who travels alone is advised, usually by men, to protect herself by avoiding bars and other "dangerous situations," by approaching her car like an Indian scout, by locking doors and windows. But these precautions aren't always enough. I spent years following them and still found myself in dangerous situations. I began to resent the idea that just because I am female, I have to be extra careful.

A few years ago, with another woman, I camped for several weeks in the West. We discussed self-defense, but neither of us had taken a course in it. She was against firearms, and local police told us Mace was illegal. So we armed ourselves with spray cans of deodorant tucked into our sleeping bags. We never used our improvised Mace because we were lucky enough to camp beside people who came to our aid when men harassed us. But on one occasion we visited a national park where our assigned space was less than 15 feet from other campers. When we returned from a walk, we found our closest neighbors were two young men. As we gathered our cooking gear, they drank beer and loudly discussed what they would do to us after dark. Nearby campers, even families, ignored them; rangers strolled past, unconcerned. When we asked the rangers point-blank if they would protect us, one of them patted my shoulder and said, "Don't worry, girls. They're just kidding." At dusk we drove out of the park and hid our camp in the woods

4

a few miles away. The illegal spot was lovely, but our enjoyment of that park was ruined. I returned from the trip determined to reconsider the options available for protecting myself.

At that time, I lived alone on the ranch and taught night classes in town. Along a city street I often traveled, a woman had a flat tire, called for help on her CB radio, and got a rapist who left her beaten. She was afraid to call for help again and stayed in her car until morning. For that reason, as well as because CBs work best along line-of-sight, which wouldn't help much in the rolling hills where I live, I ruled out a CB.

As I drove home one night, a car followed me. It passed me on a narrow bridge while a passenger flashed a blinding spotlight in my face. I braked sharply. The car stopped, angled across the bridge, and four men jumped out. I realized the locked doors were useless if they broke the windows of my pickup. I started forward, hoping to knock their car aside so I could pass. Just then another car appeared, and the men hastily got back in their car. They continued to follow me, passing and repassing. I dared not go home because no one else was there. I passed no lighted houses. Finally they pulled over to the roadside, and I decided to use their tactic: fear. Speeding, the pickup horn blaring, I swerved as close to them as I dared as I roared past. It worked: they turned off the highway. But I was frightened and angry. Even in my vehicle I was too vulnerable.

Other incidents occurred over the years. One day I glanced out a field below my house and saw a man with a shotgun walking toward a pond full of ducks. I drove down and explained that the land was post-ed. I politely asked him to leave. He stared at me, and the muzzle of the shotgun began to rise. In a moment of utter clarity I realized that I was alone on the ranch, and that he could shoot me and simply drive away. The moment passed; the man left.

One night, I returned home from teaching a class to find deep tire ruts in the wet ground of my yard, garbage in the driveway, and a large gas tank empty. A light shone in the house; I couldn't remember leaving it on. I was too embarrassed to drive to a neighboring ranch and wake someone up. An hour of cautious exploration convinced me the house was safe, but once inside, with the doors locked, I was still afraid. I kept thinking of how vulnerable I felt, prowling around my own house in the dark.

My first positive step was to take a kung fu class, which teaches evasive or protective action when someone enters your space without permission. I learned to move confidently, scanning for possible attackers. I learned how to assess danger and techniques for avoiding it without combat.

I also learned that one must practice several hours a day to be good at kung fu. By that time I had married George; when I practiced with him, I learned how *close* you must be to your attacker to use martial arts, and decided a 120-pound woman dare not let a six-foot, 220-pound attacker get that close unless she is very, very good at self-defense. I have since read articles by several women who were extremely well trained in the martial arts, but were raped and beaten anyway.

I thought back over the times in my life when I had been attacked or threatened and tried to be realistic about my own behavior, searching for anything that had allowed me to become a victim. Overall, I was convinced that I had not been at fault. I don't believe myself to be either paranoid or a risk-taker, but I wanted more protection.

With some reluctance I decided to try carrying a pistol. George had   12
always carried one, despite his size and his training in martial arts. I practiced shooting until I was sure I could hit an attacker who moved close enough to endanger me. Then I bought a license from the county sheriff, making it legal for me to carry the gun concealed.

But I was not yet ready to defend myself. George taught me that the most important preparation was mental: convincing myself I could actually *shoot a person*. Few of us wish to hurt or kill another human being. But there is no point in having a gun—in fact, gun possession might increase your danger—unless you know you can use it. I got in the habit of rehearsing, as I drove or walked, the precise conditions that would be required before I would shoot someone.

People who have not grown up with the idea that they are capable of protecting themselves—in other words, most women—might have to work hard to convince themselves of their ability, and of the necessity. Handgun ownership need not turn us into gun-slingers, but it can be part of believing in, and relying on, *ourselves* for protection.

To be useful, a pistol has to be available. In my car, it's within instant reach. When I enter a deserted rest stop at night, it's in my purse, with my hand on the grip. When I walk from a dark parking lot into a motel, it's in my hand, under a coat. At home, it's on the headboard. In short, I take it with me almost everywhere I go alone.

Just carrying a pistol is no protection; avoidance is still the best   16
approach to trouble. Subconsciously watching for signs of danger, I believe I've become more alert. Handgun use, not unlike driving, becomes instinctive. Each time I've drawn my gun—I have never fired it at another human being—I've simply found it in my hand.

I was driving the half-mile to the highway mailbox one day when I saw a vehicle parked about midway down the road. Several men were standing in the ditch, relieving themselves. I have no objection to emergency urination, but I noticed they'd dumped several dozen beer cans in the road. Besides being ugly, cans can slash a cow's feet or stomach.

The men noticed me before they finished and made quite of performance out of zipping their trousers while walking toward me. All four of them gathered around my small foreign car, and one of them demanded what the hell I wanted.

"This is private land. I'd appreciate it if you'd pick up the beer cans."

"What beer cans?" said the belligerent one, putting both hands on   20
the car door and leaning in my window. His face was inches from mine, and the beer fumes were strong. The others laughed. One tried the passenger door, locked; another put his foot on the hood and rocked the car. They circled, lightly thumping the roof, discussing my good fortune in meeting them and the benefits they were likely to bestow upon me. I felt very small and very trapped and they knew it.

"The ones you just threw out," I said politely.

"I don't see no beer cans. Why don't you get out here and show them to me, honey?" said the belligerent one, reaching for the handle inside my door.

"Right over there," I said, still being polite, "—there, and over there." I pointed with the pistol, which I'd slipped under my thigh. Within one minute the cans and the men were back in the car and headed down the road.

I believe this incident illustrates several important principles. The   24
men were trespassing and knew it; their judgment may have been impaired by alcohol. Their response to the polite request of a woman alone was to use their size, numbers, and sex to inspire fear. The pistol was a response in the same language. Politeness didn't work; I couldn't match them in size or number. Out of the car, I'd have been more vulnerable. The pistol just changed the balance of power. It worked again recently when I was driving in a desolate part of Wyoming. A man played cat-and-mouse with me for 30 miles, ultimately trying to run me off the road. When his car passed mine with only two inches to spare, I showed him my pistol, and he disappeared.

When I got my pistol, I told my husband, revising the old Colt slogan. "God made men *and women,* but Sam Colt made them equal." Recently I have seen a gunmaker's ad with a similar sentiment. Perhaps this is an idea whose time has come, though the pacifist inside me will be saddened if the only way women can achieve equality is by carrying weapons.

We must treat a firearm's power with caution. "Power tends to corrupt, and absolute power corrupts absolutely," as a man (Lord Acton) once said. A pistol is not the only way to avoid being raped or murdered in today's world, but, intelligently wielded, it can shift the balance of power and provide a measure of safety.

Topics for Critical Thinking and Writing

1. In her first eight paragraphs, Hasselstrom sketches the kinds of experiences that ultimately caused her to carry a gun. Do you find her account of those experiences persuasive? Do they, in your opinion, justify her decision? If not, why not?

2. In paragraph 13 Hasselstrom introduces an idea that perhaps takes a reader by surprise. Do you think it is true, by and large, that a person who decides to carry a gun must, by means of "rehearsing," prepare himself or herself to use it? Whether or not you think it is true, what is the effect of her introducing this idea? Does it make her account more, or less, persuasive?

3. In paragraphs 17–24 Hasselstrom recounts an episode when her gun frightened off several belligerent and probably slightly intoxicated men. Do you think that this episode serves (as Hasselstrom doubtless thinks it does) as clear support for her position? What counterargument(s) can you imagine?

4. What devices does Hasselstrom use, as a writer, to convince her reader that she is not aggressive or gun-crazy?

James Q. Wilson

James Q. Wilson is Collins Professor of Management and Public Policy at the University of California, Los Angeles. Among his books are Thinking about Crime *(1975),* Bureaucracy *(1989), and* The Moral Sense *(1993). We reprint an essay that appeared in* The New York Times Magazine *in 1994.*

Just Take Away Their Guns

The president wants still tougher gun control legislation and thinks it will work. The public supports more gun control laws but suspects they won't work. The public is right.

Legal restraints on the lawful purchase of guns will have little effect on the illegal use of guns. There are some 200 million guns in private ownership, about one-third of them handguns. Only about 2 percent of the latter are employed to commit crimes. It would take a Draconian, and politically impossible, confiscation of legally purchased guns to make much of a difference in the number used by criminals. Moreover, only about one-sixth of the handguns used by serious criminals are purchased from a gun shop or pawnshop. Most of these handguns are stolen, borrowed or obtained through private purchases that wouldn't be affected by gun laws.

What is worse, any successful effort to shrink the stock of legally purchased guns (or of ammunition) would reduce the capacity of law-abiding people to defend themselves. Gun control advocates scoff at the importance of self-defense, but they are wrong to do so. Based on a household survey, Gary Kleck, a criminologist at Florida State University, has estimated that every year, guns are used—that is, displayed or fired—for defensive purposes more than a million times, not counting their use by the police. If his estimate is correct, this means that the number of people who defend themselves with a gun exceeds the number of arrests for violent crimes and burglaries.

The available evidence supports the claim that self-defense is a   4
legitimate form of deterrence. People who report to the National Crime
Survey that they defended themselves with a weapon were less likely
to lose property in a robbery or be injured in an assault than those who
did not defend themselves. Statistics have shown that would-be bur-
glars are threatened by gun-wielding victims about as many times a
year as they are arrested (and much more often than they are sent to
prison) and that the chances of a burglar being shot are about the same
as his chances of going to jail. Criminals know these facts even if gun
control advocates do not and so are less likely to burgle occupied
homes in America than occupied ones in Europe, where the residents
rarely have guns.

Some gun control advocates may concede these points but rejoin
that the cost of self-defense is self-injury: Handgun owners are more
likely to shoot themselves or their loved ones than a criminal. Not
quite. Most gun accidents involve rifles and shotguns, not handguns.
Moreover, the rate of fatal gun accidents has been declining while the
level of gun ownership has been rising. There are fatal gun accidents
just as there are fatal car accidents, but in fewer than 2 percent of the
gun fatalities was the victim someone mistaken for an intruder.

Those who urge us to forbid or severely restrict the sale of guns
ignore these facts. Worse, they adopt a position that is politically
absurd. In effect, they say, "Your government, having failed to protect
your person and your property from criminal assault, now intends to
deprive you of the opportunity to protect yourself."

Opponents of gun control make a different mistake. The National
Rifle Association and its allies tell us that "guns don't kill, people kill"
and urge the Government to punish more severely people who use
guns to commit crimes. Locking up criminals does protect society from
future crimes, and the prospect of being locked up may deter criminals.
But our experience with meting out tougher sentences is mixed. The
tougher the prospective sentence the less likely it is to be imposed, or at
least to be imposed swiftly. If the Legislature adds on time for crimes
committed with a gun, prosecutors often bargain away the add-ons;
even when they do not, the judges in many states are reluctant to
impose add-ons.

Worse, the presence of a gun can contribute to the magnitude of the   8
crime even on the part of those who worry about serving a long prison
sentence. Many criminals carry guns not to rob stores but to protect
themselves from other armed criminals. Gang violence has become
more threatening to bystanders as gang members have begun to arm
themselves. People may commit crimes, but guns make some crimes
worse. Guns often convert spontaneous outbursts of anger into fatal
encounters. When some people carry them on the streets, others will

want to carry them to protect themselves, and an urban arms race will be underway.

Our goal should not be the disarming of law-abiding citizens. It should be to reduce the number of people who carry guns unlawfully, especially in places—on streets, in taverns—where the mere presence of a gun can increase the hazards we all face. The most effective way to reduce illegal gun-carrying is to encourage the police to take guns away from people who carry them without a permit. This means encouraging the police to make street frisks.

The Fourth Amendment to the Constitution bans "unreasonable searches and seizures." In 1968 the Supreme Court decided (*Terry v. Ohio*) that a frisk—patting down a person's outer clothing—is proper if the officer has a "reasonable suspicion" that the person is armed and dangerous. If a pat-down reveals an object that might be a gun, the officer can enter the suspect's pocket to remove it. If the gun is being carried illegally, the suspect can be arrested.

The reasonable-suspicion test is much less stringent than the probable-cause standard the police must meet in order to make an arrest. A reasonable suspicion, however, is more than just a hunch; it must be supported by specific facts. The courts have held, not always consistently, that these facts include someone acting in a way that leads an experienced officer to conclude criminal activity may be afoot; someone fleeing at the approach of an officer; a person who fits a drug courier profile; a motorist stopped for a traffic violation who has a suspicious bulge in his pocket; a suspect identified by a reliable informant as carrying a gun. The Supreme Court has also upheld frisking people on probation or parole.

Some police departments frisk a lot of people, but usually the police frisk rather few, at least for the purpose of detecting illegal guns. In 1992 the police arrested about 240,000 people for illegally possessing or carrying a weapon. This is only about one-fourth as many as were arrested for public drunkenness. The average police officer will make *no* weapons arrests and confiscate *no* guns during any given year. Mark Moore, a professor of public policy at Harvard University, found that most weapons arrests were made because a citizen complained, not because the police were out looking for guns. 12

It is easy to see why. Many cities suffer from a shortage of officers, and even those with ample law-enforcement personnel worry about having their cases thrown out for constitutional reasons or being accused of police harassment. But the risk of violating the Constitution or engaging in actual, as opposed to perceived, harassment can be substantially reduced.

Each patrol officer can be given a list of people on probation or parole who live on that officer's beat and be rewarded for making frequent stops to insure that they are not carrying guns. Officers can be trained to recognize the kinds of actions that the Court will accept as providing the "reasonable suspicion" necessary for a stop and frisk. Membership in a gang known for assaults and drug dealing could be made the basis, by statute or Court precedent, for gun frisks.

And modern science can be enlisted to help. Metal detectors at airports have reduced the number of airplane bombings and skyjackings to nearly zero. But these detectors only work at very close range. What is needed is a device that will enable the police to detect the presence of a large lump of metal someone's pocket from a distance of 10 or 15 feet. Receiving such a signal could supply the officer with reasonable grounds for a pat-down. Underemployed nuclear physicists and electronics engineers in the post-cold-war era surely have the talents for designing a better gun detector.

Even if we do all these things, there will still be complaints. Inno-   16
cent people will be stopped. Young black and Hispanic men will probably be stopped more often than older white Anglo males or women of any race. But if we are serious about reducing drive-by shootings, fatal gang wars and lethal quarrels in public places, we must get illegal guns off the street. We cannot do this by multiplying the forms one fills out at gun shops or by pretending that guns are not a problem until a criminal uses one.

Topics for Critical Thinking and Discussion

1. What is Wilson's thesis? Where does he state it?
2. In paragraph 6 Wilson offers a summary of the position of those who support severe restrictions on the sale of guns. How accurate do you think his summary is? Explain.
3. In his final paragraph Wilson recognizes that his proposal, if implemented, will cause some difficulties—will in some ways be unfair—but he brushes the difficulties or unfairnesses aside. Are you equally willing to brush them aside? Explain.
4. In a paragraph, characterize Wilson's style. Support your view with specific references or quotations.

Byron R. White

In January 1985 a majority of the United States Supreme Court, in a case called New Jersey
v. T.L.O. *(a student's initials), ruled six to three that a school official's search of a student suspected of disobeying a school regulation does not violate the Fourth Amendment's protection
against unreasonable searches and seizures.*

*The case originated thus: an assistant principal in a New Jersey high school opened the
purse of a fourteen-year-old girl who had been caught violating school rules by smoking in
the lavatory. The girl denied that she ever smoked, and the assistant principal thought that
the contents of her purse would show whether or not she was lying. The purse was found to
contain cigarettes, marijuana, and some notes that seemed to indicate that she sold marijuana to other students. The school then called the police.*

*The case went through three lower courts; almost five years after the event occurred,
the case reached the Supreme Court Associate. Justice Byron R. White wrote the majority
opinion, joined by Chief Justice Warren E. Burger and by Associate Justices Lewis F. Powell, Jr.,
William H. Rehnquist, and Sandra Day O'Connor. Associate Justice Harry A. Blackmun con-
curred in a separate opinion. Associate Justices William J. Brennan, Jr., John Paul Stevens, and
Thurgood Marshall dissented in part.*

The Majority Opinion of the Supreme Court in *New Jersey v. T.L.O* [On the Right to Search Students]

In determining whether the search at issue in this case violated the Fourth Amendment, we are faced initially with the question
whether that amendment's prohibition on unreasonable searches and
seizures applies to searches conducted by public school officials. We
hold that it does.

It is now beyond dispute that "the Federal Constitution, by virtue
of the 14th Amendment, prohibits unreasonable searches and seizures
by state officers." Equally indisputable is the proposition that the 14th
Amendment protects the rights of students against encroachment by
public school officials.

On reargument, however, the State of New Jersey has argued that
the history of the Fourth Amendment indicates that the amendment
was intended to regulate only searches and seizures carried out by law
enforcement officers; accordingly, although public school officials are
concededly state agents for purposes of the 14th Amendment, the
Fourth Amendment creates no rights enforceable against them.

But this Court has never limited the amendment's prohibition on
unreasonable searches and seizures to operations conducted by the
police. Rather, the Court has long spoken of the Fourth Amendment's
strictures as restraints imposed upon "governmental action"—that is,
"upon the activities of sovereign authority." Accordingly, we have held

4

the Fourth Amendment applicable to the activities of civil as well as criminal authorities: building inspectors, OSHA inspectors, and even firemen entering privately owned premises to battle a fire, are all subject to the restraints imposed by the Fourth Amendment.

Notwithstanding the general applicability of the Fourth Amendment to the activities of civil authorities, a few courts have concluded that school officials are exempt from the dictates of the Fourth Amendment by virtue of the special nature of their authority over schoolchildren. Teachers and school administrators, it is said, act *in loco parentis* [i.e., in place of a parent] in their dealings with students: their authority is that of the parent, not the State, and is therefore not subject to the limits of the Fourth Amendment.

Such reasoning is in tension with contemporary reality and the teachings of this Court. We have held school officials subject to the commands of the First Amendment, and the Due Process Clause of the 14th Amendment. If school authorities are state actors for purposes of the constitutional guarantees of freedom of expression and due process, it is difficult to understand why they should be deemed to be exercising parental rather than public authority when conducting searches of their students.

In carrying out searches and other disciplinary functions pursuant to such policies, school officials act as representatives of the State, not merely as surrogates for the parents, and they cannot claim the parents' immunity from the strictures of the Fourth Amendment.

To hold that the Fourth Amendment applies to searches conducted   8 by school authorities is only to begin the inquiry into the standards governing such searches. Although the underlying command of the Fourth. Amendment is always that searches and seizures be reasonable, what is reasonable depends on the context within which a search takes place.

[Standard of Reasonableness]

The determination of the standard of reasonableness governing any specific class of searches requires balancing the need to search against the invasion which the search entails. On one side of the balance are arrayed the individual's legitimate expectations of privacy and personal security; on the other, the government's need for effective methods to deal with breaches of public order.

We have recognized that even a limited search of the person is a substantial invasion of privacy. A search of a child's person or of a closed purse or other bag carried on her person, no less than a similar search carried out on an adult, is undoubtedly a severe violation of subjective expectations of privacy.

Of course, the Fourth Amendment does not protect subjective expectations of privacy that are unreasonable or otherwise "illegitimate." The State of New Jersey has argued that because of the pervasive supervision to which children in the schools are necessarily subject, a child has virtually no legitimate expectation of privacy in articles of personal property "unnecessarily" carried into a school. This argument has two factual premises: (1) the fundamental incompatibility of expectations of privacy with the maintenance of a sound educational environment; and (2) the minimal interest of the child in bringing any items of personal property into the school. Both premises are severely flawed.

Although this Court may take notice of the difficulty of maintaining   12
discipline in the public schools today, the situation is not so dire that students in the schools may claim no legitimate expectations of privacy.

[Privacy and Discipline]

Against the child's interest in privacy must be set the substantial interest of teachers and administrators in maintaining discipline in the classroom and on school grounds. Maintaining order in the classroom has never been easy, but in recent years, school disorder has often taken particularly ugly forms; drug use and violent crime in the schools have become major social problems. Accordingly, we have recognized that maintaining security and order in the schools requires a certain degree of flexibility in school disciplinary procedures, and we have respected the value of preserving the informality of the student-teacher relationship.

How, then, should we strike the balance between the schoolchild's legitimate expectations of privacy and the school's equally legitimate need to maintain an environment in which learning can take place? It is evident that the school setting requires some easing of the restrictions to which searches by public authorities are ordinarily subject. The warrant requirement, in particular, is unsuited to the school environment; requiring a teacher to obtain a warrant before searching a child suspected of an infraction of school rules (or of the criminal law) would unduly interfere with the maintenance of the swift and informal disciplinary procedures needed in the schools. We hold today that school officials need not obtain a warrant before searching a student who is under their authority.

The school setting also requires some modification of the level of suspicion of illicit activity needed to justify a search. Ordinarily, a search—even one that may permissibly be carried out without a warrant—must be based upon "probable cause" to believe that a violation of the law has occurred. However, "probable cause" is not an irreducible requirement of a valid search.

[Balancing of Interests]

The fundamental command of the Fourth Amendment is that searches   16
and seizures be reasonable, and although "both the concept of probable cause and the requirement of a warrant bear on the reasonableness of a

search, . . . in certain limited circumstances neither is required." Thus, we have in a number of cases recognized the legality of searches and seizures based on suspicions that, although "reasonable," do not rise to the level of probable cause. Where a careful balancing of governmental and private interests suggests that the public interest is best served by a Fourth Amendment standard of reasonableness that stops short of probable cause, we have not hesitated to adopt such a standard.

We join the majority of courts that have examined this issue in concluding that the accommodation of the privacy interests of school-children with the substantial need of teachers and administrators for freedom to maintain order in the schools does not require strict adherence to the requirement that searches be based on probable cause to believe that the subject of the search has violated or is violating the law.

Rather, the legality of a search of a student should depend simply on the reasonableness, under all the circumstances, of the search. Determining the reasonableness of any search involves a twofold inquiry; first, one must consider "whether the . . . action was justified at its inception," second, one must determine whether the search as actually conducted "was reasonably related in scope to the circumstances which justified the interference in the first place."

Under ordinary circumstances, a search of a student by a teacher or other school official will be "justified at its inception" when there are reasonable grounds for suspecting that the search will turn up evidence that the student has violated or is violating either the law or the rules of the school. Such a search will be permissible in its scope when the measures adopted are reasonably related to the objectives of the search and not excessively intrusive in light of the age and sex of the student and the nature of the infraction.

This standard will, we trust, neither unduly burden the efforts of   20
school authorities to maintain order in their schools nor authorize unrestrained intrusions upon the privacy of schoolchildren. By focusing attention on the question of reasonableness, the standard will spare teachers and school administrators the necessity of schooling themselves in the niceties of probable cause and permit them to regulate their conduct according to the dictates of reason and common sense. At the same time, the reasonableness standard should insure that the interests of students will be invaded no more than is necessary to achieve the legitimate end of preserving order in the schools.

There remains the question of the legality of the search in this case. We recognize that the "reasonable grounds" standard applied by the New Jersey Supreme Court in its consideration of this question is not substantially different from the standard that we have adopted today. Nonetheless, we believe that the New Jersey court's application of that standard to strike down the search of T.L.O.'s purse reflects a somewhat crabbed notion of reasonableness. Our review of the facts surrounding the search leads us to conclude that the search was in no sense unreasonable for Fourth Amendment purposes. [End of majority opinion][1]

John Paul Stevens

Dissent in the Case of *New Jersey v. T.L.O.*

The majority holds that "a search of a student by a teacher or other school official will be 'justified at its inception' when there are reasonable grounds for suspecting that the search will turn up evidence *that the student has violated or is violating either the law or the rules of the school.*"

This standard will permit teachers and school administrators to search students when they suspect that the search will reveal evidence of [violation of] even the most trivial school regulation or precatory guideline for students' behavior. For the Court, a search for curlers and sunglasses in order to enforce the school dress code is apparently just as important as a search for evidence of heroin addiction or violent gang activity.

A standard better attuned to this concern would permit teachers and school administrators to search a student when they have reason to believe that the search will uncover *evidence that the student is violating the law or engaging in conduct that is seriously disruptive of school order or the educational process.*

A standard that varies the extent of the permissible intrusion with   4
the gravity of the suspected offense is also more consistent with common-law experience and this Court's precedent. Criminal law has traditionally recognized a distinction between essentially regulatory offenses and serious violations of the peace, and graduated the response of the criminal justice system depending on the character of the violation.

Topics for Critical Thinking and Writing

1. In the majority opinion Justice White says (paragraph 14) that it is "evident that the school setting requires some easing of the restrictions to which searches by public authorities are ordinarily subject." Does White

---

[1]Questions on this selection at the bottom of this page.

offer evidence supporting what he says is "evident"? List the evidence, if you can find it in White, or if you can think of any.

2. In paragraph 20 Justice White writes of a "reasonableness standard." What does he mean by this phrase? (See paragraphs 18–20.)

3. Considering your own experience of school life as well as the arguments of Justice White and Justice Stevens, do you, on the whole, agree with the majority decision or with the dissent? What, in your opinion, are the chief issues? Explain.

4. Some forty years before this case, Justice Robert H. Jackson argued that the schools have a special responsibility for adhering to the Constitution: "That they are educating the young for citizenship is reason for scrupulous protection of constitutional freedoms of the individual, if we are not to strangle the free mind at its source and teach youth to discount important principles of our government as mere platitudes." Similarly, in 1967, in an analogous case involving another female pupil, Justice Brennan argued that "The lesson the school authorities taught her that day will undoubtedly make a greater impression than the one her teacher had hoped to convey. . . . Schools cannot expect their students to learn the lessons of good citizenship when the school authorities themselves disregard the fundamental principles underpinning our constitutional freedoms." Do you find these arguments compelling? Why or why not?

Derek Bok

Derek Bok was born in 1930 in Bryn Mawr, Pennsylvania, and was educated at Stanford and Harvard, where he received a law degree. He taught law at Harvard, then served as dean of the law school, and held the office of president of Harvard from 1971 to 1991. The essay that we give here was published in a Boston newspaper, prompted by the display of Confederate flags hung from the window of a dormitory room.

Protecting Freedom of Expression on the Campus

For several years, universities have been struggling with the problem of trying to reconcile the rights of free speech with the desire to avoid racial tension. In recent weeks, such a controversy has sprung up at Harvard. Two students hung Confederate flags in public view, upsetting students who equate the Confederacy with slavery. A third student tried to protest the flags by displaying a swastika.

These incidents have provoked much discussion and disagreement. Some students have urged that Harvard require the removal of symbols that offend many members of the community. Others reply that such symbols are a form of free speech and should be protected.

Different universities have resolved similar conflicts in different ways. Some have enacted codes to protect their communities from forms of speech that are deemed to be insensitive to the feelings of other groups. Some have refused to impose such restrictions.

It is important to distinguish between the appropriateness of such   4 communications and their status under the First Amendment. The fact that speech is protected by the First Amendment does not necessarily mean that it is right, proper, or civil. I am sure that the vast majority of Harvard students believe that hanging a Confederate flag in public view—or displaying a swastika in response—is insensitive and unwise because any satisfaction it gives to the students who display these symbols is far outweighed by the discomfort it causes to many others.

I share this view and regret that the students involved saw fit to behave in this fashion. Whether or not they merely wished to manifest their pride in the South—or to demonstrate the insensitivity of hanging Confederate flags by mounting another offensive symbol in return— they must have known that they would upset many fellow students and ignore the decent regard for the feelings of others so essential to building and preserving a strong and harmonious community.

To disapprove of a particular form of communication, however, is not enough to justify prohibiting it. We are faced with a clear example of the conflict between our commitment to free speech and our desire to foster a community founded on mutual respect. Our society has wrestled with this problem for many years. Interpreting the First Amendment, the Supreme Court has clearly struck the balance in favor of free speech.

While communities do have the right to regulate speech in order to uphold aesthetic standards (avoiding defacement of buildings) or to protect the public from disturbing noise, rules of this kind must be applied across the board and cannot be enforced selectively to prohibit certain kinds of messages but not others.

Under the Supreme Court's rulings, as I read them, the display of   8 swastikas or Confederate flags clearly falls within the protection of the free-speech clause of the First Amendment and cannot be forbidden simply because it offends the feelings of many members of the community. These rulings apply to all agencies of government, including public universities.

Although it is unclear to what extent the First Amendment is enforceable against private institutions, I have difficulty understanding why a university such as Harvard should have less free speech than the surrounding society—or than a public university.

One reason why the power of censorship is so dangerous is that it is extremely difficult to decide when a particular communication is offensive enough to warrant prohibition or to weigh the degree of offensiveness against the potential value of the communication. If we begin to forbid flags, it is only a short step to prohibiting offensive speakers.

I suspect that no community will become humane and caring by restricting what its members can say. The worst offenders will simply find other ways to irritate and insult.

In addition, once we start to declare certain things "offensive," with   12
all the excitement and attention that will follow, I fear that much ingenuity will be exerted trying to test the limits, much time will be expanded trying to draw tenuous distinctions, and the resulting publicity will
eventually attract more attention to the offensive material than would
ever have occurred otherwise.

Rather than prohibit such communications, with all the resulting
risks, it would be better to ignore them, since students would then have
little reason to create such displays and would soon abandon them. If
this response is not possible—and one can understand why—the wisest
course is to speak with those who perform insensitive acts and try to
help them understand the effects of their actions on others.

Appropriate officials and faculty members should take the lead, as
the Harvard House Masters have already done in this case. In talking
with students, they should seek to educate and persuade, rather than
resort to ridicule or intimidation, recognizing that only persuasion is
likely to produce a lasting, beneficial effect. Through such effects, I
believe that we act in the manner most consistent with our ideals as an
educational institution and most calculated to help us create a truly
understanding, supportive community.

Topics for Critical Thinking and Writing

1. In paragraph 8 Bok argues that "the display of swastikas or of Confed-
    erate flags clearly falls within the free-speech clause of the First
    Amendment and cannot be forbidden simply because it offends the
    feelings of many members of the community." Suppose someone
    replied thus: "The display of swastikas or of Confederate flags—sym-
    bols loaded with meaning—is, to a Jew or an African-American, at
    least equivalent to a slap in the face. Such a display is, in short, an act
    of violence." What would you reply, and how would you support your
    response?
2. Do you find Bok persuasive? Support your answer with evidence about
    the points of his argument and his techniques of argument.
3. What rules, if any, does your school have concerning limitations of
    speech? What rules, if any, would you propose?
4. Compare Bok with Hawley (page 544) on reasons for and against limi-
    tations on students' freedom of speech.

Edward I. Koch

Edward I. Koch, born in 1924 in New York City, was educated at City College and at New York University Law School. Active in Democratic politics, Mr. Koch served as mayor of New York from 1978 to 1989. This essay appeared in The New Republic, *a publication that usually has a liberal slant.*

Death and Justice: How Capital Punishment Affirms Life

Last December a man named Robert Lee Willie, who had been convicted of raping and murdering an 18-year-old woman, was executed in the Louisiana state prison. In a statement issued several minutes before his death, Mr. Willie said: "Killing people is wrong. . . . It makes no difference whether it's citizens, countries, or governments. Killing is wrong." Two weeks later in South Carolina, an admitted killer named Joseph Carl Shaw was put to death for murdering two teenagers. In an appeal to the governor for clemency, Mr. Shaw wrote: "Killing is wrong when I did it. Killing is wrong when you do it. I hope you have the courage and moral strength to stop the killing."

It is a curiosity of modern life that we find ourselves being lectured on morality by cold-blooded killers. Mr. Willie previously had been convicted of aggravated rape, aggravated kidnapping, and the murders of a Louisiana deputy and a man from Missouri. Mr. Shaw committed another murder a week before the two for which he was executed, and admitted mutilating the body of the 14-year-old girl he killed. I can't help wondering what prompted these murderers to speak out against killing as they entered the death-house door. Did their newfound reverence for life stem from the realization that they were about to lose their own?

Life is indeed precious, and I believe the death penalty helps to affirm this fact. Had the death penalty been a real possibility in the minds of these murderers, they might well have stayed their hand. They might have shown moral awareness before their victims died, and not after. Consider the tragic death of Rosa Velez, who happened to be home when a man named Luis Vera burglarized her apartment in Brooklyn. "Yeah, I shot her," Vera admitted. "She knew me, and I knew I wouldn't go to the chair."

During my 22 years in public service, I have heard the pros and cons of capital punishment expressed with special intensity. As a district leader, councilman, congressman, and mayor, I have represented constituencies generally thought of as liberal. Because I support the death penalty for heinous crimes of murder, I have sometimes been the subject of emotional and outraged attacks by voters who find my position reprehensible or worse. I have listened to their ideas. I have

4

weighed their objections carefully. I still support the death penalty. The reasons I maintain my position can be best understood by examining the arguments most frequently heard in opposition.

1. *The death penalty is "barbaric."* Sometimes opponents of capital punishment horrify with tales of lingering death on the gallows, of faulty electric chairs, or of agony in the gas chamber. Partly in response to such protests, several states such as North Carolina and Texas switched to execution by lethal injection. The condemned person is put to death painlessly, without ropes, voltage, bullets, or gas. Did this answer the objections of death penalty opponents? Of course not. On June 22, 1984, *The New York Times* published an editorial that sarcastically attacked the new "hygienic" method of death by injection, and stated that "execution can never be made humane through science." So it's not the method that really troubles opponents. It's the death itself they consider barbaric.

Admittedly, capital punishment is not a pleasant topic. However, one does not have to like the death penalty in order to support it any more than one must like radical surgery, radiation, or chemotherapy in order to find necessary these attempts at curing cancer. Ultimately we may learn how to cure cancer with a simple pill. Unfortunately, that day has not yet arrived. Today we are faced with the choice of letting the cancer spread or trying to cure it with the methods available, methods that one day will almost certainly be considered barbaric. But to give up and do nothing would be far more barbaric and would certainly delay the discovery of an eventual cure. The analogy between cancer and murder is imperfect, because murder is not the "disease" we are trying to cure. The disease is injustice. We may not like the death penalty, but it must be available to punish crimes of cold-blooded murder, cases in which any other form of punishment would be inadequate and, therefore, unjust. If we create a society in which injustice is not tolerated, incidents of murder—the most flagrant form of injustice—will diminish.

2. *No other major democracy uses the death penalty.* No other major democracy—in fact, few other countries of any description—are plagued by a murder rate such as that in the United States. Fewer and fewer Americans can remember the days when unlocked doors were the norm and murder was a rare and terrible offense. In America the murder rate climbed 122 percent between 1963 and 1980. During that same period, the murder rate in New York City increased by almost 400 percent, and the statistics are even worse in many other cities. A study at M.I.T. showed that based on 1970 homicide rates a person who lived in a large American city ran a greater risk of being murdered than an American soldier in World War II ran of being killed in combat. It is not surprising that the laws of each country differ according to differing conditions and traditions. If other countries had our murder problem,

the cry for capital punishment would be just as loud as it is here. And I daresay that any other major democracy where 75 percent of the people supported the death penalty would soon enact it into law.

3. *An innocent person might be executed by mistake.* Consider the work   8
of Hugo Adam Bedau, one of the most implacable foes of capital punishment in this country. According to Mr. Bedau, it is "false sentimentality to argue that the death penalty should be abolished because of the abstract possibility that an innocent person might be executed." He cites a study of the 7,000 executions in this country from 1893 to 1971, and concludes that the record fails to show that such cases occur. The main point, however, is this. If government functioned only when the possibility of error didn't exist, government wouldn't function at all. Human life deserves special protection, and one of the best ways to guarantee that protection is to assure that convicted murderers do not kill again. Only the death penalty can accomplish this end. In a recent case in New Jersey, a man named Richard Biegenwald was freed from prison after serving 18 years for murder; since his release he has been convicted of committing four murders. A prisoner named Lemuel Smith, who while serving four life sentences for murder (plus two life sentences for kidnapping and robbery) in New York's Green Haven Prison, lured a woman corrections officer into the chaplain's office and strangled her. He then mutilated and dismembered her body. An additional life sentence for Smith is meaningless. Because New York has no death penalty statute, Smith has effectively been given a license to kill.

But the problem of multiple murder is not confined to the nation's penitentiaries. In 1981, 91 police officers were killed in the line of duty in this country. Seven percent of those arrested in the cases that have been solved had a previous arrest for murder. In New York City in 1976 and 1977, 85 persons arrested for homicide had a previous arrest for murder. Six of these individuals had two previous arrests for murder, and one had four previous murder arrests. During those two years the New York police were arresting for murder persons with a previous arrest for murder on the average of one every 8.5 days. This is not surprising when we learn that in 1975, for example, the median time served in Massachusetts for homicide was less than two-and-a-half years. In 1976 a study sponsored by the Twentieth Century Fund found that the average time served in the United States for first-degree murder is ten years. The median time served may be considerably lower.

4. *Capital punishment cheapens the value of human life.* On the contrary, it can be easily demonstrated that the death penalty strengthens the value of human life. If the penalty for rape were lowered, clearly it would signal a lessened regard for the victims' suffering, humiliation, and personal integrity. It would cheapen their horrible experience, and expose them to an increased danger of recurrence. When we lower the penalty for murder, it signals a lessened regard for the value of the victim's life. Some critics of capital punishment, such as columnist Jimmy

Breslin, have suggested that a life sentence is actually a harsher penalty for murder than death. This is sophistic nonsense. A few killers may decide not to appeal a death sentence, but the overwhelming majority make every effort to stay alive. It is by exacting the highest penalty for the taking of human life that we affirm the highest value of human life.

5. *The death penalty is applied in a discriminatory manner.* This factor no longer seems to be the problem it once was. The appeals process for a condemned prisoner is lengthy and painstaking. Every effort is made to see that the verdict and sentence were fairly arrived at. However, assertions of discrimination are not an argument for ending the death penalty but for extending it. It is not justice to exclude everyone from the penalty of the law if a few are found to be so favored. Justice requires that the law be applied equally to all.

6. *Thou Shalt Not Kill.* The Bible is our greatest source of moral inspiration. Opponents of the death penalty frequently cite the sixth of the Ten Commandments in an attempt to prove that capital punishment is divinely proscribed. In the original Hebrew, however, the Sixth Commandment reads, 'Thou Shalt Not Commit Murder,' and the Torah specifies capital punishment for a variety of offenses. The biblical viewpoint has been upheld by philosophers throughout history. The greatest thinkers of the 19th century—Kant, Locke, Hobbes, Rousseau, Montesquieu, and Mill—agreed that natural law properly authorizes the sovereign to take life in order to vindicate justice. Only Jeremy Bentham was ambivalent. Washington, Jefferson, and Franklin endorsed it. Abraham Lincoln authorized executions for deserters in wartime. Alexis de Tocqueville, who expressed profound respect for American institutions, believed that the death penalty was indispensable to the support of social order. The United States Constitution, widely admired as one of the seminal achievements in the history of humanity, condemns cruel and inhuman punishment, but does not condemn capital punishment.

7. *The death penalty is state-sanctioned murder.* This is the defense with which Messrs. Willie and Shaw hoped to soften the resolve of those who sentenced them to death. By saying in effect, "You're no better than I am," the murderer seeks to bring his accusers down to his own level. It is also a popular argument among opponents of capital punishment, but a transparently false one. Simply put, the state has rights that the private individual does not. In a democracy, those rights are given to the state by the electorate. The execution of a lawfully condemned killer is no more an act of murder than is legal imprisonment an act of kidnapping. If an individual forces a neighbor to pay him money under threat of punishment, it's called extortion. If the state does it, it's called taxation. Rights and responsibilities surrendered by the individual are what give the state its power to govern. This contract is the foundation of civilization itself.

Everyone wants his or her rights, and will defend them jealously. Not everyone, however, wants responsibilities, especially the painful responsibilities that come with law enforcement. Twenty-one years ago a woman named Kitty Genovese was assaulted and murdered on a street in New York. Dozens of neighbors heard her cries for help but did nothing to assist her. They didn't even call the police. In such a climate the criminal understandably grows bolder. In the presence of moral cowardice, he lectures us on our supposed failings and tries to equate his crimes with our quest for justice.

The death of anyone—even a convicted killer—diminishes us all. But we are diminished even more by a justice system that fails to function. It is an illusion to let ourselves believe that doing away with capital punishment removes the murderer's deed from our conscience. The rights of society are paramount. When we protect guilty lives, we give up innocent lives in exchange. When opponents of capital punishment say to the state: "I will not let you kill in my name," they are also saying to murderers: "You can kill in your *own* name as long as I have an excuse for not getting involved."

It is hard to imagine anything worse than being murdered while 16 neighbors do nothing. But something worse exists. When those same neighbors shrink back from justly punishing the murderer, the victim dies twice.

Topics for Critical Thinking and Writing

1. Koch is, of course, writing an argument. He wants to persuade his readers. Beginning with paragraph 5, he states the opposition's arguments and tries to refute them. But why did he include his first four paragraphs? What, as persuasion, does each contribute?
2. In paragraph 6, Koch compares our use of capital punishment to our use of "radical surgery, radiation, or chemotherapy." Do you find this analogy impressive—or not—and why? (Note that in this paragraph Koch goes on to say that "the analogy between cancer and murder is imperfect." Should he, then, not have used it?)
3. At the end of paragraph 6, Koch says: "If we create a society in which injustice is not tolerated, incidents of murder—the most flagrant form of injustice—will diminish." Has the earlier part of the paragraph prepared us for this statement?
4. Why, or why not, are you persuaded by Koch's second argument, about the likelihood that if other countries had high rates of murder they too would enact the death penalty?
5. In paragraph 9, Koch speaks of "murder" and then of "homicide." Are these two the same? If not, *why* is Koch bringing in statistics about homicide?
6. In paragraph 12, Koch lists authorities who supported the death penalty. Some of these—for instance, Washington and Jefferson—also owned slaves. What can be said in favor of or against Koch's use of these authorities?
7. In paragraph 15, Koch puts a sentence into the mouths of his opponents. *Is* this what his opponents are in effect saying or thinking?

8. If you have read Schwarzschild's remarks (the next essay) opposing capital punishment, below, write an essay indicating which essay you think is a better piece of persuasive writing. Note that it is not a matter of which position you subscribe to; in your essay you are concerned only with the essays as examples of persuasive writing.

Henry Schwarzschild

Henry Schwarzschild was the director of the National Coalition Against the Death Penalty. The material that we print is an excerpt from his statement submitted at the hearing in 1978 before the Subcommittee on Criminal Justice of the Committee on the Judiciary, House of Representatives, 95th Congress, 2nd Session.

In Opposition to Death Penalty Legislation

You know the classic arguments about the merits of the death penalty:

Its dubious and unproved value as a deterrent to violent crime;

The arbitrariness and mistakes inevitable in any system of justice instituted and administered by fallible human beings;

The persistent and ineradicable discrimination on grounds of race, class, and sex in its administration in our country's history (including the present time);

The degrading and hurtful impulse toward retribution and revenge that it expresses;

The barbarousness of its process (whether by burning at the stake, by hanging from the gallows, by frying in the electric chair, by suffocating in the gas chamber, by shooting at the hands of a firing squad, or by lethal injection with a technology designed to heal and save lives);

Even the deeply distorting and costly effect the death penalty has upon the administration of the courts, upon law enforcement, and upon the penal institutions of the country.

Let me therefore concentrate my remarks upon a few selected issues about which much unclarity exists in the public mind, in the media, and even in many legislative chambers.

I want to discuss these issues in the context of the evident support of public opinion for the reintroduction of capital punishment in the country. Let me be candid: For the past few years, public opinion polls, whether national or regional, have tended to reflect a substantial majority of the American people affirming their support for the death penalty, to the level of between 65 percent and 75 percent—enough to make many an elected official surrender his or her religious or moral principles against capital punishment. As little as twenty years ago, the polls reflected almost precisely the opposite distribution of views in the country. It is not hard to infer what has turned the American people back toward support of so atavistic and demonstrably useless a criminal sanction. The causes are (a) the rising rate of violent crime in the past two decades, (b) the increasing panic about the rising crime rate, together with a justified (as well as exaggerated) fear for the safety of lives and property, (c) the understandable reaction to a terrible series of assassinations and attempted assassinations of our national leaders and other prominent personalities (President John Kennedy, Senator Robert Kennedy, the Rev. Dr. Martin Luther King Jr., Governor George Wallace, Malcolm X, Medgar Evers, and others), (d) the rise of international terrorism, including aircraft hijackings and the murder of prominent political and business leaders as well as the random political killings of innocent victims, (e) many years of the effective discontinuation of capital punishment and the remoteness from actual experience of its horrors, and finally (f) a largely subliminal but sometimes almost articulated racism that attributes most violent criminality to the minority community, that knows quite well that the poor and the black are most often the subjects of the death penalty, and that thinks that's just the way it ought to be.

What, then, are the rational answers to this series of partly understandable and partly impermissible misconceptions in the American public?   4

True, violent crime has risen sharply in the past two decades, but to begin with it has been abundantly demonstrated by social research that the availability of the death penalty has no effect whatsoever upon the rate of violent crime; to the contrary, there is some scientific evidence that death sentences imposed and carried out may, for peculiar reasons of social and psychic pathology, be an incentive to further acts of violence in the society. Furthermore, while the rates of most major, violent felonies have been rising—most probably by reason of increased urbanization, social mobility, economic distress, and the like—the rate of non-negligent homicide has been rising at a rate *slower* than the other major felonies, and non-negligent homicide is, of course, the only crime for which the death penalty has been declared constitutionally permissible by the Supreme Court. The crisis in violent crime, such as it is, has therefore been least acute in the area of homicide. Indeed, in the past three years, the murder rate in this country has actually been declining. Thirdly, there is an appalling number of about 20,000 non-negligent homicides in this country per year. But we would have to return to the condition of the mid–1950s to execute as many as one hundred persons per year, and even that would constitute only one in every two hundred murderers. In other words, we have always picked quite arbitrarily a tiny handful of people among those convicted of murder to be executed, not those who have committed the most heinous, the most revolting, the most destructive murders, but always the poor, the black, the friendless, the life's losers, those without competent, private attorneys, the illiterate, those despised or ignored by the community for reasons having nothing to do with their crime. Ninety-nine and one-half percent of all murderers were never executed—and the deterrent value (which very likely does not exist at all in any case) is reduced to invisibility by the overwhelming likelihood that one will not be caught, or not be prosecuted, or not be tried on a capital charge, or not be convicted, or not be sentenced to death, or have the conviction or sentence reversed on appeal, or have one's sentence commuted.

And if we took the other course and eliminated those high chances of not being executed, but rather carried out the death penalty for every murder, then we should be executing 400 persons per week, every week of the month, every month of the year—and that, Mr. Chairman, should strike even the most ardent supporters of the death penalty as a bloodbath, not as a civilized system of criminal justice.

Assassinations and terrorism are well known to be undeterrable by the threat of the death penalty. They are acts of political desperation or political insanity, always committed by people who are at least willing, if not eager, to be martyrs to their cause. Nor would executing terrorists be a preventive against the subsequent taking of hostages for the purpose of setting political assassins or terrorists free. There would of course be a considerable interval of time between arrest and execution, at least for the purpose of trial and the accompanying processes of law, and during that time their fellow activists would have a far more urgent incentive for taking hostages, since not only the freedom but the very lives of their arrested and sentenced colleagues would be at stake. Let me only respectfully add that distinguished fellow citizens of ours such as Senator Edward Kennedy and Ms. Coretta King, who have suffered terrible sadness in their lives at the hands of assassins, are committed opponents of the death penalty.

There has been only one execution in the United States since 1967, [8] that of Gary Mark Gilmore, by a volunteer firing squad in Utah on January 17, 1977. Gilmore's execution troubled the public conscience less than it might have otherwise because of his own determination to die. The public and perhaps the legislators of our states and in the Congress have forgotten in a decade that was virtually without executions what sort of demoralizing and brutalizing spectacle executions are. There are now enough people on death row in the country to stage one execution each and every single day for more than a year, to say nothing of the other people who are liable to be sentenced to death during that time. We will again know the details of men crazed with fear, screaming like wounded animals, being dragged from the cell, against their desperate resistance, strapped into the electric chair, voiding their bowels and bladder, being burned alive, almost breaking the restraints from the impact of the high voltage, with their eyeballs popping out of their sockets, the smell of their burning flesh in the nostrils of the witnesses. The ghastly experience of men being hanged, their heads half torn off their bodies, or of the slow strangulation in the gas chamber, or of the press sticking their fingers into the bloody bullet holes of the chair in which Gilmore sat to be executed by rifles, or the use of forcible injection by a paralyzing agent—these reports will not ennoble the image of the United States of America that wants to be the defender of human rights and decency in a world that has largely given up the death penalty as archaic.

No one in this Committee surely is guilty of that shoddiest of all impulses toward capital punishment, namely the sense that white, middle-class people, irrespective of their crime, in fact hardly ever get sentenced to death and in such an extremely rare case are virtually never executed. You, Mr. Chairman and Members, and I and probably everyone in this hearing room are in fact absolutely immune, no matter what ghastly crime we might commit, from the likelihood of being executed for it. The penalty of death is imposed almost entirely upon members of what the distinguished social psychologist Kenneth B. Clark has referred to as "the lower status elements of American society."

Blacks have always constituted a dramatically disproportionate number of persons executed in the United States, far beyond their share of capital crimes, and even as we sit here today they represent half of the more than 500 persons on the death rows of our state prisons. Indeed, not only the race of the criminal is directly proportional to the likelihood of his being sentenced to death and executed but the race of the victim of the crime as well. The large majority of criminal homicides are still disasters between people who have some previous connection with each other (as husband and wife, parent and child, lovers, business associates, and the like), and murder is therefore still largely an intra-racial event, i.e. black on black or white on white. Yet while half the people under sentence of death right now are black (showing egregious discrimination on the grounds of the race of the murderer), about 85 percent of their victims were white.

In other words, it is far more likely to get the murderer into the electric chair or the gas chamber if he has killed a white person than if he had killed a black person, quite irrespective of his own race. (I say "he" in this context for good reason: the death penalty is also highly discriminatory on grounds of sex. Of the 380 death-row inmates in the country today, only two are women, and even they are far more likely objects of executive commutation of their death sentences than their male counterparts.)

Let me add here that, to the extent to which fear of crime and greater exposure to it, combined with inadequate police protection and more callous jurisprudence, has made the minority communities also voice increasing support for the death penalty, they have not yet fully realized that the death penalty will not protect them from what they (and all of us) rightly fear but that their support of capital punishment will only put their brothers and husbands and sons in jeopardy of being killed by the same state that has been unable properly to protect their lives, their rights, or their property to begin with.

In sum: The public is deeply uninformed about the real social facts of the death penalty and is responding to the seemingly insoluble problem of crime by a retreat to the hope that an even more severe criminal penalty will stem the tide of violence. But it will not. We do not know what will. Judges and lawyers do not know, philosophers and criminologists don't, not even civil libertarians or legislators know the answer—if any of us did, we would have long since accomplished our purpose of reducing crime to the irreducible minimum. But legislators are not therefore entitled to suborn illusory solutions merely because they would garner widespread though uninformed public approval, in order to signal to the electorate that they are "tough on crime." Capital punishment does not deal with crime in any useful fashion and in fact deludes the public into an entirely false sense of greater security about that complex social problem. The death penalty is a legislative way of avoiding rather than dealing with the problem of crime, and the American public will come to learn this very dramatically and tragically if the Congress should unwisely enact the bill before you today.

Two final words about public support for the death penalty.

There are strong indications that the public in great numbers answers in the affirmative when asked whether they support capital punishment because they want a death penalty law on the books in the hope that this threat will deter criminals from committing violent crimes. Many, perhaps most, of the people who support the enactment of the death penalty do not want executions and would be horrified at being asked to sentence a living human being to a premeditated, ceremonial, legally sanctioned killing. They want deterrence, not electrocutions; prevention, not lethal injections; safety, not firing squads. But a reenactment by this Congress of a federal death penalty statute will give them at best only electrocutions or lethal injections or firing squads, but neither deterrence nor crime prevention nor safety from violence.

The last stand of supporters for the death penalty, when all the other arguments have been rebutted or met, is that of retribution or revenge, the proposition that a murderer has forfeited his life and that we should kill him as an act of abstract equity, irrespective of whether executions serve any social purpose whatsoever. We do not need to preach to each other here this morning, but it is important to have it said once more that civilized societies have instituted systems of justice precisely in order to overcome private acts of retribution and revenge and that they have done so with the understanding that social necessity and social usefulness will be the guideposts of their punishments. Since there has never been and cannot be a showing of social usefulness or social necessity for capital punishment, the virtually unanimous voices of the religious community of our land, our leading thinkers and social analysts, in unison with enlightened opinion for hundreds, perhaps thousands, of years should guide your actions on this matter. Whatever the understandable, bitter, vengeful impulses might be of any of us who suffer the disastrous tragedy of having someone we love or respect murdered by pathological or cruel killers, the society's laws are written not to gratify those impulses but to channel them into helpful, healing, and life-sustaining directions. Gratifying the impulse for revenge is not the business of a government that espouses the humane and liberating ideas expressed in our Declaration of Independence and Constitution. It would be rather a return to the darkest instincts of mankind. It would be arrogating unto the state, unto government, either the god-like wisdom to judge who shall live and who shall die or else the totalitarian arrogance to make that judgment. We, as a nation, have foresworn that idolatry of the state that would justify either of these grounds for the legally sanctioned killing of our fellow citizens, of any human being, except perhaps in personal or national self-defense.

Mr. Chairman: The question before the country and before the Congress ultimately is whether it is the right of the state, with premeditation, with the long foreknowledge of the victim, under color of law, in the name of all of us, with great ceremony, and to the approval of many angry people in our land, to kill a fellow citizen, a fellow human being, to do that which we utterly condemn, which we utterly abhor in him for having done. What does the penalty, after all, say to the American people and to our children? That killing is all right if the right people do it and think they have a good enough reason for doing it! That is the rationale of every pathological murderer walking the street: he thinks he is the right person to do it and has a good reason for doing his destructive deed. How can a thoughtful and sensible person justify killing people who kill people to teach that killing is wrong? How can you avert your eyes from the obvious: that the death penalty and that executions in all their bloody and terrible reality only aggravate the deplorable atmosphere of violence, the disrespect for life, and brutalization of ourselves that we need to overcome?

If the death penalty were shown, or even could be shown, to be socially necessary or even useful, I would personally still have a deep objection to it. But those who argue for its re-enactment have not and cannot meet the burden of proving its necessity or usefulness. At the very least, before you kill a human being under law, do you not have to be absolutely certain that you are doing the right thing? But how can you be sure that the criminal justice system has worked with absolute accuracy in designating this single person to be the guilty one, that this single person is the one that should be killed, that killing him is the absolutely right thing to do? You cannot be sure, because human judgment and human institutions are demonstrably fallible. And you cannot kill a man when you are not absolutely sure. You can (indeed sometimes you must) make sure that he is incapacitated from repeating his crime, and we obviously accomplish that by ways other than killing him. And while there is fallibility there also, death is different: it is final, irreversible, barbarous, brutalizing to all who come into contact with it. That it is a very hurtful model for the United States to play in the world, it is a very hurtful model for a democratic and free government to play for its people.

Topics for Critical Thinking and Writing

1. In the first paragraph, what is Schwarzschild getting at when he says that administration of the death penalty has been discriminatory?
2. In paragraph 5 Schwarzschild points out that even when capital punishment was relatively common, "ninety-nine and one-half percent of all murderers were never executed," Assuming the truth of this statement, is it inherently unjust to execute the remaining half of one percent?
3. In paragraph 8 Schwarzschild briefly describes some of the horrible physical responses of persons about to be executed. If one believes that the death penalty serves a useful purpose as a deterrent, should one argue (against Schwarzschild) that executions ought to be televised, so that they would have a maximum effect as deterrents?
4. What is Schwarzschild's chief point in paragraph 16? What counterarguments can you imagine offering?
5. What is Schwarzschild's strategy in his next-to-last paragraph?
6. Evaluate Schwarzschild's final paragraph as a piece of persuasion.
7. If you have read Koch's essay (page 649), supporting the death penalty, indicate which of Koch's arguments, if any, Schwarzschild does not address.

Katha Pollitt

Katha Pollitt (b. 1949) often writes essays on literary, political, and social topics. She is also widely known as a poet; her first collection of poems, Antarctic Traveller *(1982), won the National Book Critics Circle Award for poetry.*

Checkbook Maternity: When Is a Mother Not a Mother?

To the small and curious class of English words that have double and contradictory meanings—"moot," for example, and "cleave"—the word "mother" can now be added. Within the space of a single dazzling week this fall, this hoary old noun was redefined so thoroughly, in such mutually exclusive ways, that what it means now depends on which edition of the newspaper you read.

On October 23, in Orange County, California, Superior Court Judge Richard Parslow decided that the rightful mother of Baby Boy Johnson was not Anna Johnson, the black "gestational surrogate" who, for $10,000, carried him and birthed him, but Crispina Calvert, the womb-less Asian-born woman who provided the egg from which, after in vitro fertilization with her (white) husband's sperm and implantation in Ms. Johnson, the baby grew. Declining, he said, to play Solomon[1] and put the baby in the "crazy-making" position of having "two mothers"—or to follow California law, which defines the mother as the woman who gives birth to the child—Judge Parslow ruled that genes make the mom, as they do the dad. Anna Johnson was merely a kind of foster mother, a "home," an "environment."

One wonders what Judge Parslow would make of a headline two days later. "Menopause Is Found No Bar to Pregnancy" announced *The New York Times*, reporting that doctors had succeeded in making six prematurely menopausal women pregnant by implanting each with donated eggs fertilized in vitro with her husband's sperm. By Judge Parslow's reasoning, of course, those women are merely foster mothers, homes and environments, but so far no one has suggested this, much less called for a reevaluation of Johnson's claim in the light of new information about the value women place on pregnancy and childbirth and the persistent (if apparently erroneous) belief that the resultant babies belong to them.

To their credit, commentators have not regarded these developments with unalloyed rapture. Perhaps they learned something from

4

---

[1]**Solomon:** In 1 Kings 3.16–27 of the Hebrew Bible, Solomon, noted for his wisdom, is able to determine which of two women is a child's mother.

the Baby M fracas. In that dispute, you will remember, many intelligent people persuaded themselves that the baby's rightful mother was a woman who had *no* biological connection to it, and that its real mother, Mary Beth Whitehead, was a grasping madwoman because she did not think she was, as child psychologist Lee Salk put it, a "surrogate uterus." The New Jersey Supreme Court disagreed, restored White-head's parental rights, which the lower court had abrogated, and, lo and behold, none of the confidently predicted dire consequences ensued. Women are not regarded as too emotional to make binding contracts, as some feminists feared, nor has motherhood been more deeply consigned to the realm of instinct and mystification. The child, now a toddler, has not been destroyed or corrupted by contact with her mother: Mary Beth Whitehead, the supposed Medea[2] of the Meadow-lands, turns out to be such a good mom, in fact, that *New York Times* columnist Anna Quindlen, who observed one of the child's visits, felt moved to renounce her earlier anti-Whitehead position. Indeed, the only consequences have been positive: The child knows both her parents; paid Baby M–style arrangements have been outlawed in two states, the contracts declared unenforceable in three; Noel Keane, the infamous baby broker who boasted that he had made $300,000 in fees the year of the Baby M contract, has found another métier.

As our Eastern European friends are now reminding us, however, markets must be served. The New Jersey Supreme Court put a damper on Baby M–style contract motherhood—now known as "traditional surrogacy," as if it had come over with the Pilgrims—but it seems to have spurred science and commerce on to more ingenious devices. And so we have Baby Boy Johnson. Thanks to Baby M, we are a little sheepish, a little wiser. Ellen Goodman has called for the banning of gestational surrogacy for pay; like millions of other middle-aging moms, she wonders if being able to bear a child in one's fifties is really an unmitigated blessing. But we have not yet, as a society, begun to face the underlying ideas about class, race, children and, above all, women that the new maternities rely on.

Take class. By upholding the Johnson-Calvert contract, Judge Parslow opens the door to the sale of poor women's bodies to well-off couples. It is disingenuous to claim, as does Polly Craig of the Los Angeles Center for Surrogate Parenting, that $10,000 is not enough money to motivate a woman to sell her womb, and that gestational surrogates simply enjoy being pregnant, want to help others, or wish to atone for a past abortion. Why offer payment at all, if it serves no function? And why, if gestational surrogacy is such an occasion for pleasure, altruism and moral purification, don't prosperous women line up for it? The Calverts—she a nurse, he an insurance broker—presumably

[2]**Medea:** A woman in Greek mythology who killed her children.

possess a wide female acquaintanceship in their own income bracket, none of whom felt friendship required of them that they turn over their bodies to the Calvertian zygote. Instead the couple approached Johnson, a sometime welfare recipient, single mother and low-paid worker at Crispina Calvert's hospital.

No, money is the motivator here. Ten thousand dollars may not seem like a lot to Craig and her clients, but it's a poor person's idea of major cash—as much as 25 percent of American women earn in a whole year of full-time employment. It's quite enough to becloud good judgment. "You wave $10,000 in front of someone's face," said Anna Johnson, "and they are going to jump for it." By "someone," Johnson meant women like herself, shuttling between welfare and dead-end jobs, single, already supporting a child, with a drawerful of bills and not much hope for the future.

In a particularly nasty wrinkle, gestational surrogacy invites the singling out of black women for exploitation. It's not just that blacks are disproportionately poor and desperate, more likely to be single mothers and more likely to lack the resources to sue. It's that their visible lack of genetic connection with the baby will argue powerfully against them in court. (Indeed, about the Baby Boy Johnson case hovers the suggestion that the Calverts chose Johnson for precisely this reason.) Judge Parslow's comparison of Johnson to a foster mother is interesting in view of the fact that foster mothers who grow attached to their charges and try to keep them are regarded with much popular sympathy and sometimes even succeed. But it is safe to say that few American judges are going to take seriously the claims of a black woman to a nonblack child. Black women have, after all, always raised white children without acquiring any rights to them. Now they can breed them, too.

There are those who worry about the social implications of gestational surrogacy but who still think Judge Parslow made the right choice of homes for Baby Boy Johnson. Be that as it may, Anna Johnson wasn't suing for custody but for visitation. She wanted to be a small part of the child's life, for him to know her and for her to know him. Why would that be so terrible? As Dr. Michelle Harrison, who testified for Johnson, wrote in *The Wall Street Journal*, Judge Parslow wasn't being asked to divide the child between three parents; the Calverts had in fact so divided him when they chose to produce a baby with Johnson's help. Recent court decisions (not to mention social customs like open adoption, blended families and gay and lesbian co-parenting) have tended to respect a widening circle of adult relationships with children. Every state, for instance, gives grandparents access to grandchildren in the case of a divorce, regardless of the wishes of the custodial parent. Stepparents and lesbian co-parents are demanding their day in court. In 1986, California state courts upheld the right of a sperm donor to sue for parental rights when the artificial insemination did not involve a doctor (the old turkey-baster method). Why isn't *that* prospect too "crazy-making" for

California? Or, for that matter, mandatory joint custody, an innovation that California pioneered? Given the increasing number of children living outside the classic nuclear-family arrangement, and the equanimity with which the courts divide them up among competing adults, it seems rather late in the day to get all stuffy about Anna Johnson.

The most important and distressing aspect of Judge Parslow's decision, however, is that it defines, or redefines, maternity in a way that is thoroughly degrading to women. By equating motherhood with fatherhood—that is, defining it solely as the contribution of genetic material—he has down-graded the mother's other contributions (carrying the fetus to term and giving birth) to services rather than integral components of biological parenthood. Under this legal definition, a normally pregnant woman is now baby-sitting for a fetus that happens to be her own. "In a debate over nature vs. nurture, the winner is nature" read the *New York Times* pull-quote. But why define "nature" as DNA rather than as the physiological events of pregnancy and birth? There's nothing "natural" about egg donation, which involves the hormonal priming of an infertile woman, the extraction of an egg by delicate technology, fertilization in a dish with masturbated sperm and implantation of the zygote in another. And to call pregnancy and childbirth "nurture" seems a feeble way to describe the sharing of the body and the risking of health, well-being and even life itself that is required to bring another life into existence. Like "parenting," another fashionable buzz-word, "nurture" is a bland social-sciency word that belittles a profound relationship and masks the role of women in gender-neutral language.

The picture of pregnancy as biological baby-sitting has many sources. It's as old as Aeschylus,[3] who had Athena acquit Orestes of matricide in the *Eumenides* on the ground that mothers are merely "nurses" of men's seed, and as new as those ubiquitous photos of fetuses seeming to float in empty space. But its major proponents today are the antiabortionists. In order to maximize the claims of the fetus to personhood, they must obscure the unique status of the pregnant woman: She is not making a person, because the fertilized egg already *is* a person; she's only caring for it, or housing it, or even (as one imaginative federal judge recently wrote) holding it captive. Ironically, the movement that claims to celebrate motherhood is led by its own logic to devalue the physical, emotional and social experience of pregnancy. If unwanted pregnancy is just an "inconvenience," how serious an occasion can a *wanted* pregnancy be? If mass adoption is the answer to 1.6 million annual abortions, how strong can the ties be between mother and newborn? When ethicists fret that professional women may resort to gestational surrogacy to avoid "putting their careers on hold," they betray more than antiquated views about the capacities of pregnant

[3]**Aeschylus,** ancient Greek dramatist (525–45 B.C.).

women to get out of bed in the morning. They reveal their own assumption that pregnancy is a trivial, empty experience with nothing positive about it except the end product, the genetically connected baby. They then compound the insult by attributing this view to a demonized fantasy of working women—cold, materialistic, selfish, corrupted by "male values"—that is, those held by the ethicists themselves. Is there any evidence that working women—even M.B.A.s, even lawyers—see pregnancy this way? Who do the pundits think are mobbing infertility clinics and signing on for donated eggs? A couple needs two incomes just to pay the doctors.

Why is the primacy of genetics so attractive? At the moment, genetic determinism is having one of its periods of scientific fashion, fueling the fear that an adopted baby will never "really" be yours. At the same time, hardening class distinctions make the poor, who provide most adoptive babies, seem scary and doomed: What if junior took after his birth parents? It's not an accident that sperm donors and now egg donors are largely recruited among middle-class educated folk— they're not just white, they're successful and smart—and that the commercial aspects of the transaction ($50 for sperm, $1,500 for an egg) are disguised by calling it a "donation." You can buy a womb because wombs don't really matter, but if the all-important DNA must come from a third party, it should come as a gift between equals.

The main reason for our love affair with genes, though, is that men have them. We can't get all the way back to Aeschylus, with man as the seed sower and woman as flowerpot (although we acknowledge it in our language, when we call women "fertile" or "infertile," like farmland). Women, we now know, have seeds, too. But we can discount the aspects of procreation that women, and only women, perform. As the sociologist Barbara Katz Rothman has noted, Judge Parslow's decision follows the general pattern of our society, in which women's experiences are recognized to the extent that they are identical with men's, and devalued or ignored to the extent that they are different. Thus, Mary Beth Whitehead won back her parental rights because the New Jersey Supreme Court acknowledged her *genetic* contribution: Baby M was half hers. And the postmenopausally pregnant, egg-donated women achieve parental rights by being married to the babies' fathers, not through their own contributions.

Of the two practices—actually a single practice with two social constructions—gestational surrogacy is clearly the more repellent, but to see its real meaning it must be looked at with egg donation as its flip side. Taken together they bring pregnancy into line with other domestic tasks traditionally performed by women—housework, child care, sex. Performed within marriage, for no pay, these activities are slathered with sentimentality and declared beyond price, the cornerstone of female self-worth, family happiness and civilization itself. That is the world inhabited by prosperous married women now able to

12

undergo pregnancy thanks to egg donation. That the egg is not their own is a detail; what counts is that they are able to have a profound and transforming life experience, to bond prenatally with their baby and to reproduce the genes of their husband. But look what happens when the checkbook and the marriage certificate are in the other hand: Now the egg is the central concern, pregnancy and childbirth merely a chore, prenatal bonding a myth. Like all domestic labor performed for pay—housecleaning, baby-sitting, prostitution—childbearing in the marketplace becomes disreputable work performed by suspect, marginal people. The priceless task turns out to have a price after all: about $1.50 an hour.

What should happen now? Some suggest that new methods of parenthood require a new legal principle: pre-conception intent. Instead of socio-bio-ethical headaches—Who is the mother? Who is the father? What's best for the child? What's best for society?—we could have a simple rule of thumb: Let the seller beware. But at what cost to economic fairness, to principles of bodily integrity, to the nonmarketplace values that shape intimate life? Why not let the *buyer* beware? We cannot settle thorny questions by simply refusing to ask them.

A doctrine of pre-conception intent could, moreover, turn ordinary   16
family law into fruit salad. Most pregnancies in the United States, after all, are not intended by either partner. They occur for dozens of reasons: birth-control failure, passion, ignorance, mixed messages, fear. The law wisely overlooks these sorry facts. Instead, it says Here is a child, here are the parents, next case. Do we really want to threaten a philosophy aimed, however clumsily, at protecting children from pauperism and abandonment? If pre-conception intent caught on with the general public, no single mother would be able to win child support; no single father could win parental rights. A woman's right to abortion could be conditioned on her pre-conception intent as evidenced, for example, by her use or neglect of birth control. In fact, in several states, laws have already been proposed that would restrict abortion to women who could prove contraceptive failure (a near impossibility, if you think about it, which is probably the point).

Perhaps the biggest problem with pre-conception intent, however, is that it ignores almost everything about the actual experience of becoming a parent of either sex. Planning to have a baby is not the same as being pregnant and giving birth, any more than putting on sexy underwear is like making love. The long months of pregnancy and the intense struggle of childbirth are part of forming a relationship with the child-to-be, part of the social and emotional task of parenthood. Not the only part, or even a necessary part—I am not suggesting that adoptive parents do not "really" become mothers and fathers. But is there a woman who feels exactly the same about the baby in the ninth month, or during delivery or immediately afterward, as she did when she threw away her diaphragm? When friends and relatives assure ambivalent parents-to-be not to worry, they'll feel differently about the baby when they feel it kick, or go through Lamaze together, or first hold their newborn in their arms, are they only talking through their hats? Whether or not there is a purely biological maternal instinct, more mothers, and more fathers, fall in love with their babies than ever thought they would. Indeed, if they did not, most babies would die of neglect in their cribs. How can we respect this emotional and psychological process—indeed, rely on it—and at the same time forbid it to the Mary Beth Whiteheads and the Anna Johnsons? I don't think we can.

Pre-conception intent would wreak havoc on everyone—men, women and children—and for what? To give couples like the Calverts a risk-free shot at a genetically connected baby. It makes more sense to assimilate surrogacy to already existing values and legal principles. In my view, doing so would make payment illegal and prebirth contracts unenforceable. We don't let people sell their organs or work at slave wages; we don't hold new mothers to predelivery adoption arrangements; we don't permit the sale of children; we don't enforce contracts that violate human dignity and human rights. We respect the role of emotion and change and second thoughts in private life: We let people jilt their fiancés, and we let them divorce their spouses. True, we uphold prenuptial agreements (a mistake, in my opinion), but they're about property. If someone signed a premarital agreement never to see his children again in the case of divorce, what judge would uphold it? Those children weren't even conceived when that contract was signed, the judge would point out—and furthermore they have rights that cannot be waived by others, such as the right to contact with both parents after divorce. The children of surrogates—even nongenetic surrogates like Anna Johnson—have the right to know the women through whose body and through whose efforts they came into the world. We don't need any more disposable relationships in the world of children. They have quite enough of those already.

In order to benefit a very small number of people—prosperous womb-infertile couples who shun adoption—paid surrogacy does a great deal of harm to the rest of us. It degrades women by devaluing pregnancy and childbirth; it degrades children by commercializing their creation; it degrades the poor by offering them a devil's bargain at bargain prices. It creates a whole new class of emotionally injured children rarely mentioned in the debate: the ones the surrogate has already given birth to, who see their mother give away a newborn, or fight not to.

It is hard for Americans to see why they shouldn't have what they want if they can pay for it. We would much rather talk about individual freedoms and property rights, rational self-interest and the supposed sanctity of contracts, than about the common good or human dignity, or the depths below which no person should be allowed to sink. But even we have to call it quits somewhere. As we decided 130 years ago, the buying and selling of people is a very good place to draw the line.

Topics for Critical Thinking and Writing

1. If you are not sure of the definitions of *moot* and *cleave*, look the words up in a college dictionary. Then, with both Pollitt's argument in mind and her tone, assess her introduction.

2. In paragraph 3 Pollitt refers to the "Baby M fracas." Why does she call the case a *fracas?* Again, looking at Pollitt's tone as well as her argument, assess her views on this case. (By *tone*, we mean, for example, referring to Mary Beth Whitehead ironically as a "grasping madwoman" or "the supposed Medea of the Meadowlands," or to Noel Keane, not ironically this time, as "the infamous baby broker.")

3. In paragraph 5 Pollitt says that "we have not yet, as a society, begun to face the underlying ideas about class, race, children and, above all, women that the new maternities rely on." First of all, what are "the new maternities" that Pollitt means? And, then, what are the "underlying ideas about ... women" that she refers to? Why does Pollitt call pregnancy, for example, "biological baby-sitting"?

4. In her last paragraph Pollitt refers to our decision "130 years ago" about "the buying and selling of people." What is she referring to here? Do you find it an appropriate argument to end her essay, or does it instead cheapen it?

Mitsuye Yamada

Mitsuye Yamada, the daughter of Japanese immigrants to the United States, was born in Japan in 1923, during her mother's return visit to her native land. Yamada was raised in Seattle, but in 1942 she and her family were incarcerated and then relocated in a camp in Idaho, when Executive Order 9066 gave military authorities the right to remove any and all persons from "military areas." In 1954 she became an American citizen. A professor of English at Cypress Junior College in San Luis Obispo, California, she is the author of poems and stories.

To the Lady

The one in San Francisco who asked:
Why did the Japanese Americans let
the government put them in
those camps without protest?

4

Come to think of it I
   should've run off to Canada
   should've hijacked a plane to Algeria
   should've pulled myself up from my
bra straps
and kicked'm in the groin
should've bombed a bank
should've tried self-immolation

8

12

should've holed myself up in a
woodframe house
and let you watch me
burn up on the six o'clock news   16
should've run howling down the street
naked and assaulted you at breakfast
by AP wirephoto
should've screamed bloody murder   20
like Kitty Genovese[1]

Then
YOU would've   24
    come to my aid in shining armor
    laid yourself across the railroad track
    marched on Washington
    tatooed a Star of David on your arm   28
    written six million enraged
    letters to Congress

But we didn't draw the line   32
anywhere
law and order Executive Order 9066[2]
social order moral order internal order
                                                   36
YOU let'm
I let'm
All are punished.

                                          [1976]

Topics for Critical Thinking and Writing

1. Has the lady's question (lines 2–4) ever crossed your mind? If so, what answers did you think of?
2. What, in effect, is the speaker really saying in lines 5–21? And in lines 24–29?
3. Explain the last line.

[1]**Kitty Genovese:** In 1964 Kitty Genovese of Kew Gardens, New York, was stabbed to death when she left her car and walked toward her home. Thirty-eight persons heard her screams, but no one came to her assistance.
[2]**Executive Order 9066:** An authorization, signed in 1941 by President Franklin D. Roosevelt, allowing military authorities to relocate Japanese and Japanese-Americans who resided on the Pacific Coast of the United States.

13
IDENTITIES

Grandfather and Grandchildren Awaiting Evacuation Bus
Dorothea Lange

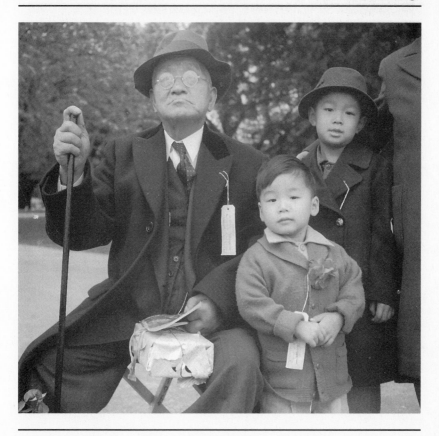

Behind the Bar, Birney, Montana
Marion Post Wolcott, 1941

Short Views

In every known society, the male's need for achievement can be recognized. Men may cook, or weave, or dress dolls or hunt hummingbirds, but if such activities are appropriate occupations of men, then the whole society, men and women alike, votes them as important. When the same occupations are performed by women, they are regarded as less important.

Margaret Mead

There is no female mind. The brain is not an organ of sex. As well speak of a female liver.

Charlotte Perkins Gilman

This has always been a man's world, and none of the reasons hitherto brought forward in explanation of this fact has seemed adequate.

Simone de Beauvoir

We all have been put into categories which fix us in a position which lasts the whole of our lives. Girls are called "feminine" beings and are taught the appropriate feminine behavior; boys are labelled "masculine" and have their behavior defined for them too. No one escapes. Failure to conform to our assigned behavior means that we feel wrong and bad about ourselves. We are not encouraged to break the laws of sex and gender; and certainly no one questions whether the demands of society are contrary to the demands of being human. There ought to be questions asked, though. For what society does is not in our best interest as persons. Society's interest is concerned with how effective we will be as economic and political and cultural supports, not how human we will be.

Heather Formaini

America is God's crucible, the great melting pot where all the races of Europe are melting and re-forming.

Israel Zangwill

676

No metaphor can capture completely the complexity of ethnic dynamics in the U. S. "Melting pot" ignores the persistence and reconfiguration of ethnicity over the generations. "Mosaic," much more apt for pluralistic societies such as Kenya or India, is too static a metaphor; it fails to take into account the easy penetration of many ethnic boundaries. Nor is "salad bowl" appropriate; the ingredients of a salad bowl are mixed but do not change. "Rainbow" is a tantalizing metaphor, but rainbows disappear. "Symphony," like "rainbow," implies near perfect harmony; both fail to take into account the variety and range of ethnic conflict in the United States.

The most accurately descriptive metaphor, the one that best explains the dynamics of ethnicity, is "kaleidoscope." American ethnicity is kaleidoscopic, i.e. "complex and varied, changing form, pattern, color . . . continually shifting from one set of relations to another; rapidly changing." When a kaleidoscope is in motion, the parts give the appearance of rapid change and extensive variety in color and shape and in their interrelationships. The viewer sees an endless variety of variegated patterns, just as takes place on the American ethnic landscape.

Lawrence Fuchs

We have room for but one language here and that is the English language, for we intend to see that the crucible turns out our people as Americans, of American nationality and not as dwellers in a polyglot boarding house, and we have room for but one loyalty and that is a loyalty to the American people.

Theodore Roosevelt

I cannot say too often—any man who carries a hyphen about him carries a dagger which he is ready to plunge into the vitals of the Republic.

Woodrow Wilson

Capitalism is a machine for the suppression of one class by another.

Vladimir I. Lenin

Through our own efforts and concerted good faith in learning to know, thus to respect, the wonderfully rich and diverse subcommunities of America, we can establish a new vision of America: a place where "community" may mean many things, yet retains its deeper spiritual significance. We may even learn to coincide with the 500th anniversary of the "discovery" of America by Columbus, that America, in its magnificent variety, has yet to be discovered.

Joyce Carol Oates

I have a dream that my four little children will one day live in a nation where they will not be judged by the color of their skin but by the content of their character.

Martin Luther King, Jr.

Dorothy Sayers

Dorothy Sayers (1893–1957), English writer was one of the first women to get a degree from Oxford University, when in 1915 she was awarded first-class honors in medieval literature. After graduating, she taught and worked as a copy writer in an advertising agency, while she was writing novels. Her first detective novel, Whose Body? *(1923), introduced Lord Peter Wimsey, who reappeared in ten later novels. His success enabled her to devote herself full-time to being a writer. Her interest in medieval literature continued, however, and she published a number of essays on the topic as well as essays on political, social, and religious matters, and a translation of most of Dante's* Divine Comedy.

When Sayers first published "Are Women Human?" in 1947, she identified it as an "Address Given to a Women's Society, 1938"

Are Women Human?

When I was asked to come and speak to you, your Secretary made the suggestion that she thought I must be interested in the feminist movement. I replied—a little irritably, I am afraid—that I was not sure I wanted to identify myself," as the phrase goes, with feminism, and that the time for "feminism," in the old-fashioned sense of the word, had gone past. In fact, I think I went so far as to say that, under present conditions, an aggressive feminism might do more harm than good. As a result I was, perhaps not unnaturally, invited to explain myself.

I do not know that it is very easy to explain, without offence or risk of misunderstanding, exactly what I do mean, but I will try.

The question of "sex-equality" is, like all questions affecting human relationships, delicate and complicated. It cannot be settled by loud slogans or hard-and-fast assertions like "a woman is as good as a man"—or "woman's place is the home"—or "women ought not to take men's jobs." The minute one makes such assertions, one finds one has to qualify them. "A woman is as good as a man" is as meaningless as to say, "a

Kaffir is as good as a Frenchman" or "a poet is as good as an engineer"
or "an elephant is as good as a racehorse"—it means nothing whatever
until you add: "at doing what?" In a religious sense, no doubt, the Kaffir is as valuable in the eyes of God as a Frenchman—but the average
Kaffir is probably less skilled in literary criticism than the average
Frenchman, and the average Frenchman less skilled than the average
Kaffir in tracing the spoor of big game. There might be exceptions on
either side: it is largely a matter of heredity and education. When we
balance the poet against the engineer, we are faced with a fundamental
difference of temperament—so that here our question is complicated
by the enormous social problem whether poetry or engineering is "better" for the State, or for humanity in general. There may be people who
would like a world that was all engineers or all poets—but most of us
would like to have a certain number of each; though here again, we
should all differ about the desirable proportion of engineering to poetry. The only provison we should make is that people with dreaming
and poetical temperaments should not entangle themselves in engines,
and that mechanically-minded persons should not issue booklets of
bad verse. When we come to the elephant and the racehorse, we come
down to bedrock physical differences—the elephant would make a
poor showing in the Derby, and the unbeaten Eclipse himself would be
speedily eclipsed by an elephant when it came to hauling logs.

That is so obvious that it hardly seems worth saying. But it is the
mark of all movements, however well-intentioned, that their pioneers
tend, by much lashing of themselves into excitement, to lose sight of the
obvious. In reaction against the age-old slogan, "woman is the weaker
vessel," or the still more offensive, "woman is a divine creature," we
have, I think, allowed ourselves to drift into asserting that "a woman is
as good as a man," without always pausing to think what exactly we
mean by that. What, I feel, we ought to mean is something so obvious
that it is apt to escape attention altogether, viz: not that every woman is,
in virtue of her sex, as strong, clever, artistic, level-headed, industrious,
and so forth as any man that can be mentioned; but, that a woman is
just as much an ordinary human being as a man, with the same individual preferences, and with just as much right to the tastes and preferences of an individual. What is repugnant to every human being is to be
reckoned always as a member of a class and not as an individual person. A certain amount of classification is, of course, necessary for practical purposes: there is no harm in saying that women, as a class, have
smaller bones than men, wear lighter clothing, have more hair on their
heads and less on their faces, go more pertinaciously to church or the
cinema, or have more patience with small and noisy babies. In the same
way, we may say that stout people of both sexes are commonly better-
tempered than thin ones, or that university dons of both sexes are more
pedantic in their speech than agricultural labourers, or that Communists of both sexes are more ferocious than Fascists—or the other way

4

round. What is unreasonable and irritating is to assume that *all* one's tastes and preferences have to be conditioned by the class to which one belongs. That has been the very common error into which men have frequently fallen about women—and it is the error into which feminist women are, perhaps, a little inclined to fall into about themselves.

Take, for example, the very usual reproach that women nowadays always want to "copy what men do." In that reproach there is a great deal of truth and a great deal of sheer, unmitigated, and indeed quite wicked nonsense. There are a number of jobs and pleasures which men have in times past cornered for themselves. At one time, for instance, men had a monopoly of classical education. When the pioneers of university training for women demanded that women should be admitted to the universities, the cry went up at once: "Why should women want to know about Aristotle?" The answer is NOT that *all* women would be the better for knowing about Aristotle—still less, as Lord Tennyson[1] seemed to think, that they would be more companionable wives for their husbands if they did know about Aristotle—but simply: "What women want as a class is irrelevant. *I* want to know about Aristotle. It is true that most women care nothing about him, and a great many male undergraduates turn pale and faint at the thought of him—but I, eccentric individual that I am, do want to know about Aristotle, and I submit that there is nothing in my shape or bodily functions which need prevent my knowing about him."

That battle was won, and rightly won, for women. But there is a sillier side to the university education of women. I have noticed lately, and with regret, a tendency on the part of the women's colleges to "copy the men" on the side of their failings and absurdities, and this is not so good. Because the constitution of the men's colleges is autocratic, old-fashioned, and in many respects inefficient, the women are rather inclined to try and cramp their own collegiate constitutions—which were mapped out on freer democratic lines—into the mediaeval mould of the men's—and that is unsound. It contributes nothing to the university and it loses what might have been a very good thing. The women students, too, have a foolish trick of imitating and outdoing the absurdities of male undergraduates. To climb in drunk after hours and get gated[2] is silly and harmless if done out of pure high spirits: if it is done "because the men do it," it is worse than silly, because it is not spontaneous and not even amusing.

Let me give one simple illustration of the difference between the right and the wrong kind of feminism. Let us take this terrible business—so distressing to the minds of bishops—of the women who go about in trousers. We are asked: "Why do you want to go about in

---

[1]**Aristotle . . . Lord Tennyson:** Aristotle (384–322 B.C.) was a Greek philosopher; Tennyson (1809–92) was a Victorian poet. (All notes to this selection are by the editors.)
[2]**Gated:** Confined within the college gates.

trousers? They are extremely unbecoming to most of you. You only do it to copy the men." To this we may very properly reply: "It is true that they are unbecoming. Even on men they are remarkably unattractive. But, as you men have discovered for yourselves, they are comfortable, they do not get in the way of one's activities like skirts and they protect the wearer from draughts about the ankles. As a human being, I like comfort, and dislike draughts. If the trousers do not attract you, so much the worse; for the moment I do not want to attract you. I want to enjoy myself as a human being, and why not? As for copying you, certainly you thought of trousers first and to that extent we must copy you. But we are not such abandoned copy-cats as to attach these useful garments to our bodies with braces. There we draw the line. These machines of leather and elastic are unnecessary and unsuited to the female form. They are, moreover, hideous beyond description. And as for indecency—of which you sometimes accuse the trousers—we at least can take our coats off without becoming the half-undressed bedroom spectacle that a man presents in his shirt and braces."

So that when we hear that women have once more laid hands upon   8
something which was previously a man's sole privilege, I think we have to ask ourselves: is this trousers or is it braces? Is it something useful, convenient, and suitable to a human being as such? Or is it merely something unnecessary to us, ugly, and adopted merely for the sake of collaring the other fellow's property? These jobs and professions, now. It is ridiculous to take on a man's job just in order to be able to say that "a woman has done it—yah!" The only decent reason for tackling any job is that it is *your* job and *you* want to do it.

At this point, somebody is likely to say: "yes, that is all very, well. But it *is* the woman who is always trying to ape the man. She *is* the inferior being. You don't as a rule find the men trying to take the women's jobs away from them. They don't force their way into the household and turn women out of their rightful occupations."

Of course they do not. They have done it already.

Let us accept the idea that women should stick to their own jobs— the jobs they did so well in the good old days before they started talking about votes and women's rights. Let us return to the middle ages and ask what we should get then in return for certain political and educational privileges which we should have to abandon.

It is a formidable list of jobs: the whole of the spinning industry, the   12
whole of the dyeing industry, the whole of the weaving industry. The whole catering industry and—which would not please Lady Astor,[3] perhaps—the whole of the nation's brewing and distilling. All the preserving, pickling, and bottling industry, all the bacon-curing. And

[3]**Lady Astor:** Nancy Astor (1879–1964), American-born British politician. She was the first woman elected to the British House of Commons. In her years as a conservative, she was known as a foe of alcohol and as a champion of women's rights and child welfare.

(since in those days a man was often absent from home for months together on war or business) a very large share in the management of landed estates. Here are the women's jobs—and what has become of them? They are all being handled by men. It is all very well to say that woman's place is the home—but modern civilisation has taken all these pleasant and profitable activities out of the home, where the women looked after them, and handed them over to big industry, to be directed and organised by men at the head of large factories. Even the dairymaid in her simple bonnet has gone, to be replaced by a male mechanic in charge of a mechanical milking plant.

Now, it is very likely that men in big industries do these jobs better than the women did them at home. The fact remains that the home contains much less of interesting activity than it used to contain. What is more, the home has so shrunk to the size of a small flat that—even if we restrict woman's job to the bearing and rearing of families—there is no room for her to do even that. It is useless to urge the modern woman to have twelve children, like her grandmother. Where is she to put them when she has got them? And what modern man wants to be bothered with them? It is perfectly idiotic to take away women's traditional occupations and then complain because she looks for new ones. Every woman is a human being—one cannot repeat that too often—and a human being *must* have occupation, if he or she is not to become a nuisance to the world.

I am not complaining that the brewing and baking were taken over by the men. If they can brew and bake as well as women or better, then by all means let them do it. But they cannot have it both ways. If they are going to adopt the very sound principle that the job should be done by the person who does it best, then that rule must be applied universally. If the women make better officeworkers than men, they must have the office work. If any individual woman is able to make a first-class lawyer, doctor, architect, or engineer, then she must be allowed to try her hand at it. Once lay down the rule that the job comes first and you throw that job open to every individual, man or woman, fat or thin, tall or short, ugly or beautiful, who is able to do that job better than the rest of the world.

Now, it is frequently asserted that, with women, the job does not come first. What (people cry) are women doing with this liberty of theirs? What woman really prefers a job to a home and family? Very few, I admit. It is unfortunate that they should so often have to make the choice. A man does not, as a rule, have to choose. He gets both. In fact, if he wants the home and family, he usually has to take the job as well, if he can get it. Nevertheless, there have been women, such as Queen Elizabeth and Florence Nightingale, who had the choice, and chose the job and made a success of it. And there have been and are many men who have sacrificed their careers for women—sometimes like Antony or Parnell,[4] very disastrously. When it comes to a *choice*, then every man or woman has to choose as an individual human being, and, like a human being, take the consequences.

As human beings! I am always entertained—and also irritated—by the newsmongers who inform us, with a bright air of discovery, that they have questioned a number of female workers and been told by one and all that they are "sick of the office and would love to get out of it." In the name of God, what human being is *not*, from time to time, heartily sick of the office and would *not* love to get out of it? The time of female officeworkers is daily wasted in sympathising with disgruntled male colleagues who yearn to get out of the office. No human being likes work—not day in and day out. Work is notoriously a curse—and if women *liked* everlasting work they would not be human beings at all. *Being* human beings, they like work just as much and just as little as anybody else. They dislike perpetual washing and cooking just as perpetual typing and standing behind shop counters. Some of them prefer typing to scrubbing—but that does not mean that they are not, as human beings, entitled to damn and blast the typewriter when they feel that way. The number of men who daily damn and blast typewriters is incalculable; but that does not mean that they would be happier doing a little plain sewing. Nor would the women.

I have admitted that there are very few women who would put their job before every earthly consideration. I will go further and assert that there are very few men who would do it either. In fact, there is perhaps only one human being in a thousand who is passionately interested in his job for the job's sake. The difference is that if that one person in a thousand is a man, we say, simply, that he is passionately keen on his job; if she is a woman, we say she is a freak. It is extraordinarily entertaining to watch the historians of the past, for instance, entangling themselves in what they were pleased to call the "problem" of Queen Elizabeth. They invented the most complicated and astonishing reasons both for her success as a sovereign and for her tortuous matrimonial policy. She was the tool of Burleigh, she was the tool of Leicester, she was the fool of Essex: she was diseased, she was deformed, she was a man in disguise. She was a mystery, and must have some extraordinary solution. Only recently has it occurred to a few enlightened people that the solution might be quite simple after all. She might be one of the rare people who were born into the right job and put that job first. Whereupon a whole series of riddles cleared themselves up by magic. She was in love with Leicester—why didn't she marry him? Well, for the very same reason that numberless kings have not married their

[4]**Antony or Parnell:** Marc Antony (c. 83 B.C.–30 B.C.), lover and political ally of Cleopatra, was conquered by Octavian. Charles Stewart Parnell (1846–91), Irish politician, fell from power because of the scandal evoked by his affair with a married woman, "Kitty" O'Shea.

lovers—because it would have thrown a spanner into the wheels of the State machine. Why was she so blood-thirsty and unfeminine as to sign the death-warrant of Mary Queen of Scots? For much the same reasons that induced King George V to say that if the House of Lords did not pass the Parliament Bill he would create enough new peers to force it through—because she was, in the measure of her time, a constitutional sovereign, and knew that there was a point beyond which a sovereign could not defy Parliament. Being a rare human being with her eye to the job, she did what was necessary; being an ordinary human being, she hesitated a good deal before embarking on unsavoury measures—but as to feminine mystery, there is no such thing about it, and nobody, had she been a man, would have thought either her statesmanship or her humanity in any way mysterious. Remarkable they were—but she was a very remarkable person. Among her most remarkable achievements was that of showing that sovereignty was one of the jobs for which the right kind of woman was particularly well fitted.

Which brings us back to this question of what jobs, if any, are women's jobs. Few people would go so far as to say that all women are well fitted for all men's jobs. When people do say this, it is particularly exasperating. It is stupid to insist that there are as many female musicians and mathematicians as male—the facts are otherwise, and the most we can ask is that if a Dame Ethel Smyth or a Mary Somerville[5] turns up, she shall be allowed to do her work without having aspersions cast either on her sex or her ability. What we ask is to be human individuals, however peculiar and unexpected. It is no good saying: "You are a little girl and therefore you ought to like dolls"; if the answer is, "But I don't," there is no more to be said. Few women happen to be natural born mechanics; but if there is one, it is useless to try and argue her into being something different. What we must *not* do is to argue that the occasional appearance of a female mechanical genius proves that all women would be mechanical geniuses if they were educated. They would not.

Where, I think, a great deal of confusion has arisen is in a failure to distinguish between special *knowledge* and special *ability*. There are certain questions on which what is called "the woman's point of view" is valuable, because they involve special *knowledge*. Women should be consulted about such things as housing and domestic architecture because, under present circumstances, they have still to wrestle a good deal with houses and kitchen sinks and can bring special knowledge to the problem. Similarly, some of them (though not all) know more about children than the majority of men, and their opinion, *as women*, is of value. In the same way, the opinion of colliers is of value about coal-mining, and the opinion of doctors is valuable about disease. But there

---

[5]**Smyth . . . Somerville:** Ethel Smyth (1858–1944), a composer of music, was a vigorous suffragist; Mary Somerville (1780–1872) wrote on astronomy and physics.

are other questions—as for example, about literature or finance—on which the "woman's point of view" has no value at all. In fact, it does not exist. No special knowledge is involved, and a woman's opinion on literature or finance is valuable only as the judgment of an individual. I am occasionally desired by congenital imbeciles and the editors of magazines to say something about the writing of detective fiction "from the woman's point of view." To such demands, one can only say, "Go away and don't be silly. You might as well ask what is the female angle on an equilateral triangle."

In the old days it used to be said that women were unsuited to sit   20
in Parliament, because they "would not be able to think imperially." That, if it meant anything, meant that their views would be cramped and domestic—in short, "the woman's point of view." Now that they *are* in Parliament, people complain that they are a disappointment: they vote like other people with their party and have contributed nothing to speak of from "the woman's point of view"—except on a few purely domestic questions, and even then they are not all agreed. It looks as though somebody was trying to have things both ways at once. Even critics must remember that women are human beings and obliged to think and behave as such. I can imagine a "woman's point of view" about town-planning, or the education of children, or divorce, or the employment of female shop-assistants, for here they have some special knowledge. But what in thunder is the "woman's point of view" about the devaluation of the franc or the abolition of the Danzig Corridor?[6] Even where women have special knowledge, they may disagree among themselves like other specialists. Do doctors never quarrel or scientists disagree? Are women really *not human,* that they should be expected to toddle along all in a flock like sheep? I think that people should be allowed to drink as much wine and beer as they can afford and is good for them; Lady Astor thinks nobody should be allowed to drink anything of the sort. Where is the "woman's point of view"? Or is one or the other of us unsexed? If the unsexed one is myself, then I am unsexed in very good company. But I prefer to think that women are human and differ in opinion like other human beings. This does not mean that their opinions, as individual opinions, are valueless; on the contrary, the more able they are the more violently their opinions will be likely to differ. It only means that you cannot ask for "the woman's point of view," but only for the woman's special knowledge—and this, like all special knowledge, is valuable, though it is no guarantee of agreement.

"What," men have asked distractedly from the beginning of time, "what on earth do women want?" I do not know that women, *as* women, want anything in particular, but as human beings they want,

---

[6]**The Danzig Corridor:** After World War I the victorious allies promised Poland access to the sea (a "corridor") through Danzig (Gdansk), a city populated chiefly by Germans.

my good men, exactly what you want yourselves: interesting occupation, reasonable freedom for their pleasures, and a sufficient emotional outlet. What form the occupation, the pleasures, and the emotion may take, depends entirely upon the individual. You know that this is so with yourselves—why will you not believe that it is so with us. The later D. H. Lawrence, who certainly cannot be accused of underrating the importance of sex and talked a good deal of nonsense upon the subject, was yet occasionally visited with shattering glimpses of the obvious. He said in one of his *Assorted Articles:*

> Man is willing to accept woman as an equal, as a man in skirts, as an angel, a devil, a baby-face, a machine, an instrument, a bosom, a womb, a pair of legs, a servant, an encyclopaedia, an ideal or an obscenity; the one thing he won't accept her as is a human being, a real human being of the feminine sex.

"Accepted as a human being!"—yes; not as a inferior class and not, I beg and pray all feminists, as a superior class—not, in fact, as a class at all, except in a useful context. We are much too much inclined in these days to divide people into permanent categories, forgetting that a category only exists for its special purpose and must be forgotten as soon as that purpose is served. There is a fundamental difference between men and women, but it is not the only fundamental difference in the world. There is a sense in which my charwoman and I have more in common than either of us has with, say, Mr. Bernard Shaw: on the other hand, in a discussion about art and literature, Mr. Shaw and I should probably find we had more fundamental interests in common than either of us had with my charwoman. I grant that, even so, he and I should disagree ferociously about the eating of meat—but that is not a difference between the sexes—on that point, that late Mr. G. K. Chesterton would have sided with me against the representative of his own sex. Then there are points on which I, and many of my own generation of both sexes, should find ourselves heartily in agreement: but on which the rising generation of young men and women would find us too incomprehensibly stupid for words. A difference of age is as fundamental as a difference of sex; and so is a difference of nationality. *All* categories, if they are insisted upon beyond the immediate purpose which they serve, breed class antagonism and disruption in the state, and that is why they are dangerous.

The other day, in the "Heart-to-Heart" column of one of our popular newspapers, there appeared a letter from a pathetic gentleman about a little disruption threatening his married state. He wrote:

> I have been married eleven years and think a great deal of the wedding anniversary. I remind my wife a month in advance and plan to make the evening a success. But she does not share my keenness, and, if I did not remind her, would let the day go by without a thought of its significance. I thought a wedding anniversary meant a lot to a woman. Can you explain this indifference?

Poor little married gentleman, nourished upon generalisations—and convinced that if his wife does not fit into the category of "a woman" there must be something wrong! Perhaps she resents being dumped into the same category as all the typical women of the comic stories. If so, she has my sympathy. "A" woman—not an individual person, disliking perhaps to be reminded of the remorseless flowing-by of the years and the advance of old age—but "a" woman, displaying the conventional sentimentalities attributed to her unfortunate and ridiculous sex.

A man once asked me—it is true that it was at the end of a very good dinner, and the compliment conveyed may have been due to that circumstance—how I managed in my books to write such natural conversation between men when they were by themselves. Was I, by any chance, a member of a large, mixed family with a lot of male friends? I replied that, on the contrary, I was an only child and had practically never seen or spoken to any men of my own age till I was about twenty-five. "Well," said the man, "I shouldn't have expected a woman [meaning me] to have been able to make it so convincing." I replied that I had coped with this difficult problem by making my men talk, as far as possible, like ordinary human beings. This aspect of the matter seemed to surprise the other speaker; he said no more, but took it away to chew it over. One of these days it may quite likely occur to him that women, as well as men, when left to themselves, talk very much like human beings also.

Indeed, it is my experience that both men and women are fundamentally human, and that there is very little mystery about either sex, except the exasperating mysteriousness of human beings in general. And though for certain purposes it may still be necessary, as it undoubtedly was in the immediate past, for women to band themselves together, as women, to secure recognition of their requirements as a sex, I am sure that the time has now come to insist more strongly on each woman's—and indeed each man's—requirements as an individual person. It used to be said that women had no *esprit de corps*;[7] we have proved that we have—do not let us run into the opposite error of insisting that there is an aggressively feminist "point of view" about everything. To oppose one class perpetually to another—young against old, manual labour against brain-worker, rich against poor, woman against man—is to split the foundations of the State; and if the cleavage runs too deep, there remains no remedy but force and dictatorship. If you wish to preserve a free democracy, you must base it—not on classes and categories, for this will land you in the totalitarian State, where no one may act or think except as the member of the category. You must base it upon the individual Tom, Dick, and Harry, on the individual Jack and Jill—in fact, upon you and me.

[7]***Esprit de corps:*** French, meaning enthusiasm among members of a group for each other and for the group

Topics for Critical Thinking and Writing

1. Sayers' talk was delivered to an English audience in 1938. Are some of her points irrelevant to an American audience in the 1990s? If so, which points?
2. In paragraph 18 Sayers assumes that there are, generally, some differences in aptitude between men and women. What examples does she offer? Do you agree that there are such differences, in these areas or others? Why or why not?
3. In paragraph 19 Sayers says that on certain issues, such as "literature and finance," the "'woman's point of view' has no value at all." Do you agree? Why or why not? (Before responding, reread the entire paragraph.)
4. In paragraph 4 Sayers writes, "What is repugnant to every human being is to be reckoned always as a member of a class and not as an individual person." If you have experienced such repugnance, recount your experience.

Stephen Jay Gould

Stephen Jay Gould, born in 1941, is a professor of geology at Harvard University, where he teaches paleontology, biology, and the history of science. The essays he has written for the magazine Natural History *have been collected in five highly readable books.*

Women's Brains

In the Prelude to *Middlemarch*, George Eliot lamented the unfulfilled lives of talented women:

> Some have felt that these blundering lives are due to the inconvenient indefiniteness with which the Supreme Power has fashioned the natures of women: if there were one level of feminine incompetence as strict as the ability to count three and no more, the social lot of women might be treated with scientific certitude.

Eliot goes on to discount the idea of innate limitation, but while she wrote in 1872, the leaders of European anthropometry were trying to measure "with scientific certitude" the inferiority of women. Anthropometry, or measurement of the human body, is not so fashionable a field these days, but it dominated the human sciences for much of the nineteenth century and remained popular until intelligence testing replaced skull measurement as a favored device for making invidious comparisons among races, classes, and sexes. Craniometry, or measurement of the skull, commanded the most attention and respect. Its unquestioned leader, Paul Broca (1824–80), professor of clinical surgery at the Faculty of Medicine in Paris, gathered a school of disciples and imitators around himself. Their work, so meticulous and apparently irrefutable, exerted great influence and won high esteem as a jewel of nineteenth-century science.

Broca's work seemed particularly invulnerable to refutation. Had he not measured with the most scrupulous care and accuracy? (Indeed, he had. I have the greatest respect for Broca's meticulous procedure. His numbers are sound. But science is an inferential exercise, not a catalog of facts. Numbers, by themselves, specify nothing. All depends upon what you do with them.) Broca depicted himself as an apostle of objectivity, a man who bowed before facts and cast aside superstition and sentimentality. He declared that "there is no faith, however respectable, no interest, however legitimate, which must not accommodate itself to the progress of human knowledge and bend before truth." Women, like it or not, had smaller brains than men and, therefore, could not equal them in intelligence. This fact, Broca argued, may reinforce a common prejudice in male society, but it is also a scientific truth. L. Manouvrier, a black sheep in Broca's fold, rejected the inferiority of women and wrote with feeling about the burden imposed upon them by Broca's numbers:

> Women displayed their talents and their diplomas. They also invoked philosophical authorities. But they were opposed by *numbers* unknown to Condorcet or to John Stuart Mill. These numbers fell upon poor women like a sledge hammer, and they were accompanied by commentaries and sarcasms more ferocious than the most misogynist imprecations of certain church fathers. The theologians had asked if women had a soul. Several centuries later, some scientists were ready to refuse them a human intelligence.

Broca's argument rested upon two sets of data: the larger brains of men in modern societies, and a supposed increase in male superiority through time. His most extensive data came from autopsies performed personally in four Parisian hospitals. For 292 male brains, he calculated an average weight of 1,325 grams; 140 female brains averaged 1,144 grams for a difference of 181 grams, or 14 percent of the male weight. Broca understood, of course, that part of this difference could be attributed to the greater height of males. Yet he made no attempt to measure the effect of size alone and actually stated that it cannot account for the entire difference because we know, a priori, that women are not as intelligent as men (a premise that the data were supposed to test, not rest upon): [4]

> We might ask if the small size of the female brain depends exclusively upon the small size of her body. Tiedemann has proposed this explanation. But we must not forget that women are, on the average, a little less intelligent than men, a difference which we should not exaggerate but which is, nonetheless, real. We are therefore permitted to suppose that the relatively small size of the female brain depends in part upon her physical inferiority and in part upon her intellectual inferiority.

In 1873, the year after Eliot published *Middlemarch,* Broca measured the cranial capacities of prehistoric skulls from L'Homme Mort cave.

Here he found a difference of only 99.5 cubic centimeters between males and females, while modern populations range from 129.5 to 220.7. Topinard, Broca's chief disciple, explained the increasing discrepancy through time as a result of differing evolutionary pressures upon dominant men and passive women:

> The man who fights for two or more in the struggle for existence, who has all the responsibility and the cares of tomorrow, who is constantly active in combating the environment and human rivals, needs more brain than the woman whom he must protect and nourish, the sedentary woman, lacking any interior occupations, whose role is to raise children, love, and be passive.

In 1879, Gustave Le Bon, chief misogynist of Broca's school, used these data to publish what must be the most vicious attack upon women in modern scientific literature (no one can top Aristotle). I do not claim his views were representative of Broca's school, but they were published in France's most respected anthropological journal. Le Bon concluded

> In the most intelligent races, as among the Parisians, there are a large number of women whose brains are closer in size to those of gorillas than to the most developed male brains. This inferiority is so obvious that no one can contest it for a moment; only its degree is worth discussion. All psychologists who have studied the intelligence of women, as well as poets and novelists, recognize today that they represent the most inferior forms of human evolution and that they are closer to children and savages than to an adult, civilized man. They excel in fickleness, inconstancy, absence of thought and logic, and incapacity to reason. Without doubt there exist some distinguished women, very superior to the average man, but they are as exceptional as the birth of any monstrosity, as, for example, of a gorilla with two heads; consequently, we may neglect them entirely.

Nor did Le Bon shrink from the social implications of his views. He was horrified by the proposal of some American reformers to grant women higher education on the same basis as men:

> A desire to give them the same education, and, as a consequence, to propose the same goals for them, is a dangerous chimera. . . . The day when, misunderstanding the inferior occupations which nature has given her, women leave the home and take part in our battles; on this day a social revolution will begin, and everything that maintains the sacred ties of the family will disappear.

Sound familiar?[1]

---

[1]When I wrote this essay, I assumed that Le Bon was a marginal, if colorful, figure. I have since learned that he was a leading scientist, one of the founders of social psychology, and best known for a seminal study on crowd behavior, still cited today (*La psychologie des foules*, 1895), and for his work on unconscious motivation.

I have reexamined Broca's data, the basis for all this derivative pro-   8
nouncement, and I find his numbers sound but his interpretation ill-
founded, to say the least. The data supporting his claim for increased
difference through time can be easily dismissed. Broca based his con-
tention on the samples from L'Homme Mort alone—only seven male
and six female skulls in all. Never have so little data yielded such far
ranging conclusions.

In 1888, Topinard published Broca's more extensive data on the
Parisian hospitals. Since Broca recorded height and age as well as brain
size, we may use modern statistics to remove their effect. Brain weight
decreases with age, and Broca's women were, on average, considerably
older than his men. Brain weight increases with height, and his average
man was almost half a foot taller than his average woman. I used multiple regression, a technique that allowed me to assess simultaneously
the influence of height and age upon brain size. In an analysis of the
data for women, I found that, at average male height and age, a
woman's brain would weigh 1,212 grams. Correction for height and
age reduces Broca's measured difference of 181 grams by more than a
third, to 113 grams.

I don't know what to make of this remaining difference because I
cannot assess other factors known to influence brain size in a major
way. Cause of death has an important effect: degenerative disease often
entails a substantial diminution of brain size. (This effect is separate
from the decrease attributed to age alone.) Eugene Schreider, also
working with Broca's data, found that men killed in accidents had
brains weighing, on average, 60 grams more than men dying of infec-
tious diseases. The best modern data I can find (from American hospitals) records a full 100-gram difference between death by degenerative
arteriosclerosis and by violence or accident. Since so many of Broca's
subjects were very elderly women, we may assume that lengthy degenerative disease was more common among them than among the men.

More importantly, modern students of brain size still have not
agreed on a proper measure for eliminating the powerful effect of
body size. Height is partly adequate, but men and women of the same
height do not share the same body build. Weight is even worse than
height, because most of its variation reflects nutrition rather than
intrinsic size—fat versus skinny exerts little influence upon the brain.
Manouvrier took up this subject in the 1880s and argued that muscular mass and force should be used. He tried to measure this elusive
property in various ways and found a marked difference in favor of
men, even in men and women of the same height. When he corrected
for what he called "sexual mass," women actually came out slightly
ahead in brain size.

Thus, the corrected 113-gram difference is surely too large; the true   12
figure is probably close to zero and may as well favor women as men.
And 113 grams, by the way, is exactly the average difference between a

5 foot 4 inch and a 6 foot 4 inch male in Broca's data. We would not (especially us short folks) want to ascribe greater intelligence to tall men. In short, who knows what to do with Broca's data? They certainly don't permit any confident claim that men have bigger brains than women.

To appreciate the social role of Broca and his school, we must recognize that his statements about the brains of women do not reflect an isolated prejudice toward a single disadvantaged group. They must be weighed in the context of a general theory that supported contemporary social distinctions as biologically ordained. Women, blacks, and poor people suffered the same disparagement, but women bore the brunt of Broca's argument because he had easier access to data on women's brains. Women were singularly denigrated but they also stood as surrogates for other disenfranchised groups. As one of Broca's disciples wrote in 1881: "Men of the black races have a brain scarcely heavier than that of white women." This juxtaposition extended into many other realms of anthropological argument, particularly to claims that, anatomically and emotionally, both women and blacks were like white children—and that white children, by the theory of recapitulation, represented an ancestral (primitive) adult stage of human evolution. I do not regard as empty rhetoric the claim that women's battles are for all of us.

Maria Montessori did not confine her activities to educational reform for young children. She lectured on anthropology for several years at the University of Rome, and wrote an influential book entitled *Pedagogical Anthropology* (English edition, 1913). Montessori was no egalitarian. She supported most of Broca's work and the theory of innate criminality proposed by her compatriot Cesare Lombroso. She measured the circumference of children's heads in her schools and inferred that the best prospects had bigger brains. But she had no use for Broca's conclusions about women. She discussed Manouvrier's work at length and made much of his tentative claim that women, after proper correction of the data, had slightly larger brains than men. Women, she concluded, were intellectually superior, but men had prevailed heretofore by dint of physical force. Since technology has abolished force as an instrument of power, the era of women may soon be upon us: "In such an epoch there will really be superior human beings, there will really be men strong in morality and in sentiment. Perhaps in this way the reign of women is approaching, when the enigma of her anthropological superiority will be deciphered. Woman was always the custodian of human sentiment, morality and honor."

This represents one possible antidote to "scientific" claims for the constitutional inferiority of certain groups. One may affirm the validity of biological distinctions but argue that the data have been misinterpreted by prejudiced men with a stake in the outcome, and that disadvantaged groups are truly superior. In recent years, Elaine Morgan has followed this strategy in her *Descent of Woman,* a speculative reconstruction of human prehistory from the woman's point of view—and as farcical as more famous tall tales by and for men.

I prefer another strategy. Montessori and Morgan followed Broca's philosophy to reach a more congenial conclusion. I would rather label the whole enterprise of setting a biological value upon groups for what it is: irrelevant and highly injurious. George Eliot well appreciated the special tragedy that biological labeling imposed upon members of disadvantaged groups. She expressed it for people like herself—women of extraordinary talent. I would apply it more widely—not only to those whose dreams are flouted but also to those who never realize that they may dream—but I cannot match her prose. In conclusion, then, the rest of Eliot's prelude to *Middlemarch:* 16

> The limits of variation are really much wider than anyone would imagine from the sameness of women's coiffure and the favorite love stories in prose and verse. Here and there a cygnet is reared uneasily among the ducklings in the brown pond, and never finds the living stream in fellowship with its own oary-footed kind. Here and there is born a Saint Theresa, foundress of nothing, whose loving heartbeats and sobs after an unattained goodness tremble off and are dispersed among hindrances instead of centering in some long-recognizable deed.

Topics for Critical Thinking and Writing

1. What is your understanding of anthropometry from paragraph 2? According to Gould, what does intelligence testing have in common with anthropometry? Characterize his attitude toward both. How does he reveal his attitude in this paragraph?

2. In paragraph 3, what does Gould mean when he says, "But science is an inferential exercise, not a catalog of facts"?

3. In paragraph 13 Gould says, "I do not regard as empty rhetoric the claim that women's battles are for all of us." What does he mean? What foundation for this opinion have this paragraph and paragraph 2 provided?

4. Who was Maria Montessori, and what does her work have to do with Gould's argument? If her relevance is not entirely clear to you, or was not on first reading, what might Gould have done to make it clearer?

5. What, according to Gould, are the social consequences of what he calls in paragraph 16 *biological labeling?* If on the whole you agree with him, what is the basis of your agreement?

6. In paragraph 13 Gould refers to the "social role of Broca and his school." What does he mean by that? On the basis of this essay (and others of Gould's that you may have read) formulate in a sentence or two the social role of Gould.

Anna Quindlen

For nearly three years Anna Quindlen wrote, for The New York Times, *"Life in the '30s," a strikingly frank column about being thirty-something. The column stopped in 1988 and later Quindlen started a new weekly column in the* Times, *"Public & Private," in which she discussed such national matters as the budget in a highly personal way. We reprint one of these columns.*

The Glass Half Empty

My daughter is 2 years old today. She is something like me, only better. Or at least that is what I like to think. If personalities had colors, hers would be red.

Little by little, in the 20 years between my eighteenth birthday and her second one, I had learned how to live in the world. The fact that women were now making 67 cents for every dollar a man makes—well, it was better than 1970, wasn't it, when we were making only 59 cents? The constant stories about the underrepresentation of women, on the tenure track, in the film industry, in government, everywhere, had become commonplace. The rape cases. The sexual harassment stories. The demeaning comments. Life goes on. Where's your sense of humor?

Learning to live in the world meant seeing the glass half full. Ann Richards was elected Governor of Texas instead of a good ol' boy who said that if rape was inevitable, you should relax and enjoy it. The police chief of Houston is a pregnant woman who has a level this-is-my-job look and a maternity uniform with stars on the shoulder. There are so many opportunities unheard of when I was growing up.

And then I had a daughter and suddenly I saw the glass half empty. 4 And all the rage I thought had cooled, all those how-dare-you-treat-us-like-that days, all of it comes back when I look at her, and especially when I hear her say to her brothers, "Me too."

When I look at my sons, it is within reason to imagine all the world's doors open to them. Little by little some will close, as their individual capabilities and limitations emerge. But no one is likely to look at them and mutter: "I'm not sure a man is right for a job at this level. Doesn't he have a lot of family responsibilities?"

Every time a woman looks at her daughter and thinks "She can be anything" she knows in her heart, from experience, that it's a lie. Looking at this little girl, I see it all, the old familiar ways of a world that still loves Barbie. Girls aren't good at math, dear. He needs the money more than you, sweetheart; he's got a family to support. Honey—this diaper's dirty.

It is like looking through a telescope. Over the years I learned to look through the end that showed things small and manageable. This is called a sense of proportion. And then I turned the telescope around, and all the little tableaus rushed at me, vivid as ever.

That's called reality.   8

We soothe ourselves with the gains that have been made. There are many role models. Role models are women who exist—and are photographed often—to make other women feel better about the fact that there aren't really enough of us anywhere, except in the lowest-paying jobs. A newspaper editor said to me not long ago, with no hint of self-consciousness, "I'd love to run your column, but we already run Ellen Goodman." Not only was there a quota, there was a quota of one.

My daughter is ready to leap into the world, as though life were chicken soup and she a delighted noodle. The work of Prof. Carol Gilligan of Harvard suggests that some time after the age of 11 this will change, that even this lively little girl will pull back, shrink, that her constant refrain will become "I don't know." Professor Gilligan says the culture sends a message: "Keep quiet and notice the absence of women and say nothing." A smart 13-year-old said to me last week, "Boys don't like it if you answer too much in class."

Maybe someday, years from now, my daughter will come home and say, "Mother, at college my professor acted as if my studies were an amusing hobby and at work the man who runs my department puts his hand on my leg and to compete with the man who's in the running for my promotion who makes more than I do I can't take time to have a relationship but he has a wife and two children and I'm smarter and it doesn't make any difference and some guy tried to jump me after our date last night." And what am I supposed to say to her?

I know?   12

You'll get used to it?

No. Today is her second birthday and she has made me see fresh this two-tiered world, a world that, despite all our nonsense about post-feminism, continues to offer less respect and less opportunity for women than it does for men. My friends and I have learned to live with it, but my little girl deserves better. She has given me my anger back, and I intend to use it well.

That is her gift to me today. Some birthday I will return it to her, because she is going to need it.

Topics for Discussion and Writing

1. In paragraph 6, after saying that we live in "a world that still loves Barbie," Quindlen clarifies her assertion by offering some bits of conversation. Drawing on your own experience, do you agree that our world "still loves Barbie"? Support your view. (If you agree, give some additional bits of conversation.)

2. In paragraph 9 Quindlen mentions Ellen Goodman, with the obvious implication that Goodman fills the editor's quota for women. Read

Goodman's article (page 424) and consider the possibility that the editor has in mind not a quota for women but a quota for a certain *kind of essay*. Argue for or against this view, calling attention to qualities in the two essays.

3. In paragraph 11 Quindlen asks what she is supposed to say to her daughter's difficult questions. What do you think she *should* say? Why?

4. Consider Quindlen's beginning and ending paragraphs, and evaluate them.

Scott Russell Sanders

Scott Russell Sanders first published this essay in Milkweek Chronicle, *Spring/Summer 1984, and then reprinted it in his book,* Paradise of Bombs.

The Men We Carry in Our Minds . . . and How They Differ from the Real Lives of Most Men

This must be a hard time for women." I say to my friend Anneke. "They have so many paths to choose from, and so many voices calling them."

"I think it's a lot harder for men," she replies.

"How do you figure that?"

"The women I know feel excited, innocent, like crusaders in a just   4
cause. The men I know are eaten up with guilt."

"Women feel such pressure to be everything, do everything," I say. "Career, kids, art, politics. Have their babies and get back to the office a week later. It's as if they're trying to overcome a million years' worth of evolution in one lifetime."

"But we help one another. And we have this deep-down sense that we're in the *right*—we've been held back, passed over, used—while men feel they're in the wrong. Men are the ones who've been discredited, who have to search their souls."

I search my soul. I discover guilty feelings aplenty—toward the poor, the Vietnamese, Native Americans, the whales, an endless list of debts. But toward women I feel something more confused, a snarl of shame, envy, wary tenderness, and amazement. This muddle troubles me. To hide my unease I say, "You're right, it's tough being a man these days."

"Don't laugh," Anneke frowns at me. "I wouldn't be a man for any-   8
thing. It's much easier being the victim. All the victim has to do is break free. The persecutor has to live with his past."

How deep is that past? I find myself wondering. How much of an inheritance do I have to throw off?

When I was a boy growing up on the back roads of Tennessee and Ohio, the men I knew labored with their bodies. They were marginal farmers, just scraping by, or welders, steelworkers, carpenters; they swept floors, dug ditches, mined coal, or drove trucks, their forearms ropy with muscle; they trained horses, stoked furnaces, made tires, stood on assembly lines wrestling parts onto cars and refrigerators. They got up before light, worked all day long whatever the weather, and when they came home at night they looked as though somebody had been whipping them. In the evenings and on weekends they worked on their own places, tilling gardens that were lumpy with clay, fixing broken-down cars, hammering on houses that were always too drafty, too leaky, too small.

The bodies of the men I knew were twisted and maimed in ways visible and invisible. The nails of their hands were black and split, the hands tattooed with scars. Some had lost fingers. Heavy lifting had given many of them finicky backs and guts weak from hernias. Racing against conveyor belts had given them ulcers. Their ankles and knees ached from years of standing on concrete. Anyone who had worked for long around machines was hard of hearing. They squinted, and the skin of their faces was creased like the leather of old work gloves. There were times, studying them, when I dreaded growing up. Most of them coughed, from dust or cigarettes, and most of them drank cheap wine or whiskey, so their eyes looked bloodshot and bruised. The fathers of my friends always seemed older than the mothers. Men wore out sooner. Only women lived into old age.

As a boy I also knew another sort of men, who did not sweat and break down like mules. They were soldiers, and so far as I could tell they scarcely worked at all. But when the shooting started, many of them would die. This was what soldiers were *for,* just as a hammer was for driving nails.

Warriors and toilers: these seemed, in my boyhood vision, to be the chief destinies for men. They weren't the only destinies, as I learned from having a few male teachers, from reading books, and from watching television. But the men on television—the politicians, the astronauts, the generals, the savvy lawyers, the philosophical doctors, the bosses who gave orders to both soldiers and laborers—seemed as remote and unreal to me as the figures in Renaissance tapestries. I could no more imagine growing up to become one of these cool, potent creatures than I could imagine becoming a prince.

A nearer and more hopeful example was that of my father, who had escaped from a red-dirt farm to a tire factory, and from the assembly line to the front office. Eventually he dressed in a white shirt and tie. He carried himself as if he had been born to work with his mind. But his body, remembering the earlier years of slogging work, began to give out on him in his fifties, and it quit on him entirely before he turned 65.

A scholarship enabled me not only to attend college, a rare enough feat in my circle, but even to study in a university meant for the children of the rich. Here I met for the first time young men who had assumed from birth that they would lead lives of comfort and power. And for the first time I met women who told me that men were guilty of having kept all the joys and privileges of the earth for themselves. I was baffled. What privileges? What joys? I thought about the maimed, dismal lives of most of the men back home. What had they stolen from their wives and daughters? The right to go five days a week, 12 months a year, for 30 or 40 years to a steel mill or a coal mine? The right to drop bombs and die in war? The right to feel every leak in the roof, every gap in the fence, every cough in the engine as a wound they must mend? The right to feel, when the layoff comes or the plant shuts down, not only afraid but ashamed?

I was slow to understand the deep grievances of women. This was   16 because, as a boy, I had envied them. Before college, the only people I had ever known who were interested in art or music or literature, the only ones who read books, the only ones who ever seemed to enjoy a sense of ease and grace were the mothers and daughters. Like the menfolk, they fretted about money, they scrimped and made do. But, when the pay stopped coming in, they were not the ones who had failed. Nor did they have to go to war, and that seemed to me a blessed fact. By comparison with the narrow, ironclad days of fathers, there was an expansiveness, I thought, in the days of mothers. They went to see neighbors, to shop in town, to run errands at school, at the library, at church. No doubt, had I looked harder at their lives, I would have envied them less. It was not my fate to become a woman, so it was easier for me to see the graces. I didn't see, then, what a prison a house could be, since houses seemed to me brighter, handsomer places than any factory. I did not realize—because such things were never spoken of—how often women suffered from men's bullying. Even then I could see how exhausting it was for a mother to cater all day to the needs of young children. But if I had been asked, as a boy, to choose between tending a baby and tending a machine, I think I would have chosen the baby. (Having now tended both, I know I would choose the baby.)

So I was baffled when the women at college accused me and my sex of having cornered the world's pleasures. I think something like my bafflement has been felt by other boys (and by girls as well) who grew up in dirt-poor farm country, in mining country, in black ghettos, in Hispanic barrios, in the shadows of factories, in Third World nations— any place where the fate of men is just as grim and bleak as the fate of women.

When the women I met at college thought about the joys and privileges of men, they did not carry in their minds the sort of men I had known in my childhood. They thought of their fathers, who were bankers, physicians, architects, stockbrokers, the big wheels of the big cities. They were never laid off, never short of cash at month's end, never lined up for welfare. These fathers made decisions that mattered. They ran the world.

The daughters of such men wanted to share in this power, this glory. So did I. They yearned for a say over their future, for jobs worthy of their abilities, for the right to live at peace, unmolested, whole. Yes, I thought, yes yes. The difference between me and these daughters was that they saw me, because of my sex, as destined from birth to become like their fathers, and therefore as an enemy to their desires. But I knew better. I wasn't an enemy, in fact or in feeling. I was an ally. If I had known, then, how to tell them so, would they have believed me? Would they now?

Topics for Critical Thinking and Writing

1. Look at Sander's introductory paragraphs (1–9). What do you think he hoped to accomplish by these paragraphs? To put it another way, suppose the essay began with paragraph 10, "When I was a boy growing up. . . ." What would be changed or lost?
2. Look at the second sentence of paragraph 10. It's a rather long sentence, with three independent clauses and lists of parallel phrases. How would you describe the verbs he uses? What effect does the structure of the sentence produce?
3. What is the topic sentence of paragraph 11? How does Sanders develop the paragraph, and what does the paragraph contribute to his argument?
4. What advantages did women enjoy that Sanders says he envied when he was a boy? What disadvantages does he mention (in paragraph 15)? What disadvantages does he *not* mention?
5. In paragraphs 16, 17, and 18, Sanders shifts from focusing on issues of gender to issues of class. How has he prepared us for this shift?
6. Evaluate Sanders' argument. How would you answer the questions he poses in his final paragraph?
7. When you were growing up, which lives seemed to have the most advantages or disadvantages, those of men or of women? Why did you think so? Did your opinion change as you grew older? Explain.

Paul Theroux

Paul Theroux was born in 1941 in Medford, Massachusetts, and was educated at the University of Maine, the University of Massachusetts, and Syracuse University. He served as a Peace Corps volunteer in Africa and has spent much of his adult life abroad, in Africa, Asia, Europe, and Central America. Though best known as a novelist and writer of travel books, he is also a poet and essayist. This essay originally appeared in The New York Times Magazine.

The Male Myth

There is a pathetic sentence in the chapter "Fetishism" in Dr. Norman Cameron's book *Personality Development and Psychopathology*. It goes: "Fetishists are nearly always men; and their commonest fetish is a woman's shoe." I cannot read that sentence without thinking that it is just one more awful thing about being a man—and perhaps it is the most important thing to know about us.

I have always disliked being a man. The whole idea of manhood in America is pitiful, a little like having to wear an ill-fitting coat for one's entire life. (By contrast, I imagine femininity to be an oppressive sense of nakedness.) Even the expression "Be a man!" strikes me as insulting and abusive. It means: Be stupid, be unfeeling, obedient and soldierly, and stop thinking. Man means "manly"—how can one think "about men" without considering the terrible ambition of manliness? And yet it is part of every man's life. It is a hideous and crippling lie; it not only insists on difference and connives at superiority, it is also by its very nature destructive—emotionally damaging and socially harmful.

The youth who is subverted, as most are, into believing in the masculine ideal is effectively separated from women—it is the most savage tribal logic—and he spends the rest of his life finding women a riddle and a nuisance. Of course, there is a female version of this male affliction. It begins with mothers encouraging little girls to say (to other adults), "Do you like my new dress?" In a sense, girls are traditionally urged to please adults with a kind of coquettishness, while boys are enjoined to behave like monkeys toward each other. The 9-year-old coquette proceeds to become womanish in a subtle power game in which she learns to be sexually indispensable, socially decorative and always alert to a man's sense of inadequacy.

Femininity—being ladylike—implies needing a man as witness and seducer; but masculinity celebrates the exclusive company of men. That is why it is so grotesque; and that is also why there is no manliness without inadequacy—because it denies men the natural friendship of women.

It is very hard to imagine any concept of manliness that does not belittle women, and it begins very early. At an age when I wanted to meet girls—let's say the treacherous years of 13 to 16—I was told to take up a sport, get more fresh air, join the Boy Scouts, and I was urged

4

not to read so much. It was the 1950's and, if you asked too many questions about sex, you were sent to camp—boy's camp, of course; the nightmare. Nothing is more unnatural or prisonlike than a boys' camp, but if it were not for them, we would have no Elks' Lodges, no poolrooms, no boxing matches, no marines.

And perhaps no sports as we know them. Everyone is aware of how few in number are the athletes who behave like gentlemen. Just as high-school basketball teaches you how to be a poor loser, the manly attitude toward sports seems to be little more than a recipe for creating bad marriages, social misfits, moral degenerates, sadists, latent rapists and just plain louts. I regard high-school sports as a drug far worse than marijuana, and it is the reason that the average tennis champion, say, is a pathetic oaf.

Any objective study would find the quest for manliness essentially right wing, puritanical, cowardly, neurotic and fueled largely by a fear of women. It is also certainly philistine. There is no book hater like a Little League coach. But, indeed, all the creative arts are obnoxious to the manly ideal, because at their best the arts are pursued by uncompetitive and essentially solitary people. It makes it very hard for a creative youngster, for any boy who expresses the desire to be alone seems to be saying that there is something wrong with him.

It ought to be clear by now that I have an objection to the way we   8 turn boys into men. It does not surprise me that when the President of the United States has his customary weekend off, he dresses like a cowboy—it is both a measure of his insecurity and his willingness to please. In many ways, American culture does little more for a man than prepare him for modeling clothes in the L. L. Bean catalogue. I take this as a personal insult because for many years I found it impossible to admit to myself that I wanted to be a writer. It was my guilty secret, because being a writer was incompatible with being a man.

There are people who might deny this, but that is because the American writer, typically, has been so at pains to prove his manliness. But first there was a fear that writing was not a manly profession—indeed, not a profession at all. (The paradox in American letters is that it has always been easier for a woman to write and for a man to be published.) Growing up, I had thought of sports as wasteful and humiliating, and the idea of manliness as a bore. My wanting to become a writer was not a flight from that oppressive role playing, but I quickly saw that it was at odds with it. Everything in stereotyped manliness goes against the life of the mind. The Hemingway personality is too tedious to go into here, but certainly it was not until this aberrant behavior was examined by feminists in the 1960's that any male writer dared question the pugnacity in Hemingway's fiction. All that bullfighting and arm-wrestling and elephant shooting diminished Hemingway as a writer: One cannot be a male writer without first proving that one is a man.

It is normal in America for a man to be dismissive or even somewhat apologetic about being a writer. Various factors make it easier. There is a heartiness about journalism that makes it acceptable—journalism is the manliest form of American writing and, therefore, the profession the most independent-minded women seek (yes, it is an illusion, but that is my point). Fiction writing is equated with a kind of dispirited failure and is only manly when it produces wealth. Money is masculinity. So is drinking. Being a drunkard is another assertion, if misplaced, of manliness. The American male writer is traditionally proud of his heavy drinking. But we are also very literal-minded people. A man proves his manhood in America in old-fashioned ways. He kills lions, like Hemingway; or he hunts ducks, like Nathanael West; or he makes pronouncements, like "A man should carry enough knife to defend himself with," as James Jones is said to have once told an interviewer. And we are familiar with the lengths to which Norman Mailer is prepared, in his endearing way, to prove that he is just as much a monster as the next man.

When the novelist John Irving was revealed as a wrestler, people took him to be a very serious writer. But what interests me is that it is inconceivable that any woman writer would be shown in such a posture. How surprised we would be if Joyce Carol Oates were revealed as a sumo wrestler or Joan Didion enjoyed pumping iron. "Lives in New York City with her three children" is the typical woman-writer's biographical note, for just as the male writer must prove he has achieved a sort of muscular manhood, the woman writer—or rather her publicists—must prove her motherhood.

There would be no point in saying any of this if it were not generally accepted that to be a man is somehow—even now in feminist-influenced America—a privilege. It is on the contrary an unmerciful and punishing burden. Being a man is bad enough; being manly is appalling. It is the sinister silliness of men's fashions that inspires the so-called dress code of the Ritz-Carlton Hotel in Boston. It is the institutionalized cheating in college sports. It is a pathetic and primitive insecurity. 12

And this is also why men often object to feminism, but are afraid to explain why: Of course women have a justified grievance, but most men believe—and with reason—that their lives are much worse.

Topics for Critical Thinking and Writing

1. In paragraph 6 Theroux says that "high school basketball teaches you how to be a poor loser." Think about this, and then write a paragraph that in effect offers a definition of a "poor loser" but that also shows how a high school sport teaches one to be a poor loser.

2. Theroux speaks of "the Hemingway personality" and of "the pugnacity in Hemingway's fiction." If you have read a work by Hemingway, write

a paragraph in which you explain (to someone unfamiliar with Hemingway) what Theroux is talking about.

3. Let's assume that a reader says he or she doesn't quite understand Theroux's final paragraph. Write a paragraph explaining it.

4. Theroux makes some deliberately provocative statements, for example:

> Nothing is more unnatural or prisonlike than a boys' camp.

> Everyone is aware of how few in number are the athletes who behave like gentlemen.

> The quest for manliness . . . [is] fueled largely by a fear of women.

Choose one such statement from the essay and consider what you would need to do to argue effectively against it. You needn't produce the argument, but simply consider how such an argument might be constructed.

Andrew Lam

Andrew Lam is an associate editor of the Pacific News Service. This essay originally appeared as an op-ed piece in The New York Times *in 1993.*

Goodbye, Saigon, Finally

Flipping through my United States passport as if it were a comic book, the customs man at the Noi Bai Airport, near Hanoi, appeared curious. "Brother, when did you leave Vietnam?"

"One day before National Defeat Day," I said without thinking. It was an exile's expression, not his.

"God! When did that happen?"

"The 30th of April, 1975."   4

"But, brother, don't you mean National Liberation Day?"

If this conversation had occurred a decade earlier, the difference would have created a dangerous gap between the Vietnamese and the returning Vietnamese-American. But this happened in 1992, when the walls were down, and as I studied the smiling young official, it occurred to me that there was something about this moment, an epiphany. "Yes, brother, I suppose I do mean liberation day."

Not everyone remembers the date with humor. It marked the Vietnamese diaspora, boat people, refugees.

On April 29, 1975, my family and I escaped from Saigon in a crowd- 8
ed C–130. We arrived in Guam the next day, to hear the BBC's tragic account of Saigon's demise: U.S. helicopters flying over the chaotic city, Vietcong tanks rolling in, Vietnamese climbing over the gate into the

U.S. Embassy, boats fleeing down the Saigon River toward the South China Sea.

In time, April 30 became the birth date of an exile's culture built on defeatism and a sense of tragic ending. For a while, many Vietnamese in America talked of revenge, of blood debts, of the exile's anguish. Their songs had nostalgic titles: "The Day When I Return" and "Oh, Mother Vietnam, We Are Still Here."

April 30, 1976: A child of 12 with nationalistic fervor, I stood in front of San Francisco City Hall with other refugees. I waved the gold flag with three horizontal red stripes. I shouted (to no one in particular): "Give us back South Vietnam!"

April 30, 1979: An uncle told me there was an American plan to retake our homeland by force: "The way Douglas MacArthur did for the South Koreans in the 50's." My 17-year-old brother declared that he would join the anti-Communist guerrilla movement in Vietnam. My father sighed.

April 30, 1983: I stayed awake all night with Vietnamese classmates   12
from Berkeley to listen to monotonous speeches by angry old men. "National defeat must be avenged by sweat and blood!" one vowed.

But through the years, April 30 has come to symbolize something entirely different to me. Although I sometimes mourn the loss of home and land, it's the American landscape and what it offers that solidify my hyphenated identity. This date of tragic ending, from an optimist's point of view, is also an American rebirth, something close to the Fourth of July.

I remember whispering to a young countryman during one of those monotonous April 30 rallies in the mid-1980's: "Even as the old man speaks of patriotic repatriation, we've already become Americans."

Assimilation, education, the English language, the American "I"— these have carried me and many others further from that beloved tropical country than the C–130 ever could. Each optimistic step the young Vietnamese takes toward America is tempered with a little betrayal of Little Saigon's parochialism, its sentimentalities and the old man's outdated passion.

When did this happen? Who knows? One night, America quietly   16
seeps in and takes hold of one's mind and body, and the Vietnamese soul of sorrows slowly fades away. In the morning, the Vietnamese American speaks a new language of materialism: his vocabulary includes terms like career choices, down payment, escrow, overtime.

My brother never made it to the Indochinese jungle. The would-be guerrilla fighter became instead a civil engineer. My talk of endless possibilities is punctuated with favorite verbs—transcend, redefine, become. "I want to become a writer," I declared to my parents one morning. My mother gasped.

April 30, 1975: defeat or liberation?

"It was a day of joyous victory," said a retired Communist official in Hanoi. "We fought and realized Uncle Ho's dream of national independence." Then he asked for Marlboro cigarettes and a few precious dollars.

Nhon Nguyen, a real state salesman in San Jose, a former South   20
Vietnamese naval officer, said: "I could never forget the date. So many
people died. So much blood. I could never tolerate Communism, you
know."

Mai Huong, a young Vietnamese woman in Saigon, said that, of
course, it was National Liberation Day. "But it's the South," she said
with a wink, "that liberated the North." Indeed, conservative Uncle Ho
has slowly admitted defeat to entrepreneurial and cosmopolitan Miss
Saigon. She has taken her meaning from a different uncle, you know,
Uncle Sam.

"April 30, 1975?" said Bobby To, my 22 year-old cousin in San Francisco. "I don't know that date. I don't remember Vietnam at all." April
29, 1992, is more meaningful to him, Bobby said. "It's when the race
riots broke out all over our country. To me it's more realistic to worry
about what's going on over here then there."

Sighing, the customs man, who offered me a ride into Hanoi, said:
"In truth, there are no liberators. We are all defeated here." There is no
job, no future, no direction, only a sense of collective malaise, something akin to the death of the national soul. He added: "You're lucky,
brother. You left Vietnam and became an American."

April 30, 1993: My friends and I plan to watch *Gone with the Wind*   24
for the umpteenth time and look for a scene of our unrequited romantic longings: Scarlett, teary-eyed with wind-blown hair, returning to
forlorn Tara. We no longer can. Children of defeat, self-liberating
adults, we promise to hug instead and recount to each other our own
stories of flight.

[1993]

Topics for Critical Thinking and Writing

1. Lam sets up at once the distinction between National Defeat Day and
   National Liberation Day and calls the moment for him *an epiphany.*
   How does he do it? And what is an epiphany?
2. In paragraph 5 Lam remembers the escape from Vietnam in 1975, and
   then April 30 in 1976, 1979, 1983. Assuming that you were not around
   to notice those dates—or even if you were—what techniques does Lam
   use to make them vivid?
3. In paragraph 15 Lam says "Each optimistic step the young Vietnamese
   takes toward America is tempered with a little betrayal of Little Saigon's
   parochialism, its sentimentalities and the old man's outdated passion."
   What does he mean?
4. At the essay's conclusion, Lam says that he and his friends will watch
   Gone with the Wind and "recount to each other our own stories of flight."
   Why do they watch *Gone with the Wind* (instead of a Vietnamese film)?
   What does Lam's choice of the film tell us?
5. If you have a story similar to Lam's, or one that in many ways is
   opposed to Lam's, try to tell it in an essay that begins with a narrative
   and may end with one too.

Dennis Altman

We print an excerpt from an article that originally appeared in the New Internationalist *in November, 1989.*

Why Are Gay Men So Feared?

Gay men are the victims of insults, prejudice, abuse, violence, sometimes murder. Why are gay men hated by so many other men? Some maintain that homosexuality is unnatural or a threat to the family. But celibacy is also unnatural, yet nuns and priests are not regularly attacked. And there is also a good case to be made that homosexuality, actually *strengthens* the family by liberating some adults from childbearing duties and so increasing the pool of adults available to look after children.

But the real objection to homosexuality (and lesbianism) is undoubtedly more deep-seated: It is threatening because it seems to challenge the conventional roles governing a person's sex, and the female and male roles in society. The assertion of homosexual identity clearly challenges the apparent naturalness of gender roles.

Men are particularly prone to use anger and violence against those they think are undermining their masculinity. And it is here that we can find at least some of the roots of homophobia and gay-bashing.

As Freud understood, most societies are built upon a set of relationships between men: Most powerful institutions like parliaments and business corporations are male-dominated. And this "male bonding" demands a certain degree of sexual sublimation.

In many societies, the links between men are much stronger than the relations that link them to women. But these bonds are social rather than individual, and for this reason need to be strictly governed. Armies, for example, depend upon a very strong sense of male solidarity, though this does not allow for too close an emotional tie between any *specific* pair of men.

Thus the most extreme homophobia is often found among tightly knit groups of men, who need to deny any sexual component to their bonding as well as boost their group solidarity by turning violently on "fags" or "queers," who are defined as completely alien. This is a phenomenon found among teenage gangs, policemen, and soldiers. A particularly prominent example of this was Germany's Nazi Party, which shortly after coming to power purged those of its members who were tempted to turn the hypermasculinity of Nazism into an excuse for overt homosexual behavior.

Many observers of sexual violence have argued that the most virulent queer-basher is attacking the homosexual potential in himself—a potential that he has learned to suppress. Because homosexuality is

706

"un-masculine," those who struggle with feelings of homosexuality (often unacknowledged) will be particularly tempted to resolve them through "masculine" expressions of violence. In court cases involving violence against gay men, the idea of preserving one's male honor is often pleaded as a defense.

Homophobia has effects that go far beyond those individuals against whom it is directed. Like racism and sexism, it is an expression of hatred that harms the perpetrator as well as the victim; the insecurities, fears, and sexual hang-ups that lead young men to go out looking for "fags" to beat up are dangerous to the entire society.

Those societies that are best able to accept homosexuals are also societies that are able to accept assertive women and gentle men, and they tend to be less prone to the violence produced by hypermasculinity.

Topics for Critical Thinking and Writing

1. Before you read this essay, had it occurred to you that gay men are "feared"? What other attitudes toward gay men does Altman suggest?
2. Does Altman believe that homosexuality is unnatural? Does he offer any evidence that it either is or is not unnatural? How, in this context, might *natural* and *unnatural* be defined?
3. In a sentence or two state the answer that Altman gives to the question that he poses in his title. How convincing do you find it?
4. Does the logic of Altman's argument lead you to infer that lesbians are feared? Do you think they *are* feared? What do you think that Altman might say in reply to this question?

Lindsy Van Gelder

Lindsy Van Gelder was born in 1942 and educated at Northwestern University and Sarah Lawrence College. After graduating, she worked as a newspaper reporter and (since 1977) as a staff writer for Ms., *where the present essay first appeared.*

Marriage as a Restricted Club

Several years ago, I stopped going to weddings. In fact, I no longer celebrate the wedding anniversaries or engagements of friends, relatives, or anyone else, although I might wish them lifelong joy in their relationships. My explanation is that the next wedding I attend will be my own—to the woman I've loved and lived with for nearly six years.

Although I've been legally married to a man myself (and come close to marrying two others), I've come, in these last six years with

Pamela, to see heterosexual marriage as very much a restricted club. (Nor is this likely to change in the near future, if one can judge by the recent clobbering of what was actually a rather tame proposal to recognize "domestic partnerships" in San Francisco.) Regardless of the *reason* people marry—whether to save on real estate taxes or qualify for married students housing or simply to express love—lesbians and gay men can't obtain the same results should they desire to do so. It seems apparent to me that few friends of Pamela's and mine would even join a club that excluded blacks, Jews, or women, much less assume that they could expect their black, Jewish, or female friends to toast their new status with champagne. But probably no other stand of principle we've ever made in our lives has been so misunderstood, or caused so much bad feeling on both sides.

Several people have reacted with surprise to our views, it never having occurred to them that gay people *can't* legally marry. (Why on earth did they think that none of us had bothered?) The most common reaction, however, is acute embarrassment, followed by a denial of our main point—that the about-to-be-wed person is embarking on a privileged status. (One friend of Pamela's insisted that lesbians are "lucky" not to have to agonize over whether or not to get married.) So wrapped in gauze is the institution of marriage, so ingrained the expectation that brides and grooms can enjoy the world's delighted approval, that it's hard for me not to feel put on the defensive for being so mean-spirited, eccentric, and/or politically rigid as to boycott such a happy event.

Another question we've fielded more than once (usually from our   4
most radical friends, both gay and straight) is why we'd want to get married in the first place. In fact, I have mixed feelings about registering my personal life with the state, but—and this seems to me to be the essence of radical politics—I'd prefer to be the one making the choice. And while feminists in recent years have rightly focused on puncturing the Schlaflyite myth of the legally protected homemaker, it's also true that marriage does confer some very real dollars-and-cents benefits. One example of inequity is our inability to file joint tax returns, although many couples, both gay and straight, go through periods when one partner in the relationship is unemployed or makes considerably less money than the other. At one time in our relationship, Pamela—who is a musician—was between bands and earning next to nothing. I was making a little over $37,000 a year as a newspaper reporter, a salary that put me in the 42 percent tax bracket—about $300 a week taken out of my paycheck. If we had been married, we could have filed a joint tax return and each paid taxes on half my salary, in the 25 or 30 percent bracket. The difference would have been nearly $100-a-week in our pockets.

Around the same time, Pamela suffered a months'-long illness which would have been covered by my health insurance if she were my spouse. We were luckier than many; we could afford it. But on top of the worry and expense involved (and despite the fact that intellectually we believe in the ideal of free medical care for everyone), we found it almost impossible to avoid internalizing a sense of personal failure—the knowledge that *because of who we are, we can't take care of each other.* I've heard of other gay people whose lovers were deported because they couldn't marry them and enable them to become citizens; still others who were barred from intensive-care units where their lovers lay stricken because they weren't "immediate family."

I would never begrudge a straight friend who got married to save a lover from deportation or staggering medical bills, but the truth is that I no longer sympathize with most of the less tangible justifications. This includes the oft-heard "for the sake of the children" argument, since (like many gay people, especially women) I *have* children, and I resent the implication that some families are more "legitimate" than others. (It's important to safeguard one's children's rights to their father's property, but a legal contract will do the same thing as marriage.)

But the single most painful and infuriating rationale for marriage, as far as I'm concerned, is the one that goes: "We wanted to stand up and show the world that we've made a *genuine* commitment." When one is gay, such sentiments are labeled "flaunting." My lover and I almost never find ourselves in public settings outside the gay ghetto where we are (a) perceived to be a couple at all (people constantly ask us if we're sisters, although we look nothing like each other), and (b) valued as such. Usually we're forced to choose between being invisible and being despised. "Making a genuine commitment" in this milieu is like walking a highwire without a net—with most of the audience not even watching and a fair segment rooting for you to fall. A disproportionate number of gay couples do.

I think it's difficult for even my closest, most feminist straight women friends to empathize with the intensity of my desire to be recognized as Pamela's partner. (In fact, it may be harder for feminists to understand than for others; I know that when I was straight, I often resented being viewed as one half of a couple. My struggle was for an independent identity, not the cojoined one I now crave.) But we are simply not considered *authentic,* and the reminders are constant. Recently at a party, a man I'd known for years spied me across the room and came over to me, arms outstretched, big happy-to-see-you grin on his face. Pamela had a gig that night and wasn't at the party; my friend's wife was there but in another room, and I hadn't seen her yet. "How's M—?" I asked the man. "Oh, she's fine," he replied, continuing to smile pleasantly. "Are you and Pam still together?"

Our sex life itself is against the law in many states, of course, and like all lesbians and gay men, we are without many other rights, both large and small. (In Virginia, for instance, it's technically against the law for us to buy liquor.) But as a gay couple, we are also most likely to be labeled and discriminated against in those very settings that, for most heterosexual Americans, constitute the most relaxed and personal parts of life. Virtually every tiny public act of togetherness—from holding hands on the street to renting a hotel room to dancing—requires us constantly to risk humiliation (I think, for example, of the two California women who were recently thrown out of a restaurant that had special romantic tables for couples), sexual harassment (it's astonishing how many men can't resist coming on to a lesbian couple), and even physical assault. A great deal of energy goes into just expecting possible trouble. It's a process which, after six years, has become second nature for me—but occasionally, when I'm in Provincetown or someplace else with a large lesbian population, I experience the *absence* of it as a feeling of virtual weightlessness.

What does all this have to do with my friends' weddings? Obviously, I can't expect my friends to live my life. But I do think that lines are being drawn in this "pro-family" Reagan era, and I have no choice about what side I'm placed on. My straight friends do, and at the very least, I expect them to acknowledge that. I certainly expect them to understand why I don't want to be among the rice-throwers and well-wishers at their weddings; beyond that, I would hope that they would commit themselves to fighting for my rights—preferably in personally visible ways, like marching in gay pride parades. But I also wish they wouldn't get married, period. And if that sounds hard-nosed, I hope I'm only proving my point—that not being able to marry isn't a minor issue.

Not that my life would likely be changed as the result of any individual straight person's symbolic refusal to marry. (Nor, for that matter, do all gay couples want to be wed.) But it's a political reality that heterosexual live-together couples are among our best tactical allies. The movement to repeal state sodomy laws has profited from the desire of straight people to keep the government out of *their* bedrooms. Similarly, it was a heterosexual New York woman who went to court several years ago to fight her landlord's demand that she either marry her live-in boyfriend or face eviction for violating a lease clause prohibiting "unrelated" tenants—and whose struggle led to the recent passage of a state rent law that had ramifications for thousands of gay couples, including Pamela and me.

The right wing has seized on "homosexual marriage" as its bottom-line scare phrase in much the same way that "Would you want your sister to marry one?" was brandished 25 years ago. *They* see marriage as their turf. And so when I see feminists crossing into that territory of respectability and "sinlessness," I feel my buffer zone slipping away. I feel as though my friends are taking off their armbands, leaving me exposed.

Topics for Critical Thinking and Writing

1. Evaluate Van Gelder's title and opening paragraph. Did the title and the first sentence attract your attention, and, if so, did the rest of the first paragraph continue to hold it? Why or why not?

2. In paragraphs 4 and 5, Van Gelder gives some concrete details to support her point that members of the club receive benefits. Do you agree that fairness requires that gay and lesbian couples (and unmarried heterosexual couples) receive the same benefits? (By the way, *why* does society grant certain benefits to married heterosexual couples? What good reasons, if any, can you think of?)

3. As paragraph 10 indicates, the essay was written during the Reagan era. Do you think the climate has changed since then?

4. In paragraph 10 Van Gelder says that she expects her friends "to understand" why she is not among the guests at their weddings. Do you understand why, or do you think she does not really explain why her inability to marry Pamela legally should influence her view of heterosexual marriage?

Zora Neale Hurston

Zora Neale Hurston (1891?–1960) was brought up in Eatonvile, Florida, a town said to be the first all-black self-governing town in the United States. Her early years were spent working at odd jobs (domestic servant, manicurist, waitress), but she managed to attend Howard University and then, with the aid of a scholarship, entered Barnard College, where she was the first black student. At Barnard, influenced by the anthropologists Franz Boas and Ruth Benedict, she set out to study the folklore of Eatonville. Later she published several volumes of folklore, as well as stories, novels, and an autobiography (the source of our selection) called Dust Tracks on a Road *(1942).*

In the 1950s her writing seemed reactionary, almost embarrassing in an age of black protest, and she herself—working as a domestic, a librarian, and a substitute teacher—was almost forgotten. She died in a county welfare home in Florida and was buried in an unmarked grave. In the 1980s Hurston was, so to speak, rediscovered, partly because of the attention given to her by Alice Walker.

A Conflict of Interest

An incident happened that made me realize how theories go by the board when a person's livelihood is threatened. A man, a Negro, came into the shop one afternoon and sank down in Banks's chair. Banks was the manager and had the first chair by the door. It was so surprising that for a minute Banks just looked at him and never said a word. Finally, he found his tongue and asked, "What do you want?"

"Hair-cut and shave," the man said belligerently.

"But you can't get no hair-cut and shave here. Mr. Robinson[1] has a fine shop for Negroes on U Street near Fifteenth," Banks told him.

---

[1]**Robinson:** George Robinson, an African American, owned a chain of barber shops. Most of his shops catered to whites in Washington, D.C. (Editors' note).

"I know it, but I want one here. The Constitution of the United   4
States—"

But by that time, Banks had him by the arm. Not roughly, but he
was helping him out of his chair, nevertheless.

"I don't know how to cut your hair," Banks objected. "I was trained
on straight hair. Nobody in here knows how."

"Oh, don't hand me that stuff!" the crusader snarled. "Don't be
such an Uncle Tom."

"Run on, fellow. You can't get waited on in here."   8

"I'll stay right here until I do. I know my rights. Things like this
have got to be broken up. I'll get waited on all right, or sue the place."

"Go ahead and sue," Banks retorted. "Go on uptown, and get your
hair cut, man. Don't be so hard-headed for nothing."

"I'm getting waited on right here!"

"You're next, Mr. Powell," Banks said to a waiting customer. "Sorry,   12
mister, but you better go on uptown."

"But I have a right to be waited on wherever I please," the Negro
said, and started towards Updyke's chair which was being emptied.
Updyke whirled his chair around so that he could not sit down and
stepped in front of it. "Don't you touch *my* chair!" Updyke glared. "Go
on about your business."

But instead of going, he made to get into the chair by force.

"Don't argue with him! Throw him out of here!" somebody in the
back cried. And in a minute, barbers, customers all lathered and hair
half cut, and porters, were all helping to throw the Negro out.

The rush carried him way out into the middle of G street and flung   16
him down. He tried to lie there and be a martyr, but the roar of oncom-
ing cars made him jump up and scurry off. We never heard any more
about it. I did not participate in the mêlée, but I wanted him thrown
out, too. My business was threatened.

It was only that night in bed that I analyzed the whole thing and
realized that I was giving sanction to Jim Crow, which theoretically, I
was supposed to resist. But here were ten Negro barbers, three porters
and two manicurists all stirred up at the threat of our living through loss
of patronage. Nobody thought it out at the moment. It was an instinctive
thing. That was the first time it was called to my attention that self-interest rides over all sorts of lines. I have seen the same thing happen hundreds of times since, and now I understand it. One sees it breaking over
racial, national, religious and class lines. Anglo-Saxon against Anglo-
Saxon, Jew against Jew, Negro against Negro, and all sorts of combinations of the three against other combinations of the three. Offhand, you
might say that we fifteen Negroes should have felt the racial thing and
served him. He was one of us. Perhaps it would have been a beautiful
thing if Banks had turned to the shop crowded with customers and
announced that this man was going to be served like everybody else
even at the risk of losing their patronage, with all of the other employees
lined up in the center of the floor shouting, "So say we all!" It would

have been a stirring gesture, and made the headlines for a day. Then we could all have gone home to our unpaid rents and bills and things like that. I could leave school and begin my wanderings again. The "militant" Negro who would have been the cause of it all, would have perched on the smuddled-up wreck of things and crowed. Nobody ever found out who or what he was. Perhaps he did what he did on the spur of the moment, not realizing that serving him would have ruined Mr. Robinson, another Negro who had got what he had the hard way. For not only would the G Street shop have been forced to close, but the F Street shop and all of his other six downtown shops. Wrecking George Robinson like that on a "race" angle would have been ironic tragedy. He always helped out any Negro who was trying to do anything progressive as far as he was able. He had no education himself, but he was for it. He would give any Howard University student a job in his shops if they could qualify, even if it was only a few hours a week.

So I do not know what was the ultimate right in this case. I do know how I felt at the time. There is always something fiendish and loathsome about a person who threatens to deprive you of your way of making a living. That is just human-like, I reckon.

Topics for Critical Thinking and Writing

1. Hurston published this account in 1942, and she was writing about an event that had taken place a couple of decades earlier. Given the period and given Hurston's analysis of her action, do you find her behavior understandable and excusable, or do you think that she is rationalizing cowardice? Explain.

2. Words like *outrageous, ironic, pathetic,* and even *tragic* probably can be appropriately applied to this episode. Would you agree, however, that, as Hurston narrates it, it also has comic elements? If so, explain.

3. Hurston argues that self-interest overrides "racial, national, religious, and class lines." Do you agree? Does she persuade you that at least in this incident it was true, or might there have been other reasons for the employees' actions?

Gloria Naylor

Gloria Naylor—university teacher, essayist, and novelist—holds an M.A. in Afro-American Studies from Yale University. Her first novel, The Women of Brewster Place *(1983), won an American Book Award. "A Question of Language" originally appeared in* The New York Times.

A Question of Language

Language is the subject. It is the written form with which I've managed to keep the wolf away from the door and, in diaries, to keep my sanity. In spite of this, I consider the written word inferior to the spoken, and much of the frustration experienced by novelists is the awareness that whatever we manage to capture in even the most transcendent passages falls far short of the richness of life. Dialogue achieves its power in the dynamics of a fleeting moment of sight, sound, smell, and touch.

I'm not going to enter the debate here about whether it is language that shapes reality or vice versa. That battle is doomed to be waged whenever we seek intermittent reprieve from the chicken and egg dispute. I will simply take the position that the spoken word, like the written word, amounts to a nonsensical arrangement of sounds or letters without a consensus that assigns "meaning." And building from the meanings of what we hear, we order reality. Words themselves are innocuous; it is the consensus that gives them true power.

I remember the first time I heard the word *nigger*. In my third-grade class, our math tests were being passed down the rows, and as I handed the papers to a little boy in back of me, I remarked that once again he had received a much lower mark than I did. He snatched his test from me and spit out that word. Had he called me a nymphomaniac or a necrophiliac, I couldn't have been more puzzled. I didn't know what a nigger was, but I knew that whatever it meant, it was something he shouldn't have called me. This was verified when I raised my hand, and in a loud voice repeated what he had said and watched the teacher scold him for using a "bad" word. I was later to go home and ask the inevitable question that every black parent must face—"Mommy, what does 'nigger' mean?"

And what exactly did it mean? Thinking back, I realize that this 4 could not have been the first time the word was used in my presence. I was part of a large extended family that had migrated from the rural South after World War II and formed a close-knit network that gravitated around my maternal grandparents. Their ground-floor apartment in one of the buildings they owned in Harlem was a weekend mecca for my immediate family, along with countless aunts, uncles, and cousins who brought along assorted friends. It was a bustling and open house with assorted neighbors and tenants popping in and out to exchange bits of gossip, pick up an old quarrel or referee the ongoing checkers game in which my grandmother cheated shamelessly. They were all there to let down their hair and put up their feet after a week of labor in the factories, laundries, and shipyards of New York.

Amid the clamor, which could reach deafening proportions—two or three conversations going on simultaneously, punctuated by the sound of a baby's crying somewhere in the back rooms or out on the street—there was still a rigid set of rules about what was said and how. Older children were sent out of the living room when it was time to get into the juicy details about "you-know-who" up on the third floor who had gone and gotten herself "p · r · e · g · n · a · n · t!" But my parents, knowing that I could spell well beyond my years, always demanded that I follow the others out to play. Beyond sexual misconduct and death, everything else was considered harmless for our young ears. And so among the anecdotes of the triumphs and disappointments in the various workings of their lives, the word *nigger* was used in my presence, but it was set within contexts and inflections that caused it to register in my mind as something else.

In the singular, the word was always applied to a man who had distinguished himself in some situation that brought their approval for his strength, intelligence, or drive:

"Did Johnny really do that?"

"I'm telling you, that nigger pulled in $6,000 of overtime last year.   8 Said he got enough for a down payment on a house."

When used with a possessive adjective by a woman—"my nigger"—it became a term of endearment for husband or boyfriend. But it could be more than just a term applied to a man. In their mouths it became the pure essence of manhood—a disembodied force that channeled their past history of struggle and present survival against the odds into a victorious statement of being: "Yeah, that old foreman found out quick enough—you don't mess with a nigger."

In the plural, it became a description of some group within the community that had overstepped the bounds of decency as my family defined it: Parents who neglected their children, a drunken couple who fought in public, people who simply refused to look for work, those with excessively dirty mouths or unkempt households were all "trifling niggers." This particular circle could forgive hard times, unemployment, the occasional bout of depression—they had gone through all of that themselves—but the unforgivable sin was lack of self-respect.

A woman could never be a *nigger* in the singular, with its connotation of confirming worth. The noun *girl* was its closest equivalent in that sense, but only when used in direct address and regardless of the gender doing the addressing. *Girl* was a token of respect for a woman. The one-syllable word was drawn out to sound like three in recognition of the extra ounce of wit, nerve or daring that the woman had shown in the situation under discussion.

"G · i · r · l, stop. You mean you said that to his face?"   12

But if the word was used in a third-person reference or shortened so that it almost snapped out of the mouth, it always involved some element of communal disapproval. And age became an important factor in these exchanges. It was only between individuals of the same generation, or from an older person to a younger (but never the other way around), that "girl" would be considered a compliment.

I don't agree with the argument that use of the word *nigger* at this social stratum of the black community was an internalization of racism. The dynamics were the exact opposite: the people in my grandmother's living room took a word that whites used to signify worthlessness or degradation and rendered it impotent. Gathering there together, they transformed *nigger* to signify the varied and complex human beings they knew themselves to be. If the word was to disappear totally from the mouths of even the most liberal of white society, no one in that room was naive enough to believe it would disappear from white minds. Meeting the word head-on, they proved it had absolutely nothing to do with the way they were determined to live their lives.

So there must have been dozens of times that the word *nigger* was spoken in front of me before I reached the third grade. But I didn't "hear" it until it was said by a small pair of lips that had already learned it could be a way to humiliate me. That was the word I went home and asked my mother about. And since she knew that I had to grow up in America, she took me in her lap and explained.

Topics for Critical Thinking and Writing

1. Why, according to Naylor (in paragraph 1) is written language inferior to spoken language? Can you think of any way or any circumstance in which written language is superior? How does Naylor's essay support her position here? Or does it?

2. In paragraph 2 Naylor says "Words themselves are innocuous; it is the consensus that gives them true power." What does this mean? In the rest of the essay Naylor discusses meanings of the word *nigger*. To what extent does her discussion demonstrate that consensus "assigns meaning" and gives words power.

3. If as a child you were the victim of an ethnic slur, explain how you reacted to it and how others (perhaps a parent or teacher) reacted to it. Or, if you ever delivered an ethnic slur, explain how you felt then and how you feel now about the incident or incidents.

Jeanne Wakatsuki Houston

Jeanne Wakatsuki, the daughter of immigrants from Japan, was born in Inglewood, California. When she was seven, the Japanese attack on Pearl Harbor aroused such fear and resentment that Japanese and Japanese Americans on the Pacific coast of the United States were relocated, and her family was forced to spend three-and-a-half years at Manzanar, a camp in Owens Valley, California. Later she graduated from San Jose State University, married James D. Houston, and took up writing as a career.

Her first book, written with her husband, was Farewell to Manzanar *(1973), a memoir of her experience of the years during World War II. We reprint an essay from a later collection,* Beyond Manzanar *(1985).*

Double Identity

The memories surrounding my awareness of being female fall into two categories: those of the period before World War II, when the family made up my life, and those after the war when I entered puberty, and my world expanded to include the ways and values of my Caucasian peers. I did not think about my Asian-ness and how it influenced my self-image as a female until I married.

In remembering myself as a small child, I find it hard to separate myself from the entity of the family. I was too young to be given "duties" according to my sex, and I was unaware that this was the organizational basis for operating the family. I took it for granted that everyone just did what had to be done to keep things running smoothly. My five older sisters helped my mother with domestic duties. My four older brothers helped my father in the fishing business. What I vaguely recall about the sensibility surrounding our sex differences was that my sisters and I all liked to please our brothers. Moreover, we tried to attract positive attention from Papa. A smile or affectionate pat from him was like a gift from heaven. Somehow, we never felt this way about Mama. We took her love for granted. But there was something special about Papa.

I never identified this as one of the blessings of maleness. After all, I played with my brother Kiyo, two years older than myself, and I never felt there was anything special about him. I could even make him cry. My older brothers were fun-loving, boisterous and very kind to me, especially when I made them laugh with my imitations of Carmen Miranda dancing, or Bonnie Baker singing "Oh, Johnny." But Papa was different. His specialness came not from being male, but from being the authority.

After the war, and the closing of the camps, my world drastically changed. The family had disintegrated, my father was no longer "God-like" despite my mother's attempt to sustain that pre-war image of him. I was spending most of my time with my new Caucasian friends and learning new values that clashed with the values of my parents. It was also time that I assumed the duties girls were supposed to do—cooking, cleaning the house, washing and ironing clothes. I remember washing and ironing my brothers' shirts, careful to press the collars correctly, try-

4

717

ing not to displease them. I cannot ever remember my brothers performing domestic chores while I lived at home. Yet, even though they may not have been working "out there," as the men were supposed to do, I did not resent it. It would have embarrassed me to see my brothers doing the dishes. Their reciprocation came in a different way. They were very protective of me and made me feel good and important for being a female. If my brother Ray had extra money, he would sometimes buy me a sexy sweater like my Caucasian friends wore, which Mama wouldn't buy for me. My brothers taught me to ride a bicycle, to drive a car, took me to my first dance, and proudly introduced me to their friends.

Although the family had changed, my identity as a female within it did not differ much from my older sisters' who grew up before the war. The males and females supported each other but for different reasons. No longer was the survival of the family as a group our primary objective; we cooperated to help each other survive "out there" in the complicated world that had weakened Papa.

We were living in Long Beach then. My brothers encouraged me to run for school office, to try out for majorette and song leader, and to run for Queen of various festivities. They were proud that I was breaking social barriers still closed to them. It was acceptable for an Oriental male to excel academically and in sports. But to gain recognition socially in a society that had been fed the stereotyped model of the Asian male as cook, houseboy or crazed *Kamikaze* pilot, was almost impossible. The more alluring myth of mystery and exotica that surrounds the Oriental female made it easier, though no less inwardly painful.

Whenever I succeeded in the *hakujin*[1] world, my brothers were supportive, whereas Papa would be disdainful, undermined by my obvious capitulation to the ways of the West. I wanted to be like my Caucasian friends. Not only did I want to look like them, I wanted to act like them. I tried hard to be outgoing and socially aggressive, and to act confidently, like my girl friends. At home I was careful not to show these traits to my father. For him it was bad enough that I did not even look very Japanese; I was too big, and I walked too assertively. My breasts were large, and besides that I showed them off with those sweaters the *hakujin* girls wore! My behavior at home was never calm and serene, but around my father I still tried to be as Japanese as I could.

As I passed puberty and grew more interested in boys, I soon   8
became aware that an Oriental female evoked a certain kind of interest from males. I was still too young to understand how or why an Oriental female fascinated Caucasian men, and of course, far too young to see then that it was a form of "not being seen." My brothers would warn me, "Don't trust the *hakujin* boys. They only want one thing. They'll treat you like a servant and expect you to wait on them hand and foot. They don't know how to be nice to you." My brothers never dated Cau-

[1]*Hakujin,* Caucasian.

casian girls. In fact, I never really dated Caucasian boys until I went to college. In high school, I used to sneak out to dances and parties where I would meet them. I wouldn't even dare to think what Papa would do if he knew.

What my brothers were saying was that I should not act towards Caucasian males as I did towards them. I must not "wait on them" or allow them to think I would, because they wouldn't understand. In other words, be a Japanese female around Japanese men and act *hakujin* around Caucasian men. This double identity within a "double standard" resulted not only in confusion of my role or roles as female, but also in who or what I was racially. With the admonitions of my brothers lurking deep in my consciousness, I would try to be aggressive, assertive and "come on strong" towards Caucasian men. I mustn't let them think I was submissive, passive and all-giving, like Madame Butterfly.[2] With Asian males I would tone down my natural enthusiasm and settle into patterns instilled in me through the models of my mother and my sisters. I was not comfortable in either role.

I found I was more physically attracted to Caucasian men. Although T.V. and film were not nearly as pervasive as they are now, we still had an abundance of movie magazines and films from which to garner our idols for crushes and fantasy. For years I was madly in love with Lon McAllister and Alan Ladd. Bruce Lee and O.J. Simpson were absent from the idol-making media. Asian men became like "family" to me: they were my brothers. Of course, no one was like my father. He was so powerful. The only men who might possess some of that power were those whose control and dominance over his life diminished his. Those would be the men who interested me.

Although I was attracted to males who looked like someone in a Coca-Cola ad, I yearned for the expressions of their potency to be like that of Japanese men, like that of my father: unpredictable, dominant, and brilliant—yet sensitive and poetic. I wanted a blond Samurai.[3]

When I met him during those college years in San Jose, I was surprised to see how readily my mother accepted the idea of our getting married. My father had passed away, but I was still concerned about her reaction. All of my married brothers and sisters had Japanese American mates. I would be the first to marry a Caucasian. "He's a strong man and will protect you. I'm all for it," she said. Her main concern for me was survival. Knowing that my world was the world of the *hakujin*, she wanted me to be protected, even if it meant marriage to one. It was 1957, and inter-racial couples were a rare sight to see. She felt that my husband-to-be was strong because he was acting against the norms of

12

---

[2]**Madame Butterfly:** In Puccini's opera with this title, a young Japanese woman falls in love with an American naval officer in Japan, becomes pregnant, and is abandoned by him.
[3]**Samurai:** A member of the Japanese warrior class.

his culture, perhaps even against his parent's wishes. From her vantage point, where family and group opinion outweighed the individual's, this willingness to oppose them was truly a show of strength.

When we first married I wondered if I should lay out his socks and underwear every morning like my mother used to do. But my brothers' warning would float up from the past: don't be subservient to Caucasian men or they will take advantage. So I compromised and laid them out whenever I thought to do it . . . which grew less and less often as the years passed. His first reaction to this wifely gesture was to be uncomfortably pleased. Then he was puzzled by its sporadic occurrence, which did not seem to be an act of apology, or a sign that I wanted something. On the days when I felt I should be a good Japanese wife, I did it. On other days, when I felt American and assertive, I did not.

When my mother visited us, as she often did, I had to be on good behavior, much to my husband's pleasure and surprise. I would jump up from the table to fill his empty water glass (if she hadn't beat me to it) or butter his roll. If I didn't notice that his plate needed refilling, she would kick me under the table and reprimand me with a disapproving look. Needless to say, we never had mother-in-law problems. He would often ask with hope in his voice "when is your mother coming to visit?"

Despite the fact that early in our marriage we had become aware of the "images" we had married and were trying to relate to each other as the real people we were, he still hoped deep in his heart that I was his exotic, mysterious but ever available *Cho-Cho san*.[4] And I still saw him as my Anglo Samurai, wielding his sword of integrity, slaying the dragons that prevented my acceptance as an equal human being in his world, now mine.

* * *

My mother dutifully served my father throughout their marriage. I   16
never felt she resented it. I served my brothers and father and did not resent it. I was made to feel not only important for performing duties of my role, but absolutely integral for the functioning of the family. I realized a very basic difference in attitude between Japanese and American culture towards serving another. In my family, to serve another could he uplifting, a gracious gesture that elevated oneself. For many white Americans it seems that serving another is degrading, an indication of dependency or weakness in character, or a low place in the social ladder. To be ardently considerate is to be "self-effacing" or apologetic.

My father used to say, "Serving humanity is the greatest virtue. Giving service of yourself is more worthy than selling the service or goods of another." He would prefer that we be maids in someone's home, serving someone well, than be salesgirls where our function would be to

---

[4]*Cho-cho san,* Madam Butterfly.

exchange someone else's goods, handling money. Perhaps it was his way to rationalize and give pride to the occupations open to us as Orientals. Nevertheless, his words have stayed with me, giving me spiritual sustenance at times when I perceived that my willingness to give was misconstrued as a need to be liked or an act of manipulation to get something.

I was talking about this subject with an Asian American woman friend, recently widowed, whose husband had also been Asian American. He had been a prominent surgeon, highly thought of in the community where we live. She is forty-two, third generation Chinese, born in San Francisco, articulate, intelligent and a professional therapist for educationally handicapped children. She "confessed" her reticence to let her Caucasian friends know she served her husband. "There is such a stereotyped view that is laid on us. They just don't understand *why* we do what we do!"

She told me of an incident when she remarked to a Caucasian friend that she polished her husband's shoes. Her friend turned on her in mock fury and said, "Don't you dare let my husband know you do that!" My friend said she felt ashamed, humiliated, that she had somehow betrayed this woman by seeming subordinate to her husband.

"I served him in many ways," she said. "Even though he was a graduate of Stanford and professionally successful, he drove himself to work harder and longer to compete because he felt he was handicapped by being Chinese. You know our Asian men, the ones raised with values from the old country are not equipped to compete like white American men. They are not conditioned to be outwardly aggressive and competitive. It was agony for my husband, and I knew he was out there doing it for us, so I tried to make it easier for him at home." As I looked at her I could see her compassion, and for a flickering moment I saw my mother. A generation had passed, but some things had not changed that much. 20

My husband and I often joke that the reason we have stayed married for so long is that we continually mystify each other with responses and attitudes that are plainly due to our different backgrounds. For years I frustrated him with unpredictable silences and accusative looks. I felt a great reluctance to tell him what I wanted or what needed to be done in the home. I was inwardly furious that I was being put into the position of having to *tell* him what to do. I felt my femaleness, in the Japanese sense, was being degraded. I did not want to be the authority. That would be humiliating for him and for me. He, on the other hand, considering the home to be under my dominion, in the American sense, did not dare to impose on me what he thought I wanted. He wanted me to tell him or make a list, like his parents.

Entertaining socially was also confusing. Up to recent times, I still hesitated to sit at one head of our rectangular dining table when my husband sat at the other end. It seemed right to be seated next to him, helping him serve the food. Sometimes I did it anyway, but only with our close friends who didn't misread my physical placement as psychological subservience.

At dinner parties I always served the men first, until I noticed the women glaring at me. I became self-conscious about it and would try to remember to serve the women first. Sometimes I would forget and automatically turn to a man. I would catch myself abruptly, dropping a bowl of soup all over him. Then I would have to serve him first anyway, as a gesture of apology. My unconscious Japanese instinct still managed to get what it wanted.

Now I just entertain according to how I feel that day. If my Japan-   24
ese sensibility is stronger I act accordingly and feel comfortable. If I want to go all-American I can do that too. I have come to accept the cultural hybridness of my personality, to recognize it as a strength and not weakness. Because I am culturally neither pure Japanese nor pure American does not mean I am less of a person. It means I have been enriched with the heritage of both.

As I look back on my marriage and try to compare it to the marriage of my parents, it seems ludicrous to do so—like comparing a sailboat to a jet airliner. Both get you there, but one depends on the natural element of wind and the other on modern technology. What does emerge as a basic difference is directly related to the Japanese concept of cooperation for group survival and the American value of competition for the survival of the individual. My Japanese family cooperated to survive economically and spiritually. Although sibling rivalry was subtly present, it was never allowed the ferocity of expression we allow our children. I see our children compete with each other. I have felt my husband and I compete with each other—not always in obvious ways, such as professional recognition or in the comparison of role responsibilities, but in attitudes toward self-fulfillment. "I love you more than you love me," or "My doing nothing is more boring than your doing nothing."

Competition does provide some challenge and excitement in life. Yet carried to extremes in personal relationships it can become destructive. How can you fully trust someone you are in competition with? And when trust breaks down, isolation and alienation set in.

I find another basic difference between my mother and myself in how we relate to sons. I try very consciously not to indulge my son, as my mother indulged my brothers. My natural inclination is to do as she did. So I try to restrain it. In fact, I find myself being harder on him, afraid that my constrained Japanese training to please the male might surface, crippling instead of equipping him for future relationships with females who may not be of my background, hampering his emotional survival in the competitive and independent world he will face when he leaves the nest.

How my present attitudes will affect my children in later years   28
remains to be seen. My world is radically different from mother's world, and all indications point to an even wider difference in our world from our children's. Whereas my family's struggle and part of my own was racially based, I do not foresee a similar struggle for our children. Their

bi-racialness is, indeed, a factor in their identity and self-image, but I feel their struggle will be more to sustain human dignity in a world rapidly dehumanizing itself with mechanization and technology. My hope is they have inherited that essential trait ethnic minorities in this country have so sharply honed: a strong will to survive.

Topics for Critical Thinking and Writing

1. In her fifth paragraph Jeanne Wakatsuki Houston recalls how her brothers and sisters cooperated to "help each other survive 'out there' in the complicated world that had weakened Papa." What do we suppose had happened to reduce Papa's "Godlike" image? And in the next paragraph, Houston speaks of how her brothers encouraged her "to run for school office, to try out for majorette and song leader, and to run for Queen of various festivities." How had her brothers encouraged her here?

2. Houston tells us in paragraph 7 that, although now past puberty, she was "still too young to understand how or why an Oriental female fascinated Caucasian men." Nowadays, Houston would probably not use the word *Oriental.* Can you explain why? (Hint: See the entry on *Orient* in "A Writer's Glossary.")

3. We are told that there are differences in the Houston household that stem from the writer and her husband coming from different cultures. Which of these differences most resemble those that are *not* a result of being a Japanese/American couple? Can you explain why?

4. In her last paragraph Houston projects some differences for her children from those of her world with her husband. What are these differences? Do you find them similar to the challenges you face or not? Explain.

5. Houston contrasts her Japanese environment, which emphasized service in her family, with the Caucasion environment, which emphasizes competition. She calls it her *cultural hybridness* and is proud of it. Compare this essay with Fan Shen's, page 281. Is he also proud of his "hybridness"? Explain.

Brent Staples

Brent Staples, born in 1951, holds a Ph.D. in psychology from the University of Chicago. He taught briefly and then turned to journalism. He is now assistant metropolitan editor at The New York Times. *We reprint an essay that appeared in this paper in 1994.*

The "Scientific" War
on the Poor

Everyone knows the stereotype of the fair-haired executive who owes the office with the view and the six-figure salary to an accident of birth—like relatives in the halls of power. What about merit, for heaven's sake? Why not give I.Q. tests, grant the best jobs to those who score well and send the laggards to the mailroom?

That would never happen, nor should it. I.Q. scores in themselves tell you almost nothing. This was clearly explained by the Frenchman Alfred Binet, who invented the first usable I.Q. test in 1905. The test had one purpose: to help identify learning-disabled children who needed special schools. Binet warned that a "brutal pessimism" would follow if his test was ever mistaken as a measure of a fixed, unchangeable intelligence.

You wouldn't know it from the I.Q. worship in progress today, but using the tests to draw finer distinctions than Binet intended amounts to overreaching, if not scientific fraud. Most scientists concede that they don't really know what "intelligence" is. Whatever it might be, paper and pencil tests aren't the tenth of it.

The fair-haired executive gets a pass for other reasons entirely.   4 First, because the world works more on insiderism and inherited privilege than on "pure merit," whatever that might be. Second, because the charge of innate stupidity has historically been reserved for the poor.

That charge surfaced during the immigrant influx of the teens and 20's, and again during the affirmative-action 60's and 70's—both times when America found "scientific" justifications of poverty very appealing. Misgivings about the "underclass" have made them appealing again. By way of example, consider Senator Daniel Patrick Moynihan's ludicrous claim that out-of-wedlock births in modern America amounted to the creation of a new species.

Alfred Binet's American imitators embraced "brutal pessimism" right away. In 1912, after Eastern and Southern Europeans began to outnumber Northern Europeans at Ellis Island, immigration authorities asked the psychologist Henry Goddard to do "quality control," through intelligence testing. Goddard and his colleagues believed that Nordic peoples were civilization's best and that the rest were genetically second-rate or worse. The test was merely a means of proving it.

Not surprisingly, Goddard's testing of what he called a representative sample of immigrants showed that 80 percent of all Jews, Italians and Hungarians and nearly 90 percent of Russians were "feeble-minded." As a result, hundreds each year were deported.

At the start of World War I, two million draftees were also tested.   8
The results showed a gap between blacks and whites, but at the time, few were interested. The passion then was proving a connection between "mental deficiency" and national origin among white immigrants. The testers didn't bother with translation; non-English-speakers were instructed in pantomime.

Once again, British immigrants were classified as first-rate, with Poles, Italians and Russians labeled stupid and undesirable. The data were published by the National Academy of Sciences in 1921, and contributed to the introduction of temporary limits on immigration. I.Q. hysteria also resulted in sterilization laws that were enforced only against the poor.

The I.Q. believers worked with messianic zeal. Like many before him, the British psychologist Sir Cyril Burt went way beyond science in defense of his beliefs. Burt alleged that intelligence was so wired into the genes, so indifferent to environment, that identical twins reared apart had virtually identical I.Q. scores. Statisticians now agree that Burt made much of it up.

The I.Q. worshipers of today remain essentially unchanged from Goddard's time. Despite the impression that there is something new in *The Bell Curve*, its authors, Charles Murray and Richard Herrnstein, have merely reasserted the long-unproven claim that I.Q. is mainly inherited. The language is calmer, the statistical gimmicks slicker, but the truth remains the same: There exist no plausible data to make the case. Belief to the contrary rests mainly on brutal preconceptions about poverty, but also on a basic confusion between pseudoscience and the real thing.

Topics for Critical Thinking and Writing

1. In his first paragraph Staples outlines the "stereotype of the fair-haired executive who owes the office with the view and the six-figure salary to an accident of birth." Why, he asks, don't we give I. Q. tests for such jobs? In the next paragraph, however, he says "That would never happen, nor should it." Why does he believe that it should *not* happen? Do *you* believe it should or should not happen? Why?
2. In paragraph 5 Staples mentions two earlier times when "'scientific'' justifications of poverty" were appealing. Why were these "justifications" appealing? Why are they appealing now? And why does Staples use quotation marks around "scientific"?
3. What happened in 1912 on Ellis Island that prompted authorities to ask Henry Goddard for "quality control." What did he do? Staples offers no examples for the "affirmative-action 60's and 70's." Should he have?

4. In his last paragraph Staples states that "brutal preconceptions about poverty" underlie arguments for I.Q. scores. If Staples had remove the word *brutal,* would the sentence remain the same?

Studs Terkel

Studs Terkel was born Louis Terkel in New York City in 1912. He was brought up in Chicago and graduated from the University of Chicago. Terkel has been an actor, playwright, colum- nist, and disc jockey, but he is best known as the man who makes books out of tape record- ings of people he gets to talk. Elsewhere in The Little, Brown Reader, *we reprint interviews from his book called* Workers *(1974); below we print an interviews from* American Dreams: Lost and Found *(1980).*

Stephen Cruz

He *is thirty-nine.*
"The family came in stages from Mexico. Your grandparents usually came first, did a little work, found little roots, put together a few bucks, and brought the family in, one at a time. Those were the days when controls at the border didn't exist as they do now."

You just tried very hard to be whatever it is the system wanted of you. I was a good student and, as small as I was, a pretty good athlete. I was well liked, I thought. We were fairly affluent, but we lived down where all the trashy whites were. It was the only housing we could get. As kids, we never understood why. We did everything right. We didn't have those Mexican accents, we were never on welfare. Dad wouldn't be on welfare to save his soul. He woulda died first. He worked during the depression. He carries that pride with him, even today.

Of the five children, I'm the only one who really got into the busi- ness world. We learned quickly that you have to look for opportunities and add things up very quickly. I was in liberal arts, but as soon as Sputnik went up, well, golly, hell, we knew where the bucks were. I went right over to the registrar's office and signed up for engineering. I got my degree in '62. If you had a master's in business as well, they were just paying all kinds of bucks. So that's what I did. Sure enough, the market was super. I had fourteen job offers. I could have had a hun- dred if I wanted to look around.

I never once associated these offers with my being a minority. I was   4 aware of the Civil Rights Act of 1964, but I was still self-confident enough to feel they wanted me because of my abilities. Looking back, the reason I got more offers than the other guys was because of the gov- ernment edict. And I thought it was because I was so goddamned bril- liant. (Laughs.) In 1962, I didn't get as many offers as those who were less qualified. You have a tendency to blame the job market. You just don't want to face the issue of discrimination.

I went to work with Procter & Gamble. After about two years, they told me I was one of the best supervisors they ever had and they were gonna promote me. Okay, I went into personnel. Again, I thought it was because I was such a brilliant guy. Now I started getting wise to the ways of the American Dream. My office was glass-enclosed, while all the other offices were enclosed so you couldn't see into them. I was the visible man.

They made sure I interviewed most of the people that came in. I just didn't really think there was anything wrong until we got a new plant manager, a southerner. I received instructions from him on how I should interview blacks. Just check and see if they smell, okay? That was the beginning of my training program. I started asking: Why weren't we hiring more minorities? I realized I was the only one in a management position.

I guess as a Mexican I was more acceptable because I wasn't really black. I was a good compromise. I was visibly good. I hired a black secretary, which was *verboten.* When I came back from my vacation, she was gone. My boss fired her while I was away. I asked why and never got a good reason.

Until then, I never questioned the American Dream. I was con- 8 vinced if you worked hard, you could make it. I never considered myself different. That was the trouble. We had been discriminated against a lot, but I never associated it with society. I considered it an individual matter. Bad people, my mother used to say. In '68 I began to question.

I was doing fine. My very first year out of college, I was making twelve thousand dollars. I left Procter & Gamble because I really saw no opportunity. They were content to leave me visible, but my thoughts were not really solicited. I may have overreacted a bit, with the plant manager's attitude, but I felt there's no way a Mexican could get ahead here.

I went to work for Blue Cross. It's 1969. The Great Society is in full swing. Those who never thought of being minorities before are being turned on. Consciousness raising is going on. Black programs are popping up in universities. Cultural identity and all that. But what about the one issue in this country: economics? There were very few management jobs for minorities, especially blacks.

The stereotypes popped up again. If you're Oriental, you're real good in mathematics. If you're Mexican, you're a happy guy to have around, pleasant but emotional. Mexicans are either sleeping or laughing all the time. Life is just one big happy kind of event. *Mañana.* Good to have as part of the management team, as long as you weren't allowed to make decisions.

I was thinking there were two possibilities why minorities were not 12 making it in business. One was deep, ingrained racism. But there was still the possibility that they were simply a bunch of bad managers who just couldn't cut it. You see, until now I believed everything I was taught about the dream: the American businessman is omnipotent and fair. If we could show these turkeys there's money to be made in hiring minorities, these businessmen—good managers, good decision makers—would respond. I naïvely thought American businessmen gave a damn about society, that given a choice they would do the right thing. I had that faith.

I was hungry for learning about decision-making criteria. I was still too far away from top management to see exactly how they were working. I needed to learn more. Hey, just learn more and you'll make it. That part of the dream hadn't left me yet. I was still clinging to the notion of work your ass off, learn more than anybody else, and you'll get in that sphere.

During my fifth year at Blue Cross, I discovered another flaw in the American Dream. Minorities are as bad to other minorities as whites are to minorities. The strongest weapon the white manager had is the old divide and conquer routine. My mistake was thinking we were all at the same level of consciousness.

I had attempted to bring together some blacks with the other minorities. There weren't too many of them anyway. The Orientals never really got involved. The blacks misunderstood what I was presenting, perhaps I said it badly. They were on the cultural kick: a manager should be crucified for saying "Negro" instead of "black." I said as long as the Negro or the black gets the job, it doesn't mean a damn what he's called. We got into a huge hassle. Management, of course, merely smiled. The whole struggle fell flat on its face. It crumpled from divisiveness. So I learned another lesson. People have their own agenda. It doesn't matter what group you're with, there is a tendency to put the other guy down regardless.

The American Dream began to look so damn complicated, I began to think: Hell, if I wanted, I could just back away and reap the harvest myself. By this time, I'm up to twenty-five thousand dollars a year. It's beginning to look good, and a lot of people are beginning to look good. And they're saying: "Hey, the American Dream, you got it. Why don't you lay off?" I wasn't falling in line.   16

My bosses were telling me I had all the "ingredients" for top management. All that was required was to "get to know our business." This term comes up all the time. If I could just warn all minorities and women whenever you hear "get to know our business," they're really saying "fall in line." Stay within that fence, and glory can be yours. I left Blue Cross disillusioned. They offered me a director's job at thirty thousand dollars before I quit.

All I had to do was behave myself. I had the "ingredients" of being the good Chicano, the equivalent of the good nigger. I was smart. I could articulate well. People didn't know by my speech patterns that I was of Mexican heritage. Some tell me I don't look Mexican, that I have a certain amount of Italian, Lebanese, or who knows. (Laughs.)

One could easily say: "Hey, what's your bitch? The American Dream has treated you beautifully. So just knock it off and quit this crap you're spreading around." It was a real problem. Every time I turned around, America seemed to be treating me very well.

Hell, I even thought of dropping out, the hell with it. Maybe get a 20 job in a factory. But what happened? Offers kept coming in. I just said to myself: God, isn't this silly? You might as well take the bucks and continue looking for the answer. So I did that. But each time I took the money, the conflict in me got more intense, not less.

Wow, I'm up to thirty-five thousand a year. This is a savings and loan business. I have faith in the executive director. He was the kind of guy I was looking for in top management: understanding, humane, also looking for the formula. Until he was up for consideration as executive v.p. of the entire organization. All of a sudden everything changed. It wasn't until I saw this guy flip-flop that I realized how powerful vested interests are. Suddenly he's saying: "Don't rock the boat. Keep a low profile. Get in line." Another disappointment.

Subsequently, I went to work for a consulting firm. I said to myself: Okay, I've got to get close to the executive mind. I need to know how they work. Wow, a consulting firm.

Consulting firms are saving a lot of American businessmen. They're doing it in ways that defy the whole notion of capitalism. They're not allowing these businesses to fail. Lockheed was successful in getting U.S. funding guarantees because of the efforts of consulting firms working on their behalf, helping them look better. In this kind of work, you don't find minorities. You've got to be a proven success in business before you get there.

The American Dream, I see now, is governed not by education, 24 opportunity, and hard work, but by power and fear. The higher up in the organization you go, the more you have to lose. The dream is *not* losing. This is the notion pervading America today: Don't lose.

When I left the consulting business, I was making fifty-five thousand dollars a year. My last performance appraisal was: You can go a long way in this business, you can be a partner, but you gotta know our business. It came up again. At this point, I was incapable of being disillusioned any more. How easy it is to be swallowed up by the same set of values that governs the top guy. I was becoming that way. I was becoming concerned about losing that fifty grand or so a year. So I asked other minorities who had it made. I'd go up and ask 'em: "Look, do you owe anything to others?" The answer was: "We owe nothing to anybody." They drew from the civil rights movement but felt no debt. They've quickly forgotten how it happened. It's like I was when I first got out of college. Hey, it's really me, I'm great. I'm as angry with these guys as I am with the top guys.

Right now, it's confused. I've had fifteen years in the business world as "a success." Many Anglos would be envious of my progress. Fifty thousand dollars a year puts you in the one or two top percent of all Americans. Plus my wife making another thirty thousand. We had lots of money. When I gave it up, my cohorts looked at me not just as strange, but as something of a traitor. "You're screwing it up for all of us. You're part of our union, we're the elite, we should govern. What the hell are you doing?" So now I'm looked at suspiciously by my peer group as well.

I'm teaching at the University of Wisconsin at Platteville. It's nice. My colleagues tell me what's on their minds. I got a farm next-door to Platteville. With farm prices being what they are (laughs), it's a losing proposition. But with university work and what money we've saved, we're gonna be all right.

The American Dream is getting more elusive. The dream is being 28 governed by a few people's notion of what the dream is. Sometimes I feel it's a small group of financiers that gets together once a year and decides all the world's issues.

It's getting so big. The small-business venture is not there any more. Business has become too big to influence. It can't be changed internally. A counterpower is needed.

Topics for Critical Thinking and Writing

1. In paragraph 9 Cruz refers to "The Great Society." What is (or was) "The Great Society," and how is it relevant to Cruz's story? If you aren't sure what The Great Society was, what can you learn about it from this paragraph or others in Cruz's account?

2. In paragraphs 13 and 14 Cruz says he discovered that "Minorities are as bad to other minorities as whites are to minorities." Does this view come as a surprise to you? Or have you had experiences that tend to confirm it? Conversely, have you had experiences that tend to refute it? Explain.

3. In paragraph 17 Cruz says, "If I could just warn all minorities and women whenever you hear 'get to know the business,' they're really saying 'fall in line.' Stay within that fence. . . ." If someone were to tell you "get to know the business," how else might you interpret it? Do you agree with Cruz that the message you were being given would depend on whether or not you were a member of a minority culture or a woman?

4. Cruz frequently cites The American Dream. What is Cruz's idea of The American Dream, and what has disillusioned him with it? Do you find yourself in sympathy with his complaints? Why or why?

5. Suppose you were in a position to offer Cruz a job in management; how would you evaluate him as a candidate? You might try to do this by writing a memo to your supervisor, arguing Cruz's strengths and weaknesses and making a recommendation to hire or not. (You can take as much license as you need to invent the company, your position in it, the job opening, and the résumé Cruz has presented.)

Courtesy Amy Tan

Amy Tan

Amy Tan was born in 1952 in Oakland, California, two-and-a-half years after her parents had emigrated from China. She attended Linfield College in Oregon and then California State University at San Jose, where she shifted her major from premedical studies to English. After earning a master's degree in linguistics from San Jose, Tan worked as a language consultant and then as a freelance business writer. In 1985, having decided to try her hand at fiction, she joined the Squaw Valley Community of Writers, a fiction workshop. In 1989 she published her first novel, The Joy Luck Club, *a collection of sixteen interwoven stories. In 1991 she published a second novel,* The Kitchen God's Wife.*

The essay that we reprint appeared in Life *magazine In April 1991.*

Snapshot: Lost Lives of Women

When I first saw this photo as a child, I thought it was exotic and remote, of a faraway time and place, with people who had no connection to my American life. Look at their bound feet! Look at that funny lady with the plucked forehead!

The solemn little girl is, in fact, my mother. And leaning against the rock is my grandmother, Jingmei. "She called me Baobei," my mother told me. "It means Treasure."

The picture was taken in Hangzhou, and my mother believes the year was 1922, possibly spring or fall, judging by the clothes. At first glance, it appears the women are on a pleasure outing.

But see the white bands on their skirts? The white shoes? They are   4
in mourning. My mother's grandmother, known to the others as

Divong, "The Replacement Wife," has recently died. The women have come to this place, a Buddhist retreat, to perform yet another ceremony for Divong. Monks hired for the occasion have chanted the proper words. And the women and little girl have walked in circles clutching smoky sticks of incense. They knelt and prayed, then burned a huge pile of spirit money so that Divong might ascend to a higher position in her new world.

This is also a picture of secrets and tragedies, the reasons that warnings have been passed along in our family like heirlooms. Each of these women suffered a terrible fate, my mother said. And they were not peasant women but big city people, very modern. They went to dance halls and wore stylish clothes. They were supposed to be the lucky ones.

Look at the pretty woman with her finger on her cheek. She is my mother's second cousin, Nunu Aiji, "Precious Auntie." You cannot see this, but Nunu Aiyi's entire face was scarred from smallpox. Lucky for her, a year or so after this picture was taken, she received marriage proposals from two families. She turned down a lawyer and married another man. Later she divorced her husband, a daring thing for a woman to do. But then, finding no means to support herself or her young daughter, Nunu eventually accepted the lawyer's second proposal—to become his number two concubine. "Where else could she go?" my mother asked. "Some people said she was lucky the lawyer still wanted her."

Now look at the small woman with a sour face (*third from left*). There's a reason that Jyou Ma, "Uncle's Wife," looks this way. Her husband, my great-uncle often complained that his family had chosen an ugly woman for his wife. To show his displeasure, he often insulted Jyou Ma's cooking. One time Great-Uncle tipped over a pot of boiling soup, which fell all over his niece's four-year-old neck and nearly killed her. My mother was the little niece, and she still has that soup scar on her neck. Great-Uncle's family eventually chose a pretty woman for his second wife. But the complaints about Jyou Ma's cooking did not stop.

Doomma, "Big Mother," is the regal-looking woman seated on a   8
rock. (The woman with the plucked forehead, far left, is a servant, remembered only as someone who cleaned but did not cook.) Doomma was the daughter of my great-grandfather and Nu-pei, "The Original Wife." She was shunned by Divong, "The Replacement Wife," for being "too strong," and loved by Divong's daughter, my grandmother. Doomma's first daughter was born with a hunchback—a sign, some said, of Doomma's own crooked nature. Why else did she remarry, disobeying her family's orders to remain a widow forever? And why did Doomma later kill herself, using some mysterious means that caused her to die slowly over three days? "Doomma died the same way she lived," my mother said, "strong, suffering lots."

Jingmei, my own grandmother, lived only a few more years after this picture was taken. She was the widow of a poor scholar, a man who had the misfortune of dying from influenza when he was about to be appointed a vice-magistrate. In 1924 or so, a rich man, who liked to collect pretty women, raped my grandmother and thereby forced her into becoming one of his concubines. My grandmother, now an outcast, took her young daughter to live with her on an island outside of Shanghai. She left her son behind, to save his face. After she gave birth to another son she killed herself by swallowing raw opium buried in the New Year's rice cakes. The young daughter who wept at her deathbed was my mother.

At my grandmother's funeral, monks tied chains to my mother's ankles so she would not fly away with her mother's ghost. "I tried to take them off," my mother said. "I was her treasure. I was her life."

My mother could never talk about any of this, even with her closest friends. "Don't tell anyone," she once said to me. "People don't understand. A concubine was like some kind prostitute. My mother was a good woman, high-class. She had no choice."

I told her I understood.   12

"How can you understand?" she said, suddenly angry. "You did not live in China then. You do not know what it's like to have no position in life. I was her daughter. We had no face! We belonged to nobody! This is a shame I can never push off my back." By the end of the outburst, she was crying.

On a recent trip with my mother to Beijing, I learned that my uncle found a way to push the shame off his back. He was the son my grandmother left behind. In 1936 he joined the Communist party—in large part, he told me, to overthrow the society that forced his mother into concubinage. He published a story about his mother. I told him I had written about my grandmother in a book of fiction. We agreed that my grandmother is the source of strength running through our family. My mother cried to hear this.

My mother believes my grandmother is also my muse, that she helps me write. "Does she still visit you often?" she asked while I was writing my second book. And then she added shyly, "Does she say anything about me?"

"Yes," I told her. "She has lots to say. I am writing it down."   16

This is the picture I see when I write. These are the secrets I was supposed to keep. These are the women who never let me forget why stories need to be told.

Topics for Critical Thinking and Writing

1. Consider the title of this essay. Why are the women's lives described as "lost lives"? Can you imagine a companion piece, "Lost Lives of Men"? If not, why not?

2. In paragraph 5, what does Tan communicate by "And they were not peasant women, but big city people, very modern"? What does she imply about the lives of those who *were* peasants?

3. In the fifth paragraph and in the last, Tan refers to "secrets" that she "was supposed to keep." What were the secrets? Why does she reveal them?
4. In the first paragraph Tan reports, "When I first saw this photo as a child, I thought it was exotic and remote, of a faraway time and place, with people who had no connection to my American life." What does she imply in this paragraph about their "connection to [her] American life" now? Where in the essay is that connection revealed or explained?
5. If you are lucky enough to have photographs of your ancestors, explore the images of the people in them and what you have been told about their lives. Do you feel "connected" or not? Explain.

Liliana Heker

Liliana Heker, born in Argentina in 1943, achieved fame in 1966 with the publication of her first book. She has continued to write fiction, and she has also been influential in her role as the editor of a literary magazine. "The Stolen Party," first published in Spanish in 1982, was translated and printed in Other Fires: Short Fiction by Latin American Women *(1985), edited and translated by Alberto Manguel.*

The Stolen Party

As soon as she arrived she went straight to the kitchen to see if the monkey was there. It was: what a relief! She wouldn't have liked to admit that her mother had been right. *Monkeys at a birthday?* her mother had sneered. *Get away with you, believing any nonsense you're told!* She was cross, but not because of the monkey, the girl thought; it's just because of the party.

"I don't like you going," she told her. "It's a rich people's party."

"Rich people go to Heaven too," said the girl, who studied religion at school.

"Get away with Heaven," said the mother. "The problem with you,   4 young lady, is that you like to fart higher than your ass."

The girl didn't approve of the way her mother spoke. She was barely nine, and one of the best in her class.

"I'm going because I've been invited," she said. "And I've been invited because Luciana is my friend. So there."

"Ah yes, your friend," her mother grumbled. She paused. "Listen, Rosaura," she said at last. "That one's not your friend. You know what you are to them? The maid's daughter, that's what."

Rosaura blinked hard: she wasn't going to cry. Then she yelled: 8 "Shut up! You know nothing about being friends!"

Every afternoon she used to go to Luciana's house and they would both finish their homework while Rosaura's mother did the cleaning.

They had their tea in the kitchen and they told each other secrets. Rosaura loved everything in the big house, and she also loved the people who lived there.

"I'm going because it will be the most lovely party in the whole world, Luciana told me it would. There will be a magician, and he will bring a monkey and everything."

The mother swung around to take a good look at her child, and pompously put her hands on her hips.

"Monkeys at a birthday?" she said. "Get away with you, believing   12
any nonsense you're told!"

Rosaura was deeply offended. She thought it unfair of her mother to accuse other people of being liars simply because they were rich. Rosaura too wanted to be rich, of course. If one day she managed to live in a beautiful palace, would her mother stop loving her? She felt very sad. She wanted to go to that party more than anything else in the world.

"I'll die if I don't go," she whispered, almost without moving her lips.

And she wasn't sure whether she had been heard, but on the morning of the party she discovered that her mother had starched her Christmas dress. And in the afternoon, after washing her hair, her mother rinsed it in apple vinegar so that it would be all nice and shiny. Before going out, Rosaura admired herself in the mirror, with her white dress and glossy hair, and thought she looked terribly pretty.

Señora Ines also seemed to notice. As soon as she saw her, she said: 16
"How lovely you look today, Rosaura."

Rosaura gave her starched skirt a slight toss with her hands and walked into the party with a firm step. She said hello to Luciana and asked about the monkey. Luciana put on a secretive look and whispered into Rosaura's ear: "He's in the kitchen. But don't tell anyone, because it's a surprise."

Rosaura wanted to make sure. Carefully she entered the kitchen and there she saw it: deep in thought, inside its cage. It looked so funny that the girl stood there for a while, watching it, and later, every so often, she would slip out of the party unseen and go and admire it. Rosaura was the only one allowed into the kitchen. Señora Ines had said: "You yes, but not the others, they're much too boisterous, they might break something." Rosaura had never broken anything. She even managed the jug of orange juice, carrying it from the kitchen into the dining room. She held it carefully and didn't spill a single drop. And Señora Ines had said: "Are you sure you can manage a jug as big as that?" Of course she could manage. She wasn't a butterfingers, like the others. Like that blonde girl with the bow in her hair. As soon as she saw Rosaura, the girl with the bow, had said:

"And you? Who are you?"   20
"I'm a friend of Luciana," said Rosaura.

"No," said the girl with the bow, "you are not a friend of Luciana because I'm her cousin and I know all her friends. And I don't know you."

"So what," said Rosaura. "I come here every afternoon with my mother and we do our homework together."

"You and your mother do your homework together?" asked the girl, laughing. 24

"I and Luciana do our homework together," said Rosaura, very seriously.

The girl with the bow shrugged her shoulders.

"That's not being friends," she said. "Do you go to school together?"

"No." 28

"So where do you know her from?" said the girl, getting impatient.

Rosaura remembered her mother's words perfectly. She took a deep breath.

"I'm the daughter of the employee," she said.

Her mother had said very clearly: "If someone asks, you say you're 32 the daughter of the employee; that's all." She also told her to add: "And proud of it." But Rosaura thought that never in her life would she dare say something of the sort.

"What employee?" said the girl with the bow. "Employee in a shop?"

"No," said Rosaura angrily. "My mother doesn't sell anything in any shop, so there."

"So how come she's an employee?" said the girl with the bow.

Just then Señora Ines arrived saying *shh shh,* and asked Rosaura if 36 she wouldn't mind helping serve out the hotdogs, as she knew the house so much better than the others.

"See?" said Rosaura to the girl with the bow, and when no one was looking she kicked her in the shin.

Apart from the girl with the bow, all the others were delightful. The one she liked best was Luciana, with her golden birthday crown; and then the boys. Rosaura won the sack race, and nobody managed to catch her when they played tag. When they split into two teams to play charades, all the boys wanted her for their side. Rosaura felt she had never been so happy in all her life.

But the best was still to come. The best came after Luciana blew out the candles. First the cake. Señora Ines had asked her to help pass the cake around, and Rosaura had enjoyed the task immensely, because everyone called out to her, shouting "Me, me!" Rosaura remembered a story in which there was a queen who had the power of life or death over her subjects. She had always loved that, having the power of life or death. To Luciana and the boys she gave the largest pieces, and to the girl with the bow she gave a slice so thin one could see through it.

After the cake came the magician, tall and bony, with a fine red 40 cape. A true magician: he could untie handkerchiefs by blowing on them and make a chain with links that had no openings. He could guess what cards were pulled out from a pack, and the monkey was his assistant. He called the monkey "partner." "Let's see here, partner," he would say, "turn over a card." And, "Don't run away, partner: time to work now."

The final trick was wonderful. One of the children had to hold the monkey in his arms and the magician said he would make him disappear.

"What, the boy?" they all shouted.

"No, the monkey!" shouted back the magician.

Rosaura thought that this was truly the most amusing party in the   44
whole world.

The magician asked a small fat boy to come and help, but the small fat boy got frightened almost at once and dropped the monkey on the floor. The magician picked him up carefully, whispered something in his ear, and the monkey nodded almost as if he understood.

"You mustn't be so unmanly, my friend," the magician said to the fat boy.

"What's unmanly?" said the fat boy.

The magician turned around as if to look for spies.   48

"A sissy," said the magician. "Go sit down."

Then he stared at all the faces, one by one. Rosaura felt her heart tremble.

"You, with the Spanish eyes," said the magician. And everyone saw that he was pointing at her.

She wasn't afraid. Neither holding the monkey, nor when the magi-   52
cian made him vanish; not even when, at the end, the magician flung his red cape over Rosaura's head and uttered a few magic words . . . and the monkey reappeared, chattering happily, in her arms. The children clapped furiously. And before Rosaura returned to her seat, the magician said:

"Thank you very much, my little countess."

She was so pleased with the compliment that a while later, when her mother came to fetch her, that was the first thing she told her.

"I helped the magician and he said to me, 'Thank you very much, my little countess.'"

It was strange because up to then Rosaura had thought that she was   56
angry with her mother. All along Rosaura had imagined that she would say to her: "See that the monkey wasn't a lie?" But instead she was so thrilled that she told her mother all about the wonderful magician.

Her mother tapped her on the head and said: "So now we're a countess!"

But one could see that she was beaming.

And now they both stood in the entrance, because a moment ago Señora Ines, smiling, had said: "Please wait here a second."

Her mother suddenly seemed worried.   60

"What is it?" she asked Rosaura.

"What is what?" said Rosaura. "It's nothing; she just wants to get the presents for those who are leaving, see?"

She pointed at the fat boy and at a girl with pigtails who were also waiting there, next to their mothers. And she explained about the presents. She knew, because she had been watching those who left before her. When one of the girls was about to leave, Señora Ines would give her a bracelet. When a boy left, Señora Ines gave him a yo-yo. Rosaura preferred the yo-yo because it sparkled, but she didn't mention that to her mother. Her mother might have said: "So why don't you ask for one, you blockhead?" That's what her mother was like. Rosaura didn't feel like explaining that she'd be horribly ashamed to be the odd one out. Instead she said:

"I was the best-behaved at the party." 64

And she said no more because Señora Ines came out into the hall with two bags, one pink and one blue.

First she went up to the fat boy, gave him a yo-yo out of the blue bag, and the fat boy left with his mother. Then she went up to the girl and gave her a bracelet out of the pink bag, and the girl with the pigtails left as well.

Finally she came up to Rosaura and her mother. She had a big smile on her face and Rosaura liked that. Señora Ines looked down at her, then looked up at her mother, and then said something that made Rosaura proud:

"What a marvelous daughter you have, Herminia." 68

For an instant, Rosaura thought that she'd give her two presents: the bracelet and the yo-yo. Señora Ines bent down as if about to look for something. Rosaura also leaned forward, stretching out her arm. But she never completed the movement.

Señora Ines didn't look in the pink bag. Nor did she look in the blue bag. Instead she rummaged in her purse. In her hand appeared two bills.

"You really and truly earned this," she said handing them over. "Thank you for all your help, my pet."

Rosaura felt her arms stiffen, stick close to her body, and then she 72
noticed her mother's hand on her shoulder. Instinctively she pressed herself against her mother's body. That was all. Except her eyes. Rosaura's eyes had a cold, clear look that fixed itself on Señora Ines's face.

Señora Ines, motionless, stood there with her hand outstretched. As if she didn't dare draw it back. As if the slightest change might shatter an infinitely delicate balance.

Topics for Critical Thinking and Writing

1. The first paragraph tells us, correctly, that Rosaura's mother is wrong about the monkey. By the time the story is over, is the mother right about anything? If so, what?
2. Characterize Señora Ines. Why does she offer Rosaura money instead of a yo-yo or a bracelet? By the way, do you assume she is speaking deceptively when she tells Rosaura that she bars other children from

the kitchen on the grounds that "they might break something"? On what do you base your view?
3. What do you make of the last paragraph? Why does Señora Ines stand with her hand outstretched, "as if she didn't dare draw it back"? What "infinitely delicate balance" might be shattered?

Pat Mora

Pat Mora did her undergraduate work at Texas Western College and then earned a master's degree at the University of Texas at El Paso, where she later served as Assistant to the Vice President for Academic Affairs, Director of the University Museum, and then (1981–89) as Assistant to the President. She has published essays on Hispanic culture as well as a children's book, Tomás and the Library Lady, *but she is best known for her books of poems. Mora has received several awards, including one from the Southwest Council of Latin American Studies.*

Immigrants

wrap their babies in the American flag,
feed them mashed hot dogs and apple pie,
name them Bill and Daisy,
buy them blonde dolls that blink blue   4
eyes or a football and tiny cleats
before the baby can even walk,
speak to them in thick English,
    hallo, babee, hallo.   8
whisper in Spanish or Polish
when the babies sleep, whisper
in a dark parent bed, that dark
parent fear, "Will they like   12
our boy, our girl, our fine american
boy, our fine american girl?"

[1986]

Topics for Critical Thinking and Writing

1. To say that someone—for example, a politician—"wraps himself in the American flag" is to suggest disapproval or even anger or contempt. What behavior does the phrase usually describe? What does Mora mean when she says that immigrants "wrap their babies in the American flag"?
2. What do you suppose is Mora's attitude toward the immigrants? Do you think the poet fully approves of their hopes? On what do you base your answer?
3. Does Mora's description of the behavior of immigrants ring true of the immigrant group you are part of or know best? What is your attitude toward their efforts to assimilate? Explain in an essay of 750–1000 words.

14
CLASSIC ESSAYS

Jonathan Swift

Jonathan Swift (1667–1745) was born in Ireland of an English family. He was ordained in the Church of Ireland in 1694, and in 1714 he became dean of St. Patrick's Cathedral, Dublin. He wrote abundantly on political and religious topics, often motivated (in his own words) by "savage indignation." It is ironic that Gulliver's Travels, the masterpiece by this master of irony, is most widely thought of as a book for children.

From the middle of the sixteenth century, the English regulated the Irish economy so that it would enrich England. Heavy taxes and other repressive legislation impoverished Ireland, and in 1728, the year before Swift wrote "A Modest Proposal," Ireland was further weakened by a severe famine. Swift, deeply moved by the injustice, the stupidity, and the suffering that he found in Ireland, adopts the disguise or persona of an economist and offers an ironic suggestion on how Irish families may improve their conditions.

A Modest Proposal
For Preventing the Children of Poor People in Ireland from Being a Burden to Their Parents or Country, and for Making Them Beneficial to the Public

[handwritten: What persona does he use?]

[handwritten: Irony: means opposite of what he says.]

It is a melancholy object to those who walk through this great town or travel in the country, when they see the streets, the roads, and cabin doors, crowded with beggars of the female sex, followed by three, four, or six children, all in rags and importuning every passenger for an alms. These mothers, instead of being able to work for their honest livelihood, are forced to employ all their time in strolling to beg sustenance for their helpless infants: who as they grow up either turn thieves for want of work, or leave their dear native country to fight for the pretender in Spain, or sell themselves to the Barbadoes.

I think it is agreed by all parties that this prodigious number of children in the arms, or on the backs, or at the heels of their mothers, and frequently of their fathers, is in the present deplorable state of the kingdom a very great additional grievance; and, therefore, whoever could find out a fair, cheap, and easy method of making these children sound, useful members of the commonwealth, would deserve so well of the public as to have his statue set up for a preserver of the nation.

But my intention is very far from being confined to provide only for the children of professed beggars; it is of a much greater extent, and shall take in the whole number of infants at a certain age who are born of parents in effect as little able to support them as those who demand our charity in the streets.

As to my own part, having turned my thoughts for many years upon this important subject, and maturely weighed the several schemes of our projectors, I have always found them grossly mistaken in their computation. It is true, a child just dropped from its dam may be supported by her milk for a solar year, with little other nourishment;

4

742

at most not above the value of 2s.,[1] which the mother may certainly get, or the value in scraps, by her lawful occupation of begging; and it is exactly at one year old that I propose to provide for them in such a manner as instead of being a charge upon their parents or the parish, or wanting food and raiment for the rest of their lives, they shall on the contrary contribute to the feeding, and partly to the clothing, of many thousands.

There is likewise another great advantage in my scheme, that it will prevent those voluntary abortions, and that horrid practice of women murdering their bastard children, alas! too frequent among us! sacrificing the poor innocent babes I doubt more to avoid the expense than the shame, which would move tears and pity in the most savage and inhuman breast.

The number of souls in this kingdom being usually reckoned one million and a half, of these I calculate there may be about 200,000 couple whose wives are breeders; from which number I subtract 30,000 couple who are able to maintain their own children (although I apprehend there cannot be so many, under the present distress of the kingdom); but this being granted, there will remain 170,000 breeders. I again subtract 50,000 for those women who miscarry, or whose children die by accident or disease within the year. There only remain 120,000 children of poor parents annually born. The question therefore is, how this number shall be reared and provided for? which, as I have already said, under the present situation of affairs, is utterly impossible by all the methods hitherto proposed. For we can neither employ them in handicraft or agriculture; we neither build houses (I mean in the country) nor cultivate land; they can very seldom pick up a livelihood by stealing, till they arrive at six years old, except where they are of towardly parts; although I confess they learn the rudiments much earlier; during which time they can, however, be properly looked upon only as probationers; as I have been informed by a principal gentleman in the county of Cavan, who protested to me that he never knew above one or two instances under the age of six, even in a part of the kingdom so renowned for the quickest proficiency in that art.

I am assured by our merchants, that a boy or a girl before twelve years old is no saleable commodity; and even when they come to this age they will not yield above 3l. or 3l. 2s. 6d. at most on the exchange; which cannot turn to account either to the parents or kingdom, the charge of nutriment and rags having been at least four times that value.

I shall now therefore humbly propose my own thoughts, which I hope will not be liable to the least objection.

8

---

[1]2s. = two shillings. Later in the essay, "£" and "l" stand for pounds and "d" for pence. (Editors' note)

I have been assured by a very knowing American of my acquaintance in London, that a young healthy child well nursed is at a year old a most delicious, nourishing, and wholesome food, whether stewed, roasted, baked, or broiled; and I make no doubt that it will equally serve in a fricassee or a ragout.

I do therefore humbly offer it to public consideration that of the 120,000 children already computed, 20,000 may be reserved for breed, whereof only one-fourth part to be males; which is more than we allow to sheep, black cattle, or swine; and my reason is, that these children are seldom the fruits of marriage, a circumstance not much regarded by our savages; therefore one male will be sufficient to serve four females. That the remaining 100,000 may, at a year old, be offered in sale to the persons of quality and fortune through the kingdom; always advising the mother to let them suck plentifully in the last month, so as to render them plump and fat for a good table. A child will make two dishes at an entertainment for friends; and when the family dines alone, the fore or hind quarter will make a reasonable dish, and seasoned with a little pepper or salt will be very good boiled on the fourth day, especially in winter.

I have reckoned upon a medium that a child just born will weigh 12 pounds, and in a solar year, if tolerably nursed, will increase to 28 pounds.

I grant this food will be somewhat dear, and therefore very proper   12
for landlords, who, as they have already devoured most of the parents, seem to have the best title to the children.

Infant's flesh will be in season throughout the year, but more plentiful in March, and a little before and after: for we are told by a grave author, an eminent French physician, that fish being a prolific diet, there are more children born in Roman Catholic countries about nine months after Lent than at any other season; therefore, reckoning a year after lent, the markets will be more glutted than usual, because the number of popish infants is at least three to one in this kingdom: and therefore it will have one other collateral advantage, by lessening the number of papists among us.

I have already computed the charge of nursing a beggar's child (in which list I reckon all cottagers, laborers, and four-fifths of the farmers) to be about 2s. per annum, rags included; and I believe no gentleman would repine to give 10s. for the carcass of a good fat child, which, as I have said, will make four dishes of excellent nutritive meat, when he has only some particular friend or his own family to dine with him. Thus the squire will learn to be a good landlord, and grow popular among the tenants; the mother will have 8s. net profit, and be fit for work till she produces another child.

Those who are more thrifty (as I must confess the times require) may flay the carcass; the skin of which artificially dressed will make admirable gloves for ladies, and summer boots for fine gentlemen.

As to our city of Dublin, shambles may be appointed for this pur-   16
pose in the most convenient parts of it, and butchers we may be assured

will not be wanting: although I rather recommend buying the children alive, and dressing them hot from the knife as we do roasting pigs.

A very worthy person, a true lover of his country, and whose virtues I highly esteem, was lately pleased in discoursing on this matter to offer a refinement upon my scheme. He said that many gentlemen of this kingdom, having of late destroyed their deer, he conceived that the want of venison might be well supplied by the bodies of young lads and maidens, not exceeding fourteen years of age nor under twelve; so great a number of both sexes in every country being now ready to starve for want of work and service; and these to be disposed of by their parents, if alive, or otherwise by their nearest relations. But with due deference to so excellent a friend and so deserving a patriot, I cannot be altogether in his sentiments; for as to the males, my American acquaintance assured me from frequent experience that their flesh was generally tough and lean, like that of our schoolboys by continual exercise, and their taste disagreeable; and to fatten them would not answer the charge. Then as to the females, it would, I think, with humble submission be a loss to the public, because they soon would become breeders themselves: and besides, it is not improbable that some scrupulous people might be apt to censure such a practice (although indeed very unjustly), as a little bordering upon cruelty; which, I confess, has always been with me the strongest objection against any project, how well soever intended.

But in order to justify my friend, he confessed that this expedient was put into his head by the famous Psalmanazar, a native of the island Formosa, who came from thence to London about twenty years ago: and in conversation told my friend, that in his country when any young person happened to be put to death, the executioner sold the carcass to persons of quality as a prime dainty; and that in his time the body of a plump girl of fifteen, who was crucified for an attempt to poison the emperor, was sold to his imperial majesty's prime minister of state, and other great mandarins of the court, in joints from the gibbet, at 400 crowns. Neither indeed can I deny, that if the same use were made of several plump young girls in this town, who without one single groat to their fortunes cannot stir abroad without a chair, and appear at the playhouse and assemblies in foreign fineries which they never will pay for, the kingdom would not be the worse.

Some persons of a desponding spirit are in great concern about that vast number of poor people, who are aged, diseased, or maimed, and I have been desired to employ my thoughts what course may be taken to ease the nation of so grievous an encumbrance. But I am not in the least pain upon that matter, because it is very well known that they are every day dying and rotting by cold and famine, and filth and vermin, as fast as can be reasonably expected. And as to the young laborers, they are now in as hopeful a condition: they cannot get work, and consequently pine away for want of nourishment, to a degree that if at any time they are accidentally hired to common labor, they have not strength to perform it; and thus the country and themselves are happily delivered from the evils to come.

I have too long digressed, and therefore shall return to my subject. 20 I think the advantages by the proposal which I have made are obvious and many, as well as of the highest importance.

(1) For first, as I have already observed, it would greatly lessen the number of papists, with whom we are yearly overrun, being the principal breeders of the nation as well as our most dangerous enemies; and who stay at home on purpose to deliver the kingdom to the Pretender, hoping to take their advantage by the absence of so many good Protestants, who have chosen rather to leave their country than stay at home and pay tithes against their conscience to an Episcopal curate.

(2) Secondly, The poor tenants will have something valuable of their own, which by law may be made liable to distress and help to pay their landlord's rent, their corn and cattle being already seized, and money a thing unknown.

(3) Thirdly, Whereas the maintenance of 100,000 children from two years old and upward, cannot be computed at less than 10s. a-piece per annum, the nation's stock will be thereby increased £50,000 per annum, beside the profit of a new dish introduced to the tables of all gentlemen of fortune in the kingdom who have any refinement in taste. And the money will circulate among ourselves, the goods being entirely of our own growth and manufacture.

(4) Fourthly, The constant breeders beside the gain of 8s. sterling per 24 annum by the sale of their children, will be rid of the charge of maintaining them after the first year.

(5) Fifthly, This food would likewise bring great custom to taverns, where the vintners will certainly be so prudent as to procure the best receipts for dressing it to perfection, and consequently have their houses frequented by all the fine gentlemen, who justly value themselves upon their knowledge in good eating; and a skilful cook who understands how to oblige his guests, will contrive to make it as expensive as they please.

(6) Sixthly, This would be a great inducement to marriage, which all wise nations have either encouraged by rewards or enforced by laws and penalties. It would increase the care and tenderness of mothers toward their children, when they were sure of a settlement for life to the poor babes, provided in some sort by the public, to their annual profit instead of expense. We should see an honest emulation among the married women, which of them would bring the fattest child to the market. Men would become as fond of their wives during the time of their pregnancy as they are now of their mares in foal, their cows in calf, their sows when they are ready to farrow; nor offer to beat or kick them (as is too frequent a practice) for fear of a miscarriage.

Many other advantages might be enumerated. For instance, the addition of some thousand carcasses in our exportation of barreled beef, the propagation of swine's flesh, and improvement in the art of making good bacon, so much wanted among us by the great destruction of pigs, too frequent at our table; which are no way comparable in taste or magnificence to a well-grown, fat, yearling child, which roasted whole will make a considerable figure at a lord mayor's feast or any other public entertainment. But this and many others I omit, being studious of brevity.

Supposing that 1,000 families in this city would be constant customers for infants' flesh, besides others who might have it at merrymeetings, particularly at weddings and christenings, I compute that Dublin would take off annually about 20,000 carcasses; and the rest of the kingdom (where probably they will be sold somewhat cheaper) the remaining 80,000.   28

I can think of no one objection that will possibly be raised against this proposal, unless it should be urged that the number of people will be thereby much lessened in the kingdom. This I freely own, and it was indeed one principal design in offering it to the world. I desire the reader will observe, that I calculate my remedy for this one individual kingdom of Ireland and for no other that ever was, is, or I think ever can be upon earth. Therefore let no man talk to me of other expedients: of taxing our absentees at 5s. a pound: of using neither clothes nor household furniture except what is of our own growth and manufacture: of utterly rejecting the materials and instruments that promote foreign luxury: of curing the expensiveness of pride, vanity, idleness, and gaming in our women: of introducing a vein of parsimony, prudence, and temperance: of learning to love our country, in the want of which we differ even from Laplanders and the inhabitants of Topinamboo: of quitting our animosities and factions, nor acting any longer like the Jews, who were murdering one another at the very moment their city was taken: of being a little cautious not to sell our country and conscience for nothing: of teaching landlords to have at least one degree of mercy toward their tenants: lastly, of putting a spirit of honesty, industry, and skill into our shopkeepers; who, if a resolution could now be taken to buy only our native goods, would immediately unite to cheat and exact upon us in the price, the measure, and the goodness, nor could ever yet be brought to make one fair proposal of just dealing, though often and earnestly invited to it.

He had advocated these earlier Irish folly

Therefore, I repeat, let no man talk to me of these and the like expedients, till he has at least some glimpse of hope that there will be ever some hearty and sincere attempt to put them in practice.

But as to myself, having been wearied out for many years with offering vain, idle, visionary thoughts, and at length utterly despairing of success, I fortunately fell upon this proposal; which, as it is wholly new, so it has something solid and real, of no expense and little trouble, full in our own power, and whereby we can incur no danger in disobliging England. For this kind of commodity will not bear exportation, the flesh being of too tender a consistence to admit a long continuance in salt, although perhaps I could name a country which would be glad to eat up our whole nation without it.

After all, I am not so violently bent upon my own opinion as to reject any offer proposed by wise men, which shall be found equally innocent, cheap, easy, and effectual. But before something of that kind shall be advanced in contradiction to my scheme, and offering a better, I desire the author or authors will be pleased maturely to consider two points. First, as things now stand, how they will be able to find food and raiment for 100,000 useless mouths and backs. And secondly, there being a round million of creatures in human figure throughout this kingdom, whose subsistence put into a common stock would leave them in debt 200,000,0001. sterling, adding those who are beggars by profession to the bulk of farmers, cottagers, and laborers, with the wives and children who are beggars in effect; I desire those politicians who dislike my overture, and may perhaps be so bold as to attempt an answer, that they will first ask the parents of these mortals, whether they would not at this day think it a great happiness to have been sold for food at a year old in the manner I prescribe, and thereby have avoided such a perpetual scene of misfortunes as they have since gone through by the oppression of landlords, the impossibility of paying rent without money or trade, the want of common sustenance, with neither house nor clothes to cover them from the inclemencies of the weather, and the most inevitable prospect of entailing the like or greater miseries upon their breed for ever.

I profess, in the sincerity of my heart, that I have not the least personal interest in endeavoring to promote this necessary work, having no other motive than the public good of my country, by advancing our trade, providing for infants, relieving the poor, and giving some pleasure to the rich. I have no children by which I can propose to get a single penny; the youngest being nine years old, and my wife past child-bearing.

Topics for Critical Thinking and Writing

1. Characterize the pamphleteer (not Swift but his persona) who offers his "modest proposal." What sort of man does he think he is? What sort of man do we regard him as? Support your assertions with evidence.
2. In the first paragraph, the speaker says that the sight of mothers begging is "melancholy." In this paragraph, what assumption does the speaker make about women that in part gives rise to this melancholy? Now that you are familiar with the entire essay, explain Swift's strategy in his first paragraph.

3. Explain the function of the "other expedients" (listed in paragraph 29).
4. How might you argue that although this satire is primarily ferocious, it also contains some playful touches? What specific passages might support your argument?

Elizabeth Cady Stanton

Elizabeth Cady Stanton (1815–1902), born into a prosperous conservative family in Johnstone, New York, became one of the most radical advocates of women's rights in the nineteenth century. In 1840 she married Henry Brewster Stanton, an ardent abolitionist lecturer. In the same year, at the World Anti-Slavery Convention in England—which refused to seat the women delegates—she met Lucretia Mott, and the two women resolved to organize a convention to discuss women's rights. Not until 1848, however, did the convention materialize. Of the three hundred or so people who attended the Seneca Falls convention, sixty-eight women and thirty-two men signed the Declaration of Sentiments, but the press on the whole was unfavorable. Not until 1920, with the passage of the Nineteenth Amendment, did women gain the right to vote. (For further details about her life and times, see Stanton's Eighty Years & More: Reminiscences 1815–1897.)

Declaration of Sentiments and Resolutions

When, in the course of human events, it becomes necessary for one portion of the family of man to assume among the people of the earth a position different from that which they have hitherto occupied, but one to which the laws of nature and of nature's God entitle them, a decent respect to the opinions of mankind requires that they should declare the causes that impel them to such a course.

We hold these truths to be self-evident: that all men and women are created equal; that they are endowed by their Creator with certain inalienable rights; that among these are life, liberty, and the pursuit of happiness; that to secure these rights governments are instituted, deriving their just powers from the consent of the governed. Whenever any form of government becomes destructive of these ends, it is the right of those who suffer from it to refuse allegiance to it, and to insist upon the institution of a new government, laying its foundation on such principles, and organizing its powers in such form, as to them shall seem most likely to effect their safety and happiness. Prudence, indeed, will dictate that governments long established should not be changed for light and transient causes; and accordingly all experience hath shown that mankind are more disposed to suffer, while evils are sufferable, than to right themselves by abolishing the forms to which they were accustomed. But when a long train of abuses and usurpations, pursuing invariably the same object, evinces a design to reduce them under absolute despotism, it is their duty to throw off such government, and to provide new guards for their future security. Such has been the patient sufferance of the women under this government, and such is now the necessity which constrains them to demand the equal station to which they are entitled.

The history of mankind is a history of repeated injuries and usurpations on the part of man toward woman, having in direct object the establishment of an absolute tyranny over her. To prove this, let facts be submitted to a candid world.

He has never permitted her to exercise her inalienable right to the   4
elective franchise.

He has compelled her to submit to laws, in the formation of which she had no voice.

He has withheld from her rights which are given to the most ignorant and degraded men—both natives and foreigners.

Having deprived her of this first right of a citizen, the elective franchise, thereby leaving her without representation in the halls of legislation, he has oppressed her on all sides.

He has made her, if married, in the eye of the law, civilly dead.   8

He has taken from her all right in property, even to the wages she earns.

He has made her, morally, an irresponsible being, as she can commit many crimes with impunity, provided they be done in the presence of her husband. In the covenant of marriage, she is compelled to promise obedience to her husband, he becoming to all intents and purposes, her master—the law giving him power to deprive her of her liberty, and to administer chastisement.

He has so framed the laws of divorce, as to what shall be the proper causes, and in case of separation, to whom the guardianship of the children shall be given, as to be wholly regardless of the happiness of women—the law, in all cases, going upon a false supposition of the supremacy of man, and giving all power into his hands.

After depriving her of all rights as a married woman, if single, and   12
the owner of property, he has taxed her to support a government which recognizes her only when her property can be made profitable to it.

He has monopolized nearly all the profitable employments, and from those she is permitted to follow, she receives but a scanty remuneration. He closes against her all the avenues to wealth and distinction which he considers most honorable to himself. As a teacher of theology, medicine, or law, she is not known.

He has denied her the facilities for obtaining a thorough education, all colleges being closed against her.

He allows her in Church, as well as State, but a subordinate position, claiming Apostolic authority for her exclusion from the ministry, and, with some exceptions, from any public participation in the affairs of the Church.

He has created a false public sentiment by giving to the world a dif-   16
ferent code of morals for men and women, by which moral delinquen-
cies which exclude women from society, are not only tolerated, but
deemed of little account in man.

He has usurped the prerogative of Jehovah himself, claiming it as
his right to assign for her a sphere of action, when that belongs to her
conscience and to her God.

He has endeavored, in every way that he could, to destroy her confidence in her own powers, to lessen her self-respect, and to make her
willing to lead a dependent and abject life.

Now, in view of this entire disfranchisement of one-half the people
of this country, their social and religious degradation—in view of the
unjust laws above mentioned, and because women do feel themselves
aggrieved, oppressed, and fraudulently deprived of their most sacred
rights, we insist that they have immediate admission to all the rights
and privileges which belong to them as citizens of the United States.

In entering upon the great work before us, we anticipate no small   20
amount of misconception, misrepresentation, and ridicule; but we shall
use every instrumentality within our power to effect our object. We
shall employ agents, circulate tracts, petition the State and National legislatures, and endeavor to enlist the pulpit and the press in our behalf.
We hope this Convention will be followed by a series of Conventions
embracing every part of the country.

[The following resolutions were discussed by Lucretia Mott,
Thomas and Mary Ann McClintock, Amy Post, Catharine A. F. Steb-
bins, and others, and were adopted:]

Whereas, The great precept of nature is conceded to be, that "man shall
pursue his own true and substantial happiness." Blackstone in his Com-
mentaries remarks, that this law of Nature being coeval with mankind, and
dictated by God himself, is of course superior in obligation to any other. It
is binding over all the globe, in all countries, and at all times; no human
laws are of any validity if contrary to this, and such of them as are valid,
derive all their force, and all their validity, and all their authority, mediate-
ly and immediately, from this original; therefore,

Resolved, That such laws as conflict, in any way, with the true and substantial happiness of woman, are contrary to the great precept of nature
and of no validity, for this is "superior in obligation to any other."

Resolved, That all laws which prevent woman from occupying such a
station in society as her conscience shall dictate, or which place her in a
position inferior to that of man, are contrary to the great precept of nature,
and therefore of no force or authority.

Resolved, That woman is man's equal—was intended to be so by the
Creator, and the highest good of the race demands that she should be recognized as such.

Resolved, That the women of this country ought to be enlightened in
regard to the laws under which they live, that they may no longer publish

their degradation by declaring themselves satisfied with their present position, nor their ignorance, by asserting that they have all the rights they want.

Resolved, That inasmuch as man, while claiming for himself intellectual superiority, does accord to woman moral superiority, it is preeminently his duty to encourage her to speak and teach, as she has an opportunity, in all religious assemblies.

Resolved, That the same amount of virtue, delicacy, and refinement of behavior that is required of woman in the social state, should also be required of man, and the same transgressions should be visited with equal severity on both man and woman.

Resolved, That the objection of indelicacy and impropriety, which is so often brought against woman when she addresses a public audience, comes with a very ill-grace from those who encourage, by their attendance, her appearance on the stage, in the concert, or in feats of the circus.

Resolved, That woman has too long rested satisfied in the circumscribed limits which corrupt customs and a perverted application of the Scriptures have marked out for her, and that it is time she should move in the enlarged sphere which her great Creator has assigned her.

Resolved, That it is the duty of the women of this country to secure to themselves their sacred right to the elective franchise.

Resolved, That the equality of human rights results necessarily from the fact of the identity of the race in capabilities and responsibilities.

Resolved, therefore, That, being invested by the Creator with the same capabilities, and the same consciousness of responsibility for their exercise, it is demonstrably the right and duty of woman, equally with man, to promote every righteous cause by every righteous means; and especially in regard to the great subjects of morals and religion, it is self-evidently her right to participate with her brother in teaching them, both in private and in public, by writing and by speaking, by any instrumentalities proper to be used, and in any assemblies proper to be held; and this being a self-evident truth growing out of the divinely implanted principles of human nature, any custom or authorities adverse to it, whether modern or wearing the hoary sanction of antiquity, is to be regarded as a self-evident falsehood, and at war with mankind.

[At the last session Lucretia Mott offered and spoke to the following resolution:]

Resolved, That the speedy success of our cause depends upon the zealous and untiring efforts of both men and women, for the overthrow of the monopoly of the pulpit, and for the securing to woman an equal participation with men in the various trades, professions, and commerce.

Topics for Critical Thinking and Writing

1. Stanton echoes the Declaration of Independence because she wishes to associate her ideas and the movement she supports with a document and a movement that her readers esteem. And of course she must have believed that if readers esteem the Declaration of Indepen-

dence, they must grant the justice of her goals. Does her strategy work, or does it backfire by making her essay seem strained?

2. The Declaration claims that women have "the same capabilities" as men (paragraph 32). Yet in 1848 Stanton and the others at Seneca Falls knew, or should have known, that history recorded no example of an outstanding woman philosopher to compare with Plato or Kant, a great composer to compare with Beethoven or Chopin, a scientist to compare with Galileo or Newton, or a creative mathematician to compare with Euclid or Descartes. Do these facts contradict the Declaration's claim? If not, why not? How else but by different intellectual capabilities do you think such facts are to be explained?

3. Stanton's Declaration is almost 150 years old. Have all of the issues she raised been satisfactorily resolved? If not, which ones remain?

4. In our society, children have very few rights. For instance, a child cannot decide to drop out of elementary school or high school, and a child cannot decide to leave his or her parents in order to reside with some other family that he or she finds more compatible. Whatever your view of children's rights, compose the best Declaration of the Rights of Children that you can.

E. M. Forster

E[dward] M[organ] Forster (1879–1970) was born in London and was graduated from King's College, Cambridge. He traveled widely and lived for a while in India, but most of his life was spent back at King's College. His best-known novel, A Passage to India *(1926), is alluded to in the first line of the essay that we reprint.*

My Wood

A few years ago I wrote a book which dealt in part with the difficulties of the English in India. Feeling that they would have had no difficulties in India themselves, the Americans read the book freely. The more they read it the better it made them feel, and a checque to the author was the result. I bought a wood with the checque. It is not a large wood—it contains scarcely any trees, and it is intersected, blast it, by a public footpath. Still, it is the first property that I have owned, so it is right that other people should participate in my shame, and should ask themselves, in accents that will vary in horror, this very important question: What is the effect of property upon the character? Don't let's touch economics; the effect of private ownership upon the community as a whole is another question—a more important question, perhaps, but another one. Let's keep on psychology. If you own things, what's their effect on you? What's the effect on me of my wood?

In the first place, it makes me feel heavy. Property does have this effect. Property produces men of weight, and it was a man of weight who failed to get into the Kingdom of Heaven. He was not wicked, that unfortunate millionaire in the parable, he was only stout; he stuck out in front, not to mention behind, and as he wedged himself this way and that in the crystalline entrance and bruised his well-fed flanks, he saw beneath him a comparatively slim camel passing through the eye of a needle and being woven into the robe of God. The Gospels all through couple stoutness and slowness. They point out what is perfectly obvious, yet seldom realized: that if you have a lot of things you cannot move about a lot, that furniture requires dusting, dusters require servants, servants require insurance stamps, and the whole tangle of them makes you think twice before you accept an invitation to dinner or go for a bathe in the Jordan. Sometimes the Gospels proceed further and say with Tolstoy that property is sinful; they approach the difficult ground of asceticism here, where I cannot follow them. But as to the immediate effects of property on people, they just show straightforward logic. It produces men of weight. Men of weight cannot, by definition, move like the lightning from the East unto the West, and the ascent of a fourteen-stone[1] bishop into a pulpit is thus the exact antithesis of the coming of the Son of Man. My wood makes me feel heavy.

In the second place, it makes me feel it ought to be larger.

The other day I heard a twig snap in it. I was annoyed at first, for I thought that someone was blackberrying, and depreciating the value of the undergrowth. On coming nearer, I saw it was not a man who had trodden on the twig and snapped it, but a bird, and I felt pleased. My bird. The bird was not equally pleased. Ignoring the relation between us, it took fright as soon as it saw the shape of my face, and flew straight over the boundary hedge into a field, the property of Mrs. Henessy, where it sat down with a loud squawk. It had become Mrs. Henessy's bird. Something seemed grossly amiss here, something that would not have occurred had the wood been larger. I could not afford to buy Mrs. Henessy out, I dared not murder her, and limitations of this sort beset me on every side. Ahab did not want that vineyard—he only needed it to round off his property, preparatory to plotting a new curve—and all the land around my wood has become necessary to me in order to round off the wood. A boundary protects. But—poor little thing—the boundary ought in its turn to be protected. Noises on the edge of it. Children throw stones. A little more, and then a little more, until we reach the sea. Happy Canute! Happier Alexander! And after all, why should even the world be the limit of possession? A rocket containing a Union Jack, will, it is hoped, be shortly fired at the moon. Mars. Sirius. Beyond which . . . But these immensities ended by saddening me. I could not suppose that my wood was the destined nucleus of universal dominion—it is so very small and contains no mineral wealth beyond

4

---

[1]**Fourteen-stone:** 196 pounds. (Editors' note)

the blackberries. Nor was I comforted when Mrs. Henessy's bird took alarm for the second time and flew clean away from us all, under the belief that it belonged to itself.

In the third place, property makes its owner feel that he ought to do something to it. Yet he isn't sure what. A restlessness comes over him, a vague sense that he has a personality to express—the same sense which, without any vagueness, leads the artist to an act of creation. Sometimes I think I will cut down such trees as remain in the wood, at other times I want to fill up the gaps between them with new trees. Both impulses are pretentious and empty. They are not honest movements towards money-making or beauty. They spring from a foolish desire to express myself and from an inability to enjoy what I have got. Creation, property, enjoyment are both very very good, yet they are often unattainable without a material basis, and at such moments property pushes itself in as a substitute, saying, "Accept me instead—I'm good enough for all three." It is not enough. It is, as Shakespeare said of lust, "The expense of spirit in a waste of shame": it is "Before, a joy proposed; behind, a dream." Yet we don't know how to shun it. It is forced on us by our economic system as the alternative to starvation. It is also forced on us by an internal defect in the soul, by the feeling that in property may lie the germs of self-development and of exquisite or heroic deeds. Our life on earth is, and ought to be, material and carnal. But we have not yet learned to manage our materialism and carnality properly; they are still entangled with the desire for ownership, where (in the words of Dante) "Possession is one with loss."

And this brings us to our fourth and final point: the blackberries.

Blackberries are not plentiful in this meager grove, but they are easily seen from the public footpath which traverses it, and all too easily gathered. Foxgloves, too—people will pull up the foxgloves, and ladies of an educational tendency even grub for toadstools to show them on the Monday in class. Other ladies, less educated, roll down the bracken in the arms of their gentlemen friends. There is paper, there are tins. Pray, does my wood belong to me or doesn't it? And, if it does, should I not own it best by allowing no one else to walk there? There is a wood near Lyme Regis, also cursed by a public footpath, where the owner has not hesitated on this point. He has built high stone walls each side of the path, and has spanned it by bridges, so that the public circulate like termites while he gorges on the blackberries unseen. He really does own his wood, this able chap. Dives in Hell did pretty well, but the gulf dividing him from Lazarus could be traversed by vision, and nothing traverses it here.[2] And perhaps I shall come to this in time. I shall wall in and fence out until I really taste the sweets of property. Enormously

---

[2]According to Christ's parable in Luke 16:19–26, the rich man (unnamed, but traditionally known as Dives) at whose gate the poor man Lazarus had begged was sent to hell, from where he could see Lazarus in heaven. (Editors' note).

stout, endlessly avaricious, pseudo-creative, intensely selfish, I shall weave upon my forehead the quadruple crown of possession until those nasty Bolshies come and take it off again and thrust me aside into the outer darkness.

Topic for Critical Thinking and Writing

Much of the strength of the essay lies in its concrete presentation of generalities. Note, for example, that the essay is called "My Wood," but we might say that the general idea of the essay is "The Effect of Property on Owners." Forster gives four effects, chiefly through concrete statements. Put these four effects into four general statements.

Virginia Woolf

Virginia Woolf (1882–1941) was born in London into an upper-middle class literary family. In 1912 she married a writer, and with him she founded the Hogarth Press, whose important publications included not only books by T. S. Eliot but her own novels.
This essay was originally a talk delivered in 1931 to The Women's Service League.

Professions for Women

When your secretary invited me to come here, she told me that your Society is concerned with the employment of women and she suggested that I might tell you something about my own professional experiences. It is true I am a woman; it is true I am employed, but what professional experiences have I had? It is difficult to say. My profession is literature; and in that profession there are fewer experiences for women than in any other, with the exception of the stage—fewer, I mean, that are peculiar to women. For the road was cut many years ago—by Fanny Burney, by Aphra Behn, by Harriet Martineau, by Jane Austen, by George Eliot—many famous women, and many more unknown and forgotten, have been before me, making the path smooth, and regulating my steps. Thus, when I came to write, there were very few material obstacles in my way. Writing was a reputable and harmless occupation. The family peace was not broken by the scratching of a pen. No demand was made upon the family purse. For ten and sixpence one can buy paper enough to write all the plays of Shakespeare—if one has a mind that way. Pianos and models, Paris, Vienna and Berlin, masters and mistresses, are not needed by a writer. The cheapness of writing paper is, of course, the reason why women have succeeded as writers before they have succeeded in the other professions.

But to tell you my story—it is a simple one. You have only got to figure to yourselves a girl in a bedroom with a pen in her hand. She had only to move that pen from left to right—from ten o'clock to one. Then it occurred to her to do what is simple and cheap enough after all—to slip a few of those pages into an envelope, fix a penny stamp in the corner, and drop the envelope in the red box at the corner. It was thus that I became a journalist; and my effort was rewarded on the first day of the following month—a very glorious day it was for me—by a letter from an editor containing a check for one pound ten shillings and sixpence. But to show you how little I deserve to be called a professional woman, how little I know of the struggles and difficulties of such lives, I have to admit that instead of spending that sum upon bread and butter, rent, shoes and stockings, or butcher's bills, I went out and bought a cat—a beautiful cat, a Persian cat, which very soon involved me in bitter disputes with my neighbors.

What could be easier than to write articles and to buy Persian cats with the profits? But wait a moment. Articles have to be about something. Mine, I seem to remember, was about a novel by a famous man. And while I was writing this review, I discovered that if I were going to review books I should need to do battle with a certain phantom. And the phantom was a woman, and when I came to know her better I called her after the heroine of a famous poem, The Angel in the House. It was she who used to come between me and my paper when I was writing reviews. It was she who bothered me and wasted my time and so tormented me that at last I killed her. You who come of a younger and happier generation may not have heard of her—you may not know what I mean by the Angel in the House. I will describe her as shortly as I can. She was intensely sympathetic. She was immensely charming. She was utterly unselfish. She excelled in the difficult arts of family life. She sacrificed herself daily. If there was chicken, she took the leg; if there was a draught she sat in it—in short she was so constituted that she never had a mind or a wish of her own but preferred to sympathize always with the minds and wishes of others. Above all—I need not say it—she was pure. Her purity was supposed to be her chief beauty—her blushes, her great grace. In those days—the last of Queen Victoria— every house had its Angel. And when I came to write I encountered her with the very first words. The shadow of her wings fell on my page; I heard the rustling of her skirts in the room. Directly, that is to say, I took my pen in hand to review that novel by a famous man, she slipped behind me and whispered: "My dear, you are a young woman. You are writing about a book that has been written by a man. Be sympathetic; be tender; flatter; deceive; use all the arts and wiles of our sex. Never let anybody guess that you have a mind of your own. Above all, be pure." And she made as if to guide my pen. I now record the one act for which I take some credit to myself, though the credit rightly belongs to some excellent ancestors of mine who left me a certain sum of money—shall we say five hundred pounds a year?—so that it was not necessary for me to depend solely on charm for my living. I turned upon her and caught her by the throat. I did my best to kill her. My excuse, if I were to be had up in a court of law, would be that I acted in self-defense. Had I not killed her she would have killed me. She would have plucked the heart out of my writing. For, as I found, directly I put pen to paper, you cannot review even a novel without having a mind of your own, without expressing what you think to be the truth about human relations, morality, sex. And all these questions, according to the Angel in the House, cannot be dealt with freely and openly by women; they must charm, they must conciliate, they must—to put it bluntly—tell lies if they are to succeed. Thus, whenever I felt the shadow of her wing or the radiance of her halo upon my page, I took up the inkpot and flung it at her. She died hard. Her fictitious nature was of great assistance to her. It is far harder to kill a phantom than a reality. She was always creeping back when I thought I had despatched her. Though I flatter myself that I killed her in the end, the struggle was severe; it took much time that had better have been spent upon learning Greek grammar; or in roaming the world in search of adventures. But it was a real experience; it was an experience that was bound to befall all women writers at that time. Killing the Angel in the House was part of the occupation of a woman writer.

But to continue my story. The Angel was dead; what then 4 remained? You may say that what remained was a simple and common object—a young woman in a bedroom with an inkpot. In other words, now that she had rid herself of falsehood, that young woman had only to be herself. Ah, but what is "herself"? I mean, what is a woman? I assure you, I do not know. I do not believe that you know. I do not believe that anybody can know until she has expressed herself in all the arts and professions open to human skill. That indeed is one of the reasons why I have come here—out of respect for you, who are in process of showing us by your experiments what a woman is, who are in process of providing us, by your failures and successes, with that extremely important piece of information.

But to continue the story of my professional experiences. I made one pound ten and six by my first review; and I bought a Persian cat with the proceeds. Then I grew ambitious. A Persian cat is all very well, I said; but a Persian cat is not enough. I must have a motor car. And it was thus that I became a novelist—for it is a very strange thing that people will give you a motor car if you will tell them a story. It is a still stranger thing that there is nothing so delightful in the world as telling stories. It is far pleasanter than writing reviews of famous novels. And yet, if I am to obey your secretary and tell you my professional experiences as a novelist, I must tell you about a very strange experience that befell me as a novelist. And to understand it you must try first to imagine a novelist's state of mind. I hope I am not giving away professional secrets if I say that a novelist's chief desire is to be as unconscious as possible. He has to induce in himself a state of perpetual lethargy. He wants life to proceed with the utmost quiet and regularity. He wants to see the same faces, to read the same books, to do the same things day after day, month after month, while he is writing, so that nothing may break the illusion in which he is living—so that nothing may disturb or disquiet the mysterious nosings about, feelings round, darts, dashes and sudden discoveries of that very shy and illusive spirit, the imagination. I suspect that this state is the same both for men and women. Be that as it may, I want you to imagine me writing a novel in a state of trance. I want you to figure to yourselves a girl sitting with a pen in her hand, which for minutes, and indeed for hours, she never dips into the inkpot. The image that comes to my mind when I think of this girl is the image of a fisherman lying sunk in dreams on the verge of a deep lake with a rod held out over the water. She was letting her imagination sweep unchecked round every rock and cranny of the world that lies submerged in the depths of our unconscious being. Now came the experience, the experience that I believe to be far commoner with women writers than with men. The line raced through the girl's fingers. Her imagination had rushed away. It had sought the pools, the depths, the dark places where the largest fish slumber. And then there was a smash. There was an explosion. There was foam and confusion. The imagination had dashed itself against something hard. The girl was roused from her dream. She was indeed in a state of the most acute and difficult distress. To speak without figure she had thought of something, something about the body, about the passions which it was unfitting for her as a woman to say. Men, her reason told her, would be shocked. The consciousness of what men will say of a woman who speaks the truth about her passions had roused her from her artist's state of unconsciousness. She could write no more. The trance was over. Her imagination could work no longer. This I believe to be a very common experience with women writers—they are impeded by the extreme conventionality of the other sex. For though men sensibly allow themselves great freedom in these respects, I doubt that they realize or can control the extreme severity with which they condemn such freedom in women.

These then were two very genuine experiences of my own. These were two of the adventures of my professional life. The first—killing the Angel in the House—I think I solved. She died. But the second, telling the truth about my own experiences as a body, I do not think I solved. I doubt that any woman has solved it yet. The obstacles against her are still immensely powerful—and yet they are very difficult to define. Outwardly, what is simpler than to write books? Outwardly, what obstacles are there for a woman rather than for a man? Inwardly, I think the case is very different; she has still many ghosts to fight, many prejudices to overcome. Indeed it will be a long time still, I think, before a woman can sit down to write a book without finding a phantom to be slain, a rock to be dashed against. And if this is so in literature, the freest of all professions for women, how is it in the new professions which you are now for the first time entering?

Those are the questions that I should like, had I time, to ask you. And indeed, if I have laid stress upon these professional experiences of mine, it is because I believe that they are, though in different forms, yours also. Even when the path is nominally open—when there is nothing to prevent a woman from being a doctor, a lawyer, a civil servant— there are many phantoms and obstacles, as I believe, looming in her way. To discuss and define them is I think of great value and importance; for thus only can the labor be shared, the difficulties be solved. But besides this, it is necessary also to discuss the ends and the aims for which we are fighting, for which we are doing battle with these formidable obstacles. Those aims cannot be taken for granted; they must be perpetually questioned and examined. The whole position, as I see it— here in this hall surrounded by women practising for the first time in history I know not how many different professions—is one of extraordinary interest and importance. You have won rooms of your own in the house hitherto exclusively owned by men. You are able, though not without great labor and effort, to pay the rent. You are earning your five hundred pounds a year. But this freedom is only a beginning; the room is your own, but it is still bare. It has to be furnished; it has to be decorated; it has to be shared. How are you going to furnish it, how are you going to decorate it? With whom are you going to share it, and upon what terms? These, I think, are questions of the utmost importance and interest. For the first time in history you are able to ask them; for the first time you are able to decide for yourselves what the answers should be. Willingly would I stay and discuss those questions and answers— but not tonight. My time is up; and I must cease.

Topics for Critical Thinking and Writing

1. How would you characterize Woolf's tone, especially her attitude toward her subject and herself, in the first paragraph?
2. What do you think Woolf means when she says (paragraph 3): "It is far harder to kill a phantom than a reality"?
3. Woolf conjectures (paragraph 6) that she has not solved the problem of "telling the truth about my own experiences as a body." Is there any reason to believe that today a woman has more difficulty than a man in telling the truth about the experiences of the body?
4. In paragraph 7, Woolf suggests that phantoms as well as obstacles impede women from becoming doctors and lawyers. What might some of these phantoms be?
5. This essay is highly metaphoric. Speaking roughly (or, rather, as precisely as possible), what is the meaning of the metaphor of "rooms" in the final paragraph? What does Woolf mean when she says: "The

room is your own, but it is still bare. . . . With whom are you going to share it, and upon what terms?"

6. Evaluate the last two sentences. Are they too abrupt and mechanical? Or do they provide a fitting conclusion to the speech?

May Sarton

May Sarton (1912–1995), born in Belgium, was brought to the United States in 1916 and in 1924 she became a citizen. A teacher of writing and a distinguished writer herself, she has received numerous awards for her fiction, poetry, and essays.

The Rewards of Living a Solitary Life

The other day an acquaintance of mine, a gregarious and charming man, told me he had found himself unexpectedly alone in New York for an hour or two between appointments. He went to the Whitney and spent the "empty" time looking at things in solitary bliss. For him it proved to be a shock nearly as great as falling in love to discover that he could enjoy himself so much alone.

What had he been afraid of, I asked myself? That, suddenly alone, he would discover that he bored himself, or that there was, quite simply, no self there to meet? But having taken the plunge, he is now on the brink of adventure; he is about to be launched into his own inner space, space as immense, unexplored, and sometimes frightening as outer space to the astronaut. His every perception will come to him with a new freshness and, for a time, seem startlingly original. For anyone who can see things for himself with a naked eye becomes, for a moment or two, something of a genius. With another human being present vision becomes double vision, inevitably. We are busy wondering, what does my companion see or think of this, and what do I think of it? The original impact gets lost, or diffused.

"Music I heard with you was more than music."[1] Exactly. And therefore music *itself* can only be heard alone. Solitude is the salt of personhood. It brings out the authentic flavor of every experience.

"Alone one is never lonely: the spirit adventures, walking/In a   4 quiet garden, in a cool house, abiding single there."

Loneliness is most acutely felt with other people, for with others, even with a lover sometimes, we suffer from our differences of taste,

---

[1]**"Music . . . music":** A line from Conrad Aiken's *Bread and Music* (1914).

temperament, mood. Human intercourse often demands that we soften the edge of perception, or withdraw at the very instant of personal truth for fear of hurting, or of being inappropriately present, which is to say naked, in a social situation. Alone we can afford to be wholly whatever we are, and to feel whatever we feel absolutely. That is a great luxury!

For me the most interesting thing about a solitary life, and mine has been that for the last twenty years, is that it becomes increasingly rewarding. When I can wake up and watch the sun rise over the ocean, as I do most days, and know that I have an entire day ahead, uninterrupted, in which to write a few pages, take a walk with my dog, lie down in the afternoon for a long think (why does one think better in a horizontal position?), read and listen to music, I am flooded with happiness.

I am lonely only when I am overtired, when I have worked too long without a break, when for the time being I feel empty and need filling up. And I am lonely sometimes when I come back home after a lecture trip, when I have seen a lot of people and talked a lot, and am full to the brim with experience that needs to be sorted out.

Then for a little while the house feels huge and empty, and I won- 8 der where my self is hiding. It has to be recaptured slowly by watering the plants, perhaps, and looking again at each one as though it were a person, by feeding the two cats, by cooking a meal.

It takes a while, as I watch the surf blowing up in fountains at the end of the field, but the moment comes when the world falls away, and the self emerges again from the deep unconscious, bringing back all I have recently experienced to be explored and slowly understood, when I can converse again with my hidden powers, and so grow, and so be renewed, till death do us part.

Topics for Critical Thinking and Writing

1. The essay opens with an anecdote about an acquaintance of the author's. Why are we told at the outset that he is "a gregarious and charming man"?

2. In paragraph 2 Sarton compares inner space with outer space. And in paragraph 3 she writes, "Solitude is the salt of personhood." How do you interpret these metaphors? How do they enrich her main point, that solitude is rewarding?

3. What does Sarton mean when in her first paragraph she says, "Anyone who can see things for himself with a naked eye becomes, for a moment or two, something of a genius"? Does your own experience confirm her comment? Explain.

4. What phrase in the last paragraph connects the ending with the first paragraph?

5. Drawing on Sarton's essay, in a paragraph explain the distinction between being "alone" and being "lonely."

6. In an essay of about five hundred words explain the difference between loving and being in love.

Martin Luther King, Jr.

Martin Luther King, Jr. (1929–68), clergyman and civil rights leader, achieved national fame in 1955–56 when he led the boycott against segregated bus lines in Montgomery, Alabama. His policy of passive resistance succeeded in Montgomery, and King then organized the Southern Christian Leadership Conference in order to extend his efforts. In 1963 Dr. King was arrested in Birmingham, Alabama, for participating in a march for which no parade permit had been issued by the city officials. In jail he wrote a response to a letter that eight local clergymen had published in a newspaper. Their letter titled "A Call for Unity" is printed here, followed by King's response. In 1964 he was awarded the Nobel Peace Prize, but he continued to encounter strong opposition. On April 4, 1968, while in Memphis to support striking sanitation workers, he was shot and killed.

Letter from Birmingham Jail
In Response to "A Call for Unity"

A Call for Unity

April 12, 1963

We the undersigned clergymen are among those who, in January, issued "An Appeal for Law and Order and Common Sense," in dealing with racial problems in Alabama. We expressed understanding that honest convictions in racial matters could properly be pursued in the courts, but urged that decisions of those courts should in the meantime be peacefully obeyed.

Since that time there had been some evidence of increased forebearance and a willingness to face facts. Responsible citizens have undertaken to work on various problems which cause racial friction and unrest. In Birmingham, recent public events have given indication that we all have opportunity for a new constructive and realistic approach to racial problems.

However, we are now confronted by a series of demonstrations by some of our Negro citizens, directed and led in part by outsiders. We recognize the natural impatience of people who feel that their hopes are slow in being realized. But we are convinced that these demonstrations are unwise and untimely.

We agree rather with certain local Negro leadership which has called for honest and open negotiation of racial issues in our area. And we believe this kind of facing of issues can best be accomplished by citizens of our own metropolitan area, white and Negro, meeting with their knowledge and experience of the local situation. All of us need to face that responsibility and find proper channels for its accomplishment.

4

Just as we formerly pointed out that "hatred and violence have no sanction in our religious and political traditions," we also point out that such actions as incite to hatred and violence, however technically peaceful those actions may be, have not contributed to the resolution of our local problems. We do not believe that these days of new hope are days when extreme measures are justified in Birmingham.

We commend the community as a whole, and the local news media and law enforcement officials in particular, on the calm manner in which these demonstrations have been handled. We urge the public to continue to show restraint should the demonstrations continue, and the law enforcement officials to remain calm and continue to protect our city from violence.

We further strongly urge our own Negro community to withdraw support from these demonstrations, and to unite locally in working peacefully for a better Birmingham. When rights are consistently denied, a cause should be pressed in the courts and in negotiations among local leaders, and not in the streets. We appeal to both our white and Negro citizenry to observe the principles of law and order and common sense.

C.C.J. Carpenter, D.D., L.L.D., Bishop of Alabama; Joseph A. Durick, D.D., Auxiliary Bishop, Diocese of Mobile-Birmingham; Rabbi Milton L. Grafman, Temple Emanu-El, Birmingham, Alabama; Bishop Paul Hardin, Bishop of the Alabama–West Florida Conference of the Methodist Church; Bishop Nolan B. Harmon, Bishop of the North Alabama Conference of the Methodist Church; George M. Murray, D.D., L.L.D., Bishop Coadjutor, Episcopal Diocese of Alabama; Edward V. Ramage, Moderator, Synod of the Alabama Presbyterian Church in the United States; Earl Stallings, Pastor, First Baptist Church, Birmingham, Alabama.   8

Letter from Birmingham Jail

April 16, 1963

My Dear Fellow Clergymen:

While confined here in the Birmingham city jail, I came across your recent statement calling my present activities "unwise and untimely."[1] Seldom do I pause to answer criticism of my work and ideas. If I sought to answer all the criticisms that cross my desk, my secretaries would have little time for anything other than such correspondence in the course of the day, and I would have no time for constructive work. But since I feel that you are men of genuine good will and that your criticisms are sincerely set forth, I want to try to answer your statement in what I hope will be patient and reasonable terms.

---

[1]This response to a published statement by eight fellow clergymen from Alabama (Bishop C.C.J. Carpenter, Bishop Joseph A. Durick, Rabbi Milton L. Grafman, Bishop Paul Hardin, Bishop Nolan B. Harmon, the Reverend George M. Murray, the Reverend Edward V. Ramage, and the Reverend Earl Stallings) was composed under somewhat constricting circumstances. Begun on the margins of the newspaper in which the statement appeared while I was in jail, the letter was continued on scraps of writing paper supplied by a friendly Negro trusty, and concluded on a pad my attorneys were eventually permitted to leave me. Although the text remains in substance unaltered, I have indulged in the author's prerogative of polishing it for publication. [King's note]

I think I should indicate why I am here in Birmingham, since you have been influenced by the view which argues against "outsiders coming in." I have the honor of serving as president of the Southern Christian Leadership Conference, an organization operating in every southern state, with headquarters in Atlanta, Georgia. We have some eighty-five affiliated organizations across the South, and one of them is the Alabama Christian Movement for Human Rights. Frequently we share staff, educational, and financial resources with our affiliates. Several months ago the affiliate here in Birmingham asked us to be on call to engage in a nonviolent direct-action program if such were deemed necessary. We readily consented, and when the hour came we lived up to our promise. So I, along with several members of my staff, am here because I was invited here. I am here because I have organizational ties here.

But more basically, I am in Birmingham because injustice is here. Just as the prophets of the eighth century B.C. left their villages and carried their "thus saith the Lord" far beyond the boundaries of their home towns, and just as the Apostle Paul left his village of Tarsus and carried the gospel of Jesus Christ to the far corners of the Greco-Roman world, so am I compelled to carry the gospel of freedom beyond my own home town. Like Paul, I must constantly respond to the Macedonian call for aid.

Moreover, I am cognizant of the interrelatedness of all communities and states. I cannot sit idly by in Atlanta and not be concerned about what happens in Birmingham. Injustice anywhere is a threat to justice everywhere. We are caught in an inescapable network of mutuality; tied in a single garment of destiny. Whatever affects one directly, affects all indirectly. Never again can we afford to live with the narrow, provincial "outside agitator" idea. Anyone who lives inside the United States can never be considered an outsider anywhere within its bounds.   12

You deplore the demonstrations taking place in Birmingham. But your statement, I am sorry to say, fails to express a similar concern for the conditions that brought about the demonstrations. I am sure that none of you would want to rest content with the superficial kind of social analysis that deals merely with effects and does not grapple with underlying causes. It is unfortunate that demonstrations are taking place in Birmingham, but it is even more unfortunate that the city's white power structure left the Negro community with no alternative.

In any nonviolent campaign there are four basic steps: collection of the facts to determine whether injustices exist; negotiation; self-purification; and direct action. We have gone through all these steps in Birmingham. There can be no gainsaying the fact that racial injustice engulfs this community. Birmingham is probably the most thoroughly segregated city in the United States. Its ugly record of brutality is widely known. Negroes have experienced grossly unjust treatment in the courts. There have been more unsolved bombings of Negro homes and churches in Birmingham than in any other city in the nation. These are the hard, brutal facts of the case. On the basis of these conditions, Negro leaders sought to negotiate with the city fathers. But the latter consistently refused to engage in good-faith negotiation.

Then, last September, came the opportunity to talk with leaders of Birmingham's economic community. In the course of the negotiations, certain promises were made by the merchants—for example, to remove the stores' humiliating racial signs. On the basis of these promises, the Reverend Fred Shuttlesworth and the leaders of the Alabama Christian Movement for Human Rights agreed to a moratorium on all demonstrations. As the weeks and months went by, we realized that we were the victims of a broken promise. A few signs, briefly removed, returned; the others remained.

As in so many past experiences, our hopes had been blasted, and   16
the shadow of deep disappointment settled upon us. We had no alternative except to prepare for direct action, whereby we would present our very bodies as a means of laying our case before the conscience of the local and the national community. Mindful of the difficulties involved, we decided to undertake a process of self-purification. We began a series of workshops on nonviolence, and we repeatedly asked ourselves: "Are you able to accept blows without retaliating?" "Are you able to endure the ordeal of jail?" We decided to schedule our direct-action program for the Easter season, realizing that except for Christmas, this is the main shopping period of the year. Knowing that a strong economic-withdrawal program would be the by-product of direct action, we felt that this would be the best time to bring pressure to bear on the merchants for the needed change.

Then it occurred to us that Birmingham's mayoralty election was coming up in March, and we speedily decided to postpone action until after election day. When we discovered that the Commissioner of Public Safety, Eugene "Bull" Connor, had piled up enough votes to be in the run-off, we decided again to postpone action until the day after the run-off so that the demonstrations could not be used to cloud the issues. Like many others, we waited to see Mr. Connor defeated, and to this end we endured postponement after postponement. Having aided in this community need, we felt that our direct-action program could be delayed no longer.

You may well ask: "Why direct action? Why sit-ins, marches, and so forth? Isn't negotiation a better path?" You are quite right in calling for negotiation. Indeed, this is the very purpose of direct action. Nonviolent direct action seeks to create such a crisis and foster such a tension that a community which has constantly refused to negotiate is forced to confront the issue. It seeks so to dramatize the issue that it can no longer be ignored. My citing the creation of tension as part of the work of the nonviolent resister may sound rather shocking. But I must confess that I am not afraid of the word "tension." I have earnestly opposed violent tension, but there is a type of constructive, nonviolent tension which is necessary for growth. Just as Socrates felt that it was necessary to create a tension in the mind so that individuals could rise from the bondage of myths and half-truths to the unfettered realm of creative analysis and objective appraisal, so must we see the need for nonviolent gadflies to create the kind of tension in society that will help men rise from the dark depths of prejudice and racism to the majestic heights of understanding and brotherhood.

The purpose of our direct-action program is to create a situation so crisis-packed that it will inevitably open the door to negotiation. I therefore concur with you in your call for negotiation. Too long has our beloved Southland been bogged down in a tragic effort to live in monologue rather than dialogue.

One of the basic points in your statement is that the action that I 20 and my associates have taken in Birmingham is untimely. Some have asked: "Why didn't you give the new city administration time to act?" The only answer that I can give to this query is that the new Birmingham administration must be prodded about as much as the outgoing one, before it will act. We are sadly mistaken if we feel that the election of Albert Boutwell as mayor will bring the millennium to Birmingham. While Mr. Boutwell is a much more gentle person than Mr. Connor, they are both segregationists, dedicated to maintenance of the status quo. I have hope that Mr. Boutwell will be reasonable enough to see the futility of massive resistance to desegregation. But he will not see this without pressure from devotees of civil rights. My friends, I must say to you that we have not made a single gain in civil rights without determined legal and nonviolent pressure. Lamentably, it is an historical fact that privileged groups seldom give up their privileges voluntarily. Individuals may see the moral light and voluntarily give up their unjust posture; but as Reinhold Niebuhr[2] has reminded us, groups tend to be more immoral than individuals.

We know through painful experience that freedom is never voluntarily given by the oppressor; it must be demanded by the oppressed. Frankly, I have yet to engage in a direct-action campaign that was "well timed" in the view of those who have not suffered unduly from the disease of segregation. For years now I have heard the word "Wait!" It rings in the ear of every Negro with piercing familiarity. This "Wait" has almost always meant "Never." We must come to see, with one of our distinguished jurists, that "justice too long delayed is justice denied."[3]

We have waited for more than 340 years for our constitutional and God-given rights. The nations of Asia and Africa are moving with jet-like speed toward gaining political independence, but we still creep at

---

[2]**Reinhold Niebuhr** (1892–1971). Minister, political activist, author, and professor of applied Christianity at Union Theological Seminary. [This and the following notes are the editors'.]

[3]**Justice . . . denied:** A quotation attributed to William E. Gladstone (1809–1898), British statesman and prime minister.

horse-and-buggy pace toward gaining a cup of coffee at a lunch counter. Perhaps it is easy for those who have never felt the stinging darts of segregation to say, "Wait." But when you have seen vicious mobs lynch your mothers and fathers at will and drown your sisters and brothers at whim; when you have seen hate-filled policemen curse, kick, and even kill your black brothers and sisters; when you see the vast majority of your twenty million Negro brothers smothering in an airtight cage of poverty in the midst of an affluent society; when you suddenly find your tongue twisted and your speech stammering as you seek to explain to your six-year-old daughter why she can't go to the public amusement park that has just been advertised on television, and see tears welling up in her eyes when she is told that Funtown is closed to colored children, and see ominous clouds of inferiority beginning to form in her little mental sky, and see her beginning to distort her personality by developing an unconscious bitterness toward white people; when you have to concoct an answer for a five-year-old son who is asking: "Daddy, why do white people treat colored people so mean?"; when you take a cross-country drive and find it necessary to sleep night after night in the uncomfortable corners of your automobile because no motel will accept you; when you are humiliated day in and day out by nagging signs reading "white" and "colored"; when your first name becomes "nigger," your middle name becomes "boy" (however old you are) and your last name becomes "John," and your wife and mother are never given the respected title "Mrs."; when you are harried by day and haunted by night by the fact that you are a Negro, living constantly at tiptoe stance, never quite knowing what to expect next, and are plagued with inner fears and outer resentments; when you are forever fighting a degenerating sense of "nobodiness"—then you will understand why we find it difficult to wait. There comes a time when the cup of endurance runs over, and men are no longer willing to be plunged into the abyss of despair. I hope, sirs, you can understand our legitimate and unavoidable impatience.

You express a great deal of anxiety over our willingness to break laws. This is certainly a legitimate concern. Since we so diligently urge people to obey the Supreme Court's decision of 1954 outlawing segregation in the public schools, at first glance it may seem rather paradoxical for us consciously to break laws. One may well ask: "How can you advocate breaking some laws and obeying others?" The answer lies in the fact that there are two types of laws: just and unjust. I would be the first to advocate obeying just laws. One has not only a legal but a moral responsibility to obey just laws. Conversely, one has a moral responsibility to disobey unjust laws. I would agree with St. Augustine that "an unjust law is no law at all."

Now, what is the difference between the two? How does one determine whether a law is just or unjust? A just law is a man-made code that squares with the moral law or the law of God. An unjust law is a code

24

that is out of harmony with the moral law. To put it in the terms of St. Thomas Aquinas: An unjust law is a human law that is not rooted in eternal law and natural law. Any law that uplifts human personality is just. Any law that degrades human personality is unjust. All segregation statutes are unjust because segregation distorts the soul and damages the personality. It gives the segregator a false sense of superiority and the segregated a false sense of inferiority. Segregation, to use the terminology of the Jewish philosopher Martin Buber, substitutes an "I-it" relationship for an "I-thou" relationship and ends up relegating persons to the status of things. Hence segregation is not only politically, economically, and sociologically unsound, it is morally wrong and sinful. Paul Tillich[4] has said that sin is separation. Is not segregation an existential expression of man's tragic separation, his awful estrangement, his terrible sinfulness? Thus it is that I can urge men to obey the 1954 decision of the Supreme Court, for it is morally right; and I can urge them to disobey segregation ordinances, for they are morally wrong.

Let us consider a more concrete example of just and unjust laws. An unjust law is a code that a numerical or power majority group compels a minority group to obey but does not make binding on itself. This is *difference* made legal. By the same token, a just law is a code that a majority compels a minority to follow and that it is willing to follow itself. This is *sameness* made legal.

Let me give another explanation. A law is unjust if it is inflicted on a minority that, as a result of being denied the right to vote, had no part in enacting or devising the law. Who can say that the legislature of Alabama which set up that state's segregation laws was democratically elected? Throughout Alabama all sorts of devious methods are used to prevent Negroes from becoming registered voters, and there are some counties in which, even though Negroes constitute a majority of the population, not a single Negro is registered. Can any law enacted under such circumstances be considered democratically structured?

Sometimes a law is just on its face and unjust in its application. For instance, I have been arrested on a charge of parading without a permit. Now, there is nothing wrong in having an ordinance which requires a permit for a parade. But such an ordinance becomes unjust when it is used to maintain segregation and to deny citizens the First Amendment privilege of peaceful assembly and protest.

I hope you are able to see the distinction I am trying to point out. In no sense do I advocate evading or defying the law, as would the rabid segregationist. That would lead to anarchy. One who breaks an unjust law must do so openly, lovingly, and with a willingness to accept the   28

---

[4]**Paul Tillich:** Tillich (1886–1965), born in Germany, taught theology at several German universities, but in 1933 he was dismissed from his post at the University of Frankfurt because of his opposition to the Nazi regime. At the invitation of Reinhold Niebuhr, he came to the United States and taught at Union Theological Seminary.

penalty. I submit that an individual who breaks a law that conscience tells him is unjust, and who willingly accepts the penalty of imprisonment in order to arouse the conscience of the community over its injustice, is in reality expressing the highest respect for law.

Of course, there is nothing new about this kind of civil disobedience. It was evidenced sublimely in the refusal of Shadrach, Meshach, and Abednego to obey the laws of Nebuchadnezzar, on the ground that a higher moral law was at stake. It was practiced superbly by the early Christians, who were willing to face hungry lions and the excruciating pain of chopping blocks rather than submit to certain unjust laws of the Roman Empire. To a degree, academic freedom is a reality today because Socrates practiced civil disobedience. In our own nation, the Boston Tea Party represented a massive act of civil disobedience.

We should never forget that everything Adolf Hitler did in Germany was "legal" and everything the Hungarian freedom fighters did in Hungary was "illegal." It was "illegal" to aid and comfort a Jew in Hitler's Germany. Even so, I am sure that, had I lived in Germany at the time, I would have aided and comforted my Jewish brothers. If today I lived in a Communist country where certain principles dear to the Christian faith are suppressed, I would openly advocate disobeying that country's anti-religious laws.

I must make two honest confessions to you, my Christian and Jewish brothers. First, I must confess that over the past few years I have been gravely disappointed with the white moderate. I have almost reached the regrettable conclusion that the Negro's great stumbling block in his stride toward freedom is not the White Citizen's Counciler or the Ku Klux Klanner, but the white moderate, who is more devoted to "order" than to justice; who prefers a negative peace which is the absence of tension to a positive peace which is the presence of justice; who constantly says: "I agree with you in the goal you seek, but I cannot agree with your methods or direct action"; who paternalistically believes he can set the timetable for another man's freedom; who lives by a mythical concept of time and who constantly advises the Negro to wait for a "more convenient season." Shallow understanding from people of good will is more frustrating than absolute misunderstanding from people of ill will. Lukewarm acceptance is much more bewildering than outright rejection.

I had hoped that the white moderate would understand that law 32 and order exist for the purpose of establishing justice and that when they fail in this purpose they become the dangerously structured dams that block the flow of social progress. I had hoped that the white moderate would understand that the present tension in the South is a necessary phase of the transition from an obnoxious negative peace, in which the Negro passively accepted his unjust plight, to a substantive and positive peace, in which all men will respect the dignity and worth of human personality. Actually, we who engage in nonviolent direct action are not the creators of tension. We merely bring to the surface the hidden tension that is already alive. We bring it out in the open, where it can be seen and dealt with. Like a boil that can never be cured so long as it is covered up but must be opened with all its ugliness to the natural medicines of air and light, injustice must be exposed, with all the tension its exposure creates, to the light of human conscience and the air of national opinion before it can be cured.

In your statement you assert that our actions, even though peaceful, must be condemned because they precipitate violence. But is this a logical assertion? Isn't this like condemning a robbed man because his possession of money precipitated the evil act of robbery? Isn't this like condemning Socrates because his unswerving commitment to truth and his philosophical inquiries precipitated the act by the misguided populace in which they made him drink hemlock? Isn't this like condemning Jesus because his unique God-consciousness and never-ceasing devotion to God's will precipitated the evil act of crucifixion? We must come to see that, as the federal courts have consistently affirmed, it is wrong to urge an individual to cease his efforts to gain his basic constitutional rights because the quest may precipitate violence. Society must protect the robbed and punish the robber.

I had also hoped that the white moderate would reject the myth concerning time in relation to the struggle for freedom. I have just received a letter from a white brother in Texas. He writes: "All Christians know that the colored people will receive equal rights eventually, but it is possible that you are in too great a religious hurry. It has taken Christianity almost two thousand years to accomplish what it has. The teachings of Christ take time to come to earth." Such an attitude stems from a tragic misconception of time, from the strangely irrational notion that there is something in the very flow of time that will inevitably cure all ills. Actually, time itself is neutral; it can be used either destructively or constructively. More and more I feel that the people of ill will have used time much more effectively than have the people of good will. We will have to repent in this generation not merely for the hateful words and actions of the bad people but for the appalling silence of the good people. Human progress never rolls in on wheels of inevitability; it comes through the tireless efforts of men willing to be co-workers with God, and without this hard work, time itself becomes an ally of the forces of social stagnation. We must use time creatively, in the knowledge that the time is always ripe to do right. Now is the time to make real the promise of democracy and transform our pending national elegy into a creative psalm of brotherhood. Now is the time to lift our national policy from the quicksand of racial injustice to the solid rock of human dignity.

You speak of our activity in Birmingham as extreme. At first I was rather disappointed that fellow clergymen would see my nonviolent efforts as those of an extremist. I began thinking about the fact that I stand in the middle of two opposing forces in the Negro community. One is a force of complacency, made up in part of Negroes who, as a result of long years of oppression, are so drained of self-respect and a sense of "somebodiness" that they have adjusted to segregation; and in part of a few middle-class Negroes who, because of a degree of academic and economic security and because in some ways they profit by segregation, have become insensitive to the problems of the masses. The other force is one of bitterness and hatred, and it comes perilously close to advocating violence. It is expressed in the various black nationalist groups that are springing up across the nation, the largest and best-known being Elijah Muhammad's Muslim movement. Nourished by the Negro's frustration over the continued existence of racial discrimination, this movement is made up of people who have lost faith in America, who have absolutely repudiated Christianity, and who have concluded that the white man is an incorrigible "devil."

I have tried to stand between these two forces, saying that we need   36
emulate neither the "do-nothingism" of the complacent nor the hatred and despair of the black nationalist. For there is the more excellent way of love and nonviolent protest. I am grateful to God that, through the influence of the Negro church, the way of nonviolence became an integral part of our struggle.

If this philosophy had not emerged, by now many streets of the South should, I am convinced, be flowing with blood. And I am further convinced that if our white brothers dismiss as "rabble-rousers" and "outside agitators" those of us who employ nonviolent direct action, and if they refuse to support our nonviolent efforts, millions of Negroes will, out of frustration and despair, seek solace and security in black-nationalist ideologies—a development that would inevitably lead to a frightening racial nightmare.

Oppressed people cannot remain oppressed forever. The yearning for freedom eventually manifests itself, and that is what has happened to the American Negro. Something within has reminded him of his birthright of freedom, and something without has reminded him that it can be gained. Consciously or unconsciously, he has been caught up by the *Zeitgeist*,[5] and with his black brothers of Africa and his brown and yellow brothers of Asia, South America, and the Caribbean, the United States Negro is moving with a sense of great urgency toward the promised land of racial justice. If one recognizes this vital urge that has engulfed the Negro community, one should readily understand why public demonstrations are taking place. The Negro has many pent-up resentments and latent frustrations, and he must release them. So let him march; let him make prayer pilgrimages to the city hall; let him go on freedom rides—and try to understand why he must do so. If his

[5]*Zeitgeist:* German for "spirit of the age."

repressed emotions are not released in nonviolent ways, they will seek expression through violence; this is not a threat but a fact of history. So I have not said to my people: "Get rid of your discontent." Rather, I have tried to say that this normal and healthy discontent can be channeled into the creative outlet of nonviolent direct action. And now this approach is being termed extremist.

But though I was initially disappointed at being categorized as an extremist, as I continued to think about the matter I gradually gained a measure of satisfaction from the label. Was not Jesus an extremist for love: "Love your enemies, bless them that curse you, do good to them that hate you, and pray for them which despitefully use you, and persecute you." Was not Amos an extremist for justice: "Let justice roll down like waters and righteousness like an ever-flowing stream." Was not Paul an extremist for the Christian gospel: "I bear in my body the marks of the Lord Jesus." Was not Martin Luther an extremist: "Here I stand; I cannot do otherwise, so help me God." And John Bunyan: "I will stay in jail to the end of my days before I make a butchery of my conscience." And Abraham Lincoln: "This nation cannot survive half slave and half free." And Thomas Jefferson: "We hold these truths to be self-evident, that all men are created equal. . . ." So the question is not whether we will be extremists, but what kind of extremists we will be. Will we be extremists for hate or for love? Will we be extremists for the preservation of injustice or for the extension of justice? In that dramatic scene on Calvary's hill three men were crucified. We must never forget that all three were crucified for the same crime—the crime of extremism. Two were extremists for immorality, and thus fell below their environment. The other, Jesus Christ, was an extremist for love, truth, and goodness, and thereby rose above his environment. Perhaps the South, the nation, and the world are in dire need of creative extremists.

I had hoped that the white moderate would see this need. Perhaps   40
I was too optimistic; perhaps I expected too much. I suppose I should have realized that few members of the oppressor race can understand the deep groans and passionate yearnings of the oppressed race, and still fewer have the vision to see that injustice must be rooted out by strong, persistent, and determined action. I am thankful, however, that some of our white brothers in the South have grasped the meaning of this social revolution and committed themselves to it. They are still all too few in quantity, but they are big in quality. Some—such as Ralph McGill, Lillian Smith, Harry Golden, James McBride Dabbs, Ann Braden, and Sarah Patton Boyle—have written about our struggle in eloquent and prophetic terms. Others have marched with us down nameless streets of the South. They have languished in filthy, roach-infested jails, suffering the abuse and brutality of policemen who view them as "dirty nigger-lovers." Unlike so many of their moderate brothers and sisters, they have recognized the urgency of the moment and

sensed the need for powerful "action" antidotes to combat the disease of segregation.

Let me take note of my other major disappointment. I have been so greatly disappointed with the white church and its leadership. Of course, there are some notable exceptions. I am not unmindful of the fact that each of you has taken some significant stands on this issue. I commend you, Reverend Stallings, for your Christian stand on this past Sunday, in welcoming Negroes to your worship service on a nonsegregated basis. I commend the Catholic leaders of this state for integrating Spring Hill College several years ago.

But despite these notable exceptions, I must honestly reiterate that I have been disappointed with the church. I do not say this as one of those negative critics who can always find something wrong with the church. I say this as a minister of the gospel, who loves the church; who was nurtured in its bosom; who has been sustained by its spiritual blessings and who will remain true to it as long as the cord of life shall lengthen.

When I was suddenly catapulted into the leadership of the bus protest in Montgomery, Alabama, a few years ago, I felt we would be supported by the white church. I felt that the white ministers, priests, and rabbis of the South would be among our strongest allies. Instead, some have been outright opponents, refusing to understand the freedom movement and misrepresenting its leaders; all too many others have been more cautious than courageous and have remained silent behind the anesthetizing security of stained-glass windows.

In spite of my shattered dreams, I came to Birmingham with the hope that the white religious leadership of this community would see the justice of our cause and, with deep moral concern, would serve as the channel through which our just grievances could reach the power structure. I had hoped that each of you would understand. But again I have been disappointed.   44

I have heard numerous southern religious leaders admonish their worshipers to comply with a desegregation decision because it is the law, but I have longed to hear white ministers declare: "Follow this decree because integration is morally right and because the Negro is your brother." In the midst of blatant injustices inflicted upon the Negro, I have watched white churchmen stand on the sideline and mouth pious irrelevancies and sanctimonious trivialities. In the midst of a mighty struggle to rid our nation of racial and economic injustice, I have heard many ministers say: "Those are social issues, with which the gospel has no real concern." And I have watched many churches commit themselves to a completely otherworldly religion which makes a strange, unbiblical distinction between body and soul, between the sacred and the secular.

I have traveled the length and breadth of Alabama, Mississippi, and all the other southern states. On sweltering summer days and crisp autumn mornings I have looked at the South's beautiful churches with their lofty spires pointing heavenward. I have beheld the impressive outlines of her massive religious-education buildings. Over and over I have found myself saying: "What kind of people worship here? Who is their God? Where were their voices when the lips of Governor Barnett dripped with words of interposition and nullification? Where were they when Governor Wallace gave a clarion call for defiance and hatred? Where were their voices of support when bruised and weary Negro men and women decided to rise from the dark dungeons of complacency to the bright hills of creative protest?"

Yes, these questions are still in my mind. In deep disappointment I have wept over the laxity of the church. But be assured that my tears have been tears of love. There can be no deep disappointment where there is not deep love. Yes, I love the church. How could I do otherwise? I am in the rather unique position of being the son, the grandson, and the great-grandson of preachers. Yes, I see the church as the body of Christ. But, Oh! How we have blemished and scarred that body through social neglect and through fear of being nonconformists.

There was a time when the church was very powerful—in the time 48 when the early Christians rejoiced at being deemed worthy to suffer for what they believed. In those days the church was not merely a thermometer that recorded the ideas and principles of popular opinion; it was a thermostat that transformed the mores of society. Whenever the early Christians entered a town, the people in power became disturbed and immediately sought to convict the Christians for being "disturbers of the peace" and "outside agitators." But the Christians pressed on, in the conviction that they were "a colony of heaven," called to obey God rather than man. Small in number, they were big in commitment. They were too God-intoxicated to be "astronomically intimidated." By their effort and example they brought an end to such ancient evils as infanticide and gladiatorial contests.

Things are different now. So often the contemporary church is a weak, ineffectual voice with an uncertain sound. So often it is an archdefender of the status quo. Far from being disturbed by the presence of the church, the power structure of the average community is consoled by the church's silent—and often even vocal—sanction of things as they are.

But the judgment of God is upon the church as never before. If today's church does not recapture the sacrificial spirit of the early church, it will lose its authenticity, forfeit the loyalty of millions, and be dismissed as an irrelevant social club with no meaning for the twentieth century. Every day I meet young people whose disappointment with the church has turned into outright disgust.

Perhaps I have once again been too optimistic. Is organized religion too inextricably bound to the status quo to save our nation and the world? Perhaps I must turn my faith to the inner spiritual church, the church within the church, as the true *ekklesia* and the hope of the world. But again I am thankful to God that some noble souls from the ranks of organized religion have broken loose from the paralyzing chains of conformity and joined us as active partners in the struggle for freedom. They have left their secure congregations and walked the streets of Albany, Georgia, with us. They have gone down the highways of the South on tortuous rides for freedom. Yes, they have gone to jail with us. Some have been dismissed from their churches, have lost the support of their bishops and fellow ministers. But they have acted in the faith that right defeated is stronger than evil triumphant. Their witness has been the spiritual salt that has preserved the true meaning of the gospel in these troubled times. They have carved a tunnel of hope through the dark mountain of disappointment.

I hope the church as a whole will meet the challenge of this decisive hour. But even if the church does not come to the aid of justice, I have no despair about the future. I have no fear about the outcome of our struggle in Birmingham, even if our motives are at present misunderstood. We will reach the goal of freedom in Birmingham and all over the nation, because the goal of America is freedom. Abused and scorned though we may be, our destiny is tied up with America's destiny. Before the pilgrims landed at Plymouth, we were here. Before the pen of Jefferson etched the majestic words of the Declaration of Independence across the pages of history, we were here. For more than two centuries our forebears labored in this country without wages; they made cotton king; they built the homes of their masters while suffering gross injustice and shameful humiliation—and yet out of a bottomless vitality they continue to thrive and develop. If the inexpressible cruelties of slavery could not stop us, the opposition we now face will surely fail. We will win our freedom because the sacred heritage of our nation and the eternal will of God are embodied in our echoing demands.

Before closing I feel impelled to mention one other point in your statement that has troubled me profoundly. You warmly commended the Birmingham police force for keeping "order" and "preventing violence." I doubt that you would have so warmly commended the police force if you had seen its dogs sinking their teeth into unarmed, nonviolent Negroes. I doubt that you would so quickly commend the policemen if you were to observe their ugly and inhumane treatment of Negroes here in the city jail; if you were to watch them push and curse old Negro women and young Negro girls; if you were to see them slap and kick old Negro men and young boys; if you were to observe them, as they did on two occasions, refuse to give us food because we wanted to sing our grace together. I cannot join you in your praise of the Birmingham police department.

It is true that the police have exercised a degree of discipline in handling the demonstrators. In this sense they have conducted themselves rather "nonviolently" in public. But for what purpose? To preserve the evil system of segregation. Over the past few years I have consistently preached that nonviolence demands that the means we use must be as pure as the ends we seek. I have tried to make clear that it is wrong to use immoral means to attain moral ends. But now I must affirm that it

52

is just as wrong, or perhaps even more so, to use moral means to pre-serve immoral ends. Perhaps Mr. Connor and his policemen have been rather nonviolent in public, as was Chief Pritchett in Albany, Georgia, but they have used the moral means of nonviolence to maintain the immoral end of racial injustice. As T. S. Eliot has said: "The last tempta-tion is the greatest treason: To do the right deed for the wrong reason."

I wish you had commended the Negro sit-inners and demonstrators of Birmingham for their sublime courage, their willingness to suffer, and their amazing discipline in the midst of great provocation. One day the South will recognize its real heroes. They will be the James Merediths, with the noble sense of purpose that enables them to face jeering and hostile mobs, and with the agonizing loneliness that characterizes the life of the pioneer. They will be old, oppressed, battered Negro women, symbolized in a seventy-two-year-old woman in Montgomery, Alaba-ma, who rose up with a sense of dignity and with her people decided not to ride segregated buses, and who responded with ungrammatical profundity to one who inquired about her weariness: "My feets is tired, but my soul is at rest." They will be the young high school and college students, the young ministers of the gospel and a host of their elders, courageously and nonviolently sitting in at lunch counters and willing-ly going to jail for conscience' sake. One day the South will know that when these disinherited children of God sat down at lunch counters, they were in reality standing up for what is best in the American dream and for the most sacred values in our Judaeo-Christian heritage, thereby bringing our nation back to those great wells of democracy which were dug deep by the founding fathers in their formulation of the Constitu-tion and the Declaration of Independence.

Never before have I written so long a letter. I'm afraid it is much too long to take your precious time. I can assure you that it would have been much shorter if I had been writing from a comfortable desk, but what else can one do when he is alone in a narrow jail cell, other than write long letters, think long thoughts, and pray long prayers? 56

If I have said anything in this letter that overstates the truth and indicates an unreasonable impatience, I beg you to forgive me. If I have said anything that understates the truth and indicates my having a patience that allows me to settle for anything less than brotherhood, I beg God to forgive me.

I hope this letter finds you strong in the faith. I also hope that cir-cumstances will soon make it possible for me to meet each of you, not as an integrationist or a civil-rights leader but as a fellow clergyman and a Christian brother. Let us all hope that the dark clouds of racial prejudice will soon pass away and the deep fog of misunderstanding will be lifted from our fear-drenched communities, and in some not too distant tomorrow the radiant stars of love and brotherhood will shine over our great nation with all their scintillating beauty.

Yours for the cause of Peace and Brotherhood,

Martin Luther King, Jr.

Topics for Critical Thinking and Writing

1. In his first five paragraphs how does King assure his audience that he is not a meddlesome intruder but a man of good will?
2. In paragraph 3 King refers to Hebrew prophets and to the Apostle Paul, and later (paragraph 10) to Socrates. What is the point of these references?
3. In paragraph 11 what does King mean when he says that "our beloved Southland" has long tried to "live in monologue rather than dialogue"?
4. King begins paragraph 23 with "I must make two honest confessions to you, my Christian and Jewish brothers." What would have been gained or lost if he had used this paragraph as his opening?
5. King's last three paragraphs do not advance his argument. What do they do?
6. Why does King advocate breaking unjust laws "openly, lovingly" (paragraph 20)? What does he mean by these words? What other motives or attitudes do these words rule out?
7. Construct two definitions of *civil disobedience,* and explain whether and to what extent it is easier (or harder) to justify civil disobedience, depending on how you have defined the expression.
8. If you feel that you wish to respond to King's letter on some point, write a letter nominally addressed to King. You may, if you wish, adopt the persona of one of the eight clergymen whom King initially addressed.
9. King writes (paragraph 46) that "nonviolence demands that the means we use must be as pure as the ends we seek." How do you think King would evaluate the following acts of civil disobedience: (a) occupying a college administration building in order to protest the administration's unsatisfactory response to a racial incident on campus, or in order to protest the failure of the administration to hire minority persons as staff and faculty; (b) sailing on a collision course with a whaling ship to protest against whaling; (c) trespassing on an abortion clinic to protest abortion? Set down your answer in an essay of five hundred words.

Peter Singer

Peter Singer teaches philosophy at Monash University in Melbourne, Australia. This essay originally appeared in 1973 as a review of Animals, Men and Morals, *edited by Stanley and Roslind Godlovitch and John Harris.*

Animal Liberation

I

We are familiar with Black Liberation, Gay Liberation, and a variety of other movements. With Women's Liberation some thought we had come to the end of the road. Discrimination on the basis of sex, it has been said, is the last form of discrimination that is universally accepted and practiced without pretense, even in those liberal circles which have long prided themselves on their freedom from racial discrimination. But one should always be wary of talking of "the last remaining form of discrimination." If we have learned anything from the liberation movements, we should have learned how difficult it is to be aware of the ways in which we discriminate until they are forcefully pointed out to us. A liberation movement demands an expansion of our moral horizons, so that practices that were previously regarded as natural and inevitable are now seen as intolerable.

Animals, Men and Morals is a manifesto for an Animal Liberation movement. The contributors to the book may not all see the issue this way. They are a varied group. Philosophers, ranging from professors to graduate students, make up the largest contingent. There are five of them, including the three editors, and there is also an extract from the unjustly neglected German philosopher with an English name, Leonard Nelson, who died in 1927. There are essays by two novelist/critics, Brigid Brophy and Maureen Duffy, and another by Muriel the Lady Dowding, widow of Dowding of Battle of Britain fame and the founder of "Beauty Without Cruelty," a movement that campaigns against the use of animals for furs and cosmetics. The other pieces are by a psychologist, a botanist, a sociologist, and Ruth Harrison, who is probably best described as a professional campaigner for animal welfare.

Whether or not these people, as individuals, would all agree that they are launching a liberation movement for animals, the book as a whole amounts to no less. It is a demand for a complete change in our attitudes to nonhumans. It is a demand that we cease to regard the exploitation of other species as natural and inevitable, and that, instead, we see it as a continuing moral outrage. Patrick Corbett, Professor of Philosophy at Sussex University, captures the spirit of the book in his closing words:

> ... We require now to extend the great principles of liberty, equality and fraternity over the lives of animals. Let animal slavery join human slavery in the graveyard of the past.

The reader is likely to be skeptical. "Animal Liberation" sounds   4
more like a parody of liberation movements than a serious objective. The reader may think: We support the claims of blacks and women for equality because blacks and women really are equal to whites and males—equal in intelligence and in abilities, capacity for leadership, rationality, and so on. Humans and nonhumans obviously are not equal in these respects. Since justice demands only that we treat equals equally, unequal treatment of humans and nonhumans cannot be an injustice.

This is a tempting reply, but a dangerous one. It commits the non-racist and non-sexist to a dogmatic belief that blacks and women really are just as intelligent, able, etc., as whites and males—and no more. Quite possibly this happens to be the case. Certainly attempts to prove that racial or sexual differences in these respects have a genetic origin have not been conclusive. But do we really want to stake our demand for equality on the assumption that there are no genetic differences of this kind between the different races or sexes? Surely the appropriate response to those who claim to have found evidence for such genetic differences is not to stick to the belief that there are no differences, whatever the evidence to the contrary; rather one should be clear that the claim to equality does not depend on IQ. Moral equality is distinct from factual equality. Otherwise it would be nonsense to talk of the equality of human beings, since humans, as individuals, obviously differ in intelligence and almost any ability one cares to name. If possessing greater intelligence does not entitle one human to exploit another, why should it entitle humans to exploit nonhumans?

Jeremy Bentham expressed the essential basis of equality in his famous formula: "Each to count for one and none for more than one." In other words, the interests of every being that has interests are to be taken into account and treated equally with the like interests of any other being. Other moral philosophers, before and after Bentham, have made the same point in different ways. Our concern for others must not depend on whether they possess certain characteristics, though just what that concern involves may, of course, vary, according to such characteristics.

Bentham, incidentally, was well aware that the logic of the demand for racial equality did not stop at the equality of humans. He wrote:

> The day *may* come when the rest of the animal creation may acquire those rights which never could have been withholden from them but by the hand of tyranny. The French have already discovered that the blackness of the skin is no reason why a human being should be abandoned without redress to the caprice of a tormentor. It may one day come to be recognized that the number of the legs, the villosity of the skin, or the termination of the *os sacrum*, are reasons equally insufficient for abandoning a sensitive being to the same fate. What else is it that should trace the insuperable line? Is it the faculty of reason, or perhaps the faculty of discourse? But a full-grown horse or dog is beyond comparison a more rational, as well as a more conversable animal, than an infant of a day, or a week, or even a month, old. But suppose they were otherwise, what would it avail? The question is not, Can they *reason?* nor Can they *talk?* but, Can they *suffer?*[1]

Surely Bentham was right. If a being suffers, there can be no moral justification for refusing to take that suffering into consideration, and, indeed, to count it equally with the like suffering (if rough comparisons can be made) of any other being.

[1]*The Principles of Morals and Legislation*, ch. XVII, sec. 1, footnote to paragraph 4.

So the only question is: Do animals other than man suffer? Most people agree unhesitatingly that animals like cats and dogs can and do suffer, and this seems also to be assumed by those laws that prohibit wanton cruelty to such animals. Personally, I have no doubt at all about this and find it hard to take seriously the doubts that a few people apparently do have. The editors and contributors of *Animals, Men and Morals* seem to feel the same way, for although the question is raised more than once, doubts are quickly dismissed each time. Nevertheless, because this is such a fundamental point, it is worth asking what grounds we have for attributing suffering to other animals.   8

It is best to begin by asking what grounds any individual human has for supposing that other humans feel pain. Since pain is a state of consciousness, a "mental event," it can never be directly observed. No observations, whether behavioral signs such as writhing or screaming or physiological or neurological recordings, are observations of pain itself. Pain is something one feels, and one can only infer that others are feeling it from various external indications. The fact that only philosophers are ever skeptical about whether other humans feel pain shows that we regard such inference as justifiable in the case of humans.

Is there any reason why the same inference should be unjustifiable for other animals? Nearly all the external signs which lead us to infer pain in other humans can be seen in other species, especially "higher" animals such as mammals and birds. Behavioral signs—writhing, yelping, or other forms of calling, attempts to avoid the source of pain, and many others—are present. We know, too, that these animals are biologically similar in the relevant respects, having nervous systems like ours which can be observed to function as ours do.

So the grounds for inferring that these animals can feel pain are nearly as good as the grounds for inferring other humans do. Only nearly, for there is one behavioral sign that humans have but nonhumans, with the exception of one or two specially raised chimpanzees, do not have. This, of course, is a developed language. As the quotation from Bentham indicates, this has long been regarded as an important distinction between man and other animals. Other animals may communicate with each other, but not in the way we do. Following Chomsky, many people now mark this distinction by saying that only humans communicate in a form that is governed by rules of syntax. (For the purposes of this argument, linguists allow those chimpanzees who have learned a syntactic sign language to rank as honorary humans.) Nevertheless, as Bentham pointed out, this distinction is not relevant to the question of how animals ought to be treated, unless it can be linked to the issue of whether animals suffer.

This link may be attempted in two ways. First, there is a hazy line of philosophical thought, stemming perhaps from some doctrines associated with Wittgenstein, which maintains that we cannot meaningfully attribute states of consciousness to beings without language. I have not   12 seen this argument made explicit in print, though I have come across it in conversation. This position seems to me very implausible, and I doubt that it would be held at all if it were not thought to be a consequence of a broader view of the significance of language. It may be that the use of a public, rule-governed language is a precondition of conceptual thought. It may even be, although personally I doubt it, that we cannot meaningfully speak of a creature having an intention unless that creature can use a language. But states like pain, surely, are more primitive than either of these, and seem to have nothing to do with language.

Indeed, as Jane Goodall points out in her study of chimpanzees, when it comes to the expression of feelings and emotions, humans tend to fall back on non-linguistic modes of communication which are often found among apes, such as a cheering pat on the back, an exuberant embrace, a clasp of hands, and so on.[2] Michael Peters makes a similar point in his contribution to *Animals, Men and Morals* when he notes that the basic signals we use to convey pain, fear, sexual arousal, and so on are not specific to our species. So there seems to be no reason at all to believe that a creature without language cannot suffer.

The second, and more easily appreciated way of linking language and the existence of pain is to say that the best evidence that we can have that another creature is in pain is when he tells us that he is. This is a distinct line of argument, for it is not being denied that a non-language-user conceivably could suffer, but only that we could know that he is suffering. Still, this line of argument seems to me to fail, and for reasons similar to those just given. "I am in pain" is not the best possible evidence that the speaker is in pain (he might be lying) and it is certainly not the only possible evidence. Behavioral signs and knowledge of the animal's biological similarity to ourselves together provide adequate evidence that animals do suffer. After all, we would not accept linguistic evidence if it contradicted the rest of the evidence. If a man was severely burned, and behaved as if he were in pain, writhing, groaning, being very careful not to let his burned skin touch anything, and so on, but later said he had not been in pain at all, we would be more likely to conclude that he was lying or suffering from amnesia than that he had not been in pain.

Even if there were stronger grounds for refusing to attribute pain to those who do not have a language, the consequences of this refusal might lead us to examine these grounds unusually critically. Human infants, as well as some adults, are unable to use language. Are we to deny that a year-old infant can suffer? If not, how can language be crucial? Of course, most parents can understand the responses of even very young infants better than they understand the responses of other

---

[2]Jane van Lawick-Goodall, *In the Shadow of Man* (Boston: Houghton Mifflin, 1971), p. 225.

animals, and sometimes infant responses can be understood in the light of later development.

This, however, is just a fact about the relative knowledge we have 16 of our own species and other species, and most of this knowledge is simply derived from closer contact. Those who have studied the behavior of other animals soon learn to understand their responses at least as well as we understand those of an infant. (I am not referring to Jane Goodall's and other well-known studies of apes. Consider, for example, the degree of understanding achieved by Tinbergen from watching herring gulls.[3] Just as we can understand infant human behavior in the light of adult human behavior, so we can understand the behavior of other species in the light of our own behavior (and sometimes we can understand our own behavior better in the light of the behavior of other species).

The grounds we have for believing that other mammals and birds suffer are, then, closely analogous to the grounds we have for believing that other humans suffer. It remains to consider how far down the evolutionary scale this analogy, holds. Obviously it becomes poorer when we get further away from man. To be more precise would require a detailed examination of all that we know about other forms of life. With fish, reptiles, and other vertebrates the analogy still seems strong, with molluscs like oysters it is much weaker. Insects are more difficult, and it may be that in our present state of knowledge we must be agnostic about whether they are capable of suffering.

If there is no moral justification for ignoring suffering when it occurs, and it does occur in other species, what are we to say of our attitudes toward these other species? Richard Ryder, one of the contributors to *Animals, Men and Morals,* uses the term "speciesism" to describe the belief that we are entitled to treat members of other species in a way in which it would be wrong to treat members of our own species. The term is not euphonious, but it neatly makes the analogy with racism. The non-racist would do well to bear the analogy in mind when he is inclined to defend human behavior toward nonhumans. "Shouldn't we worry about improving the lot of our own species before we concern ourselves with other species?" he may ask. If we substitute "race" for "species" we shall see that the question is better not asked. "Is a vegetarian diet nutritionally adequate?" resembles the slave-owner's claim that he and the whole economy of the South would be ruined without slave labor. There is even a parallel with skeptical doubts about whether animals suffer, for some defenders of slavery professed to doubt whether blacks really suffer in the way whites do.

[3]N. Tinbergen, *The Herring Gull's World* (New York: Basic Books, 1961).

I do not want to give the impression, however, that the case for Animal Liberation is based on the analogy with racism and no more. On the contrary, *Animals, Men and Morals* describes the various ways in which humans exploit nonhumans, and several contributors consider the defenses that have been offered, including the defense of meat-eating mentioned in the last paragraph. Sometimes the rebuttals are scornfully dismissive, rather than carefully designed to convince the detached critic. This may be a fault, but it is a fault that is inevitable, given the kind of book this is. The issue is not one on which one can remain detached. As the editors state in their Introduction:

> Once the full force of moral assessment has been made explicit there can be no rational excuse left for killing animals, be they killed for food, science, or sheer personal indulgence. We have not assembled this book to provide the reader with yet another manual on how to make brutalities less brutal. Compromise, in the traditional sense of the term, is simple unthinking weakness when one considers the actual reasons for our crude relationships with the other animals.

The point is that on this issue there are few critics who are genuinely detached. People who eat pieces of slaughtered nonhumans every day find it hard to believe that they are doing wrong; and they also find it hard to imagine what else they could eat. So for those who do not place nonhumans beyond the pale of morality, there comes a stage when further argument seems pointless, a stage at which one can only accuse one's opponent of hypocrisy and reach for the sort of sociological account of our practices and the way we defend them that is attempted by David Wood in his contribution to this book. On the other hand, to those unconvinced by the arguments, and unable to accept that they are merely rationalizing their dietary preferences and their fear of being thought peculiar, such sociological explanations can only seem insultingly arrogant.

II

The logic of speciesism is most apparent in the practice of experimenting on nonhumans in order to benefit humans. This is because the issue is rarely obscured by allegations that nonhumans are so different from humans that we cannot know anything about whether they suffer. The defender of vivisection cannot use this argument because he needs to stress the similarities between man and other animals in order to justify the usefulness to the former of experiments on the latter. The researcher who makes rats choose between starvation and electric shocks to see if they develop ulcers (they do) does so because he knows that the rat has a nervous system very similar to man's, and presumably feels an electric shock in a similar way.

Richard Ryder's restrained account of experiments on animals made me angrier with my fellow men than anything else in this book. Ryder, a clinical psychologist by profession, himself experimented on animals before he came to hold the view he puts forward in his essay. Experimenting on animals is now a large industry, both academic and commercial. In 1969, more than 5 million experiments were performed in Britain, the vast majority without anesthetic (though how many of these involved pain is not known). There are no accurate U.S. figures, since there is no federal law on the subject, and in many cases no state law either. Estimates vary from 20 million to 200 million. Ryder suggests that 80 million may be the best guess. We tend to think that this is all for vital medical research, but of course it is not. Huge numbers of animals are used in university departments from Forestry to Psychology, and even more are used for commercial purposes, to test whether cosmetics can cause skin damage, or shampoos eye damage, or to test food additives or laxatives or sleeping pills or anything else.

A standard test for foodstuffs is the "LD50." The object of this test is to find the dosage level at which 50 percent of the test animals will die. This means that nearly all of them will become very sick before finally succumbing or surviving. When the substance is a harmless one, it may be necessary to force huge doses down the animals, until in some cases sheer volume or concentration causes death.

Ryder gives a selection of experiments, taken from recent scientific journals. I will quote two, not for the sake of indulging in gory details, but in order to give an idea of what normal researchers think they may legitimately do to other species. The point is not that the individual researchers are cruel men, but that they are behaving in a way that is allowed by our speciesist attitudes. As Ryder points out, even if only 1 percent of the experiments involve severe pain, that is 50,000 experiments in Britain each year, or nearly 150 every day (and about fifteen times as many in the United States, if Ryder's guess is right). Here then are two experiments:

> O. S. Ray and R. J. Barrett of Pittsburgh gave electric shocks to the feet of 1,042 mice. They then caused convulsions by giving more intense shocks through cup-shaped electrodes applied to the animals' eyes or through pressure spring clips attached to their ears. Unfortunately some of the mice who "successfully completed Day One training were found sick or dead prior to testing on Day Two." [*Journal of Comparative and Physiological Psychology,* 1969, vol. 67, pp. 110–116]

> At the National Institute for Medical Research, Mill Hill, London, W. Feldberg and S. L. Sherwood injected chemicals into the brains of cats—"with a number of widely different substances, recurrent patterns of reaction were obtained. Retching, vomiting, defaecation, increased salivation and greatly accelerated respiration leading to panting were common features.". . .

The injection into the brain of a large dose of Tubocuraine caused the cat to jump "from the table to the floor and then straight into its cage, where it started calling more and more noisily whilst moving about restlessly and jerkily . . . finally the cat fell with legs and neck flexed, jerking in rapid clonic movements, the condition being that of a major [epileptic] convulsion . . . within a few seconds the cat got up, ran for a few yards at high speed and fell in another fit. The whole process was repeated several times within the next ten minutes, during which the cat lost faeces and foamed at the mouth."

This animal finally died thirty-five minutes after the brain injection. [*Journal of Physiology,* 1954, vol. 123, pp. 148–167]

There is nothing secret about these experiments. One has only to open any recent volume of a learned journal, such as the *Journal of Comparative and Physiological Psychology,* to find full descriptions of experiments of this sort, together with the results obtained—results that are frequently trivial and obvious. The experiments are often supported by public funds.

It is a significant indication of the level of acceptability of these practices that, although these experiments are taking place at this moment on university campuses throughout the country, there has, so far as I know, not been the slightest protest from the student movement. Students have been rightly concerned that their universities should not discriminate on grounds of race or sex, and that they should not serve the purposes of the military or big business. Speciesism continues undisturbed, and many students participate in it. There may be a few qualms at first, but since everyone regards it as normal, and it may even be a required part of a course, the student soon becomes hardened and, dismissing his earlier feelings as "mere sentiment," comes to regard animals as statistics rather than sentient beings with interests that warrant consideration.

Argument about vivisection has often missed the point because it has been put in absolutist terms: Would the abolitionist be prepared to let thousands die if they could be saved by experimenting on a single animal? The way to reply to this purely hypothetical question is to pose another: Would the experimenter be prepared to experiment on a human orphan under six months old, if it were the only way to save many lives? (I say "orphan" to avoid the complication of parental feelings, although in doing so I am being overfair to the experimenter, since the nonhuman subjects of experiments are not orphans.) A negative answer to this question indicates that the experimenter's readiness to use nonhumans is simple discrimination, for adult apes, cats, mice, and other mammals are more conscious of what is happening to them, more self-directing, and, so far as we can tell, just as sensitive to pain as a human infant. There is no characteristic that human infants possess that adult mammals do not have to the same or a higher degree.

(It might be possible to hold that what makes it wrong to experiment on a human infant is that the infant will in time develop into more than the nonhuman, but one would then, to be consistent, have to oppose abortion, and perhaps contraception, too, for the fetus and the egg and sperm have the same potential as the infant. Moreover, one would still have no reason for experimenting on a nonhuman rather than a human with brain damage severe enough to make it impossible for him to rise above infant level.)

The experimenter, then, shows a bias for his own species whenever he carries out an experiment on a nonhuman for a purpose that he would not think justified him in using a human being at an equal or lower level of sentience, awareness, ability to be self-directing, etc. No one familiar with the kind of results yielded by these experiments can have the slightest doubt that if this bias were eliminated the number of experiments performed would be zero or very close to it.

III

If it is vivisection that shows the logic of speciesism most clearly, it is the use of other species for food that is at the heart of our attitudes toward them. Most of *Animals, Men and Morals* is an attack on meat-eating—an attack which is based solely on concern for nonhumans, without reference to arguments derived from considerations of ecology, macrobiotics, health, or religion.

The idea that nonhumans are utilities, means to our ends, pervades our thought. Even conservationists who are concerned about the slaughter of wild fowl but not about the vastly greater slaughter of chickens for our tables are thinking in this way—they are worried about what we would lose if there were less wildlife. Stanley Godlovitch, pursuing the Marxist idea that our thinking is formed by the activities we undertake in satisfying our needs, suggests that man's first classification of his environment was into Edibles and Inedibles. Most animals came into the first category, and there they have remained.

Man may always have killed other species for food, but he has never exploited them so ruthlessly as he does today. Farming has succumbed to business methods, the objective being to get the highest possible ratio of output (meat, eggs, milk) to input (fodder, labor costs, etc.). Ruth Harrison's essay "On Factory Farming" gives an account of some aspects of modern methods, and of the unsuccessful British campaign for effective controls, a campaign which was sparked off by her *Animal Machines* (Stuart: London, 1964).

Her article is in no way a substitute for her earlier book. This is a pity since, as she says, "Farm produce is still associated with mental pictures of animals browsing in the fields . . . of hens having a last forage before going to roost. . . ." Yet neither in her article nor elsewhere in *Animals, Men and Morals* is this false image replaced by a clear idea of

32

the nature and extent of factory farming. We learn of this only indirectly, when we hear of the code of reform proposed by an advisory committee set up by the British government.

Among the proposals, which the government refused to implement on the grounds that they were too idealistic, were: *"Any animals should at least have room to turn around freely."*

Factory farm animals need liberation in the most literal sense. Veal calves are kept in stalls five feet by two feet. They are usually slaughtered when about four months old, and have been too big to turn in their stalls for at least a month. Intensive beef herds, kept in stalls only proportionally larger for much longer periods, account for a growing percentage of beef production. Sows are often similarly confined when pregnant, which, because of artificial methods of increasing fertility, can be most of the time. Animals confined in this way do not waste food by exercising, nor do they develop unpalatable muscle.

"A dry bedded area should be provided for all stock." Intensively kept   36
animals usually have to stand and sleep on slatted floors without straw, because this makes cleaning easier.

"Palatable roughage must be readily available to all calves after one week of age." In order to produce the pale veal housewives are said to prefer, calves are fed on an all-liquid diet until slaughter, even though they are long past the age at which they would normally eat grass. They develop a craving for roughage, evidenced by attempts to gnaw wood from their stalls. (For the same reason, their diet is deficient in iron.)

"Battery cages for poultry should be large enough for a bird to be able to stretch one wing at a time." Under current British practice, a cage for four or five laying hens has a floor area of twenty inches by eighteen inches, scarcely larger than a double page of the *New York Review of Books.* In this space, on a sloping wire floor (sloping so the eggs roll down, wire so the dung drops through) the birds live for a year or eighteen months while artificial lighting and temperature conditions combine with drugs in their food to squeeze the maximum number of eggs out of them. Table birds are also sometimes kept in cages. More often they are reared in sheds, no less crowded. Under these conditions all the birds' natural activities are frustrated, and they develop "vices" such as pecking each other to death. To prevent this, beaks are often cut off, and the sheds kept dark.

How many of those who support factory farming by buying its produce know anything about the way it is produced? How many have heard something about it, but are reluctant to check up for fear that it will make them uncomfortable? To non-speciesists, the typical consumer's mixture of ignorance, reluctance to find out the truth, and vague belief that nothing really bad could be allowed seems analogous to the attitudes of "decent Germans" to the death camps.

There are, of course, some defenders of factory farming. Their argu-   40
ments are considered, though again rather sketchily, by John Harris.

Among the most common: "Since they have never known anything else, they don't suffer." This argument will not be put by anyone who knows anything about animal behavior, since he will know that not all behavior has to be learned. Chickens attempt to stretch wings, walk around, scratch, and even dustbathe or build a nest, even though they have never lived under conditions that allowed these activities. Calves can suffer from maternal deprivation no matter at what age they were taken from their mothers. "We need these intensive methods to provide protein for a growing population." As ecologists and famine relief organizations know, we can produce far more protein per acre if we grow the right vegetable crop, soy beans for instance, than if we use the land to grow crops to be converted into protein by animals who use nearly 90 percent of the protein themselves, even when unable to exercise.

There will be many readers of this book who will agree that factory farming involves an unjustifiable degree of exploitation of sentient creatures, and yet will want to say that there is nothing wrong with rearing animals for food, provided it is done "humanely." These people are saying, in effect, that although we should not cause animals to suffer, there is nothing wrong with killing them.

There are two possible replies to this view. One is to attempt to show that this combination of attitudes is absurd. Roslind Godlovitch takes this course in her essay, which is an examination of some common attitudes to animals. She argues that from the combination of "animal suffering is to be avoided" and "there is nothing wrong with killing animals" it follows that all animal life ought to be exterminated (since all sentient creatures will suffer to some degree at some point in their lives). Euthanasia is a contentious issue only because we place some value on living. If we did not, the least amount of suffering would justify it. Accordingly, if we deny that we have a duty to exterminate all animal life, we must concede that we are placing some value on animal life.

This argument seems to me valid, although one could still reply that the value of animal life is to be derived from the pleasures that life can have for them, so that, provided their lives have a balance of pleasure over pain, we are justified in rearing them. But this would imply that we ought to produce animals and let them live as pleasantly as possible, without suffering.

At this point, one can make the second of the two possible replies   44
to the view that rearing and killing animals for food is all right so long as it is done humanely. This second reply is that so long as we think that a nonhuman may be killed simply so that a human can satisfy his taste for meat, we are still thinking of nonhumans as means rather than as ends in themselves. The factory farm is nothing more than the application of technology to this concept. Even traditional methods involve castration, the separation of mothers and their young, the breaking up of herds, branding or ear-punching, and of course transportation to the abattoirs and the final moments of terror when the animal smells blood

and senses danger. If we were to try rearing animals so that they lived and died without suffering, we should find that to do so on anything like the scale of today's meat industry would be a sheer impossibility. Meat would become the prerogative of the rich.

I have been able to discuss only some of the contributions to this book, saying nothing about, for instance, the essays on killing for furs and for sport. Nor have I considered all the detailed questions that need to be asked once we start thinking about other species in the radically different way presented by this book. What, for instance, are we to do about genuine conflicts of interest like rats biting slum children? I am not sure of the answer, but the essential point is just that we do see this as a conflict of interests, that we recognize that rats have interests too. Then we may begin to think about other ways of resolving the conflict—perhaps by leaving out rat baits that sterilize the rats instead of killing them.

I have not discussed such problems because they are side issues compared with the exploitation of other species for food and for experimental purposes. On these central matters, I hope that I have said enough to show that this book, despite its flaws, is a challenge to every human to recognize his attitudes to nonhumans as a form of prejudice no less objectionable than racism or sexism. It is a challenge that demands not just a change of attitudes, but a change in our way of life, for it requires us to become vegetarians.

Can a purely moral demand of this kind succeed? The odds are certainly against it. The book holds out no inducements. It does not tell us that we will become healthier, or enjoy life more, if we cease exploiting animals. Animal Liberation will require greater altruism on the part of mankind than any other liberation movement, since animals are incapable of demanding it for themselves, or of protesting against their exploitation by votes, demonstrations, or bombs. Is man capable of such genuine altruism? Who knows? If this book does have a significant effect, however, it will be a vindication of all those who have believed that man has within himself the potential for more than cruelty and selfishness.

Topics for Critical Thinking and Writing

1. Reread Singer's first seven paragraphs carefully, observing how he leads us to see that "animal liberation" is not a joke. It will help you to understand his strategy if for each of his paragraphs you write one sentence either summarizing the paragraph or commenting on what it accomplishes in his argument.
2. What grounds does Singer find for attributing suffering to nonhumans? List the arguments he offers to dismiss the relevance of a developed language. Why does he find it necessary to offer these arguments?
3. Does Singer attribute the capacity to feel pain to all species? Explain.

4. How does Singer define *speciesism?* To what extent does he use the analogy of speciesism to racism?
5. What is vivisection? Why, according to Singer, *must* defenders of vivisection also defend speciesism? Why do many of us who would not be willing to defend speciesism tolerate or even participate in experiments on animals?
6. What use of animals does Singer analyze beginning with paragraph 30? Why does he reserve this discussion for the last part of his essay? Why does he offer more detailed and more concrete examples in this section than in the second part, beginning with paragraph 21?
7. When Singer wrote "Animal Liberation," more than 20 years ago, he used language that would now be described as sexist. In paragraph 8, for example, he wrote "Do animals other than man suffer?" where he might today write "Do animals other than human beings suffer?" How would you revise his concluding paragraph to avoid sexist language?

APPENDIX

A Writer's Glossary

analogy. An analogy (from the Greek *analogos,* proportionate, resembling) is a kind of comparison. Normally an analogy compares substantially different kinds of things and reports several points of resemblance. A comparison of one city with another ("New York is like Chicago in several ways") does not involve an analogy because the two things are not substantially different. And a comparison giving only one resemblance is usually not considered an analogy ("Some people, like olives, are an acquired taste"). But if we claim that a state is like a human body, and we find in the state equivalents for the brain, heart, and limbs, we are offering an analogy. Similarly, one might construct an analogy between feeding the body with food and supplying the mind with ideas: the diet must be balanced, taken at approximately regular intervals, in proper amounts, and digested. An analogy may be useful in explaining the unfamiliar by comparing it to the familiar ("The heart is like a pump . . . "), but of course the things compared are different, and the points of resemblance can go only so far. For this reason, analogies cannot prove anything, though they are sometimes offered as proof.

analysis. Examination of the parts and their relation to the whole.

argument. Discourse in which some statements are offered as reasons for other statements. Argument, then, like emotional appeal and wit, is a form of persuasion, but argument seeks to persuade by appealing to reason. (See Chapter 4, and *deduction,* pages 794–95.)

audience. The writer's imagined readers. An essay on inflation written for the general public—say, for readers of *Newsweek*—will assume less specialized knowledge than will an essay written for professional economists—say, the readers of *Journal of Economic History*. In general, the imagined audience in a composition course is *not* the instructor (though in fact the instructor may be the only reader of the essay); the imagined audience usually is the class, or, to put it a little differently, someone rather like the writer but without the writer's specialized knowledge of the topic.

cliché. Literally, a *cliché* was originally (in French) a stereotype or an electrotype plate for printing; in English the word has come to mean an oft-repeated expression such as "a sight for sore eyes," "a heartwarming experience," "the acid test," "a meaningful relationship," "last but not least." Because these expressions implicitly claim to be impressive

793

or forceful, they can be distinguished from such unpretentious common expressions as "good morning," "thank you," and "see you tomorrow." Clichés in fact are not impressive or forceful; they strike the hearer as tired, vague, and unimaginative.

compare/contrast. Strictly speaking, to compare is to examine in order to show similarities. (It comes from the Latin *comparare*, "to pair," "to match.") To contrast is to set into opposition in order to show differences. (It comes from the Latin *contra*, "against," and *stare*, "to stand.") But in ordinary usage a comparison may include not only similarities but also differences. (For a particular kind of comparison, emphasizing similarities, see *analogy*.) In comparing and contrasting, a writer usually means not simply to list similarities or differences but to reveal something clearly, by calling attention either to its resemblances to something we might not think it resembles, or to its differences from something we might think it does resemble.

connotation. The associations that cluster around a word. *Mother* has connotations that *female parent* does not have, yet both words have the same denotation or explicit meaning.

convention. An agreed-on usage. Beginning each sentence with a capital letter is a convention.

deduction. Deduction is the process of reasoning from premises to a logical conclusion. Here is the classic example: "All men are mortal" (the major premise); "Socrates is a man" (the minor premise); "therefore Socrates is mortal" (the conclusion). Such an argument, which takes two truths and joins them to produce a third truth, is called a *syllogism* (from Greek for "a reckoning together"). Deduction (Latin for "lead down from") moves from a general statement to a specific application; it is, therefore, the opposite of *induction* (page 797), which moves from specific instances to a general conclusion.

Notice that if a premise of a syllogism is not true, one can reason logically and still come to a false conclusion. Example: "All teachers are members of a union"; "Jones is a teacher"; "therefore Jones is a member of a union." Although the process of reasoning is correct here, the major premise is false—all teachers are *not* members of a union—and so the conclusion is worthless. Jones may or may not be a member of the union.

Another point: some arguments superficially appear logical but are not. Let's take this attempt at a syllogism: "All teachers of Spanish know that in Spanish *hoy* means *today*" (major premise); "John knows that in Spanish *hoy* means *today*" (minor premise); "therefore John is a teacher of Spanish" (conclusion). Both of the premises are correct, but the conclusion does not follow. What's wrong? Valid deduction requires that the subject or condition of the major premise (in this case, teachers of Spanish) appear also in the minor premise, but here it does not. The minor premise should be "John is a teacher of Spanish," and the valid conclusion, of course, would be "therefore John knows that *hoy* means *today.*"

denotation. The explicit meaning of a word, as given in a dictionary, without its associations. *Daytime serial* and *soap opera* have the same denotation, though *daytime serial* probably has a more favorable connotation (see *connotation*).

description. Discourse that aims chiefly at producing a sensory response (usually a mental image) to, for example, a person, object, scene, taste, smell, and so on. A descriptive essay, or passage in an essay, uses concrete words (words that denote observable qualities such as *hair* and *stickiness*) and it uses specific language (words such as *basketball* rather than *game*, and *steak, potatoes, and salad* rather than *hearty meal*).

diction. Choice of words. Examples: between *car, auto*, and *automobile*, between *lie* and *falsehood*, between *can't* and *cannot*.

euphemism. An expression such as *passed away* for *died*, used to avoid realities that the writer finds unpleasant. Thus, oppressive governments "relocate people" (instead of putting them in concentration camps).

evaluation. Whereas an interpretation seeks to explain the meaning, an evaluation judges worth. After we interpret a difficult piece of writing we may evaluate it as not worth the effort.

explication. An attempt to reveal the meaning by calling attention to implications, such as the connotations of words and the tone conveyed by the brevity or length of a sentence. Unlike a paraphrase, which is a rewording or rephrasing in order to set forth the gist of the meaning, an explication is a commentary, that makes explicit what is implicit. If we paraphrased the beginning of the Gettysburg Address (page 480), we might turn "Four score and seven years ago our fathers brought forth" into "Eighty-seven years ago our ancestors established," or some such statement. In an explication, however, we would mention that *four score* evokes the language of the Bible, and that the biblical echo helps to establish the solemnity and holiness of the occasion. In an explication we would also mention that *fathers* initiates a chain of images of birth, continued in *conceived in liberty, any nation so conceived,* and *a new birth.* (See Highet's explication of the Gettysburg Address, page 481.)

exposition. An expository essay is chiefly concerned with giving information—how to register for classes, the causes of the French Revolution, or the tenets of Zen Buddhism. The writer of exposition must, of course, have a point of view (an attitude or a thesis), but because exposition—unlike persuasion—does not assume that the reader's opinion differs from the writer's, the point of view in exposition often is implicit rather than explicit.

general and **specific** (or **particular**). A general word refers to a class or group; a specific (particular) word refers to a member of the class or group. Example: *vehicle* is general compared with *automobile* or with *motorcycle*. But *general* and *specific* are relative. *Vehicle* is general when compared to *automobile,* but *vehicle* is specific when compared to *machine,* for *machine* refers to a class or group that includes not only vehicles but clocks, typewriters, and dynamos. Similarly, although *automobile* is specific in comparison with *vehicle, automobile* is general in comparison with *Volkswagen* or *sportscar.*

generalization. A statement relating to every member of a class or category, or, more loosely, to most members of a class or category. Example: "Students from Medford High are well prepared." Compare: (1) "Janet Kuo is well prepared" (a report of a specific condition); (2) "Students from Medford High are well prepared" (a low-level generalization, because it is limited to one school); (3) "Students today are well prepared" (a high-level generalization, covering many people in many places).

imagery and **symbolism.** When we read *rose,* we may more or less call to mind a picture of a rose, or perhaps we are reminded of the odor or texture of a rose. Whatever in a piece of writing appeals to any of our senses (including sensations of heat and pressure as well as of sight, smell, taste, touch, sound) is an image. In short, images are the sensory content of a work, whether literal (the roses discussed in an essay on rose-growing) or figurative (a comparison, in a poem, of a girl to a rose). It is usually easy to notice images in literature, particularly in poems, which often include comparisons such as "I wandered lonely as a cloud," "a fiery eye," and "seems he a dove? His feathers are but borrowed." In literature, imagery (again, literal as well as figurative) plays a large part in communicating the meaning of the work. For instance, in *Romeo and Juliet* abundant imagery of light and dark reenforces the conflict between life and death. Juliet especially is associated with light (Romeo says, "What light through yonder window breaks? It is the east and Juliet is the sun"), and at the end of the play, when the lovers have died, we are told that the morning is dark: "The sun for sorrow will not show his head."

   If we turn from imaginative literature to the essay, we find, of course, that descriptive essays are rich in images. But other kinds of essays, too, may make use of imagery—and not only by literal references to real people or things. Such essays may use figures of speech, as Thoreau does when he says that the imagination as well as the body should "both sit down at the same table." The imagination, after all, does not literally sit down at a table—but Thoreau personifies the imagination, seeing it as no less concrete than the body.

The distinction between an image and a symbol is partly a matter of emphasis and partly a matter of a view of reality. If an image is so insisted on that we feel that the writer sees it as highly significant in itself and also as a way of representing something else, we can call it a symbol. A symbol is what it is, and yet it is also much more. We may feel that a passage about the railroad, emphasizing its steel tracks and its steel cars, its speed and its noise, may be not only about the railroad but also about industrialism and, even further, about an entire way of life—a way of thinking and feeling—that came into being in the nineteenth century.

A symbol, then, is an image so loaded with significance that it is not simply literal, and it does not simply stand as a figure for something else; it is both itself *and* something else that it richly suggests, a kind of manifestation of something too complex or too elusive to be otherwise revealed. Still, having said all of this, one must add that the distinction between *image* and *symbol* is not sharp, and usage allows us even to say such things as, "The imagery of light symbolizes love," meaning that the imagery stands for or represents or is in part about love.

induction. Reasoning from the particular to the general, or drawing a conclusion about all members of a class from a study of some members of the class. Every elephant I have seen is grayish, so by induction (from Latin, "lead into," "lead up to") I conclude that all elephants are grayish. Another example: I have met ten graduates of Vassar College and all are females, so I conclude that all Vassar graduates are females. This conclusion, however, happens to be incorrect; a few years ago Vassar began to admit males, and so although male graduates are relatively few they do exist. Induction is valid only if the sample is representative.

Because one can rarely be certain that it is representative, induced conclusions are usually open to doubt. Still, we live our lives largely by induction; we have dinner with a friend, we walk the dog, we write home for money—all because these actions have produced certain results in the past and we assume that actions of the same sort will produce results consistent with our earlier findings. Nelson Algren's excellent advice must have been arrived at inductively: "Never eat at a place called Mom's, and never play cards with a man called Doc."

interpretation. An explanation of the meaning. If we see someone clench his fist and tighten his mouth, we may interpret these signs as revealing anger. When we say that in the New Testament the passage alluding to the separation of sheep from goats is to be understood as referring to the saved and the damned, we are offering an interpretation.

irony. In *verbal irony,* the meaning of the words intentionally contradicts the literal meaning, as in "that's not a very good idea," where the intended meaning is "that's a terrible idea."

Irony, in distinction from sarcasm, employs at least some degree of wit or wryness. Sarcasm reveals contempt obviously and heavily, usually by asserting the opposite of what is meant: "You're a great guy" (if said sarcastically) means "It's awful of you to do this to me." Notice that the example of irony we began with was at least a trifle more ingenious than this sarcastic remark, for the sarcasm here simply is the opposite of what is meant, whereas our example of verbal irony is not quite the opposite. The opposite of "that's not a very good idea" is "that is a very good idea," but clearly (in our example) the speaker's meaning is something else. Put it this way: sarcasm is irony at its crudest, and finer irony commonly uses over-statement or especially understatement, rather than a simple opposite. (For a brief discussion of the use of irony in satire, see *satire,* pages 800–01.)

If the speaker's words have an unintentional double meaning, the irony may be called *dramatic irony:* a character, about to go to bed, says, "I think I'll have a sound sleep," and dies in her sleep. Similarly, an action can turn dramatically ironic: a character seeks to help a friend and unintentionally harms her. Finally, a situation can be ironic: thirsty sailors are surrounded by water that cannot be drunk.

All these meanings of irony are held together, then, by the sense of a somewhat bitter contrast.

jargon. Technical language used inappropriately or inexactly. *Viable* means *able to survive.* To speak of *a viable building* is to use jargon. "A primary factor in my participation in the dance" is jargon if what is meant is "I dance because. . . ."

metaphor. Words have literal meanings: a lemon is a yellow, egg-shaped citrus fruit; to drown is to suffocate in water or other fluid. But words can also have metaphoric meanings: we can call an unsatisfactory automobile a *lemon,* and we can say that we are *drowning* in paperwork. Metaphoric language is literally absurd; if we heed only the denotation it is clearly untrue, for an automobile cannot be a kind of citrus fruit, and we cannot drown in paperwork. (Even if the paper literally suffocated someone, the death could not be called a drowning.) Metaphor, then, uses not the denotation of the word but the associations, the connotations. Because we know that the speaker is not crazy, we turn from the literal meaning (which is clearly untrue) to the association.

myth. (1) A traditional story dealing with supernatural beings or with heroes, often accounting for why things are as they are. Myths tell of the creation of the world, the creation of man, the changes of the season, the achievements of heroes. A Zulu myth, for example, explains that rain is the tears of a god weeping for a beloved slain bird. *Mythology* is a system or group of such stories, and so we speak of Zulu mythology, Greek mythology, or Norse mythology. (2) Mark Schorer, in *William Blake,* defines myth as "a large controlling image that gives philosophic meaning to the facts of ordinary life. . . . All real convictions involve a mythology. . . . Wars may be described as the clash of mythologies." In this sense, then, a myth is not a traditional story we do not believe, but any idea, true or false, to which people subscribe. Thus, one can speak of the "myth" of democracy or of communism.

narration. Discourse that recounts a real or a fictional happening. An anecdote is a narrative, and so is a history of the decline and fall of the Roman Empire. Narration may, of course, include substantial exposition ("four possible motives must be considered") and description ("the horse was an old gray mare"), but the emphasis is on a sequence of happenings ("and then she says to me, . . . ").

parable. A parable is a short narrative from which a moral or a lesson can be drawn. A parable may, but need not, be an allegory wherein, say, each character stands for an abstraction that otherwise would be hard to grasp. Usually the parable lacks the *detailed* correspondence of an allegory.

paradox. An apparent self-contradiction, such as "He was happiest when miserable."

paraphrase. A rewording of a passage, usually in order to clarify the meaning. A paraphrase is a sort of translating within the same language; it can help to make clear the gist of the passage. But one must recognize the truth of Robert Frost's charge that when one paraphrases a line of good writing one puts it "in other and worse English." Paraphrase should not be confused with *explication,* pages 795–96.

parody. A parody (from the Greek *counter song*) seeks to amuse by imitating the style—the diction, the sentence structure—of another work, but normally the parody substitutes a very different subject. Thus, it might use tough-guy Hemingway talk to describe not a bullfighter but a butterfly catcher. Often a parody of a writer's style is a good-natured criticism of it.

persona. The writer or speaker in a role adopted for a specific audience. When Abraham Lincoln wrote or spoke, he sometimes did so in the persona of commander in chief of the Union army, but at other times he did so in the persona of the simple man from Springfield, Illinois. The persona is a mask put on for a performance (*persona* is the Latin word for *mask*). If *mask* suggests insincerity, we should remember that whenever we speak or write we do so in a specific role—as friend, or parent, or teacher, or applicant for a job, or whatever. Although Lincoln was a husband, a father, a politician, a president, and many other things, when he wrote a letter or speech he might write solely as one of these; in a letter to his son, the persona (or, we might say, personality) is that of father, not that of commander in chief. The distinction between the writer (who necessarily fills many roles) and the persona who writes or speaks a work is especially useful in talking about satire, because the satirist often invents a mouthpiece very different from himself. The satirist—say, Jonathan Swift—may be strongly opposed to a view, but his persona (his invented essayist) may favor the view; the reader must perceive that the real writer is ridiculing the invented essayist.

persuasion. Discourse that seeks to change a reader's mind. Persuasion usually assumes that the writer and the reader do not agree, or do not fully agree, at the outset. Persuasion may use logical argument (appeal to reason), but it may also try to win the reader over by other means— by appeal to the emotions, by wit, by geniality.

rhetoric. Although in much contemporary usage the word's meaning has sadly decayed to "inflated talk or writing," it can still mean "the study of elements such as content, structure, and cadence in writing or in speech." In short, in the best sense rhetoric is the study of the art of communicating with words.

satire. A work ridiculing identifiable objects in real life, meant to arouse in the reader contempt for its object. Satire is sometimes distinguished from comedy in that comedy aims simply to evoke amusement, whereas satire aims to bring about moral reform by ridicule. According to Alexander Pope, satire "heals with morals what it hurts with wit." Satire sometimes uses invective (direct abuse), but if the invective is to entertain the reader it must be witty, as in a piling up of ingenious accusations. Invective, however, is probably less common in satire than is irony, a device in which the tone somehow contradicts the words. For instance, a speaker may seem to praise ("well, that's certainly an original idea that you have"), but we perceive that she is ridiculing a crackpot idea. Or the satirist may invent a naive speaker (a persona) who praises, but the praise is really dispraise because a simpleton offers it; the persona is sincere, but the writer is ironic and satiric. Or, adopting another strategy, the writer may use an apparently naive persona to represent the voice of reason; the persona dispassionately describes actions that we take for granted (a political campaign), and through this simple, accurate, rational description we see the irrationality of our behavior. (For further comments on *irony*, see page 798.)

style. A distinctive way of expression. If we see a picture of a man sitting on a chair, we may say that it looks like a drawing for a comic book, or we may say that it looks like a drawing by Rembrandt, Van Gogh, or Andrew Wyeth. We have come to recognize certain manners of expression—independent of the content—as characteristic of certain minds. The content, it can be said, is the same—a man sitting in a chair—but the creator's way of expressing the content is individual.

Similarly, "Four score and seven years ago" and "Eighty-seven years ago" are the same in content; but the styles differ, because "Four score and seven years ago" distinctively reflects a mind familiar with the Bible and an orator speaking solemnly. Many people (we include ourselves) believe that the content is not the same if the expression is not the same. The "content" of "Four score and seven years ago" includes suggestions of the Bible and of God-fearing people not present in "eighty-seven years ago." In this view, a difference in style is a difference in content and therefore a difference in meaning. Surely it is true that in the work of the most competent writers, those who make every word count, one cannot separate style and content.

Let C. S. Lewis have the next-to-last word: "The way for a person to develop a style is (a) to know exactly what he wants to say, and (b) to be sure he is saying exactly that. The reader, we must remember, does not start by knowing what we mean. If our words are ambiguous, our meaning will escape him. I sometimes think that writing is like driving sheep down a road. If there is any gate open to the left or the right the readers will most certainly go into it." And let the Austrian writer Karl Kraus have the last word: "There are two kinds of writers, those who are and those who aren't. With the first, content and form belong together like soul and body; with the second, they match each other like body and clothes."

summary. The word *summary* is related to *sum,* to the total something adds up to. (The Greeks and Romans counted upward, and wrote the total at the top.) A summary is a condensation or abridgment briefly giving the reader the gist of a longer work. Here are a few principles that govern summaries:

1. A summary is much briefer than the original. It is not a paraphrase—a word-by-word translation of someone's words into your own—for a paraphrase is usually at least as long as the original, whereas a summary is rarely longer than one-fourth the original, and may even be much briefer, perhaps giving in a sentence or two an entire essay.

2. A summary usually achieves its brevity by omitting almost all the concrete details of the original, presenting only the sum that the details add up to.

3. A summary is accurate; it has no value if it misrepresents the point of the original.

4. The writer of a summary need not make the points in the same order as that of the original. In fact, a reader is occasionally driven to write a summary because the original author does not present the argument in an orderly sequence; the summary is an attempt to disengage the author's argument from the confusing presentation.

5. A summary normally is written in the present tense, because the writer assumes that although the author wrote the piece last year or a hundred years ago, the piece speaks to us today. (In other words, the summary is explicitly or implicitly prefaced by "He says," and all that follows is in the present tense.)

6. Because a summary is openly based on someone else's views, not your own, you need not use quotation marks around any words that you take from the original.

Here is a summary of this entry on *summary:*

A summary is a condensation or abridgment. These are some characteristics: 1) it is rarely more than one-fourth as long as the original; 2) its brevity is usually achieved by leaving out most of the concrete details of the original; 3) it is accurate; 4) it may rearrange the organization of the original, especially if a rearrangement will make things clearer; 5) it normally is in the present tense; 6) quoted words need not be enclosed in quotation marks.

thesis. The writer's position or attitude; the proposition advanced.

thesis statement. A sentence or two summarizing the writer's position or attitude. An essay may or may not have an explicit thesis statement.

tone. The prevailing spirit of an utterance. The tone may be angry, bitter, joyful, solemn, or expressive of any similar mood or emotion. Tone usually reflects the writer's attitude toward the subject, the audience, and the self. (For further comments on tone, see pages 20–22.)

INDEX